Handbook of NeuroLeadership

Dr. David Rock
and
Dr. Al H Ringleb

ISBN-10: 1483925331
ISBN-13: 9781483925332

Contents

Introduction

I am pleased to introduce the first *Handbook of NeuroLeadership*. Since our first NeuroLeadership Summit in 2007 in Asolo, Italy, interest in the field has grown tremendously, with seven international summits now held, hundreds of research projects underway, and four journals published.

This handbook represents the best journal papers since the first *NeuroLeadership Journal* was published in 2008 and focuses on the big ideas in the field.

The research has been divided into the four domains of neuroleadership: decision making and problem solving, regulating emotions, collaborating with others, and facilitating change. This handbook presents important foundational research in each section about each domain. It also includes a section that explores the bigger ideas of the field itself and a section on case studies, which will no doubt grow in further editions.

A big thank you to the journal team in putting this together, including coeditor Dr. Al Ringleb, Tony Pottle, Steven Poelmans, Rivka Louwen (editing), Alison Forte (design), and all the contributors to the work.

SECTION I:
The Field of Neuroleadership

1. The emerging field of neuroleadership

Dr. Al H. Ringleb and Dr. David Rock

Al H. Ringleb, Director, CIMBA, Asolo, Italy
Cofounder, NeuroLeadership Institute; Editor, *NeuroLeadership Journal*
ringleb@cimba.it

David Rock, CEO, NeuroLeadership Group, New York, USA
Faculty, CIMBA; Cofounder, NeuroLeadership Institute; Editor, *NeuroLeadership Journal*
david@neuroleadership.com

Introduction

Although management and leadership research in the past century has significantly enhanced our understanding of human workplace behavior, recent developments in neuroscience with the potential to significantly advance that research remain largely untapped. Standing on this rapidly developing body of neuroscience research, and particularly social-cognitive neuroscience research, we propose the formalization of a specific new field dedicated and committed to exploring the processes in the brain that underlie or influence human decisions, behaviors, and interactions in the workplace and beyond.

Called neuroleadership, this interdisciplinary field explores the neural basis of leadership and management practices, effectively bringing about the interface between the tools of social-cognitive and affective neuroscience, cognitive neuroscience, integrative neuroscience, neurobiology, and other domains within neuroscience, and the questions and theories from the leadership and management social sciences. The research objective of this field is to improve leadership effectiveness within institutions and organizations by developing a science for leadership and leadership development that directly takes into account the physiology of the mind and the brain.

The formalization of neuroleadership is driven by the overarching need worldwide for the efficient and effective development of leaders and of processes for continuous improvement in leadership quality (Boston Consulting Group 2008). In the ongoing search for alternative solutions to this leadership crisis, the underlying subtleties and complexities of the leadership development process due to individual differences in the efficiency and sensitivity of brain structures are increasingly becoming understood and appreciated (Lieberman 2003). Much of this new comprehension is flowing from a rapid expansion in research on the biological underpinnings of social processes driven by the advent of functional neuroimaging and other technologies (Ochsner and Lieberman 2001; Adolphs 2003). In this light, there are clearly significant benefits to reframing traditional leadership and leadership development theories and concepts through the lens of neuroscience.

The formalization of neuroleadership is driven by the overarching need worldwide for the efficient and effective development of leaders...

First, neuroscience provides evidence-based "hard" science to assist leadership theorists in the development of those leadership skills traditionally considered "soft" skills or "soft" science. As a "soft" science, leadership skills development has typically been ignored as being beyond the reach of traditional business education and training, with contemporary managers and leadership educators making limited use of the significant and substantial "hard-science" evidence provided by neuroscience and psychology on behaviors relevant and applicable to effective organizational and leadership practices (Rousseau and McCarthy 2007; Pfeffer and Sutton 2006). Second, by identifying the active biological "ingredients" in leadership interventions, the efficacy of those leadership development efforts can be significantly improved. Third, neuroscience provides the necessary scientific rigor to promote the discovery of new and important insights into the leadership development process going forward.

History and definition of neuroleadership

Neuroleadership focuses on how individuals in a social environment make decisions and solve problems, regulate their emotions, collaborate with and influence others, and facilitate change; that is, neuroleadership engages the "people," as opposed to the functional (Minzberg 2004) side of business. As a field, neuroleadership is emerging in parallel with developments in research technologies that provide researchers with the ability to directly observe brain activity. Those technologies are providing researchers with both confirmation of and new insights into long-held theories and concepts, which to date have largely focused on social psychology theories (Ochsner and Lieberman 2001). The adaptation of this research to other social sciences in general, and to leadership and leadership development more specifically, is moving much more slowly.

Neuroleadership engages the "people," as opposed to the functional side of business.

Developments in the neuroscience domain

The neuroscience world is vast, with over 30,000 scientists worldwide studying a wide range of issues. Based on existing research, the neuroscience fields with the most potential to impact neuroleadership include cognitive neuroscience, integrative neuroscience, neurobiology, neurophysiology, and particularly social-cognitive and affective neuroscience. The strong potential interface between the leadership and neuroscience domains of study has come about as a direct consequence of several interrelated developments within the neuroscience domain over the past decade. First, neuroscience researchers began to move away from describing what brain functions are impaired in brain-damaged patients, and began applying more sophisticated experimental methods to normal, healthy individuals. Focusing on processes involved in normal social cognition, the second development was the expanded use of the fMRI to explore and study social cognition. Although used by neuroscientists in the 1990s, the fMRI really only began to play an integral role in social psychological research after 2000. Since then, social-cognitive neuroscience research has grown exponentially, covering such diverse topics as empathy, social rejection, self-awareness, social factors in economic decision making, theory of mind, social connection, and emotion regulation—all of which are of significant interest to leadership theorists.

Developments in the leadership domain

Although several individual leadership and leadership development practitioners made informal links to neuroscience in the 1990s and early 2000s (Goleman, Boyatzis, and McKee 2002; Wolfe and Brandt 1998; Masters 2001), the first reference in the broader academic business literature was in the *Harvard Business Review* in 2005 (Bennis and O'Toole 2005). There, in an article focused on the limitations of traditional MBA programs in developing students for leadership roles, leadership experts Bennis and O'Toole specifically pointed to the need for neuroleadership, stating: "Oddly, despite B schools' scientific emphasis, they do little in the areas of contemporary science that probably hold the greatest promise for business education: cognitive science and neuroscience" (103). In 2006, Rock and Schwartz published an article that first began to define the field. Titled "The Neuroscience of Leadership," the article became one of the most downloaded articles in *strategy+business* magazine's history, clearly articulating both frustration with the nature and direction of traditional leadership research and a decided hunger for more effective tools and techniques (Rock and Schwartz 2006). Within the academic business community, economics and, to a more limited extent, marketing both began to cite neuroscience research in support of their theories and concepts and to utilize neuroimaging in research (Dickhaut 2005; Rustichini 2005; Camerer, Lowenstein, and Prelec 2005).

Sponsored by an executive coaching company, a business school consortium now led by the University of Iowa, and several consulting firms, the first conference on neuroleadership convened in Asolo, Italy, and brought together scientists and practitioners to discuss the development of the field. After the conference, the field began drawing the attention of mainstream business publications—"The Business Brain in

Close Up" (*Bloomberg Businessweek* 2007) and "The Brain at Work" (Fox 2008)—the business community, and business schools (Petersen et al. 2008). In 2008, neuroleadership conferences were held to wider audiences in Sydney, Australia, and in New York. Interest in the field is growing rapidly and broadly; an Internet search using the word "neuroleadership" yielded fewer than 10 hits in 2004, but more than 8,700 hits today.

Organizing the field

A general overview of each domain reveals that neuroscience, and particularly social-cognitive neuroscience, has many of the same research objectives as leadership and leadership development. The fundamental difference lies in the research tools brought to bear on those objectives. Understanding the comparative advantages and disadvantages of the primary research tools used in each of the domains can assist in organizing the neuroleadership field and identifying research questions of interest going forward.

Using fMRI, social-cognitive neuroscience experiments seek to identify the brain region or regions involved in a process of interest—essentially, where the brain "lights up" when engaging in a specified social psychological process. There can be no face-to-face interactions with fMRIs—research subjects must keep their heads absolutely still during imaging and cannot speak. Typical fMRI experiments require the research subjects to watch through video goggles and respond to tasks by pressing buttons on a small computer keypad. Because the signals the fMRI detects in the brain during the performance of such tasks are "noisy" signals, a number of subjects normally must perform the same task several times before good information is extracted. In situations where the research objective will depend on a large number of research subjects each performing a task one time, this task repetition may result in loss of meaning. As a consequence, some leadership and leadership development questions cannot be addressed easily through the use of fMRI research data.

On the other hand, fMRI research data can make significant contributions to leadership and leadership development research in several ways. For example, there are leadership situations that practically and experimentally produce similar behavioral results but actually rely on different underlying brain mechanisms. In very meaningful ways, fMRI research allows the researcher to clearly distinguish between those two underlying brain mechanisms, something very difficult to do using traditional social-science behavioral methods, which often rely on self-reported and reaction-time measures to test hypotheses. Similarly, fMRI research allows leadership researchers to identify processes that one would not believe rely on the same brain mechanisms but in fact do. Finally, in contrast to traditional behavioral research, fMRI research may allow the researcher to infer the mental processes in which a subject is engaged just from looking at the activity of the subject's brain, as opposed to interrupting the subject and asking, "How do you feel?" to determine the mental state. Relative to traditional social-science experiments, this should prove useful because subjects may not want to report their mental state, may not accurately remember what state they were in before the researcher asked, and, perhaps more importantly to the validity of the underlying experiment, simply reporting their mental state may change subjects' current state or affect how they performs on the remainder of the experiment.

> *Neuroscience, and particularly social-cognitive neuroscience, has many of the same research objectives as leadership and leadership development.*

With this general understanding of research methodologies, after first reviewing separately and then comparing leadership and neuroscience research topics of interest, four general issue categories of mutual research interest emerged:

- Decision making and problem solving
- Regulating emotion
- Collaborating with and influencing others; and,
- Facilitating change

Decision making and problem solving

In traditional leadership and management research, decision making and problem solving have focused on the nature of decision making (Harrison 1999), the types of decisions to be made (Huber 1980; Collins, Ryan, and Mutuski 1999), decision-making conditions (Miller and Starr 1976; Hodgkinson et al. 1999), and a leader's decision-making style, focusing on subordinate participation in the decision-making process (Vroom and Yetton 1973; Vroom and Jago 1988; Vroom 2000). Research first focused on probabilistic or prescriptive models equating good decision making with probabilistic reasoning, with decision making a matter of carrying out rational calculations, logical operations, and statistical computations that view the human brain as a complex machine (Edwards 1954; Gigerenzer 2000; Mullen and Roth 1991). More recently, focus has shifted to behavioral models, arguing that a person's computational ability was limited, and has begun to explore the heuristics and biases decision makers commonly employ in making decisions, many of which were understood to operate below the level of conscious awareness (Simon 1945; Simon 1987; Kahneman, Slovic, and Tversky 1982; Bazerman 2005; Plous 1993). Further inquiries within the bounds of the behavioral models have looked to the roles that intuition (Brousseau et al. 2006; Hayashi, 2001), commitment (Shaw and Ross 1988; Bobocel and Meyer 1994), and risk propensity (McNamara and Bromiley 1999) play in a leader's decision-making process.

Innovation is another important leadership and management thinking process.

How can neuroscience add to the body of traditional leadership research on problem solving and decision making? There is a tendency in the leadership and management literature (and in the real world) to view decision making and problem solving as identical activities (Huber 1986), with the terms often used interchangeably (Costello and Zalkind 1963). If we view decision making as a managerial response to the question "What are my choices?" and problem solving as a managerial response to the question "What has gone wrong?" can neuroscience tell us whether the brain uses the same algorithm in bringing about a solution? Can knowing this answer assist leaders in getting the most from organizational members' mental resources?

Several theorists suggest a more systematic-process approach to decision making and problem solving to combat the implicit nature of these processes in group settings (Hammond, Keeney, and Raiffa 1999; Kepner and Tregoe 1965). Although decision making in social settings has only just begun to receive attention among neuroscientists (Izuma, Saito, and Sadato 2008), a number of important questions with potential to significantly impact leadership and leadership development have emerged. Does "making thinking visible" through the use of such processes when explicated serve to overcome the processing limits of the prefrontal cortex and increase performance within those limits (Shiffrin and Nosofsky 1994; Miller 2001; Halford, Cowan, and Andrews 2007; Halford et al. 2005; Pashler and Christian 1994; Gailliot et al. 2007; Pashler, Johnston, and Ruthruff 2001)? With leadership and management theorists showing that an overwhelming majority of top managers consider it a sign of immaturity to express sentiments during decision-making meetings (Argyris 1966; Argyris 1971; Holloman 1992; Martin 1993), what does social-cognitive neuroscience have to say about the use of suppression mechanisms to inhibit personal feelings, particularly in those situations where personal values and organizational objectives conflict (Ray et al. 2005)?

As evidenced by the volume of leadership and management literature and research spent to define it, innovation is another important leadership and management thinking process. As in decision making and problem solving, the creative process is in large measure an implicit one. To the extent that performance gains can be had by making these processes explicit (Herbig, Muller, and Petrovic 2007; Bussing and Herbig 2003), how can cognitive neuroscience assist us in the explication process?

To the extent the explication process proves difficult, can neuroscience assist leadership theorists in developing ways to maximize unconscious processes to better facilitate breakthrough thinking (Bowden et al. 2005; Ohlsson et al. 1984; Kounios et al. 2006; Lehrer 2008; Rock 2006)? In the same regard, can neuroscience assist leadership theorists in better understanding the role of dopamine (interest) and norepinephrine (alertness) in mental performance, and their management through novelty, reward, visualization, and other tools (Vijayraghavan et al. 2007; Schultz 2001; Waelti, Dickinson, and Schultz 2001)?

Regulating emotion

Early research on leaders' emotions and emotion regulation focused on identifying those personal traits and behaviors that, among other things, allowed effective leaders to stay cool and confident under pressure (Yukl 1981; Kohs and Irle 1960; Kirkpatrick and Locke 1991; Likert 1961; Likert 1967; Stogdill and Coons 1957). Advancements in the field of psychology led to the use of aptitude and personality tests in the 1950s and 1960s, allowing investigators to probe deeper for insights into the leader mind (Stogdill 1948). Broadly speaking, this early lineage of research focused on conflict management and stress management as personal traits that seemed to contribute most to effective leadership (Stogdill 1974; Bass 1990). This inquiry was extended in the 1980s to teams and teambuilding, again with considerable attention placed on conflict and conflict management at both the organization and organizational-member level (Rahim 1990).

Organizational members experience conflict most in situations or circumstances that bring about role conflict...

It was generally concluded that organizational members experience conflict most in situations or circumstances that bring about role conflict (Kahn et al. 1964; Tubre and Collins 2000) or role ambiguity (Kets de Vries 1989; Van Sell, Brief, and Schuler 1981). This interpersonal conflict was seen as being dysfunctional by creating anger, distrust, fear, rejection, or resentment in and among organizational members (Filley 1975; Blake and Mouton 1984). In working to develop effective leadership skills, theorists observed conflict-management styles representing various combinations of assertiveness and cooperativeness a leader might use in a conflict situation (Van de Vliert and Kabanoff 1990; Likert and. Likert 1976; Lee 1990). More recently, certain kinds of conflict have come to be viewed as beneficial, with the leader's goal being to find and maintain the optimal amount of conflict that best fosters organizational-member or group performance, as the case may be (Eisenhardt, Kahwajy, and Bourgeois III 1997; Pinkley and Northcraft 1994).

In defining work-related stress, research initially observed leaders (and also followers) subjected to extreme conflicts, ambiguity, or the ineffective conflict-management styles of others (Matteson and Ivancevich 1987). Stress was understood to create a nonspecific response in the leader, which meant that certain emotional, physical, and cognitive responses occurred unconsciously (Selye 1980). Individual stress-management actions included, among other things, disciplining oneself not to overreact emotionally, learning how to relax, exercising, and modifying one's behaviors and attitudes in confronting stressful situations (Nelson, Quick, and Quick 1989; Williams 1989; Swanbrow 1989; Baron 1989). Organizational stress-management actions included setting clear objectives to reduce ambiguity, providing emotional support, and developing "wellness" programs (Nykodym and George 1980; Jayaratne and Chess 1984; Baron 1989).

More recently, both leadership researchers and psychologists have come to explicitly recognize the importance of emotion and emotional stability in effective leadership (Goleman 1998). This lineage of research suggests that emotion, more than intellectual ability, drives a leader's thinking in decision making and interpersonal relationships (Goleman, Boyatzis, and McKee 1995; Goleman 1995; Boyatzis and McKee 2005; Goleman 2006). The leadership literature characterizes a leader who is emotionally stable as someone who handles stress well, is able to manage criticism, and generally does not take mistakes personally (Daft 2008). Emotional intelligence has come to refer to a person's abilities to perceive, identify, understand, and successfully manage his or her emotions and the emotions of others. In this sense, it is generally understood that effective leaders harness and direct the power of emotion to build trust and improve follower satisfaction, morale, and motivation, and thus enhance overall organizational effectiveness. Current research is focusing on understanding the role of a leader's emotion and emotion-management skills and abilities in change management (Megerian and Sosik 1996; Ashkanasy and Daus 2002), motivation (Hatfield, Cacioppo, and Rapson 1994), and leadership development (Boyatzis, Smith and Blaize 2006).

Current research is focusing on understanding the role of a leader's emotion and emotion-management skills and abilities in change management.

How can neuroscience add to the body of traditional leadership research on emotion regulation? Social-cognitive neuroscientists and psychologists have begun to more clearly articulate the deleterious consequences of stress (Dickerson and Kennedy 2004; Ray 2004; Segerstom and Miller 2004), and responsive management theories and approaches are beginning to emerge (Boyatzis and McKee 2005). With stress clearly a driver for arousing the limbic system (McClelland and Jemmott 1980; Sapolsky 1996; McEwen 1998; LeDoux 2002), how can neuroscience assist leadership theorists in better understanding the "minimize danger–maximize reward response," and particularly the strength of the "minimize danger" response (Gordon 2000; Baumeister, Bratslavsky, and Vohs 2001; Klein 2002; Fredrickson 2001; Naccache et al. 2005)? Can it assist leadership theorists in better understanding optimal levels of stress and productivity in the workplace (Vijayraghavan et al. 2007)?

Leadership researchers have come to understand that managing emotions does not mean suppressing or denying them...

With leadership and management beginning to more fully explore and address the behavioral, psychological, and medical consequences of workplace stress and its impact on performance (Landy, Quick, and Kasl 1994), how can neuroscience research on the complex dynamic between the prefrontal cortex and the limbic system and on how limbic system arousal impacts thinking and performance more clearly define this important area of leadership and leadership-development research (Mather et al. 2006; Hariri, Bookheimer, and Mazziotta 2000; Phelps 2006; Arnsten 1998; Birnbaum et al. 2004)? With a growing recognition in the leadership literature of emotions and emotional stability as core ingredients in the effective leadership process, how will neuroscience's understanding of the effects and consequences of those experiences that generate strong emotions in organizational members—including experiences that create strong, negative autobiographical memories (LeDoux 1998), uncertainty (Hedden and Gabrieli 2006; Mason, Norton, Van Horn, Wegner, Grafton and Macrae et al., 2007), and a lack of autonomy (Donny, Bigelow, and Walsh, 2006; Dworkin, Mirkis, and Smith, 1995; Mineka and Hendersen, 1985) – —impact leadership and leadership- development research? Leadership researchers have come to understand that managing emotions does not mean suppressing or denying them, but rather means understanding them and using that understanding to deal with situations productively (Weisinger, 1998). In this sense, how can the neuroscience-validated techniques of mindfulness (Farb et al. 2007; Tang et al. 2007; Slagter et al. 2007), labeling (Lieberman et al. 2007), and reappraisal (Ray et al. 2005; Gross and John 2003; Ochsner et al. 2004; Richards and Gross 2006) provide leaders with greater personal control over negative emotionality and stress, and thereby enhance well-being?

Collaborating with and influencing others

Leadership theorists initially placed research focus on the leader's power and influence, defining power as "an individual's ability to influence another person to bring about desired outcomes" and influence as "the affect a person's actions had on the attitudes, values, beliefs or actions of others" (Burns 1978; Hitchner 1992; Dahl 1957). Much of the early work was small-group, sociological research on roles (Katz and Kahn 1978; Stewart and Barrick 2000), norms (Feldman 1984), cohesiveness (Bishop and Scott 1997), and group size (Lawless 1972). Within the context of leading and leadership, theorists then explored influence and collaboration by examining teams and teamwork, looking first to the reasons why people join and why they behave as they do in groups or teams (Shaw 1985; Roethlisberger and Dickson 1939; Homans 1950; Maier 1967), and then later to group dynamics and stages of group development (Tuckman 1965). Building on research on motivation (Maslow 1943), research moved toward behavioral models to build theories of leadership that focused on differences in the actions or behaviors of effective versus ineffective leaders and how those behaviors influence teams or followers (McGregor 1960). From the 1980s, research moved toward participative management and team building (Block 1994; McCarthy, Faerman, and Hart 1995), leading to more recent inquiries into the concept of high-performance teams (Pfeffer 1994; Katzenbach and Smith 1993).

What can neuroleadership add to the body of traditional leadership research on collaborating with and influencing others? The potential contributions in this area are particularly interesting, with current neuroscience research overlapping a broad range of leadership behavior. The driving force of social-cognitive neuroscience research is the simple principal that the brain is "deeply social" (Ochsner and Lieberman 2001). From this perspective, social-cognitive neuroscientists argue persuasively that "belongingness" is misplaced in the middle of Maslow's needs hierarchy and would be more accurately positioned at its very foundation (Lieberman 2007). Seemingly consistent with this social-cognitive neuroscience belief, both the academic and business communities recognize the need to be a team player is so strong today that many organizations actively resist hiring someone who does not want to work with others ("How to Avoid Hiring the Prima Donnas," *Wall Street Journal*, February 15, 2000).

Brain scans are clearly showing there is relatively little difference between physical pain and social pain...

Brain scans are clearly showing there is relatively little difference between physical pain and social pain (Eisenberger and Lieberman 2004). If social pain has evolved much like hunger, thirst, or any other form of pain—as a signal to change behavior—and, as in the case of hunger or thirst, if the social pain goes unheeded it takes a serious toll on mind and biology and becomes increasingly difficult to overcome, then what can social-cognitive neuroscience tell us about the key drivers of social pain (and pleasure) in the workplace and particularly from the standpoint of workplace status (Zink et al. 2008; Eisenberger and Lieberman 2004; Chiao, Bordeaux, and Ambady 2004), relatedness (Cacioppo and Patrick 2008; Kosfeld et al. 2005; Mitchell, Macrae, and Banaji 2006), and fairness (Tabibnia, Satpute, and Lieberman 2008; Seymour, Singer, and Dolan 2007)? Can social-cognitive neuroscience assist leadership and leadership-development research by offering a deeper understanding of the workplace consequences of various leadership styles, and particularly as differences in those styles relate to how the work environment and thus performance is impacted (Baumeister, Twenge, and Nuss 2002)? With neuroscience research showing that disruptions in the social environment most affect an individual's higher-order thinking (Baumeister et al. 2002), what does it tell leadership theorists about the impacts of such a workplace environment on creativity and innovation? With much of an organization's culture and workplace cohesion driven by trust, integrity, and shared values (Whitmire 2005; Kouzes and Pozner 1993), how can neuroscience research on values (Takahashi et al. 2008) and trust (Zahn et al. 2008) guide leadership and leadership-development theorists in building more productive work environments?

Within the leadership literature, social awareness relates to one's ability to understand others—socially aware leaders practice empathy, which means being able to put oneself in other people's "shoes," sense their emotions, and understand their perspective. Clearly, our brains respond to other people in ways that are involuntary and automatic. As Adam Smith observed more than three hundred years ago, we all wince when someone else cuts his or her finger (Smith 1752). Neuroscientists refer to this phenomenon in the brain as "mirror neurons" (Rizzolatti et al. 1999). That is, observing an action being performed by another activates the observer's mirror neuron system, bringing about a reaction in the observer's brain very much the same as in the person performing the action. Importantly, the mirror neuron system is activated not only through the observation of a physical act, but also through facial expressions associated with such emotions as guilt or embarrassment (Wicker et al. 2003).

Clearly, our brains respond to other people in ways that are involuntary and automatic.

How can an understanding of mirror neurons assist leaders in better interpreting and appreciating facial expressions, body language, intonation in speech, and other social cues that allow them to form impressions of other people, including the ability to adapt another person's perspective and assign mental states and intentions to that person (Phillips et al. 1997; Norris and Cacioppo 2007; Iacoboni et al. 2005; Montgomery and Haxby 2008)? And, how is that impacted by the degree to which a person is in social pain (Gardner et al. 2005) or, as in the case of a business meeting, performance evaluation, or other incidences of feedback, in *expectation* of social pain (Pickett and Gardner 2005)? In the same sense, with social interaction leading to social cohesion, can social-cognitive neuroscience assist leadership theorists in understanding what effects the increased use of e-mail, texting, and particularly video conferencing are having on both organizational and organizational-member performance (Kraut et al. 1999)?

It is well understood and appreciated that providing feedback to subordinates about their performances is one of the most important tasks confronting any leader.

To illustrate that research overlaps more specifically, it is well understood and appreciated that providing feedback to subordinates about their performances is one of the most important tasks confronting any leader. Giving and receiving feedback is often difficult for both leaders and followers, with leaders being concerned that even the slightest criticism will provoke anger or tears and subordinates terrified they will hear nothing but complaints (Jackman and Strober 1987; Eisenberg and Witten 1987). While the leadership literature does recognize that proper training can assist leaders in conducting more effective feedback interviews (Nathan, Mohrman, and Milliman 1991), can the social-cognitive neuroscience concept of social pain resulting from feedback's impact on the status and relatedness of the follower receiving it give leadership theorists insights into different and more effective feedback techniques? If organizations profit when followers at any level seek feedback and are able to deal well with criticism, can the neuroscience concepts of "labeling" and "reappraisal" discussed in the "Regulating emotion" section above further impact the development of those same feedback techniques from the follower's perspective? If empathy is truly one of the leader's most powerful tools during the feedback process (Daft 2008), can the neuroscience concept of mirror neurons assist leaders in understanding and accentuating this important leadership attribute both inside and outside the feedback process (Carr et al. 2003)?

Facilitating change

Research on change initially focused on organizational change (Armenakis and Bedeian 1999), examining the forces of change (Hitt 2000; Beer and Nohria 2000), and processes for bringing about change within the organization (Lewin 1951; Porras and Silvers 1991; Weick and Quinn 1999). To understand the success or failure of an organization to change, attention focused on the organization's resistance to change and the programs that could be put in place to promote acceptance (Lawrence 1954; Kotter and Schlesinger 1979; Sculley 1987; Drucker 1989). More recently, theorists have focused on the processes and key characteristics of leaders who accomplish successful change projects (Kotter 1996; Vas 2001). In drawing a distinction between leading for change and leading for stability, theorists have defined a "transformational leader" as one with the ability to bring about significant change by focusing on such qualities as vision and shared values to build relationships, rather than on the use of rules, directions, and incentives (Burns 1985; Tichy and Devanna 1986; Kuhnert and Lewis 1987).

Whether from a management or a leadership perspective, much of the research on facilitating change has focused on motivating organizational-member behavior (Vroom 1964). That is, much of the research has been behavior-based, focused on investigating the psychological nature of organizational-member behavior, including studies on key personality traits (Goldberg 1990; Mount, Barrick, and Strauss 1994; Judge, Martocchio, and Thoreson 1997), functional differences (Jung 1971; McCrae and Costa 1989), attitudes (Smith, Kendal, and Hulin 1969; Steers 1977; George and Jones 1996), perceptions (Kelley 1971), and creativity (Woodman, Sawyer, and Griffin 1993; Tabak 1997). A clearer understanding of organizational-member behavior was thought to provide leaders with the ability to motivate people appropriately in the interest of organizational change and performance (Pfeffer 1998). This lineage of research focused first on economic gain (Taylor 1911) and then on the social needs of the individual (Mayo 1945; Roethlisberger and Dickson 1939). A variety of models were offered by motivational theorists (Alderfer 1972; Herzberg 1987), and research identified individual needs such as achievement, affiliation, and power as important drivers (McClelland 1961).

Much of the research on facilitating change has focused on motivating organizational-member behavior.

Concerns about how motivation occurs generated considerable research on the process of motivation, emphasizing expectations (Vroom 1964; Porter and Lawler III 1968), fairness (Adams 1963), goal setting (Locke 1968; Latham and Baldes 1975; Fried and Slowik 2004), and reinforcement (Skinner 1971; Luthans and Kreitner 1985; Stajlovis and Luthans 1997) in explaining the various approaches used by leaders to bring about behavioral change. Research into the application of motivational strategies focused on empowerment (Quinn, Gretchen, and Spreitzer 1997), participation (Glew et al. 1995), alternative forms of work arrangements (Sewell 1996; Cohen and Gadon 1978), and performance-based rewards systems (Wiley 1993; DeMatteo, Eby, and Sundstrom 1998).

How can neuroscience add to the body of traditional leadership research on facilitating change? With estimates that some two-thirds of all organizational change efforts fail or at best deliver mediocre results (Beer and Nohria 2000; Kotter 1996), leadership theorists assert that both organizations and organizational members view such initiatives as being more threat than opportunity (Gilbert and Bower 2002). In assisting leadership theorists in understanding organizational members' perceptions and expectations of change initiatives, how can neuroscientific understanding of the brain's approach-avoidance response—its fundamental organizing principle to "minimize danger and maximize reward"—provide insight (Gordon 2000; Coghill, McHaffie, and Yen 2003; Arslan 2006; Beauregard 2007)? With leadership research showing that communication helps organizational members cope with change (Jaffe, Scott, and Tobe 1994; Schweiger and DeNisi 1991), how can social-cognitive neuroscience research on uncertainty (Hedden and Gabrieli 2006), autonomy (Donny, Bigelow, and Walsh 2006), and status (Zink et al. 2008; Chiao, Bordeaux, and Ambady 2003) improve leadership theorists' understanding of what makes such communications effective in reducing organizational members' resistance? With most organizational change models or frameworks emphasizing the importance of establishing and communicating the goals and objectives of the change initiative (Kotter 1996), how can social-cognitive neuroscience and its research on the importance of goals on brain function impact the importance of goals and goal setting in leading change (Berkman and Lieberman, forthcoming)? Or, similarly, by explaining functional differences in leader communications that would move organizational-member thinking away from a resistive problem-solving orientation toward a far more receptive goal orientation (Darnon et al. 2007)?

Getting people to change long-entrenched habits, such as changing the way they work together in an organization, is not easy.

Through their research on resistance to change, leadership theorists understand that getting people to change long-entrenched habits, such as changing the way they work together in an organization, is not easy. In providing guidance to organizations in overcoming such resistance, theorists have long touted the importance of organizational learning (Simon 1997; Senge 1990; Garvin, Edmondson, and Gino 2008) through such tools and techniques as coaching (Boyatzis, Smith, and Blaize 2006; Donde and Rock 2008; Passmore 2007; Feldman 2005), mentoring (Bell 2000; Kram 1988; Roche 1979), training (Huselid, Jackson, and Schuler 1997), employee-development programs (Jacobs and Washington 2003), executive-development programs (Griffin 2003; Kaiser and Kaplan 2006), work assignments (Brown and Reich 1997), and corporate universities (Meister 1998) as efforts to bring about improved employee performance and therefore to facilitate organizational change. In each case, the underlying research suggests that the success of such programs is some function of the organizational member's level of self-awareness—a personal sense of strengths and weaknesses and vision of continuous advancement and personal growth. How can neuroscience's growing understanding of the relationship between cognitive control and mindfulness assist theorists in defining more effective leadership-development change tools and techniques (Bishop et al. 2004; Brown and Reich 1997; Schwartz, Stapp, and Beauregard 2005; Libet 1999)? How can neuroscience's growing understanding of neuroplasticity in the context of volition, interest, and attention provide insights and guidance to leadership theorist's development quest, particularly in the growth areas of coaching and mentoring (Schwartz and Begley 2002; Schwartz 1999)?

Neuroscience is very rapidly beginning to show the anatomy and physiology of the social-science research on leadership.

Conclusion

Although the research linkages between psychology and leadership are long held and productive, the formal research linkages between leadership and neuroscience are much less developed. Still, the contributions that social-cognitive neuroscience research have and can make to social psychology differ little from the contributions it can make to furthering and deepening our understanding of leadership and leadership development. The potential for substantive advances in both domains is significant and important.

Neuroscience is very rapidly beginning to show the anatomy and physiology of social-science research on leadership. Still, while the interface between neuroscience and leadership research seems clear, a quick survey of the leading management textbooks and a leading leadership textbook shows few if any cites to neuroscience literature and research. Given the potential benefits to both domains, the authors would like to emulate the words of the leading social-cognitive neuroscientist Matthew Lieberman: "It may be time for leadership theorists to take a neuroscientist to lunch."

References

Adams, J. S. 1963. "Towards an Understanding of Inequity." *Journal of Abnormal and Social Psychology* 67(5): 422–436.

Adolphs, R. 2003. "Cognitive Neuroscience of Human Social Behavior." *Nature Reviews Neuroscience* 4: 165–178.

Alderfer, C. P. 1972. *Existence, Relatedness, and Growth*. New York: Free Press.

Argyris, C. 1966. "Interpersonal Barriers to Decision-Making." *Harvard Business Review* (March-April): 84–97.

Argyris, C. 1971. "Management Information Systems: The Challenge to Rationality and Emotionality." *Management Science* (February) 17(6): 275–292.

Armenakis, A. A., and Bedeian, A. G. 1999. "Organizational Change: A Review of Theory and Research in the 90s." *Journal of Management* 25(3): 293–315.

Arnsten, A. F. T. 1998. "The Biology of Being Frazzled." *Science* 280(5370): 1711–1712.

Arslan, A. 2006. "Even Black-and-White Bananas Look Yellow: Experiment Reveals How Expectation Interferes with Perception." Published online, October 15, 2006. doi:10.1038/news061009-13. Article referring to Hansen, T., Olkonnen, M., Walter, S., and Gegenfurtner, K. R. 2006. "Memory Modulates Color Appearance." *Nature Neuroscience* 9(11): 1367.

Ashkanasy, N. M., and Daus, C. S. 2002. "Emotion in the Workplace: A New Challenge for Managers." *Academy of Management Executive* 16(1): 76–86.

Baron, R. A. 1989. "Personality and Organizational Conflict: Effects of the Type A Behavior Pattern and Self-Monitoring." *Organizational Behavior and Human Decision Processes* 44(2): 281–296.

Bass, B. M. 1990. *Bass and Stogdill's Handbook of Leadership: Theory, Research, and Managerial Applications.* 3rd ed. New York: Free Press.

Baumeister, R. F., Bratslavsky, E., and Vohs, K. D. 2001. "Bad Is Stronger than Good." *Review of General Psychology* 5(4): 323–370.

Baumeister, R. F., Twenge, J. M., and Nuss, C. K. 2002. "Effects of Social Exclusion on Cognitive Processes: Anticipated Aloneness Reduces Intelligent Thought." *Journal of Personality and Social Psychology* 83(4): 817–827.

Bazerman, M. H. 2005. *Judgment in Managerial Decision-Making*. 6th ed. New York: John Wiley & Sons.

Beauregard, M. 2007. "Mind Does Really Matter: Evidence from Neuroimaging Studies of Emotional Self-Regulation, Psychotherapy, and Placebo Effect." *Progress in Neurobiology* 81: 218–236.

Beer, M., and Nohria, N. 2000. "Cracking the Code of Change." *Harvard Business School Press* 78(3): 133–144.

Bell, C.R. 2000. "The Mentor as Partner." *Training and Development* 54(2): 52-56.

Bennis, W., and O'Toole, J. 2005. "How Business Schools Lost Their Way." *Harvard Business Review* 83(5): 96–104.

Berkman, E., and Lieberman, M. D. Forthcoming. "The Neuroscience of Goal Pursuit: Bridging Gaps Between Theory and Data." In *Goals,* edited by G. Moskowitz. Guilford.

Birnbaum, S. G., Yuan, P. X., Wang, M., Vijayraghavan, S., Bloom, A. K., Davis, D.J., Gobeske, K. T., Sweatt, J. D., Manji, H. K., and A. F. T. Arnsten. 2004. "Protein Kinase C Overactivity Impairs Prefrontal Cortical Regulation of Working Memory." *Science* 306(5697): 882–884.

Bishop, J. W., and Scott, K. D. 1997. "How Commitment Affects Team Performance." *Human Resources Magazine* 42(2): 107–111.

Bishop, S. R., Lau, M., Shapiro, S., Carlson, L., Anderson, N. D., Carmody, J., Segal, Z. V., Abbey, S., Speca, M., Velting, D., and Devins, G. 2004. "Mindfulness: A Proposed Operational Definition." *Clinical Psychology: Science and Practice* 11(3): 230–241.

Blake, R. R., and Mouton, J. S. 1984. *Solving Costly Organizational Conflicts.* San Francisco: Jossey-Bass.

Block, P. 1994. "Reassigning Responsibilities." *Sky* (February) 26–31.

Bobocel, R., and Meyer, J. 1994. "Escalating Commitment to a Failing Cause of Action: Separating the Roles of Choice and Justification." *Journal of Applied Psychology* 79: 360–363.

Boston Consulting Group. World Federation of Personnel Management Associations, and Society for Human Resource Management 2008. "Creating People Advantage: How to Address HR Challenges Worldwide through 2015." Presented at WFPMA World HR congress, London April 14, 2008.

Bowden, E. M., Jung-Beeman, M., Fleck, J., and Kounios, J. 2005. "New Approaches to Demystifying Insight." *Trends in Cognitive Sciences* 9(7): 322–328.

Boyatzis, R., and McKee, A. 2005. *Resonant Leadership.* Boston: Harvard Business School Press.

Boyatzis, R., Smith, M., Blaize, N. 2006. "Developing Sustainable Leaders through Coaching and Compassion." *Academy of Management Learning and Education* 5(1): 8–24.

Briggs Myers, I., and Myers, P. 1980. *Gifts Differing: Understanding Personality Type.* Mountain View, CA: Davies-Black.

Brousseau, K., Driver, M., Hourihan, G., and Larsson, R. 2006. "The Seasoned Executive's Decision-Making Style." *Harvard Business Review* 84(2): 111–112.

Brown, C., and Reich, M. 1997. "Micro-macro Linkages in High-Performance Employment systems." *Organizational Stufies* 18: 765-781.

Brown, K. W., Ryan, R. M. 2007. "Mindfulness: Theoretical Foundations and Evidence for its Salutary Effects." *Psychological Inquiry* 18(4): 211–237.

Burns, J. M. 1978. *Leadership.* New York: Harper & Row.

Burns, J. M. 1985. "Leadership: Good, Better, Best." *Organizational Dynamics* 13(3): 26–40.

"Business Brain in Close Up." 2007. *Business Week* (July 23). http://www.businessweek.com/magazine/content/07_30/b4043084.htm.

Cacioppo, J. T., and Patrick, B. 2008. *Loneliness: Human Nature and the Need for Social Connection*. New York: W. W. Norton.

Camerer, C., Lowenstein, G., and D. Prelec. 2005. "Neuro-economics: How Neuroscience Can Inform Economics." *Journal of Economic Literature* 43(1): 9–64.

Carr, L., Iacoboni, M., Dubeau, M. C., Mazziota, J. C., and Lenzi, G. L. 2003. "Neural Mechanisms of Empathy in Humans: A Relay from Neural Systems for Imitation to Limbic Areas." *Proceedings of the National Academy of Sciences, USA* 100: 5497–5502.

Chiao, J. Y., Bordeaux, A. R., and Ambady, N. 2004. "Mental Representations of Social Status." *Cognition* 93: 49–57.

Coghill, R. C., McHaffie, J. G., Yen, Y. 2003. "Neural Correlates of Inter-Individual Differences in the Subjective Experience of Pain. *Proceedings of the National Academy of Sciences, USA* 100: 8538–8542.

Cohen, A.R., and Gadon, H. 1978. *Alternative Work Schedules: Integrating Individuals and Organizational Needs*. Reading, MA: Addison-Wesley Publishing Company.

Collins, P. D., Ryan, L. V., and Matusik, S. F. 1999. "Programmable Automation and the Locus of Decision-Making Power." *Journal of Management* 25(1): 29–53.

Costello, T. W., and Zalkind, S. S., eds. 1963. *Psychology in Administration: A Research Orientation*. Englewood Cliffs, NJ: Prentice Hall.

Daft, D. 2008. *The Leadership Experience*. 2nd ed. Boston: Thomson/South-Western.

Dahl, R. A. 1957. "The Concept of Power." *Behavioral Science* 2(3): 201–215.

Darnon, C., Harackiewicz, J.M., Butera, F., Mugny, G., and Quizmzade, A. 2007. "Performance-Approach and Performance-Avoidance Goals: When Uncertainty Makes a Difference." *Personality and Social Psychology Bulletin* 33(6): 813-827.

Dematteo, J.S., Eby, L.T., and Sundstrom, E. 1998. "Team-based rewards: Current empirical evidence and directions for future research." *Research in Organizational Behavior* 20: 141-183.

Dickerson, S. S., and Kennedy, M. E. 2004. "Acute Stressors and Cortisol Responses: A Theoretical Integration and Synthesis of Laboratory Research." *Psychological Bulletin* 130(3): 355–391.

Dickhaut, J. 2005. "A Brain Imaging Study of the Choice Procedure." *Games and Economic Behavior* 52(2): 257–282.

Donde, R., and Rock, D. 2008. "Driving Organizational Change with Internal Coaching Programmes: Part one and Part two." *Industrial and Commercial Training* 40(2): 75-80.

Donny, E. C., Bigelow, G. E., and Walsh, S. L. 2006. "Comparing the Physiological and Subjective Effects of Self-Administered vs. Yoked Cocaine in Humans." *Psychopharmacology* (Berl.) 186(4): 544–52.

Drucker, P. F. 1989. *The New Realities: In Government and Politics/In Economics and Business/In Society and World View*. New York: Harper & Row.

Dunbar, R. I. M., and Schultz, S. 2007. "Evolution in the Social Brain." *Science* 317(5843): 1344–1347.

Dworkin, S. I., Mirkis, S., and Smith, J. E. 1995. "Response-dependent Versus Response-independent Presentation of Cocaine: Differences in the Lethal Effects of the Drug." *Psychopharmacology* 117: 262–266.

Edwards, W. 1954. "The Theory of Decision Making." *Psychological Bulletin* 51: 380–417.

Eisenberg, E. M., and Witten, E. G. 1987. "Reconsidering Openness in Organizational Communication." *Academy of Management Review* 12(3): 418–426.

Eisenberger, N. I., and Lieberman, M. D. 2004. "Why Rejection Hurts: A Common Neural Alarm System for Physical and Social Pain." *Trends in Cognitive Sciences* 8: 294–300.

Eisenberger, N. I., Lieberman, M. D., and Williams, K. D. 2003. "Does Rejection Hurt? An fMRI Study of Social Exclusion." *Science* 302(5643): 290–292.

Eisenhardt, K. M., Kahwajy, J. L., and Bourgeois III, L. J. 1997. "How Management Teams Can Have a Good Fight." *Harvard Business Review* 75(4): 77–89.

Farb, N. A. S., Segal, Z. V., Mayberg, H., Bean, J., McKeon, D., Fatima, Z., and Anderson, A. K. 2007. "Attending to the Present: Mindfulness Meditation Reveals Distinct Neural Modes of Self-reference." *Social Cognitive and Affective Neuroscience* 2(4): 313–322.

Feldman, D. C. 1984. "The Development and Enforcement of Group Norms." *Academy of Management Review* 9(1): 47–53.

Filley, A.C. 1975. *Interpersonal Conflict Resolution*. Glenview, IL: Scott Foresman.

Fox, A. 2008. "The Brain at Work." *Society for Human Resource Management* 53(3). http://www.shrm.org/hrmagazine/articles/0308/0308fox.asp.

Fredrickson, B. L. 2001. "The Role of Positive Emotions in Positive Psychology: The Broaden-and-Build Theory of Positive Emotions." *American Psychologist* 56(3): 218–226.

Fried, Y., and Slowik, L. H. 2004. "Enriching Goal-Setting Theory with Time." *Academy of Management Review* 29(3): 404–422.

Gailliot, M. T., Baumeister, R. F., DeWall, C. N., Maner, J. K., Plant, E. A., Tice, D. M., Brewer, L. E., and Schmeichel, B. J. 2007. "Self-Control Relies on Glucose as a Limited Energy Source: Willpower Is More than a Metaphor." *Journal of Personality and Social Psychology* 92, 325–336.

Gallese, V., Keysers, C., Rizzolatti, G. 2004. "A Unifying View of the Basis of Social Cognition." *Trends Cognitive Science* 8(9): 396–403.

Gardner, W. L., Pickett, C. L., Jefferies, V., and Knowles, M. 2005. "On the Outside Looking in: Loneliness and Social Monitoring." *Personality and Social Psychology Bulletin* 31(11): 1549–1560.

Garvin, D.A., Edmondson, A.C., and Gino, F. 2008. "Is Yours a Learning Organization?" *Harvard Business Review* (March) 109–116.

George, J. M., and Jones, G. R. 1996. "The Experience of Mood and Turnover Intentions: Interactive Effects of Value Attainment, Job Satisfaction, and Positive Mood." *Journal of Applied Psychology* 81(3): 318–325.

Gigerenzer, G. 2000. *Adaptive Thinking: Rationality in the Real World*. Oxford: Oxford University Press.

Gilbert, C. and Bower, J. 2002. "Disruptive Change: When Trying Harder is Part of the Problem." *Harvard Business Review* 80(5): 94-101.

Glew, D.J., O'Leary-Kelly, A.M., Griffin, R.W., and Van Fleet, D.D. 1995. "Participation in Organizations: A Preview of the Issues and Proposed Framework for Future Analysis." *Journal of Management* 21(3): 395-421.

Goldberg, L. R. 1990. "An Alternative ' Description of Personality': The Big Five Factor Structure." *Journal of Personality and Social Psychology* 59(6): 1216–1229.

Goleman, D. 1995. *Emotional Intelligence: Why It Can Matter More than IQ*. New York: Bantam Books.

Goleman, D. 2006. *Social Intelligence: The New Science of Human Relationships*. New York: Bantam Books.

Goleman, D., Boyatzis, R. E., and McKee, A. 2002. *Primal Leadership: Realizing the Power of Emotional Intelligence*. Boston: Harvard Business School Press.

Gordon, E., ed. 2000. *Integrative Neuroscience: Bringing Together Biological, Psychological and Clinical Models of the Human Brain*. Harwood.

Griffin, N.S. 2003. "Personlize your Management Development." *Harvard Business Review* 81(3): 113-119.

Gross, J. J., and John, O. P. 2003. "Individual Differences in Two Emotion Regulation Processes: Implications for Affect, Relationships, and Well-Being." *Journal of Personality and Social Psychology* 85(2): 348 –362.

Halford, G. S., Baker, R., McCredden, J., and Bain, J. D. 2005. "How Many Variables Can Humans Process?" *Psychological Science* 16(1): 70–76.

Halford, G. S., Cowan, N., and Andrews, G. 2007. "Separating Cognitive Capacity from Knowledge: A New Hypothesis. " *Trends in Cognitive Sciences* 11(6): 236–242.

Hammond, J. S., Keeney, R.L., and Raiffa, H. 1999. *Smart Choices: A Practical Guide to Making Better Decisions*. Boston: Harvard Business School Press.

Hariri, A. R., Bookheimer, S. Y., Mazziotta, J. C. 2000. "Modulating Emotional Responses: Effects of a Neocortical Network on the Limbic System." *Neuroreport* 11: 43–48.

Harrison, E. F. 1999. *The Managerial Decision-Making Process*. 5th ed. Boston: Houghton Mifflin.

Hatfield, E., Cacioppo, J. T., and Rapson, R. L. 1994. *Emotional Contagion*. New York: Cambridge University Press.

Hayashi, A. M. 2001. "When to Trust Your Gut." *Harvard Business Review* 79(2): 58–65.

Hedden, T., and Gabrieli, J. D. E. 2006. "The Ebb and Flow of Attention in the Human Brain." *Nature Neuroscience* 9(7): 863–865.

Herbig, B., Muller, A., and Petrovic, K. 2007. "Implicit Knowledge in the Product Innovation Process." In eds. *Innovationsforschung: Ansätze, Methoden, Grenzen und Perspektiven*, edited by H. Hof and U. Wenganroth. Hamburg, Germany: Lit Verlag, 2007. A. Bussing and B. Herbig, "Implicit Knowledge and Experience in Work and Organizations," *International Review of Industrial and Organizational Psychology* 18, S, 239–280.

Herzberg, F. 1987. "One More Time: How Do You Motivate Employees?" *Harvard Business Review* 65(5): 109–120. Reprinted 2003, *Harvard Business Review* 46(1): 87–98.

Hitchner, E. 1992. "The Power to Get Things Done." *National Productivity Review* 12(1): 117–122.

Hitt, M. A. 2000. "The New Frontier: Transformation of Management for the New Millennium." *Organizational Dynamics* 29(4): 7–17.

Hodgkinson, G. P., Brown, N. J., Maule, A. J., Glaister, K. W., and Pearman, A. J. 1999. "Breaking the Frame: An Analysis of Strategic Cognition and Decision-Making under Uncertainty." *Strategic Management Journal* 20: 977–985.

Holloman, C. R., 1992. "Using Both Head and Heart in Managerial Decision-Making." *Industrial Management* 34(6): 7–10.

Homans, G. C. 1950. *The Human Group*. New York: Harcourt, Brace.

Huber, G. P. 1980 *Managerial Decision-Making*. Glenview, IL: Scott Foresman.

Huber, O. 1986. "Decision-Making as a Problem Solving Process." In *New Directions in Research on Decision-Making*, edited by B. Brehmer, H. Jungermann, P. Lourens, and G. Sevon, 108–138. New York: Elsevier.

Huselid, M.A., Jackson, S.E., and Schuler, R.S. 1997. "Technical and Strategic Human Resources Management Effectiveness as Determinants of Firm Performance. *Academy of Management Journal* 40(1): 171-188.

Iacoboni, M., Molnar-Szakacs, I., Gallese, V., Buccino, G., . Mazziotta, J.C., and Rizzolatti, G. 2005. "Grasping the Intentions of Others with One's Own Mirror Neuron System." *PLoSBiology* 3(3): 79.

Izuma, K., Saito, D. N., and Sadato, N. 2008. "Processing of Social and Monetary Rewards in the Human Striatum." *Neuron* 58(2): 284–294.

Jackman, J. M., and Strober, M. H. 2003. "Fear of Feedback." *Harvard Business Review* 81(4): 101–108.

Jacobs, R., and Washington, C. 2003. "Employees Development and Organizational Performance: A Review of Literature and Directions for Future Research." *Human Resource Development International* 6(3): 343-354.

Jaffe, D., Scott, C., and Tobe, G. 1994. *Rekindling Commitment: How to Revitalize Yourself, Your Work and Your Organization.* San Francisco: Jossey-Bass.

Janis, I. L. 1972. *Victims of Groupthink*. Boston: Houghton Mifflin.

Jayaratne, S., and Chess, W. A. 1984. "The Effects of Emotional Support of Perceived Job Stress and Strain." *Journal of Applied Behavioral Science* 20: 141–153.

Judge, T. A., Martocchio, J. J., and Thoreson, C. J. 1997. "Five Factor Model of Personality and Employee Absence." *Journal of Applied Psychology* 82: 745–755.

Jung, G. C. 1971. "Psychological Types." In *Collected Works of C.G. Jung*, vol. 6. Princeton, NJ: Princeton University Press.

Kahn, R., Wolf, D., Quinn, R., and Snoek, J. 1964. *Organizational Stress: Studies in Role Conflict and Ambiguity.* New York: John Wiley & Sons.

Kahneman, D., Slovic, P., and Tversky, A., eds. 1982. *Judgment under Uncertainty: Heuristics and Biases*. Cambridge: Cambridge University press.

Kaiser, R.B., and Kaplan, R.E. 2006. *The Versatile Leader: Make the Most of Your Strengths Without Overdoing it*. San Francisco, CA: Pfeiffer.

Katz, D., and Kahn, R. L. 1978. *The Social Psychology of Organizations.* 2nd ed. New York: John Wiley & Sons.

Katzenbach, J. R., and Smith, D. K. 1993. *The Wisdom of Teams: Creating the High-Performance Organization*. New York: HarperBusiness.

Kelley, H.H. 1971. *Attribution in Social Interaction*. New York: General Learning Press.

Kepner, C. H., and Tregoe, B. B. 1965. *The Rational Manager*. New York: McGraw-Hill.

Kets de Vries, M. F. 1989. "Leaders Who Self-Destruct: The Causes and Cures." *Organizational Dynamics* 17(4): 5–17.

Kirkpatrick, S. A., and Locke, E. A. 1991. "Leadership: Do Traits Matter?" *Academy of Management Executive* 5(2): 48–60.

Klein, S. 2002. *The Science of Happiness*. New York: Avalon.

Kohs S. C., and Irle, K. W. 1920. "Prophesying Army Promotions." *Journal of Applied Psychology* 4: 73–87.

Kosfeld, M., Heinrichs, M., Zak, P. J., Fischbacher, U., and Fehr, E. 2005. "Oxytocin Increases Trust in Humans." *Nature* 435: 673–676.

Kotter, J. P. 1996. *Leading Change*. Boston: Harvard Business School Press.

Kotter, J. P., and Schlesinger, L. A. 1979. "Choosing Strategies for Change." *Harvard Business Review* 57(2): 106–114.

Kounios, J., Frymiare, J. L., Bowden, E. M., Fleck, J. I., Subramaniam, K., Parrish, T. B., and Jung-Beeman, M. 2006. "The Prepared Mind: Neural Activity Prior to Problem Presentation Predicts Subsequent Solution by Sudden Insight." *Psychological Science* 17: 882–890.

Kouzes J. M., and Posner, B. C. 1993. *Credibility: How Leaders Gain and Lose It*. San Francisco, CA: Jossey-Bass.

Kraut, R., Patterson, M., Lundmark, V., and Keisler, S. 1999. "Internet Paradox: A Social Technology that Reduces Social Involvement and Psychological Well-Being?" *American Psychologist* 53(9): 1017–31.

Kram, K.E. 1985. *Mentoring at Work: Developmental Relationships in Organizational Life*. Lanham, MD: University Press of America.

Kuhnert, K.W., and Lewis, P. 1987. "Transactional and Transformational Leadership: A Constructive/Developmental Analysis." *Academy of Management Review* 12(4): 648–657.

Landy, F., Quick, J. C., and Kasl, S. 1994. "Work, Stress, and Well-Being." *International Journal of Stress Management* 1(1): 33–73.

Latham, G. P., and Baldes, J. J. 1975. "The Practical Significance of Locke's Theory of Goal Setting." *Journal of Applied Psychology* 60: 122–124.

Lawless, D. J. 1972. *Effective Management: A Social Psychological Approach*. Englewood Cliffs, NJ: Prentice Hall.

Lawrence, P. R. 1954. "How to Deal with Resistance to Change." *Harvard Business Review* 32(3): 49–57.

LeDoux, J. 1998. *The Emotional Brain: The Mysterious Underpinnings of Emotional Life*. New York: Simon & Schuster.

LeDoux, J. 2002. *Synaptic Self: How Our Brains Become Who We Are*. New York: Viking.

Lee, C. W. 1990. "Relative Status of Employees and Styles of Handling Interpersonal Conflict: An Experimental Study with Korean Managers." *International Journal of Conflict Management* 1(4): 327–340.

Lehrer, J., 2008. "The Eureka Hunt." *The New Yorker Annals of Science*, July 28, 40.

Lewin, K. 1951. *Field Theory in Social Science*. New York: Harper & Row.

Libet, B. 1999. "Do We Have Free Will?" *Journal of Consciousness Studies* 6(8–9): 47–57.

Lieberman, M. D. 2003. "Reflective and Reflexive Judgment Processes: A Social Cognitive Neuroscience Approach." In *Social Judgments: Implicit and Explicit Processes*, edited by J. P. Forgas, K. R. Williams, and W. von Hippel, 44–67. New York: Cambridge University Press.

Lieberman, M. D. 2007. "Social Cognitive Neuroscience: A Review of Core Processes." *Annual Review of Psychology* 58: 259–289.

Lieberman, M. D., Eisenberger, N., Crockett, M., Tom, S., Pfeifer, J., and Way, B. 2007. "Putting Feelings into Words: Affect Labelling Disrupts Amygdala Activity in Response to Affective Stimuli. *Psychological Science* 18(5): 421–428.

Likert, R. 1961. *New Patterns of Management*. New York: McGraw-Hill.

Likert, R. 1967. *The Human Organization*. New York: McGraw-Hill.

Likert R., and Likert, J. G. 1976. *New Ways of Managing Conflict*. New York: McGraw-Hill.

Locke, E. A. 1968. "Toward a theory of task motivation and incentives." *Organizational Behavior and Human Performance* 3: 157–189.

Luthans, F., and Kreitner, R. 1985. *Organizational Behavior Modification and Beyond: An Operant and Social Learning Approach*. Glenview, IL: Scott Foresman.

Maier, N. R. F. 1967. "Assets and Liabilities in Group Problem-Solving: The Need for an Integrative Function." *Psychology Review* 74(4): 239–249.

Martin, C. L. 1993. "Feelings, Emotional Empathy, and Decision-Making: Listening to the Voices of the Heart." *Journal of Management Development* 12(5): 33–45.

Mason, M. F., Norton, M. I., Van Horn, J. D., Wegner, D. M., Grafton, S. T., and Macrae, C. N. 2007. "Wandering Minds: The Default Network and Stimulus-Independent Thought." *Science* 315: 393–395.

Maslow, A. H. 1943. "A Theory of Human Motivation." *Psychological Review* 50: 370–96.

Masters, R. D. 2001. "Cognitive Neuroscience, Emotion, and Leadership." In *Citizens and Politics: Perspectives from Political Psychology*, edited by J. H. Kuklinski. New York: Cambridge University Press.

Mather, M., Mitchell, K. J., Raye, C. L., Novak, D. L., Greene, E. J. and Johnson, M. K. 2006. "Emotional Arousal Can Impair Feature Binding in Working Memory." *Journal of Cognitive Neuroscience* 18: 614–625.

Matteson, M. T., and Ivancevich, J. M. 1987. *Controlling Work Stress*. San Francisco, CA: Jossey-Bass.

Mayo, E. 1945. *The Social Problems of Industrial Civilization*. Boston: Harvard University Press.

McCarthy, D. P., Faerman, S. R., and Hart, D. W. 1995. "The Appeal and Difficulty of Participative Systems." *Organization Science* 6(6): 603–627.

McClelland, D. C. 1961. *The Achieving Society*. Princeton, NJ: Van Nostrand.

McClelland, D. C. 1975. Power: *The Inner Experience*. New York: Irvington.

McClelland, D. C., and Jemmott, J. B. III. 1980. "Power, Motivation, Stress, and Physical Illness." *Journal of Human Stress* 6(4): 6–15.

McCrae, R. R., and Costa, P.T. Jr. 1989. "Reinterpreting the Myers-Briggs Type Indicator from the Perspective of the Five-Factor Model of Personality." *Journal of Personality* 57: 17–40.

McEwen, B. S. 1998. "Protective and Damaging Effects of Stress Mediators." *New England Journal of Medicine* 338(3): 171–179.

McGregor, D. 1960 *The Human Side of Enterprise*. New York: McGraw Hill.

McNamara, G., and. Bromiley, P. 1999. "Risk and Return in Organizational Decision-Making." *Academy of Management Journal* 42(3): 330–339.

Megerian, L. E., and Sosik, J. J. 1996. "An Affair of the Heart: Emotional Intelligence and Transformational Leadership." *The Journal of Leadership and Organizational Studies* 3(3): 31–48.

Meister, J.C. 1998. *Corporate Universities: Lessons in Building a World-Class Work Force*. New York: McGraw-Hill.

Miller, E. K., and Cohen, J. D. 2001. "An Integrative Theory of Prefrontal Cortex Function." *Annual Review of Neuroscience* 24: 167–202.

Miller, D. W., and Starr, M. K. 1967. *The Structure of Human Decisions*. Englewood Cliffs, NJ: Prentice Hall.

Mintzberg, H. 2004. *Managers Not MBAs*. San Francisco, CA: Berrett-Koehler.

Mineka, S., and Hendersen, R. W. 1985. "Controllability and Predictability in Acquired Motivation." *Annual Review of Psychology* 36: 495–529.

Mitchell, J. P., Macrae, C. N., and Banaji, M. R. 2006. "Dissociable Medial Prefrontal Contributions to Judgments of Similar and Dissimilar Others." *Neuron* 50: 655–663.

Montgomery, K. J., and Haxby, J. V. 2008. "Mirror Neuron System Differentially Activated by Facial Expressions and Social Hand Gestures: A Functional Magnetic Resonance Imaging Study." *Journal of Cognitive Neuroscience* 20: 1866–1877.

Mount, M. K., Barrick, M. R., and Strauss, J. P. 1994. "Validity of Observer Ratings of the Big Five Personality Factors." *Journal of Applied Psychology* 79: 272–280.

Mullen, J., and Roth, B. 1991. *Decision-Making: Its Logic and Practice*. Savage, MD: Rowman and Littlefield.

Naccache, L., Gaillard, R. L., Adam, C., Hasboun, D., Clemenceau, S., Baulac, M., et al. 2005. "A Direct Intracranial Record of Emotions Evoked by Subliminal Words." *Proceedings of the National Academy of Sciences, USA* 102(21): 7713–7717.

Nathan, B. R., Mohrman, A., and Milliman, J. 1991. "Interpersonal Relations as a Context for the Effects of Appraisal Interviews on Performance and Satisfaction: A Longitudinal Study." *Academy of Management Journal* 34: 352–369.

Nelson, D. L., Quick, J. C., Quick, J. D. 1989. "Corporate Warfare: Preventing Combat Stress and Battle Fatigue." *Organizational Dynamics* 18(1): 65–79.

Norris, C. J., and Cacioppo, J. T. 2007. "I Know How You Feel: Social and Emotional Information Processing in the Brain." In *Social neuroscience*, edited by Harmon-Jones, E., and Winkielman, P., 84–105. New York: Guilford.

Nykodym, N., and George, K. 1980. "Stress Busting on the Job." *Personnel* 9: 56–59.

Ochsner, K. N., and Lieberman, M. D. 2001. "The Emergence of Social Cognitive Neuroscience." *American Psychologist* 56: 717–734.

Ochsner, K. N., Ray, R. D., Cooper, J. C., Robertson, E. R., Chopra, S., Gabrieli, J. D. E., et al. 2004. "For Better or for Worse: Neural Systems Supporting the Cognitive Down-and Up-Regulation of Negative Emotion." *NeuroImage* 23: 483–499.

Ohlsson, S., Carter, C. S., Macdonald, A. M., Botvinick, M., Ross, L. L., Stenger, V.A., and Noll, D. 1984. "Restructuring Revisited: II. An Information Processing Theory of Restructuring and Insight." *Scandinavian Journal of Psychology* 25: 17–129.

Pashler, H., and Christian, C. L. 1994. *Center for Human Information Processing Technical Report: Bottlenecks in Planning and Producing Vocal, Manual and Foot Responses.* La Jolla, CA: University of California, San Diego. http://www.pashler.com/manuscripts.html.

Pashler, H., Johnston, J. C., and Ruthruff, E. 2001. "Attention and Performance." *Annual Review of Psychology* 52: 629–51.

Passmore, J. 2007. "Addressing Deficit Performance Through Coaching: Using Motivational Interviewing for Performance Improvement in Coaching." *International Coaching Psychology Review* 2(3): 265-279.

Petersen, S. J., Waldman, D. A., Balthazard, P. A., and Thatcher, R. W. 2008. "Neuroscientific Applications of Psychological Capital: Are the Brains of Optimistic, Hopeful, Confident, and Resilient Leaders Different?" *Organizational Dynamics* 37(4): 342–353.

Pfeffer, J. 1994. *Competitive Advantage through People: Unleashing the Power of the Work Force*. Boston: Harvard Business School Press.

Pfeffer, J. 1998. *The Human Equation*. Boston: Harvard Business School Press.

Pfeffer, J., and Sutton, R. I. 2006. "Evidence-Based Management." *Harvard Business Review* 84(1): 62–75.

Phelps, E. A., 2006. " Emotion and Cognition: Insights from Studies of the Human Amygdala." *Annual Review of Psychology* 57: 27–53.

Phillips, M. L., Young, A. W., Senior, C., Brammer, M., Andrew, C., Calder, A. J., et al. 1997. "A Specific Neural Substrate for Perceiving Facial Expressions of Disgust." *Nature* 389(6650): 495–498.

Pickett, C. L., and Gardner, W. L. 2005. "The Social Monitoring System: Enhanced Sensitivity to Social Cues as an Adaptive Response to Social Exclusion." In *The Social Outcast: Ostracism, Social Exclusion, Rejection, and Bullying*, edited by K. Williams, J. Forgas, and W. von Hippel. New York: Psychology Press.

Pinkley, R., and Northcraft, G. 1994. "Conflict Frames of Reference: Implications for Dispute Processes and Outcomes." *Academy of Management Journal* 37(1): 193–205.

Plous, S. 1993. *The Psychology of Judgment and Decision-Making*. Philadelphia: Temple University Press.

Porras, J. I., and Silvers, R. C. 1991. "Organizational Development and Transformation." *Annual Review of Psychology* 42: 51–78.

Porter, L. W., and Lawler III, E. E. 1968. *Managerial Attitudes and Performance*. Homewood, IL: Irwin-Dorsey.

Quinn, R.E and Spreitzer, G.M. 1997. "The Road to Empowerment: Seven Questions Every Leader Should Consider." *Organizational Dynamics* 26(2): 37-49.

Rahim, M. A., ed. 1990. *Theory and Research in Conflict Management*. New York: Praeger.

Ray, O. 2004. "How the Mind Hurts and Heals the Body." *American Psychologist* 59(1): 29–40.

Ray, R. D., Ochsner, K. N., Cooper, J. C., Robertson, E. R., Gabrieli, J. D. E., and Gross, J. J. 2005. "Individual Differences in Trait Rumination and the Neural Systems Supporting Cognitive Reappraisal." *Cognitive, Affective, and Behavioral Neuroscience* 5(2): 156–168.

Richards, J. M., and Gross, J. J. 2006. "Personality and Emotional Memory: How Regulating Emotion Impairs Memory for Emotional Events." *Journal of Research in Personality* 40(5): 631–651.

Rizzolatti, G., Fadiga, L., Fogassi, L., Gallese, V. 1999. "Resonance Behaviors and Mirror Neurons." *Archives Italiennes de Biologie* 137: 85–100.

Roberts, M., and Harris, T. G. 1989. "Wellness at Work." *Psychology Today* 23: 54–58.

Roche, G.R. 1979. "Much Ado about Mentors." *Harvard Business Review* 57(1): 14-31.

Rock, D. 2006. *Quiet Leadership*. New York: Collins.

Rock, D., and Schwartz, J. M. 2006. "The Neuroscience of Leadership." *Strategy+Business* 43: 71–81.

Roethlisberger, F. J., and Dickson, W. J. 1939. *Management and the Worker*. Cambridge: Harvard University Press.

Rousseau, D. M., and McCarthy, S. 2007. "Educating Managers from an Evidence-Based Perspective." *Academy of Management Learning and Education* 6(1): 84–101.

Rustichini, A. 2005. "Neuroeconomics: Present and Future." *Games and Economic Behavior* 52(2): 201–212.

Sapolsky, R. M. 1996. "Why Stress Is Bad for Your Brain." *Science* 273(5276): 749–750.

Sewell, G. 1996. "A Japanese "Cure" to a British "Disease"? Cultural Dimensions to the Development of Workplace Surveillance Technologies." *Information Technology and People* 9(3): 12-29.

Schultz, W. 2001. "Reward Signalling by Dopamine Neurons." *Neuroscientist* 7(4): 293–302.

Schwartz, J. M. 1999. "A Role for Volition and Attention in the Generation of New Brain Circuitry." *Journal of Consciousness Studies* 6(8–9): 115–142.

Schwartz, J. M., and Begley, S. 2002. *The Mind and the Brain*. New York: Regan Books.

Schwartz, J. M., Stapp, H. P., and Beauregard, M. 2005. "Quantum Physics in Neuroscience and Psychology: A neurophysical Model of Mind-Brain Interaction." *Philosophical Transactions of the Royal Society* (June) 360(1458): 1309–1327. doi:10.1098/rstb2004.1598.

Schweiger, D.M., and DeNisi, A.S. 1991. "Communication with Employees Following a Merger: A longtudional field experiment." *Academy of Management Journal* 34(1): 110-135.

Sculley, J. 1987. *Odyssey*. New York: Harper & Row.

Segerstom, S. C., and Miller, G. E. 2004. "Psychological Stress and the Human Immune System: A Met-Analytical Study of 30 Years of Inquiry." *Psychological Bulletin* 130(3): 601–630.

Seymour, B., Singer, T., and Dolan, R. 2007. "The Neurobiology of Punishment." *Nature Reviews Neuroscience* 8: 300–311.

Selye, H. 1980. "The Stress Concept Today." In Kutash, I. L., Schlesinger, L. B., and Associates, eds. *Handbook on Stress Anxiety*. San Francisco, CA: Jossey-Bass, 127–143.

Shaw, B. M., and Ross, J. 1988. "Good Money after Bad." *Psychology Today* 22: 30–33.

Shaw, M. E. 1985. *Group Dynamics: The Psychology of Small Group Behavior*. 4th ed. New York: McGraw-Hill.

Shiffrin, R. M., and Nosofsky, R. M. 1994. "Seven Plus or Minus Two: A Commentary on Capacity Limitations." *Psychological Review* 101(2): 357–361.

Simon, H. A. 1945. *Administrative Behavior*. New York: Free Press.

Simon, H. A. 1987. "Making Management Decisions: The Role of Intuition and Emotion." *Academy of Management Executive* (February): 57–63.

Simon, H. A. 1977. *The New Science of Management Decision*. Englewood Cliffs, NJ: Prentice-Hall.

Skinner, B. F. 1971. *Beyond Freedom and Dignity*. New York: Knopf.

Slagter, H. A., Lutz, A., Greischar, L. L., Francis, A. D., Nieuwenhuis, S., Davis, J. M., et al. 2007. "Mental Training Affects Distribution of Limited Brain Resources." *Public Library of Sciences Biology* 5(6): 138.

Smith, A. 1752. *The Theory of Moral Sentiments.* Reprinted 2002. Cambridge: Cambridge University Press.

Smith, P. C., Kendal, L. M., and Hulin, C., 1969. *The Measurement of Satisfaction in Work and Retirement.* Chicago: Rand-McNally.

Stajlovis, A. D., and Luthans, F. 1997. "A Meta-Analysis of the Effects of Organizational Behavior Modification on Task Performance." *Academy of Management Journal* 40(5): 1122–1149.

Steers, R. M. 1977. "Antecedents and Outcomes of Organizational Commitment." *Administrative Science Quarterly* 22: 46–56.

Stewart, G. L., and Barrick, N. R. 2000. "Team Structure and Performance: Assessing the Meditating Role of Intrateam Process and the Moderating Role of Task Type." *Academy of Management Journal* 43(2): 135–148.

Stogdill, R. M. 1948. "Personal Factors Associated with Leadership: A Survey of the Literature." *Journal of Psychology* 25: 35–71.

Stogdill, R. M., and Coons, A. E., eds.1957. *Leadership Behavior: Its Description and Measurement.* Columbus, OH: Bureau of Business Research, Ohio State University.

Stogdill, R. M. 1974. *Handbook of Leadership: A Survey of the Literature.* New York: Free Press.

Swanbrow, D. 1989. "The Paradox of Happiness." *Psychology Today* 22: 37–39.

Tabak, F. 1997. "Employee Creative Performance: What Makes It Happen?" *Academy of Management Executive* 11(1): 119–122.

Tabibnia, G., Satpute, A. B., and Lieberman, M. D. 2008. "The Sunny Side of Fairness: Preference for Fairness Activates Reward Circuitry (and Disregarding Unfairness Activates Self-control Circuitry)." *Psychological Science* 19: 339–347.

Takahashi, H., Kato, M., Matsuura, M., Koeda, M., Yahata, N., Suhara, T., et al. 2008. "Neural Correlates of Human Virtue Judgment." *Cerebral Cortex* 18(8): 1886–1891.

Tang, Y., Ma, Y., Wang, J., Fan, Y., Feng, S., Lu, Q., Yu, Q., Sui, D., Rothbart, M. K., Fan, M., Posner, M. I. 2007. "Short-term Meditation Training Improves Attention and Self-regulation." *Proceedings of the National Academy of Sciences, USA* 104(43): 17152–17156.

Taylor, F. W. 1911. *The Principles of Scientific Management.* New York: Harper & Brothers.

Tichy, N. M., and Devanna, M. A. 1986. *The Transformational Leader.* New York: John Wiley & Sons.

Tubre, T. C., and Collins, J. M. 2000. Jackson and Schuler 1985. "Revisited: A Meta-Analysis of the Relationships Between Role Ambiguity, Role Conflict, and Job Performance." *Journal of Management* 26(1): 155–169.

Tuckman, B. W. 1965. "Developmental Sequence in Small Groups." *Psychological Bulletin* 63(6): 384–399.

Van Sell, M., Brief, A.P., and Schuler, R. S. 1981. "Role Conflict and Role Ambiguity: Integration of Literature and Directions for Future Research." *Human Relations* 34: 43–71.

Van de Vliert, E., and Kabanoff, B. 1990. "Toward Theory-Based Measures of Conflict Management." *Academy of Management Journal* 33(1): 199–209.

Vas, A. 2001. "Top Management Skills in a Context of Endemic Organizational Change: The Case of Belgacom." *Journal of General Management* 27(1): 70–89.

Vijayraghavan, S., Wang, M., Birnbaum, S. G., Williams, G. V., and Arnsten, A. 2007. "Inverted-Udopamine D1 Receptor Actions on Prefrontal Neurons Engaged in working Memory." *Nature Neuroscience* 10: 376–384.

Vroom, V. H. 1964. *Work and Motivation*. New York: John Wiley & Sons.

Vroom, V. H., and Yetton, P. H. 1973. *Leadership and Decision-Making*. Pittsburgh: University of Pittsburgh Press.

Vroom, V. H., and Jago, A. G. 1988. *The New Leadership*. Englewood Cliffs, NJ: Prentice Hall.

Vroom, V. H. 2000. "Leadership in the Decision-Making Process." *Organizational Dynamics* 28(4): 82–94.

Waelti, P., Dickinson, A., and Schultz, W. 2001. "Dopamine Responses Comply with Basic Assumptions of Formal Learning Theory." *Nature* 412: 43–48.

Weick, K. E., and Quinn, R. E. 1999. "Organizational Change and Development." *Annual Review of Psychology* 50: 381–386.

Weisinger, H. 1998. *Emotional Intelligence at Work*. San Francisco: Jossey-Bass.

Whitmire, K. 2005. "Leading through Shared Values." *Leader to Leader* 37: 48–54.

Wicker, B., Keysers, C., Plailly, J., Royet, J. P., Gallese, V., and Rizzolatti, G. 2003. "The Common Neural Basis of Seeing and Feeling Disgust." *Neuron* 40(3): 655–664.

Williams, R. 1989. *The Trusting Heart: Great News about Type A Behavior*. New York: Random House.

Wolfe, P., and Brandt, R. 1998. "What Do We Know from Brain Research?" *Educational Leadership* 56(3): 8–13.

Woodman, R. W. Sawyer, J. E. and Griffin, R. W. 1993. "Toward a Theory of Organizational Creativity." *Academy of Management Review* 18: 293–321.

Yukl, G. A. 1981. *Leadership in Organizations*. Englewood Cliffs, NJ: Prentice Hall.

Zahn, R., Moll, J., Paiva, M., Garrido, G., Krueger, F., Huey, E. D., et al. 2008. "The Neural Basis of Human Social Values: Evidence from Functional MRI." *Cerebral Cortex* 10(3): 308–317.

Zink, C. F., Tong, Y., Chen, Q., Bassett, D. S., Stein, J. L., and Meyer-Lindenberg, A. 2008. "Know Your Place: Neural Processing of Social Hierarchy in Humans." *Neuron* 58: 273–283.

2. Defining neuroleadership as a field

Dr. David Rock and Dr. Al H. Ringleb

David Rock, CEO, NeuroLeadership Group, New York, USA
Faculty, CIMBA; Cofounder, NeuroLeadership Institute; Editor, *NeuroLeadership Journal*
david@neuroleadership.com

Al H. Ringleb, Director, CIMBA, Asolo, USA
Cofounder, NeuroLeadership Institute; Editor, *NeuroLeadership Journal*
ringleb@cimba.it

Introduction

At the start of any new field of study, there are important discussions about how to organize the ideas within that field and the overall value that field may have. In the opening paper of the first *NeuroLeadership Journal*, we outlined an organizing framework for the neuroleadership field based on four domains: decision making and problem solving, regulating emotions, collaboration, and facilitating change (Ringleb and Rock 2008). This organization appears to be standing the test of time as a robust way of dividing up the areas of interest within neuroleadership. The goals of this chapter are to provide an understanding of why leadership scholars should study the brain, to assist researchers and practitioners to understand the deeper philosophical debates that exist in this leadership subfield of study, and to point to additional issues that may need further discussion or research.

As a starting point, it is fair to assume that both leadership scholars and practitioners would agree that studying the brain for its own sake does not provide sufficient rationale for creating a neuroleadership subfield. Conversely, it is equally fair to assume that both leadership scholars and practitioners would agree that if neuroscience measures are able to better assist people in managing themselves and improving performance and well-being, that would provide sufficient rationale for its creation. As a starting point, we would like to look at what it means for neuroleadership to be a subfield of the leadership field of study, as well as some of the challenges facing it and other fields of study as neuroscience research continue to provide interesting insights.

Neuroleadership as a subfield of leadership study

The placement of the term "neuro" in front of an existing field of study, as in neuroeconomics or neuromarketing, typically focuses the scientific inquiry on people's emotions in situations involving the subject of the existing field, often using fMRI technology.

At the start of any new field of study, there are important discussions about how to organize the ideas within that field and the overall value that field may have.

For example, "neuro" in front of the existing field of marketing becomes neuromarketing and is defined as the study of how people's brains respond to advertising and other marketing messages by scientifically monitoring brain-wave activity. Neuroeconomics involves the study of people's brain systems in economic situations—in current research typically as the person makes decisions.

Traditional leadership scholars have the choice to consider or not consider information on the brain that flows from the neurosciences.

The intent of the research is to understand the mental activity associated with a person's interaction with the subject of the field, including mental representations, emotions, expectations, learning, memory, and behavior. As a scientific discipline, the intent of research is to observe social phenomena, collect data relating to the observations, establish workable theories to explain the phenomena, test hypotheses about the validity of those theories, and develop models for applications of the new learning to improve performance. Scientists publish their work so that other scientists can perform similar experiments to double-check conclusions. The results of this process enable a better understanding of past events, with the expectation of better predicting future events of the same kind.

Relative to existing fields of study, the rate of knowledge acquisition in neuro-based subfields is considerably slower. This slower rate is explained in part by the fact that most of these subfields are less than a decade old, so there are relatively few social scientists with the credentials to undertake neuro-based research without the assistance of a neuroscientist. In the area of neuroeconomics, for example, there are fewer than 200 neuroscientists and economists active in the field, with a 2:1 mix of neuroscientists to economists. Further compounding personnel limitations are the costs associated with neuro-based experiments; a well-constructed neuroscience experiment can cost in excess of $100,000. As a consequence, much of the thinking is being driven by both practitioners and those scientists who are taking neuroscience and social psychology findings and proposing interventions, explanations, and models consistent with (some would argue) a field of practice, as opposed to a field of study.

Within the leadership field of study, neuroleadership is a subfield. The leadership field of study involves undertaking scientific research on "the interpersonal influence relationship among leaders and followers who intend real changes and outcomes which reflect their shared purposes" (Rost 1993). Neuroleadership can be defined as the study of the biological microfoundations of that relationship. As in other fields, the number of active neuroleadership scholars is quite small relative to the number of traditional leadership scholars. Given the significantly larger outlays by business on leadership development relative to other disciplines, it would not be surprising to find the number of practitioners calling themselves "leadership consultants" to also be larger. With the typical neuroscience-based experiment into specific leadership hypotheses being considerably more expensive than typical social-science experiments on the same or similar issues, it is not surprising to find practitioner "inquiries" to be exceeding scholarly "inquiries." Still, those same leadership scholars are accustomed to building hypotheses based on research in psychology, social psychology, and sociology, among other fields, where research findings have an influential effect on leadership theory. As is the case with those influential fields, traditional leadership scholars have the choice to consider or not consider information on the brain that flows from the neurosciences. In viewing neuroleadership as a subfield of leadership in its infancy, those scholars and others have made the following arguments for and against the inclusion of brain-based research in traditional leadership research.

Traditional arguments against creating the subfield

Not surprising, in the informal process of getting recognized as a field of study, nearly all neuro-based subfields found, or are finding, themselves simultaneously both embraced by curiosity and repelled by skepticism. The skeptics in any field of study can be formidable and resistive, stonewalling serious consideration of perspectives or viewpoints novel to the field's core knowledge. For example, with the advent of behavior economics in the last two decades, economics has begun to once again embrace insights from psychology after nearly a century of separation (Camerer, Lowenstein, and Prelec 2005). In the particular case of neuro-based subfields, skepticism is further fueled by the degree of expertise required to conduct meaningful research, all but necessitating interdisciplinary research teams. Generally speaking, resistive assertions to the development of subfields take one of the following directions:

- This subfield would only repackage existing knowledge.

- This subfield would be interesting but would not create new knowledge.
- This subfield generates information that may be interesting in the lab but is not appropriate for the real world.
- This subfield is not supported by empirical data sufficient to drive research.

Subfield would only repackage existing knowledge

Of all assertions, the "repackaging existing knowledge" assertion seems the least compelling. Many practitioners and academicians, including the authors, have noted anecdotally that students more firmly grasp the traditional leadership development notion of personal intentional change when it is couched in discussions about their brain (Rock 2009a). Similarly, empirical research has shown findings that when a research article includes a picture of the brain, the article is considered by readers to be more authoritative and compelling (Miller 2008). If we make the difficult assumption that neuroleadership will not add to existing knowledge on leadership and leadership development, then the empirical question still remains as to whether presenting traditional leadership concepts through the lens of neuroscience increases a person's confidence in those concepts and thus brings about improved results.

Students more firmly grasp the traditional leadership development notion of personal intentional change when it is couched in discussions about their brain...

Subfield would not create new knowledge

The authors are aware that most traditional leadership concepts do not meet expectations (Boston Consulting Group 2008) and most change initiatives in companies are unsuccessful (Beer and Nohria 2000). However, these facts alone are not sufficient to warrant the assertion that new knowledge will not be created, and an extensive discussion of the need for leadership, the leadership "crisis," leadership "meltdown," or leadership "vacuum" is of little value here. Most readers are quite familiar with the need for leadership and leadership development based on its coverage in the media, the number of business schools placing the word "leader" in their mission statement (Snook 2007), the number of executive development programs containing the word "leadership" in their title (DeAngelis 2008), and the number of books defining its laws (Maxwell 2007), authenticity (George 2007), accountability (Dive 2008), secrets (Slater 2002), important questions (Young 2008), experience (Thomas 2008), principles (Adair 2009), and other attributes.

Most readers are quite familiar with the need for leadership and leadership development based on its coverage in the media...

There are more than 50,000 neuroscientists in the world, and knowledge is being gained rapidly. According to *Nature Neuroscience* magazine, "It has now been more than two decades since the first fMRI paper was published. In 1992 just four such papers were published; in 2007 there were eight published per day." (Editorial 2009). With eight studies a day being published, we are able to make more than just basic statements about the functioning of the brain and its applications to neuroleadership.

Subfield will generate information interesting only in the lab

This assertion has its origins in the belief that as the ultimate "black box," the actual functioning of the brain would very likely not be known, or more precisely, not be capable of being measured directly. Social scientists in the leadership area, as in other social-science areas, devised experiments with the intent to indirectly measure human feelings. Neuroscience research tools have effectively opened the door a little to this black box and have given us the ability to more closely measure human feelings.

Using an fMRI, social-cognitive neuroscience experiments seek to identify the brain region or regions involved in a process of interest—essentially, where the brain "lights up" when engaging in a specified social-psychological process. There can be no face-to-face interactions with fMRIs—research subjects must keep their heads absolutely still during imaging and cannot speak. Typical experiments require the research subject to watch through video goggles and respond to computer tasks by pressing buttons on a small keypad. Because the signals the fMRI detects in the brain during the performance of such tasks are "noisy" signals, a subject normally must perform the same task several times before good information is extracted. In situations where the research objective will depend on a large number of research subjects each performing a task one time, this task repetition may result in loss of meaning. As a consequence, some leadership and leadership development questions cannot be addressed easily through the use of fMRI research data.

The use of fMRI research data makes significant contributions to leadership and leadership development research.

On the other hand, there are several ways in which the use of fMRI research data makes significant contributions to leadership and leadership development research. For example, there are leadership situations that practically and experimentally produce similar behavioral results but actually rely on different underlying brain mechanisms. In very meaningful ways, fMRI research allows the researcher to clearly distinguish between those two underlying brain mechanisms, something very difficult to do using traditional social-science behavioral methods, which often rely on self-reported measures and reaction-time measures to test hypotheses. Similarly, fMRI research allows leadership researchers to identify processes that one would not believe rely on the same brain mechanisms, when in fact they do.

fMRI research may allow the researcher to infer some of the mental processes in which a subject is engaged just from looking at the activity of his/her brain...

Finally, in contrast to traditional behavioral research, fMRI research may allow the researcher to infer some of the mental processes in which a subject is engaged just from looking at the activity of his/her brain, rather than interrupting the subject and asking how he or she feels to determine mental state. This should prove useful because the subject may not want to report his/her mental state or may not accurately remember what state he/she was in before the researcher asked, and, perhaps more importantly, simply reporting his/her current state may change the subject's current state or affect how the subject performs on the remainder of the experiment. In this way, fMRI research can be combined with more traditional experimental and survey methods to gain a better understanding of social and affective processes.

At the same time, many neuroscience studies have recently been replicated in social settings, specifically by the social-cognitive neuroscience field (Ochsner and Lieberman 2001). For example, Butler et al. (2003) repeated James Gross's studies on emotion regulation, showing that suppression increased limbic arousal, this time in real settings. It will be important for neuroleadership principles to focus on research that has come from real settings, not just from fMRI experiments.

Subfield is not supported by empirical data sufficient to drive research

With eight studies a day being published, we are able to make some basic statements about the brain. For example, there is enough evidence to say that current ways of trying to bring people to insight are likely to be ineffective, whereas questions that enable people to notice subtle signals are more likely to work (Jung-Beeman, Collier, and Kounios 2008). We also now have ways of testing the brain to validate interventions. These tests are thoroughly validated themselves (Gordon 2008). Another example is the way suppressing the expression of emotions actually increases limbic system arousal, which inhibits clear thinking (Ochsner 2008a). Yet suppression is the strategy of choice for many leaders.

There is enough evidence to say that current ways of trying to bring people to insight are likely to be ineffective, whereas questions that enable people to notice subtle signals are more likely to work...

Brain research is providing fresh insights about maximizing attention (Rock and Schwartz 2006), managing expectations (Coghill, McHaffie, and Yen 2003), increasing innovation (Jung-Beeman, Collier, and Kounios 2008), regulating emotions (Ochsner 2008a), and many other leadership skills. Within the research are discoveries about the brain that open up ideas for new types of interventions to improve the content of leadership programs. For example, a study showed that just 100 minutes of mindfulness training in a week created a 30% to 50% reduction in cortisol levels, a marker of stress, against a control group (Tang and Posner 2008). Before this study, it was generally understood that benefits from mindfulness took significantly longer to realize. Mindfulness can give leaders deep benefits toward emotion regulation and help them make better decisions. As another example, research on the social brain points to the real pain of social threat (Lieberman and Eisenberger 2008), which in turn points to the central driver of why performance reviews are often ineffective and how we could improve their effectiveness (Rock 2009a).

Mindfulness can give leaders deep benefits toward emotion regulation and help them make better decisions.

Laboratory research is also providing hard data, rigorously tested, that is applicable to the real world. One example is the MyBrainSolutions brain training tool. Based on the world's largest database of brain research, this system is able to assess an individual's brain functioning, then give the person activities for improving specific skills, delivered by Internet only (Gordon 2008). This kind of neuroleadership research is highly applicable and scalable. It gives people the ability to understand and change their brain, based on solid brain research.

There is significant value to be gained in exploring leadership and leadership development through the lens of neuroscience.

Conclusion

In summary, we propose that although the field is still emerging, there is significant value to be gained in exploring leadership and leadership development through the lens of neuroscience. While indeed talking about the brain provides some "marketing" value, there is clearly significant value above and beyond marketing. By having neuroscience as a framework, we can increase the effectiveness of existing interventions, be able to show hard evidence of the impact of interventions, develop new delivery mechanisms for interventions, and develop totally new leadership interventions. All of this can help us create more effective leaders who can create better functioning organizations that can then deliver more fully on their promises.

References

Adair, J. 2009. *Leadership and Motivation: The Fifty-Fifty Rule and the Eight Key Principles of Motivating Others*. London: Kogan Page.

Baumeister, R. F., Bratslavsky, E., Finkenauer, C., and Vohs, K. D. 2001. "Bad is Stronger than Good." *General Psychology* 5(4): 323–370.

Beer, M., and Nohria, N. 2000. "Cracking the Code of Change." *Harvard Business Review* 78(3): 133–144.

Bennis, W., and O'Toole, J. 2005. "How Business Schools Lost their Way." *Harvard Business Review* 83(5): 96–104.

Block-Lerner, J., Adair, C., Plumb, J. C., Rhatigan, D. L., and Orsillo, S. M. 2007. "The Case for Mindfulness-Based Approaches in the Cultivation of Empathy: Does Nonjudgmental, Present-Moment Awareness Increase Capacity for Perspective-Taking and Empathic Concern?" *Journal of Marital and Family Therapy* 33(4): 501–516.

Boston Consulting Group, World Federation of Personnel Management Associations, and Society for Human Resource Management. 2008. "Creating People Advantage: How to Address HR Challenges Worldwide through 2015." Presented at WFPMA World HR Congress, London, April 14.

Brefczynski-Lewis, J. A., Lutz, A., Schaefer, H. S., Levinson, D. B., and Davidson R. J. 2003. "Neural Correlates of Attentional Expertise in Long-Term Meditation Practitioners." *National Academy of Sciences, USA* 104(27): 11483–11488.

Bromberg-Martin, E., and Hikosaka, O. 2009. "Midbrain Dopamine Neurons Signal Preference for Advance Information about Upcoming Rewards." *Neuron* 63(1): 119–126.

Brown, K. W., and Ryan, R. M. 2003. "The Benefits of Being Present: Mindfulness and its Role in Psychological Well-Being." *Journal of Personality and Social Psychology* 84(4): 822–848.

Butler, E.A., Egloff, B., Erickson, E.A., Gross, J.J., Smith, N.C., and Wilhelm, F.H. 2003. "The Social Consequences of Expressive Suppression." *Emotion* 3(1): 48-67.

Cacioppo, J. T., and Patrick, B. 2008. *Loneliness: Human Nature and the Need for Social Connection*. New York: W. W. Norton.

Camerer, C., Loewenstein, G., and Prelec, D. 2005. "Neuroeconomics: How Neuroscience Can Inform Economics." *Journal of Economic Literature* 43(1): 6–94.

Coghill, R. C., McHaffie, J. G., and Yen, Y. 2003. "Neural Correlates of Inter-Individual Differences in the Subjective Experience of Pain." *Proceedings of the National Academy of Sciences, USA* 100: 8538–8542.

Creswell, J. D., Way, B. M., Eisenberger, N. I., and Lieberman, M. D. 2007. "Neural Correlates of Dispositional Mindfulness During Affect Labelling." *Psychosomatic Medicine* 69: 560–565.

DeAngelis, T., ed. 2008. "Bricker's International Directory 2009: Executive Education and Development Programs." Lawrenceville, NJ: Peterson's.

Dempster, C., and Moran, J. 2007. *EDS case study. Presented at Conference Board Executive Coaching Summit*, New York City, January.

Dive, B. 2008. *The Accountable Leader: Developing Effective Leadership through Managerial Accountability*. London: Kogan Page.

Editorial: Connecting the dots. 2009. *Nature Neuroscience* 12(2): 99.

Farb, N. A. S., Segal, Z. V., Mayberg, H., Bean, J., McKeon, D., Fatima, Z., and Anderson, A. K. 2007. "Attending to the Present: Mindfulness Meditation Reveals Distinct Neural Modes of Self-Reference." *Social Cognitive Affective Neuroscience* 2: 313–322.

Fredrickson, B. L. 2001. "The Role of Positive Emotions in Positive Psychology: The Broaden-and-Build Theory of Positive Emotions." *American Psychologist* 56: 218–226.

Gordon, E. 2008. "Neuroleadership and Integrative Neuroscience: "It's About Validation Stupid!"" *NeuroLeadership Journal* 1: 71–80.

Green, C. H. 2007. "Is Neuroleadership More Than Reinventing Wheels?" *Trust Matters Blog*, Trusted Advisor Associates website (July 26). Accessed August 13, 2009. http://trustedadvisor.com/trustmatters/184/Is-NeuroLeadership-More-Than-Reinventing-Wheels.

Hassed, C. 2008. "Mindfulness, Well-Being, and Performance." *NeuroLeadership Journal* 1: 53–60.

Heath, C., and Heath, D. 2007. *Made to Stick: Why Some Ideas Survive and Others Die*. New York: Random House.

Hsu, M., Bhatt, M., Adolphs, R., Tranel, D., and Camerer, C. F. 2005. "Neural Systems responding to Degrees of Uncertainty in Human Decision Making." *Science* 310: 1681–1683.

Jung-Beeman, M., Collier, A., and Kounios, J. 2008. "How Insight Happens: Learning from the Brain." *NeuroLeadership Journal* 1: 20–25.

Kabat-Zinn, J. 2008. *Clinical Handbook of Mindfulness*. London: Springer.

Knoblich, G., Ohlsson, S., Haider, H., and Rhenius, D. 1999. "Constraint Relaxation and Chunk Decomposition in Insight Problem Solving." *Journal of Experimental Psychology: Learning, Memory, and Cognition* 25(6): 1534–1555.

Kounios, J., Frymiare, J. L., Bowden, E. M., Fleck, J. I., Subramaniam, K., Parrish, T. B., and Jung-Beeman, M. 2006. "The Prepared Mind: Neural Activity Prior to Problem Presentation Predicts Solution by Sudden Insight." *Psychological Science* 17: 882–890.

Lieberman, M., and Eisenberger, N. 2008. "The Pains and Pleasures of Social Life: A Social Cognitive Neuroscience Approach." *NeuroLeadership Journal* 1: 38-43.

Maxwell, J. C. 2007. *The 21 Irrefutable Laws of Leadership: Follow Them and People Will Follow You*. 10th ed. New York: Thomas Nelson.

Miller, G. 2008. "Neuroimaging: Don't be Seduced by the Brain." *Science* 320(5882): 1413.

Moran, J. 2007. Coaching Leaders to be Coaches at EDS. Global Business and Organizational Excellence 26(6): 55–62.

Ochsner, K. N. 2008a. "Staying Cool Under Pressure: Insights from Social Cognitive Neuroscience and their Implications for Self and Society." *NeuroLeadership Journal* 1: 26–32.

Ochsner, K. N. 2008b. Interview filmed at Ochsner's home in early 2008.

Ochsner, K. N., and Gross, J. J. 2005. "The Cognitive Control of Emotion. Trends in Cognitive." *Sciences* 9(5): 242–249.

Ochsner, K. N., and Lieberman, M. D. 2001. "The Emergence of Social Cognitive Neuroscience." *American Psychologist* 56: 717–734.

Reader comments. 2007. "The Business Brain in Close-Up: Can Neuroscience Offer Insights into the 'Soft" Art of Leadership?" *BusinessWeek* (July 22). Accessed August 13, 2009. http://www.businessweek.com/magazine/content/07_30/b4043084.htm.

Ringleb, A., and Rock, D. 2008. "The Emerging Field of Neuroleadership." *NeuroLeadership Journal* 1: 3–19.

Rock, D. 2008a. Presentation at Conference Board ROI Summit. Accessed August 13, 2009. http://www. conference-board.org/conferences/conference.cfm?id=1636.

Rock, D. 2008b. Presentation at Conference Board Summits. Accessed August 13, 2009. http://www.conferenceboard.org/conferences/conference.cfm?id=1636.

Rock, D. 2008c. "SCARF: A Brain-Based Model for Collaborating with and Influencing Others." *NeuroLeadership Journal* 1: 44–52.

Rock, D. 2009a. *Your Brain at Work*: Strategies for Overcoming Distraction, Regaining Focus, and Working Smarter All Day Long. New York: HarperBusiness.

Rock, D. 2009b. "Managing with the Brain in Mind." *StrategyBbusiness Magazine* 56: 58–67.

Rock, D., and Donde, R. 2008. "Driving Organizational Change with Internal Coaching Programs: Part one and Part two." *Industrial and Commercial Training* 40(1): 10–18.

Rock, D., and Schwartz, J.M. 2006. "The Neuroscience of Leadership." *Strategy and Business Magazine* 43(2): 2-10.

Rost, J. C. 1993. *Leadership for the 21st Century*. Westport, CT: Praeger.

Siegel, D. J. 2007. *The Mindful Brain: Reflection and Attunement in the Cultivation of Well-Being*. New York: W. W. Norton.

Slater, R. 2002. *29 Leadership Secrets from Jack Welch*. New York: McGraw-Hill.

Snook, S. A. 2007. "Leader(ship) Development." *Harvard Business School Case Note*. http://www.hbsp.harvard.edu.

Subramaniam, K., Kounios, J., Parrish, T. B., and Jung-Beeman, M. 2009. "A Brain Mechanism for Facilitation of Insight by Positive Affect." *Journal of Cognitive Neuroscience* 21: 415–432.

Tang, Y. Y., and Posner, M. I. 2008. "The Neuroscience of Mindfulness." *NeuroLeadership Journal* 1: 33–37.

Thomas, R. J. 2008. *Crucibles of Leadership: How to Learn from Experience to Become a Great Leader*. Cambridge, MA: Harvard Business School Press.

Uddin, L. Q., Iacoboni, M., Lange, C., and Keenan, J. P. 2007. "The Self and Social Cognition: The Role of Cortical Midline Structures and Mirror Neurons." *Trends in Cognitive Sciences* 11(4): 153–157.

Young, R. J. 2008. *The Five Essential Leadership Questions: Living with Passion, Leading through Trust*. Charlotte, NC: Keane.

3. Neuroleadership in 2011 and 2012

Dr. Al H. Ringleb and Dr. David Rock and Chris Ancona

Al H. Ringleb, Director, CIMBA, Asolo, Italy
Cofounder, NeuroLeadership Institute; Editor, *NeuroLeadership Journal*
ringleb@cimba.it

David Rock, CEO, NeuroLeadership Group, New York, USA
Faculty, CIMBA; Cofounder, NeuroLeadership Institute; Editor, *NeuroLeadership Journal*
david@neuroleadership.com

Chris Ancona, Senior Research Associate, NeuroLeadership Labs
Faculty, CIMBA
ancona@cimba.it

Introduction

Neuroscience is one of the fastest growing areas of interest in contemporary science. As it has from its inception, the NeuroLeadership Institute continues to work both in organizing and disseminating neuroscience findings applicable to the effective practice of leadership and in supporting practitioners in their personal and leadership development efforts. Within the NeuroLeadership Institute, enrollment in its education programs, institute membership, summit attendance, requests for institute and summit materials, and participation in local chapters worldwide are following a similar growth pattern. Outside the institute, research scientists continue to publish both scholarly works in the interest of expanding the field of knowledge and practitioner works in the interest of expanding its field of use and application.

Due in large measure to rapidly advancing technology that both defines and supports brain-imaging research and allows its seemingly instantaneous distribution, practitioners can easily be overwhelmed by the breadth and depth of insights that seem to arrive on a daily basis. As of early 2012, more than 60 labs in the United States alone focused on social or affective neuroscience, a field from which neuroleadership draws heavily.

To assist in that specific regard, this chapter looks back over 2011 and 2012 and reflects on neuroscience and social-psychology research relevant to neuroleadership and its practitioners. In reviewing the available research, and guided by suggestions from the scientists, we will categorize the research based on the four domains set out in the initial *NeuroLeadership Journal* (Ringleb and Rock 2008): decision making and problem solving, regulating emotions, collaborating with others, and facilitating change.

In selecting research for inclusion, the following basic criteria were applied to the extent possible: significance to the field of neuroleadership; likelihood of significantly expanding or creating research linkages between neuroscience and the practices of leadership and leadership development; impacts on current thinking as driven by social-science research; and, perhaps most importantly, relevance to the interests of practitioners in this growing field.

Neuroscience is one of the fastest-growing areas of interest in contemporary science.

Decision-making and problem-solving domain

In 2010 the decision-making and problem-solving domain was broadened to encompass the neural bases of the processes and procedures a leader uses to produce results (Ringleb, Rock, and Conser 2010).

As noted by practitioners, this delineation closely accords with the *do* (or *doing*) component of the generally accepted Be-Know-Do leadership model (Hesselbein and Shinseki 2004). This change also provided a more consistent representation of what this domain means to the fields of both neuroleadership and traditional leadership, defined, at a minimum, as groups making decisions and solving problems in the *doing* sense.

Neuroscience teaches us to appreciate the brain-efficiency gains provided by express (versus implicit) processes...

Given the highly complex social environments in which leaders must operate, many of a leader's most important decisions are additionally dependent on the concomitant choices of others (Rilling and Sanfey 2011). In this sense, this broader definition serves to distinguish neuroleadership from the fields of neuroeconomics and neuromarketing, both of which are more focused on how an individual makes decisions. In contrast, neuroleadership research (and much of social psychology and neuroscience) is more likely to make explicit efforts to measure rather than control for SCARF (Status, Certainty, Autonomy, Relatedness, Fairness) affects inherent in effective leadership's social interactions.

Decision making and SCARF

Neuroscience teaches us to appreciate the brain-efficiency gains provided by explicit (versus implicit) processes (Herbig, Muller, and Petrovic 2007) in overcoming the working limitations of the prefrontal cortex (PFC) (Halford, Cowan, and Andrews 2007) by tempering negative and promoting positive SCARF affects in social interactions (Rock 2008). The leader's objective in using express *doing* processes and procedures is to increase overall organizational engagement and employee performance and well-being (Rock and Tang 2009). Difficult issues eliciting conflict between emotion and reason (Frith and Singer 2008) addressed in teams through the use of implicit, unstructured processes and procedures are highly susceptible to emotional contagion (Johnson 2008). Those emotional contagions arouse "SCARF emotions" and impose measureable negative consequences on limited team cognitive resources. Increasingly, traditional neuroscience and social-psychology research are finding the management of SCARF emotions to be an important determinant of the success of collaborative activities (e.g., Li, Liang, and Michael 2010; Rilling and Sanfey 2011). At the NeuroLeadership Labs, we have consistently observed reductions of 50 percent and more in group emotion (as measured by aggregate individual skin conductance) when we compare group performance on statistically similar decision tasks, the first completed without an explicit process (using any approach the group chooses) and the second completed with an explicit process (Kepner-Tregoe's PSDM rational process tools), all of which we attribute to team control over SCARF emotions brought about by the use of explicit versus implicit process.

Neuroscience and social-psychology research in 2011 continued to implicitly highlight the functional simplicity of SCARF...

Neuroscience and social-psychology research in 2011 continued to implicitly highlight the functional simplicity of SCARF and support its applications in collaborative *doing* activities, among other applications and uses. Traditional research conducted in the decision-making domain typically makes use of models based on game theory, with decision makers being studied as they interact with one another (Neumann and Morgenstern 1947).

The most commonly used research models are the Prisoner's Dilemma, the Trust Game, the Ultimatum Game, the Dictator Game, and the Iowa Gambling Task. In addition to these models in their classic designs, a number of recent studies have employed creative adaptations to examine other aspects of social interaction, such as social conformity (Klucharev et al. 2009), norm-abiding social behavior (Spitzer et al. 2007), revenge and altruistic punishment (De Quervain et al. 2004; Singer et al. 2006), and reputation management (Izuma et al. 2008). Taken together, the characteristics being studied—trust, fairness, altruism, social conformity, norm-abiding social behavior, and others—map comfortably and consistently into NeuroLeadership's SCARF® model.

Sleep-deprived people may make risky decisions based on too much optimism.

For example, Nguyen et al. (2011) used the Ultimatum Game to ferret out differences between the "rational" and "irrational" response patterns in the game. In considering a wide variety of demographic (age, gender, education), cognitive (intelligence, attention/working memory, speed, language, memory, executive functions), and personality ("Big Five," positive affect, negative affect) variables, they found that the personality variables of trust (for the "rational" response) and negative affect such as anger and contempt (for the "rational" response)—SCARF's status, relatedness, and fairness—were the only variables that differentiated the two response patterns. Demographic and cognitive factors did not differ between rational and irrational players. The study accentuates the importance of affect in our understanding of individual differences in decision making and other *doing* processes and procedures—what we at the NeuroLeadership Labs refer to as individual differences in "SCARF profiles." Such a profile provides insights into an individual's hypersensitivities and suggests the situations and circumstances that might lead to unproductive and unhealthy choices.

Researchers are also confirming that a variety of factors can influence SCARF sensitivities, and thus influence an individual's ability to make reasoned decisions. Such factors include exercise, sleep, relationships, and mindfulness, among others (see the discussion of the Healthy Mind Platter in the facilitating-change domain section). Regarding the impact of sleep, Venkatraman et al. (2011) used fMRI data to show that a night of sleep deprivation leads to increased brain activity in those brain regions that assess positive outcomes and decreased activity in brain regions that process negative outcomes. In other words, sleep-deprived people may make risky decisions based on too much optimism. Participants in the study tended to make decisions that emphasized monetary gain and were less likely to make choices that reduced loss. One of the study's authors, Professor Jessica Payne, presented these and other findings at the NeuroLeadership Summit in San Francisco. We will discuss more about her work in subsequent sections.

The NeuroLeadership Summit provided a forum for after-session discussions about the role of individual values in the SCARF model and ethical decision making. Some discussion arose about the need for a sixth category in the model to account explicitly for values, while others asserted that values were accounted for implicitly in the current categories. The discussion offered a rich opportunity to raise some of the interesting issues discussed at the 2010 Boston Summit by Professor Joshua Greene.

Researchers are also confirming that a variety of factors can influence SCARF sensitivities, and thus influence an individual's ability to make reasoned decisions.

In looking at the role of emotions in ethical decision making, a team of German researchers considered the effect of stress on moral decision making (Starck et al. 2010). The study compared performances between a stress-induced group of 20 participants and a controlled second group of 20 participants on moral-decision-making tasks in which everyday moral dilemmas were described. Consistent with the notion that values may be implicitly accounted for in the current SCARF categories, the results showed that the two groups did not differ significantly in everyday moral decision making. However, and consistent with the notion that emotion in decision making is important, the study did show an association between an individual's cortisol stress response and egotistical decision making in high emotional situations.

In another interesting study on moral decision making using fMRI data, Decety, Michalska, and Kinzler (2012) showed that an individual's moral responses to similar situations change as they age. According to the authors, the different responses between children and adults correlate with the various stages of neurodevelopment. As the brain ages, it becomes better equipped to make reasoned judgments and integrate an understanding of the mental states of others with the outcome of their actions. In the discussion of the collaborating-with-others domain, and consistent with this finding, we will take a look at interesting research showing that the development of our social-awareness circuitry begins in infancy and that its development seems to occur in advance of our self-awareness circuitry.

Decision making, emotions, and emotion regulation

Decision research in economics, business, psychology, and neuroscience now readily accepts that emotions play a significant role in decision making. Several neurological theories have been developed to explain the emotion–decision-making relationship, including the somatic marker (Lawrence et al. 2009), risk-as-feeling (Loewenstein et al. 2001), anticipatory affect (Kuhnen and Knutson 2005), and, from marketing, net emotional response strength (Hansen and Christensen 2007) theories. Much of the controversy among the theories centers on the neuroanatomy of the decision-making process, with somatic marker theory's more holistic analysis (Reimann and Bechara 2010) arguably a better fit with SCARF and current neuroleadership thinking on emotion and its management.

Specifically, somatic marker theory asserts that decision making incorporates a multitude of brain areas involved in emotion (amygdala, ventromedial PFC) and memory (hippocampus, dorsolateral PFC). With the amygdala long recognized for its involvement in emotion, both Gospic et al. (2011) and Gupta et al. (2011) looked to explore more deeply the role of the amygdala in decision making, and to differentiate its contributions from those of other functionally connected neural regions. In Gospic et al. (2011), the research team used a benzodiazepine treatment to damp down amygdala activity and thus participant response to somatic marker cues as they played the Ultimatum Game.

In Gupta et al. (2011), the research team used patients with amygdala damage who were known to lack autonomic responses to reward and punishment and, consequently, could not utilize somatic marker cues to guide future decision making. Somatic marker cues include emotion-related signals, such as changes in heart rate, blood pressure, gut motility, and glandular secretion, that assist cognitive processes in implementing decisions. Using the Iowa Gambling Task model as a laboratory proxy for the real world, they observed deficiencies in decision making in patients with bilateral amygdala damage consistent with the real-world difficulties they were experiencing.

The research teams theorized that the amygdala is part of an impulsive, habit-type system that triggers emotional responses to immediate outcomes. Implicit in the application of these research findings is the importance of either express process and/or emotional-regulation strategies (such as mindfulness, discussed below with regard to decision making and more generally under facilitating change) in situations where emotion and habitual responses to it may lead to unproductive or unhealthy choices.

> *Decision research in economics, business, psychology, and neuroscience now readily accepts that emotions play a significant role in decision making.*

In 2010, several studies added to our understanding of "collective intelligence." Social psychologists found convincing evidence of a collective intelligence factor (as opposed to the psychologist's general intelligence applied to individuals) that seemingly explains group performance differences (Woolley et al. 2010). One of the study's authors, Dr. Alex Pentland, explained at the 2010 Boston NeuroLeadership Summit that while collective intelligence is not strongly correlated with the average or maximum individual intelligence of group members, it is correlated with the average social sensitivity of group members (the ability to read and understand the emotion of others). Groups with higher social sensitivity shared criticism constructively, were more open-minded, were less autocratic, and had leaders who more effectively managed conversational turn-taking—in neuroLleadership terms, they undertook express efforts to control negative SCARF influences.

Taking as a given the importance of social sensitivity to effective group success, the MIT study raises interesting questions for practitioners: Is team success a function of social sensitivity for the purpose of controlling unproductive emotion? Could a well-defined, express process or procedure play a similar, more consistent role in the control of group emotions? The distinction may be more fundamental than is apparent in that the study's participants were given a well-defined set of tasks to perform. The answers are important in light of the authors' hypothesis that a collective intelligence test—in essence, a test for social sensitivity—might be a strong predictor of a sales or top-management team's long-term effectiveness. Consider the Mojzisch and Schulz-Hard (2010) study noted in the 2010 review. Their study demonstrated that, in the case of unstructured decision-making processes that opened with team members sharing initial preferences, team members pay less attention to relevant information during subsequent group discussion and thereby risk reaching suboptimal decisions. Avni-Babad (2011) showed us that if the process involved is "routine," group members are more likely to feel comfortable, confident, and safe—again, neuroleadership terms, a positive SCARF environment.

Groups with higher social sensitivity shared criticism constructively, were more open-minded, were less autocratic...

In an interesting fMRI study, Reverberi et al. (2012) showed that the parts of the brain used differ depending on the type of reasoning involved in the process. If we take this result as a given, what can we say about the emotional state of the team as it wrestles with the uncertainty as to which rational-process thinking tools to use: is it a decision (choice), problem (cause), strategy (visioning), situation appraisal (information gathering), or potential problem (planning)? Reverberi et al. suggest that each thinking process may have its own reasonably independent circuitry. Is it feasible to hypothesize that such an emotional state brought about by explicit process would eliminate the wrestling (thereby firmly moving the brain from a "mentalizing" to an "analyzing" state, a concept discussed in detail under the collaboration domain), calm the brain, and lead to greater social sensitivity and, derivatively, greater productivity? The implications for the application of this line of research make the resolution of this question fundamental.

Participants who successfully used cognitive emotion regulation made fewer risky choices...

Consistent with the growing interest in emotion across disciplines generally, a number of studies considered the impact of emotion on decision making and on varying efforts to manage those emotions. Martin and Delgado (2011) investigated the efficacy of cognitive emotion regulation strategies during decision making under risk. Prior studies had largely focused on the efficacy of such strategies in reward-expectation environments (e.g., Tom et al. 2007). The research team found that participants who successfully used cognitive emotion regulation made fewer risky choices in comparison with trials where decisions were made in the absence of such regulation.

On the basis of extensive observations of equity, bond, and derivative traders in the City of London, Fenton-O'Creevy et al. (2011) found that high-performing traders made greater and more effective use of both their intuitions (a notion consistent with somatic marker theory) and their emotion-regulation strategies than did their lower-performing colleagues. The study provides important insights into the role of emotion and emotion management in what would seemingly be a highly rational profession. In a somewhat related study, Bollen, Mao, and Zeng (2011) found that "public mood" (defined as, in essence, a relatively long-lasting emotional state held in common by the public) was a reasonably accurate predictor of the stock market. The research team made creative use of the content from a large number of Twitter feeds to develop its "public mood" measure. The study is supportive of the notion that SCARF engagement environments are both scalable and similar in their impacts on productivity and well-being across a wide variety of situations.

A number of studies looked at a specific emotion and its impact on decision efficacy. For example, Thiel, Connelly, and Griffith (2011) explored the relationship between anger and ethical decision making. Kligyte et al. (2009) had found that incidental anger negatively influenced ethical decision making. The study found that angry individuals were less likely to thoroughly evaluate ethical dilemmas, more likely to make punitive judgments of others, and increasingly deceptive in making ethical choices.

Thiel et al. (2011) observed that the cognitive evaluations made by angry individuals during the decision-making process seemed to resemble anger appraisals identified in the appraisal literature (e.g., Kuppens et al. 2007; according to the appraisal theory of emotions, how we feel about a certain situation is determined by our appraisal or evaluation of the event).

The study showed that appraisals of certainty are the primary driving mechanism behind the negative relationship between anger and ethical decision making. Certainty appraisals led to less application of ethical-decision-making promotional strategies and more unethical social motives. Such appraisals cause an individual to feel certain about who caused the event, why the event occurred, and the future outcomes directly or indirectly related to the affective event.

Certainty appraisals led to less application of ethical-decision-making promotional strategies and more unethical social motives.

The study sheds light on how certain emotional states can disrupt ethical decision making through the underlying appraisals and social motives, suggesting the need to focus efforts in training initiatives that address these factors and provide strategies for overcoming them.

Decision making and gender

Several interesting studies looked to the neural bases for gender differences in decision making, either by experimental design or as an observation of research intended for other purposes. In the previously mentioned study by Gupta et al. (2011), which looked to explore the role of the amygdala in decision making, they found evidence for a differing interaction between males and females and laterality of amygdala functioning: unilateral damage to the right amygdala results in greater deficits in decision making and social behavior in men, while left amygdala damage seems to be more detrimental for women.

Gender differences in behavior are associated with differences in activity in the insula and dorsal striatum, the brain regions involved in computing risk and preparing to take action.

Lighthall et al. (2011) found that under stress, men and women respond differently to risky decision making. Under stress, males take more risk and females take less risk. These gender differences in behavior are associated with differences in activity in the insula and dorsal striatum, the brain regions involved in computing risk and preparing to take action. Interestingly, when stress was absent, their behavior and brain activation was more similar. The authors assert that men and women faced with difficult decisions might improve the outcome by waiting until a stressful situation has passed—that is, until the emotion has subsided. Again, we see the same potential result coming from the use of express process and/or emotion-regulation strategies. One possible practical implication of this finding is that practitioners may want to recommend mixed teams in situations where the issue being confronted carries with it significant emotion.

Neuroscience and social psychology continue to develop and define the relationship between self-awareness and self-regulation...

Decision making, self-awareness, self-regulation, and mindfulness

Neuroscience and social psychology continue to develop and define the relationship between self-awareness and self-regulation, as well as the influential impact that mindfulness can have on strengthening that relationship. With regard to self-awareness, Dunn et al. (2010) investigated the way interoception (the ability to detect subtle changes in somatic marker signals, including muscles, skin, joints, and viscera) shapes emotional experience and intuitive decision making. Interestingly, the research team demonstrated that the more accurately participants could track their heartbeat, the stronger was the observed link between their heart-rate reactions and their subjective arousal ratings of emotional images. In other words, the more self-aware the participants (as measured by their ability to sense and interpret their somatic marker signals), the greater was their ability to assess their emotions and predict their cognitive consequences. In building on this finding, the group found that increasing interoception ability either helped or hindered adaptive intuitive decision making, depending on whether the anticipatory bodily signals generated favored advantageous or disadvantageous choices (a result consistent with prior studies looking into the accuracy of intuitive decision making; see, for example, Myers 2004; Shiv et al. 2005)—in other words, to the extent an intuitive decision relies on more than an awareness of physiology.

Over the past five years, self-regulation has garnered more and more attention from both scientists and practitioners. Here, we will limit our discussion to self-regulation as it impacts decision making and other *doing* processes, with a more detailed discussion on this important topic in the section on the facilitating-change domain. An interesting study in that regard involved the ego-depletion aspect of self-regulation and its impact on decision making. Within the Ego Depletion or Limited Resource Model, leading self-regulation scholars argue that self-regulation is a finite resource (e.g., Hagger et al. 2010). In the context of this model, Danziger, Levav, and Avnaim-Pesso (2011) examined more than 1,100 judicial rulings to see if extraneous factors beyond legal reasoning were influencing the decisions. They found that the percentage of favorable rulings drops gradually from about 65 percent to nearly 0 percent within each decision session and then returns abruptly to about 65 percent after a break. Given that a meal was served at each of the breaks, the research team was cautious about asserting this was the cause for the decision pattern (the effect of glucose on mental resource replenishment as the Ego Depletion Model would assert) or whether simply the period of rest resulted in the restoration of the judges' mental resources.

Still, on the basis of the data available, the study suggests that decisions can be swayed by extraneous variables, most arguably when they carry emotion, which perhaps should have no bearing on the choices being made. Again, as we have argued previously, with decisions in this case seemingly driven by the idiosyncratic process of each judge and therefore open to varying extraneous influences affecting emotion and emotion regulation, would the result be different if the decision-making process were expressed with criteria open and understood by all for the purpose of holding such influences constant? Or perhaps the judges could engage an emotion-regulation strategy?

Leading self-regulation scholars argue that self-regulation is a finite resource...

In that specific regard, Alfonso et al. (2011) examined the effect of mindfulness training on the decision-making competence of polysubstance abusers (defined as individuals diagnosed with an addiction who have used at least three different drug types indiscriminately over a 12-month period). The study enrolled 18 participants in a mindfulness program and compared them with a control group of 16 participants who undertook standard treatment. The results showed that individuals enrolled in the mindfulness program significantly improved their performance on a variety of neuropsychological measures, including decision making as measured by performance on the Iowa Gambling Task.

Clearly, and as we shall see in the next section, research to date on the use and application of emotion-regulation tools and techniques strongly suggests practitioners consider their inclusion—and particularly when coupled with mindfulness meditation—in personal and leadership-development interventions.

Emotion-regulation domain

Effective leadership is in large part defined by the leader's ability to perceive, identify, understand, and successfully manage both his or her emotions and the emotions of others. Effective leaders harness and direct the power of emotion to build trust and improve follower satisfaction, morale, and motivation, and thus enhance overall organizational effectiveness (Rock and Tang 2009; Riggio and Reichard 2008). In prior reviews, we considered the neuroscience-validated techniques of mindfulness (Farb et al. 2007), meditation (Tang et al. 2007), labeling (Lieberman et al. 2007), and reappraisal (Ray et al. 2005) as vehicles for leaders to gain greater personal control over emotionality. Given its significant potential in leadership development and intervention strategies, it is not surprising that emotion regulation has garnered considerable interest among both practitioners and researchers. At the center of much of this research is Professor James Gross, who shared many of his insights at the 2011 NeuroLeadership Summit in San Francisco.

Effective leaders harness and direct the power of emotion to build trust and improve follower satisfaction, morale, and motivation...

Research on emotion

As we discussed at length in the 2010 review, it has been nearly 60 years since Skinner (1953; 1974) declared that emotion was on the list of fictional causes to which an individual's behavior is commonly ascribed. Over the past two decades, leadership scholars have expressly recognized the importance of emotion and emotion regulation in effective leadership and have begun to define its core elements and components (Gooty et al. 2010; Rajah, Song, and Arvey 2011), with this interest paralleling that in neuroscience and social psychology (Izard 2010). Research studies in neuroscience and social psychology continue to provide leadership-development practitioners with insights into the necessary tools and techniques to make emotion and emotion regulation integral components of consistent, effectual intervention and development strategies. Interestingly, virtually all disciplines are confronting research obstacles in the form of competing models and differing terminology.

The ability to process facial expressions assists in the regulation of behavior and social perception...

Consistent with Heatherton (2011) and the NeuroLeadership Lab's Social Brain Theory of Leadership (discussed as part of the collaborating domain), Niedenthal and Brauer (2012) provide important insights into the fundamental importance of emotion processing for successful social living. Importantly, the authors note its importance regardless of the size of the social unit being examined—from dyads to large social groups. In looking to the question, "What are human emotions for?" the authors assert that the ability to process facial expressions assists in the regulation of behavior and social perception in "a dense and efficient way" and is thus a social necessity (as we see in the collaborating domain discussion, this ability develops in infancy and more rapidly than self-awareness).

Vicarious emotions—where one individual feels an emotion because he or she observes another individual experiencing an emotion or observes the other individual in an emotionally evocative situation—play a fundamental role in learning. The authors note that both neuroscience and social-psychology research are finding that group emotions and group-based emotions seem to serve the more abstract goals of group cohesion and collective action. Because group emotions can be triggered by powerful leaders and generated in increasing intensity over time, they are considered an important focus of future research.

Our growing ability to measure emotion has elevated its importance in a wide variety of disciplines, including the academic disciplines of leadership, management, and organizational behavior. As to emotion and the state of leadership science, Gooty et al. (2010) and Rajah, Song, and Arvey (2011) provided an in-depth overview of the progress that has been made in bringing emotion and emotion regulation to the forefront of our understanding of leadership. Similarly, from the perspective of neuroscience and social psychology, Gross and Barrett (2011) tell us that in 1990 only 4 publications contained the phrase "emotion regulation," while by 2005 some 671 publications contained the phrase—a more than 150-fold increase in citations over a 15-year period, clearly showing the growing popularity of this topic. Still, it came as somewhat of a surprise to us that the definitions and models of emotion, emotion generation, and emotion regulation vary from discipline to discipline, or perhaps more precisely, from research purpose to research purpose (Niedenthal and Brauer 2012). This lack of consensus is needlessly inhibiting the pace of research efforts in this area of growing importance to practitioners (Izard 2010).

Our growing ability to measure emotion has elevated its importance in a wide variety of disciplines...

With specific regard to the concept of "emotion regulation," Thompson (2011) argues that it should be studied not in terms of uniquely dedicated neurobiological or executive cognitive processes, but rather as multifaceted influences on emotion that assume a regulatory function depending on the context. Gross and Barrett (2011) argue that disagreements about the nature of the processes that regulate emotion and whether such processes are meaningfully distinct from those that are typically considered to constitute emotion reside in the different ways in which emotion is scientifically defined. More specifically, it depends on the scientific perspectives taken on emotion generation and regulation. Through a thorough review of the literature, the authors showed that four reasonably distinct models of emotion have evolved and that emotion regulation has flourished under two of those models (Basic and Appraisal) and has been limited or nonexistent under the other two (Psychological Construction and Social Construction). At the NeuroLeadership Labs, we find ourselves more aligned with the former, but this divergence in opinion is certainly slowing the development and integration of emotion into the leadership, management, and organizational-behavior literature. As summarized by Gross and Barrett (2011, 14–15):

> We believe that once differences in perspective are made explicit, it is more likely the researchers and theoreticians from diverse perspectives will be able to surmount terminological differences and join together in addressing shared concerns...We believe that this effort must be extended to the many other disciplines which have so much to contribute to our understanding of emotion and other mental states, including linguistics, philosophy, history, communications, sociology, anthropology, cognitive science, physiology, economics, neuroeconomics, and computer science. Acknowledging and respecting differences in terminology and perspective is a critical first step, and the sooner we join together in shared purpose the better.

As if to drive this point home, in introducing a special issue of *Emotion Review*, Greene (2011) focuses our attention on the scientific study of morality. You may recall that Professor Joshua Greene was a speaker at the 2010 NeuroLeadership Summit in Boston. He notes that moral psychology has been influenced by two dramatic changes, the first being that it has become broadly interdisciplinary (including many of the disciplines listed in the quote above) and the second being that emotion now plays a central role in moral psychology research. Again, emotion and its measurement are moving to center stage.

Despite these obstacles, the body of research on emotion is growing. In an interesting study highlighting the consequences of deficiencies in emotion regulation, Aldwin et al. (2011) conclude that men who experience persistently moderate or high levels of stressful life events over a number of years have a 50 percent higher mortality rate. The study used longitudinal data surveying almost 1,000 middle-class and working-class men for an 18-year period, from 1985 to 2003.

Keeping your major stress events to a minimum, being married, and having a glass of wine every night is the secret to a longer life.

All the men in the study were picked because they were in good health when they first signed up to be part of an aging study in the 1960s. Those in the low-stress group experienced an average of two or fewer major life events in a year, compared with an average of three for the moderate group and up to six for the high-stress group. One of the study's most surprising findings was that the mortality risk was similar for the moderate- and the high-stress groups. The study also showed that married men and moderate drinkers lived longest, leading the authors to conjecture that keeping your major stress events to a minimum, being married, and having a glass of wine every night is the secret to a longer life. The "keeping your major stress events to a minimum" criterion leads to our discussion of emotion-regulation strategies. Importantly in this regard, McRae et al. (2012) found a positive relationship between reappraisal ability, reappraisal frequency, working memory capacity, and well-being.

Emotion-regulation strategies

In reviewing leadership research over the past decade, scholars have begun to place increased emphasis on emotional reasoning over intelligence (see, e.g., Gilkey, Caceda, and Kilts 2010)—often reaching contradictory results (Gooty et al. 2010) in large measure due to terminology conflicts similar to those undermining research efforts in neuroscience and psychology (Gross and Barrett 2011). In looking at the literature, two general themes seem to be forming: a focus on "self issues" (leader emotional competence and emotion management, particularly as it relates to stress management) and "social issues" (mirrored emotional contagion and workplace outcomes). In relation to the neuroscience and social-psychology literature, and consistent with the way we have mapped those topics into neuroleadership domains, the "social issues" would be discussed in the collaborating domain, while "self issues" are covered in this, the emotion-regulation domain. Due in large measure to differences in research design, the principal social-science experimental design used in leadership studies has typically focused on observed consequences. With specific regard to emotion regulation, for example, the social-science research is more likely to look into the consequences of leader-suppressed and leader-faked emotions on followers, as opposed to neuroscience and social psychology's interest in the effectiveness of the emotion-regulation strategies the leader or followers actually employ, with effectiveness measured using brain imaging technology. While often reaching similar conclusions, observing and understanding the neural basis for a particular activity provides valuable insights into the complexity of human behavior: what else is lighting up when...?

Traditional leadership research tells us that emotion regulation and interactions between leaders and followers may affect the relationship, as well as job satisfaction...

To illustrate, traditional leadership research tells us that emotion regulation and interactions between leaders and followers may affect the relationship, as well as job satisfaction (Glasø and Einarsen 2008); followers tend to recall more negative emotional displays from leaders and rate them more negatively as a consequence (Dasborough 2006); followers interpret leaders' intentions as more sincere when the leader is in a positive mood (Dasborough and Ashkanasy 2002); and leaders are more positively rated when their facial expressions are congruent with the message being delivered (Newcombe and Ashkanasy 2002).

In neuroleadership, the focus is more on looking to neuroscience and social-psychology research to assist the leader in understanding the most effective means of bringing about that positive mood, both for the leader and the followers.

Emotional expressiveness, defined as the ability to convey emotional messages to others, is an important skill/behavior for successful leaders...

For example, Stoeber and Janssen (2011) found that positive reframing, acceptance, and humor (see also Samson and Gross 2012) are the most effective coping strategies for people dealing with failure. The least effective were using social support, denial, venting, behavioral disengagement, and self-blame. The study found that positive reframing (seeing things in a more positive light, looking for something good in what happened) was particularly beneficial for individuals high in perfectionistic concerns, a group more likely to perceive and exaggerate failure.

McRae et al. (2011) undertook to see if the motive for emotion generation influences emotion regulation. The intent was to determine whether certain emotion-regulation strategies are more effective when performed on emotions generated in similar ways. In the workplace, emotions can be elicited in a variety of ways, ranging from an unexpected encounter with an angry customer or superior ("bottom-up" emotion generation, influences from the limbic system to higher cortical regions; elicited from perceptions) to conclusions drawn from an interpretation of a social interaction ("top-down" emotion generation, influences from the PFC to the amygdala; elicited by cognitions). The study found that top-down-generated emotions are more successfully down-regulated by a reappraisal than are bottom-up emotions, and that using cognitive reappraisal to decrease bottom-up-generated emotions may even be counterproductive. The study provides important insights for those practitioners actively engaged in creating and implementing intervention strategies to assist in leader development.

Traditional leadership research tells us that emotional expressiveness, defined as the ability to convey emotional messages to others, is an important skill/behavior for successful leaders (Riggio and Reichard 2008). Emotionally expressive leaders are perceived as being both more charismatic and more effective (Groves 2006), and the expression of certain emotions, such as anger, can affect follower processing of social information. Tiedens and Linton (2001) showed that expression of anger increases status, while expression of sadness decreases it. In examining the essence of the former, et al. (2012) found that once individuals have adjusted their attitude toward someone, they are not disturbed by that person's anger the next time it appears. Conversely, when individuals are told to just feel the emotion brought on by the person's anger, they continue to be upset. The social environment, and particularly the workplace, requires people to quickly form contextually appropriate social evaluations. This study suggests that controlled processes, such as reappraisal, can quickly and substantially modulate early evaluative processes in the context of biologically significant social stimuli.

Positive reappraisal and mindfulness appear to serially and mutually enhance one another.

Bridging this domain and the discussion in the section on the change domain, which follows, Garland, Gaylord, and Fredrickson (2011) investigated the relationship between mindfulness and positive reappraisal. In prior reviews we have examined the stress-reductive effects of mindfulness practice (Farb et al. 2007; Tang et al. 2007). In observing more than 300 participants undergoing an eight-week mindfulness-based management course in which some of the participants received both pre- and postinterventions involving positive reappraisal, the authors found that positive reappraisal and mindfulness appear to serially and mutually enhance one another. Again, the study's findings have interesting implications for developing more effective personal-coaching and leadership-intervention strategies.

Growing interest in implicit emotion regulation

Research on emotion regulation has historically focused on effortful (explicit) attempts to alter the course and intensity of emotional responses. Specifically, explicit emotion regulation is defined as those processes that require conscious effort for initiation, demand some level of monitoring during implementation, and are associated with some level of insight and awareness. More recently, researchers have started to describe less effortful and more automatic (implicit) forms of emotion regulation. Implicit processes are believed to be evoked automatically by the stimulus itself, run to completion without monitoring, and can happen without insight and awareness (Gyurak, Gross, and Etkin 2011).

Both forms of regulation are considered necessary for well-being. This basic distinction is presented here in large measure because of potential implications for coaching and leadership-development interventions. Implicit emotion regulation includes explicit emotion-regulation strategies that have become habitual (Gross, Richards, and John 2006), affect labeling (Lieberman et al. 2007), and emotion regulatory goals and values (Schweiger-Gallo et al. 2009), among others.

Research in this area is showing the significance of implicit emotion regulation in psychological adaptation, goal-directed behavior, interpersonal behavior, personality functioning, and mental health (Koole and Rothermund 2011). For example, a study by DeWall et al. (2011) showed that acute social exclusion sets in motion an automatic emotion-regulation process in which positive emotions become highly accessible, which in turn relates to positive mental health. Compared with nonexcluded participants, excluded participants recalled more positive memories from childhood, gave greater weight to positive emotion in their judgments of word similarity, and completed more ambiguous word stems with happy words. As we will see in the discussion of the collaborating domain, the brain makes remarkable adaptations to relieve the anxiety and other social pains associated with social exclusion (real or perceived).

Emotion regulation and gender

Several interesting studies addressed the question, are there gender differences in emotion-regulation strategies? Although asserting that the literature on emotion regulation is likely missing vital information on how men specifically regulate their emotions, Nolen-Hoeksema's (2012) review of the literature on this topic showed that women report using emotion-regulation strategies more than men do. According to the study, women ruminate more than men, which accounts for greater depression and anxiety in women, compared with men; men have a greater tendency to use alcohol to cope, which partially accounts for more alcohol misuse in men than in women. Nolen-Hoeksema and Aldao (2011) showed that the use of emotion-regulation strategies decreases with age, with two notable exceptions: (1) the use of suppression increased with age for women, but not for men; and (2) the use of acceptance did not decrease with age for women.

In a study with implications for implicit emotion regulation, Galli, Wolpe, and Otten (2011) showed that men and women differ in the way they anticipate an unpleasant emotional experience, thereby influencing the effectiveness with which that experience is committed to memory. By measuring electrical brain activity, scientists were able to predict whether an unpleasant image would be remembered, and found that it would be remembered by men but not by women. The authors speculated that on anticipating an unpleasant event, women may spontaneously engage in emotion-regulation strategies to counter the impact of negative emotions.

Excluded participants recalled more positive memories from childhood...

Collaborating-with-others domain

In reviewing the research from 2011 and 2012 in this important domain, we were assisted by an interesting article written by Professor Todd Heatherton (2011). Consistent with the views of the NeuroLeadership Labs, Heatherton provides a detailed discussion of the neural bases of self and self-regulation. Internally, the NeuroLeadership Labs refers to a theory similar to that proffered by Professor Heatherton as the Social Brain Theory of Leadership. According to Heatherton's theory, the human brain had to adapt to a complex social environment to survive, and so it evolved dedicated neural mechanisms acutely sensitive to social context—particularly to any signal (real or perceived) that one's social inclusion was somehow at risk. The neural drivers for controlling oneself to be a good group member imply a need for dedicated neural circuitries to enhance social awareness (mentalizing, theory of mind, mirror neurons, SCARF), threat and reward detection (social pain), self-awareness, and self-regulation. To the brain, survival means acceptance by the social group, with the consistent underperformance of any one of those component circuitries leading to social exclusion and "death." Moderated by self-regulation (research on this important topic is reviewed in the discussion of the facilitating change domain), the adaptive challenges of the social environment include adherence to group values and beliefs and the SCARF elements of Status, Certainty, Autonomy, Relatedness, and Fairness (Rock 2008). In that specific regard, in this domain's discussion, we are largely concerned with research on social awareness and threat- and reward-detection circuitries. An understanding of these critical circuitries can assist practitioners in focusing coaching interventions more specifically and in creating and maintaining engaged work environments more generally.

Social awareness circuitry

Developing research on social awareness strongly suggests that our need to understand the emotions of others may have evolved a neural circuitry more refined than the circuitry dedicated to evaluating our own emotions, our self-awareness circuitry. The authors (Vazire and Carlson 2011) make a compelling case for 360-degree feedback assessments. Additionally, although our first impressions of others seem to vary in accuracy and misperception, research is showing that people do very well at sensing when their first impressions are correct (Biesanz et al. 2011). These and other studies from 2011 suggest that our social-awareness circuitry has demanded the brain's greater attention and thus is more developed than our self-awareness circuitry.

To the brain, survival means acceptance by the social group...

Seemingly consistent with this conclusion but coming from another direction is research that is beginning to suggest we are socially aware well before we are self-aware; that is, our social-awareness circuitry develops sooner and more rapidly than our self-awareness circuitry. The investigations suggesting this conclusion largely involve creative research with infants. Research by Hamlin et al. (2011) showed that from as early as three months, infants prefer a person who helps others over someone who hinders. At the age of eight months, infants learn to judge an action not simply on the basis of whether it helps or harms a person, but also on whether the person deserves it. Research by Lou (2011) indicates that at ten months, babies start to understand another person's thought processes, a skill referred to as mentalizing or having "theory of mind" (see Amodio and Frith 2006). Mentalizing allows people to be aware that other people have emotions and also attempts to understand the context of those emotions. Ultimately, this allows people to empathize with others and predict their judgments or behaviors. The study results indicate that, like adults, even preverbal infants have the ability to consider others' mental states when making inferences about others' actions.

Research is beginning to suggest that we are socially aware well before we are self-aware...

An important tool supporting this social awareness is our ability to read and interpret faces. According to a study by Germine, Duchaine, and Nakayama (2011), our facial recognition and interpretation abilities do not peak until our early thirties. In the study, a large sample of 44,000 people between ten and seventy years of age completed an online, face-learning test that required them to study several unfamiliar faces. They then had to identify those faces from among further unfamiliar faces. Performance at the task increased steadily through adolescence, peaked among participants aged 31.4 years, and then declined slowly (the average performance by 16-year-olds matched the average performance of those aged 65).

Additional studies by the research team controlled for growth and development in general memory and cognitive abilities in order to eliminate them as possible alternative explanations for the phenomenon observed. While group adaptive challenges are arguably different now, the impacts on available cognitive resources remain much the same. A group member with an aroused threat response is likely to find him- or herself mentalizing about that threat response at the expense of performance and well-being (Hambrick and Meinz 2011), and particularly so if the person considers him- or herself to be a "lower-level" employee (Stellar et al. 2011).

Miron-Spektor et al. (2011) examined whether and how observing anger influences thinking processes and problem-solving ability. Interestingly, the authors found that creativity was dampened by observing anger but enhanced by observing sarcasm. In three studies involving 375 engineering students, the authors showed that participants who listened to an angry customer were more successful in solving analytic problems but less successful in solving creative problems, compared with participants who listened to an emotionally neutral customer. In subsequent studies, the authors further showed that observing anger communicated through sarcasm actually enhances complex thinking and the solving of creative problems. An engineer's "prevention orientation" was asserted as the characteristic that served to mediate the effect of observing anger on complex thinking. The researchers suspected that the humor of sarcasm makes it less overtly threatening and thus less likely to trigger prevention orientation.

Observing anger communicated through sarcasm actually enhances complex thinking and the solving of creative problems.

In the 1960s and '70s, anthropologists began to take note that mammals who lived in larger social groups had significantly larger brains, in terms of both absolute size and brain size scale to body size (see, e.g., Alexander 1989; Holloway 1967). They argued persuasively that our ancestors reached a point at which social competition became the primary selective pressure driving human brain evolution, a concept now known as the social-brain hypothesis (Dunbar 2003). Advocates of this hypothesis assert that expanding populations provided evolutionary advantages to social, cognitive, and brain adaptations to support individuals in functioning in large cooperative groups, which in turn then competed against other groups for control of resources and social dynamics (Bailey and Geary 2009). In building on this research, neuroscientists in Sallet et al. (2011) found that macaque monkeys housed in larger groups showed increases in the amount of gray matter in several parts of the brain involved in social cognition—the mid-superior temporal sulcus and rostral prefrontal cortex, as well as the frontal and temporal cortex used for interpreting facial expressions and gestures and for predicting what other individuals intend to do. Specifically, monkeys who lived in the most socially complex groups had an average increase of 20 percent more neocortical growth than monkeys housed individually. The research team also found correlations between gray matter volume and a monkey's dominance rank within its group, suggesting that increased neural circuitry in certain brain areas promotes or enables social success.

This growing scientific support for the social-brain hypothesis leads to an interesting question: does having more Facebook friends make you smarter? Facebook, Twitter, Google+, and other social networks have clearly become an integral part of life. In an interesting collaboration between neuroscientists and anthropologists, a research team examined social media users, specifically Facebook, to see how such activity affected brain size (Kanai et al. 2012). The researchers considered differences between individuals in the number of both their online network of friends and their real-world friends, as well as the size of the neocortical brain regions involved in social behavior. Interestingly, while the research team was able to identify a strong correlation between the volume of three specific neocortical brain regions and the number of that individual's Facebook friends, those three brain regions (the right superior temporal sulcus, left middle temporal gyrus, and entorhinal cortex—areas previously implicated in social perception and associative memory) had no statistical relationship to the real-world social networks of those individuals. One area, the amygdala, did show a correlation between gray matter density and both forms of social networking; however, the other brain regions seem to be specifically wired for the web. Future research will need to ferret out whether online social networking technology allows some individuals to express a form of social behavior that has seemingly emerged to adapt to Internet technology but has been underutilized until now—perhaps providing some sense of relief to those concerned with the interpersonal consequences of the "overuse" of social networking technologies (see e.g., Carr 2010).

People of higher social classes are worse than people of lower social classes at reading the emotional states of others.

Several researchers investigated the extent to which our social-awareness circuitry may be limited or constrained. Hurley and Frank (2011) examined whether subjects could control facial behavior while under the scrutiny of a "lie catcher." The researchers found that facial actions—eyebrow movements or smiles—could be reduced but not eliminated.

Kraus, Piff, and Keltner (2011a) found that people of higher social classes are worse than people of lower social classes at reading the emotional states of others. People with a college education or who reported themselves as belonging to a high socioeconomic group did not perform as well at gauging the emotions of strangers, either in person or by looking at pictures, compared with people who had not graduated from college or who classified themselves as belonging to a lower socioeconomic group. The researchers speculated that this difference in empathy could be explained by the fact that people in higher social classes can solve problems without relying on others, so they are less dependent on the people around them; less attention on such social-awareness circuitry brings about less development.

In a follow-on study, Kraus et al. (2011b) theorized that lower-class individuals, because of their lower rank in society, are more vigilant regarding social threats relative to their upper-class counterparts and that the difference would shape the emotional content of social interactions in systematic ways. The researchers found that lower-class participants (measured in terms of social class rank in society and within the friendship) more accurately tracked the hostile emotions of their friends and, as a result, experienced more hostile emotion contagion. In addition, lower-class participants showed more hostile reactivity to ambiguous social scenarios relative both to upper-class participants and to lower-class participants experiencing elevated socioeconomic rank. The results suggest that class affects expectations, perception, and the experience of hostile emotion, particularly in situations where lower-class individuals perceive their subordinate rank.

Interestingly, the two studies are consistent with research findings showing that empathy among college students (higher social class) has declined by more than 30 percent over the past 10 years, something that has generally been attributed to social networking and other technologies that reduce opportunities for young people to interact in person, as well as a decline in the amount of time spent reading (Konrath, O'Brien, and Hsing 2011).

Using EEG recordings, Senholzi and Kubota (2011) showed that the brain works differently when memorizing the face of a person from one's own race than when memorizing a face from another race. The study sheds light on a well-documented psychology finding known as the "other-race effect," which holds that people are less likely to remember a face from a racial group different from their own. The outstanding question remaining before this study was not that the effect existed but why. The study found that brain activity increases in the very first 200 to 250 milliseconds upon seeing both same-race and other-race faces. Interestingly, they found that the amplitude of that increased brain activity only predicts whether an other-race face (not a same-race face) is later remembered. Why is individuation so fragile for other-race faces? One possibility, the researchers say, is that many people simply have less practice seeing and remembering other-race faces—again, less attention on that social-awareness circuitry brings about less development.

Social pain

As Heatherton (2011) points out, one of the four psychological components necessary to be an acceptable group member is an active and responsive threat and reward circuitry. As we have discussed in *NeuroLeadership Journal* articles (Rock 2008; Lieberman and Eisenberger 2008), neuroleadership places considerable significance on social pain as a driver for that circuitry. Building on research on the default brain state (e.g., Ossandon et al. 2011), researchers are beginning to accumulate evidence of the existence of two additional states—the "mentalizing" and "analyzing" brain states. As we discussed above, mentalizing involves circuitry used to predict other people's emotional or intentional states and is influenced by social pain (real or perceived). The circuitry for thinking analytically allows us to think about concepts, ideas, and the future. As Professor Matt Lieberman pointed out at the NeuroLeadership Summit in San Francisco in 2010, while we may be reasonably efficient at sensing other people's emotions, the first challenge with this circuitry is that we are not good at mentalizing about their thoughts. The second is that the use of analyzing circuitry switches off mentalizing circuitry, and vice versa.

Mentalizing involves circuitry used to predict other people's emotional or intentional states...

As we have seen for other aspects of our social-awareness circuitry, people who spend a lot of time being analytical, conceptual, or goal-focused may have diminished mentalizing circuitry simply due to lack of use. That is, leaders who spend too much time analyzing and strategizing may find it difficult to activate their rarely used social-awareness circuitry involved in mentalizing. In addition, as we discussed earlier in the section on the decision-making domain, a leader's lack of an explicit rational process for issue resolution (e.g., defined and understood decision-making, problem-solving, innovation, and other critical-thinking processes) causes followers to move back and forth between the analyzing and mentalizing brain states, detracting from their ability to deeply focus cognitive resources on the issue being addressed.

In 2011, a number of interesting studies were conducted to more clearly define and characterize social pain and its consequences. Accumulating evidence demonstrates that experiences of social and physical pain actually rely on some of the same neurobiological and neural substrates. To the extent that being ostracized from a social group is detrimental to survival, feeling hurt by this separation may have been our brain's adaptive way to prevent it. Over the course of our evolutionary history, social pain may have assisted us in avoiding social rejection, increasing our connection with others, enhancing our probabilities for inclusion in the social group, and ultimately increasing our chances of survival. In this sense, social pain, though distressing in the moment, is an adaptation that ensures social bonding and ultimately survival (Eisenberger and Lieberman 2004; Eisenberger 2011).

Experiences of social and physical pain actually rely on some of the same neurobiological and neural substrates.

Williams and Nida (2011) showed that while ostracism or social exclusion may not leave external bruises, it can cause pain that is often deeper and longer lasting than a physical injury. More than five thousand people participated in their study, which made use of a computer game Williams designed to show how just 2 or 3 minutes of ostracism can produce lingering negative feelings. The researchers confirmed the use of the same neurobiological and neural substrates in the brain for both physical injury and social pain, and they noted that the process of ostracism includes three stages: the initial acts of being ignored or excluded, coping, and resignation, with important individual differences in each stage. Ostracism threatens psychological needs (belonging, self-esteem, control, and meaningful existence), and it unleashes a variety of physiological, affective, cognitive, and behavioral responses.

We often overlook detrimental consequences that can flow from social events that generate positive valence.

Several important studies looked into the consequences of social exclusion and social pain. Miner and Eischeid (2012) found that workers who witnessed incivility toward colleagues felt negative emotions (specifically, anger, demoralization, fear, and anxiety), especially when incivilities were directed toward others of the same sex. Perhaps not surprisingly, De Ruddere et al. (2011) found that the valence of that negative emotional response was significantly influenced by how much that colleague was liked (influenced by how egotistical, hypocritical, or arrogant he or she was perceived to be). The more the person was disliked, the less sympathetic others were to the colleague's social pain. According to Berger (2011), whether the incivility event will be shared with others depends more on how physically or emotionally stimulated people were when they processed the information about the event and not its actual emotional content.

A study by Ferguson (2011) showed that stress created by incivility in the workplace can be so intense that, at the end of the day, it is taken home by the worker and has an impact on the well-being of the worker's family and partner, who in turn takes that stress to his/her workplace. The author notes the importance of controlling this ripple effect. The study also found that such stress also negatively affected the worker's and partner's marital satisfaction. In an interesting article that reviewed recent psychological research on social acceptance and rejection, DeWall et al. (2011) noted research showing that those experiencing social rejection feel isolated and lonely, tend to have poorer physical health, do not sleep well, have lower immune response, and tend to die sooner than people who enjoy social inclusion (whether real or perceived).

Because of a natural proclivity to be drawn to the negative, we often overlook detrimental consequences that can flow from social events that generate positive valence.

In an interesting study conducted by Wood, McInnes, and Norton (2011), the research team looked at the incidence of traffic fatalities after sporting events. The analysis showed that major sporting events in which the game is decided by a close margin result in an increase in traffic deaths, compared with games decided by large margins ("blowouts"). The authors hypothesize that close games may be more dangerous because they increase the competition-associated testosterone, which then spills over into aggressive driving. The authors further speculate that the results indicate benefits for losing in that those fans may enjoy a safer drive home. It is interesting to ponder whether these results could be generalized to such activities as negotiations, sales, or other such competitive events in the business world.

Concepts related to SCARF play an important role in understanding and explaining how brain activity in response to social stimuli manifests in observable behavior.

Continuing development of SCARF

Within NeuroLeadership, we categorize those social events that can activate mentalizing by causing social pain through the SCARF (Status, Certainty, Autonomy, Relatedness, Fairness) model (Rock 2008). Several interesting strands of research in 2010 further developed and defined the model. SCARF and concepts related to SCARF play an important role in understanding and explaining how brain activity in response to social stimuli manifests in observable behavior.

For example, at the NeuroLeadership Labs, we expressly consider individual differences in SCARF through what we refer to as an individual's SCARF profile. An individual who shows hypersensitivity to status-related issues is likely to require a different intervention strategy, for example, than an individual showing a less sensitive response to such issues. As practitioners, the more we understand about the kind of stimuli that generate a particular SCARF response, the better we are able to assist individuals and organizations in their development efforts.

Status

Liew et al. (2011) found that, in contrast to the Chinese who responded fastest to pictures of their direct supervisor, white Americans responded faster to pictures of their own face than to pictures of their boss. Interestingly, the American tendency toward individualism is less pronounced if the supervisor is considered someone with high social status. That is, for Americans, status as a social motivator may be influenced more by one's social status than one's hierarchical position as a boss. The authors point out that while we are quicker to react to faces we think are important, which most of the time is our own face, certain individuals—those with real or perceived social status—may interfere with how we think about ourselves.

Allen and Sherman (2011) showed that when people feel bad about themselves, they are more likely to show bias toward people who are different; it makes us feel better about ourselves. Allen and Sherman used the Implicit Association Test (IAT)—a task designed to assess people's automatic reactions to words and/or images—to investigate their hypothesis. In a follow-on study involving the authors (Gonsalkorale et al. 2011), the research team found that individuals who are primarily internally motivated to respond without prejudice show less bias on implicit measures than individuals who are externally motivated or unmotivated to respond without prejudice, again suggesting a role for individual differences in self-regulation as an explanation for individual differences in hypersensitivities to SCARF's social motivations.

In addition to showing bias toward others to feel better about ourselves, Mercier and Sperber (2011) assert that we do the same when we enter into arguments. The authors take on generally accepted philosophical theory, which holds that reasoning exists to allow people to reach beyond mere perception in search of truth, to make better decisions, or to gain scientific enlightenment. Rather, according to the authors' argumentative theory of reasoning, reasoning is a social phenomenon that evolved to assist us in convincing others and in being careful when others attempt to convince us—in social brain theory terms, a social adaptation that enables one group to persuade (and defeat) another, regardless of how far the argument may depart from the truth. In this sense, arguing becomes little more than a hard-wired compulsion to triumph in the debating arena, to gain or avoid losing social status.

One study of great interest to status research (though not in the neuroscience lab directly) showed that "localized" status, or the status you feel in the group you are surrounded by, is more important to your happiness than your socioeconomic status is (Anderson et al. 2012). Prior research on status had shown that monkeys will direct their attention to others of higher or lower status depending on their own position in the group. Ly et al. (2011) conducted a study to see if this principle also holds in humans.

FMRI was used to measure brain activity in the ventral striatum (prominently implicated in processing value and salience), while research participants of varying social status were shown information about someone of relatively higher status and information about someone of relatively lower status. The study showed that the brain's response to status cues varies depending on an individual's own subjective perception of their status. Individuals of higher subjective socioeconomic status showed greater brain activity in the ventral striatum in response to other high-ranked individuals, while those with a lower status perception had a greater response to other low-status individuals. In other words, if we consider ourselves high status, we both listen to and place greater value on information from higher-status individuals; if we consider ourselves lower status, we listen to and value information from both higher- and lower-status individuals.

The study raises a variety of interesting questions. Of particular note is the fact that individual differences create varying levels of sensitivity to this social motivator. With hypersensitive individuals likely to see their perceived status shifting over time for better or for worse, how their brain responds to such changes in the context of this research is an intriguing question for future study.

Individual differences create varying levels of sensitivity to this social motivator.

Certainty

In the SCARF model, the concept of certainty deals with the human need for clarity and predictability; ambiguity activates threat circuitry. Roets and Van Hiel (2011) assert that individuals with a hypersensitive need for certainty are more likely to show signs of prejudice. According to the authors, people who are prejudiced have a stronger need to make quick, firm judgments and decisions in order to reduce ambiguity. Being hypersensitive to ambiguity, they are more prone to quickly rely on the most obvious information, often the first information they come across, to reduce their anxiety. They also favor authority and social norms, which make it easier to make such decisions. Once they have made a choice, they adamantly stick to their decisions even in the face of new, contradictory information—all generally done unconsciously. In this sense, sources of prejudice are not ideology but rather a basic human need and a way of thinking. The authors' proposed solution: provide information—say, by bringing groups together—to find an alternative, more positive source of "first" information on which to rely.

People who are prejudiced have a stronger need to make quick, firm judgments and decisions in order to reduce ambiguity.

Autonomy

In the SCARF model, the concept of autonomy deals with the human need for a sense of control over events. Reduced autonomy activates threat circuitry; increasing autonomy activates reward circuitry. Inesi et al. (2011) showed that this control aspect of autonomy forms a critical shared foundation for an individual's power over others and the ability to make choices in their lives. The study showed that power and choice in this sense are substitutable—less of one increases the desire for the other to offset the anxiety of the loss (and the social pain associated with it). Further, the authors found that power and choice exhibited a "threshold effect"—once an individual had one source of autonomy/control, additions of the other source yielded diminishing returns. Practitioners will see that the interchangeability of power and choice can provide useful insights into workplace design and team development.

Leotti and Delgado (2011) showed that in addition to exercising control by making choices to satisfy a need for autonomy, the opportunity to exercise control may also be similarly adaptive because it activates the areas of the brain associated with rewards (corticostriatal regions, particularly the ventral striatum, involved in affective and motivational processes). Combined with Inesi et al.'s (2011) results above, these findings may have important applications for understanding the role of perception of control in self-regulatory processes intent on changing habits.

The study showed that power and choice in this sense are substitutable...

Relatedness

In the SCARF model, the concept of relatedness involves our sense of safety with others, of being with "friends" rather than "foes." Its impact on our sense of self is important. Cwir et al. (2011) showed that even superficial feelings of connectedness with a stranger are enough to lead to a mirroring of their emotions and even their heart rate. Walton et al. (2012) illustrated that mere belonging, a minimal social connection, to another person or group increased task motivation by creating socially shared goals around the task.

In a demonstration of the interconnectedness of the SCARF elements, Lount and Pettit (2011) showed that high-status people tended to trust people more in initial encounters than did people with lower status—higher status people rated others as more benevolent, which led them to trust more (in other words, the boss is likely to trust a new hire more than the new hire is likely to trust the boss). Kogan et al. (2011) found that it can take just 20 seconds to detect whether a stranger is inclined to be trustworthy, kind, or compassionate. The authors argue that humans are wired—in fact, may be genetically predisposed—to recognize strangers as more likely to help them out in difficult situations. We will discuss the importance of first impressions in the section on the facilitating change domain.

Fairness

In the SCARF model, the concept of fairness relates to our sense of perception of fair exchanges with people. How to distribute available resources among members of a group is a central aspect of social life. Gospic et al. (2011) showed that the brain has built-in mechanisms that trigger an automatic reaction to someone who refuses to share. Using brain imaging, the study provided neuroscience data to support the universal human behavior to react with instant aggression whenever a person behaves unfairly and in a manner that is not in the best interests of the group. The researchers saw that the brain region more active during such decisions was the amygdala, and not the prefrontal cortex and insula as had previously been identified.

At what age do we develop the sense that resource distributions are inequitable? A study by Geraci and Surian (2011) suggests that infants aged 12 to 18 months (mean age 16 months) pay attention to the outcomes of distributive actions in order to evaluate the distributor's actions and to reason about the distributor's disposition. And the consequences of such unfair distributions? Robbins, Ford, and Tetrick (2011) conducted a meta-analysis to examine the effects of unfairness perceptions on health. The results suggest that perceptions of unfairness are associated with negative impacts on physical and mental health, particularly in those situations where the unfairness breaches a psychological contract held by group members.

Another chapter in this book offers a deeper discussion by Rock and Cox (2012) of research that has emerged about SCARF in the five years since it was launched by Rock. (See chapter 18, "SCARF in 2012: Updating the social neuroscience of collaborating with others").

The results suggest that perceptions of unfairness are associated with negative impacts on physical and mental health...

Social interaction and gender

A considerable body of research demonstrates that social interactions are affected by gender. In adding to that research, Van Honk et al. (2011) found that an administration of testosterone under the tongue of volunteers negatively affected an individual's ability to mentalize, an indication of empathic ability. The researchers conjectured that this may help explain why on average women perform better than men on tests requiring the subject to infer what a person is feeling from photographs of facial expressions that emphasize the eyes.

While stereotypes suggest that women are more cooperative than men, Balliet et al. (2011), in a meta-analysis of 50 years of research, showed that men are equally cooperative in situations involving a social dilemma that pits an individual's interests against the group's interests. Interestingly, the study also showed that men cooperate better with other men than women cooperate with each other; women tend to cooperate more than men when interacting with the opposite sex.

Reuben et al. (2011) conducted an experiment in which groups were required to select a leader. The research team found that women are selected less often as leaders than is suggested by their individual past performances. While looking for explanations for this underrepresentation of women, the authors found that men's overconfidence was the driving force behind the observed prevalence of male representation.

Workplace engagement

Workplace engagement involves the degree to which people put discretionary effort and care into their job. Workplaces driven by positive emotions would elicit more of such discretionary effort than would negative environments. Traditional business research has focused on the impact of engagement on organizational performance; only in the last few years have we seen inquiries into the neurological drivers of engagement. Organizational theorists have only recently begun to incorporate neuroscience into investigations of workplace behavior (Becker, Cropanzano, and Sanfey 2011). In looking for the implications of brain science on workplace behavior, the NeuroLeadership Labs has been guided by a mapping of Gallup's "Q12" assessments into SCARF (Rock and Tang 2009; Ringleb 2009). This mapping provides a convenient means by which to tie neuroscience research to the business concept of engagement.

Only in the last few years have we seen inquiries into the neurological drivers of engagement.

In neuroscience terms, a leader increases workplace engagement by increasing SCARF—by increasing employee status, certainty, autonomy, relatedness, and fairness. In addition to the seemingly obvious performance benefits from an engaged work force, such a work force also enjoys significant health benefits. In a 20-year follow-up study of predictors of mortality, Shirom et al. (2011) found that employees who believe they have the personal support of their peers at work are more likely to live a longer life (even after controlling for such psychological, behavioral, or physiological risk factors as smoking, obesity, and depression).

Employees who believe they have the personal support of their peers at work are more likely to live a longer life...

Several studies with engagement implications warrant consideration by practitioners. Bault et al. (2011) investigated why an individual would take a risk when all other colleagues are watching but would never take if alone. According to the study findings, the brain places more value on winning in a social setting than it does on winning when alone. The researchers found that the striatum, a part of the brain associated with rewards, showed higher activity when an individual beat a peer in the lottery, as opposed to when that individual won while alone. The medial prefrontal cortex, a part of the brain associated with social reasoning, was also more active.

Waytz and Young (2012) asked the question, "When something goes wrong, who gets the blame: the person or the group?" The researchers found that the more cohesive the group, the more likely it is that people in the group will hold its members less responsible for their individual actions. Interestingly, the researchers speculated that the more people judge a group to have a mind—a "group mind" (that is, the ability to think or plan)—the less they seem to judge a member of that group as having his or her own capacity to think or plan. The research raises interesting questions about decision-making, blame, and moral judgment.

Researchers in a variety of other fields also provided interesting insights into the engagement equation. Wood and De Menezes (2011) used a large database to show that when employees are given greater independence (autonomy) in their jobs and when management readily shares information and consults with them, employees feel both less stress and more satisfied. The study also showed that performance-related pay, a highly used management tenet of high-performance work systems, makes no difference in satisfaction or stress.

In an interesting study with broad applications, Xie et al. (2011) found that when just 10 percent of a community holds an unshakable belief, the majority of the society will always adopt their belief. The percentage of committed opinion holders remains at approximately 10 percent, regardless of how or where that opinion starts and is spread in the community/society. The fundamental characteristic of these opinion holders is that they are completely set in their views and unflappable in modifying them. At the NeuroLeadership Labs, we found this study to be particularly interesting in that it is consistent with our anecdotal observations of when leadership-development interventions in MBA and undergraduate groups are more or less successful.

Facilitating-change domain

While we recognize the importance of research in organizational change, little research has been done up to now involving neuroscience tools or theories to inform our understanding of how complex systems change. This is largely due to the complexity of change efforts, the difficulties of isolating success factors in change, and the challenges of current brain-imaging technologies. We hope in the future to see greater research by neuroscientists into organizational change. In this review, we are focusing on new research about individual change.

Leadership, psychology, and neuroscience scholars all recognize the challenges in changing long-entrenched personal habits.

Leadership, psychology, and neuroscience scholars all recognize the challenges in changing long-entrenched personal habits. As we have seen in our discussions in the other domains, recent research in neuroscience and social psychology continues to reveal the importance of emotion and emotion management as fundamental ingredients in effective social interactions. While practitioners will be the first to express their appreciation for the importance of technically trained leaders, they will also be the first to express their frustration with the effectiveness of skills- or content-based approaches to personal and leadership development, which typically leave out, or at best hold constant, emotion variables in the change equation.

The ability to inhibit prepotent impulses is a core feature of self-regulation...

In virtually all disciplines relevant to neuroleadership, individual change has become associated with an individual's level of self-awareness—a personal sense of strengths and weaknesses and a vision of continuous advancement and personal growth. As we discussed above in the collaborating-domain section, controlling oneself to be socially accepted involves an awareness of how one is thinking, feeling, or behaving and the ability to alter any of those to satisfy the expectations of the social group. The ability to inhibit prepotent impulses is a core feature of self-regulation and refers to a process by which individuals initiate, adjust, interrupt, stop, or otherwise change thoughts, feelings, or actions to effect the realization of personal goals or plans or to maintain current standards (Bauer and Baumeister 2011). In the broadest sense, self-regulation refers to intentional or purposeful acts directed from within the individual. From this perspective, learning, physiology, and culture predispose certain behaviors, thoughts, or emotions in specific circumstances, but self-regulation allows the individual to change or overcome them.

Learning, habits, and individual change

Neuroscience and social-psychology research is now outlining the important consequences of individual differences in working-memory capacity for learning (Alloway, Banner, and Smith 2010) and in responses to emotional events and cognitive performance (Beal and Ghandour 2011). If we take the discussions from the collaborating and emotion-regulation domains and bring them together here, emotions clearly have an impact on working-memory capacity. To that end, McRae et al. (2012) showed us that individual differences in reappraisal ability are positively correlated with differences in working-memory capacity; the greater an individual's reappraisal ability, the greater his or her working-memory capacity. From the practitioner's standpoint, this line of research strongly supports the notion that change efforts focused on increasing emotion regulation will increase working-memory capacity and thereby improve cognitive functioning.

Given our need to be good group members, it seems reasonable to assume that certain life experiences that brought into question our social inclusion (real or perceived) would stay with us and influence our emotional "set points" as adults (Kendler et al. 2011). To the extent that those life experiences involved top-down emotion generation, the brain would likely adapt and form habitual responses to similar experiences with the intent to maintain social group survival (the goal). At NeuroLeadership Labs, when such a habitual response is unhealthy or unproductive, we refer to the top-down emotion generated as being a "deceptive brain message" (Schwartz and Gladding 2011). According to Neal et al. (2011a), and as many coaches and leadership-development practitioners have experienced, if the habit formed is strong, the individual's perception of recurring context cues will activate the response in memory, deactivate alternative responses, and be relatively uninfluenced by changes in motivational states. Regarding personal-development interventions, Duhigg (2012) in his book *The Power of Habit* argues that the issue becomes how to bring about change in such circumstances. In a thorough review of the relevant literature, he showed that social psychologists and neuroscientists are developing more effective and person-specific intervention strategies to assist people in overcoming unproductive and unhealthy habits. Our intent is to review some of the more important contributions from this past year.

> *Recent research offers several insights into what triggers habits and how they respond to motivational influences.*

Recent research offers several insights into what triggers habits and how they respond to motivational influences. Neal et al. (2011b) investigated the factors that can alter habit performance. They conducted experiments by varying the conditions under which people consume popcorn at a movie theater. Some participants in their research had strong habits of eating popcorn at the theater (i.e., a history of frequent popcorn consumption in that setting), whereas others had weaker habits. Some participants were given fresh popcorn, while others were given seven-day-old, stale popcorn. To test the effects of changes in motivations introduced by the stale popcorn, researchers first controlled for hunger, the degree to which participants liked the popcorn, and habit strength. Striking differences emerged in eating patterns.

Strong-habit participants, when they could eat automatically with their dominant hand, repeated past responses, regardless of the palatability of the popcorn. However, when strong-habit participants were forced to eat in an atypical way, their behavior was brought under intentional control, and—like the weak-habit participants in all conditions—they ate little of the stale popcorn. Specifically, the use of the non-dominant hand raised self-awareness sufficiently to allow the individual time to make a conscious choice as to whether to eat the stale popcorn (Baumeister et al. 2006). In subsequent sections below, we will look at this relationship between mindfulness, self-awareness, and self-regulation and the growing body of research supporting those relationships.

Personal characteristics and individual change

A variety of recent studies described the kind of personal characteristics that seem to generate the most success, perhaps providing some guidance as to the direction a change effort might want to travel.

Johnson, Rowatt, and Petrini (2011) showed us that those individuals who possess the combination of honesty and humility have better job performance. In fact, the combination predicted job performance better than any of the traditional five personality traits. Similarly, LaBouff et al. (2012) found that those same people are more likely than an arrogant person to offer their time to someone in need.

Johnson and Fowler (2011) showed that self-deception in the form of a mistakenly inflated belief that we can easily meet a challenge or win a conflict may actually be good for us. Their model demonstrates that when competing for resources, a weaker, yet more confident competitor is more likely to take control over larger portion of disputed resources than a competitor who is more able, yet humble. This bias in human judgement is adaptive precisely because it *deceives* an individual into fitness-maximizing behavior.

Chance et al. (2011) took on the notion that although people seem to have an endless capacity for rationalizing what they have done, they do not know they are deceiving themselves. The research team found that not only do they deceive themselves, but they are largely oblivious to their self-deception.

Gawronski et al. (2010) found there is more than a literal truth to the saying "you never get a second chance to make a first impression." To bring about a change in that first impression, they found it is necessary for the first impression to be challenged in multiple different contexts; as long as a first impression is challenged only within the context in which it was developed, it will continue to dominate. How does making an effort to create a positive impression on others affect the accuracy of those impressions? Human et al. (2012) showed that making a positive self-presentation facilitates more accurate impressions, indicating that putting one's best self forward helps reveal one's true self. The research team showed that when done this way, impressions were more in line with participants' self-reported personality traits and IQ test scores.

Self-deception in the form of a mistakenly inflated belief that we can easily meet a challenge or win a conflict may actually be good for us.

This growing body of research begs an important question: as we direct interventions toward the most productive and healthy characteristics, do we need to be concerned about whether nice guys finish last? According to Judge, Livingston, and Hurst (2012), nice guys really do finish last, or at least make less money. Overall, they are less likely to get fired and just as likely to supervise others; however, they are less inclined to negotiate pay increases and other personal rewards to which they may be entitled.

Healthy Mind Platter

In looking to improve human performance and well-being from a neurobiological, as opposed to a psychological, perspective, Dr. Dan Siegel and Dr. David Rock created the Healthy Mind Platter. The Platter, conceived in the wake of the US government's revised food pyramid, has "7 essential mental activities necessary for optimal mental health in daily life." Those seven essential daily mental activities are:

1. **Focus Time:** when we focus closely on tasks in a goal-oriented way, taking on challenges that make deep connections in the brain
2. **Play Time:** when we allow ourselves to be spontaneous or creative, playfully enjoying novel experiences, which helps make new connections in the brain
3. **Connecting Time:** when we connect with other people, ideally in person, or take time to appreciate our connection to the natural world around us or to a world bigger than we are, richly activating the brain's relational circuitry
4. **Physical Time:** when we move our bodies, aerobically if medically possible, which strengthens the brain in many ways
5. **Time-in:** when we quietly reflect internally, focusing on sensations, images, feelings, and thoughts, helping to better integrate the brain
6. **Downtime:** when we are nonfocused, without any specific goal, and let our mind wander or simply relax, which helps our brain recharge
7. **Sleep Time:** when we give the brain the rest it needs to consolidate learning and recover from the experiences of the day

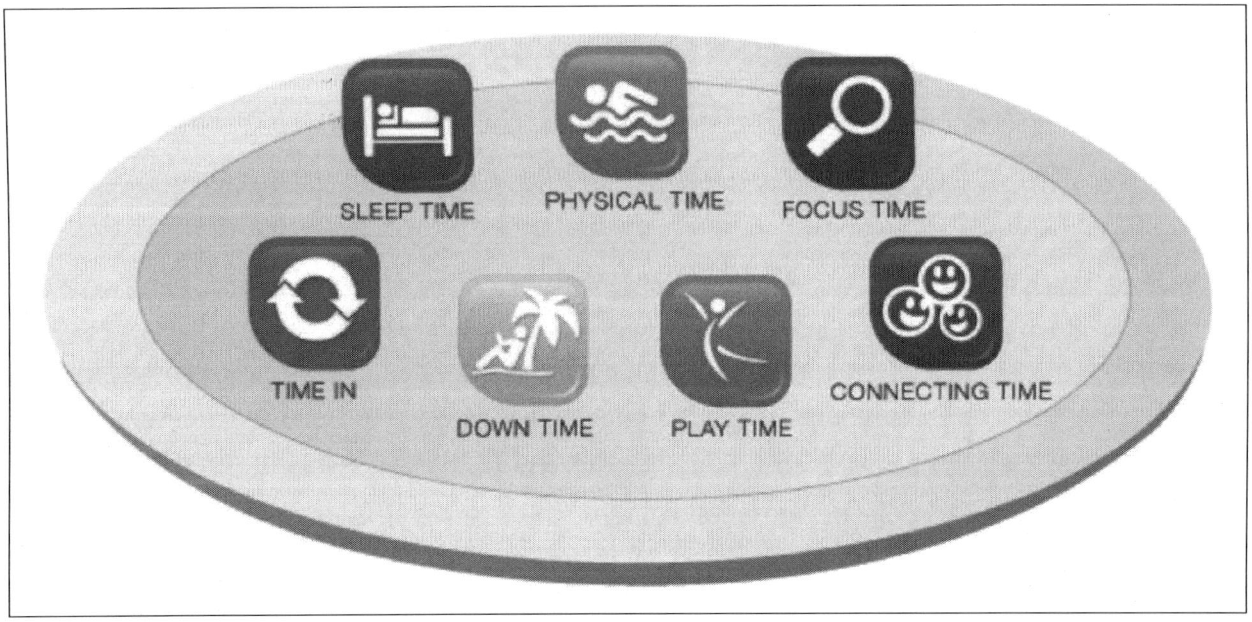

Figure 1. Ingredients of the Healthy Mind Platter

In the past year, considerable research has been done on several of these ingredients, substantiating their importance for human performance and well-being. Beginning with research at the most general level, social influences are among the influences on brain structure and function that are most powerful in inducing plastic change. Although the precise mechanisms of plasticity are still not fully understood, moderate to severe stress appears to increase the growth of several sectors of the amygdala, whereas the effects in the hippocampus and prefrontal cortex tend to be opposite (McEwen 2007). With the amygdala and PFC and their interconnections strongly implicated in emotion regulation (Wager et al. 2008) and well-being (Davidson 2004), adaptations to those social influences can drive unproductive and unhealthy habits.

Using data from the Framingham Heart Study, an investigation of residents of the Massachusetts town ongoing since 1948, Debette et al. (2011) showed that smoking, hypertension, obesity, and diabetes all caused brains to shrink in size, leading to a decline in the brain's executive function, among other things. Several interventions suggested implicitly by the Healthy Mind Platter have been shown to promote prosocial behavior and well-being and are likely to induce plasticity-related changes in the brain. That is, those interventions would lead to an increase in brain size and an increase in the brain's executive function (such as self-regulation), as well as promote changes driven by healthy habits (Hölzel et al. 2010).

Smoking, hypertension, obesity, and diabetes all caused brains to shrink in size, leading to a decline in the brain's executive function...

Support for the importance of "connected time" can be seen in the works of Coan, Schaefer, and Davidson (2006) and Eisenberger et al. (2007), previously reviewed in this and other contexts. Regarding "physical time," studies demonstrated the importance of exercise both for brain health and cognition (Voss et al. 2011) and for changes in the brain consistent with improved stress management and memory (Erickson et al. 2011).

"Time-in," or mindfulness meditation, has found considerable scientific support for its beneficial attributes to physical well-being and brain heath. In a controlled longitudinal study to investigate pre and post changes in brain gray matter concentration attributable to participation in a Mindfulness-Based Stress Reduction (MBSR) program, Hölzel et al. (2011) found that participation is associated with changes in gray-matter concentration in brain regions involved in learning and memory processes, emotion regulation, self-referential processing, and perspective taking.

At the 2011 NeuroLeadership Summit in San Francisco, Professor Jessica Payne showed us the relationship between stress, mood, and sleep. When a person has high levels of stress and negative mood, resulting in poor sleep, the consequence is significant cognitive impairment, affecting basic perception as well as judgment and decision making. Consistent with other ingredients in the Healthy Mind Platter, Payne and Kensinger (2011) found that lack of sleep leads to a shift from the employment of a diffuse memory-retrieval network (including widespread activity in the lateral prefrontal and parietal cortices) to a more refined network of regions (including the amygdala and ventromedial PFC). Additional research on sleep demonstrated the positive relationship between sleep and self-control (Barnes et al. 2011) and the benefits of a short nap on both performance (Wamsley et al. 2010) and sensitivity to emotion (Gujar et al. 2010). There is a deeper summary of the Healthy Mind Platter in a later chapter, "The Healthy Mind Platter" (Rock, Siegel, Poelmans and Payne 2012).

Self-regulation

While emotion regulation (see above discussion of that domain) is an aspect of self-regulation, self-regulation relates to the broader issue of personal change, including regulating a wider set of behaviors and processes than just emotion. Self-regulation—and its relationship to self-awareness and mindfulness—is the subject of a rapidly growing body of research. As Heatherton (2011) points out, and which the NeuroLeadership Labs' Social Brain Theory of Leadership concurs with, self-regulation is an indispensable psychological ingredient in successful social interactions. The past year has seen serious research on the consequences of individual differences in self-regulatory ability, its neural constructs, and a number of its most important characteristics, particularly the rate and the conditions under which it is depleted.

The relationship between self-regulation and delayed gratification is generally attributed to a landmark study by Dr. Walter Mischel in the late 1960s, in which Mischel used marshmallows and cookies to assess the ability of preschool children to delay gratification (Mischel, Shoda, and Rodriguez 1989). In that study, the children were told that if they held off on the temptation to eat a treat, they would be rewarded with more treats later. Some of the children were able to resist, while others were not. (At the NeuroLeadership Labs, we assert that the group is normally distributed.) In Casey et al. (2011), the research team (which included Mischel) recruited 59 adults who had participated as young children in the original study and who represented both extremes of the delayed-ratification spectrum. Because marshmallows are less rewarding to adults, the researchers used robust psychometric tests to reveal whether the aptitude for delayed gratification was consistent among the participants from childhood into adulthood. When the test was repeated while participants' brains were being scanned using fMRI, the results showed that the brain's prefrontal cortex was more active in "high delayers" and the ventral striatum (an area linked to addictions) was more active in "low delayers."

The study showed that participants with poor childhood self-regulatory ability were more likely in adulthood to be a single parent, to have credit and health problems, and to have been convicted of a criminal offense...

In a study following the original hypothesis proposed by Casey et al., Moffitt et al. (2011) systematically assessed the self-regulatory ability of 1000 New Zealand children at the ages of three, five, seven, nine, and 11, and then interviewed them when they had reached age of 32. In a result consistent with Mitchell, the study showed that participants with poor childhood self-regulatory ability were more likely in adulthood to be a single parent, to have credit and health problems, and to have been convicted of a criminal offense—even after controlling for intelligence and social class.

Given that the relationship between childhood self-regulatory ability and adult outcomes held across a full range of self-control scores, the researchers recommend introducing into the core school curriculum universal intervention strategies intended to assist students in raising self-regulatory ability. On the basis of the evidence, why not consider it an integral part of all personal-development interventions?

In looking to more fully understand the neural basis of self-regulation, Figner et al. (2010) were, for the first time, causally able to show that self-regulatory ability is rooted in the prefrontal cortex, and specifically the left lateral prefrontal cortex (LPFC). The research team used a noninvasive brain-stimulation technique called low-frequency repetitive transcranial magnetic stimulation, or rTMS, to temporarily disrupt the function of the lateral prefrontal cortex in a group of 52 healthy volunteers. One-third of the group received stimulation to the left lateral prefrontal cortex; one-third to the right lateral prefrontal cortex; and one-third, the control group, received a sham stimulation. After the stimulation, the volunteers were asked to make choices between smaller, immediate rewards or larger, later rewards. Those subjects whose left lateral prefrontal cortex had been disrupted by the simulation increased the choice of immediate rewards over larger delayed rewards; both those receiving the sham simulation and those receiving right lateral prefrontal cortex stimulation did not.

Wanless et al. (2011) showed that self-regulation can be formally trained, as well as measured, at a young age. The study involved children aged three to six years in four countries. It showed that children who regularly participated in a Simon Says type of game designed to improve self-regulation (called the Head-Toes-Knees-Shoulders task) improved their academic achievement. Importantly, and as the primary intent of the study, academic gains were seen in students in countries already known to have stronger self-regulation than US students (i.e., Taiwan, China, and South Korea).

Ego depletion

Ego-depletion theory assumes that activities requiring self-control consume a limited mental resource, the so-called "limited resource" theory (Baumeister, Muraven, and Tice 2000). According to the theory, even relatively small exertions lead to a reduction in this mental resource, and self-control-related tasks and activities carried out immediately after such exertions will demonstrate diminished performance. In the past year, several studies tested this general proposition from a number of perspectives. Within the greater discipline, there has been some conjecture that ego depletion is merely a result of fatigue.

There has been some conjecture that ego depletion is merely a result of fatigue.

In a study involving a group of participants, half of whom were sleep deprived, Vohs et al. (2011) found that performance on a task requiring self-control was influenced by whether the participant had completed a prior task requiring self-control and not by whether the participant was sleep deprived, lending support to the limited resource model. In two interesting studies where the experiential task involved focusing on an emotion, Hill, DelPriore, and Vaughan (2011) (envy) and Xu, Beguea, and Bushman (2011) (guilt) both found that depleted participants (brought about through experiments intended to elicit the specific emotion of interest) showed lower self-regulatory ability during subsequent acts of volition.

Prior research has shown that money in the form of actual cash rewards can counteract ego depletion...

Prior research has shown that money in the form of actual cash rewards can counteract ego depletion (Muraven and Slessareva 2003). Boucher and Kofos (2012) went an additional step and found that the idea of money similarly buffers ego-depletion effects. With implications for employee motivation, the research team found that the concept of money evokes a focus on individual goals and performance and confers the feelings of efficacy needed to confront challenges and attain important outcomes. Interestingly, the idea of money did not impart extra self-control ability among nondepleted participants; that is, money-primed nondepleted participants did no better than neutral-primed nondepleted participants on subsequent self-control-related tasks and activities.

In a study with potentially broad applications, Fennis (2011) looked to the impact of ego depletion on perspective taking and its associated prosocial behavior (willingness to assist others). Prior research has found that perspective taking requires the self-regulatory energy to override the tendency to maintain an egocentric perspective. Fennis showed that, compared to nondepleted participants, depleted participants exhibited considerably reduced willingness to undertake perspective taking and the prosocial behaviors associated with it.

Perspective taking requires the self-regulatory energy to override the tendency to maintain an egocentric perspective.

Although the independent bodies of research supporting self-awareness, self-regulation, and mindfulness have grown substantially over the past decade, research formally linking them together is moving more slowly. An important question in that regard, for example, is whether self-regulatory failure resulting from ego depletion can be circumvented. Alberts, Martijn, and De Vries (2011) looked specifically at whether ego depletion can be circumvented by increasing self-awareness. Building on research developed independently in the areas of self-regulation (ego depletion) and self-awareness, the research team showed that nondepleted and depleted participants who had been given a self-awareness prime performed equally well on a subsequent task and considerably better than depleted participants who had received a neutral prime. An interesting question in the application of this research, and one that leads us into the next section is, what role does or could mindfulness play as a "self-awareness prime"?

Glucose may be one factor in ego depletion...

Finally, there is an intriguing argument emerging that glucose may be one factor in ego depletion but not the only factor. Job, Dweck, and Walton (2010) found that one's beliefs about willpower played a key role in whether willpower was influenced by glucose. Another study showed that thinking about something one values positively in between willpower tasks mitigates the glucose-depletion effect (Schmeichel and Vohs 2009). A number of other studies are pointing to the role of both beliefs and the general threat/reward state of the brain as key factors in the ego-depletion model. At the time of writing, the debate continues on this topic.

Mindfulness

At NeuroLeadership Labs, we refer to mindfulness as the ability to directly experience the world in the present, in an accepting way. Sometimes we refer to it simply as "direct experience." Mindfulness as we discuss it here is not a Buddhist or religious capacity but an innate human capacity that varies across populations, but that can be increased with practice. In recent years, mindfulness has moved from being largely supported through anecdotal evidence to building a strong scientific foundation. The benefits of mindfulness are gaining empirical support in both psychology (e.g., Shapiro et al. 2008) and neuroscience (e.g., Tang et al. 2007). The growing evidence suggests that mindfulness practice is associated with neuroplastic changes in the anterior cingulate cortex, insula, temporoparietal junction, fronto-limbic network, and default mode network structures (Hölzel et al. 2011). An increasing amount of work explains the elements that make mindfulness effective, showing that it likely combines attention regulation, body awareness, emotion regulation (including reappraisal and exposure, extinction, and reconsolidation), and change in perspective of the self (Hölzel et al. 2011).

Mindfulness as we discuss it here is not a Buddhist or religious capacity but an innate human capacity that varies across populations...

Several recent studies have produced findings that may assist practitioners in making mindfulness an integral part of personal- and leadership-development intervention strategies. Zeidan et al. (2010) undertook a study to compare the effects of a brief mindfulness-meditation intervention compared with a sham mindfulness-meditation intervention. The study consisted of three groups (meditation, sham meditation, and a control), each of which underwent three consecutive days of training for 20 minutes a day. The mindfulness-meditation group was trained by a facilitator with eight years of training in mindfulness-meditation interventions. Although told they were "meditating," the sham mindfulness-meditation group received instruction based on relaxation techniques emphasizing breathing exercises. Members of the control group were led to believe they were registering for mindfulness intervention, then sat in a chair for 20 minutes each session and were allowed to speak to one another. Each of the three groups was broken down into smaller groups of between five and eight participants to receive their training. Heart rate, blood pressure, and psychological variables (Profile of Mood States, State Anxiety Inventory) were assessed before and after the three-day intervention.

The research team found that the mindfulness intervention was more effective at reducing negative mood, depression, fatigue, confusion, and heart rate when compared with the sham meditation and control groups. The authors concluded that brief meditation training has beneficial effects on mood and cardiovascular variables that go beyond the demand characteristics of a sham meditation intervention.

"Is mindfulness a measurable quality in people who do not practice mindfulness-based meditation?"

At the NeuroLeadership Labs, considerable research effort is placed on understanding how individual differences, particularly in self-regulatory ability, affect intervention strategies. In looking at all aspects of leadership and personal development, the beginning notion is that a particular characteristic or attribute is normally distributed across the population. Against this line of thinking, one hypothesis was that the ability to be mindful is also normally distributed across nonmeditators. If this hypothesis is true, then one would further hypothesize that the upper end of the distribution of nonmeditators would compare favorably in level of mindfulness with that of meditators, at least with those meditators at the lower end of the distribution of meditators.

Hollis-Walker and Colosimo (2011) tested the hypothesis, "Is mindfulness a measurable quality in people who do not practice mindfulness-based meditation?" Further, they looked to see if mindfulness could also be a predictor of well-being among nonmeditators as it is among meditators. They found that nonmeditating participants who scored high on mindfulness also tended to score high on self-compassion, psychological well-being, agreeableness, extraversion, openness, and conscientiousness, and low on neuroticism, in line with the mindfulness literature describing meditators. They conjectured that nonmeditating individuals high in this construct are better equipped to recognize, manage, and resolve day-to-day conflicts, which promotes a healthy mind. The ability to notice moment-to-moment experience, with compassion, facilitates insight, clarity, and acceptance. We see this study as saying that such individuals are at an advantage in recognizing an emotional conflict (more self-aware) and thus are able to utilize their self-regulatory abilities and then to pause and plan (rather than fight or flight) in devising strategies for management and resolution (as opposed to returning repeatedly to ingrained, maladaptive habits).

More mindful participants were better able to recognize a broader range of stimuli sufficiently in advance to allow a more reasoned, flexible response...

Coaches and other practitioners working in personal and leadership development have noticed that while individuals trained on a task will typically improve on that very task, other tasks, even very similar ones, often show little or no improvement. This is particularly troublesome in working to overcome a habit that has general as well as specific consequences. That is, training benefits often seem to be stimulus or content-specific, rather than process-specific. At the NeuroLeadership Labs, we have seen that individuals typically adopt one of three self-regulation strategies in working to confront or change a habit: (1) setting a goal and garnering support; (2) fixing a "mental state" in advance of the stimulus that elicits the unproductive or unhealthy habitual response; and (3) through a process we have labeled "habitualization," physically or mentally practice a more productive or healthy response to a stimulus in the hope of overriding an ingrained habit should the stimulus be confronted. This last strategy is similar to the setting of implementation intentions, as outlined by Dixon, Ochsner, and Rock (2010), in which specific, concrete new behaviors are defined. This is one of the more effective strategies for individual behavior change.

In each case, we observed that the strategies were situation or stimulus specific. In contrast, we observed that more mindful participants were better able to recognize a broader range of stimuli sufficiently in advance to allow a more reasoned, flexible response (something we labeled "pause and plan"). On this basis, we began to see mindfulness as a far more effective strategy in terms of providing the meditator with the ability to recognize and manage a broader array of stimuli—to provide process-specific learning. Slagter, Davidson, and Lutz (2011) is the first study to consider whether neuroscience can provide important insights into the potential for mindfulness-meditation training to both strengthen cognitive skills and, more importantly, identify the factors that contribute to and the mechanisms that underlie process-specific learning. We believe this study, and the research it will certainly generate, are going to have a profound impact on the nature and direction of coaching strategies in personal- and leadership-development environments in the near future.

It is evident that significant and impressive progress has been made in defining and detailing the developing field of neuroleadership.

Conclusion

In bringing together and reflecting on the breadth and depth of recent research in neuroscience and social psychology, it is evident that significant and impressive progress has been made in defining and detailing the developing field of neuroleadership. The applications of this research by neuroleadership scholars and practitioners are clarifying thinking, motivating creativity, inspiring learning, enhancing productivity, and promoting well-being—making the difference we all anticipated just six short years earlier when the discipline was first considered. Much work has been done; much is yet to begin.

Still, with the growing recognition of emotion's indispensable role in personal and leadership development, it is becoming increasingly evident that social psychologists, neuroscientists, organizational-behavior and leadership theorists, and leadership practitioners need to be working together more closely to break down terminology barriers where they are needlessly inhibiting advancements in new thinking and applications. A functional co-mingling of concepts ranging from definitions to terminology to functioning models among these disciplines will serve to focus the usefulness of those tools and have the beneficial effect of accelerating "time-to-market" for working practitioners.

With what we see in the research pipeline and what we anticipate, a large body of compelling work is forthcoming. In light of this anticipation and our expectations, perhaps the best advice we can give is still the same as we offered in our initial review of research and have offered in all subsequent reviews: "Now continues to be a good time to take a neuroscientist to lunch."

References

Alberts, H. J. E. M., Martijn, C., and De Vries, N. K. 2011. "Fighting Self-Control Failure: Overcoming Ego Depletion by Increasing Self-Awareness." *Journal of Experimental Social Psychology* 47(1): 58–62.

Aldwin, C. M., Molitor, N-T, Spiro, A., Levenson, M. R., Molitor, J., and Igarashi, H. 2011. "Do Stress Trajectories Predict Mortality in Older Men?" Longitudinal findings from the VA normative aging study. *Journal of Aging Research*.

Alexander, R. D. 1989. "Evolution of the Human Psyche." In *The Human Revolution: Behavioral and Biological Perspectives on the Origins of Modern Humans*, edited by P. Mellars, and C. Stringer, 455–513. Princeton, NJ: Princeton University Press.

Alfonso, J. P., Caracuel, A., Delgado-Pastor, L. C., and Verdejo- Garcíab, A. 2011. "Combined Goal Management Training and Mindfulness Meditation Improve Executive Functions and Decision-Making Performance in Abstinent Polysubstance Abusers." *Drug and Alcohol Dependence* 117: 78–81.

Allen, T. J., and. Sherman, J. W. 2011. "Ego Threat and Intergroup Bias: A test of Motivated-activation Versus Self-Regulatory Accounts." *Psychological Science* 22(3): 331–333.

Alloway, T. P., Banner, G. E., and Smith, P. 2010. "Working Memory and Cognitive Styles in Adolescents' Attainment." *British Journal of Educational Psychology* 80: 567–581.

Amodio, D. M., and Frith, C. D. 2006. "Meeting of the Minds: The Medial Frontal cortex and Social Cognition." *Nature* 7: 268–77.

Anderson, C., Kraus, M. W., Galinsky, A. D., and Keltner, D. 2012. "The Local-Ladder Effect: Social Status and Subjective Well-Being." *Psychological Science*, May 31.

Avni-Babad, D. 2011. "Routine and Feelings of Safety, Confidence, and Well-Being." *British Journal of Psychology* 102(2): 223–244.

Bailey, D. H., and Geary, D. C. 2009. "Hominid Brain Evolution: Testing Climatic, Ecological, and Social Competition Models." *Human Nature* 20: 67–79.

Balliet, D., Li, N. P., Macfarlan, S. J., and Van Vugt, M. 2011. "Sex Differences in Cooperation: A Meta-Analytic Review of Social Dilemmas." *Psychological Bulletin* 137(6): 881–909.

Barnes, C. M., Schaubroeck, J., Huth, M., and Ghumman, S. 2011. "Lack of Sleep and Unethical Conduct." *Organizational Behavior and Human Decision Processes* 115(2): 169–180.

Bauer, I. M., and Baumeister, R. F. 2011. "Self-Regulatory Strength." In *Handbook of Self-Regulation*, edited by K. D. Vohs, and R. F. Baumeister, 64–82. New York: Guilford.

Bault, N., Joffily, M., Rustichini, A., and Coricelli, G. 2011. "Medial Prefrontal Cortex and Striatum Mediate the Influence of Social Comparison on the Decision Process." *Proceedings of the National Academy of Sciences, USA* 108(38): 16044–16049.

Baumeister, R. F., Gailliot, M. T., DeWall, C. N., and Oaten, M. 2006. "Self-Regulation and Personality: How Interventions Increase Regulatory Success, and How Depletion Moderates the Effects of Traits on Behavior." *Journal of Personality* 74: 1773–1801.

Baumeister, R. F., Muraven, M., and Tice, D. M. 2000. "Ego-Depletion: A Resource Model of Volition, Self-Regulation, and Controlled Processing." *Social Cognition* 18: 130–150.

Beal, D., and Ghandour, L. 2011. "Stability, Change, and the Stability of Change in Daily Workplace Affect." *Journal of Organizational Behavior* 32(4): 526–546.

Becker, W. J., Cropanzano, R., and Sanfey, A. G. 2011. "Organizational Neuroscience: Taking Organizational Theory Inside the Neural Black Box." *Journal of Management* 37(4): 933–961.

Berger, J. 2011. "Arousal Increases Social Transmission of Information." *Psychological Science* 22(7): 891–893.

Biesanz, J. C., Human, L. J., Paquin, A. C., Chan, M., Parisotto, K. L., Sarracino, J., et al. 2011. "Do We Know When Our Impressions of Others Are Valid? Evidence for Realistic Accuracy Awareness in First Impressions of Personality." *Social Psychological and Personality Science* 2(5): 452–459.

Blechert, J., Sheppes, G., Di Tella, C., Williams, H., and Gross, J. J. 2012. "See What you Think: Reappraisal Modulates Behavioral and Neural Responses to Social Stimuli." *Psychological Science* 23(4): 346–353.

Bollen, J., Mao, H., and Zeng, X. J. 2011. "Twitter Mood Predicts the Stock Market." *Journal of Computational Science* 2(1): 1–8.

Boucher, H. C., and Kofos, M. N. 2012. "The Idea of Money Counteracts Ego Depletion Effects." *Journal of Experimental Social Psychology*, forthcoming.

Carr, N. 2010. *The Shallows: What the Internet Is Doing to Our Brains.* New York: W. W. Norton.

Casey, B. J., Somerville, L. H., Gotlib, I. H., Ayduk, O., Franklin, N. T., Askren, M. K., et al. 2011. "Behavioral and Neural Correlates of Delay of Gratification 40 years later." *Proceedings of the National Academy of Sciences, USA* 108(36): 14998–15003.

Chance, Z., Norton, M. I., Gino, F., and Ariely, D. 2011. "Temporal View of the Costs and Benefits of Self-Deception." *Proceedings of the National Academy of Sciences, USA* 108(3): 15655–15659.

Coan, J. A., Schaefer, H. S., and Davidson, R. J. 2006. "Lending a Hand: Social Regulation of the Neural Response to Threat." *Psychological Science* 17: 1032–1039.

Cwir, D., Carr, P., Walton, G., and Spencer, S. 2011. "Your Heart Makes My Heart Move: Cues of Social Connectedness Cause Shared Emotions and Physiological States Among Strangers." *Journal of Experimental Social Psychology* 47(3): 661–664.

Danziger, S., Levav, J., and Avnaim-Pesso, L. 2011. "Extraneous Factors in Judicial Decisions." *Proceedings of the National Academy of Sciences, USA* 108: 6889–6892.

Dasborough, M. T. 2006. "Cognitive Asymmetry in Employee Emotional Reactions to Leadership Behaviors." *Leadership Quarterly* 17: 163–178.

Dasborough, M. T., and Ashkanasy, N. M. 2002. "Emotion and Attribution of Intentionality in Leader–Member Relationships." *Leadership Quarterly* 13: 615–634.

Davidson, R. J. 2004. "Well-Being and Affective Style: Neural Substrates and Biobehavioural Correlates." *Philosophical Transactions of the Royal Society B: Biological Sciences* 359: 1395–1411.

Debette, S., Metso, T., Pezzini, A., Abboud, S., Metso, A., Leys, D., Bersano, A., et al. 2011. "Association of Vascular Risk Factors With Cervical Artery Dissection and Ischemic Stroke in Young Adults." *Circulation* 123(14): 1537–1544.

Debette, S., Seshadri, S., Beiser, A., Au, R., Himali, J.J., Palumbo, C., Wolf, P.A., et al. 2011. "Midlife Vascular Risk Factor Exposure Accelerates Structural Brain Aging and Cognitive Decline." *Neurology* 77(5): 461–468.

Decety, J., Michalska, K. J., and Kinzler, K. D. 2012. "The Contribution of Emotion and Cognition to Moral Sensitivity: A Neurodevelopmental Study." *Cerebral Cortex* 22(1): 209–220.

De Quervain, D. J., Fischbacher, U., Treyer, V., Schellhammer, M., Schnyder, U., Buck, A., et al. 2004. "The Neural Basis of Altruistic Punishment." *Science* 305: 1254–1258.

De Ruddere, L., Goubert, L., Prkachin, K. M., Stevens, M. A. L., Van Ryckeghem, D. M. L., and Crombez, G. 2011. "When you Dislike Patients, Pain is taken Less Seriously." *Pain* 152(10): 2342–2347.

DeWall, C. N., and Bushman, B. J. 2011. "Social Acceptance and Rejection: The Sweet and the Bitter." *Current Directions in Psychological Science* 20(4): 256–260.

DeWall, C. N., Twenge, J. M., Koole, S. L., Baumeister, R. F., Marquez, A., and Reid, M. W. 2011. "Automatic Emotion Regulation after Social Exclusion: Tuning to Positivity." *Emotion* 11(3): 623–636.

Dixon, P., Ochsner, K. N., and Rock, D. 2010. "Turn the 360 Around." *NeuroLeadership Journal* 3: 78–86.

Duhigg, C. 2012. *The Power of Habit: Why We Do What We Do in Life and Business.* New York: Random House.

Dunbar, R. 2003. "Evolution of the Social Brain." *Science* 302: 1160–1161.

Dunn, B. D, Galton, H. C., Morgan, R., Evans, D., Oliver, C., Meyer M., et al. 2010. "Listening to Your Heart: How Interoception Shapes Emotion Experience and Intuitive Decision-Making." *Psychological Science* 21(12): 1835–1844.

Eisenberger, N. I. 2011. "Broken Hearts and Broken Bones: A Neural Perspective on the Similarities Between Social and Physical Pain." *Current Directions in Psychological Science* 21(1): 42–47.

Eisenberger, N. I., and Lieberman, M. D. 2004. "Why Rejection Hurts: The Neurocognitive Overlap Between Physical and Social Pain." *Trends in Cognitive Sciences* 8: 294–300.

Eisenberger, N. I., Taylor, S. E., Gable, S. L., Hilmert, C. J., and Lieberman, M. D. 2007. "Neural Pathways Link Social Support to Attenuated Neuroendocrine Stress Response." *NeuroImage* 35: 1601–1612.

Erickson, K. I., Voss, M. W., Prakash, R. S., Basak, C., Szabo, A., Chaddock, L., et al. 2011. "Exercise Training Increases Size of Hippocampus and Improves Memory." *Proceedings of the National Academy of Sciences, USA* 108: 3017–3022.

Farb, N. A. S., Segal, Z. V., Mayberg, H., Bean, J., McKeon, D., Fatima, Z., et al. 2007. "Attending to the Present: Mindfulness Meditation Reveals Distinct Neural Modes of Self-Reference." *Social Cognitive and Affective Neuroscience* 2(4): 313–322.

Fennis, B. M. 2011. "Can't Get Over Me: Ego Depletion Attenuates Prosocial Effects of Perspective Taking." *European Journal of Social Psychology* 41(5): 580–585.

Fenton-O'Creevy, M., Soane, E., Nicholson, N., and Willman, P. 2011. "Thinking, Feeling and Deciding: The Influence of Emotions on the Decision-Making and Performance of Traders." *Journal of Organizational Behavior* 32: 1044–1061.

Ferguson, M. 2011. "You Cannot Leave it at the Office: Spillover and Crossover of Coworker Incivility." *Journal of Organizational Behavior* 33(4): 571–588.

Figner, B., Knoch, D., Johnson, E. J., Krosch, A. R., Lisanby, S. H., Fehr, E., et al. 2010. "Lateral Prefrontal Cortex and Self-Control in Intertemporal Choice." *Nature Neuroscience* 13(5): 538–539.

Frith, C. D., and Singer, T. 2008. "The Role of Social Cognition in Decision-Making." *Philosophical Transactions of the Royal Society B: Biological Sciences* 363: 3875–3886.

Galli, G., Wolpe, N., and Otten, L. J. 2011. "Sex Differences in the Use of Anticipatory Brain Activity to Encode Emotional Events." *Journal of Neuroscience* 31(34): 12364–12370.

Garland, E. L., Gaylord, S. A., and Fredrickson, B. K. 2011. "Positive Reappraisal Mediates the Stress-Reductive Effects of Mindfulness: An Upward Spiral Process." *Mindfulness* 2: 59–67.

Gawronski, B., Rydell, R. J., Vervliet, B., and De Houwer, J. 2010. "Generalization Versus Contextualization in Automatic Evaluation." *Journal of Experimental Psychology: General* 139(4): 683–701.

Geraci, A., and Surian, L. 2011. "The Developmental Roots of Fairness: Infants' Reactions to Equal and Unequal Distributions of Resources." *Developmental Science* 14(5): 1012–1020.

Germine, L., Duchaine, B., and Nakayama, K. 2011. "Where Cognitive Development and Aging Meet: Face Learning Ability Peaks After Age 30." *Cognition* 118(2): 201–210.

Gilkey, R., Caceda, R., and Kilts, C. 2010. "When Emotional Reasoning Triumphs Over IQ." *Harvard Business Review* 88(9): 27.

Glasø, L., and Einarsen, S. 2008. "Emotional Regulation in Leader-Follower Relationships." *European Journal of Work and Organizational Psychology* 17: 482–500.

Gonsalkorale, K., Sherman, J. W., Allen, T. J., Klauer, K. C., and Amodio, D. M. 2011. "Accounting for Successful Control of Implicit Racial Bias: The Roles of Association Activation, Response Monitoring, and Overcoming Bias." *Personality and Social Psychology Bulletin* 37(11): 1534–1545.

Gooty, J., Connelly, S., Griffith, J., and Gupta, A. 2010. "Leadership, Affect, and Emotions. A State of the Science Review." *Leadership Quarterly* 21(6): 979–1004.

Gospic, K., Mohlin, E., Fransson, P., Petrovic, P., Johannesson, M., and Ingvar, M. 2011. "Limbic Justice: Amygdala Involvement in Immediate Rejection in the Ultimatum Game." *PLoS Biology* 9(5).

Greene, J. D. 2011. "Emotion and Morality: A Tasting Menu." *Emotion Review* 3(3): 1–3.

Gross, J. J., and Barrett, L. F. 2011. "Emotion Generation and Emotion Regulation: One or two Depends on your Point of View." *Emotion Review* 3(1): 8–16.

Gross, J. J., Richards, J. M., and John, O. P. 2006. "Emotion Regulation in Everyday Life." In *Emotion Regulation in Couples and Families: Pathways to Dysfunction and Health*, edited by D. K. Snyder, J. Simpson, and J. N. Hughes, 13–35. Washington, DC: American Psychological Association.

Groves, K. S. 2006. "Leader Emotional Expressivity, Visionary Leadership, and Organizational Change." *Leadership and Organization Development Journal* 27: 566–583.

Gujar, N., McDonald, S., Nishida, M., and Walker, M. 2010. "A Role for REM Sleep in Recalibrating the Sensitivity of the Human Brain to Specific Emotions." *Cerebral Cortex* 21(1): 115–123.

Gupta, R., Koscik, T. R., Bechara, A., and Tranel, D. 2011. "The Amygdala and Decision-Making." *Neuropsychologia* 49(4): 760–766.

Gyurak, A., Gross, J. J., and Etkin, A. 2011. "Explicit and Implicit Emotion Regulation: A Dual-Process Framework." *Cognition and Emotion* 25(3): 400–412.

Hagger, M. S., Wood, C., Stiff, C., and Chatzisarantis, N. L. D. 2010. "Ego Depletion and the Strength Model of Self-Control: A Meta-Analysis." *Psychological Bulletin* 136(4): 495–525.

Halford, G. S., Cowan, N., and Andrews, G. 2007. "Separating Cognitive Capacity from Knowledge: A New Hypothesis." *Trends in Cognitive Sciences* 11(6): 236–242.

Hambrick, D. Z., and Meinz, E. J. 2011. "Limits on the Predictive Power of Domain-Specific Experience and Knowledge in Skilled Performance." *Current Directions in Psychological Science* 20(5): 275–279.

Hamlin, J. K., Wynn, K., Bloom, P., and Mahajan, N. 2011. "How Infants and Toddlers React to Antisocial Others." *Proceedings of the National Academy of Science, USA* 108(50): 19931–19936.

Hansen, F., and Christensen, S. R. 2007. *Emotions Advertising and Consumer Choice*. Copenhagen, Denmark: Copenhagen Business School Press.

Heatherton, T. F. 2011. "Neuroscience of Self and Self-Regulation." *Annual Review of Psychology* 62: 363–390.

Herbig, B., Muller, A., and Petrovic, K. 2007. "Implicit Knowledge in the Product Innovation Process." *In Innovationsforschung: Ansätze, methoden, grenzen und perspektiven*, edited by Hof, H., and Wenganroth, U., 239–280. Hamburg, Germany: Lit Verlag.

Hesselbein, F., and Shinseki, E. K. 2004. *Be-Know-Do: Leadership the Army Way*. San Francisco, CA: Jossey-Bass.

Hill, S. E., DelPriore, D. J., and Vaughan, P. W. 2011. "The Cognitive Consequences of Envy: Attention, Memory, and Self-Regulatory Depletion." *Journal of Personality and Social Psychology* 101(4): 653–666.

Hollis-Walker, L., and Colosimo, K. 2011. "Mindfulness, Self-Compassion, and Happiness in Nonmeditators: A theoretical and Empirical Examination." *Personality and Individual Differences* 50: 222–227.

Holloway, R. L., Jr. 1967. "The Evolution of the Human Brain: Some Notes Toward a Synthesis between Alexander Neural Structure and the Evolution of Complex Behavior." *General Systems* 12: 3–19.

Hölzel, B. K, Carmody, J., Vangel, M., Congleton, C., Yerramsetti, S .M., Gard, T., and Lazar, S. 2011. "Mindfulness Practice Leads to Increases in Regional Brain Gray Matter Density." *Psychiatry Research: Neuroimaging* 191(1): 36–43.

Human, L. J., Biesanz, J. C., Parisotto, K. L., and Dunn, E. W. 2012. "Your Best Self Helps Reveal Your True Self: Positive Self-Presentation Leads to More Accurate Personality impressions." *Social Psychological and Personality Science* 3(1): 23–30.

Hurley, C. M., and Frank, M. G. 2011. "Executing Facial Control During Deception Situations." *Journal of Nonverbal Behavior* 35(2): 119–131.

Inesi, M. E., Botti, S., Dubois, D., Rucker, D. D., and Galinsky, A. D. 2011. "Power and Choice: Their Dynamic Interplay in Quenching the Thirst for Personal Control." *Psychological Science* 22(8): 1042–1048.

Izard, C. E. 2010. "Emotion Theory and Research: Highlights, on Answered Questions, and Emerging Issues." *Annual Review of Psychology* 60: 1–25.

Izuma, K., Saito, D. N., and Sadato, N. 2008. "Processing of Social and Monetary Rewards in the Human Striatum." *Neuron* 58: 284–294.

Job, V., Dweck, C. S., and Walton, G. M. 2010. "Ego Depletion—Is it all in Your Head? Implicit Theories about Willpower Affect Self-Regulation." *Psychological Science* 21(11): 1686–1693, November.

Johnson, S.K. 2008. "I Second that Emotion: Effects of Emotional Contagion and Affect at Work on Leader and Follower Outcomes." *The Leadership Quarterly* 19: 1-19.

Johnson, D. D. P., and Fowler, J. H. 2011. "The Evolution of Overconfidence." *Nature* 477: 317–320.

Johnson, M. K., Rowatt, W. C., and Petrini, L. 2011. "A New Trait on the Market: Honesty-Humility as a Unique Predictor of Job Performance." *Personality and Individual Differences* 50(6): 857–862.

Judge, T. A., Livingston, B. A., and Hurst, C. 2012. "Do Nice Guys—and Gals—Really Finish Last? The Joint Effects of Sex and Agreeableness on Income." *Journal of Personality and Social Psychology* 102(2): 390–407.

Kanai, R., Bahrami, B., Roylance, R., and Rees, G. 2012. "Online Social Network Size is Reflected in Human Brain Structure." *Proceedings of the Royal Society B: Biological Sciences* 279(1732): 1327–1334.

Kendler, K. S., Eaves, L. J., Loken, E. K., Pedersen, N. L., Middeldorp, C. M., Reynolds, C., et al. 2011. "The Impact of Environmental Experiences on Symptoms of Anxiety and Depression Across the Life Span." *Psychological Science* 22(10): 1343–1352.

Kligyte, V., Connelly, S., Thiel, C. E., Devenport, L. D., Brown, R. P., and Mumford, M. D. 2009. "Influence of Emotions and Emotion Regulation Strategies on Ethical Decision-Making." Paper presented at the Annual Meeting of the Society for Industrial and Organizational Psychology, New Orleans, LA.

Klucharev, V., Hytonen, K., Rijpkema, M., Smidts, A., and Fernandez, G. 2009. "Reinforcement Learning Signal Predicts Social Conformity." *Neuron* 6: 140–151.

Kogan, A., Keltner, D., Impett, E., Oveis, C., and Saturn, S. 2011. "Thin-Slicing Study of the Oxytocin Receptor (OXTR) Gene and the Evaluation and Expression of the Prosocial Disposition." *Proceedings of the National Academy of Sciences, USA* 108(48): 19189–19192.

Konrath, S. H., O'Brien, E. H., and Hsing, C. 2011. "Changes in Dispositional Empathy in American College Students Over Time: A Meta-Analysis." *Personality and Social Psychology Review* 15(2): 180–198.

Koole, S. L., and Rothermund, K. 2011. "'I Feel Better But I Don't Know Why': The Psychology of Implicit Emotion Regulation." *Cognition and Emotion* 25(3): 389–399.

Kraus, M. W., Piff, P. K., and Keltner, D. 2011a. "Social Class as Culture: The Convergence of Resources and Rank in the Social Realm." *Current Directions in Psychological Science* 100: 246–250.

Kraus, M. W., Horberg, E. J., Goetz, J. L., and Keltner, D. 2011b. "Social Class Rank, Threat Vigilance, and Hostile Reactivity." *Personality and Social Psychology Bulletin* 37: 1376–1388.

Kuhnen, C. M., and Knutson, B. 2005. "The Neural Basis of Financial Risk Taking." *Neuron* 47: 763–770.

Kuppens, P., Van Mechelen, I., Smits, D. J. M., De Boeck, P., and Ceulemans, E. 2007. "Individual Differences in Patterns of Appraisal and Anger Experience." *Cognition and Emotion* 21: 689–713.

LaBouff, J. P., Rowatt, W. C., Johnson, M. K., Tsang, J., and Willerton, G. M. 2012. "Humble Persons are More Helpful than Less Humble Persons: Evidence from Three Studies." *Journal of Positive Psychology* 7(1): 16–29.

Lawrence, N. S., Jollant, F., O'Daly, O., Zelaya, F., and Phillips, M. L. 2009. "Distinct Roles of Prefrontal Cortical Subregions in the Iowa Gambling Task." *Cerebral Cortex* 19: 1134–1143.

Leotti, L. A., and Delgado, M. R. 2011. "The Inherent Reward of Choice." *Psychological Science* 22(10): 1310–1318.

Li, N., Liang, J., and Michael, C. J. 2010. "The Role of Proactive Personality in Job Satisfaction and Organizational Citizenship Behavior: A Relational Perspective." *Journal of Applied Psychology* 95(2): 395–404.

Lieberman, M. D., and Eisenberger, N. I. 2008. "The Pains and Pleasures of Social Life: A Social Cognitive Neuroscience Approach." *NeuroLeadership Journal* 1: 38–43.

Lieberman, M. D., Eisenberger, N. I., Crockett, M. J., Tom, S. M., Pfeifer, J. H., and Way, B. M. 2007. "Putting Feelings into Words: Affect Labeling Disrupts Amygdala Activity in Response to Affective Stimuli." *Psychological Science: A Journal of the American Psychological Society* 18(5): 421–428.

Liew, S. L., Ma, Y., Han, S., and Aziz-Zadeh, L. 2011. "Who's Afraid of the Boss: Cultural Differences in Social Hierarchies Modulate Self-Face Recognition in Chinese and Americans." *PLoS one*, 6(2): e16901. doi:10.1371/journal.pone.0016901.

Lighthall, N. R., Sakaki, M., Vasunilashorn, S., Nga, L., Somayajula, S., Chen, E. Y., et al. 2011. "Gender Differences in Reward-Related Decision Processing Under Stress." *Social Cognitive and Affective Neuroscience*, forthcoming.

Lou, Y. 2011. "Do 10-Month-Old Infants Understand Others' False Beliefs?" *Cognition* 121(3): 289–298.

Lount, R. B., and Pettit, N. C. 2012. "The Social Context of Trust: The Role of Status." *Organizational Behavior and Human Decision Processes* 117(1): 15–23.

Loewenstein, G. F., Weber, E. U., Hsee, C. K., and Welch, N. 2001. "Risk as Feelings." *Psychological Bulletin* 127: 267–286.

Ly, M., Haynes, M. R., Barter, J. W., Weinberger, D. R., and Zink, C. F. 2011. "Subjective Socioeconomic Status Predicts Human Ventral Striatal Responses to Social Status Information." Current Biology 21(9): 794–797.

Martin, L. N., and Delgado, M. R. 2011. "The Influence of Emotion Regulation on Decision-Making Under Risk." *Journal of Cognitive Neuroscience* 23(9): 2569–2581.

McEwen, B. S. 2007. "Physiology and Neurobiology of Stress and Adaptation: Central Role of the Brain." *Physiological Reviews*. 87: 873–904.

McRae, K., Jacobs, S. E., Ray, R. D., John, O. P., and Gross, J. J. 2012. "Individual Differences in Reappraisal Ability: Links to Reappraisal Frequency, Well-Being, and Cognitive Control." *Journal of Research in Personality* 46: 2–7.

McRae, K., Misra, S., Prasad, A. K., Pereira, S. C., and Gross, J. J. 2011. "Bottom-up and Top-down Emotion Generation: Implications for Emotion Regulation." *Social Cognitive and Affective Neuroscience* 7(3): 253–262.

Mercier, H., and Sperber, D. 2011. "Why do Humans Reason? Arguments for an Argumentative Theory." *Behavioral and Brain Sciences* 34: 57–111.

Miner, K. N., and Eischeid, A. 2012. "Observing Incivility Toward Coworkers and Negative Emotions: Do Gender of the Target and Observer Matter?" *Sex Roles* 66(7–8): 492–505.

Miron-Spektor, E., Efrat-Treister, D., Rafaeli, A., and Schwarz-Cohen, O. 2011. "Others' Anger Makes People Work Harder Not Smarter: The Effect of Observing Anger and Sarcasm on Creative and Analytic Thinking." *Journal of Applied Psychology* 96(5): 1065–1075.

Mischel, W., Shoda, Y., and Rodriguez, M. I. 1989. "Delay of Gratification in Children." *Science* 244: 933–938.

Moffitt, T., Arseneault, L., Belsky, D., Dickson, N., Hancox, R., Harrington, H., et al. 2011. "A Gradient of Childhood Self-Control Predicts Health, Wealth, and Public Safety." *Proceedings of the National Academy of Sciences, USA* 108(7): 2693–2698.

Mojzisch, A., and Schulz-Hard, S. 2010. "Knowing Others' Preferences Degrades the Quality of Group Decisions." *Journal of Personality and Social Psychology* 98(5): 794–808.

Muraven, M., and Slessareva, E. 2003. "Mechanisms of Self-Control Failure: Motivation and Limited Resources." *Personality and Social Psychology Bulletin* 29: 894–906.

Myers, D. G. 2004. *Intuition: Its Powers and Perils*. New Haven, CT: Yale University Press.

Neal, D. T., Wood, W., Labrecque, J., and Lally, P. 2011a. "How do Habits Guide Behavior? Perceived and Actual Triggers of Habits in Daily Life." *Journal of Experimental Social Psychology* forthcoming.

Neal, D. T., Wood, W., Wu, M., and Kurlander, D. 2011b. "The Pull of the Past: When do Habits Persist Despite Conflict with Motives?" *Personality and Social Psychology Bulletin* 37(11): 1428–1437.

Neumann, J. V., and Morgenstern, O. 1947. *Theory of Games and Economic Behavior*. Princeton, NJ: Princeton University Press.

Newcombe, M. J., and Ashkanasy, N. M. 2002. "The Role of Affect and Affective Congruence in Perceptions of Leaders: An Experimental Study." *Leadership Quarterly* 13: 601–614.

Niedenthal, P. M., and Brauer, M. 2012. "Social Functionality of Human Emotion." *Annual Review of Psychology* 63: 259–285.

Nguyen, C. M., Koenigs, M., Yamada, T. H., Teo, S. H., Cavanaugh, J. E., Tranel, D., et al. 2011. "Trustworthiness and Negative Affect Predict Economic Decision-Making." *Journal of Cognitive Psychology* 23(6): 748–759.

Nolen-Hoeksema, S. 2012. "Emotion Regulation and Psychopathology: The Role of Gender." *Annual Review of Clinical Psychology* 8: 161–187.

Nolen-Hoeksema, S., and Aldao, A. 2011. "Gender and Age Differences in Emotion Regulation Strategies and their Relationship to Depressive Symptoms." *Personality and Individual Differences* 51(6): 704–708.

Ossandon, T., Jerbi, K., Vidal, J. R., Bayle, D. J., Henaff, M. A., Jung, J., et al. 2011. "Transient Suppression of Broadband Gamma Power in the Default-Mode Network is Correlated with Task Complexity and Subject Performance." *Journal of Neuroscience* 31(41): 14521–14530.

Pashler, H., McDaniel, M., Rohrer, D., and Bjork, R. 2008. "Learning Styles: Concepts and Evidence." *Psychological Science in the Public Interest* 9(3): 105–119.

Payne, J. D., and Kensinger, E. A. 2011. "Sleep Leads to Qualitative Changes in the Emotional Memory Trace: Evidence from fMRI." *Journal of Cognitive Neuroscience* 23(6): 1285–1297.

Rajah, R., Song, Z., and Arvey, R. D. 2011. "Emotionality and Leadership: Taking Stock of the Past Decade of Research." *Leadership Quarterly* 22: 1107–1119.

Ray, R. D., Ochsner, K. N., Cooper, J. C., Robertson, E. R., Gabrieli, J. D. E., and Gross, J. J. 2005. "Individual Differences in Trait Rumination and the Neural Systems Supporting Cognitive Reappraisal." *Cognitive, Affective, and Behavioral Neuroscience* 5(2): 156–168.

Reimann, M., and Bechara, A. 2010. "The Somatic Marker Framework as a Neurological Theory of Decision-Making: Review, Conceptual Comparisons, and Future Neuroeconomics Research." *Journal of Economic Psychology* 31: 767–776.

Reuben, E., Rey-Biel, P., Sapienza, P., and Zingales, L. 2011. "The Emergence of Male Leadership in Competitive Environments." *Journal of Economic Behavior and Organization*, forthcoming.

Reverberi, C., Bonatti, L. L., Frackowiak, R. S. J., Paulesu, E., Cherubini, P., and Macaluso, E. 2012. "Large Scale Brain Activations Predict Reasoning Profiles." *NeuroImage* 59(2): 1752–1764.

Riggio, R. E., and Reichard, R. J. 2008. "The Emotional and Social Intelligences of Effective Leadership: An Emotional and Social Skill Approach." *Journal of Managerial Psychology* 23: 169–185.

Rilling, J. K., and Sanfey, A. G. 2011. "The Neuroscience of Social Decision-Making." *Annual Review of Psychology* 62: 23–48.

Ringleb, A. 2009. "Building Quality in the Work Force: Understanding the Neuroscience of Engagement." Paper presented at Kakovost ustvarja razliko (Quality Makes the Difference), 18th Annual Conference, Portorož, Slovenia, November 12.

Ringleb, A., and Rock, D. 2008. "NeuroLeadership in 2008." *NeuroLeadership Journal* 1: 1–10.

Ringleb, A., Rock, D., and Conser, J. 2010. "NeuroLeadership in 2010." *NeuroLeadership Journal* 3: 1–12.

Robbins, J. M., Ford, M. T., and Tetrick, L. E. 2011. "Perceived Unfairness and Employee health: A Meta-Analytic Integration." *Journal of Applied Psychology* 97(2): 235–272.

Rock, D. 2008. "SCARF: A Brain-Based Model for Collaborating with and Influencing Others." *NeuroLeadership Journal* 1: 44–52.

Rock, D., and Cox, C. 2012. "SCARF in 2012: Updating the Social Neuroscience of Collaborating with Others." *NeuroLeadership Journal* 4: 129-142.

Rock, D., Siegel, D., Poelmans, S.A.Y., and Payne, J. 2012. "The Healthy Mind Platter." *NeuroLeadership Journal* 4: 40-62.

Rock, D., and Tang, Y. 2009. "Neuroscience of Engagement." *NeuroLeadership Journal* 2: 15–22.

Roets, A., and Van Hiel, A. 2011. "Allport's Prejudiced Personality Today: Need for Closure as the Motivated Cognitive Basis of Prejudice." *Current Directions in Psychological Science* 20(6): 349–354.

Sallet, J., Mars, R. B., Noonan, M. P., Andersson, J. L., O'Reilly, J. X., Jbabdi, S., et al. 2011. "Social Network Size Affects Neural Circuits in Macaques." *Science* 4: 697–700.

Samson, A. C., and Gross, J. J. 2012. "Humour as Emotion Regulation: The Differential Consequences of Negative Versus Positive Humour." *Cognition and Emotion* 26(2): 375–384.

Schmeichel, B. J., and Vohs, K. 2009. "Self-Affirmation and Self-Control: Affirming Core Values Counteracts Ego Depletion." *Journal of Personality and Social Psychology* 96: 770–782.

Schwartz, J., and Gladding, R. 2011. *You Are Not Your Brain: The 4-Step Solution for Changing Bad Habits, Ending Unhealthy Thinking, and Taking Control of Your Life*. New York: Avery.

Schweiger-Gallo, I., Keil, A., McCulloch, K. C., Rockstroh, B., and Gollwitzer, P. M. 2009. "Strategic Automation of Emotion Regulation." *Journal of Personality and Social Psychology* 96(1): 11–31.

Senholzi, K. B., and Kubota, J. T. 2011. "Knowing you Beyond Race: The Importance of Individual Feature Encoding in the Other-Race Effect." *Frontiers in Human Neuroscience* 5(33): 1.

Shapiro, S., Oman, D., Thoresen, C., Plante, T., and Flinders, T. 2008. "Cultivating Mindfulness: Effects on Well-Being." *Journal of Clinical Psychology* 64: 840–862.

Shirom, A., Toker, S., Alkaly, Y., Jacobson, O., and Balicer, R. 2011. "Work-Based Predictors of Mortality: A 20-year Followup of Healthy Employees." *Health Psychology* 30(3): 268–275.

Shiv, B., Loewenstein, G., Bechara, A., Damasio, H., and Damasio, A.R. 2005. "Investment Behavior and the Negative Side of Emotion." *Psychological Science* 16: 435–439.

Singer, T., Seymour, B., O'Doherty, J. P., Stephan, K. E., Dolan, R. J., and Frith, C. D. 2006. "Empathic Neural Responses are Modulated by the Perceived Fairness of Others." *Nature* 439: 466–469.

Spitzer M., Fischbacher U., Herrnberger B., Gron G., and Fehr E. 2007. "The Neural Signature of Social Norm Compliance." *Neuron* 56: 185–96

Slagter, H. A., Davidson, R. J., and Lutz, A. 2011. "Mental Training as a Tool in the Neuroscientific Study of Brain and Cognitive Plasticity." *Frontiers in Human Neuroscience* 5: 1–12.

Starck, K., Polzer, C., Wolf, O. T., and Brand, M. 2010. "Does Stress Alter Everyday Moral Decision-Making?" *Psychoneuroendocrinology* 36: 210–219.

Stellar, J. E., Manzo, V. M., Kraus, M. W., and Keltner, D. 2011. "Class and Compassion: Socioeconomic Factors Predict Responses to Suffering." *Emotion* (no pagination provided).

Stoeber, J., and Janssen, D. P. 2011. "Perfectionism and Coping with Daily Failures: Positive Reframing Helps Achieve Satisfaction at the End of the Day." *Anxiety, Stress and Coping* 24(5): 477–497.

Tang, Y. Y., Yinghua, M., Wang, W., et al. 2007. "Short-Term Meditation Training Improves Attention and Self-Regulation." *Proceedings of the National Academy of Sciences, USA* 104: 17152–17156.

Thiel, C. E., Connelly, S., and Griffith, G. A. 2011. "The Influence of Anger on Ethical Decision-Making: Comparison of a Primary and Secondary Appraisal." *Ethics and Behavior* 21(5): 380–403.

Thompson, R. A. 2011. "Emotion and Emotion Regulation: Two Sides of the Developing Coin." *Emotion Review* 3(1): 53–61.

Tiedens, L. Z., and Linton, S. 2001. "Judgment under Emotional Certainty and Uncertainty: The Effects of Specific Emotions on Information Processing." *Journal of Personality and Social Psychology* 81: 973–988.

Tom, S. M., Fox, C. R., Trepel, C., and Poldrack, R. A. 2007. "The Neural Basis of Loss Aversion in Decision-Making Under Risk." *Science* 315: 515–518.

Van Honk, J., Schutter, D. J., Bos, P. A., Kruijt, A. W., Lentjes, E. G., and Baron-Cohen, S. 2011. "Testosterone Administration Impairs Cognitive Empathy in Women Depending on Second-to-Fourth Digit Ratio." *Proceedings of the National Academy of Sciences, USA* 108(8): 3448–3452.

Vazire, S., and Carlson, E. N. 2011. "Others Sometimes Know Us Better Than We Know Ourselves." *Current Directions in Psychological Science* 20(2): 104–108.

Venkatraman, V., Huettel, S. A., Chuah, L. Y. M., Payne, J. W., and Chee, M. W. L. 2011. "Sleep Deprivation Biases the Neural Mechanisms Underlying Economic Preferences." *Journal of Neuroscience* 31(10): 3712–3718.

Vohs, K. D., Glass, B. D., Maddox, W. T., and Markman, A. B. 2011. "Ego Depletion is not Just Fatigue." *Social Psychological and Personality Science* 2: 166–173.

Voss, M. W., Nagamatsu, L. S., Liu-Ambrose, T., and Kramer, A. F. 2011. "Exercise, Brain, and Cognition Across the Life Span." *Journal of Applied Physiology* 111(5): 1505–1513.

Wager, T. D., Davidson, M. L., Hughes, B. L., Lindquist, M. A., and Ochsner, K. N. 2008. "Prefrontal-Subcortical Pathways Mediating Successful Emotion Regulation." *Neuron* 59: 1037–1050.

Wamsley, E. J., Tucker, M. A., Payne, J. D., and Stickgold, R. 2010. "A Brief Nap is Beneficial for Human Route Learning: The Role of Initial Skill Level and EEG Spectral Power." *Learning and Memory* 17: 332–336.

Wanless, S. B., McClelland, M. M., Acock, A. C., Ponitz, C. C., Son, S. H., Lan, X., et al. 2011. "Measuring Behavioral Regulation in Four Societies." *Psychological Assessment* 23(2): 364–378.

Waytz, A., and Young, L. 2012. "The Group-Member Mind Trade-Off: Attributing Mind to Groups Versus Group Members." *Psychological Science* 23(1): 77–85.

Williams, K. D., and Nida, S. A. 2011. "Ostracism: Consequences and Coping." *Current Directions in Psychological Science* 20(2): 71–75.

Wood, S., and De Menezes, L. M. 2011. "High Involvement Management, High Performance Work Systems and Well-Being." *International Journal of Human Resource Management* 22(7): 1585–1608.

Wood, S., McInnes, M. M., and Norton, D. A. 2011. "The Bad Thing About Good Games: The Relationship Between Close Sporting Events and Game-Day Traffic Fatalities." *Journal of Consumer Research* 38(4): 611–621.

Woolley, A. W., Chabris, C. F., Pentland, A., Hashmi, N., and Malone, T. W. 2010. "Evidence for a Collective Intelligence Factor in the Performance of Human Groups." *Science* 330(6004): 686–688.

Xie, J., Sreenivasan, S., Korniss, G., Zhang, W., Lim, C., and Szymanski, B. K. 2011. "Social Consensus Through the Influence of Committed Minorities." *Physical Review E.* 84(1).

Xu, H., Bègue, L., and Bushman, B. J. 2012. "Too Fatigued to Care: Ego Depletion, Guilt, and Prosocial Behavior." *Journal of Experimental Social Psychology* forthcoming.

Zeidan, F., Johnson, S. K., Gordon, N. S., and Goolkasian, P. 2010. "Effects of Brief and Sham Mindfulness Meditation on Mood and Cardiovascular Variables." *Journal of Alternative and Complementary Medicine* 16(8): 867–873.

4. Neuroleadership and integrative neuroscience: "it's about validation, stupid!"

Dr. Evian Gordon
Evian Gordon, Chairman/CEO, Brain Resource Company
Founding Director, The Brain Dynamics Centre, Westmead Millennium Institute and University of Sydney, Westmead Hospital, Sydney, Australia
Associate Editor, *Journal of Integrative Neuroscience*
eviang@brainresource.com

Introduction

The field of "neuroleadership" (Rock 2006) has captured the attention of diverse stakeholders in the corporate sector because if its potential materializes, it will result in significant cost reductions and enhanced productivity.

The overarching goal of neuroleadership is to distill and apply what neuroscience is telling us about leadership, beyond common sense or pop psychology. Many reports now extol the potential virtues of neuroleadership for providing leaders and employees with brain insights to improve their performance.

Essentially, the brain insights concern an understanding of self or dealing with others. The specific proposed benefits of neuroleadership include improvements in thinking and learning; making more effective decisions; overcoming negativity biases; finding more creative solutions; increasing the capacity for attention to key tasks and goals; dealing more effectively with stress; and having a more positive attitude, optimal motivation, engagement, and outcome focus in the workplace.

These are lofty expectations. Can current neuroscience insights deliver these pragmatic outcomes?

Understandably, there is considerable skepticism about the "neuro" in neuroleadership, especially since it is still at an embryonic stage. Such skepticism is not new; rather, it is evident at the early stages of most emerging areas. The recurring criticisms from skeptics (who are often stakeholders with a vested interest in retaining their premier status in a related field) include claims that the data have been "overhyped," "oversimplified," "not new, just repackaged," "over interpreted," "oversold and underdelivered," "misused," and "with unproven benefits."

The onus is on the field of neuroleadership to address this skepticism, and that can only be done with solid evidence. That is, the key predictions of the neuroleadership field require validation (or disconfirmation) in empirical studies with large cohorts, studied longitudinally. Without validation, neuroleadership could be another passing fad. This would be rather ironic, given the brain's role in information processing and behavior.

This chapter provides an overview of an exemplar "integrative neuroscience validation infrastructure for neuroleadership." It consists of the first global standard for brain assessment that provides the framework for testing hypotheses concerning the specific aspects of behavioral change targeted within neuroleadership programs. A brief outline of potential hypotheses to be tested within the field of neuroleadership is also suggested.

Integrative neuroscience validation infrastructure for neuroleadership

This validation infrastructure has been created under the auspices of Brain Resource (www.brainresource.com), which set up the first standardized international database on the human brain. This infrastructure was initially set up for "personalized medicine," to identify the best gene-brain-cognition markers that predict individual treatment response (Gordon 2007). An exclusive partnership between Brain Resource and Optum Health Solutions (United Behavioral Health) has resulted in an extension of this infrastructure to include Optum's USA corporate clients.

The standardized infrastructure emerged from several decades of intensive scientific research, which now forms the basis of Brain Resource's academic partner, BRAINnet (www.BRAINnet.net). BRAINnet is a network of more than 150 scientists globally that operates independently to draw on the standardized international database for research purposes, providing ongoing scientific insights.

This validation infrastructure consists of a series of interrelated platforms, from theory to assessment to application in the "real world" (summarized in fig. 1). At the level of theory, it is based on an "integrative neuroscience" model, which brings together the essential commonalities in brain theory across disciplines. This theory underlies the choice of standardized assessments of brain function and behavior. With standardization, these data sources have also been pooled and have formed an international database on human brain and behavior that is the first of its kind.

The summary below reflects the potential use of this infrastructure to deliver the efficiency benefits of standardized assessments, as well as also examines the validation of predicted neuroleadership outcomes.

Integrative neuroscience model

The brain is a highly interconnected system. Yet most brain models still focus on the microscopic scale of genes, single neurons, and specialized networks. However, despite the importance of this detailed information, there are real limits on the extent to which mechanisms operating at microscopic scale can be extrapolated into useful models of the whole brain, where phenomena result from the collective behavior of many highly connected, interacting networks.

Without validation, neuroleadership could be another passing fad.

The fragmentation has begun to change in a very distinctive way. Multidisciplinary efforts have provided the impetus to break down the boundaries and encourage a more "integrative neuroscience" that serves to formulate and test working models of the whole brain, which bring together key organizing principles across scales of brain function (Gordon 2000).

Despite huge deficits of knowledge, sufficient facts about the brain already exist for an integrative neuroscience to begin to lift us clear of the jungle of detail and shed light on the workings of the brain as a system.

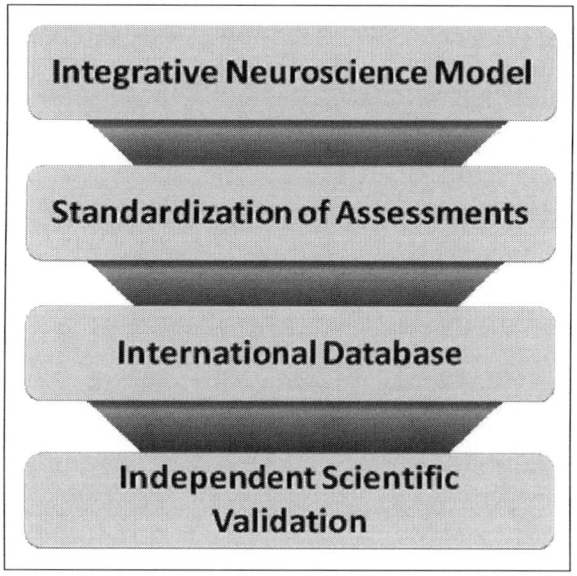

Figure 1. Outline of the neuroleadership validation infrastructure.

The brain model used as a frame of reference in the infrastructure is the INTEGRATE Model (fig. 2; Gordon et al. 2008; Williams et al. 2008; Williams and Gordon 2007), which is based in integrative neuroscience and the evidence base it has established (e.g., Gordon 2000; Gordon et al. 2005; Gordon et al. 2008). The model outlines the brain's core motivations, key modes of function, and diverse implications on many aspects of health care and productivity in the workplace.

The INTEGRATE Model is an integration of many models across disciplines and scale. It brings together five separations:

1. The separation of emotion and thinking
2. The separation of nonconscious and conscious processing
3. The separation of cortical and subcortical activities
4. The separation of spatial and temporal processes and networks
5. The separation of brain and body interactions

The key elements of the model that are most relevant to neuroleadership validation studies are summarized below.

The core motivation underlying all brain processing and behaviors is to **"minimize danger and maximize reward."** This motivation drives brain organization by determining what is significant at each point in time. For instance, at short time scales, a sudden loud noise will signal danger and trigger our reflexive "fight or flight" reactions, whereas at longer time scales, the drive to find reward from meaning could shape our behaviors to find a new job.

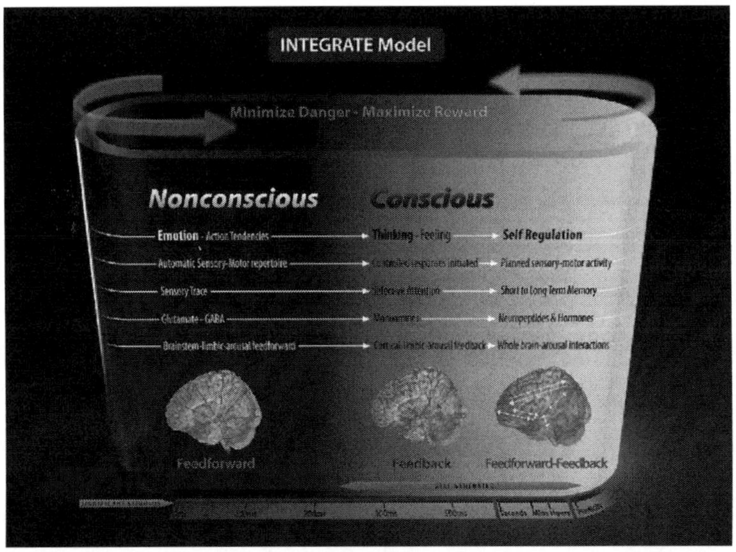

Figure 2. The INTEGRATE Continuum Model of brain organization. In this model, the core motivation to minimize danger–maximize reward is the key organizing principle of the brain. This motivation drives emotion, thinking and self-regulation along a continuum of time and associated nonconscious and conscious modes of brain and body activity. At early time scales (< 200 milliseconds), emotion is reflected in "action tendencies" that are triggered automatically and nonconsciously by basic signals of potential danger or reward. These emotional action tendencies rely on autonomic sensory-motor repertoires, low-level sensory input (sensory store) that engages fast latency "feed-forward" mode of brain and body activity. Rapid-acting neurotransmitters (GABA-Glutamate) are involved at this early time scale. At longer time scale (200–500 ms), thinking and feeling emerge with conscious awareness that relies on "feedback" from brain and body. Thinking supports the initiation of voluntary actions and selective attention and involves more detailed sensory processing with feedback from higher brain areas and from the body. Thinking typically occurs in combination with feeling, which also relies on brain-body feedback. Brain chemicals that modulate thinking and feeling include monoamines (dopamine, serotonin, noradrenaline, and acetylcholine). At longer time scales of seconds, minutes, and beyond, there is a capacity for self-generated as well as stimulus-related processing. Self-regulation is aimed at achieving longer-term and more abstract goals related to minimize danger–maximize reward, and relies on planned behaviors, memory, and ongoing cycles of feed-forward/feedback brain-body interactions. Self-regulation is modulated by slower-acting brain chemicals, such as hormones and neuropeptides. With ongoing outcomes from emotion–thinking–self-regulation, both brain and behavior are constantly adapting, and this is reflected in brain "plasticity" and the potential to generate new behavioral habits.

Cognition encompasses all aspects of information processing. The INTEGRATE Model makes explicit the manner in which key processes of emotion, thinking, and self-regulation continuously interact in a parallel-processing continuum. A further emphasis in this model is on the modes of parallel nonconscious (feed-forward) and conscious (feedback) processes, which are continuously interacting from second to second across the life-span. Modes of processing emphasize the type of processing, rather than the brain region. In the model, the brain's specialized single neuron, networks, and processes are all integral elements of the ongoing brain and body excitation-inhibition interactions.

Emotions are "action tendencies" triggered automatically and without awareness by signals of potential danger and reward that we react to in the absence of conscious awareness. They are supported by a "feed-forward" mode of brain and body activity. For example, a sudden loud noise will trigger an automatic startle response ("jump") which is the action tendency of fear that prepares us to flee.

At longer time scales (from a fifth to approximately half a second), "feedback" from brain and body supports the emergence of conscious awareness and the capacity for thinking and feeling.

Thinking is when you can identify information to yourself in words or images. **Feeling** is when you can identify to yourself the emotion you are experiencing. Thinking and feeling allow you to selectively attend to information, extract its context, make voluntary decisions and responses, and link these to what you know and remember. They occur to minimize danger–maximize reward. Thinking and feeling rely on conscious awareness, and a "feedback" mode of brain-body activity. For example, with feedback and awareness, you can identify the loud noise (car backfiring), your emotion (fear), and their context (cars backfiring are not harmful and you don't need to be afraid)—and choose to inhibit your fear-related action tendencies.

Self-regulation is the shaping, planning and monitoring of behaviors over time, to minimize danger–maximize reward. It encompasses emotion regulation. For example, if you find that you have excessive fear reactions to signals in your environment, you can train your breathing so you can better inhibit these reactions and ensure they do not interfere with your reward-related behaviors.

With ongoing outcomes from emotion, thinking, and self-regulation, both brain and behavior are constantly adapting, and this is reflected in your brain's "plasticity."

Standardization of assessments

Brain Resource's standardized methodology brings together complementary information to capture the essence of the brain's inordinate complexity. Measures normally assessed in isolation are brought together, including cognition (thinking, feeling, self-regulation), personal experience, brain function (EEG, ERP, fMRI) and structure (MRI), and genomics (fig. 3).

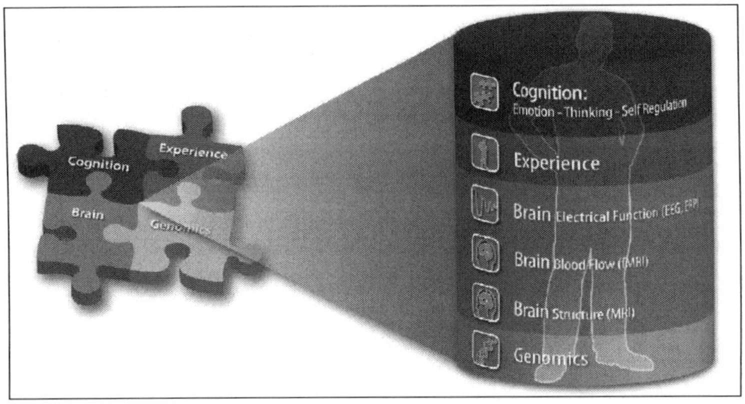

Figure 3. Brain Resource brings together complementary measures of the brain and behavior in a standardized manner.

Standardization allows pooling of the data and the consequent statistical power that is more likely to lead to robust testing of neuroleadership predictions.

For the first phase of neuroleadership validation, measures of emotion, thinking, and self-regulation can be delivered via web-based assessments. These web-based assessments also incorporate functional outcome measures of workplace attitude and performance. These web-based assessments and the scores they generate are briefly outlined below.

Cognition encompasses all aspects of information processing.

Emotion, thinking, self-regulation

Cognition includes all aspects of information processing. The web-based standardized assessment focuses on emotion, thinking, and self-regulation.

Emotion

- Emotion recognition: conscious identification of facial emotions. Variations in the time and accuracy with which emotions are identified indicate specific changes in core emotional function.
- Emotion bias: nonconscious emotional biases to fear, sad, disgust, surprise, happy, and neutral emotions.

Thinking

- Memory: aspects of memory that require learning of new information, holding information "online" (like a telephone number), and recalling it later.

- Sustained attention: focusing on the main task and resisting distractions over time.
- Impulsivity: balance between automatic responses and suppressing these responses as the task situation changes.
- Executive function: planning, monitoring, and using feedback to adjust and organize behavior to meet goals.

Self-regulation

- Negativity bias: the tendency to see yourself and your world as negative. It is associated with sensitivity to stress and emotional stability.
- Positivity bias: the tendency to see the opportunity and solutions rather than the problems in yourself and your external situations.
- Social skills: capacity for social relationship building relies on the ability to understand other people's emotions and intentions.
- Emotional intelligence (EI): defined by Salovey and Mayer (1990) as the "ability to monitor one's own and others' feelings and emotions, to discriminate amongst them and use them to guide one's thinking and actions." Brain Resource's validated EI assessment has three scores that assess empathy/intuition, social skills, and self-esteem (Kemp et al. 2005).
- Emotional resilience: capacity for coping with life and feeling confident in yourself and your opinions, especially during times of negativity and volatility.

Additional workplace-related assessments

Likelihood of a stress-related problem

Screening scores of stress, anxiety, and depression are also acquired (Lovibond and Lovibond 1995).

Functional outcome measures

Health and work performance questionnaire (HPQ)

The HPQ is a widely validated assessment of absenteeism, presenteeism, and productivity levels of members within an organization (Kessler et al. 2003).

Workplace evaluation (WE) 360

WE360 (Hermens 2001) assesses employees' self-evaluation compared with other appropriate staff's ratings of them in 4 key dimensions of performance (fig. 5):

- Relationship management: ability to deal effectively with customers
- Technical competence: ability to use organizational tools and systems

- Value focus: personal approach to bottom-line issues
- Emotional awareness: willingness to accept and undergo change

Standardization is critical

All assessment hardware, software, activation tasks, scoring, and analyses are undertaken in an identical fashion. The virtues of standardized assessments have been replicated in many fields. For example, in medicine, standardizing assessments has been found to increase accuracy and reliability by an average of 15% (Kawamoto et al. 2005; Reilly et al. 2002). This is due to diminishing the random errors.

The Brain Resource international database has thousands of subjects' scores on the key assessments. Many of the subjects also have information on their brain measures, including functional magnetic resonance imaging (fMRI), event-related potentials (ERP), electroencephalogram (EEG), all acquired during a range of standardized activation tasks.

This amount of data allows examination of interrelationships between the web-based assessments and what they reflect in terms of actual brain function (in other words, their "construct validity"). Equally importantly, this integrative neuroscience approach, allows interpretation of the web assessments to be maximized, in that they are able to extend what these measures mean in terms of functional outcomes, such as workplace performance and behavior ("predictive validity").

All subjects in the database also have their personality trait scores (extroversion-introversion, neuroticism, openness, agreeableness, conscientiousness) assessed using the NEO FFI (Cost and McCrae 1997). Interrelationships between emotional intelligence scores (summarized above), personality traits, cognition, brain, and genetics are similarly examined with respect to their real-world utility in workplace performance.

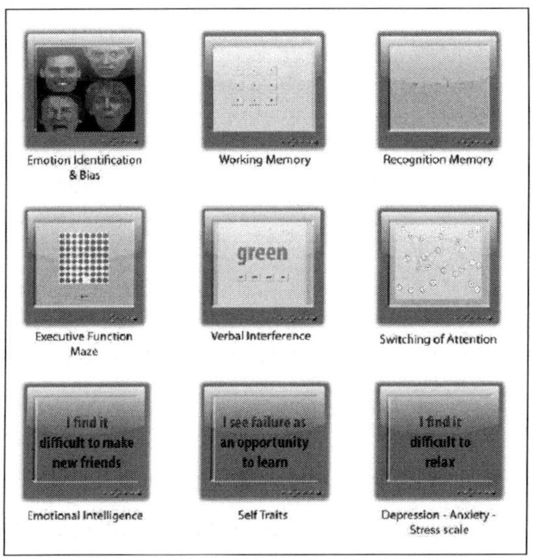

Figure 4. Emotion, thinking, self-regulation web assessments.

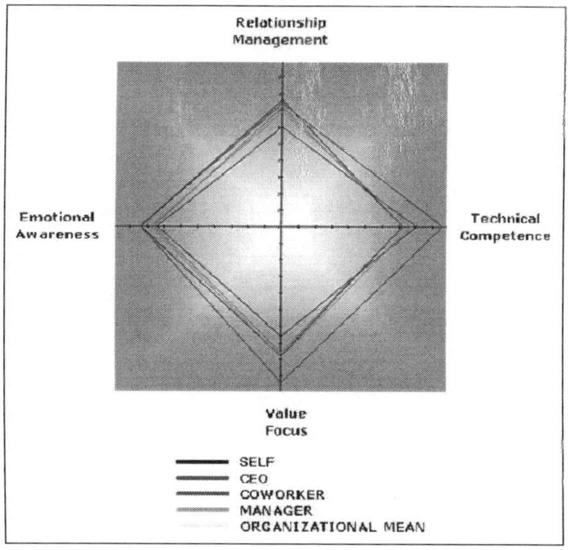

Figure 5. Relative self-scores of a leader or employee, compared with their closest colleagues' evaluation of them. Mismatches provide an evidence base for intervention. Average score changes within a company allow the cost-benefit of an intervention to be determined.

Figure 6. A snapshot of the BRAINnet members' page that lists the options available to members, including submitting a new project proposal and requesting data from the international database (www.BRAINnet.net).

International database

All these measures are taken in each individual. Standardization allows pooling of subject numbers (in a de-identified manner; no names of people, only ID codes enter the database).

Companies have total control over the use of their own data and make all decisions about if and when their data should be examined independently.

In parallel, Brain Resource undertakes its own research, acquiring its own data internationally, which goes into the database.

Independent scientific validation

Scientific integrity of the neuroleadership findings will be researched by an independent scientific network: the Brain Research and Integrative Neuroscience Network (BRAINnet; http://www.BRAINnet.net). It is the first e-science infrastructure for large-scale sharing of human neuroscience data and testing hypotheses generated from integration of theory (fig. 6).

BRAINnet was formed as an independent collaborative to coordinate scientific use of Brain Resource's international database. The milestone of 150 peer-reviewed publications was reached in 2007 (total 187). On average, one publication was published per week during 2008. There are more than 180 scientific members from the USA, Europe, and Australia.

The goal is to extend BRAINnet as a platform for facilitating efforts in applied areas—for instance, to bring together applied researchers from complementary disciplines into a neuroleadership international research consortium aimed at testing programs and hypotheses using this standardized assessment methodology, with the integrative neuroscience database as the frame of reference.

The integrative neuroscience-neuroleadership infrastructure allows for testing programs and selective hypotheses and is also an iterative learning system. This infrastructure may be employed to test a series of neuroleadership objectives in a programmatic manner. One proposed set of objectives using the integrative model and standardized assessments is the following:

1. **To establish the "construct validity" of the key concepts in neuroleadership.** For instance, do those individuals classified as "effective leaders" perform better on measures of stress resilience, positivity versus negativity, bias, and attention to key tasks (captured by the continuum of objective emotion, thinking, and self-regulation measures) than those classified as "poorer leaders"? From there, one might test whether these measures relate to underlying brain differences.

2. **To establish the "predictive validity" of the key concepts.** Do the objective measures associated with leadership and styles of leadership (for example, hierarchical control versus shared leadership models) predict functional outcomes, such as workplace performance?

3. **To establish the "efficacy" of NeuroLeadership programs**. Do these programs lead to significant improvements in functional outcomes and are these improvements related to the constructs established in objectives 1 and 2? If yes, these measures can be used as markers to assess and predict neuroleadership.

4. **To replicate the results in the above three objectives**. Replicating these results across companies using the standardized assessments in independent samples would also be important in determining their robustness.

Statistically significant changes using the standardized assessments would provide a "proof of efficacy" for any neuroleadership intervention.

The design of a validation study would then need to consider "effectiveness" or conventional randomized, controlled trial designs. Effectiveness designs are based on the presumption that the most ecologically valid protocol is one that mirrors normal practice as much as possible. The conventional view remains that unambiguous validation of a training program would require a double-blind, placebo-controlled study with sufficient subject numbers to ensure high statistical power.

Standardization allows multiple researchers to undertake the identical research in different companies simultaneously, thereby expediting the speed of replication.

Experience from current international studies in integrative neuroscience and health care using this infrastructure has shown that it is prudent to initially focus on relatively straightforward hypotheses before testing questions with multiple interactions and subtle underlying mechanisms.

With respect to the proposed neuroleadership predictions relevant to the four objectives above, the following exemplars (A–E) are proposed:

A. Standardized assessments to determine the efficacy of NeuroLeadership programs.

NeuroLeadership programs such as David Rock's *Quiet Leadership* program (to help people think better—don't tell them what to do; Rock 2006), John Medina's *Brain Rules* (Medina 2008), and others are readily examined to determine the extent of benefits. From there, more detailed predictions might concern which forms of a neuroleadership program the brain best responds to, versus those that the brain "resists." Evidence from these types of studies would help shape NeuroLeadership programs and provide a base for assessing their impact and cost-benefits.

Standardization allows multiple researchers to undertake the identical research...

Any emerging brain-based NeuroLeadership program could also be directly compared (using the standardized assessments) with the stated benefits of more long-standing training programs that have to some extent been driven by brain processes. These include, for example, multiple intelligences (Gardner 2007), theory of mind (Baron-Cohen et al. 2000), emotional intelligence (Goleman 2000), and many others. Existing programs have a defined area of proposed benefit and have contentious extents of replicated validation.

A further sobering context when considering the validation of an emerging field such as neuroleadership is that despite their widespread use by HR personnel in many corporations, psychometric tests of psychological function (including of cognition and personality) have little construct validity. They are often used with significant "subjective inference" about "personal capacity" to select and stream people for specific executive and nonexecutive positions. To my knowledge, there is no database of longitudinal results using mainstream psychometric assessments in corporations that has unambiguous replicated "personalized" validation and predictive validity with respect to individual leaders or employees.

B. Assessing the relative interactions among key elements in NeuroLeadership programs

Can a small activity sometimes make a big difference, and vice versa? A rather telling example of this point is provided (in a personal communication, 2008) by Dr. Eugene Baker (vice president, Employee Assistance Programs at Optum Health Solutions):

> There are some interventions in which the learning curve accelerates early and tapers off, while there are other situations in which learning is slow at first and plateaus later. Some interventions achieve the results from only a small portion of the program. For example, speed reading programs often successfully teach people to move along a pointer as they read and then charge for techniques that have relatively less marginal utility. The assessment framework could help personalize learning profiles and identify the key ingredients in interventions.

C. Examining the best pathway for behavioral change

The brain's "plasticity" (Kilgard and Merzenich 1998) and the importance of diminishing chronic stress to enhance well-being (Seligman 2007) have generated considerable optimism across all areas of behavioral change (including in the neuroleadership literature) of the capacity for people to change. Yet, in reality, change is hard. It remains unknown whether some programs will be more effective than others in making change possible.

The principle of change pathways is, "If you can't measure it, you can't manage it" (Mimma Mason; personal communication, 2008).

Meaningful long-term change requires objective measurement of *what* to change. Mastery of *how* to change begins with overcoming "motivational ambivalence" (Miller and Rollnick 2002). Dr. Roy Sugarman (personal communication, 2008), summarizes the essence of this step as follows: "No one fully believes or acts upon anything unless it comes out of their own mouth." Once the motivation is "owned," the implementation of the change pathway could include "small steps" of positive reinforcement and the "Gordon 1,000 rule" to practice, visualize, or simulate the change more than a 1,000 times until it becomes an automatic nonconscious habit. Monitoring the *extent* of change (using standardized assessments) ensures that personalized change is happening to a meaningful extent.

The "Gordon 1,000 rule" comes out of decades of independent science using the integrative infrastructure, for which the evidence points to the large amount of practice needed to achieve genuine change. On the other hand, the emotional, thinking, and self-regulation measures show that periods of high emotional arousal can facilitate change more rapidly.

Comparative studies between both programs and individuals could tease out "personalized" capacities and best pathways for change.

Comparative studies between both programs and individuals could tease out "personalized" capacities and best pathways for change.

D. Testing specific aspects of performance in leaders and employees

The INTEGRATE Model provides many possible testable performance variables. One example, which cuts across all aspects of information processing, is decision making.

The relevance to neuroleadership is that converging evidence is showing that most leaders and employees are unaware that their decision making is likely to be significantly flawed by systematic biases.

Decision making involves every time frame along the continuum of the INTEGRATE Model. It is simply the way in which processing options or reactions become iteratively narrowed down over time. All decision making is affected by the same core motivational drive to minimize danger and maximize reward. All biases are part of the same process.

For example, a "confirmation bias" is simply a nonconscious threat contradicting a person's prediction that the world is safe or consistent. On the other hand, an "exposure effect bias" (that people like things that are more familiar) is a form of safety (reward), which is a reason why people nonconsciously like what they are used to; newness can be threatening.

Decision making exemplifies an area that requires integration of the growing multidisciplinary literature, which extends from biological models (Ernst and Paul 2005; Doya 2008; Bechara, Damasio and Damasio 2000; Lee 2008), to mathematical decision theory (Goodwyn and Wright 2004), to the use of "heuristics" (Tversky and Kahneman 1974; Kahneman 2003).

Validation of the best interventions to enhance decision making in leaders and employees would provide a significant neuroleadership benefit.

These models and insights can be reconciled as "intuitive versus rational" decision making in the INTEGRATE Model and tested using the standardized assessments, including the conscious "thinking" executive functions and planning scores from the "maze" assessment, and nonconscious bias indices (as described previously and in point E, below).

E. Ultimately, emotions that operate nonconsciously are key to understanding and predicting neuroleadership qualities

The INTEGRATE Model highlights the importance of nonconscious emotion processing and its effects on behavior. Details about the recent objective measures of nonconscious processing is beyond the scope of this chapter, but can be found in a number of publications (Williams et al. 2004; Liddell et al. 2005; Williams et al. 2006a, b; Williams et al. 2007; Williams et al. forthcoming).

One example of a nonconscious measure from the integrative neuroscience infrastructure is of "emotional bias," which captures the degree to which an individual automatically focuses on negative and threat-related emotions, versus positive ones. A greater automatic bias toward the negative is difficult to control and has been associated with higher anxiety, suboptimal decision making, and what drives the "pushback" issues in leader-employee dynamics.

This area of research shows promise for elucidating the underlying mechanisms of leadership, which to date have been underexplored.

Studies of relative change also highlight the importance of "personalized" insights into what styles of neuroleadership are best suited to which program. Studies that compare programs should allow for tailoring each program to the individuals concerned, as well as to the needs of each corporation.

The onus is on neuroleadership researchers and practitioners to embrace this harsh reality.

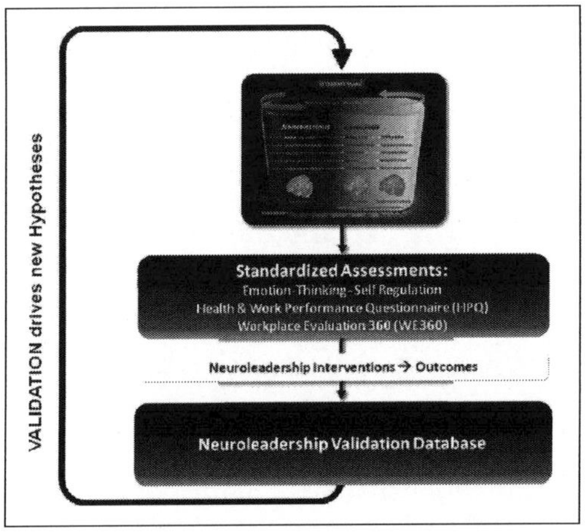

Figure 7. The integrative neuroscience neuroleadership validation infrastructure allows testing of programs and hypotheses and also becomes an iterative learning system.

The neuroleadership infrastructure acts as a strategic decision-making database to select which validated programs provide the best cost-benefit ratio. It also has the capacity to learn on the basis of the evidence, so the cumulative insights and outcomes could help neuroleadership scientists to iteratively extend the model and generate new hypotheses and programs.

Conclusion

I have attempted to provide some context of the complexities that demand a rigorous approach to validating findings from the emerging field of neuroleadership.

I have also attempted to summarize an exemplar standardized infrastructure that might be employed to validate neuroleadership programs and hypotheses.

Data will be the only final arbiter for the *validation* of which programs and key elements of neuroleadership really work, in a cost-effective manner.

References

Baron-Cohen, S., Tager-Flusberg, H., and Cohen, D. J. 2000. *Understanding Other Minds: Perspectives from Developmental Cognitive Neuroscience*. New York: Oxford University Press.

Bechara, A. 2004. "The Role of Emotion in Decision-Making: Evidence from Neurological Patients with Orbitofrontal Damage." *Brain and Cognition* 55: 30–40.

Bechara, A., Damasio, H., and Damasio, A.R. 2000. "Emotion, Decision Making and the Orbitofrontal Cortex." *Cerebral Cortex* 10(3): 295-307.

Costa, P., and McCrae, R. 1997. "Stability and Change in Personality Assessment: The Revised NEO Personality Inventory in the Year 2000." *Journal of Personality Assessment* 68(1): 86–94.

Doya, K. 2008. "Modulators of Decision Making." *Nature Neuroscience* 11(4): 410–416.

Ernst, M., and Paulus, M. 2005. "Neurobiology of Decision Making: A Selective Review from a Neurocognitive and Clinical Perspective." *Biological Psychiatry* 58(8): 597–604.

Gardner, H. 2007. *Five Minds for the Future*. Cambridge, MA: Harvard Business School Press.

Goleman, D. 2000. *Working with Emotional Intelligence*. New York: Bantam.

Goodwyn, P., and Wright, G. 2004. *Decision Analysis for Management Judgement*. London: John Wiley & Sons.

Gordon, E., ed. 2000. *Integrative Neuroscience: Bringing together Biological, Psychological, and Clinical Models of the Human Brain*. Reading, UK: Harwood Academic Publications.

Gordon, E., Cooper, N., Rennie, C. J., Hermens, D., and Williams, L. M. 2005. "Integrative Neuroscience: The Role of the Standardized Database." *Clinical EEG and Neuroscience* 36(2): 64–75.

Gordon, E. 2007. "Genomics and Neuromarkers are Both Required for the Era of Brain Related 'Personalized Medicine.'" *Personalized Medicine* 4(2): 201–215.

Gordon, E., Barnett. K.J., Cooper. N.J., Tran, N. and Williams, L. 2008. "An 'Integrative Neuroscience' Platform: Application to Profiles of Negativity and Positivity Bias." *Journal of Integrative Neuroscience* (September).

Hermens, G. 2001."Culture and Psychology." *Culture and the Dialogical Self: Theory, Method, and Practice* 7(3): 243–408.

Kahneman D. 2003. "A Perspective on Judgment and Choice: Mapping Bounded Rationality." *American Psychologist* 58(9): 697–720.

Kawamoto, K., Houlihan, C. A., Balas, E. A., Lobach, D. F. 2005. "Improving Clinical Practice Using Clinical Decision Support Systems: A Systematic Review of Trials to Identify Features Critical to Success." *British Medical Journal*. http://www.ncbi.nlm.nih.gov/pmc/.

Kemp, A., Cooper, N., Hermens, G., Gordon, E., Bryant, R., and Williams, L. 2005. "Toward an Integrated Profile of Emotional Intelligence: Introducing a Brief Measure." *Journal of Integrative Neuroscience* 41: 41–61.

Kessler, R., Barber, C., Beck, A., Berglund, P., Cleary, P., McKenas, D., Pronk, N., Simon, G., Stang, P., Ustun, T., and Wang, P. 2003. "The World Health and Work Performance Questionnaire (HPQ)." *Journal of Occupational and Environmental Medicine* 45(2): 156–174.

Kilgard, M. P., and Merzenich, M. 1998. "Cortical Map Reorganization Enabled by Nucleus Basalis Activity." *Science* 279(5357): 1715–1718.

Lee, D. 2008. "Game Theory and the Neural Basis of Social Decision." *Nature Neuroscience* 11(4): 404–409.

Liddell, B. J., Brown, K. J., Kemp, A. H., Barton, M. J., Pritha, D., Peduto, A., Gordon, E., and Williams, L. M. 2005." *Neuroimage* 24: 235–243.

Lovibond, P., and Lovibond, S. 1995. "The Structure of Negative Emotional States: Comparison of the Depression Anxiety Stress Scales (DASS) with the Beck Depression and Anxiety Inventories." *Behaviour Research and Therapy* 33: 335–343.

Medina, J. 2008. *Brain Rules*. Seattle, WA: Pear Press.

Miller, W., and Rollnick, S. 2002. *Motivational Interviewing: Preparing People to Change*. New York: Guilford.

Reilly, B. M., Evans, A. T., Schaider, J. J., and Want, Y. 2002. "Triage of Patients with Chest Pain in the Emergency Department: A Comparative Study of Physicians' Decisions." *American Journal of Medicine* 112: 95–103.

Rock, D. 2006. *Quiet Leadership: Six Steps to Transforming Performance at Work*. New York: Harper Collins.

Salovey, P., and Mayer, J. 1990. "Emotional Intelligence." *Imagination, Cognition, and Personality* 9: 185–211.

Seligman, M. E. P. 2007. *What You Can Change and What You Can't: The Complete Guide to Successful Self-Improvement*. London: Vintage.

Tversky, A., and Kahneman, D. 1974. "Judgment Under Uncertainty: Heuristics and Biases. Biases in Judgments Reveal Some Heuristics of Thinking Under Uncertainty." *Science, New Series* 185(4157).

Williams, L. M., and Gordon E. 2007. "The Dynamic Organization of the Emotional Brain: Responsivity, Stability, and Instability." *Neuroscientist* 13: 349–370.

Williams, L. M., Liddell, B. J., Rathjen, J., Brown, K. J., Shevrin, H., Gray, J. A., Phillips, M., Young, A., and Gordon, E. 2004. "Mapping the Time Course of Nonconscious and Conscious Perception of Fear: An Integration of Central and Peripheral Measures." *Human Brain Mapping* 21: 64–74.

Williams, L. M., Liddell, B. J., Kemp, A. H., Bryant, R. A., Peduto, A. S., Meares, R. A., and Gordon, E. 2006a. "An Amygdala-Prefrontal Dissociation of Subliminal and Supraliminal Fear." *Human Brain Mapping* 27: 652–661.

Williams, L. M., Das, P., Liddell, B. J., Kemp, A. H., Rennie, C. J., and Gordon, E. 2006b. "Awareness for Fear Depends on Mode of Connectivity in Amygdala Pathways." *Journal of Neuroscience* 26: 9264–9271.

Williams, L. M., Gatt, J.M., Hatch, A., Palmer, D.M., Nagy, M., Rennie, C., et al. 2008. "The Integrated Model of Emotion, Thinking and Self Regulation: An Application to the 'Paradox of Aging'." *Journal of Integrative Neuroscience* 7(3): 367-404..

SECTION II:
Make Decisions and Solve Problems

5. How insight happens: learning from the brain

Dr. Mark Jung-Beeman, Dr. Azurii Collier, and Dr. John Kounios

Mark Jung-Beeman, Department of Psychology, Northwestern University, Illinois, USA
mjungbee@northwestern.edu

Azurii Collier, [1]Northwestern University, Illinois, USA

John Kounios, Department of Psychology, Drexel University, Pensylvannia, USA
john.kounios@gmail.com

Introduction

This chapter briefly summarizes recent research investigating how the brain achieves insight—the sudden solution to a long-vexing problem, sudden recognition of a new idea, or sudden understanding of a complicated situation. The notion that important insights can come in a sudden *Aha!* moment is widespread and ingrained across many cultures. Since the time—legend has it—that Archimedes first shouted, "Eureka!" ("I have found it!"), sudden insight has been colloquially described in countless ways: these are ideas that come like a bolt of lightning, out of the blue, out of thin air, or even hit like a ton of bricks. Scientific and business lore are chock-full of anecdotes describing how a single sudden insight yielded great advances—or profits.

Insight is considered an important component of creativity and contributes to many creative ideas. These days, not a week goes by without seeing a headline touting the importance of creativity and innovation. There is increasing pressure on nearly all organizations for increased creativity: for developing new products, streamlining delivery systems, optimizing managerial structure, and—not least—dealing with personnel and clients. Creating conditions conducive to insight is one way to enhance organizational creativity, and leaders who are able to do this will be intrinsically valuable to their organization. Moreover, insight may be an important agent of change (e.g., for helping people change their habits and ways of thinking) because of the enhanced and perhaps distinctive way in which people remember ideas achieved through insight.

Yet, for all the attention lavished on insight, it has, until recently, remained poorly understood by science. Two roadblocks have been the involvement of unconscious—therefore unreportable—processing leading to insight (c.f., Bowden and Beeman 1998) and the seemingly subjective nature of defining insight (Sternberg and Davidson 1995). In fact, some have claimed that insight does not differ from more methodical problem solving, and that it merely feels different (Weisberg 1994)—although that begs the question of why some problem solutions "feel different" from others. Recent advances in brain science have opened new avenues for investigating this important topic. It is hoped that, eventually, elucidating the brain bases of insight will foster new ways to facilitate it. Already, evidence from brain science is beginning to illuminate the core processes involved in achieving insight. The goal is not to simply map brain areas involved in insight, but to use information about brain activity to inform and constrain cognitive theories of insight and predictions about how to facilitate it.

Brain activity at the Aha! moment

Semantic integration

Examining brain activity for sudden insight presents several challenges. Even if we knew who the "next Einstein" was, we couldn't simply put her in a brain scanner and wait for her to have a great insight. Even if she were willing, we wouldn't learn much, because that one observation would be inadequate to interpret scientifically. Current neuroimaging techniques—ways of assessing brain activity—require averaging many observations of highly similar events, and comparing this average against that of a similar but contrasting type of event. Even many classic psychology experiments cannot be simply converted into neuroimaging experiments. These classic psychology experiments typically compared how people solved a very small number (from one to six) of insight problems (identified in earlier experiments as problems that were usually solved with some report or characteristic of insight) with a small number of analytic problems (usually solved more methodically). More observations are needed for effective neuroimaging. Furthermore, analytic problems that are of comparable difficulty to insight problems usually place a very high load on working memory (i.e., keeping various facts in mind while performing additional operations). Comparing these two classes of problems would undoubtedly show increased activity in working-memory brain areas during analytic solving, which would overshadow the critical operations of insight.

In the first study to isolate brain activity at the moment people solve with insight (Jung-Beeman et al. 2004), we were able to overcome these challenges by using a large set of simple word problems that can be solved either with insight or more analytically. The problems were modeled on the Remote Associates Test (Mednick 1962), which has been used as a test of creativity. In our version, called Compound Remote Associate (CRA) problems, people view three problem words, such as storm, wave, drain. They have to think of a solution word that can form a compound or a common two-word phrase with each of the problem words. For instance, rainstorm works, but rain doesn't fit with the others; similarly, heat wave works, and drain plug works, but neither heat nor plug fits with the other words. However, brain can fit with all three words (brainstorm, brain wave, brain drain).

After each solution (people solved about half within 30 seconds), participants pressed a button to indicate how they solved the problem. About 40–50% of the time, people solved these problems by methodically generating compounds for one problem word (picking the one that seems most constraining) and testing it out with the other problem words. When they succeeded this way, participants pressed a button to indicate that they solved the problem analytically, without insight. The remaining 50–60% of the time, people were thinking about the problem in one way, when suddenly a different word popped into mind, and instantly they "just knew" this word fit with all three problem words. This sudden obviousness is a hallmark of insight, so when this happened, participants pressed buttons indicating they solved with insight.

While people performed this task, we measured brain activity in two ways: in one experiment with functional magnetic resonance imaging (fMRI), and in another with electroencephalography (EEG). Somewhat indirectly (through blood oxygenation changes), fMRI provides excellent information about which brain areas are more active during some events compared with other events. The fMRI signals corresponding to the second or two preceding a solution revealed distinct patterns of brain activity corresponding to insight, versus analytic solutions. Several critical brain areas were more active when people solved problems with insight than when they solved the same types of problems analytically.

In the initial study (Jung-Beeman et al. 2004), this effect was statistically reliable in only one area, and in subsequent replication (Subramaniam et al. 2009), this area remained the most robust differentiator between insight and noninsight solutions. The area identified was in the anterior temporal lobe of the right hemisphere. Importantly, this is not an "insight area"; it is an area that, among other functions, participates in integrating semantic information—with the right hemisphere area likely integrating information that is relatively distantly related. This was exactly as predicted, given that a critical feature of insight is seeing new connections and the answer coming as a whole—that is, already integrated.

It should be noted that fMRI provides very poor information about the timing of neural activity, so that data alone could not pinpoint decisively whether the observed activity occurred before or slightly after the participants solved the problems with insight. However, a parallel study using EEG demonstrated that the onset of the critical activity began just over 300 milliseconds before the response—perfect timing for the sudden (and confident) recognition of the solution (Smith and Kounios 1996). Also, although EEG by itself does not provide incontrovertible spatial information, the location of this burst of EEG activity perfectly corresponded with that provided by fMRI. Finally, EEG also provides another dimension: the frequency of the neural activity. The right temporal activity preceding the solution was in the gamma band, a high-frequency (40 Hz) activity usually associated with binding information into a coherent representation—consistent with the interpretation that it reflected the emergence into consciousness of the solution idea.

Memory

Other areas of stronger activity for insight than noninsight solutions that we reported in the initial study, and were strongly verified in a later study (Subramaniam et al. 2009), included the hippocampus and the anterior and posterior cingulate cortex. The hippocampus is involved in both memory formation and retrieval—and past reports have suggested that insight solutions are better remembered than analytical solutions (Wills et al. 2000). Moreover, we believe that insight could be involved in reorganizing memory. A classic characteristic of solving with insight is that it requires cognitive restructuring—a reorganization or reinterpretation of the way one views a problem. In this way, an insight is akin to understanding a joke—usually, a premise is followed by a punch line that makes the listener reinterpret the joke. Yet, it is often hard to remember—or at least retell—jokes. Why? Because it's too easy to confuse and combine the punch line with the premise. Later, we'll return to the idea that this reorganization can be a useful agent of change.

Cognitive control

Both the anterior and posterior cingulate cortex are more active when people solve problems with insight than when they solve problems without insight (Jung-Beeman et al. 2004; Subramaniam et al. 2009). These deep midline brain areas are involved in cognitive control and attention (Botvinick, Cohen, and Carter 2004), helping people switch their focus of attention from one aspect of processing to another. It is not surprising to see some aspects of the cognitive control system engaged for insight, as people must shift their processing from one train of thought—often being stuck on a strong but incorrect association—to another. Based only on the fact that these regions are more active at insight than at analytical solutions, the precise role of each region is not entirely clear. However, a few additional pieces of information described below add to the picture.

Quiet before the brainstorm

Although the burst of gamma band activity in the right temporal lobe occurs at the moment of solution, another component of the EEG signal precedes it (Jung-Beeman et al. 2004). About one second before insight solutions (and not analytical ones), an increase in alpha-band (10–12 Hz) activity is measured over posterior occipital-parietal cortex (slightly to the right side), near areas where visual information is passed to other brain areas. This posterior alpha activity persists until precisely the time the gamma band activity bursts in the right temporal lobe. What does this tell us? Alpha band activity is like brain idling; it increases at rest. When such activity occurs over the visual cortex, it is thought to reflect visual gating (Worden et al. 2001). We interpret the posterior alpha activity as quieting visual input (from the problem words) so that solvers can better detect and switch attention to fragile internal activation, which may lead them to a solution. If this weak activation integrates all the relevant problem elements, it is particularly useful for solutions and will likely be experienced as an insight (the whole solution emerging into consciousness all at once).

Interestingly, the fact that visual gating is employed at that moment implies the use of cognitive control; further, it implies that some neural system detected the presence of some brain activity potentially related to (or useful for) the solution. We believe that system is the cognitive control system and involves the anterior cingulate cortex. Importantly, this doesn't mean the anterior cingulate "knows" the answer, just that it detects some competing thought (focus of brain activity) that seems potentially relevant.

The idea that cognitive control can help an individual switch from one association (sometimes a strong but incorrect one) to a weak, even unconscious, one is consistent with the long-standing idea that insight involves unconscious processing.

Insight seems quite sudden. It feels, in part, as if one moment you were either not thinking of the problem or were thinking of it entirely incorrectly, and then suddenly the idea pops into your head from nowhere. Psychologists asking people to make "warmth" ratings about how close they are to solving problems have observed distinct patterns for insight versus analytic problems. When working on analytic problems, warmth ratings gradually increase until solution is achieved; for insight problems, warmth ratings remain stable (though probably not at zero), then suddenly jump at solution (Metcalfe and Weibe 1987).

Intuition

Insight solving can lead to another type of metacognition—thinking about thinking, or in this case, about solving. Like experiencing an insight, intuition seems to involve unconscious processing. Both phenomena reflect related phases of unconscious processing: intuition as the faint presence of widespread unconscious activation, and insight as the shift to consciousness at the Aha! moment. Just as with insight, most people have experienced a moment of intuition, and we are all aware of this distinct feeling of "knowing without knowing."

Oftentimes, when people are unaware of a problem's solution and don't feel as if they're progressing toward solution (so warmth ratings don't increase), they may feel or intuit that a problem is solvable. Indeed, people can guess whether insight-like problems are solvable long before they can solve them (Bowers et al. 1990; Bolte, Goschke, and Kuhl 2003). Moreover, they may have an intuitive hunch or tip-of-the-tongue experience, feeling that the solution—or a better solution path—lurks beneath consciousness. Such hunches are associated with better solving, eventually. When given CRA problems to solve and a twenty-four-hour break from the problems, individuals solved more problems on Day 2 if on Day 1 they experienced an intuitive hunch that they could (eventually) solve it. Moreover, on Day 2 participants were more likely to solve the old (unsolved Day 1) problem with a moment of insight if they experienced an intuitive hunch related to that problem on Day 1.

Understanding which intuitions are correct versus those that are incorrect is critical to identifying which hunches are most useful in certain situations. On average, people's intuitions have validity but are far from perfect. In at least some instances, correct intuitive judgments of solvability were associated with increased activity in the right superior temporal cortex (Ilg et al. 2007). Thus, intuition and insight seem to share similar regions of neural activity; moreover, the processing advantage of the right hemisphere is evident in both phenomena. Further research into differentiating valid versus invalid intuition and fostering the ability to discern the two could also relate to insight; at the least, valid intuitions that a solution is near would signal opportune situations for facilitating insight (see below).

Whereas neuroimaging measures provide information about which brain and mental processes seem to be engaged, they do not provide much information about the content of those processes. However, some behavioral measures can do that. If an intuition that a solution lurks beneath consciousness is valid, then even if people fail to solve a problem, they should show priming—that is, they should be able to process the solution word quickly if they see it. Indeed, this is the case: people read solution words faster than control words Moreover, this is especially true when the words are presented to the left visual field so that they are initially processed in the right hemisphere—further confirmation that the right hemisphere is particularly sensitive to the types of associations on which insight solutions are built (Bowden and Beeman 1998). In fact, this right hemisphere advantage in priming, and in speed to make solution decisions, happens only when people recognize the solutions with a sense of insight—an Aha!, or immediate recognition that the word fits for all problem words (Bowden and Jung-Beeman 2003).

However, keep in mind that the processing that led to solution priming remained largely unconscious; hence, participants did not solve those problems. When the insight solution does come into consciousness, it does so quickly, seems quite obvious, and the solver is very confident about it.

But what happens to allow the sudden boost from unconscious to conscious levels of processing? We suggest that the cognitive control system detects weak (unconscious) neural activity and engages a switch of attention to the new target, bringing it into awareness. This provides a target for the facilitation of insights: variables that improve the ability to detect weak associations may improve insight solving.

Preparatory state and mood

In another experiment, we observed a remarkable precursor of insight. We examined brain activity during a preparatory period preceding each problem people tried to solve (Kounios et al. 2006). This was a resting period, before people even knew what the next problem would be (although they knew it would be another CRA problem). We contrasted the pattern observed before the problems they eventually solved with insight to the same period before problems later solved analytically. Both conditions were successful, but in different ways.

Several brain areas were more active during insight preparation than during analytic preparation (leaving aside whether the type of preparation was intentional). These areas included temporal lobe areas on both sides of the brain, which suggests that before insight, people were prepared to engage two types of semantic processing (Jung-Beeman 2005): close associations (left-hemisphere semantic processing) and more remote associations (right-hemisphere semantic processing). The other brain areas involved in insight preparation were anterior and posterior cingulate cortex, suggesting that being ready to engage these components of the cognitive control system is conducive to insight. Several interpretations of this activity are possible, but again, we currently interpret the anterior cingulate cortex activation as being prepared to detect competing associations, allowing other components to direct attention toward them.

Variables that improve the ability to detect weak associations may improve insight solving.

As for the reverse comparison, in general, only visual brain areas were more active during analytic preparation than during insight preparation. This suggests that when people were prepared to pay more direct attention to the visual input rather than the chain of evoked internal associations, then they were more likely to solve analytically than with insight.

The preparatory states described above varied from trial to trial within individuals. However, other factors that vary more slowly, or may be intrinsic to individuals, could make them better able to solve with insight. For instance, we have also observed that when people have no task to perform and can simply think whatever they want, and indeed don't even know what task they will later perform, distinct patterns of resting-state brain activity are associated with individuals who preferentially solve anagrams with insight, compared with those who solve anagrams more analytically (Kounios et al. 2008).

At least one factor appears to directly affect the preparatory brain activity described above: mood. It has long been reported that people in a relatively positive mood, whether naturally occurring or induced experimentally, are better able to solve insight or creative problems (Isen, Daubman, and Nowicki 1987; Ashby, Isen, and Turken 1999, for reviews). Likewise, we observed that the amount of positive mood participants reported when entering our experiment correlated with the number of CRA problems solved, as well as with the degree to which they solved the problems with insight (Subramaniam et al. 2009), and participants solved more problems, and more with insight, after watching comedy films that increased their positive mood than after watching neutral films.

Positive mood has also been shown to broaden attention (Gasper and Clore 2002), and at least one study has demonstrated both effects simultaneously (Rowe, Hirsch, and Anderson 2007). Broader, less-focused attention should be well suited to detecting weak associations in the brain, enabling insight, so we predicted that the mechanism by which positive mood facilitates insight would relate to cognitive control and attention. Indeed, when we examined brain activity during the preparatory period described above, people in a positive mood showed the same pattern in anterior cingulate that was associated on a trial-by-trial basis with insight preparation. That is, across all problems, the amount of activity in the anterior cingulate during the preparatory period directly correlated with positive mood (Subramaniam et al. 2009). To some extent, anxiety had the opposite effect: fewer problems solved with insight and decreased preparatory activity in the anterior cingulate.

Facilitating insight: beyond positive mood

Clearly, positive mood can facilitate insight, and therefore the aspect of problem solving, creativity, and innovation that depend on insight. In reality, most problems worth solving require more than a single Aha! moment. They require dedicated analysis revealing the critical elements of the problem before the Aha! moment and often require further analysis afterward. There may be times when it is particularly useful to elicit a positive mood, such as when someone is stuck but has an intuition that a solution lurks beneath consciousness. Regardless, the mechanism of positive mood's facilitation of insight may point the way to other methods. For instance, we are currently experimenting with tasks that demand particular and distinct modes of attention and observing that participating in these simple visual-spatial tasks alters (for better or worse) the ability to solve verbal problems with insight. One task that appears particularly helpful for insight is called rapid identification: pictures of objects are flashed on the screen much too quickly for normal recognition but are still possible to occasionally identify after some delay. What happens during the delay? The observer must attend not to the visual input (since the stimulus has disappeared) but to weak associations evoked by the vanished stimulus. After performing this task, participants solve more CRA problems, specifically with insight. In contrast, after engaging in a task that demands highly focused attention, they solve more problems analytically rather than with insight (Wegbreit et al 2012).

It could be that any behavior that encourages people to attend to their own quiet thoughts will be somewhat helpful for insight. David Rock of Results Coaching Systems (and the *NeuroLeadership Journal*) engages clients in problem-solving sessions during which some participants coach other individuals to consider a problem on which they are stuck. When the coaches ask questions probing their companion's metacognition—their thoughts about their thoughts, such as, how long has this been a problem? how often does this enter your thinking? and so on—Rock claims there is a marked increase in the number of Aha! moments experienced by those presenting the problems. It's not that all problems are solved, but that some new insight is gained about the nature of the problem. Such techniques remain to be rigorously tested under tight control, but they are consistent with some of the results observed in the problem-solving brain.

It could be that any behavior that encourages people to attend to their own quiet thoughts will be somewhat helpful for insight.

One mental behavior potentially related to insight and creativity is mind-wandering, or spontaneous thought. Mind wandering is somewhat similar to daydreaming. It occurs when an individual begins to attend to internal thoughts rather than externally driven tasks. It can happen in the absence of a task, or when a person's thoughts drift away from a task—particularly monotonous repetitive tasks. It's what happens when you are driving on the highway and after a while realize that you are thinking deeply about something else and barely attending to the road (hopefully enough to respond, if need be). Legend has it that Thomas Edison would routinely sit in a comfortable chair and rest, allowing his mind to wander as he perhaps headed toward sleep. However, he would do this while balancing a spoon over a pie plate, so that should he fall asleep, the spoon would drop and the resulting clang would awaken him. He would then write down his thoughts during that period, in the belief that they were often creative. A recent neuro-imaging study of mind wandering—itself a creative endeavor—revealed that spontaneous off-task thinking shared features of both "default state" brain activity and purposeful semantic processing (Christoff, Ream, and Gabrieli 2004). In today's hectic environment, there may a relative paucity of time for simple, but potentially creative, mind wandering.

Conclusions

Recent research has been elucidating the brain bases of insight. The anatomical structures involved, the timing of the activity, and the type of neural activity all have implications for theories of insight and how to facilitate it. The Aha! moment itself seems to reflect the sudden emergence into consciousness of a representation or thought that brings together all the necessary problem elements and is likely to involve right-hemisphere semantic integration that connects distantly related concepts. This sudden emergence tends to be preceded by weak, subconscious processing of the integrating information and usually requires a sudden shift of attention from a stronger association (or solution path). This shift, in turn, requires the engagement of cognitive control systems, particularly the anterior cingulate, and is further enhanced by a quieting or gating of sensory input to better detect the weakly active internal concept. Brain states conducive to insight can begin long before problem-solving efforts and can vary from trial to trial, be modulated by moods, and probably also differ across individuals. Behaviors that encourage attention to internal states over external stimuli seem to be beneficial for achieving an Aha! moment. As brain research continues to illuminate the enigma of insight, leadership research can both capitalize on this research and add to it by investigating real-world instances of insight and common practices for facilitating it.

References

Amabile, T. M., Barsade, S. G., Mueller, J. S., and Staw, B. M. 2005. "Affect and Creativity at Work." *Administrative Science Quarterly* 50: 367–403.

Ashby, F. G., Isen, A. M., and Turken, U. 1999. "A Neuropsychological Theory of Positive Affect and its Influence on Cognition." *Psychological Review* 106: 529–550.

Bolte, A., Goschke, T., and Kuhl, J. 2003. "Emotion and Intuition: Effects of Positive and Negative Mood on Implicit Judgments of Semantic Coherence." *Psychological Science* 14: 416–421.

Botvinick, M. M., Cohen, J. D., and Carter, C. S. 2004. Conflict Monitoring and Anterior Cingulate Cortex: An update." *Trends in Cognitive Sciences* 8: 539–546.

Bowden, E.M., and Beeman, M.J. 1998. "Getting the Right Idea: Sematic Activation in the Right Hemisphere May Help Solve Insight Problems." *Psychological Science* 6: 435–440.

Bowden, E. M., and Jung-Beeman, M. 2003. "Aha! Insight Experience Correlates with Solution Activation in the Right Hemisphere." *Psychonomic Bulletin and Review* 10: 730–737.

Bowers, K. S., Regehr, G., Balthazard, C., and Parker, K. 1990. "Intuition in the Context of Discovery." *Cognitive Psychology* 22: 72–110.

Christoff, K., Ream, J. M. and Gabrieli, J. D. E. 2004. "Cognitive and Neural Basis of Spontaneous Thought Processes." *Cortex* 40: 623–630.

Gasper, K., and Clore, G. L. 2002. "Attending to the Big Picture: Mood and Global Versus Local Processing of Visual Information." *Psychological Science* 13: 34–40.

Ilg, R., Vogeley, K., Goschke, T., Bolte, A., Shah, J. N., Poppel, E., and Fink, G. R. 2007. "Neural Processes Underlying Intuitive Coherence Judgments as Revealed by fMRI on a Semantic Judgment Task." *Neuroimage* 38: 228–38.

Isen, A. M., Daubman, K. A., and Nowicki, G. P. 1987. "PA Facilitates Creative Problem Solving." *Journal of Personality and Social Psychology* 32: 112–1131.

Jung-Beeman, M. 2005. "Bilateral Brain Processes for Comprehending Natural Language." *Trends in Cognitive Sciences* 9: 512–518.

Jung-Beeman, M., Bowden, E. M., Haberman, J., Frymiare, J. L., Arambel-Liu, S., Greenblatt, R., Reber, P. J., and Kounios, J. 2004. "Neural Activity When People Solve Verbal Problems with Insight." *PLoS Biology* 2: 500–510.

Kounios, J., Frymiare, J. L., Bowden, E. M., Fleck, J. I., Subramaniam, K., Parrish, T. B., and Jung-Beeman, M. J. 2006. "The Prepared Mind: Neural Activity Prior to Problem Presentation Predicts Subsequent Solution by Sudden Insight." *Psychological Science* 17: 882–890.

Kounios, J., Fleck, J. I., Green, D. L., Payne, L., Stevenson, J. L., Bowden, M., and Jung-Beeman, M. 2008. "The Origins of Insight in Resting-State Brain Activity." *Neuropsychologia* 46: 281–291.

Mednick, S. A. 1962. "The Associative Basis of the Creative Process." *Psychological Review* 69: 220–232.

Metcalfe, J., and Weibe, D. 1987. "Intuition in Insight and Noninsight Problem Solving." *Memory and Cognition* 15: 238–246.

Rowe, G., Hirsch, J. B., and Anderson, A. K. 2007. "Positive Affect Increases the Breadth of Attentional Selection." *Proceedings of the National Academy of Sciences, USA* 104(1): 383–388.

Smith, R. W., and Kounios, J. 1996. "Sudden insight: All-or-None Processing Revealed by Speed Accuracy Decomposition." *Journal of Experimental Psychology: Learning, Memory, and Cognition* 22: 1443–1462.

Sternberg, R. J., and Davidson, J. E., eds. 1995. *The Nature of Insight*. Cambridge, MA: MIT Press.

Subramaniam, K., Kounios, J., Parrish, T. B., and Jung-Beeman, M. 2009. "A Brain Mechanism for Facilitation of Insight by Positive Affect." *Journal of Cognitive Neuroscience* 3: 415-432.

Wegbreit, E., Suzuki, S., Grabowecky, M., Kounios, J., and Beeman, M. 2012. "Visual Attention Modulates Insight Versus Analytic Solving of Verbal Problems." *The Journal of Problem Solving* 4(2): Article 6. DOI:http://dxdoi.org/10.7771/1932-6246.1127.

Weisberg, R. W. 1994. "Genius and Madness? A Quasi-Experimental Test of the Hypothesis that Manic-Depression Increases Creativity." *Psychological Science* 5: 361–367.

Wills, T. W., Soraci, S. A., Chechile, R. A., and Taylor, H. A. 2000. "'Aha' Effects in the Generation of Pictures." *Memory and Cognition* 28: 939–948.

Worden, M. S., Foxe, J. J., Wang, N., and Simpson, G. V. 2001. "Anticipatory Biasing of Visuospatial Attention Indexed by Retinotopically Specific Alpha-Band Electroencephalography Increases Over Occipital Cortex." *Journal of Neuroscience* 20: 61–66.

6. The Healthy Mind Platter

Dr. David Rock, Dr. Daniel J. Siegel, Dr. Steven A. Y. Poelmans, and Dr. Jessica Payne

David Rock, CEO, NeuroLeadership Group, New York, USA
Faculty, CIMBA; Cofounder, NeuroLeadership Institute; Coeditor, *NeuroLeadership Journal*
david@neuroleadership.com

Daniel J. Siegel, Mindsight Institute, California, USA
UCLA: Center for Culture, Brain, and Development, Mindful Awareness Research Center, Clinical Professor, School of Medicine, California, USA

Steven A. Y. Poelmans, EADA Business School, Barcelona, Spain
Coaching Competency Center

Jessica Payne, University of Notre Dame, Indiana, USA

Introduction

The last few decades have witnessed a growing awareness of the importance of nutrition as a basis for health within the general population. In the United States and Europe, governments have created nutrition recommendations. Published as charts, such as healthy-food pyramids, which indicate that different food groups provide important nutrients, these guidelines recommend that citizens follow a "complete" diet that provides all the essentials the body needs. Because the body needs a wide variety of ingredients for optimal health, the basic underlying principles are variation and complementarity. This suggests that always eating the same food, even if it is healthy, does not provide the body with a wide enough variety of ingredients for optimal health.

Spurred on in 2011 by the US government's relaunch of the food pyramid as a "healthy eating plate," we decided to explore a framework for understanding the ideal diet for our brain. We chose to coin this the "Healthy Mind Platter." We do not refer literally to substances like glucose, which is an essential nutrient for the functioning of the brain, but to a set of everyday activities that on the whole optimize "brain health."

Based on our literature review, we hypothesize that there are seven activities, each of which has different and beneficial effects on the mind and complements the others, together providing a well-balanced "mental diet" for optimal neurocognitive functioning and well-being. We propose that, just as with food, people can do without some of these activities, but that this lack of behavior will be associated with sub-optimal levels of functioning or ill health. Further research is needed to determine the exact quantity and quality of each activity required for optimal health, but we propose that each activity makes a unique and positive contribution to mental productivity and well-being. As such, the objective of the Healthy Mind Platter is to propose a framework for creating and maintaining mental well-being, summarizing and integrating distinct strands of neuroscience and psychology research, which can be used to inform groups such as schools, organizations, governments, and communities, as well as families and individuals, about best practices for promoting mental health.

Why the Healthy Mind Platter

Throughout the world, driven by advances in information technology and automation, our economy is gradually shifting to a knowledge- and service-driven economy, where increasingly the basic production factor of muscle power is being replaced by brainpower. Although it is often compared to a muscle, the brain's anatomy and physiology is fundamentally different from those of muscles. Whereas a combination of exercise, rest, and nutrition can be sufficient to produce physical strength and resilience, these clearly are not sufficient conditions for an alert, creative, and resilient mind. In line with the principles and purpose of positive psychology, we want to move beyond studying and summarizing what is needed to avoid pathology, and make clear and useful what is needed to promote health. Though awareness is now being raised of how an unhealthy physical diet can result in serious pathologies and epidemics, such as obesity, many people are hardly aware of the costs of an unhealthy mental diet, such as massive losses in productivity, exhaustion, burnout, and stress. Explicating the constituent activities for a healthy mind is therefore timely and important, especially since developed countries are reaching the limits of economic growth.

One can daily observe on the news the catastrophic consequences of being deprived of food and basic housing, but society is relatively unaware of what happens when individuals or large communities are deprived of play (think of entire generations of children working under conditions of forced labor), good quality sleep (think of the vast number of people regularly taking sleep medications), or satisfying time to focus and sustain clear attention without distraction (think of population groups suffering unemployment or underemployment, or the vast number of people who fill their time with junk media). Most members of the general population know little about how the constant interruptions and distractions caused by communication devices and the bombardment of information and publicity sent out by the media impacts our mental well-being. They have minimal awareness of the negative effects of the sense of isolation and lack of relatedness that can occur in large cities built without regard for our need for a sense of community. Finally, what we have to gain as a species from the generalized practice of reflective practices is not readily apparent to the general population unaware of the research pointing to its positive impacts.

With stress, the brain will disconnect more often from the task at hand, and we may find ourselves staring at the computer screen, experiencing a momentary state of reverie or trance.

Consider the current state of how most people manage—cultivate and maintain—their mental well-being. We have all experienced the challenge of maintaining focus over prolonged periods and know how it can cause fatigue. We all know that our attention is even more limited if we had little sleep the night before. With stress, the brain will disconnect more often from the task at hand, and we may find ourselves staring at the computer screen, experiencing a momentary state of reverie or trance. As soon as we become aware of our disconnection, we may want to return to the task, but we might feel an urge to stand up, go for a walk, and get a snack. Basically, our brain is demanding a minimum level of physical motion and important nutrients to be able to operate well. On our way to the vending machine, we may encounter a colleague, and although we are cognizant of the pile of work waiting for us on our desk, we connect with a bystander to exchange a chat and a joke.

Following a healthy mind diet can provide us with the physical and mental well-being necessary to establish and maintain relationships with family, friends, and colleagues...

Once again, our brain is automatically driving us to socialize even without our awareness or conscious intention, distracting us, and delaying the time before we return to work. Once we are back at our desk we may be able to focus again, but we seem to lack the necessary creativity to resolve the problem. None of the techniques we know seem to help in producing a satisfactory solution. Frustrated by this impasse, we may lean back in our chair and suddenly remember the joke our colleague told half an hour ago. We internally laugh at the joke, not realizing that thanks to this playful mental intermezzo, our brain is capable of having a sudden insight that will help us solve the problem. In the case described above, the person is basically stumbling from activity to activity, driven by the needs of the brain, without any level of awareness of why this chain of events is occurring. We may even return home that night believing we had a productive working day, ignorant of the fact that the reason we are irritable is not because our spouse is being unreasonable, but because we are mentally exhausted.

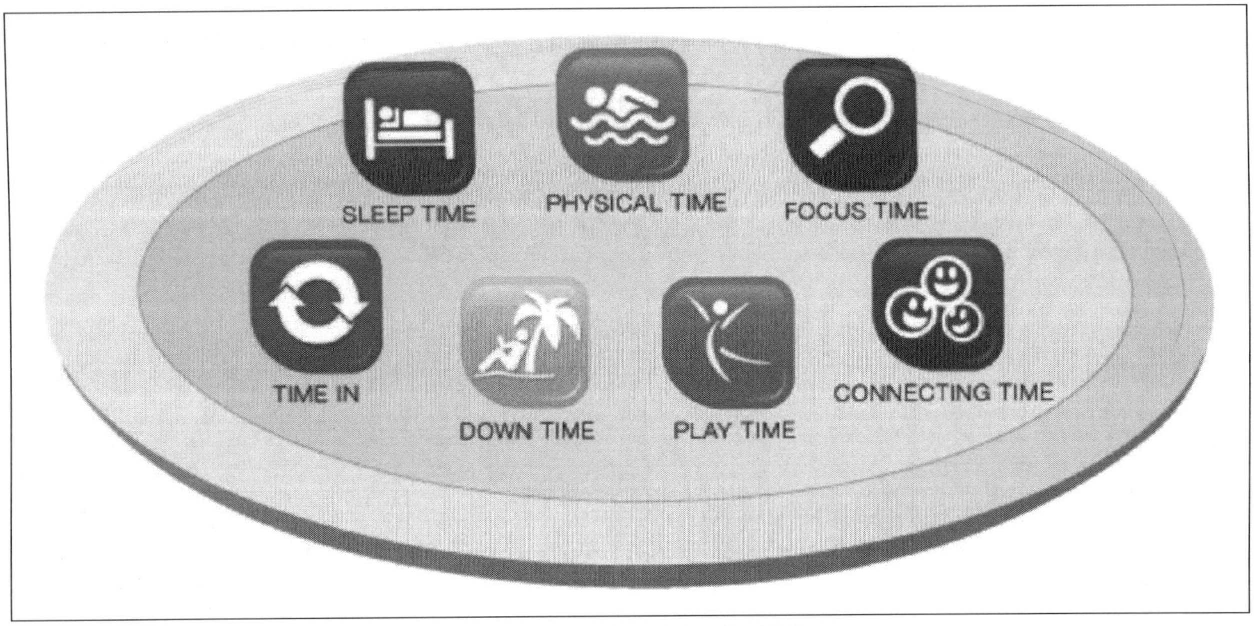

Figure 1. Ingredients of the Healthy Mind Platter.

Now consider how different things *could* be. What would happen if we were to start the day after a good night's sleep with half an hour of reflective practice, taking advantage of the rested and centered mind to prioritize the activities of the day? We might consciously plan to take a break over lunch, allowing for downtime or even a brief nap, and arrange for a tennis game with a friend right after work, thus combining connecting time and physical activity. When we arrive at work, we might mindfully schedule the day's meetings to alternate individual focus time with meetings with colleagues to have a day with variation in brain activity. The result might be that when we go home, we actually have sufficient reserves to connect and play with our children, completing the list of healthy activities for the day before dinnertime. Following a healthy mind diet can provide us with the physical and mental well-being necessary to establish and maintain relationships with family, friends, and colleagues, and efficiently realize the tasks and responsibilities at school, at work, and in our communities.

In the next paragraphs, we will provide the scientific foundations for the Healthy Mind Platter, synthesizing what we have learned from clinical work, behavioral research, affective and social neuroscience, and psychology.

First we will review the neuro-cognitive benefits of seven key activities: (1) sleep time; (2) playtime; (3) time-in (meditation or reflective practice); (4) downtime; (5) connecting time; (6) physical time; and (7) focus time. We will explicate their relationships with outcome variables such as creativity, health, and cognitive performance. Second, we will present the Healthy Mind Platter model, representing the complex relationships between its elements as antecedents and moderators for the three variables: creativity, (mental) health, and cognitive performance. This approach can serve as both a model with hypotheses for future research and a framework for brain health practice.

Seven neuro-cognitive activities that nurture the mind

1. Sleep time: refreshing mind and body and consolidating memory

Sleep is a highly complex and vital process that is essential for the biological balance of the mammalian organism (Benington 2000) and thought to be critical for homeostatic restoration, thermo-regulation, tissue repair, immunity, memory processing, and emotion regulation. Accordingly, sleep deprivation can be more lethal than food deprivation.

According to the 2008 Sleep in America poll on sleep, performance, and the workplace, conducted by the National Sleep Foundation, Americans said they wake up, on average, around 5:35 a.m. on workdays and around 7:12 a.m. on nonworkdays.

Depression associated with long work hours is primarily a result of sleep deprivation...

Overall, respondents reported an average sleep time of six hours and 40 minutes on workdays, with 44% getting less than seven hours of sleep on workdays. About three in ten respondents (29%) reported falling asleep or becoming very sleepy while at work in the past month, and just more than one in ten (12%) were late to work in the past month due to sleepiness or a sleep problem.

In the United States, drowsy drivers are responsible for a fifth of all motor vehicle accidents and some 8,000 deaths annually. It is estimated that 80,000 drivers fall asleep at the wheel every day; 10 percent of those drivers run off the road, and every two minutes, one of them crashes (Czeisler and Fryer 2006).

A study of work hours, sleep, and depression in 2,643 Japanese citizens who were employed full time showed that participants working more than 10 hours per day, sleeping less than six hours per day, and reporting insufficient sleep were, respectively, 37%, 43%, and 97% more likely to be depressed than those working six to eight hours per day, sleeping six to eight hours per day, and reporting sufficient sleep. The study concluded that depression associated with long work hours is primarily a result of sleep deprivation (Nakata 2011).

These statistics do not take into account the vast opportunity costs that sleep deprivation has on the quality and quantity of performance at work. Since Aristotle and until the middle of last century, sleep was considered a passive state that simply counteracted sleepiness (Payne 2011). Now, half a century later, there is a general consensus that sleep not only allows us to rest and recuperate strength for the next day but is also a highly active state that is important for cognitive processes such as memory consolidation, semantic integration, learning, and processing emotions (Stickgold 2005; Ibañez et al. 2008; Payne 2011).

Generally a distinction is made between two main types of sleep: rapid eye movement (REM) sleep and non-REM sleep. REM sleep occurs in roughly 90-minute cycles and alternates with four additional stages (stages 1–4, in order of increasing depth) known collectively as non-REM sleep. Slow-wave sleep (SWS) is the deepest of the non-REM phases and is characterized by high-amplitude, low-frequency brain oscillations. REM sleep, on the other hand, is a lighter state of sleep characterized by eye movements, decreased muscle tone (which inhibits the acting out of dreams), and low-amplitude, fast brain oscillations. In fact, REM-sleep is a neurophysiological state that is more similar to wakefulness (Hobson and Pace-Schott 2002) than non-REM states. More than 80% of SWS is concentrated in the first half of the night, whereas the second half of the night contains roughly twice as much REM sleep than the first half (fig. 1).

Sleep and the body

One proposed theory of sleep, especially slow-wave sleep, involves homeostatic restoration; that is, after a day of "use," sleep restores chemical and physiological processes that have become depleted during the day. Supporting this idea, the amount and power of slow-wave sleep in the first half of the night is strongly related to the amount of prior sleep and wakefulness, and thereby represents a marker of homeostatic sleep regulation (called "Process S"). The more hours spent awake, the more sleep pressure one accumulates and the more intense and abundant subsequent slow-wave sleep will be. This "slow-wave sleep rebound" may reflect a mandatory period of recovery or restoration for multiple biological systems as they recover from the "wear and tear" of waking activities, which is an idea supported by the surge in growth hormone that parallels slow-wave sleep early in the sleep cycle. Growth hormone is critical not only in early development but also in continued growth and maintenance of bone and tissues throughout life (Payne 2011).

The more hours spent awake, the more sleep pressure one accumulates and the more intense and abundant subsequent slow-wave sleep will be.

Sleep and the mind/brain

As important as sleep is for the body, evidence suggests that it may be even more critical for the brain. There is strong evidence that sleep's role extends beyond the body and includes critical brain functions, such as memory function, creative processing, and emotion regulation. Recent studies suggest that sleep is critical for solidifying or "consolidating" memories so that we integrate what we learn into long-term knowledge. Recent studies have shown that during sleep, neuronal populations previously engaged in a learning task are reactivated.

As important as sleep is for the body, evidence suggests that it may be even more critical for the brain.

This reactivation during sleep is a key process for stabilizing memory traces (Diekelmann and Born 2010). Examples include motor-sequence learning (Walker et al. 2002; Cohen et al. 2005), visual-discrimination learning (Stickgold, James, and Hobson 2000), perceptual learning of language (Fenn, Nusbaum, and Margoliash 2003), and declarative memory (Stickgold 2005). For instance, learning to navigate a maze during the day is associated with activation in the hippocampus, a structure essential for normal memory function. During subsequent sleep, there is a reactivation or "replay" of this hippocampal activation, as if the brain is reprocessing recently learned information. A compelling relationship exists between the increase in hippocampal activation during sleep and the amount of improvement in the maze task the next day. Moreover, if people dream about the maze task, their performance improves still further. This suggests that the reexpression of hippocampal activation during sleep reflects the offline processing of memory traces, which in turn leads to the strengthening of network connections in the brain, resulting in improved memory performance.

REM sleep in particular has been associated with insight and creativity, which is perhaps not surprising given that the most bizarre, fragmented, sometimes emotional, and certainly creative dreams happen during REM sleep. A recent report showed that a nap with REM sleep improves a person's ability to integrate unassociated information for creative problem solving (Cai et al. 2009). During sleep, our brains integrate information in highly novel ways and make connections that we simply are not capable of seeing during wakefulness (Payne 2011). In addition, several studies have shown that suppression of sleep produces deficits in cognitive and emotional processing during wakefulness (Gais and Born 2004; Durmer and Dinges 2005; Stickgold and Walker 2005; Tassi et al. 2006). Even a single night of sleep deprivation can render one more negative and more emotionally unregulated the next day than is experienced with a full night of restorative sleep. Based on this research, the expression of "to sleep on it" gains a whole new meaning and the idea that little or no mental activity occurs during sleep is unfounded. Instead, sleep is a highly dynamic and active collection of brain states that are critical for physical, cognitive, and emotional health.

But how much sleep should an individual get? It turns out that while the answer is, on average, 8 hours, it varies among individuals. Sleep need follows a normal distribution, or bell curve function, with the bulk of individuals requiring seven to nine hours of sleep. However, some individuals require as few as four or as many as twelve. While these people are outside the common range of distribution and very rare, they should not be considered to have a disorder.

Even very brief naps can help boost cognitive performance and help us feel more alert.

Understanding one's sleep needs and ensuring these are managed properly is central to a healthy body, brain, and mind. What can one do if short on sleep? It turns out even a short nap can help; studies have shown that a day's worth of sleep need not be acquired in a single nocturnal chunk. Siesta cultures show us that sleep can be divided into a night of five to seven hours and a daytime nap spanning one to two hours. What seems important is that the so-called 90-minute "ultradian cycles" are preserved. Alternatively, however, even very brief naps can help boost cognitive performance and help us feel more alert. In our "sleep-sick" society, napping has become a regular and sometimes necessary part of our daily lives.

Research investigating the benefits associated with napping holds potential for informing workplace practices and individual functioning.

To get the positive effects of a nap right away, a brief nap is most effective.

In an informative study, Brooks and Lack (2006) assess the benefits of different lengths of naps (5, 10, 20, and 30 minutes). Interestingly, the 10 -minute nap conferred the biggest benefit in alertness and performance both immediately after and up to three hours later. The five-minute nap was not quite enough to confer a significant benefit, and while the 20 and 30 minute naps were helpful, the benefits did not emerge until several hours later, arguably due to the effects of sleep inertia. To get the positive effects of a nap right away, a brief nap is most effective. This is because brief naps are more likely to contain light sleep (largely stage 2 non-REM sleep) and are short enough to prevent one from delving into slow-wave sleep, which is restorative but difficult to awaken from. It is also important to recognize that napping can be learned (with enough practice and diligence); this is key because evidence suggests that regular nappers may glean more benefits from napping than those who only nap out of necessity when absolutely exhausted. Clearly, recent research strongly points to the fact that sleep is far more important than is generally recognized, and though people do not get enough of it, there are easy steps to take to start remedying this problem. Adding a nap to one's day, or an extra 20 minutes to one's sleep cycle (or both) can yield major benefits to cognition, emotion regulation, and general performance.

2. Play time: the joy of experimenting with life

> *"Playfulness enhances the capacity to innovate, adapt, and master changing circumstances. It is not just an escape. It can help us integrate and reconcile difficult or contradictory circumstances. And, often, it can show us a way out of our problems."* —Stuart Brown, National Institute for Play

Play, which may seem like a frivolous, unimportant behavior with no apparent purpose, has earned new respect as biologists, neuroscientists, psychologists, and others see that play is indeed serious business and is perhaps equally important to other basic drives of sleep, rest, and food (Frost 1998). Neuroscience research reveals that play-joy is a basic emotional system and essential in child development and adult creativity and learning (Panksepp and Biven 2012). It has been suggested that play is an important behavioral tendency that does not require learning, and is an "experience-expectant" process that has adaptive neuro-developmental effects that promote later adaptive behaviors and help program higher brain regions involved in emotional behaviors (Gordon et al. 2003).

The play-joy system is one of the basic emotional systems in human beings, similar to rage, fear, expectancy, panic, lust, and the maternal nurturance-acceptance system...

According to a report from the American Academy of Pediatrics (AAP), free and unstructured play is healthy and in fact essential for helping children reach important social, emotional, and cognitive developmental milestones, as well as helping them manage stress and become resilient. Forces threatening free play and unscheduled time include changes in family structure, the increasingly competitive college admissions process, and federal education policies that have led to reduced recess and physical education in many schools. Play is not, however, only vital for children; it also appears to generate cognitive benefits for adults.

Based on his extensive research of play, Panksepp proposes that the play-joy system is one of the basic emotional systems in human beings, similar to rage, fear, expectancy, panic, lust, and the maternal nurturance-acceptance system (Panksepp 1991; 1992). Research on roughhousing play in mammals, both sapient and otherwise, clearly indicates that the sources of play and laughter in the brain are instinctive and subcortical (Panksepp 1998). Panksepp's research revealed that if rats are tickled in a playful way, they readily emit 50-kHz chirps (1998; 2003). Given that these chirps are indicative of positive affect and joy, they are probably comparable to human laughter (Panksepp and Burgdorf 2003; Panksepp 2005). Although the human capacity for verbal joking probably requires more refined cortically dependent cognitive skills, language likely "tickles" the ancient play circuits of our minds and causes joy to occur (Panksepp 2005). The rats that were tickled became socially bonded to the experimenters and were rapidly conditioned to seek tickles. The effect of juvenile isolation on these behaviors appears mainly due to deprivation of play (van den Berg et al. 1999a). Therefore, play may serve to prepare for more adaptive social behaviors in adulthood. The early games and frivolity of animals and humans equip them for the skills they will need in later life (Angier 1992; Brown 1994).

Indeed, human play and laughter is fundamentally a social phenomenon. The reason one cannot tickle oneself may be because the underlying neural systems are controlled by social cues and interactions. These are factors that help weave individuals into the social fabric in which they reside, reflecting different levels of position and dominance (Panksepp and Burgdorf 2003). After multiple play bouts, juvenile rats develop dominance hierarchies that remain relatively stable over the juvenile period (Meaney and Stewart 1981; Panksepp, Siviy, and Normansell 1984). Preventing male rats from playing has lasting consequences on social (Hol et al. 1999; van den Berg et al. 1999a; van den Berg et al. 1999b), aggressive, and sexual behavior (van den Berg et al. 1999b). In human children, playing only in isolation has also been associated with social problems (Coplan et al. 1994).

Neuroscientist and play expert Panksepp suggests that one reason for the increasing incidence of attention deficit hyperactivity disorder (ADHD) may be the diminishing availability of opportunities for preschool children to engage in natural self-generated social play. He suggests that instead of psychostimulants, at-risk children should be stimulated through play to facilitate frontal lobe maturation and the healthy development of prosocial minds (2007; see also Panksepp and Biven 2012). Psychiatrist Stuart Brown, founder of the National Institute for Play, became interested in play when he found that 90 percent of the 26 murderers he studied had a common history of play deprivation or abnormal play (Brown 1994; Brown and Vaughan 2010). This is a sensible conclusion in light of all the above because play seems to serve an important role in establishing relationships with positive effects. It is a safe way of learning about the "rules of the game" and developing adaptive social behavior. This is of vital importance in children, but is equally important in adults.

Human play and laughter is fundamentally a social phenomenon.

An important benefit of play is that it can facilitate learning. Research in rats has shown that play behavior is considered to be rewarding, as the opportunity to play can be used as an incentive for maze learning (Humphreys and Einon 1981; Normansell and Panksepp 1990). Just as in rats, the reward circuits in the brain light up during human mirth (Mobbs et al. 2003). States of engaged attention between infants and their caregivers tend to be associated with play, states of joy, and general experiences of positive affect (Gottman, Katz, and Hooven 1997). Play-joy stimulates the reward centers in the brain and is associated with the release of dopamine, which facilitates the establishment and consolidation of new neuronal pathways, which in turn is important for creativity (new connections) and memory (lasting connections). A study by Garaigordobil Landazabal (2005) focusing on the impact of play on the intellectual development of schoolchildren aged 10–11 years demonstrated a significant effect of play on verbal intelligence—the ability to form concepts or define words—and on the capacity for verbal associative thinking. The intervention program consisted of a weekly 2-hour play session throughout the academic year.

In their review, Spinka, Newberry, and Bekoff (2005) propose that play enables animals to develop flexible emotional responses to unexpected events in which they experience a sudden loss of control. This loss of control has more than a symbolic significance for humans. Indeed, it has been identified as one of the major causes of stress (Karasek and Theorell 1990; Spector et al. 2002). In the same way that animals play to increase the versatility of movements to recover from sudden shocks such as loss of balance and falling over, young children learn to cope emotionally with unexpected stressful situations by "training for the unexpected." Spinka and his colleagues suggest that the playful switching between in-control and out-of-control elements is cognitively demanding and is accompanied by neuroendocrinological responses that produce a complex emotional state known as "having fun."

In other words, Mother Nature has provided us with a naturally rewarding activity—play—that allows both animals and humans to experiment with the demands of life itself and practice spontaneous and novel motor and social skills that will prove essential for survival in the concrete jungle.

3. Downtime: disconnecting for integration and insight

When explaining "downtime" in workshops, we found that this is the most counterintuitive component of the Healthy Mind Platter and needs quite a bit of explaining. Downtime does not correspond to "leisure time" exactly, which is a much broader term and which may refer to hobbies and sports. In the Healthy Mind Platter, hobbies are more likely to come under "focus time" and sports under "physical time." With downtime we refer to a very specific type of "activity": inactivity, or doing absolutely nothing that has a predefined goal. Think of downtime as literally being un-goal-focused. Downtime is hanging out, being with one's surroundings, being spontaneous, having no particular goal or focus, as one might do on a lazy Sunday morning with no plans. Downtime is more about "being" in the moment with spontaneous emergence of whatever activity may or may not arise rather than "doing" a preplanned activity with a goal or preset agenda.

Downtime is actually intentionally having no intention, consciously engaging in doing nothing specific...

We have many words in our vocabulary that seem to refer to downtime, such as idling, hanging around, loafing, lazing, goofing off, and chilling out. These terms suggest that downtime is not very well understood nor highly regarded. In our definition, downtime is actually intentionally having no intention, consciously engaging in doing nothing specific or "preplanned," a process of disconnecting from intended directions and surrendering to daydreaming, letting our minds wander off in no particular direction with spontaneity and freedom. Downtime may occur between activities: while waiting for an appointment or an airplane, while listening to music or sifting through a magazine—that is, if we do not really pay sustained, focused attention to what is heard or written. If we consciously choose to spend downtime, we might find a comfortable chair, in the comfort of our living room or in the shadow of a tree, and disconnect from an intentional, linear focus on our environment. During those periods of downtime, we do much more than slumber, rest, and go "offline." During the "inactive" state of wakeful rest or daydreaming, the default neuronal network (or task-negative network) activates. This mode has been found to be characterized by activity in the medial temporal lobe (for memory), the medial prefrontal cortex (for theory of mind and sense of self), the posterior cingulate (related to autobiographical reflection), and the lateral parietal cortex (for integration) (Buckner, Andrews-Hanna, and Schacter 2008).

Unconscious thought produces better decisions than when people decide immediately using conscious, logical reasoning...

Researchers have shown that insight is preceded and aided by disconnecting from deliberate, goal-directed, conscious thinking. In many ways, downtime permits a sorting through of many disparate elements of our mental lives, permitting a process called integration—the linkage of differentiated parts—to naturally unfold. The research of Dijksterhuis and his colleagues (2004; 2006) found that unconscious thinkers outperform conscious analysts when making complex decisions. A meta-analysis across many studies confirmed that unconscious thought produces better decisions than when people decide immediately using conscious, logical reasoning (Strick et al. 2010). Unconscious thought leads to clearer, more integrated representations in memory (Dijksterhuis et al. 2006). What has long been dismissed as reverie and distraction now turns out to be a necessary precursor of insight in complex decision making. Recent research is showing that not just any "distraction" works, though. Maarten Bos and his colleagues (2008) found that "distraction with a goal" produced better results than "mere distraction." A break in the attentive activity devoted to a problem—also referred to as "incubation"—may eventually facilitate the solution process. Research showed that a break from close, focused, effortful attention improves performance with insight problem solving and that its length does not make a difference (Segal, 2004).

The very fact that unconscious thought and incubation time is conducive to better decision making and insight has profound implications for self-leadership.

In their book *The Breakout Principle*, Benson and Proctor (2003) explain that the best way to solve a thorny issue or complex problem is first to struggle with it, through problem analysis or fact gathering, up to the point where one stops feeling productive and starts feeling anxious and stressed. This is the signal for the second step: "distracting" oneself from the problem. There are many ways of doing this, including visiting a museum, taking a hot shower, or listening to some calming music. According to the authors, the key is "to stop analyzing, surrender control, and completely detach [oneself] from the stress producing thoughts." This typically leads to what the authors call "the breakout": a sudden insight or a new perspective that sheds a whole new light on the problem at hand.

The very fact that unconscious thought and incubation time is conducive to better decision making and insight has profound implications for self-leadership. Under pressure of deadlines, quarterly results, and shareholders, incubation time is squeezed out of the system, and so is the essential juice of creativity. Caught up in the rat race, laboring under the pressure of demanding objectives, creativity is pushed out of the equation. In this age of the knowledge and service economy, regular breaks on a daily basis, weekends, or a monthly basis, and sabbaticals on a long-term basis should not be viewed as a luxury at all. Such breaks are needed to sort and integrate important elements of our minds and permit creativity to emerge. Organizations need "positive turbulence" to build continuous renewal into their cultures (Gryskiewicz 1999) and develop supportive cultures that foster creative behaviors in employees (Rao, Wilson, and Watkinson 2009).

Whereas analytical thinking requires an increase and maintenance of (visual) attention, insight is characterized by less-focused, inward-directed, more open forms of attention. We propose that downtime moderates the relationship between previous knowledge/experience and the generation of new insights. Not just any downtime, idle-time, or daydream-time will do. It is important that our brain disconnects and "unfocuses" from the task at hand and its millions of distractions to connect with something entirely different, as a condition to have insights on a whole different level. Insight, contrary to analytic thinking, is fast and manifests as sudden awareness or understanding. Sternberg and Davidson (1995) define insight as a "sudden comprehension that can result in a new interpretation of a situation and that can point to the solution to a problem." In light of the previous paragraphs, this "suddenness" is misleading. It is the result of previously collecting the pieces of the puzzle and allowing time to let them connect in new and perhaps more integrated ways nonconsciously—new assemblies that are outside of awareness.

Downtime moderates the relationship between previous knowledge/experience and the generation of new insights.

Psychologists have been studying insight for nearly a century, but more recent advances in neuroscience are demonstrating that insight is the culmination of a series of brain states and processes operating at different time scales (Kounios and Jung-Beeman 2009). Bowden and Jung-Beeman (2003) propose that semantic activation in both hemispheres cooperatively contributes to problem solving, but weak solution activation that contributes to the Aha! experience is more likely to occur with neural activations in the right hemisphere than in the left hemisphere.

The right anterior cingulate cortex is involved in directing attention to detect weakly activated, nonconscious solutions (Kounios and Jung-Beeman 2009). Kounios et al. (2006) suggest that the activity observed in the anterior cingulate cortex (ACC) before an insight may reflect increased readiness to monitor for competing responses and to apply cognitive control mechanisms as needed to (a) suppress extraneous thoughts, (b) initially select prepotent solution spaces or strategies, and, if these prove ineffective, (c) subsequently shift attention to a nonprepotent solution or strategy. Such shifts are characteristic of insight.

People are more likely to solve problems with insight if they are in a positive mood.

Understanding the precursors of insight is important, as it may point to interventional opportunities for the facilitation of insight (Kounios and Jung-Beeman 2009). For instance, Subramaniam et al. (2009) found that people are more likely to solve problems with insight if they are in a positive mood. Jill Bolte Taylor's fascinating tale *My Stroke of Insight* (2009) clearly describes how the right hemisphere is "openminded and thinks out of the box. It's not limited by the rules and regulations established by my left mind that created that box" (148). This right brain is present in the moment and integrates and nuances thoughts as the left-brain constant chatter is silenced. Segal goes one step further, stating that "the default state has a large emphasis on stimulus-independent thought—mind-wandering, chatter that cannot be cut off—and the deviation from that to a place where people aren't controlled by ongoing internal speech is a place where people are able to find some calm and respite" (2009). Ian McGilchrist (2009) notes that the right hemisphere contributes to a way of being that senses context and the interrelated, whole nature of reality, whereas the left focuses on text and the individual parts that comprise the world. Downtime may permit integration across the hemispheres and in particular enable the less-vocal and less-assertive right hemisphere's synthetic processing to be sensed and expressed.

For leadership, the relevance of understanding the antecedents of insight is great since it is a process that, from a neurological point of view, is extremely cost-effective. It allows connecting very diffuse information in a "moment of genius," where everything becomes suddenly clear with relatively little effort. Such intuition allows experienced managers to make decisions much more quickly, which in times of constant change is an enormous advantage. Certain decisions, such as buying or selling stock, depend on so many interrelated and complex factors, which are in constant flux, that using sequential, analytical cognition alone will not suffice. Managers do not always have the opportunity to scrutinize all information, weigh in on all options with conscious deliberation, and think through all solutions. Their "bounded rationality" (Simon 1991) and limited time forces them to trust their more intuitive, sudden insights.

Based on what we are learning from the neurosciences, we need to be more cautious in creating the proper conditions for insight. We can intentionally cultivate a positive atmosphere while encouraging the development of mindfulness to stabilize the mind, quiet the internal chatter, and block out external distractions so that what emerges spontaneously can be seen clearly. With intention, we can invite people to respect nonconscious thought and incubation time and enable genius and "thinking outside the box" to bubble up from the wells of experience and relaxation.

We can intentionally cultivate a positive atmosphere while encouraging the development of mindfulness to stabilize the mind...

4. Time-in: reflection, attunement, mindfulness

Various studies cited by the National Institute for Occupational Safety and Health in the report *Stress at Work* indicate that between 26% and 40% of all workers today feel stressed or burnt out by work (NIOSH, Publication No. 99–101). Roughly 60% of doctor visits stem from stress-related complaints and illnesses (Kroenke and Mangelsdorff 1989). Confronted with pressure or stress, the brain strives to reestablish and maintain homeostasis through the coordinated activation and control of neuroendocrine and autonomic stress systems. Stress responses are mediated by largely overlapping circuits in the limbic forebrain—the hypothalamus and the brainstem—so that the respective contributions of the neuroendocrine and autonomic systems are tuned in accordance with stressor modality and intensity (Ulrich-Lai and Herman 2009). Sabine Sonnentag and her colleagues have extensively studied the dynamic of recovery experiences and distinguish between psychological detachment from work (i.e., not thinking about job-related issues or problems), relaxation (a process characterized by decreased sympathetic activation), and mastery experiences (challenging off-job experiences that provide opportunities for learning and success) (Sonnentag and Fritz 2007). Their research showed that low psychological detachment from work during the evening predicted negative activation and fatigue, whereas mastery experiences during the evening predicted positive activation and relaxation predicted serenity. Sleep quality showed positive relations with all affective states. In our Healthy Mind Platter, we refer to mastery experiences under "focus time" and to "psychological detachment" under "downtime." For "time-in" we focus on reflection, relaxation, and mindfulness.

In his classic work *The Relaxation Response* (1975), Herbert Benson explored the importance and practice of relaxation to a broad business audience. Relaxation is a process characterized by decreased sympathetic activation and becomes evident in a decrease in heart rate and muscle tension (Benson 1975). There are many relaxation techniques, including progressive muscle relaxation (Jacobson 1938) and various forms of meditation (Grossman et al. 2004). Yet there are also many "everyday activities" that can result in responses similar to relaxation, such as a walk in nature (Hartig et al. 2003) or listening to music (Pelletier 2004). A wide body of research now shows the beneficial effects of relaxation, such as the reduction of tension (Van der Klink et al. 2001), and the increase of positive affective states (Stone, Kennedy-Moore, and Neale 1995; Parkinson and Totterdell 1999; Fredrickson 2000).

Yet when we talk about "time-in" in the Healthy Mind Platter, we refer to much more than relaxation. Relaxation is actually only one of the aspects or benefits of the broader practice of meditation—a way of training the mind—defined as an intentional self-regulation of attention, in the service of self-inquiry, in the here and now (Masion et al.1995). There are many forms of meditation. Descriptions of meditation vary and are often expressed in behavioral terms; they include (1) relaxation, (2) concentration, (3) altered state of awareness, (4) suspension of logical thought processes, and (5) maintenance of a self-observing attitude (Perez-de-Albeniz and Holmes 2000).

One particular type of meditation that has been scrutinized by neuroscientists in increasing ways recently is mindfulness meditation. Mindfulness has been described as "paying attention in a particular way: on purpose, in the present moment, and non-judgmentally" (Kabat-Zinn 1994). Bishop et al. (2004) propose an operational definition distinguishing two components: (1) self-regulation of attention focused on immediate experience and (2) orientation toward one's experiences in the present moment, characterized by curiosity, openness, and acceptance. Rather than changing the environment or the appraisal of the situation, mindfulness aims at becoming aware and accepting thoughts, feelings, and bodily sensations. According to Creswell et al. (2007), part of the positive effect of mindfulness may be due to labeling affect.

Mindfulness in trained individuals has been associated with increased engagement of a right lateralized network, comprising the lateral prefrontal cortex (PFC) and viscera-somatic areas such as the insula, secondary somatosensory cortex, and inferior parietal lobule (Farb et al. 2007). According to Chiesa and Serretti (2009a), mindfulness meditation activates the PFC and the anterior cingulate cortex (ACC). Long-term meditation practice is associated with an enhancement of cerebral areas related to attention and emotion regulation (Lazar et al. 2005; Luders et al. 2009). Meta-analytic studies of the impact of mindfulness-based stress reduction seem to suggest that these programs may help a broad range of individuals to cope with their clinical and nonclinical problems, such as pain, cancer, heart disease, depression, anxiety, and stress (Grossman et al. 2004; Chiesa and Serretti 2009a; 2009b). A meta-analysis of the effect of mindfulness-based therapy (MBT) on anxiety and depression concluded that MBT improves symptoms of anxiety and depression across a relatively wide range of severity, even when these symptoms are associated with other disorders, such as medical problems (Chiesa and Serretti 2009b; Hoffmann et al. 2010).

Mindfulness has been described as "paying attention in a particular way: on purpose, in the present moment, and non-judgmentally."

To conclude, "time-in" is characterized by a very particular type of conscious, focused attention on the inner life of the self in the here and now. Time-in focuses attention on one's intentions and highlights awareness of awareness itself—the two fundamental elements of being mindful (Siegel 2007). Time-in develops the capacity to be present with experience. Presence, in turn, has been found to be associated with improvements in a number of processes, including the levels of the enzyme telomerase, which maintains the telomere caps at the ends of chromosomes within the nucleus of our cells (see Parker et al., forthcoming). Time-in focuses on acceptance of process rather than content (Perez-de-Albeniz and Holmes 2000) and can be generally seen to be related to a range of benefits if practiced on a regular basis: in addition to being a wakeful hypometabolic physiological state, it has physiological (e.g., balance of parasympathetic and sympathetic function, health), cognitive (e.g., attention, flexible perspective), emotional (e.g., self-control, stress management), and social (e.g., compassion, empathy) benefits. Regular time-in can therefore be counted among the seven vital activities on the Mental Health Platter.

5. Connecting time: the healing power of relationships

> *"Pleasant words are a honeycomb, sweet to the soul and healing to the bones."* —Solomon, 1000 BC, Proverbs 16:24

According to Matthew Lieberman, one of the founders of social-cognitive neuroscience, our "evolutionary wiring predisposes us to be social," actually causing a sense of physical pain if we are socially rejected (Eisenberger, Lieberman, and Williams 2003; Eisenberger and Lieberman 2004). Thus one could argue that social connection is a basic human need, very much like water, food, and shelter. Social support is a well-documented antecedent of well-being. A landmark study by Berkman and Syme (1979) found that the status and extent of social relationships predicts mortality over a nine-year follow-up after controlling for sociodemographic, physical health, and health behavior variables. Based on these epidemiological findings, researchers have proposed specific relationships between interpersonal functioning, biological processes, and disease (Pettit, Grover, and Lewinsohn 2007).

Cohen, Gottlieb, and Underwood (2000) proposed two processes through which social relationships affect health. One process involves the provision or exchange of emotional, informational, or instrumental resources in response to the perceptions that others are in need of aid. The other process focuses on the health benefits that accrue from participation in one or more distinct social groups. Others can influence cognitions, emotions, behaviors, and biological responses in ways beneficial to health and well-being through interactions that are not explicitly intended to exchange help or support—for example, increased self-esteem, personal control, and conformity to behavioral norms that have implications for our health (Cohen, Gottlieb, and Underwood 2000). A review of 81 studies revealed that social support is reliably related to beneficial effects on aspects of the cardiovascular, endocrine, and immune systems (Uchino et al. 1999). Social support has been associated with positive effects on various diseases, such as cardiovascular reactivity and blood pressure (Spitzer et al. 1992; Uchino et al. 1999; Gallo, Smith, and Kircher 2000; Steptoe 2000; Evans and Steptoe 2001; Uno, Uchino, and Smith 2002) and depression (Hays et al. 2001; Sayal et al. 2002). Reviews of the social-support literature (e.g., Berkman 1984; Cohen and Wills 1985; House, Landis, and Umberson 1988) conclude that social integration and perceived emotional support are directly and positively related to physical and mental health, including lower mortality (Thoits 1995). The most powerful measure of social support is whether a person has an intimate, confiding relationship, typically with a spouse or a lover; friends or relatives function similarly but less powerfully (Cohen and Wills 1985).

Social support is reliably related to beneficial effects on aspects of the cardiovascular, endocrine, and immune systems...

Given that stress is an important cause of sleep problems and cognitive impairment, the buffering effect of social support on stress is pertinent to our discussion of the Healthy Mind Platter. Impaired social functioning may represent a form of stress (Cohen 2004) that impacts physical health indirectly via emotional experiences (Kiecolt-Glaser et al. 2002) and directly through physiological pathways. Social support is one of the pillars of the job-demand-support model developed by Karasek and Theorell (1990) and adopted by the World Health Organization for predicting stress, cardiovascular disease, and productivity. According to a meta-analytic review, social support has a threefold effect on work stressor–strain relations (Viswesvaran, Sanchez, and Fisher 1999): social support reduces the strains experienced, mitigates perceived stressors, and moderates the stressor–strain relationship.

Lonely individuals may experience higher levels of perceived stress, react more negatively to stress, and benefit less from social interactions...

Cacioppo et al. (2000) found that satisfying social relationships are associated with more positive outlooks on life, more secure attachments and interactions with others, more flexible autonomic activation when confronting acute psychological challenges, and more efficient restorative behaviors. Individuals who were chronically lonely had elevated mean salivary cortisol levels across the course of a day, suggesting more discharges of corticotropin-releasing hormone and elevated activation of the hypothalamic-pituitary-adrenocortical axis. Lonely individuals may experience higher levels of perceived stress, react more negatively to stress, and benefit less from social interactions (Cacioppo et al. 2002; Hawkley et al. 2003). Lonely individuals experience less efficient and less effective sleep that may interfere with the restorative processes of sleep (Cacioppo et al. 2002), another crucial element of the Healthy Mind Platter.

In contrast to impaired social functioning, the perception that others are available to provide assistance and emotional support buffers the negative effects of stress on health. The presence of positive social support reduces the likelihood of negative health outcomes in the wake of stressful events (Rosengren et al. 1993). In addition, the extent to which individuals actively participate in social activities and hold social roles prospectively predicts health outcomes (Cohen et al. 1997).

Another interesting strand of research studying the interplay between stress, health, and social support looks at the impact of neuropeptides such as oxytocin. Oxytocin is an evolutionarily highly preserved nonapeptide released from the paraventricular nucleus of the hypothalamus through the posterior pituitary (Buijs et al. 1983). In nonhuman mammals, oxytocin is a key mediator of complex emotional and social behaviors, including attachment, social recognition, and aggression. Oxytocin reduces anxiety and impacts on fear conditioning and extinction (Kirsch et al. 2005). Heinrichs et al. (2003) designed a placebo-controlled, double-blind study, in which 37 men were exposed to the Trier Social Stress Test and were randomly assigned to receive intranasal oxytocin or a placebo, as well as social support from their best friend during the preparation period or no such presence of a friend for support. They found that salivary free cortisol levels remained low with social support in response to stress. The combination of oxytocin and social support exhibited the lowest cortisol concentrations, as well as increased calmness and decreased anxiety during stress (Heinrichs et al. 2003).

> *From our earliest days of life, our connections to others provide a source of feeling seen, safe, and secure.*

Oxytocin administration in humans was shown to increase trust, suggesting involvement of the amygdala, a central component of the neuro-circuitry of fear and social cognition that has been linked to trust (Winston et al. 2002; Kosfeld et al. 2005). In their study, Kirsch et al. (2005) showed that human amygdala function is strongly modulated by oxytocin. They used fMRI to image amygdala activation by fear-inducing visual stimuli after the intranasal application of a placebo or oxytocin. Compared with the placebo, oxytocin potently reduced activation of the amygdala and reduced coupling of the amygdala to brainstem regions involved in autonomic and behavioral manifestations of reactive fear (Kirsch et al. 2005).

From our earliest days of life, our connections to others provide a source of feeling seen, safe, and secure (Siegel 2012a). Our profoundly social brains may require ongoing connections with close and reliable others in order to maintain the physiologic and emotional balance that such relationships establish from the beginning of life. To conclude, the link between social support and health is well documented, but the exact neural mechanisms of social cognition in the human brain and the beneficial effects of social supports are complex and need further research drawing from a wide range of disciplines, such as social-cognitive neuroscience, neuro-immuno-endocrinology, and occupational health psychology.

6. Physical time: improving the brain's plasticity through exercise

In an article in the *New York Times*, Sandra Aamodt and Sam Wang, respectively editor in chief of *Nature Neuroscience* and associate professor of molecular biology and neuroscience at Princeton, take a critical look at computer programs to improve brain performance. The digital brain health and fitness software market is a booming business. According to the 2010 industry report *Transforming Brain Health with Digital Tools to Assess, Enhance, and Treat Cognition across the Lifespan: The State of the Brain Fitness Market 2010*, the size of the worldwide market in 2009 was $295 million, a 35% growth since 2008 and representing an annualized growth rate of 31% since 2005. According to Aamodt and Wang (2007):

> "Advertising for these products often emphasizes the claim that they are designed by scientists or based on scientific research. To be charitable, we might call them inspired by science—not to be confused with actually proven by science. One form of training, however, has been shown to maintain and improve brain health—physical exercise."

Exercise can help to achieve and maintain brain health and plasticity throughout life (Cotman and Berchtold 2002). The clinical literature has recognized for years that exercise affects overall health and brain function, especially in later life (Berkman et al. 1993; Blomquist and Danner 1987; Rogers, Meyer, and Mortel 1990; Hill et al. 1993; Laurin et al. 2001). Exercise is associated with enhanced metabolism of energy throughout the body (Gomez-Pinilla 2008).

Studies in humans have demonstrated the beneficial effects of exercise on cognitive function (Suominen-Troyer et al. 1986; Kramer et al. 1999). Exercise has the capacity to enhance learning and memory (Suominen-Troyer et al. 1986; Rogers, Meyer, and Mortel 1990; van Praag, Kempermann, and Gage 1999b) under a variety of conditions, ranging from counteracting the mental decline associated with aging (Kramer et al. 1999) to aiding recovery in patients suffering from brain injury or disease (Bohannon 1993; Lindvall et al. 1994; Grealy, Johnson, and Rushton 1999). Cardiovascular fitness training improves overall cognitive function, regardless of task type (Colcombe et al. 2004). Exercise improves "executive functions," the set of abilities (e.g., response speed and working memory) that allows us to select appropriate behavior, inhibit inappropriate behavior, and focus despite distractions (Aamodt and Wang 2007; Davis et al. 2007). Moderate aerobic-type exercise also reduces stress, decreases anxiety, and alleviates depression (Salmon 2001). Overall, physical activity has a significant positive and global impact on mental functioning.

Exercise can help to achieve and maintain brain health and plasticity throughout life...

Studies by neuroscientists are strengthening the premise that exercise can benefit brain function and are encouraging additional clinical studies in this area (Cotman and Berchtold 2002). Research reporting human brain activity during exercise is sparse but consolidates the data in the animal literature, showing that the simple act of moving activates a large percentage of the brain involving sensory/perceptual processes, autonomic regulation, and motor output (Dietrich 2006). A PET study found that increased brain activation was recorded in the "primary sensory cortex, primary motor cortex, supplementary motor cortex as well as the anterior part of the cerebellum" in response to cycling (Christensen et al. 2000). Another study using single-photon-emission computed tomography found increases in regional cerebral blood flow (CBF) in the supplementary motor area, medial primary sensorimotor area, striatum, visual cortex, and cerebellar vermis during walking (Fukuyama et al. 1997).

Physical activity has a significant positive and global impact on mental functioning.

Exercise is an activity that, if practiced on a regular basis, activates molecular and cellular cascades that support and maintain brain plasticity. It induces the expression of genes associated with plasticity and promotes brain vascularization, neurogenesis, functional changes in neuronal structure, and neuronal resistance to injury (Cotman and Berchtold 2002). Exercise activates mechanisms that protect the brain from damage. Studies in animals have shown that physical activity, in the form of voluntary wheel running, can increase levels of brain-derived neurotrophic factor (BDNF), a molecule that enhances synaptic growth, increases neuronal survival, promotes learning, and protects against cognitive decline. It also increases other growth factors, stimulates neurogenesis, increases resistance to brain insult, improves learning and mental performance, and induces gene expression changes in the brain (Cotman and Engesser-Cesar 2002; Cotman and Berchtold 2002).

The finding that exercise increases BDNF levels in the hippocampus—an area vital for memory formation and learning—has provided insight about the possible molecular mechanisms responsible for the positive effects of exercise on cognition (Neeper et al. 1995; Gomez-Pinilla et al. 2002; Vaynman, Ying, and Gomez-Pinilla 2004). By inducing BDNF and other molecules, exercise strengthens neuronal growth and interconnected synaptic linkages among neurons and facilitates synaptic transmission, thus priming activated cells for encoding into long-term storage (Cotman and Berchtold 2002).

7. Focus time: attention management for performance

Today's business context is characterized by a number of tendencies that, combined, have radically increased the fragmentation of time. Developments in communication and information technology have multiplied and made more immediate and intricate the nature of our connectivity. Globalization has intensified competition, and with it, customers increasingly expect 24/7 access, just-in-time deliveries, and minimum waiting times. In turn, firms expect their managers to be flexible, mobile, and available to meet customer expectations. With a steady increase of women in the labor force, dual-earner families have become the norm, and juggling work and family responsibilities is now a concern for both men and women.

In this context, time is being fragmented and focus scattered. Less time is available for more tasks and responsibilities. Since time is a scarce resource, those skilled in (re-)focusing quickly and staying focused within fragments of time will thrive and be more successful. This requires the capacity to manage one's attention: to focus entirely on the person or task at hand while also exerting self-control to block out interferences. The central component of the Healthy Mind Platter for those concerned not just with brain health but also performance is undoubtedly focus time: the time we are able to focus, stay focused, and refocus efficiently and effectively.

Focusing attention involves several functions, including alerting, orienting, and executive control (Tang and Posner 2009). The executive capacity to focus depends on a well-developed PFC, also referred to as the executive part of the brain, responsible for most of the higher cognitive functions that organize actions, both physical and mental. The PFC's functions are wide and varied; they include capacities such as: (1) working memory, involved in organizing and structuring information, remembering self, and creating images of the possible future for consequence evaluation and long-term planning; and (2) processes for monitoring behavior and inhibiting prepotent responses, including emotion regulation and self-observation (Siegel 2010). Our executive functions allow us to reconsider the environment moment to moment and make choices that may be different from our automatic responses.

Developments in communication and information technology have multiplied and made more immediate and intricate the nature of our connectivity.

When we focus, we activate working memory long enough to allow other recombinant processes to occur within this "chalkboard of the mind." The process consists of encoding the information through the activity of the hippocampus and parts of the cortex to create linkages among aspects of experience that encode both context and the explicit elements of factual and autobiographical memory. Ultimately, these forms of explicit memory can be flexibly retrieved, enabling us to have a context for the present and an understanding of the past, and to more effectively plan for the future as we harness the power of the prefrontal cortex.

To focus is to pay close attention. Attention is a complex process involving multiple parts of the brain related to perception, arousal, emotion, and memory. The attention process, akin to putting a spotlight on something, consists of three stages that involve different parts of the brain and different systems (norepinephrine and dopamine): (1) alerting (reticular activating system, brainstem, thalamus), activated by fear or novelty; (2) orienting (thalamus, superior colliculus, parietal cortex), to orient or direct the focus of processing on input from the sensory organs or internally generated neural activity from the cortex; and (3) executive functions (PFC, ACC, striatum) that can hold information in mind and make choices about processes as they occur (Carter 1998, 305).

A lack of stimulation (boredom) and overstimulation (stress) both lead to impairment of executive functions, distraction, and lack of focus.

These higher cognitive functions mediated by the PFC have been found to require adequate levels of catecholamines, which in turn are altered by levels of arousal or stress. A lack of stimulation (boredom) and overstimulation (stress) both lead to impairment of executive functions, distraction, and lack of focus. In these conditions, the brain can be altered to enter a state of hypo- or hypervigilance that can impair performance. Attention can therefore be considered to be dependent on a state of optimal arousal that activates the body and mind to process incoming information and respond adequately.

For a person to function at optimal levels of arousal, predictability and a sense of control are necessary. Deep breathing, mindfulness (openness and acceptance to what arises in the field of attention), and framing the stressor as controllable or transient can also help maintain or bring a person back to optimal levels of arousal and attentional focus. In short, there is a direct relationship between stress, focus, and health. One could even propose that the capacity to focus attention is an ongoing indicator of mental fitness. Many mental difficulties, such as attention deficit hyperactivity disorder (ADHD), schizophrenia, and Alzheimer's disease, are characterized by attention problems.

Another aspect of focus time is sustaining attention, or staying focused, which is a function of self-control. This important function of motoric, cognitive, and emotional control is mediated by activity in the (ventrolateral) prefrontal cortex (areas 44, 45, and 47). Lesions or dysfunction in this area are associated with obsessive-compulsive behavior and addictions. The exertion of self-control appears to depend on a limited resource. Just as a muscle gets tired from exertion, acts of self-control cause short-term impairments (mental depletion) in subsequent self-control, even on unrelated tasks. Research has supported this strength framework for understanding the possible challenges in the domains of eating, drinking, spending, sexuality, intelligent thought, making choices, and interpersonal behavior (Baumeister, Vohs, and Tice 2007). These authors note that motivational or framing factors can temporarily block the deleterious effects of being in a state of mental depletion, and that blood glucose is a component of the energy required for effective executive control.

Last but not least is the capacity to refocus after distraction or during multitasking. Given the limited capacity of our working memory, rather than processing multiple sources of information simultaneously, we continuously switch our spotlight of attention back and forth between different stimuli. As a consequence, we divide attention, allocating less time to each task or distributing a given focus in divided ways over a longer time span. The logical consequence is that multitasking impairs performance, also referred to as "dual task interference." According to Meyer et al., multitasking requires multiple cognitive microprocesses (1998) involving multiple regions of the brain (1997), including the dorsolateral PFC for goal shifting and refocusing attention, the posterior parietal lobe for activating the task's procedural rules, the anterior cingulate cortex (ACC) for error monitoring, and the premotor cortex for anticipatory movement preparation. The time required for executing all these microprocesses depends on a series of criteria but in general increases with the number of interruptions, switching from one task to the other (Rubinstein, Evans, and Meyer 1994).

In the Healthy Mind Platter, focus time involves the application of a singular attentional focus on a task that permits a sense of mastery and completion. Focus time enables an individual to avoid the sense of being overwhelmed and incomplete that so often accompanies multitasking. Focus time is both a cognitive process necessary for effective performance and an intentional effort that requires self-control, both of which require energy and the management of stress. This has important implications for self-management—keeping down the "switching-time costs" of multitasking, which diminishes cognitive performance. In these ways, focus time is helpful for a sense of efficacy in the outcome of efforts and the effective sense of contributing to work output.

Discussion and conclusion

In this chapter we introduced the Healthy Mind Platter, a framework for managing our lives and promoting mental, relational, and brain health. This approach may be useful in informing schools, organizations, governments, and communities about the necessary "mental nutrients" for the daily mental activities that promote well-being. The ingredients of the Healthy Mind Platter are sleep time, play time, time-in, downtime, connecting time, physical time, and focus time. The Healthy Mind Platter can be used as a simple visual framework to promote and increase the awareness of mental health in our daily lives. Following a healthy mind "diet" can provide us with the physical and mental well-being necessary to establish and maintain relationships with family, friends, and colleagues and to efficiently complete the tasks and responsibilities at school, at work, and in our communities. The mind can be seen to emerge from both body and relationships, and so the Healthy Mind Platter focuses on our bodies, our social connections, and how we focus our minds themselves (see Siegel 2012a and 2012b).

Following a healthy mind "diet" can provide us with the physical and mental well-being necessary to establish and maintain relationships...

Although we have introduced the different factors constituting the Healthy Mind Platter individually, there are many direct and indirect and sometimes complex interrelations between them. All ingredients have clear and well-documented relationships with one or several of the outcome variables: creativity, mental health, and cognitive performance. Downtime, play time, connecting time, time-in, and focus time are associated with creativity. All factors are related to mental health.

Focus time has complex relationships with many other variables. First, focus time is a logical antecedent of cognitive performance. Focusing involves a coordinated constellation of cognitive processes necessary for thinking or acting consciously and intelligently in general. If focus time is characterized by "flow" or engagement, according to positive psychologists such as Seligman (2011) and Csikszentmihalyi (1990), it has many beneficial effects for health. For instance, active leisure time is an example of focus time that allows us to completely distract ourselves from work and reconnect with a refreshed mind. The relationship between focus time and cognitive performance is moderated by sleep time, downtime, and time-in. Without sufficient rest and breaks, people may be quite challenged to maintain focus. Without alternating focus time with instances of reflection within (time-in), for example, attention fades and the level of processing may be restricted to only surface considerations.

Moments before an insight, we unfocus visually and mentally to enable an idea to bubble to the surface.

The relationship between focus time and creativity is a complex one. As mentioned in the section on downtime, insight often does not occur without previous processes of analysis (focus time) and incubation (downtime, sleep time, time-in), for the pieces to come together in a creative "aha" way or within a complex decision-making process. Moments before an insight, we unfocus visually and mentally to enable an idea to bubble to the surface. Interestingly, EEG assessments of gamma waves suggest this cognitive event resembles moments of deep meditation. In other words, in some cases, different ingredients in the Healthy Mind Platter (e.g., focus time, downtime, time-in) alternate with each other instantaneously to produce yet another phenomenon (e.g., a transient state of insight or creativity).

A second complex relationship is between physical time and cognitive performance, which we discussed in the section on physical time. According to the transient hypofrontality hypothesis, during exercise and exertion of effort, cognitive performance decreases because blood is disproportionally concentrated in the muscles. Following exercise and long afterward, however, physical activity practice should increase cognitive performance, thanks to improved blood distribution to the brain and enhanced neuroplasticity after exercise. In addition, downtime and sleep time moderate the relationships between physical time and mental health. Both incessant physical activity without rest and a general lack of exercise can endanger (mental) health. While we have not listed amounts of time, ratios, or proportions of time to be spent in these activities, each individual and each program harnessing the Healthy Mind Platter can apply reflective reasoning to include each of these activities on a daily basis in a range of time that may depend on the day and the individual. Sleep time, for example, may vary depending on age, but for the average adult, seven to eight hours are the typical amount often needed. For children and adolescents, this time is often greater; though modern life makes teenagers challenged to achieve the eight to nine hours of sleep that may be needed for optimal functioning and well-being, ideally such important healthy priorities should be achieved if possible.

Further research is needed to understand which combinations are needed and in what order, proportion, and relationship to produce optimal levels of creativity, health, and performance. From our review, we can conclude that, as we are writing, neuroscientists, psychologists, molecular biologists, and many other researchers around the world are independently investigating the physical and mental substrates underlying the relationships between the elements of the Healthy Mind Platter and a variety of health outcomes. A range of disciplines may contribute meaningfully to research required to study which different constellations among these elements represent the best recipes for public health and individual and organizational performance.

As for the field of neuroleadership, the Healthy Mind Platter offers a theoretical model for studying and optimizing the mental well-being, brain health, creativity, and performance of leaders. For families, schools, and our wider society, the Healthy Mind Platter offers a framework to open the conversation and facilitate the work of public health policy makers, health practitioners, educators, coaches, organizational consultants, and many other professionals to develop and evaluate interventions. As the brain takes more of a central stage in health management, science, and society at large, we need to integrate insights generated in laboratories around the globe to confront one of the biggest scientific, public health, and economic challenges of the twenty-first century: improving brain health and plasticity to deal with the increasing complexity and uncertainty unfolding around us.

References

Aamodt, S., and Wang, S. 2007. "Exercise on the Brain." *New York Times* (November) 8.

Angier, N. 1992. "The Purpose of Playful Frolics: Training for Adulthood." *New York Times* (October) 20, B5–B6.

Baumeister, R. F., Vohs, K. D., and Tice, D. T. 2007. "The Strength Model of Self-Control." *Current Directions in Psychological Science* 16(6): 351–355.

Benington, J. 2000. "Sleep Homeostasis and the Function of Sleep." *Sleep* 23: 959–966.

Benson, H. 1975. *The Relaxation Response*. New York: Morrow.

Benson, H., and Proctor. 2003. *The Breakout Principle*. New York: Scribner.

Berkman, L.F. 1984. "Assessing the Physical Health Effects of Social Networks and Social Support." *Annual Review of Public Health* 5: 413-432.

Berkman, L. F., Seeman, T.E., and Albert, M.1993. "High, Usual and Impaired Functioning in Community-Dwelling Older Men and Women: Findings from the MacArthur Foundation Research Network on Successful Aging." *Journal of Clinical Epidemiology* 46: 1129–1140.

Berkman, L. F., and Syme, L. S. 1979. "Social Networks, Host Resistance, and Mortality: A Nine-Year Follow-up Study of Alameda County Residents." *American Journal of Epidemiology* 109: 186–204.

Bishop, S. R., Lau, M., Shapiro, S., Carlson, L., Anderson, N. D., Carmody, J., Segal, Z.V. et al. 2004. "Mindfulness: A proposed Operational Definition." *Clinical Psychology: Science and Practice* 11(3): 230–241.

Blomquist, K. B., and Danner, F. 1987. "Effects of Physical Conditioning on Information Processing Efficiency." *Perceptual Motor Skills* 65: 175–186.

Bohannon, R. W. 1993. "Physical Rehabilitation in Neurologic Diseases." *Current Opinion in Neurology* 6: 765–772.

Bolte, Taylor, J. 2009. *My Stroke of Insight*. London: Penguin Books.

Bos, M. W., Dijksterhuis, A., and van Baaren, R. B. 2008. "On the Goal-Dependency of Unconscious Thought." *Journal of Experimental Social Psychology* 44: 1114-1120.

Bowden, E. M., and Jung-Beeman, M. 1998. "Getting the Right Idea: Semantic Activation in the Right Hemisphere May Help Solve Insight Problems." *Psychological Science* 6: 435–440.

Bowden, E. M., and Jung-Beeman, M. 2003. "Aha! Insight Experience Correlates with Solution Activation in the Right Hemisphere." *Psychonomic Bulletin and Review* 10: 730–737.

Bowden, E. M., and Jung-Beeman, M. 2003. "One Hundred Forty-Four Compound Remote Associate Problems: Short Insight-Like Problems with One-Word Solutions." *Behavioral Research, Methods, Instruments, and Computers* 35: 634–639.

Brooks, A., and Lack, L. 2006. "A Brief Afternoon Nap Following Nocturnal Sleep Restriction: Which Nap Duration is Most Recuperative?" *Sleep* 29 6: 831–840.

Brown, S. L. 1994. "Animals at Play." *National Geographic* 186: 2–35.

Brown, S. L., and Vaughan, C. 2010. *Play: How It Shapes the Brain, Opens Imagination, and Invigorates the Soul.* New York: Avery.

Buckner, R. L., Andrews-Hanna, J. R., and Schacter, D. L. 2008. "The Brain's Default Network: Anatomy, Function, and Relevance to Disease." *Annual New York Academy of Science* 1124: 1–38.

Buijs, R. M., De Vries, G. J., Van Leeuwen, F. W., and Swaab, D. F. 1983. "Vasopressin and Oxytocin: Distribution and Putative Functions in the Brain." *Progressive Brain Research* 60: 115–122.

Cacioppo, J. T., Ernst, J. M., Burleson, M. H., McClintock, M. K., Malarkey, W. B., Hawkley, L. C., Kowaleswski, R.B., et al 2000. "Lonely Traits and Concomitant Physiological Processes: The MacArthur Social Neuroscience Studies." *International Journal of Psychophysiology* 35(2–3): 143–154.

Cacioppo, J. T., Hawkley, L. C., Crawford, L. E., Ernst, J. M., Burleson, M. H., Kowalewski, R. B., Malarkey, W.B., et al 2002. "Loneliness and Health: Potential Mechanisms." *Psychosomatic Medicine* 64(3): 407–417.

Cai, D.J., Mednick, S.A., Harrison, E.M., Kanady, J.C., and Mednick, S.C. 2009. "REM, Not Incubation, Improves Creativity by Priming Associative Networks." *Proceedings of the National Academy of Sciences, USA* 106(25): 10130-10134.

Carter, R. 1998. *Mapping the Mind.* London: Phoenix.

Chiesa, A., and Serretti, A. 2009a. "Mindfulness-Based Stress Reduction for Stress Management in Healthy People: A Review and Meta-Analysis." *Journal of Alternative and Complementary Medicine* 15(5): 593–600.

Chiesa, A., and Serretti, A. 2009b. "A Systematic Review of Neurobiological and Clinical Features of Mindfulness Meditations." *Psychological Medicine* 27: 1–14.

Christensen, L. O., Johannsen, P., Sinkjaer, N., Peterson, N., Pyndt, H. S., and Nielsen, J. B. 2000. "Cerebral Activation During Bicycle Movements in Man." *Experimental Brain Research* 135: 66–72.

Cohen, D. A., Pascual-Leone, A., Press, D. Z., and Robertson, E. M. 2005. "Off-line Learning of Motor Skill Memory: A Double Dissociation of Goal and Movement." *Proceedings of the National Academy of Sciences, USA* 102: 18237–18241.

Cohen, S. 2004. "Social Relationships and Health." *American Psychologist* 59: 676–684.

Cohen, S., Doyle, W. J., Skoner, D. P., Rabin, B. S., and Gwaltney, J. M. 1997. "Social Ties and Susceptibility to the Common Cold." *Journal of the American Medical Association* 277: 1940–1944.

Cohen, S., Gottlieb, B., and Underwood, L. 2000. Social Relationships and Health. In *Measuring and Intervening in Social Support*, edited by S. Cohen, L. Underwood, and B. Gottlieb, New York: Oxford University Press.

Cohen, S., and Wills, T. A. 1985. "Stress, Social Support, and the Buffering Hypothesis." *Psychological Bulletin* 98: 310–357.

Colcombe, S. J., Kramer, A. F., Erickson, K. I., Scalf, P., McAuley, E., Cohen, N. J., et al. 2004. "Cardiovascular Fitness, Cortical Plasticity, and Aging." *Proceedings of the National Academy of Sciences, USA* 101: 3316–3321.

Coplan, R. J., Rubin, K. H., Fox, N. A., Calkins, S. D., and Stewart, S. L. 1994. "Being Alone, Playing Alone, and Acting Alone: Distinguishing Among Reticence and Passive and Active Solitude in Young Children." *Child Development* 65: 129–137.

Cotman, C. W., and Engesser-Cesar, C. 2002. "Exercise Enhances and Protects Brain Function." *Exercise Sport Science Review* 30(2): 75–79.

Cotman, C. W., and Berchtold, N. C. 2002. "Exercise: A Behavioral Intervention to Enhance Brain Health and Plasticity." *Trends in Neuroscience* 25(6): 295–301.

Creswell, J.D., Way, B.M., Eisenberger, N.I., Lieberman, M.D. 2007. "Neural Correlates of Dispositional Mindfulness During Affect Labeling." *Psychomatic Medicine* 69(6): 560–565.

Csikszentmihalyi, M. 1990. *Flow: The Psychology of Optimal Experience*. New York: Harper & Row.

Davis, C. L., Tomporowski, P. D., Boyle, C. A., Waller, J .L., Miller, P. H., and Naglieri, J. A. 2007. "Effects of Aerobic Exercise on Overweight Children's Cognitive Functioning: A Randomized Controlled Trial." *Research Quarterly for Exercise and Sport* 78(5): 510–519.

Diekelmann, S., and Born, J. 2010. "The Memory Function of Sleep." *Nature Reviews Neuroscience* 11(2): 114–126.

Dietrich A. 2006. "Transient Hypofrontality as a Mechanism for the Psychological Effects of Exercise." *Psychiatry Research* 145(1): 79–83.

Dijksterhuis, A. 2004. "Think Different: The Merits of Unconscious Thought in Preference Development and Decision-Making." *Journal of Personality and Social Psychology* 87: 586–598.

Dijksterhuis, A., Bos, M. W., Nordgren, L. F., and van Baaren, R. B. 2006. "On Making the Right Choice: The Deliberation Without Attention Effect." *Science* 311: 1005–1007.

Durmer, J. S., and Dinges, D. F. 2005. "Neurocognitive Consequences of Sleep Deprivation." *Seminars in Neurology* 25: 117–129.

Eisenberger, N. I., and Lieberman, M. D. 2004. "Why Rejection Hurts: A Common Neural Alarm System for Physical and Social Pain." *Trends in Cognitive Sciences* 8: 294–300.

Eisenberger, N. I., Lieberman, M. D., and Williams, K. D. 2003. "Does Rejection Hurt? An fMRI Study of Social Exclusion." *Science* 302: 290–292.

Evans, O., and Steptoe, A. 2001. "Social Support at Work, Heart Rate, and Cortisol: A Self-Monitoring Study." *Journal of Occupational Health Psychology* 6: 361–370.

Farb, N. A. S., Segal, Z. V., Mayberg, H., Bean, J., McKeon, D., Fatima, Z., and Anderson, A. K. 2007. "Attending to the Present: Mindfulness Meditation Reveals Distinct Neural Modes of Self-Reference." *Social Cognitive and Affective Neuroscience* 2(4): 313–322.

Fenn, K. M., Nusbaum, H. C., and Margoliash, D. 2003. "Consolidation During Sleep of Perceptual Learning of Spoken Language." *Nature* 425: 614–616.

Fredrickson, B. 2000. "Cultivating Positive Emotions to Optimize Health and Well-Being." *Prevention and Treatment* 3(1).

Frost, J. 1998. "Neuroscience, Play, and Child Development." Paper presented at the IPA/USA Triennial National Conference, Longmont, CO.

Fyer, B. 2006. "Sleep Deficit: The Performance Killer." *The Harvard Business Review* 10: 55–56.

Fukuyama, H., Ouchi, Y., Matsuzaki, S., Nagahama, Y., Yamauchi, H., Ogawa, M., Kimura, J., et al. 1997. "Brain Functional Activity During Gait in Normal Subjects: A SPECT Study." *Neuroscience Letters* 228: 183–186.

Gais, S., and Born, J. 2004. "Declarative Memory Consolidation: Mechanisms Acting During Human Sleep." *Learning and Memory* 11: 679–685.

Gallo, L. C., Smith, T. W., and Kircher, J. C. 2000. "Cardiovascular and Electrodermal Responses to Support and Provocation: Interpersonal Methods in the Study of Psychophysiological Reactivity." *Psychophysiology* 37: 289–301.

Garaigordobil Landazabal, M. 2005. "Prosocial and Creative play: Effects of a Programme on the Verbal and Nonverbal Intelligence of Children aged 10–11 years." *International Journal of Psychology* 40(3): 176–188.

Gomez-Pinilla, F. 2008. "The Influences of Diet and Exercise on Mental Health Through Hormesis." *Ageing Research Review* (January) 7(1): 49–62.

Gomez-Pinilla, F., Ying, Z., Roy, R. R., Molteni, R., and Edgerton, V. R. 2002. "Voluntary Exercise Induces a BDNF-Mediated Mechanism that Promotes Neuroplasticity." *Journal of Neurophysiology* 88: 2187–2195.

Gordon, N. S., Burke, S., Akil, H., Watson, S. J., and Panksepp, J. 2003. "Socially-Induced Brain "Fertilization": Play Promotes Brain Derived Neurotrophic Factor Transcription in the Amygdala and Dorsolateral Frontal Cortex in Juvenile Rats." *Neuroscience Letters* 341(1): 17–20.

Gottman, J. M., Katz, L. F., and Hooven, C. 1997. *Meta-Emotion: How Families Communicate Emotionally*. Mahwah: Lawrence Erlbaum Associates.

Grealy, M. A., Johnson, D. A., and Rushton, S. K. 1999. "Improving Cognitive Function after Brain Injury: The Use of Exercise and Virtual Reality." *Archives of Physical Medicine and Rehabilitation* 80: 661–667.

Grossman, P., Niemann, L., Schmidt, S., and Walach, H. 2004. "Mindfulness-Based Stress Reduction and Health Benefits: A Meta-Analysis." *Journal of Psychosomatic Research* 57: 35–43.

Gryskiewicz, S. 1999. *Positive Turbulence: Developing Climates for Creativity, Innovation, and Renewal*. San Francisco, CA: Jossey-Bass.

Hartig, T., Evans, G. W., Jamner, L. D., Davis, D. S., and Gärling, T. 2003. "Tracking Restoration in Natural and Urban Field Settings." *Journal of Environmental Psychology* 23: 109–123.

Hays, J. C., Steffens, D. C., Flint, E. P., Bosworth, H. B., and George, L. K. 2001. "Does Social Support Buffer Functional Decline in Elderly Patients with Unipolar Depression?" *American Journal of Psychiatry* 158: 1850–1855.

Hawley, L.C., Burleson, M.H., Bernston, G.G., and Cacioppo, J.T 2007. "Loneliness in Everyday Life: Cadriovascular Activity, Psychosocial Context, and Health Behaviors." *Journal of Personality and Social Psychology* 85: 105–120.

Heinrichs, M., Baumgartner, T., Kirschbaum, C., and Ehlert, U. 2003. "Social Support and Oxytocin Interact to Suppress Cortisol and Subjective Responses to Psychosocial Stress." *Biological Psychiatry* 54: 1389–1398.

Hernández-Peón, R., and Sterman, M. B. 1966. "Brain Functions." *Annual Review of Psychology* 17: 363–394.

Hill, R. D., Storandt, M., **and** Malley, M. 1993. "The Impact of Long-Term Exercise Training on Psychological Function in Older Adults." *Journal Gerontology* 48: 12–17.

Hobson, J. A., Pace-Schott, E. F., Stickgold, R., and Kahn, D. 1998. "To Dream or Not to Dream? Relevant Data from New Neuroimaging and Electrophysiological Studies." Current Opinion in *Neurobiology* 8: 239–244.

Hobson, J. A., and Pace-Schott, E. F. 2002. "The Cognitive Neuroscience of Sleep: Neuronal Systems, Consciousness, and Learning." *Nature Reviews Neuroscience* 3(9): 679–693.

Hofmann, S. G., Sawyer, A. T., Witt, A. A., and Oh, D. 2010. "The Effect of Mindfulness-Based Therapy on Anxiety and Depression: A Meta-Analytic Review." *Journal of Consulting Clinical Psychology* 78(2): 169–183.

Hol, T., Van den Berg, C. L., Van Ree, J. M., and Spruijt, B. M. 1999. "Isolation During the Play Period in Infancy Decreases Adult Social Interactions in Rats." *Behavioral Brain Research*, 100: 91–97.

House, J. S., Landis, K. R., and Umberson, D. 1988. "Social Relationships and Health." *Science* 241: 540-545.

Humphreys, A. P., and Einon, D. F. 1981. "Play as a Reinforcer for Maze-Learning in Juvenile Rats." *Animal Behavior* 29: 259–270.

Ibañez, A., San Martin, R., Dufey, M., Bacquet, S., and Lopez, V. 2008. "ERP Studies of Cognitive Processing During Sleep." *International Journal of Psychology* 44(4): 290–304.

Jacobson, E. 1938. *Progressive Relaxation*. Chicago: University of Chicago Press.

Kabat-Zinn, J. 1994. *Wherever You Go, There You Are: Mindfulness Meditation in Everyday Life*. New York: Hyperion.

Karasek, R. A., and Theorell, T. G. 1990. *Health, Work, Stress, Productivity, and the Reconstruction of Working Life*. New York: Basic Books.

Kiecolt-Glaser, J. K., McGuire, L., Robles, T. F., and Glaser, R. 2002. "Emotions, Morbidity, and Mortality: New Perspectives from Psychoneuroimmunology." *Annual Review of Psychology* 53: 83–107.

Kirsch, P., Esslinger, C., Chen, Q., Mier, D., Lis, S., Siddhanti, S., Gruppe, H., et al. 2005. "Oxytocin Modulates Neural Circuitry for Social Cognition and Fear in Humans." *Journal of Neuroscience* 25(49): 11489–11493.

Kramer, A. F., Hahn, S., Cohen, N. J., Banich, M. T., McAuley, E., Harrison, C.R., Chason, J. et al.1999. "Ageing, Fitness, and Neurocognitive Function." *Nature* 400: 418–419.

Kolb, D. A. 1984. *Experiential Learning*. Englewood Cliffs, NJ: Prentice Hall.

Kosfeld, M., Heinrichs, M., Zak, P. J., Fischbacher, U., and Fehr, E. 2005. "Oxytocin Increases Trust in Humans." *Nature* 435: 673–676.

Kounios, J., and Jung-Beeman, M. 2009. "Aha! The Cognitive Neuroscience of Insight." *Current Directions in Psychological Science* 18: 210–216.

Kroenke, K., and Mangelsdorff, A. D. 1989. "Common Symptoms in Ambulatory Care: Incidence, Evaluation, Therapy, and Outcome." *American Journal of Medicine* 86: 262–266.

Laurin, D., Verreault, R., Lindsay, J., MacPherson, K., Rockwood, K.. 2001 "Physical Activity and Risk of Cognitive Impairment and Dementia in Elderly Persons." *Archives of Neurology* 58: 498–504.

Lazar, S. W., Kerr, C., Wasserman, R. H., Gray, J. R., Greve, D., Treadway, M. T., McGavey, M., et al..2005. "Meditation Experience is Associated with Increased Cortical Thickness." *NeuroReport* 16(17): 1893–1897.

Lindvall, O., Kokaia, Z., Bengzon, J., Elmer, E., and Kokaia, M. 1994. "Neurotrophins and Brain Insults." *Trends in Neurosciences* 17: 490–496.

Luders, E., Narr, K. L., Thompson, P. M., and Toga, A. W. 2009. "Neuroanatomical Correlates of Intelligence." *Intelligence* 37(2): 156–163.

Masion, A. O., Teas, J., Herbert, J. R., Werheimer, M. D., and Kabat-Zinn, J. 1995. "Meditation, Melatonin and Breast/ Prostate Cancer: Hypotheses and Preliminary Data." *Medical Hypotheses* 44: 39–46.

McGilchrist, I. 2009. *The Master and His Emissary*. New Haven: Yale University Press.

Meaney, M. J., and Stewart, J. 1981. "A Descriptive Study of Social Development in the Rat (rattus norvegicus)." *Animal Behavior* 29: 34–45.

Meyer, D. E., Evans, J. E., Lauber, E. J., Gmeindl, L., Rubinstein, J., Junck, L., and Koeppe, R. A. 1998. "The Role of Dorsolateral Prefrontal Cortex for Executive Cognitive Processes in Task Switching." Poster presented at meeting of Cognitive Neuroscience Society (San Francisco, CA, April). Abstract published in *Journal of Cognitive Neuroscience* 10.

Meyer, D. E., Evans, J. E., Lauber, E. J., Rubinstein, J., Gmeindl, L., Junck, L., and Koeppe, R. A. 1997. "Activation of Brain Mechanisms for Executive Mental Processes in Cognitive Task Switching." Poster presented at meeting of Cognitive Neuroscience Society (Boston, MA, March). Abstract published in *Journal of Cognitive Neuroscience* 9.

Mobbs, D., Greicius, M. D., Abdel-Azim, E., Menon, V., and Reiss, A. L. 2003. "Humor Modulates the Mesolimbic Reward Centers." *Neuron* 40(5): 1041–1048.

Nakata, A. 2011. "Work Hours, Sleep Sufficiency, and Prevalence of Depression Among Full-Time Employees: A Community-Based Cross-Sectional Study [CME]." *Journal of Clinical Psychiatry* 72(5): 605-614.

National Institute for Occupational Safety and Health. Stress at work. DHHS (NIOSH) Publication No. 99–101. http://www.cdc.gov/niosh/docs/99-101/.

Neeper, S. A., Gómez-Pinilla, F., Choi, J., and Cotman, C. 1995. "Exercise and Brain Neurotrophins." *Nature* 373: 109.

Normansell, L., and Panksepp, J. 1990. "Effects of Morphine and Naloxone on Play-Rewarded Spatial Discrimination in Juvenile Rats." *Developmental Psychobiology* 23: 75–83.

Panksepp, J. 1991. "Affective Neuroscience: A Conceptual Framework for the Neurobiological Study of Emotions." In *International reviews of studies in emotions*, edited by K. Strongman, 1: 59–99. Chichester: Wiley.

Panksepp, J. 1992. "A Critical Role for "Affective Neuroscience" in Resolving what is Basic About Basic Emotions. *Psychological Review* 99(3): 554–60.

Panksepp, J. 1998. *Affective Neuroscience*. New York: Oxford University Press.

Panksepp, J. 2005. "Beyond a Joke: From Animal Laughter to Human Joy?" *Science* 308: 62–63.

Panksepp, J. 2007. "Can Play Diminish ADHD and Facilitate the Construction of the Social Brain?" *Journal of the Canadian Academy of Child and Adolescent Psychiatry* 16(2): 57–66.

Panksepp, J., and Biven, L. 2012. *Archaeology of Mind*. New York: W. W. Norton.

Panksepp, J., and Burgdorf, J. 2003. "'Laughing' Rats and the Evolutionary Antecedents of Human Joy?" *Physiological Behavior* 79: 533–547.

Panksepp, J., Siviy, S., and Normansell, L. 1984. "The Psychobiology of Play: Theoretical and Methodological Perspectives." *Neuroscience Biobehavioral Review* 8: 465–492.

Parker, S. C., Nelson, B. W., Epel, E. S., and Siegel, D. J. (forthcoming). "The Science of Presence: A Central Mediator of the Interpersonal Benefits of Mindfulness." Handbook of Mindfulness: Theory and Research.

Parkinson, B., and Totterdell, P. 1999. "Classifying Affect-Regulation Strategies." *Cognition and Emotion* 13: 277–303.

Payne, J. D. 2011. "Learning, Memory and Sleep in Humans." *Sleep Medicine Clinics* 6(1): 15–30.

Payne, L., and Kounios, J. 2009. "Coherent Oscillatory Networks Supporting Short-Term Memory Retention." *Brain Research* 1247: 126–132.

Pelletier, C. L. 2004. "The Effect of Music on Decreasing Arousal Due to Stress: A Meta-Analysis." *Journal of Music Therapy* 41: 192–214.

Perez-de-Albeniz, A., and Holmes, J. 2000. "Meditation: Concepts, Effects, and Uses in Therapy." *International Journal of Psychotherapy* 5(1): 49–58.

Pettit, J. W., Grover, K. E., and Lewinsohn, P. M. 2007. "Interrelations Between Psychopathology, Psychosocial Functioning, and Physical Health: An Integrative Perspective." *International Journal of Clinical Health Psychology* 7(2): 453-476.

Tang, Y. Y., and Posner, M. I. 2009. "Attention Training and Attention State Training." *Trends in Cognitive Sciences* 13(5): 222–227.

Rao, J., Wilson, J., and Watkinson, J. 2009. "Culture Drives Innovation, Not Ideas!" *Innovation at Work (blog)*. http://innovationatwork.wordpress.com/2009/06/05/culture-drives-innovation-not-ideas/.

Rogers, R. L., Meyer, J. S., and Mortel, K. F. 1990. "After Reaching Retirement Age Physical Activity Sustains Cerebral Perfusion and Cognition." *Journal of the American Geriatric Society* 38: 123–128.

Rosengren, A., Orth-Gomer, K., Wedel, H., and Wilhelmsen, L. 1993. "Stressful Life Events, Social Support, and Mortality in Men Born in 1933." *British Medical Journal* 307: 1102–1105.

Rubinstein, J., Evans, J., and Meyer, D. E. 1994. "Task Switching in Patients with Prefrontal Cortex Damage." Poster presented at meeting of Cognitive Neuroscience Society (San Francisco, CA, March). Abstract published in *Journal of Cognitive Neuroscience* 6.

Salmon, P. 2001. "Effects of Physical Exercise on Anxiety, Depression, and Sensitivity to Stress: A Unifying Theory." *Clinical Psychology Review* 21: 33–61.

Sayal, K., Checkley, S., Rees, M., Jacobs, C., Harris, T., Papadopoulos, A., and Poon, L. 2002. "Effects of Social Support During Weekend Leave on Cortisol and Depression Ratings: A Pilot Study." *Journal of Affective Disorders* 71: 153–157.

Segal, E. 2004. "Incubation in Insight Problem-Solving." *Creativity Research Journal* 16(1): 141–148.

Segal, Z. 2009. "Happiness and the Brain." *The Agenda with Steve Paikin,* TVO, January 13. www.TVO.org.

Seligman, M. E. P. 2011. *Flourish: A Visionary New Understanding of Happiness and Well-Being*. New York: Free Press.

Siegel, D.J. 2007. "Mindfulness Training and Neural Integration: Differentiation of Distinct Streams of Awareness and the Cultivation of Well-Being." *Social Cognitive Affect Neuroscience* 2(4): 259–263.

Siegel, D.J. 2010. *Mindsight: The New Science of Personal Transformation*. New York: Bantam.

Siegel, D. J. 2012a. *The Developing Mind: How Relationships and the Brain Interact to Shape Who We Are*. 2nd ed. New York: Guilford.

Siegel, D. J. 2012b. *Pocket Guide to Interpersonal Neurobiology: An Integrative Handbook of the Mind.* New York: W. W. Norton.

Simon, H. 1991. "Bounded Rationality and Organizational Learning." *Organization Science* 2(1): 125–134.

Sonnentag, S., and Fritz, C. 2007. "The Recovery Experience Questionnaire: Development and Validation of a Measure Assessing Recuperation and Unwinding at Work." *Journal of Occupational Health Psychology* 12: 204–221.

Spector, P., Cooper, C. L., Sanchez, J. I., Sparks, K., Bernin, P., Büssing, A., Dewe, P., et al 2002. "A 24 Nation/Territory Study of Work Locus of Control, Well-Being, and Individualism: How Generalizable are Western Work Findings?" *Academy of Management Journal* 45(2): 453–466.

Spinka, M., Newberry, R. C., and Bekoff, M. 2005. "Mammalian Play: Training for the Unexpected." *Quarterly Review of Biology* 76(2): 141-68.

Spitzer, S. B., Llabre, M. M., Ironson, G. H., Gellman, M. D., and Schneiderman, N. 1992. "The Influence of Social Situations on Ambulatory Blood Pressure." *Psychosomatic Medicine* 54: 79–86.

Steptoe, A. 2000. "Stress, Social Support, and Cardiovascular Activity Over the Working Day." *International Journal of Psychophysiology* 37: 299–308.

Sternberg, R. J., and Davidson, J. E., eds. 1995. *The Nature of Insight.* Cambridge: MIT Press.

Stickgold, R. 2005. "Sleep-Dependent Memory Consolidation." *Nature* 437: 1272–1278.

Stickgold, R., and Walker, M. P. 2005. "Sleep and Memory: The Ongoing Debate." *Sleep* 28: 1225–1227.

Stickgold, R., James, L., and Hobson, J. A. 2000. "Visual Discrimination Learning Requires Sleep After Training." *Nature Neuroscience* 3: 1237–1238.

Stickgold, R., and Walker, M. P. 2005. "Sleep and Memory: The Ongoing Debate." *Sleep* 28: 1225–1227.

Stone, A. A., Kennedy-Moore, E., and Neale, J. M. 1995. "Association Between Daily Coping and End-Of-Day Mood." *Health Psychology* 14: 341–349.

Strick, M., Dijksterhuis, A., Bos, M. W., Sjoerdsma, A., Van Baaren, R. B., and Nordgren, L .F. 2010. "A Meta-Analysis on Unconscious Thought Effects." Unpublished manuscript.

Subramaniam, K., Kounios, J., Bowden, E. M., Parrish, T. B., and Jung-Beeman, M. 2009. "Positive Mood and Anxiety Modulate Anterior Cingulate Activity and Cognitive Preparation for Insight." *Journal of Cognitive Neuroscience* 21: 415–432.

Subramaniam, K., Kounios, J., Parrish, T. B., and Jung- Beeman, M. 2009. "A Brain Mechanism for Facilitation of Insight by Positive Affect." *Journal of Cognitive Neuroscience* 21: 415–432.

Suominen-Troyer, S., Davis, K. J., Ismail, A. H., and Salvendy, G. 1986. "Impact of Physical Fitness on Strategy Development in Decision-Making Tasks." *Perceptual and Motor Skills* 62: 71–77.

Tassi, P., Bonnefond, A., Engasser, O., Hoeft, A., Eschenlauer, R., and Muzet, A. 2006. "EEG Spectral Power and Cognitive Performance During Sleep Inertia: The Effect of Normal Sleep Duration and Partial Sleep Deprivation." *Physiology and Behavior* 87: 177–184.

Thoits, P. A. 1995. "Stress, Coping, and Social Support Processes: Where Are We? What Next?" *Journal of Health and Social Behavior* 35: 53–79.

Uchino, B. N. 2006. "Social Support and Health: A Review of Physiological Processes Potentially Underlying Links to Disease Outcomes." *Journal of Behavioral Medicine* 29: 377–387.

Uchino, B. N. 2009. "Understanding the Links Between Social Support and Physical Health: A Lifespan Perspective with Emphasis on the Separability of Perceived and Received Support." *Perspectives in Psychological Science* 4: 236–255.

Uchino, B. N., Cacioppo, J. T., and Kiecolt-Glaser, J. K. 1996. "The Relationship Between Social Support and Physiological Processes: A Review with Emphasis on Underlying Mechanisms and Implications for Health." *Psychological Bulletin* 119: 488–531.

Uchino, B. N., Holt-Lunstad, J., Uno, D., Betancourt, R., and Garvey, T. S. 1999. "Social Support and Age-Related Differences in Cardiovascular Function: An Examination of Potential Mediators." *Annual Behavioral Medicine* 21: 135–142.

Ulrich-Lai, Y. M., and Herman, J. P. 2009. "Neural Regulation of Endocrine and Autonomic Stress Responses." *Nature Reviews Neuroscience* 10: 397–409.

Uno, D., Uchino, B. N., Smith, T. W. 2002. "Relationship Quality Moderates the Effect of Social Support Given by Close Friends on Cardiovascular Reactivity in Women." *International Journal of Behavioral Medicine* 9:243–262.

Van den Berg, C. L., Van Ree, J. M., Spruijt, B. M., and Kitchen, I. 1999a. "Effects of Juvenile Isolation and Morphine Treatment on Social Interactions and Opioid Receptors in Adult Rats: Behavioural and autoradiographic studies." *European Journal of Neuroscience* 11: 3023–3032.

Van den Berg, C. L., Hol, T., Van Ree, J. M., Spruijt, B. M., Everts, H., and Koolhaas, J. M. 1999b. "Play is Indispensable for an Adequate Development of Coping with Social Challenges in the Rat." *Developmental Psychobiology* 34: 129–138.

Van der Klink, J. J. L., Blonk, R. W. B., Schene, A. H., and van Dijk, F. J. H. 2001. "The Benefits of Interventions for Work-Related Stress." *American Journal of Public Health* 91: 270–276.

van Praag, H. 2008. "Neurogenesis and Exercise: Past and Future Directions." *Neuromolecular Medicine* 10: 128–40.

van Praag, H., Kempermann, G., and Gage, F.H. 1999b. "Running Increases Cell Proliferation and Neurogenesis in the Adult Mouse Dentate Gyrus." *Nature Neuroscience* 2: 266–270.

Vaynman, S., Ying, Z., and Gomez-Pinilla, F. 2004. "Hippocampal BDNF Mediates the Efficacy of Exercise on Synaptic Plasticity and Cognition." *European Journal of Neuroscience* 20: 2580–2590.

Viswesvaran, C., Sanchez, J. I, and Fisher, J. 1999. "The Role of Social Support in the Process of Work Stress: A Meta-Analysis." *Journal of Vocational Behavior* 54(2): 314–334.

Walker, M. P., Brakefield, T., Morgan, A., Hobson, J. A., and Stickgold, R. 2002. "Practice with Sleep Makes Perfect: Sleep-Dependent Motor Skill Learning." *Neuron* 35: 205–211.

Winston, J. S., Strange, B. A., O'Doherty, J., and Dolan, R. J. 2002. "Automatic and Intentional Brain Responses During Evaluation of Trustworthiness of Faces." *Nature Neurosciences* 5: 277–283.

7. Using the whole brain to improve strategic reasoning

Dr. Roderick Gilkey, Dr. Ricardo Cáceda, Andrew Bate, MBA, Dr. Diana Robertson, and Dr. Clint Kilts

Roderick Gilkey, Goizueta Business School, Emory University, Georgia, USA Rick_Gilkey@bus.emory.edu

Ricardo Cáceda, Department of Psychiatry and Behavioral Sciences, University of Miami Miller School of Medicine, Florida, USA
RCaceda@med.miami.edu

Andrew Bate, MBA, Goizueta Business School, Emory University, Georgia, USA
Andrew@trustedguests.com

Diana Robertson Wharton School, University of Pennsylvania, Pennsylvania, USA robertsd@wharton.upenn.edu

Clint Kilts, Psychiatric Research Institute, University of Arkansas for Medical Sciences, Arkansas, USA
CDKilts@uams.edu

Introduction

Traditional views of strategic reasoning have emphasized the role of cognitive analytic processes, often to the neglect of affective and social behavioral functions. This bias has influenced both the theory and the practice of strategic planning. Neuroscientific research holds the promise of identifying a much broader range of human capacities that contribute to the ability to engage and excel in strategic reasoning. Our study of the strategic-reasoning performance of a group of midcareer business leaders identified the engagement of social and emotional brain processes that play an important role in strategic-thinking ability. In identifying the neural processing correlates of strategic and tactical thinking, we hope to expand and revise the theories of strategic thinking and help develop models for more effective application. We suggest that understanding and engaging the brain's fuller range of information-processing capacity in accomplishing strategic expertise is itself an important strategy for enhancing the performance of individuals and organizations. We also explore the need to create brain-friendly organizational environments to enhance human performance.

Background

Despite the heavy and costly emphasis on cognitive approaches to enhancing strategic-planning ability, outcomes remain disappointingly mixed. For example, a recent report in the *Economist* (2011) examined 197 companies and found only 63% of them reporting positive anticipated results from their strategic-planning initiatives. This disconnect carries a hefty price tag. The annual expenditure for consulting services in the United States was approximately $170 billion in 2011, with strategic consulting accounting for approximately 12% (or about $20 billion) of the total (First Research 2012). The expenditures associated with strategic consulting represent conservative estimates because the bulk of these expenses are incurred by high-end private firms that do not make their revenues public. Despite these investments, strategic-planning efforts produce what appear to be disappointing or uncertain results. While there are many explanations for this suboptimal performance, including poor downstream implementation processes, the prime cause may lie upstream, the result of a flawed or limited understanding of the very nature of strategic thinking and planning itself. We would be well advised to ask if our emphasis on cognitive, linear, and analytic approaches to strategic thinking is misplaced and contributes to underperformance.

Could our failure to appreciate the emotional/affective, social, or deliberative (versus automated) elements of strategy explain why so many strategic initiatives fail because of lack of engagement and execution? From a neuroscience perspective, we might ask if the current model of strategic thinking—involving a selective and limited use of some brain capacities (reflective or analytically focused) without drawing on other perspectives and brain capabilities—affective, social, and reflexive—could be the source of failed strategies. Can it be that the first challenge in strategic planning is to reconceptualize and expand our definition and understanding of strategic thinking? Eisenhardt and Zbaracki, in their seminal paper "Strategic Decision-Making" (1992), advocate for such a reformulation of our view of strategy:

> We...propose a broader agenda. Part of that agenda involves creating a more realistic view of strategic decision-making by opening up our conceptions of cognition...to include insight, intuition, (and) emotion. (35)

The authors are responding to what has become the gold standard for defining and creating strategy, first espoused by Michael Porter (1996). Porter describes strategic thinking as a rational decision-making process that focuses on getting the right data, avoiding biases, and choosing activities that differentiate a firm from its competitors. While this rational, linear, highly cognitive model has been the defining model for strategic thinking and analysis, it does not address other forms of reasoning that can inform strategic thinking. In an effort to offer a broader conception of strategy and strategic thinking, we define strategic thinking as the ability to sense and assess complex, ambiguous, and conflicting alternatives from multiple (cognitive/emotional) perspectives, make informed choices and recommendations, and formulate compelling implementation plans that facilitate effective action.

We view our preliminary investigation of the neural substrates of strategic thinking and the potential role of social-emotional reasoning as consistent with a broader research agenda in neuroscience. For example, in the political arena, Drew Westen has written a well-recognized book, *The Political Brain: The Role of Emotion in Deciding the Fate of the Nation* (2007). In neuromarketing, Dan Ariely, a well-recognized behavioral economist, has written a number of books, including *Predictably Irrational: The Hidden Forces that Shape Our Decisions* (2009). We hope this pilot research helps promote a stream of continued research in this area with increasingly refined instrumentation and larger samples.

The study

With these questions in mind, we engaged in a functional magnetic resonance imaging (fMRI) pilot study of midcareer executives, focused on strategic and tactical thinking and moral reasoning (for details on design of the study see Robertson et al. [2007]). fMRI is a neuroscience technology that explores the relation of the brain to human behavior and defines, noninvasively, the functional brain states that encode ongoing behaviors. The pilot study consisted of a two-part process: interviews and assessments of each of 16 healthy, male, midlevel executives who were enrolled in the Emory executive MBA program were followed by fMRI while subjects responded to reasoning tasks posed by a series of narratives and questions about a fictional employee in a corporate setting engaged in a series of strategic (6), tactical (6), neutral (17), and ethical dilemmas (12) (Robertson et al. 2007; Cáceda et al. 2010). All subjects were exposed to the same stimuli, a protocol based on a narrative account of a firm involved in assessing strategic options and choices. In the first phase, we used standard interview protocol (the Bate scale; Bate et al. 2010) we developed to assess the relative performance of each subject on a series of strategic-thinking questions and identify the most and least proficient strategic thinkers on a continuum.

The study was organized in the following sequence: (1) Identify subjects from an executive MBA leadership course and conduct a brief interview to obtain information on their history (early and current, including their management role) and clinical status (including any past or current medication use). (2) Interview the resulting pool of qualified subjects using a standardized protocol designed for this pilot study on a variety of management strategic challenges. The subjects were presented with a number of scenarios in which a consumer products company had to make critical strategic decisions about whether to compete in certain markets and which products they would introduce to those markets. They were then queried about their analysis and recommendations. These interviews were then transcribed. (3) Analyze the data using an instrument developed for this exploratory study, the Bate Scale (2010). The investigators involved in this analysis were not involved in analyzing the subsequent fMRI data that was obtained. (4) Have all subjects undergo fMRI scanning during which they responded to another standardized protocol consisting of different scenarios involving strategic challenges and questions. This data was analyzed independently using a median split analysis based on the distribution of scores on the Bate Scale. The results are summarized below.

fMRI is a neuroscience technology that explores the relation of the brain to human behavior...

After acquisition of the task-related fMRI data, the second part of the process used imaging analysis to focus on the comparison of neural responses for strategic dilemmas and its correlation with strategic scores. Significance was set at $p \leftarrow 0.005$ and $k = 5$ (Robertson et al. 2007; Cáceda et al. 2010; Cáceda et al. 2011).

Findings

We initially believed that this study would elucidate the predicted roles in strategic reasoning of the prefrontal cortex, the locus of diverse executive functions associated with planning, decision making, attentional control, risk assessment, goal representation, and probabilistic reasoning. The role of the frontal lobes in executive functioning has been well documented and described; particularly noteworthy is Elkhonon Goldberg's *The New Executive Brain: Frontal Lobes in a Complex World* (2009), where he traces the history of research in this area dating back to his teacher Alexander Luria. Thus our hypothesis was that we would see consistent and enduring activations in the frontal lobes while they were engaged in strategic reasoning. We were surprised, however, to observe that while all subjects displayed prefrontal activations of some magnitude, this was not the dominant strategic-reasoning-related pattern of brain response for all subjects. The less adept strategic thinkers did exhibit consistent activations in the executive areas of the dorsal lateral prefrontal cortex (DLPFC) and the dorsal medial prefrontal cortex (DMPFC). However, the more proficient strategic thinkers displayed a significantly different pattern of brain response related to strategic reasoning; in their case, the prefrontal cortex response (see fig. 1) was one of relative deactivation. That is, PFC activations were quickly supplanted by more expansive activations of primitive limbic areas of the brain, such as the insula, as well as the superior temporal sulcus (STS) (Gilkey, Cáceda, and Kilts 2010). Thus, in comparing the two subgroups, we found that the more proficient strategic thinker had higher activations in the insula and STS and lower activations in the PFC areas, while the less proficient strategic thinkers had higher levels of sustained activations in the PFC areas and lower activations in the insula and STS. This unexpected result implicates social and emotional processing in expertise related to strategic reasoning.

...when asked about the internal processes associated with developing the theory of relativity, Einstein observed that the concept began as a physical sensation...

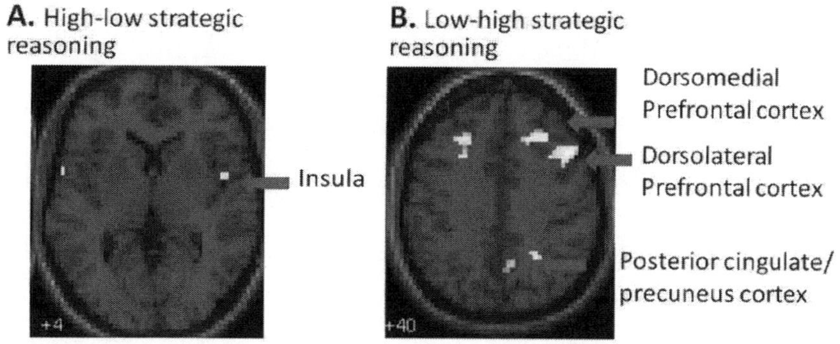

Figure 1. Neural activations in strategic-neutral contrast found in male executives with high -low (A) and low- high (B) strategic reasoning scores. P<0.005; k=5.

The insula is associated with proprioceptive (sensing–intuitive) processes, essentially "tuning in" to one's internal body states associated with feelings and emotions and their role in decision making. While it might seem incongruous that the substrate of higher cognitive thinking might involve lower-level limbic processes, there are precedents supporting this theory. Interestingly, when asked about the internal processes associated with developing the theory of relativity, Einstein observed that the concept began as a physical sensation and later became visual images and ultimately words he could use to describe his insights. In this context it is plausible to view the neural activity of our most accomplished strategic thinkers as reflecting a "deep dive" involving the use of older, more primordial parts of the brain. This is consistent with clinical insights of the psychoanalytic tradition where Freud and later Ernst Kris identified the use of regression in thought and feeling to serve higher creative processes. Kris's (1999) work focused on a two-part dynamic involving inspiration (the deep dive) and elaboration (understanding-application-action). His research documented how particularly creative thinkers and artists were able to temporarily suspend normal, daily forms of reasoning to access earlier, nonverbal capacities to achieve higher-order insights and performance.

The very presence of emotion as a motivational force has profound implications for strategic planning and implementation.

Kris described an array of internal feeling states and affective experiences artists and visionaries used that allowed them to ultimately connect to the external world in deeply effective ways. Kris's work explored the difference between the creativity of artists and the psychotic disorganization of patients who could conjure up novel ideas but not refine or apply them. Lest these examples appear to be too far afield from the corporate realities we are trying to understand, note that Walt Disney brought groups of patients with schizophrenia into the Disney studios to provide novel ideas (inspiration) to his production staff, who could use the material to produce an artistic product (elaboration). In fact, Disney used this process to create Disney Studio's first breakthrough animation, *Fantasia* (Giroux 1999). Kris's work pointed to the use of neural capacities and dynamics that provide clues to the linkage between artistic creativity and innovative, high-level strategic reasoning.

"Emotional intelligence isn't a luxury you can dispense with in tough times."

While identifying the emotional substrates of cognitive reasoning is an important part of our findings, the very presence of emotion as a motivational force has profound implications for strategic planning and implementation. Daniel Goleman's insights into the importance of the emotional circuitry of the brain in leadership are vitally important in areas such as strategic decision making. Referring to a patient described by Antonio Damasio (2003), a lawyer who had suffered a brain lesion that made it impossible for him to connect his thoughts with his feelings and therefore make any decisions, Goleman observes, "In order to make a good decision we need to have feelings about our thoughts" (2011). This inner intrapersonal process of accessing feelings in order to have clear thoughts and make good decisions has far-reaching impacts interpersonally.

While failure to process and incorporate feelings and emotional reasoning can have adverse effects on individual performance, it can also have negative consequences on organizational performance, notably in the area of strategic leadership. Jeanne Liedtka (2011) has argued persuasively that the gap between strategic rhetoric and strategic action reflects a lack of emotional connections that foster engagement and action. She observes:

> I have come to believe that an even more fundamental and seemingly obvious cause may underlie the long-standing failure to align word with deed: nobody really cares about these strategies. Leaders must move beyond incorporating solid strategic thinking and effective communication in order to succeed: decisive strategies must be felt as personally meaningful and compelling by the members of the organization who must adopt new behaviors in order to execute them. And thinking alone won't get you there. (30)

While the role of emotions and the internal representations of their drive states/effects in strategic reasoning would seem self-evident, they have in fact been discounted and disregarded in most models of strategic ability. Regarding emotional processing as "soft" or as "noise" compared with the "signal" of cognitive reasoning results in a limited understanding of both strategy and leadership. As Goleman pointed out in a recent interview, "Emotional intelligence, it turns out, isn't...soft. If emotional obliviousness jeopardizes your ability to perform, fend off aggressors, or be compassionate in a crisis, no amount of attention to the bottom line will protect your career. Emotional intelligence isn't a luxury you can dispense with in tough times. It's a basic tool that deployed with finesse is the key to professional success." The case for "limbic leadership"—that is, developing emotionally literate and intelligent leaders—is a logical consequence of the results of an emerging area of neuroscience research (Brown, Swart, and Meyler 2009; Ringleb and Rock 2009).

Brain regions associated with proficient strategic reasoning

The role of insula activation in decision making is dominated by the "somatic marker" hypothesis (Damasio 1999; 2003), in which internal proprioceptive signals bias and inform decisions. A further function of the insula is attentional deployment, helping us to create and maintain focus. By its connectivity with other neural networks involving planning and memory, the insula enables the capacity to both think and act strategically.

This capacity to link attention, memory, and action was described by David Ingvar, a Swedish psychiatrist and neuroscientist, as the brain's capacity to generate "memories of the future" (Ingvar 1985; Goldberg 2009). Ingvar suggests that our ability as human beings to be proactive and capable of planning a future involves generating and internalizing representations of the desired future state, which are used as templates for guiding and informing action. The need for an iterative strategic process of using forward thinking informed by reflective memories of a desired future to take effective action was described by Stephen Haines (2012) as follows: "Thinking backwards in order to move forward to grow your business is what outstanding strategic thinkers do, time after time, day after day." Using memory systems in the service of forward-thinking strategic reasoning is supported by the insula. Thus, in addition to encoding the somatic state of social emotions, the insula also supports strategic reasoning ability by biasing and focusing the attentional capacities and memory systems necessary to guide strategic action.

Another area of strategic reasoning-related neural activation observed in our top-performing subjects involved the superior temporal sulcus (STS). This neural region is associated with, among other functions, the attribution of mental states to others, referred to as theory of mind or mentalizing (Frith and Frith 2003; Saxe and Wexler 2005), as well as the perception and expression of social emotions such as trustworthiness (Moll et al. 2002; Winston et al. 2002), cooperation (Rilling et al. 2002), altruism (Tankersley, Stowe, and Huettel 2007), and empathy (Carr et al. 2003). Our interpretation of the observed STS activation is that the higher-performing strategic thinkers integrated an assessment of their own inner thoughts and feelings with reactions of other stakeholders (Schultz et al. 2004).

A story thus begins to emerge that suggests that effective strategic thinking involves both a clear understanding of one's own feelings about a given idea and an appraisal of how other people may react to such an idea. It was not surprising to us that these STS activations were also seen in response to subjects' reactions to moral dilemmas embedded in our research protocol. In both strategy and ethics, one of the ultimate litmus tests for deciding the appropriateness and efficacy of a decision is appraising the effects it has on others (Greene et al. 2001).

Effective strategic thinking involves both a clear understanding of one's own feelings about a given idea and an appraisal of how other people may react to such an idea.

The gap between knowing and doing in strategy

In reformulating our understanding of strategy, we are well advised to focus on a major symptom of strategic-performance problems—lack of execution. This is such a universally recognized problem that there is even an acronym for it: SPOTS, or "strategic plans on the shelf." Somehow amid all the analysis, charting, meeting, and planning, a fundamental element of executing strategy is lost. As Professor Brad Killaly (2010) suggests, "Strategy is a verb." His point is a response to what Alfred North Whitehead (1925) once referred to as "the fallacy of misplaced concreteness," the tendency of human beings to create a map and then mistake it for the reality it is supposed to represent.

In studying the brain's antecedent activities before taking action (the cognitive and emotional neural substrates of strategic thinking), we are reminded of the narrow reductionist theories and models that inform contemporary strategic practice. Current models of strategic planning emphasize only some of the brain's (cognitive front-lobe-based) capacities, largely ignoring the engagement of other capabilities, such as the limbic processes of instincts and social awareness. Brown, Swart, and Meyler (2009) put it succinctly when they stated (paraphrasing Damasio 1999), "If reason makes the lists but emotion makes the decisions, then the integration of thinking and feeling becomes a key area for the development of effective executive functioning."

Identifying a comprehensive assembly of neural processes and brain capacities associated with effective strategic thinking creates the possibility of executive-education strategies focusing on a broad, multi-functional approach to engaging the brain for optimized strategic decision making. While our research, like most scientific research, raises more questions than answers, we can at minimum infer that identifying critical brain capacities associated with optimal strategic thinking holds the promise of expanding our understanding and practice to improve strategic thinking and leadership performance.

Building brain-friendly environments to enhance strategic thinking and performance

Building a brain-centric organizational capability has been a driving interest in our research. Consequently, we have tried to explore and identify the variables that optimize brain and thus behavioral performance. From the time of Heisenberg's Uncertainty Principle in 1927, in his studies of the motion of electrons, it has been well recognized that experimental conditions affect outcomes and results. A basic component of our research design was to create a neurobiologically motivated environment in our offices and laboratory that was positive, motivating, and stress minimizing. We accomplished this in two ways: first, we developed a deliberate, intentional, and systematic approach to managing the experience of the subjects (particularly necessary because of the nonnaturalistic, confining, and noisy environment of the fMRI scanner); and second, we did everything possible to provide cognitive clarity and emotional support to diminish subjects' stress responses. These very basic efforts have been supplemented by our own continued research and by other neuroscience-influenced research efforts, including those of David Rock, who developed the SCARF® model for facilitating engagement based on addressing five key variables: status, certainty, autonomy, relatedness, and fairness (Rock 2008). Such neurobiologically based frameworks provide a promising avenue for leaders to create more productive, engaging, and brain-friendly environments.

Conclusions

A small but growing body of evidence suggests an "expertise effect" in neural functioning across disparate brain activities, including language, archery, chess, and cello playing (e.g., Seo et al. 2012). This research, which is based on neural assessments of experts, versus nonexperts, identifies consistent patterns of neural activation and deactivation in these different populations. The findings from these studies suggest that, with experience and acquired expertise, the brain gains neural and cognitive efficiency by using less neural space and less-complex networks to perform practiced higher-level tasks. These gains in neuroefficiency also allow the brain to operate more effectively by increasing the brain's available computational workspace to facilitate access to other neural resources. Our research reinforces and supports the findings of these studies. The more proficient strategic thinkers in our sample had developed highly efficient algorithms or activation patterns that allowed them to access a broader range of neural competencies and connections (prompting them to activate both cognitive and emotional capacities) than their less proficient counterparts in the study.

Future research agendas should continue to investigate strategic thinking with a larger, broader sample of subjects to better understand and optimize the brain's capacity to build strategic expertise. Finally, neuroscientific research needs to address the challenge of building brain-friendly organizational environments to enhance human performance.

References

Ariely, D. 2009. *Predictably Irrational: The Hidden Forces that Shape Our Decisions*. New York: HarperCollins.

Bate, A., Gilkey, R., Cáceda, R., Robertson, D., and Kilts, C. 2010. "The Bate Scale for Differentiating the Quality of Strategic Reasoning Among Professional Managers." Working paper, Goizueta Business School, Emory University, Atlanta, GA.

Brown, P., Swart, T., and Meyler, J. 2009. "Emotional Intelligence." *NeuroLeadership Journal* 2: 74–75.

Cáceda, R., James, G. A., Ely, T., Bate, A., Gilkey, R., Robertson, D., and Kilts, C. D. 2010. "Are Ethics Really Incompatible with Strategic Thinking?" Paper presented at 2010 Human Brain Mapping Annual Meeting, Barcelona, Spain. June 6–10.

Cáceda, R., James, A., Ely, T. D., Snarey, J., and Kilts, C. D. 2011. "Mode of Effective Connectivity Within a Putative Neural Network Differentiates Moral Cognitions related to Care and Justice Ethics." *PLoS One* 6: e14730.

Carr, L., Iacoboni, M., Dubeau, M. C., Mazziotta, J. C., and Lenzi, G. L. 2003. "Neural Mechanisms of Empathy in Humans: A Relay from Neural Systems for Imitation to Limbic Areas." *Proceedings of the National Academy of Sciences, USA* 100: 5497–5502.

Damasio, A. 1999. *The Feeling of What Happens*. London: Heinemann.

Damasio, A. 2003. *Looking for Spinoza: Joy, Sorrow, and the Feeling Brain*. New York: Harcourt, Brace.

Economist. 2011 "Consulting Bounces Back: Advice for Consultants." June 3.

Eisenhardt, K. M., and Zbaracki, M. J. 1992. "Strategic Decision-Making." *Strategic Management Journal* 13: 17–37.

First Research. 2012. Library Education Academic Research Network Affiliates, Full Industry Profile. Consulting services. July 9.

Frith, U., and Frith, C. D. 2003. "Development and Neurophysiology of Mentalizing." *Philosophical Transactions of the Royal Society of London. Series B: Biological Sciences* 358: 459–473.

Gilkey, R., Cáceda, R., and Kilts, C. 2010. "Strategy and Execution: When Emotional Reasoning Trumps IQ." *Harvard Business Review* (September).

Giroux, H. A. 1999. *The Mouse that Roared: Disney and the End of Innocence*. New York: Rowan and Littlefield.

Goldberg, E. 2009. *The New Executive Brain: Frontal Lobes in a Complex World*. New York: Oxford University Press.

Goleman, D. 2011. *The Brain and Emotional Intelligence: New insights*. Northampton, MA: More Than Sound.

Greene, J. D., Sommerville, R. B., Nystrom, L. E., Darley, J. M., and Cohen, J. D. 2001. "An fMRI Investigation of Emotional Engagement in Moral Judgment." *Science* 293: 2105–2108.

Haines, S. 2012. *Becoming a Strategic Thinker on a Daily Basis: Raising Your Strategic IQ for 21st-Century Success*. San Diego, CA: Centre for Strategic Management.

Ingvar, D. H. 1985. "Memory of the future: An Essay on the Temporal Organization of Conscious Awareness." *Human Neurobiology* 127–136.

Killaly, B. 2010. "Leading Strategically." Executive Presentation at Goizueta Business School, Emory University, Atlanta, GA.

Kircher, T. T., Senior, C., Phillips, M. L., Benson, P. J., Bullmore, E. T., Brammer, M., Simmons, A. et al. 2000. "Towards a Functional Neuroanatomy of Self Processing: Effects of Faces and Words. Brain Research." *Cognitive Brain Research* 10: 133–144.

Kris, E. 1999. *Psychoanalytic Explorations in Art*. New York: International Universities Press.

Lawson, A., and Fouts, G. 2004. "Mental Illness in Disney Animated Films." *Canadian Journal of Psychiatry* 49(5): 165–169.

Liedtka, J. 2011. *Beyond Business Strategy: Strategy as Experienced*. Toronto: Rotman Management.

Moll, J., de Oliveira-Souza, R., Bramati, I. E., and Grafman, J. 2002. "Functional Networks in Emotional Moral and Nonmoral Social Judgments." *Neuroimage* 16: 696–703.

Porter, M. E. 1996 "What is strategy?" *Harvard Business Review* 74(6): 61–78.

Rilling, J., Gutman, D., Zeh, T., Pagnoni, G., Berns, G., and Kilts, C. 2002. "A Neural Basis for Social Cooperation." *Neuron* 35: 395–405.

Ringleb A. H., and Rock, D. 2009. "Neuroleadership in 2009." *NeuroLeadership Journal* 2: 2–8.

Robertson, D. C., Snarey, J., Ousley, O., Harenski, K., Bowman, F. D., Gilkey, R., and Kilts, C. 2007. "The Neural Processing of Moral Sensitivity to Issues of Justice and Care." *Neuropsychologia* 45: 755–766.

Rock, D. 2008. "SCARF: A Brain-Based Model for Collaborating with and Influencing Others." *NeuroLeadership Journal* 1: 44–52.

Saxe, R., and Wexler, A. 2005. "Making Sense of Another Mind: The Role of the Right Temporo-Parietal Junction." *Neuropsychologia* 43: 1391–1399.

Schultz, J., Imamizu, H., Kawato, M., and Frith, C. D. 2004. "Activation of the Human Superior Temporal Gyrus During Observation of Goal Attribution by Intentional Objects." *Journal of Cognitive Neuroscience* 16: 1695–1705.

Seo, J., Kim, Y. T., Song, H. J., Lee, H. J., Lee, J., Jung, T.D. et al. 2012. "Stronger Activation and Deactivation in Archery Experts of Differentiated Cognitive Strategic Visual Spatial Working Memory Processing." *Behavioral Brain Research* 229: 185–193.

Tankersley, D., Stowe, C. J., and Huettel, S. A. 2007. "Altruism is Associated with an Increased Neural Response to Agency." *Nature Neuroscience* 10: 150–151.

Westen, D. 2007 *The Political Brain: The Role of Emotion in Deciding the Fate of the Nation*. New York: PublicAffairs, Perseus.

Whitehead, A. N. 1925. *Science and the Modern World*. New York: Free Press.

Winston, J. S., Strange, B. A., O'Doherty, J., and Dolan, R. J. 2002. "Automatic and Intentional Brain Responses During Evaluation of Trustworthiness of Faces." *Nature Neuroscience* 5: 277–283.

8. Neural substrates of corporate decision making

Dr. Ulrich Kirk

Ulrich Kirk, Research Assistant Professor, Human Neuroimaging Lab, Computational Psychiatry Unit, Virginia Tech Carilion Research Institute, Roanoke, Virginia, USA

Cofounder, Headspin LLC

ukirk@vtc.vt.edu

Introduction

Which behavioral characteristics bring out true leadership? A fundamental requirement for promoting sustainable and resilient leadership in organizations, governments, and society is self-awareness and self-control. A self-aware leader integrates achievement, creativity, drive, emotional intelligence, and team-building skills. Using neuroimaging tools, modern neuroscience allows us to investigate how our brains generate models of ourselves, others around us, and the decisions we make. A daunting reality of corporate leadership is that critical decisions made by intelligent, responsible people with the best information and intentions can be hopelessly flawed.

A self-aware leader integrates achievement, creativity, drive, emotional intelligence, and team-building skills.

In this chapter we elaborate on novel neuroimaging experiments examining the neural substrates of human decision-making. We demonstrate that mindfulness training enhances our self-awareness and self-control by decreasing susceptibility to bias blind spots, emotional reactivity in social domains, and reward prediction responses. Together, the experiments discussed in this chapter show that mindfulness training can change decision-making parameters by influencing competing decision-making networks in the brain.

We discuss the potential of mindfulness training in corporate leadership and the potential of profiling individual decision makers. Such neural profiling of decision making may minimize misleading influences on decision-making processes.

Self-awareness and decision making

Human brain tissue contains approximately 100 billion neurons. Despite such abundance of information processors, we are subjectively mostly unaware of what our minds are doing (Eagleman 2011). The brain's ability for introspection relies on how well we can "tune in" to self-observation of our thoughts and emotions and make such information available for conscious deliberation and for guiding the decisions we make. Such abilities have been framed as emotional intelligence (Goleman 1998; 2004). Behind the headline of emotional intelligence are tangible neurobiological constructs such as self-awareness and self-control. A new quest that has emerged in recent years in brain-imaging research is uncovering the neural foundation of self-control and self-awareness, bearing the promise of a more quantitative way to assess how individuals utilize self-control and self-awareness in decision-making domains (Kirk, Downar, and Montague 2011; Kirk, Harvey, and Montague 2011).

In today's corporate climate, it is of paramount importance that corporate leadership increase self-awareness (Rock 2008) and cultivate an ability to exert self-control (Goleman 2004) to optimize decision-making processes and avoid flawed decision making.

Consider a study from Harvard psychologist Ellen Langer (2005) that illustrates the importance of self-awareness in decision making. Research participants were engaged in a betting game against either a self-assured, well-dressed opponent or a shy and poorly dressed opponent. Langer found that her subjects bet far more aggressively when they played against a shy and badly dressed opponent. Participants looked at their awkward opponent and thought, "I'm better than he is." Yet the game was pure chance: all each player did was draw cards randomly from a deck of cards to see who had the high hand. This study illustrates the "introspection illusion" that arises when we lack introspective insight into whether we are in control of the situation. When introspective ability or self-awareness is low, we tend to judge our degree of control by a process that is often unreliable (e.g., the opponent's appearance, in the case of the Langer experiment). As a consequence, we see ourselves as responsible for events that essentially may be random or without causality.

It is of paramount importance that corporate leadership increase self-awareness and cultivate an ability to exert self-control...

Biological substrates govern our emotional impulses. However, research shows that we can do much to manage them. Self-control is a key component in the vast emotion-regulation literature (e.g., Ochsner et al. 2002). Self-control frees us from being prisoners of our feelings and emotions, and research shows that utilizing emotion-regulation strategies can change behavior in dramatic ways—even in the context of monetary rewards (Delgado, Gillis, and Phelps 2008; Sokol-Hessner et al. 2009). Neuroeconomics research has in recent years confronted the importance of self-control processes in decision making (Hare, Camerer, and Rangel 2009; Kirk, Downar, and Montague, 2011; Kirk, Harvey, and Montague, 2011). Consider the case of "temporal discounting" to contextualize the importance of self-control in decision making.

We frequently make decisions that promise a benefit in the short run but turn out to be disadvantageous in the long run. For example, someone offered the choice between twenty dollars today and twenty-one dollars tomorrow might be tempted to choose the immediate option. However, if asked today to choose between twenty dollars in a year and twenty-one dollars in a year and a day, the same person is likely to prefer the slightly delayed but larger amount.

Biological substrates govern our emotional impulses... research shows that we can do much to manage them.

We have also developed more or less efficient ways to manage the temptation of instant gratification whenever the immediate outcomes of a choice are less desirable than the future prospects. These two dispositions that govern decisions about future consequences are called "impulsivity" and "self-control." Impulsive decision making is defined as the preference for a small, immediate reward over a large, delayed reward, while self-control leads to the preference for a large, delayed reward.

Studies from neuroeconomics have investigated the neural underpinnings of self-control and impulsive decision making, using temporal discounting paradigms. A functional magnetic resonance imaging (fMRI) study involving choices between rewards with different delays showed that choices for immediate rewards recruited brain areas associated with dopamine functions, including the ventral striatum (nucleus accumbens) and the ventromedial prefrontal cortex (VMPFC), whereas lateral prefrontal cortex (LPFC) and the posterior parietal cortex were activated while making choices independent of the delay (McClure et al. 2004). The authors concluded that impatience associated with the prospect of an immediate reward was mediated by striatum and VMPFC, brain areas encoding both emotional values and reward size. In contrast, rational and economic planning and time-reward trade-off were mediated by LPFC and parietal cortex. This conclusion is consistent with the idea of several competing decision-making networks or systems in the brain (McClure et al. 2004; Tanaka et al. 2004; Sanfey et al. 2006).

We are currently studying human decision making in real time using neuroimaging tools such as fMRI. Our studies show measurable changes in the brain, allowing us to visualize and quantify introspection abilities and map the neural mechanisms behind concepts such as self-awareness and self-control and to track the impact of these concepts on decision-making parameters. The remainder of this chapter will summarize some of these findings and discuss the relevance of these studies in the context of corporate leadership.

Neural mechanisms of mindful decision making

Decision making has a biological foundation and is shaped through experience that ultimately reflects the way we value the world around us. The questions of how we can—and how we should—make decisions and judgments were once the sole domain of philosophers and sociologists. Times have changed. In recent years, neuroscience research is applying neuroimaging technology that allows probing the brain's response to everyday decision-making processes in social and economic domains. This movement has established a melting pot of interdisciplinary research, such as neuroaesthetics, neuroeconomics, neuroleadership, and mindful decision making.

The worldwide popularity of mindfulness practice has become mainstream only in the last decade or so. Mindfulness is being applied in areas such as health care and corporate settings. Accumulating evidence demonstrates that mindfulness has measurable effects on brain and health-related behavior (Davidson and McEwen 2012). For example, mindfulness has a positive effect on heart rate, blood pressure, and immune function, as well as on subjectively perceived stress levels and psychological well-being (Brown and Ryan 2004; Davidson et al. 2003; Ryan, Bernstein, and Brown 2010; Zeidan et al. 2010; 2011). One reason for the impact of mindfulness compared with other psychological techniques might be that mindfulness uses an outsider's perspective on one's subjective experiences, rather than changing the content (distraction) or context (reframing). This means that mindfulness is a technique independent from distraction ("think happy thoughts") and reframing ("look on the bright side") and one that seems to work in many people where the other two techniques have failed. Despite the widespread acceptance of mindfulness, it was only recently that scientists started to investigate the effects of mindfulness, or direct-experience training, in the context of decision making.

Neuroscience research is applying neuroimaging technology that allows probing the brain's response to everyday decision-making processes in social and economic domains.

In the next section we will discuss brain imaging experimental findings that highlight the novelty and potential of mindful decision-making by describing how mindfulness training can optimize the way we make decisions. These specific experimental questions are driven by the author's interest in mapping brain regions involved in mindful decision making. Some of these enticing experimental questions are: Does mindfulness reduce your susceptibility to bias when making choices? Can mindfulness make you less irrational in the face of financial loss? Does mindfulness increase self-control in the context of financial incentives?

Social neuroscience and neuroeconomics have developed experimental techniques to quantitatively study brain responses to financial loss, gain, material desires, unfairness, and so on. Neuroimaging studies have demonstrated that emotional processes, which may lead to suboptimal decisions, can compromise cognitive processes that are involved in rational decision making (Sanfey et al. 2003).

One idea is that mindfulness presents a way to avoid this competition between rational and emotional processes in the brain. This idea is based on research showing that the insular cortex is of great importance in mindfulness as this brain region is activated during meditative states (Farb et al. 2007; Holzel et al. 2008; Lazar et al. 2005; Lutz et al. 2008), which are interpreted as an increased awareness of bodily states, specifically interoceptive states and global visceral awareness (Critchley et al. 2004). Interoceptive awareness refers to subjective awareness of inner feelings. The inter-subjective variability in the degree of self-awareness is enormous; some people have more direct "access," while others have very sparse access to self-awareness. As the insular cortex encodes awareness of one's bodily responses, it may be the case that increased bodily awareness can be intentionally achieved through mindfulness and guide decision making in other directions than would otherwise be the case. For example, could mindfulness training rewire the brain so that decision making is processed through a neural route that increases one's interoceptive or bodily awareness, as opposed to primarily being guided by rational or emotional processes? As mindfulness gives rise to a heightened awareness of the self, one hypothesis might be that such increased self-awareness will "regulate" responses when facing, for instance, anticipation of monetary loss and when exposed to social unfairness.

Neurobiology of leadership

We believe that insights from neuroscience can inform companies interested in leadership development. These insights can help protect corporations from flawed and suboptimal decision making. Three lines of scientific findings support the idea that corporate mindfulness training can optimize decision making: (1) Reliance on exogenous information in value judgments can be diminished. This means that decision-making processes can become less susceptible to bias effects and increase awareness of bias blind spots. (2) Mindfulness training increases the ability to respond rationally by being able to control the urge to react to negative emotions during economic decision making. (3) Bias toward either negative or positive rewards can be diminished. This frees up decision-making processes by enabling a less restrained and more explorative and creative focus on problem solving. These three findings are described in detail in the following sections.

Bias blind spots—how to safeguard against misleading judgments

It is well known that people are enormously influenced by external and sometimes unrelated factors in making judgments. For example the "mere exposure effect" (Zajonc 1968) was the first psychological experiment showing that people are not always aware of the influences that bias their judgments. Several recent neuroimaging studies have examined the presence of bias in many domains of decision making, even without people being aware of its influence.

Experiments have begun to shed light on the neural mechanisms of social exchange...

Take, for example, a recent experiment from our lab where we investigated how external social value can manipulate value judgments for abstract rewards. A particularly salient real-world example is the use of monetary favors to influence preferences. Bias may be rooted in biological mechanisms that subvert cognitive control. For example, social gestures from a sender to a receiver are known to bias decisions made by the recipient, especially when the decision relates to the sender—a feature of social exchange known as reciprocity. Recent experiments have begun to shed light on the neural mechanisms of social exchange (King-Casas et al. 2005; Sanfey et al. 2003; Li et al. 2009); however, little is known about the influence of an "open-loop" favor where there is no possibility for reciprocating interactions between the sender and the receiver.

We designed an experiment by providing monetary favors to participants as they came to the lab expecting normal compensation (twenty to forty dollars) (Harvey et al. 2010). However, our experimental manipulation was that we told them they would receive three hundred dollars and this money had been provided by one of the two sponsoring companies. We expected to see that such monetary favors would bias subjective preference for the sponsoring logo, even for objects unrelated to the favor itself. We conducted the experiment as follows: An agent sent a monetary favor to a subject. We then tested the influence of this favor on subjects' preference for art, a domain where there is no objectively "correct" answer and no economic relationship exists between the favor and the preference judgment. During fMRI scanning, subjects passively viewed images of artwork paired with company logos, one of which was one of the companies "sponsoring" the subjects' participation in the experiment. After scanning, the subjects provided preference ratings for all the paintings.

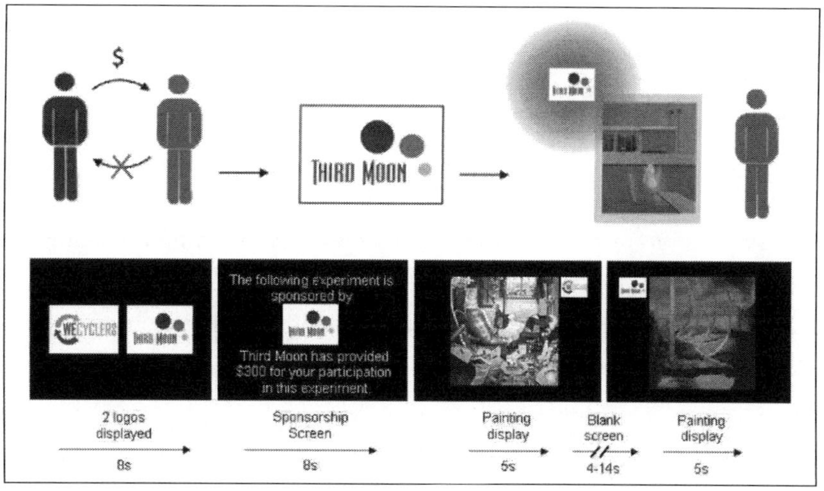

Figure 1. Monetary favor paradigm. A monetary gesture ($300) is encoded in a representative logo. The logo acts as a value proxy for the gesture and presumably acquires a "value field." The value field transmits gesture to objects in spatial and temporal proximity to the logo such that object value (e.g., painting) is influenced by proximity to the logo. In the scanner, participants are initially presented with two logos: a sponsoring and a nonsponsoring logo. One of two company logos was associated with the funds ($300) that participants received for study compensation. The sponsorship screen is subsequently shown once at the beginning of the scanning cycle for 8seconds. Participants are subsequently presented with 60 paintings displayed on different trials with either the sponsoring or the nonsponsoring logo during a scanning session. In a subsequent behavioral session (not shown), participants provide preference responses for each painting.

The behavioral results showed that preference for paintings paired with the sponsoring company's logo was higher than those paired with the nonsponsor's logo (Harvey et al. 2010). The functional imaging results revealed that activity in the VMPFC tracked the sponsorship category of the painting.

This imaging study is the first to show that a monetary favor transfers value to a proxy and influences judgment of objects in spatial proximity, with corresponding changes in brain activity as measured by fMRI. The results raise the important possibility that monetary favors bias judgments by acting on existing valuation mechanisms, and individuals may have difficulty detecting influence of the favor over their subjective preferences, even for objects seemingly unrelated to the favor. We refer to this influence as a bias blind spot.

Consider for a moment the daily routines we go through where our decisions are tinged by favoritism, rules of thumb, partiality, heuristics, and so on. Our biases come into play with every decision we make and every tactic we execute. A highly salient question in the context of corporate decision making is whether there might be ways to recognize our own biases so decision makers become increasingly aware and thereby counteract the impact of bias blind spots. In other words, can we develop strategies that may instigate disruption of external influences and increase the capacity to attribute more weight to internal parameters in guiding decision making?

Our biases come into play with every decision we make and every tactic we execute.

Does self-awareness training mitigate bias blind spots?

In a follow-up experiment, we examined whether the biasing effects of the social gesture on valuation judgments could be mitigated. To test this directly, we recruited a group of participants who had been trained in mindfulness programs to perform the favor task outlined in the previous section.

The hypothesis was that training in self-awareness may insulate participants against the biasing gesture of the sponsoring company. Specifically, we asked whether people with mindfulness training are able to employ mindfulness techniques such as nonidentification and nonjudgmental observations to regulate potential bias effects. If so, there should be neurobiological correlates tracking the behavioral difference between individuals.

Training in self-awareness may insulate participants against the biasing gesture of the sponsoring company.

In contrast with the previous study, the results showed that people with mindfulness training had no differences in preference for the sponsor's paintings over the nonsponsor's paintings (Kirk and Montague, in prep). We found that normal controls exhibited activity in the VMPFC that correlated linearly with painting preference for all paintings. The next question to investigate based on the behavioral results was: which region(s) in the brain might be involved in insulating against the bias-effect in people with mindfulness training? We found that those with mindfulness training displayed greater activity in the anterior insular cortex.

As discussed previously, the insula (especially the anterior portion) mediates explicit awareness of internal bodily processes. It has been argued that a sense of "self" is grounded in homeostatic bodily responses (Damasio 1999), and thus subjective feeling states and emotions might arise from representations of somatic processes (Naqvi et al. 2007; Montague 2007). A consequence of these accounts is that mindfulness might give rise to heightened emotional self-awareness that essentially protects such individuals against bias blind spots.

One idea emerging from these results, which we are now pursuing in a commercial setting, relates to the following two aspects that our experiments uncovered: (1) bias-effects subvert cognitive control, even without people's subjective awareness of the influences; and (2) mindfulness training can raise self-awareness to continuously regulate bias susceptibility. Based on these findings, it has become possible to extract neural measures in individuals, before and after mindfulness training, to quantify training effects. Specifically, one might use the anterior insular cortex as a seed region to objectively assess the impact that bias might exert on decision making. Thus, such neural profiling of individual decision makers carries the promise of identifying individuals who are susceptible to bias and importantly of applying corporate training such as mindfulness to track the neural impact of training as a way to safeguard against biased decision making.

Why does a Buddhist meditator make more rational economic decisions than a business manager?

In a rational account of human behavior, if a person is offered the choice of gaining a reward versus gaining nothing, they should always choose the reward. While this is typically true in a nonsocial context, this account often breaks down during social interactions. In the classic example of the Ultimatum Game, a "proposer" offers to split a sum of money with a "responder" in a two-person exchange. If the responder rejects the offer, both players get nothing. Hence, according to rational choice theory, responders should accept all nonzero offers. In reality, responders are rarely so magnanimous. They typically reject offers in which the proposer's share exceeds 80% of the total, preferring to gain nothing rather than to accept an inferior share of the winnings (Guth, Schmittenberger, and Schwarze 1982; Bolton and Zwick 1995).

Mindfulness might give rise to heightened emotional self-awareness that essentially protects such individuals against bias blind spots.

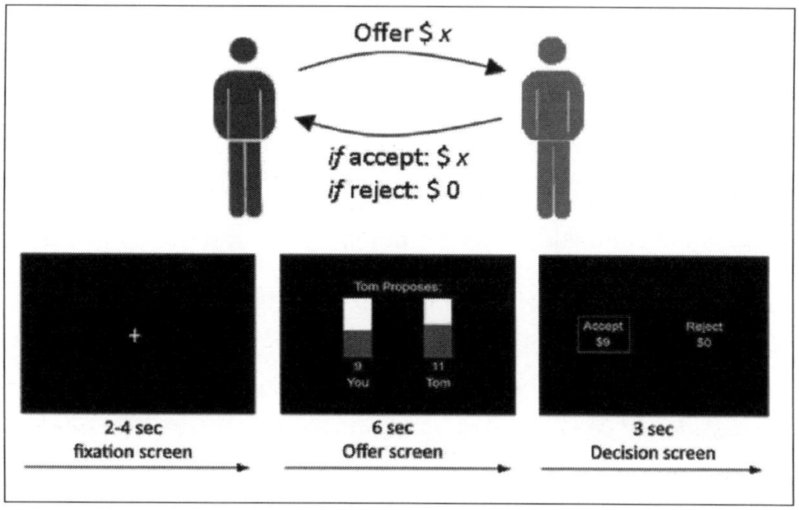

Figure 2. Ultimatum Game paradigm. Participants played as responders in the Ultimatum Game. Participants choose on each round to accept or reject a monetary split of $20 made by a new partner on each round. Trial outline for the Ultimatum Game is displayed. Each trial starts with a fixation period (2-4 seconds) followed by an offer to split $20 (6 seconds). Finally, subjects indicate the decision to accept or reject the offer (3 seconds). A red box highlights the choice being made by each participant on each trial while in the fMRI magnet.

So why do human beings turn a perfectly good reward into a disappointment when others are getting more? One proposal is that the superficially "irrational" rejection of inferior shares is a costly but effective means of enforcing social norms (Boyd et al. 2003). Ultimately, the costs of giving up inferior shares are presumably outweighed by the long-term benefits of establishing a cooperative social environment (Fehr and Gachter 2002; de Quervain et al. 2004). Although this may be so, the strategy of measuring one's own gains against others also has a downside. Even in wealthy societies, a comfortable income can become unsatisfactory if compared with an extravagant one: the millionaire envies the billionaire, and the billionaire envies still richer billionaires. This arms race of reward can in itself lead to inequity and social unrest.

The human tendency to see rewards in socially relative terms may therefore be a mixed blessing. If so, the question arises as to whether some people are capable of ignoring social considerations and assessing a reward based on its intrinsic qualities alone. The willingness to sacrifice money to punish an unfair proposer has specific neural correlates, identified in neuroimaging studies of social exchange. Unfair offers elicit greater activation in the anterior insula (King-Casas et al. 2005; Rilling et al. 2002; Sanfey et al. 2003), an area we mentioned earlier and that is linked to interoceptive awareness (Craig 2002; 2009; Critchley et al. 2004) and in particular to the emotion of disgust (Calder, Lawrence, and Young 2001). Anterior insula activation scales inversely with offer size and predicts whether an unfair offer will be rejected (Sanfey et al. 2003). These results suggest that rejection of unfair offers in the Ultimatum Game is driven by negative emotional reactions.

The human tendency to see rewards in socially relative terms may therefore be a mixed blessing.

In a recent neuroimaging study, we demonstrated that people with mindfulness training have an ability to uncouple emotional reactions from their behavior while playing the Ultimatum Game (Kirk, Downar, and Montague 2011). What we found was that people with mindfulness training experience a reduced conflict between cognitive (accept) and emotional (reject) motives.

Our results are important in that we have identified that mindfulness training enables people to behave more like rational economic agents when playing the Ultimatum Game. Specifically, they are roughly twice as likely as controls to say yes to a free dollar over no money at all, rather than reject the reward due to its unfavorable social context. Proximately, mindfulness practitioners seem to avoid generating aversive responses in the anterior insula during unfair offers. In controls, such responses are powerful predictors of rejecting offers during social interaction.

Our results suggest that, instead of the anterior insula, the lower-level interoceptive representation in the posterior insula is recruited based on a person's level of mindfulness experience. Presumably, by engaging the posterior insula, people are focusing more on the physiological condition of the body (Craig 2009), as opposed to generating aversive responses in the anterior insula. When assessing unfair offers, people with mindfulness training activate an almost entirely different network of brain areas than do normal controls. Controls draw on areas involved in theory of mind, prospection, and episodic memory. In contrast, mindfulness training enables people to instead draw on areas involved in interoception and attention to the present moment.

Mindfulness practitioners seem to avoid generating aversive responses in the anterior insula during unfair offers.

In a subsequent analysis, we looked at the brain response that correlates with self-control. Self-control in this context is the ability to remain rational and accept an unfair offer by controlling the urge to reject such an offer. We found that rational controls recruited the dorso-lateral PFC, which has in the literature been shown to be involved in cognitive control and emotion regulation (Hare, Camerer, and Rangel 2009; Ochsner et al. 2002; Wagner et al. 2001). This result provides an anatomical base for successful self-control in rational controls. However, the mindfulness group displayed activity in a different set of regions, including the somatosensory cortex. The somatosensory cortex is reported in studies requiring mapping of subjective feeling states arising from bodily responses (Critchley et al. 2004; Lutz et al. 2008). It is striking to observe that the mindfulness group employs a different set of brain regions to accomplish self-control than does the control group.

This study (Kirk, Harvey, and Montague 2011) is relevant for corporate leadership in that it showed that self-control can indeed be trained with distinct neural correlates and brought online during decision making. The study furthermore suggests that the trick may lie not in rational calculation but in steering away from what-if scenarios and concentrating on the qualities that accompany any reward, no matter how small.

Individual rationality index

In a follow-up study of the Ultimatum Game, we are currently developing a way to calculate an individual rationality index. By engaging participants in mindfulness-training programs that include neuroimaging scanning at baseline (i.e., before the training) and posttraining, we can calculate behavioral and neural change parameters in individual participants. Such a neural assay has potential as a training tool for corporate leadership in that it allows for an objective and quantitative metric of the impact of a leadership-training program tailored to individual participants. This concept may also have potential, beyond novelty, in that it provides "360-degree feedback" and evaluations that derive from subjective choice parameters using covert neural measures. For example, in corporate leadership training that includes neural-profiling, participants can gain insights about the impact that self-awareness and self-control exert on behavior and the brain. The ancient notion of "know thyself" and the concept of self-knowledge remain a strong predictor of accomplishment in life and leadership (Goleman 1998; 2004). Modern neuroscience now provides techniques that allow us to investigate, using neuroimaging tools, how our brains generate models of ourselves, others around us, and the decisions we make.

Creative focus—the concept of neural reward prediction and valuation

Learning from environmental cues that predict future rewards elicits positive sensations ("pleasure") across several species, including humans. A major role of dopamine neurons in the brain is to encode anticipation of both the magnitude and timing of rewards. Dopamine governs people's reactions to any type of reward, from monetary rewards to the rewarding aspects of pleasant taste and smell.

Human neuroimaging studies have identified activity in target brain areas of dopamine neurons in the striatum that is indicative of a role for this structure in mediating learning of expected rewards (McClure, Berns, and Montague 2003; O'Doherty et al. 2003; Pagnoni et al. 2002). However, the striatum is a protagonist in developing "valuation diseases" (Montague 2007). For example, an elevated dopaminergic function represents a biological substrate of vulnerability to addiction (Dagher and Robbins 2009), as well as to selection bias in compulsive behavior (Voon et al. 2010). Impulsivity is associated with greater activity in areas innervated by the dopamine system, including the striatum (McClure et al. 2004; Pine et al. 2010). Pathological gambling is associated with decision-making impairments such as greater impulsive choices and disadvantageous choices on gambling tasks (Goudriaan et al. 2005; Petry 2001).

Taken together, these studies suggest that a hyperactive dopaminergic system may potentially cause suboptimal choice formation, as well as develop into more serious pathologies, such as addiction. Despite advances in understanding how the brain assigns value to the expectation of rewards, it is poorly understood how to control or regulate hypervaluation of reward-prediction signals. The downside of the reward-signaling mechanism is that people tend to overvalue events, as the studies on valuation disease above reveal.

Cognitive flexibility and even creativity arise from an evolved adaptation toward flexible reward exploratory behavior...

Our hypothesis is that the bases of cognitive flexibility and even creativity arise from an evolved adaptation toward flexible reward exploratory behavior, enabling freedom from reflexive/stimulus-driven responses through broader, more reflective processing. This would imply that the dopamine signals do not over-value particular choices, but that responses are attenuated, thus allowing for creativity or play to flourish among a richer reward space. We propose that cognitive flexibility and creativity is associated with activation of dopaminergic "play/exploration," as opposed to "seeking/exploitation" systems. Similarly, in the corporate world, it may in some circumstances be beneficial to engage a flexible mind-set and explore different options available to any decision maker, rather than exploit one particular option that, based on habit-learning, is associated with a positive outcome or reward.

We designed an experiment to investigate if mindfulness training strategies exert effects on the reward-prediction circuitry in the human brain. If so, this type of training could potentially be applied as an antidote to impulsivity and selection bias in decision making. Our results (Kirk and Montague, in prep.) showed that mindfulness training recruits the dopaminergic "play/exploration" system, illustrated by a decreased neural response in the reward system of the brain. Reward seeking/exploitation of both negative and positive rewards is diminished, which frees up decision-making processes by enabling a less restrained and more explorative and creative focus on problem solving.

Outlook—the potential of mindful corporate decision making

Any corporate executive needs to maintain peak performance. Suboptimal decision making from key executives can be disastrous for corporations. For example, relying on emotional processes without realizing that such processes bias economic decisions can be disastrous for individuals as well as corporations. In this chapter, we have (1) reviewed the potential of fMRI as a technique to profile individual decision makers while engaged in economic and social decision making; (2) demonstrated that fMRI can visualize brain responses when emotional processes have captured our decision-making abilities; and, most critically, (3) shown that mindfulness training can "recalibrate" decision-making processes. The potential for corporations is that extracting covert neural responses while a person is engaged in decision making can help executives gain intimate knowledge about what type of decision maker he or she is and how to improve decision making. We can now eavesdrop on brain activity and extract multidimensional and covert neural responses that are more sensitive and reliable than any behavioral measure alone. The studies discussed in this chapter have demonstrated a framework to quantify self-control and self-awareness and to measure the impact of such processes on decision making. Such neural markers can be utilized to gain insights about the biology of leadership from a first-person perspective in the context of corporate training programs. Ultimately, such an approach will more objectively assess an executive's ability to improve decision making and protect against flawed decision making[1].

[1]Headspin LLC (www.headspinllc.com) is a spin-off company that takes advantage of cutting-edge neuroscience technology to gain neural and behavioral insight into decision-making parameters in individual clients while quantifying their ability to change entrenched decision-making patterns.

References

Bolton, G. E., and Zwick, R. 1995. "Anonymity Versus Punishment in Ultimatum Bargaining." *Games and Economic Behavior* 10: 95–121.

Boyd, R., Gintis, H., Bowles, S., and Richerson, P. J. 2003. "The Evolution of Altruistic Punishment." *Proceedings of the National Academy of Sciences, USA* 100: 3531–3535.

Brown, K. W., and Ryan, R. M. 2004. "Fostering Healthy Self-Regulation from Within and Without: A Self Determination Theory Perspective." In *Positive Psychology in Practice*, edited by P. A. Linley and S. Joseph, 105–124. New York: John Wiley & Sons.

Calder, A. J., Lawrence, A. D., and Young, A. W. 2001. "Neuropsychology of Fear and Loathing." *Nature Reviews Neuroscience* 2(5): 352–363.

Craig, A. D. 2002. "How Do You Feel? Interoception: The Sense of the Physiological Condition of the Body." *Nature Reviews Neuroscience* 3(8): 655–666.

Craig, A. D. 2009. "How Do You Feel—Now? The Anterior Insula and Human Awareness." *Nature Reviews Neuroscience* 10(1): 59–70.

Critchley, H. D., Wiens, S., Rotshtein, P., Ohman, A., and Dolan, R. J. 2004. "Neural Systems Supporting Interoceptive Awareness." *Nature Neuroscience* 7(2): 189–195.

Dagher, A., and Robbins, T. W. 2009. "Personality, Addiction, Dopamine: Insights from Parkinson's Disease." *Neuron* 61(4): 502–510.

Damasio, A. R. 1999. *The Feeling of What Happens: Body and Emotion in the Making of Consciousness*. Boston: Houghton Mifflin Harcourt.

Dani, J. A., and Montague, P. R. 2007. "Disrupting Addiction Through the Loss of Drug-Associated Internal States." *Nature Neuroscience* 10(4): 403–404.

Davidson, R. J., Kabat-Zinn, J., Schumacher, J., Rosenkranz, M., Muller, D., Santorelli, S.F., Urbanowski F. et al. 2003. "Alterations in Brain and Immune Function Produced by Mindfulness Meditation." *Psychosomatic Medicine* 65(4): 564–570.

Davidson, R. J., and McEwen, B. S. 2012. "Social Influences on Neuroplasticity: Stress and Interventions to Promote Well-Being." *Nature Neuroscience* 15(5): 689–695.

Delgado, M. R., Gillis, M. M., and Phelps, E. A. 2008. "Regulating the Expectation of Reward Via Cognitive Strategies." *Nature Neuroscience* 11(8): 880–881.

De Quervain, D. J., Fischbacher, U., Treyer, V., Schellhammer, M., Schnyder, U., Buck, A., and Fehr, E. 2004. "The Neural Basis of Altruistic Punishment." *Science* 305(5688): 1254–1258.

Eagleman, D. 2011. *Incognito: The Secret Lives of the Brain*. New York: Pantheon Books.

Farb, N. A., Segal, Z. V., Mayberg, H., Bean, J., McKeon, D., Fatima, Z., and Anderson, A. K. 2007. "Attending to the Present: Mindfulness Meditation Reveals Distinct Neural Modes of Self-Reference." *Social, Cognitive, and Affective Neuroscience* 2(4): 313–322.

Fehr, E., and Gachter, S. 2002. "Altruistic Punishment in Humans." *Nature* (415): 137–140.

Goleman, D. 1998. *Working with Emotional Intelligence*. New York: Bantam Books.

Goleman, D. 2004. "What Makes a Great Leader?" *Harvard Business Review* 82(1): 1–11.

Goudriaan, A. E., Oosterlaan, J., de Beurs, E., and van den Brink, W. 2005. "Decision-Making in Pathological Gambling: A Comparison Between Pathological Gamblers, Alcohol Dependents, Persons with Tourette Syndrome, and Normal Controls." *Cognitive Brain Research* 23(1): 137–151.

Guth, W., Schmittenberger, R., and Schwarze, B. 1982. "An Experimental Analysis of Ultimatum Bargaining." *Journal of Economic Behavior and Organization* (3): 376.

Hare, T. A., Camerer, C. F., and Rangel, A. 2009. "Self-Control in Decision-Making Involves Modulation of the vmPFC Valuation System." *Science* 324(5927): 646–648.

Harvey, A., Kirk, U., Denfield, G., and Montague, P. R. 2010. "Monetary Favors and their Influence on Neural Responses and Revealed Preference." *Journal of Neuroscience* (30): 9597–9602.

Holzel, B. K., Ott, U., Gard, T., Hempel, H., Weygandt, M., Morgen, K., and Vaitl, D. 2008. "Investigation of Mindfulness Meditation Practitioners with Voxel-Based Morphometry." *Social, Cognitive, and Affective Neuroscience* 3(1): 55–61.

King-Casas, B., Tomlin, D., Anen, C., Camerer, C. F., Quartz, S. R., and Montague, P. R. 2005. "Getting to Know You: Reputation and Trust in a Two-Person Economic Exchange." *Science* 308(5718): 79–83.

Kirk, U., Downar, J., and Montague, P. R. 2011. "Interoception Drives Increased Rational Decision-Making in Meditators Playing the Ultimatum Game." *Frontiers in Neuroscience* 5(4): 49.

Kirk, U., Harvey, A. H., and Montague, P. R. 2011. "Domain Expertise Insulates Against Judgment Bias by Monetary Favors Through a Modulation of Ventromedial Prefrontal Cortex. " *Proceedings of the National Academy of Sciences, USA* 108: 10332–10336.

Kirk, U., and Montague, P. R. (forthcoming). "Buddhist Meditators Display Attenuated Prediction Error Signaling in Human Striatum."

Langer, E. J. 2005. *On Becoming an Artist*. New York: Ballantine Books.

Lazar, S. W., Kerr, C. E., Wasserman, R. H., Gray, J. R., Greve, D. N., Treadway, M.T., McGarvey, M. et al. 2005. "Meditation Experience is Associated with Increased Cortical Thickness." *Neuroreport* (16): 1893–1897.

Li, J., Xiao, E., Houser, D., and Montague, P. R. 2009. "Neural Responses to Sanction Threats in Two-Party Economic Exchange. " *Proceedings of the National Academy of Sciences, USA* 106: 16835–16840.

Lutz, A., Slagter, H. A., Dunne, J. D., Davidson, R. J. 2008. "Attention Regulation and Monitoring in Meditation." *Trends in Cognitive Science* 12(4): 163–169.

McClure, S. M., Berns, G. S., and Montague, P. R. 2003. "Temporal Prediction Errors in a Passive Learning Task Activate Human Striatum." *Neuron* 38(2): 339–346.

McClure, S. M., Laibson, D. I., Loewenstein, G., and Cohen, J. D. 2004. "Separate Neural Systems Value Immediate and Delayed Monetary Rewards." *Science* 306(5695): 503–507.

Montague, P. R. 2007. "Neuroeconomics: A View from Neuroscience." *Functional Neurology* 22(4): 219–234.

Naqvi, N. H., Rudrauf, D., Damasio, H., and Bechara, A. 2007. "Damage to the Insula Disrupts Addiction to Cigarette Smoking." *Science* 315(5811): 531–534.

Ochsner, K. N., Bunge, S. A., Gross, J. J., and Gabrieli, J. D. 2002. "Rethinking Feelings: An fMRI Study of the Cognitive Regulation of Emotion." *Journal of Cognitive Neuroscience* 14(8): 1215–1229.

O'Doherty, J. P., Dayan, P., Friston, K., Critchley, H., and Dolan, R. J. 2003. "Temporal Difference Models and Reward-Related Learning in the Human Brain." *Neuron* 38(2): 329–337.

Pagnoni, G., Zink, C. F., Montague, P. R., and Berns, G. S. 2002. "Activity in Human Ventral Striatum Locked to Errors of Reward Prediction." *Nature Neuroscience* 5(2): 97–98.

Petry, N. M. 2001. "Pathological Gamblers, With and Without Substance Use Disorders, Discount Delayed Rewards at High Rates." *Journal of Abnormal Psychology* 110(3): 482–487.

Pine, A., Shiner, T., Seymour, B., and Dolan, R. J. 2010. "Dopamine, Time, and Impulsivity in Humans." *Journal of Neuroscience* 30(26): 8888–8896.

Rilling, J., Gutman, D., Zeh, T., Pagnoni, G., Berns, G., and Kilts, C. 2002. "A Neural Basis for Social Cooperation." *Neuron* 35(2) 395–405.

Rock, D. 2008. "SCARF: A Brain-Based Model for Collaborating With and Influencing Others." *Neuroleadership Journal* 1: 1–9.

Ryan, R. M., Bernstein, J., and Brown, K. W. 2010. "Weekends, Work and Well-Being: Psychological Need Satisfactions and Day of the Week Effects on Mood, Vitality, and Physical Symptoms." *Journal of Social and Clinical Psychology* 29: 95–122.

Sanfey, A. G., Rillig, J. K., Aronson, J. A., Nystrom, L. E., and Cohen, J. D. 2003. "The Neural Basis of Economic Decision-Making in the Ultimatum Game." *Science* 300(5626): 1755–1758.

Sanfey, A. G., Loewenstein, G., McClure, S. M., and Cohen, J. D. 2006. "Neuroeconomics: Cross-Currents in Research on Decision-Making." *Trends in Cognitive Science* 10(3): 108–116.

Sokol-Hessner, P., Hsu, M., Curley, N. G., Delgado, M. R., Camerer, C. F., and Phelps, E. A. 2009. "Thinking Like a Trader Selectively Reduces Individuals' Loss Aversion." *Proceedings of the National Academy of Sciences, USA* 106(13): 5035–5040.

Tanaka, S. C., Doya, K., Okada, G., Ueda, K., Okamoto, Y., and Yamawaki, S. 2004. "Prediction of Immediate and Future Rewards Differentially Recruits Cortico-Basal Ganglia Loops." *Nature Neuroscience* 7(8): 887–893.

Voon, V., Pessiglione, M., Brezing, C., Gallea, C., Fernandez, H. H., Dolan, R. J., and Hallett, M. 2010. "Mechanisms Underlying Dopamine-Mediated Reward Bias in Compulsive Behaviors." *Neuron* 65(1): 135–142.

Wagner, A. D., Maril, A., Bjork, R. A., and Schacter, D. L. 2001. "Prefrontal Contributions to Executive Control: fMRI Evidence for Functional Distinctions Within Lateral Prefrontal Cortex." *Neuroimage* 14: 1337–1347.

Zajonc, R. B. 1968. "Attitudinal Effects of Mere Exposure." *Journal of Personality and Social Psychology* 9 (2, Pt.2): 1–27.

Zeidan, F., Johnson, S. K., Diamond, B. J., David, Z., and Goolkasian, P. 2010. "Mindfulness Meditation Improves Cognition: Evidence of Brief Mental Training." *Consciousness and Cognition* 19(2): 597–605.

Zeidan, F., Martucci, K. T., Kraft, R. A., Gordon, N. S., McHaffie, J. G., and Coghill, R. C. 2011. "Brain Mechanisms Supporting the Modulation of Pain by Mindfulness Meditation." *Journal of Neuroscience* 31(14): 5540–5548.

SECTION III:
Regulating Emotions

9. Staying cool under pressure: insights from social-cognitive neuroscience and their implications for self and society

Dr. Kevin Ochsner
Kevin Ochsner, Department of Psychology, Columbia University, New York, USA
kochsner@paradox.psych.columbia.edu

Introduction

If you were to ask a group of average Americans what they fear most, what do you think would be the answer?

With some reliability, the answer is public speaking, which ranks number one above even the fear of death. This fact prompted the comedian Jerry Seinfeld to joke that this must mean that at a funeral, you would rather be the person inside the coffin than the guy in front of it giving the eulogy.

Beyond public speaking and death, of course, life is full of a myriad of other things that make us afraid, stress us out, or make us anxious. Whether it is our daily commute, airline travel, workplace conflicts or disagreements with spouses, serious challenges to our emotional equilibrium are many and varied. The goal of this chapter is to provide a quick overview of how we can manage our emotional responses to these challenges so that our equilibrium is maintained.

Toward that end, this chapter has four parts. The first briefly describes what emotions are and what triggers them. This provides the backdrop for the second section, which describes five different ways you can regulate your emotion. In each section, I'll provide examples from both neuroscience and behavioral research to illustrate both how emotions are generated and how regulatory strategies enable you to regulate your emotions. The third section provides concrete examples of a select subset of strategies. And the final section considers the broader implications of emotion-regulation research for how you interact with others in your daily life.

The nature of emotion

Popular culture is full of examples of the commonsense view of emotion. One of my favorites comes from the 1970s hit TV show *The Odd Couple*. On one hand, the character Oscar epitomizes this commonsense ideal: Oscar is impulsive, messy, guttural, and passionate. His needs overtake him and can barely be controlled. The subtext is that this is what emotions are like in general.

On the other hand, cognition is epitomized by Felix, Oscar's supposed opposite. Felix is deliberate, precise, rational, and distant. In this view, cognition and emotion only make contact with one another when cognition is trying to clean up emotion's messes after the fact.

Despite its intuitive appeal, this commonsense view of emotion as being totally separate from cognition is fundamentally wrong. Cognition—or thinking—is, in fact, is integral to both the generation and regulation of emotion. To see why that might be, let's lay out a simple model of emotion generation and regulation that was first proposed by James Gross from Stanford University, has since been elaborated on in a variety of ways (Gross 1998; Ochsner and Gross 2007), and is based on appraisal theories of emotion (Scherer, Schorr, and Johnstone 2001).

The process of generating an emotion starts when you are presented with a situation that includes various kinds of stimuli. For example, if you are engaged in public speaking, the stimuli might include the lecture hall and all members of the audience, including the actions they might take—scratching their heads, looking down at their notes, staring at the ceiling, falling asleep, making facial expressions, and so on. At the next step of the emotion-generation process, you use selective attention to take in only some of those social cues from the audience; for example, you may fixate on just particular people, such as someone who looks particularly bored. At the next and most critical step, you appraise the meaning of that bored expression in the context of your current goals, wants, and needs. You might quickly assess whether this is someone who just did not get a lot of sleep last night or whether it reflects negatively in some way on the presentation you are giving. If you appraise the expression as resulting from something you are doing, you might feel threatened and afraid that perhaps you need to change what you are doing. Once you have made this appraisal, a response is triggered that includes changes in experience (feeling afraid), behavior (freezing), and physiology (palms sweating).

Two brain systems are critical for appraising something as a threat and mobilizing various aspects of an emotional response. One is the amygdala, which means *almond* in Greek. The amygdala is a little cluster of nuclei buried in the depths of your temporal lobe. In evolutionary terms it is a very old structure whose function is to detect stimuli in the world that have innate or learned affective significance, with a special emphasis on identifying those who are—or might be—threatening (LeDoux 2000; Ochsner and Barrett 2001; Phelps 2006).

The second structure is the insula, which is a cortical region folded underneath the frontal and temporal lobes. The insula has a viscerotopic map of what is going on in your internal organs and how they change when you are responding emotionally, including information about painful sensations (Craig 2002). The insula is involved especially in negative emotions that have a strong bodily component, such as disgust.

Beyond public speaking and death, of course, life is full of a myriad of other things that make us afraid...

Finally, it is important to note that emotions do not just start and stop, but rather are continuously generated by a cyclical process that is constantly taking place. Emotions are effected not only by stimulus inputs, but also by whatever responses you make to a situation and the effects your behavior has on those things in the world. If you were particularly afraid when speaking in public, for example, and ran out of the room, all the stimuli you perceive would change, as would your actions and bodily state, thereby changing all the inputs to your emotion system. Every action you take can change what you are attending to, how you are appraising it, how you are responding, and so on. The key is to view emotional responses as continuously updated readouts of the personal affective meaning of your current environment.

Five ways to regulate emotion

With that model of emotion in place, let's now talk about different ways to regulate it. The critical idea is that different strategies impact different stages of generating an emotion and that you can understand their efficacy and impact in terms of the stage of the emotion-generative process they influence (Gross 1998; Ochsner and Gross 2007).

The first strategy, *situation selection*, involves acting in anticipation of something you know might be emotionally arousing. Here you simply put yourself in a situation that promotes the emotions you want to have, and you take yourself out of situations that promote the emotions you do not want to have. A simple example is that if you are on a diet and trying to avoid a craving and desire for sweets, you could either not buy them or not go in the kitchen (if you already have sweets at home). In the case of fear of public speaking, you could choose to not give a speech, but instead to meet individuals one-on-one, or to only put your thoughts in writing. This, of course, may not be adaptive for people who are in a leadership position, which might lead you to try one of the next four strategies.

The second strategy is known as *situation modification*. The idea is that if you cannot keep yourself away from the thing that makes you emotional, you can attempt to change it in some way to promote the kind of feelings you want to have. In the case of fear of public speaking, you might familiarize yourself with your audience and venue and might also practice your talk enough that it is on autopilot. To the extent that your presentation and the audience are familiar and their potential reactions and evaluations can be counted on, you will worry less that they might be critical and that your relationship with them might hinge on their assessment of your public speaking.

If you cannot effectively change the situation, you might use the third attention-deployment strategy to *change the focus of your attention or awareness.* Whatever you attend to is processed more deeply and has greater access to behavior, and by diverting attention from an emotionally arousing input, you can temporarily lessen your response to it. For example, if you are a nervous speaker, you might selectively focus on the wall behind your audience or look at friendly people in the audience you already know who are nodding along with what you are saying. Instead of changing the outward focus of attention, you might also change your inward focus by distracting yourself with thoughts about something less anxiety provoking. Of course, in the case of public speaking and many other performance contexts (such as a big meeting), you would only do that in preparation to lessen your anticipatory anxiety about what could happen, because in the moment you need to devote all your attention to the task at hand.

The fourth strategy is the one that beats all the others in one key way: you can deploy it no matter what situation you are in, and it is almost universally applicable. Victor Frankl, the psychoanalyst and a Holocaust survivor, wrote about *reappraisal* in his book *Man's Search for Meaning*. He described the capacity for cognitive change as the one thing you can never take away from people, no matter what their circumstances, noting that their capacity to cognitively change the meaning of what is happening to them is their most essential personal freedom. The most well-known kind of cognitive change is known as reappraisal (Lazarus 1991), which involves reinterpreting the meaning of a stimulus or event in a way that changes its emotional impact.

Of the many ways of doing this, three have received the most attention. The first method involves reframing or reinterpreting events in either more or less emotional terms. Old aphorisms, such as "look on the bright side" or "every cloud has a silver lining," encapsulate the essence of this kind of reappraisal to lessen the punch of unpleasant experiences.

The second form of reappraisal involves adopting an acceptance and allowance perspective that involves the realization that your emotions are fleeting mental events, interpretations of the world that need not define you. In the case of public speaking, you might realize that it is OK to be anxious or afraid, and by letting this emotion pass through, you do not have a secondary reaction to it—such as being frustrated that you are anxious—that perpetuates your initial response. You might think of this as the "bend like a reed in the wind" strategy in the sense that it is similar to certain tenets of specific Eastern meditation practices that emphasize a separation of the self from the emotional response. It is not that you do not experience an emotion fully, but you maintain awareness of how and why you are responding and allow yourself to have emotions that are situationally appropriate.

The third type of reappraisal involves distancing yourself from the situation quite literally, imagining that you imagine are experiencing an event not in the first person but in the third person. It is as if you watch an event unfold from the perspective of the proverbial fly on the wall. As I will describe later, this method is particularly effective when you are recollecting a troubling emotional event that happened in the past. Deliberately recollecting the event from the third-person perspective gives you the psychological space to gain insights into the causes of your feelings. In this way, distancing works well in combination with the reinterpretive reappraisals previously mentioned to enable you to see beyond the immediate, visceral meaning of an event and to promote positive insights about its meaning.

The fifth and last strategy for regulating emotions, known as *response modulation*, involves suppressing or enhancing the behavioral manifestation of an emotion. Suppression involves trying to hide your feelings so nobody else knows what you are feeling on the inside. The old saying, "never let them see you sweat" captures some of the essence of this strategy. As described below, although this strategy is effective for short periods, it is particularly pernicious in the long run. The other option in response modulation is to attempt to enhance your emotion expressive behavior by, for example, deliberately smiling and nodding and producing other cues that amplify the expression of whatever emotion you are feeling.

The ability to implement these five strategies depends on brain systems generally involved in the control of behavior, which includes, most importantly, portions of your prefrontal cortex (Ochsner and Gross 2005; 2007; 2008). The prefrontal cortex is generally involved in higher executive control. Subregions on its lateral surface are thought to carry out specific processes associated with retrieving, maintaining, and manipulating information in memory. Subregions on the medial wall are thought to be important for reasoning about the mental states of yourself or someone else. Depending on the strategy you employ, different combinations of regions will be recruited to support your use of it. To see how this might work, we turn to a few concrete examples, described in the next section.

Examples from current research

Let us consider four examples of research examining the mechanisms of emotion regulation. The first study examined the use of expressive suppression as a form of response modulation. Expressive suppression involves trying to hide your feelings from someone so they cannot tell what you are feeling inside. In this particular experiment, James Gross and his graduate student Emily Butler had two people come into the laboratory and sit together while watching an emotionally upsetting video clip (Butler et al. 2003). Both people were told that after watching the film together, they would be asked to have a conversation about it. They were videotaped having the conversation, and measures of autonomic physiology (e.g., blood pressure) were also taken from each person. Afterward, each participant was asked a few questions about how they felt about their partner. Critically, one of the participants was secretly given one of two instructions. In the control group, that person was told to just have a conversation naturally. In the suppression group, participants were told to hide their emotions from their partner during the conversation. Of course, because they had just seen an emotionally upsetting film, it would be natural to be emotionally expressive when having a conversation about it. Participants in the suppression group, however, kept their faces a mask and their voices a monotone.

So what happens experientially and physiologically for each conversation partner? Those who are trying to suppress their emotions are successful in hiding their feelings—they say fewer emotional things, display fewer facial expressions. But their partners rate them as being not very responsive in the conversation, which makes sense, given that they would not respond to an emotional comment with a similarly emotional sentiment. Critically, however, suppressing one's emotion takes a toll in three ways. First, suppressors feel distracted because they are trying to do two things at once—have a conversation and also hide their feelings. Second, and more importantly, suppressors' blood pressure goes up relative to participants in the control group, suggesting that trying to keep a lid on your feelings is actually more physiologically arousing than going ahead and expressing what you feel. Third, not only does the suppressors' blood pressure go up, but so does the blood pressure of their partners. It seems that hiding your feelings in a context where it would make sense to be emotional makes your conversation partner aroused. If you continue to suppress over time, this arousal will have a cumulative effect, taking a long-term toll on your cardiovascular health.

Now let's consider a second example that compares suppression with another regulatory strategy—reappraisal—which targets a different aspect of the emotional response and has different consequences for emotional responding and physical health. As a form of cognitive change, reappraisal involves changing one's interpretation of an emotionally evocative event so as to divert the generation of an emotional response before it has begun. Emotional response suppression is like trying to close the barn door while an agitated horse is trying to get out; reappraisal is like calming the horse down so it never wants to leave.

In this second experiment, James Gross and one of his postdoctoral fellows, Philippe Goldin, had participants watch disgusting video clips while in a functional magnetic resonance imaging scanner (Goldin et al. 2008). This allowed the researchers to visualize brain activity as participants were regulating their emotion. For some of the clips, participants were asked to suppress the disgusted facial expression that would naturally be elicited by watching each film. For other clips they were asked to reappraise the film by imagining that they were a detached third-person observer while viewing it. To make sure the participants were not moving their faces when being asked to suppress, Goldin and Gross watched each participant's face with a little camera inside the scanner.

So what happens when people try to suppress or reappraise their disgust reactions? Although in both cases participants showed fewer facial expressions of disgust, they were probably doing so for different reasons. When suppressing, participants reported continuing to feel disgust, whereas when reappraising, they felt much less disgusted. In the former case, suppression is merely trying to keep an emotion from being expressed; it does not divert the impulse that generates it. In the latter case, reappraisal succeeds in derailing the emotional response, lessening the disgusting punch of a film clip.

Emotional response suppression is like trying to close the barn door as an agitated horse is trying to get out...

Now, what is happening in the brain? As might be expected, both strategies activate and depend on the kinds of prefrontal control systems described previously. When suppressing, participants are using these control systems to inhibit motor movements, and when reappraising, they are using control systems to generate and apply a neutralizing cognitive perspective. What differentiates the two strategies is the response in brain systems such as the amygdala and insula that are involved in generating the emotional response. Strikingly, suppression increases activity in these two brain systems, whereas reappraisal reduces activity in them. This is intriguing because the amygdala, as noted above, serves as an alarm that alerts you if something affectively arousing has been detected. In this study, and many others like it, amygdala activity dropped during reappraisal, suggesting that reappraisal is successful in changing what the amygdala "sees"—that is, it no longer detects an arousing and aversive event. When you are suppressing, however, amygdala and insula activity goes up, as if they are trying to amp up the affective arousal because you have failed to respond appropriately to the stimulus by expressing disgust toward it. Although this study did not demonstrate it directly, it is likely that increased amygdala and insula activity during suppression are the culprits in boosting physiological arousal and negatively impacting physical health.

For the third example, let us consider a case where reappraisal does not necessarily make you feel better. In fact, the cognitive change processes involved in reappraisal are often used to enhance or augment emotional responses. Imagine, for example, that you visit a friend in the hospital who has been in a car accident. Your natural emotional impulse is to feel sad about your friend's plight and fearful that his or her health might not improve. So as not to feel sad or fearful, you might reappraise with the goal of reducing your negative emotion. Thus you might say to yourself, "Well, my friend is probably more tired than he is in pain, he's got a strong constitution, and he'll be right as rain come morning." By looking at the bright side, you feel less sad and fearful. However, that is not what we always do. Sometimes we elaborate negative events in ways that amplify our feelings about them, adding cognitive insult to perceived injury. In this case, you might say to yourself, "My friend really is in a lot of pain, might not be able to pull through, and could suffer serious disability—or worse!" Here you are turning an emotional molehill into an emotional mountain.

Sometimes we elaborate negative events in ways that amplify our feelings about them, adding cognitive insult to perceived injury.

We studied the ability of college undergraduates to use reappraisal in both these ways and found robust activity in prefrontal control regions, whether they were using reappraisal to turn up or turn down their negative emotion (Ochsner et al. 2004). This suggests that there is a common neural machinery we use to generate and maintain cognitive frames for or cognitive appraisals of situations and that these frames/appraisals critically determine our emotional response. This can be seen both in participants' self-reports of how negative they felt, which went up or down according to their reappraisal goal, and in changes in amygdala activity, which also went up or down in accordance with the reappraisal goal.

This same basic prefrontal-amygdala dynamic that we and others have found holds across a variety of reappraisal contexts (for reviews see Ochsner and Gross 2005; 2007; 2008). For present purposes, the most interesting is when you perceive an ostensibly neutral event but imagine the worst about it. To study this tendency to cognitively generate negative emotions, we asked participants to tell negative stories about images that on average most people would have said were neutral (Ochsner et al., under review). Here again, we see the basic prefrontal-amygdala dynamic: prefrontal regions involved in the controlled generation of a reappraisal activation led people to feel unpleasant and to show activation in the amygdala where otherwise there would have been none.

For the fourth and final example, let us consider what happens when you are trying to reappraise your own life experiences. The ability to reappraise life events is, of course, critically important to our long-term mental and physical well-being. Ethan Kross and Ozlem Ayduk studied this ability by asking participants to recollect a series of unpleasant personal memories of times they had been distraught about the loss of a loved one, upset about a breakup, and so on (Kross and Ayduk 2008). For some of the memories, participants were instructed to relive them from the first-person perspective, as if they were reliving the event as seen through their own eyes. When using this immersion strategy, emotional responses were particularly strong. For other memories, participants were asked to recollect the memory from the perspective of a third-person observer, watching themselves in the event as if they were a video camera. This distancing strategy diminished negative affect significantly. In the final condition, participants were instructed to recollect their unpleasant memories and then distract themselves with unrelated thoughts. This distraction strategy also diminished negative affect significantly. These data suggest that either distancing or distraction can be effective for reducing unpleasant emotion in the short term. But things look a little bit different one week later. When feelings about the event are reassessed after a one-week delay, negative feelings continue to be lower only for the memories that were recollected in the distancing condition. Critically, distraction had no long-term benefit. When those memories were recollected again, they elicited negative feelings that were just as strong as if participants had never attempted to regulate their responses to them.

In recent work I have conducted with Ethan Kross (Kross et al., forthcoming), we have found that this method of distancing oneself from unpleasant memories depends on the same kinds of prefrontal systems described earlier, but differs importantly from the studies discussed above in one way: recollecting a highly self-relevant and unpleasant memory activated not the amygdala, but rather a portion of the brain known as the subgenual anterior cingulate cortex (sgACC). This is a cortical region that lies directly underneath (hence the "sub") the genu (the front part) of the corpus callosum (the fiber bundle connecting the two hemispheres of your brain). The sgACC is known to be dysfunctional in depression, although its specific functional role in human behavior has remained somewhat elusive. The behavioral and imaging work we have done on regulating responses to personal experiences has shown that activity in this region tracks with the strength of one's negative emotion during recollection. In combination with clinical research suggesting that cognitive strategies are one of the most effective treatments for depression, these data highlight the power of cognitive reappraisal for buffering us against negative emotion in the short term so that we do not develop long-term emotional disorders such as depression.

Implications

Let's end by taking a step back and considering three important big-picture implications of the research we've described.

The first is the power that comes from realizing that our emotions are defined by the way we appraise the meaning of situations. The fact that emotional responses are fundamentally interpretations enables us to take control of this interpretive process, to reappraise the meaning of emotional events, and thereby take control of our emotional lives. This fact highlights the distinction between your reaction to a situation and what the situation actually is. Or put another way, if someone's actions make you angry, it doesn't necessarily mean their actions will always provoke anger in you or anyone else—you interpreted them at that moment in such a way that you became angry, and you or others might not interpret them that way again. Plus, emotional reactions to the same ostensive event may vary across time and across individuals as a function of our goals, wants, and needs.

In the extreme, an inability to separate one's interpretation of a situation from the situation itself is a hallmark of certain forms of psychopathology, such as borderline personality disorder, in which a person has a tendency to think of people and events in the world solely in terms of their emotional impact on him or her.

The second implication follows from the first. If how you appraise the meaning of something determines how you respond to it and that appraisal is not constant and can vary across individuals, then we should be aware of the factors that determine these appraisals. As a case in point, consider the famous Pepsi challenge from the 1970s, which asked consumers to taste samples of Coke and Pepsi. When the samples were given in unmarked containers, Pepsi was preferred, in part because it is sweeter. When the samples were given in marked containers, Coke was preferred, in part because it has greater brand cachet. This is a classic example of how effective marketing can control your appraisals.

Appraisals controlled by marketing can be much more consequential than those that determine our preference for a canned soft drink. The placebo effect in medicine, for example, accounts for a large percentage of the efficacy of any drug, presumably due to your belief that it should help change something—your headache, your itch, or what have you. Imaging research conducted by Tor Wager has shown that the brain regions involved in maintaining the belief that a placebo is effective are very much like those used when people reappraise. In both cases, activity in regions of prefrontal cortex determine your emotional or placebo response. The difference is that in the case of reappraisal, the beliefs come from within, whereas in the case of the placebo, the beliefs come from without.

This suggests that you need to be mindful of who controls the nature of your appraisals; for example, do not give away your power over them to marketers or others who might want to control your emotional responses—such as politicians. Politicians call the control over your appraisal "spin," and they are masters at it. The late Susan Sontag wrote a book about this, *Regarding the Pain of Others*, in which she recounts the ways in which politicians have used spin during wartime to control the public's reaction to the horrors of war. Her message, like mine, is simple: be the controller of your appraisals rather than letting them be controlled for you.

Finally, it's important to recognize that the knowledge that one can take control over one's own emotional life comes with the responsibility to use this power and to use it wisely. The consequence of failing to successfully reappraise or to effectively implement any of the other regulatory strategies described are both personal and societal. On the personal level, you will experience greater stress and your mental and physical well-being will take a hit. Repeated failures compound the problem and can lean to long-term psychological and physical health problems, ranging from anxiety and depression to diabetes and cardiovascular disease. On the societal level, the costs of caring for those who have failed to regulate themselves effectively are certainly financial, but they are experiential as well. As the experiment on the social consequences of suppression suggests, when we fail to use the most adaptive emotion-regulation strategy, that failure is felt by others. The toll on human welfare taken by unchecked anger, stress, and fear cannot be measured in dollars alone.

This toll is perhaps greatest for the youngest among us. On the one hand, children who are the victims of impoverished environments or emotional and physical abuse may suffer self-regulatory problems throughout their life. On the other hand, society may not do enough to prepare children for the emotion-regulation obstacles they face. Few programs exist at the national level to help promote self-regulatory capacities and emotional awareness. And yet the presence of these capacities in young children has been shown to predict important life outcomes in adulthood. This has been shown convincingly in the work of Walter Mischel, who conducted studies of self-regulation in Bing nursery school at Stanford University in the 1960s.

Mischel presented children with a simple delay-of-gratification dilemma. Each child sat at a table on which was placed a Styrofoam tray. On this tray was placed an assortment of cookies, marshmallows, or other tempting treats. The experimenter, who was sitting across the table, informed the child that in a few minutes they would play a game. But first the experimenter needed to leave the room for a few minutes. While she was gone, the child was to not eat any of the treats. If he or she could refrain indulging until the experimenter returned, the child would be allowed to have two treats. But if the child could not wait, he or she could eat one treat, as long as the child rang a bell (that also was sitting on the table) to alert the experimenter in the next room that a treat had been eaten. Mischel and his colleagues simply measured the amount of time a child could wait before taking the treat. They then continued to follow these children for the next 40 years, measuring various measures of life success, including education, income, substance abuse (or lack thereof), quality of personal relationships, and so on.

Even after accounting for differences in age, education, and economic status of the children and their parents, the simple amount of time a child could wait before taking a treat strongly correlated with these measures of adult attainment. What this suggests is that children's capacity to self-regulate, which is probably a combination of temperament and social learning from their environment, likely determines their capacity to deal with life stressors, to roll with life's proverbial punches, and ultimately to be successful no matter what obstacles life puts in their way.

Imagine how many more children could delay gratification for longer periods—and by extension experience greater life success—if only there were effective programs to train them from an early age to understand the nature of their emotional responses and to regulate them effectively. Now imagine the consequences of failing to have such programs. Clearly, the onus is on all of us to not only regulate our own emotions but to help each other—and our children—regulate theirs.

References

Butler, E. A., Egloff, B., Wilhelm, F. H., Smith, N. C., Erickson, E. A., and Gross, J. J. 2003. "The Social Consequences of Expressive Suppression." *Emotion* 3(1): 48–67.

Craig, A. D. 2002. "How Do You Feel? Interoception: The Sense of the Physiological Condition of the Body." *Nature Reviews Neuroscience* 3(8): 655–666.

Goldin, P. R., McRae, K., Ramel, W., and Gross, J. J. 2008. "The Neural Bases of Emotion Regulation: Reappraisal and Suppression of Negative Emotion." *Biological Psychiatry* 63(6): 577–586.

Gross, J. J. 1998. "The Emerging Field of Emotion Regulation: An Integrative Review." *Review of General Psychology* 2: 271–299.

Kross, E., and Ayduk, O. 2008. "Facilitating Adaptive Emotional Analysis: Distinguishing Distanced-Analysis of Depressive Experiences from Immersed-Analysis and Distraction." *Personality and Social Psychology Bulletin* 34(7): 924–938.

Kross, E., Davidson, M., Weber, J., and Ochsner, K. N. (forthcoming). "Coping with Emotions Past: The Neural Bases of Regulating Affect Associated with Negative Autobiographical Memories." *Biological Psychiatry* 65: 361–366.

Lazarus, R. S. 1991. *Emotion and Adaptation*. Oxford, UK: Oxford University Press.

LeDoux, J. E. 2000. "Emotion Circuits in the Brain." *Annual Review Neuroscience* 23: 155–184.

Ochsner, K. N., and Barrett, L. F. 2001. "A Multiprocess Perspective on the Neuroscience of Emotion." In *Emotions: Current Issues and Future Directions*, edited by T. J. Mayne and G. A. Bonanno, 38–81. New York: Guilford.

Ochsner, K. N., and Gross, J. J. 2005. "The Cognitive Control of Emotion." *Trends in Cognitive Sciences* 9(5): 242–249.

Ochsner, K. N., and Gross, J. J. 2007. "The Neural Architecture of Emotion Regulation." In *The Handbook of Emotion Regulation*, edited by J. J. Gross and R. H. Thompson, 87–109. New York: Guilford.

Ochsner, K. N., and Gross, J. J. 2008. "Cognitive Emotion Regulation: Insights from Social Cognitive and Affective Neuroscience." *Currents Directions in Psychological Science* 17(1): 153–158.

Ochsner, K. N., Ray, R., Hughes, B., McRae, K., Cooper, J., Weber, J., et al. (under review). "Bottom-Up and Top-Down Processes in Emotion Generation." *Psychological Science*.

Ochsner, K. N., Ray, R. D., Cooper, J. C., Robertson, E. R., Chopra, S., Gabrieli, J. D. E., et al. 2004. "For Better or for Worse: Neural Systems Supporting the Cognitive Down- and Up-Regulation of Negative Emotion." *Neuroimage* 23(2): 483–499.

Phelps, E. A. 2006. "Emotion and Cognition: Insights from Studies of the Human Amygdala." *Annual Review of Psychology* 57: 27–53.

Scherer, K. R., Schorr, A., and Johnstone, T., eds. 2001. *Appraisal Processes in Emotion: Theory, Methods, Research*. New York: Oxford University Press.

This chapter is an edited version of a presentation delivered at the North American NeuroLeadership Summit, New York City, October 29, 2008.

10. The brain's braking system (and how to "use your words" to tap into it)

Dr. Matthew Lieberman
Matthew Lieberman, Associate Professor, UCLA Department of Psychology, California, USA
lieber@ucla.edu

Introduction

"I dragged myself out of bed." "I made myself go to the gym." "I kept my cool and did not yell at my boss (even though I really wanted to)." Our capacity for self-control is unquestionably one of the things that separates humans from beasts, and yet, like most psychological capacities, it is typically taken for granted. This capacity is unique, complex, and responsible for most human accomplishments being accomplishments instead of half-baked ideas that never leave the drawing board. Self-control allows us to persist in the face of other appealing options and to adapt, rather than be slaves to our impulses.

Self-control may also get you into the college of your choice. In the 1970s, Walter Mischel ran a series of studies in which he confronted young children with a straightforward dilemma: "You can have one marshmallow now or any time before I return by ringing this bell, or you can wait until I return and I'll give you two marshmallows." There are adorable videos of the children doing everything they can to resist chowing down the one marshmallow that is already sitting in front of them. Just like adults, children logically know that two is better than one, and so they want to wait it out. But you can see they are fighting against something: themselves. And whoever wins this battle of the selves (the self who wants immediate gratification versus the self who appreciates the big picture) has real consequences. Those children who were able to wait the full 15 minutes went on to score more than 200 points higher on their SATs a decade later than those who immediately gobbled up the first marshmallow. Self-control at age five sets you on a career to greater or lesser success for the rest of your life.

Motor self-control and perspective-taking self-control are as different as can be, and yet both of these rely on the same neural mechanism.

At first blush, the kind of self-control needed to resist marshmallows seems very different from the kind of self-control involved in performing well on standardized tests. However, neuroscientists are demonstrating how disparate forms of self-control all rely on a common neural mechanism. Indeed, the kinds of self-control that depend on this system vary much more widely than the marshmallow and SAT cases. Imagine driving in a foreign country where they drive on the opposite side of the road. It takes enormous motor self-control to override your normal driving habits. At the other extreme of the self-control spectrum, imagine watching a sporting event with someone who is rooting for the team you are rooting against. Trying to accept this person's perspective on the event also involves great self-control as you attempt to inhibit your own way of seeing things. Motor self-control and perspective-taking self-control are as different as can be, and yet both of these rely on the same neural mechanism.

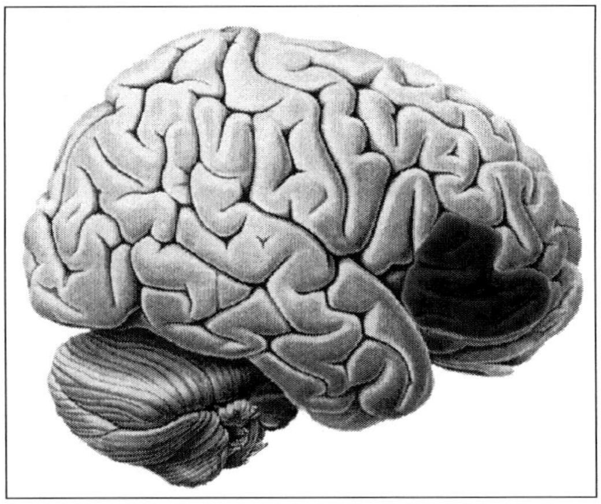

Figure 1. The anatomical outlines of right ventrolateral prefrontal cortex (RVLPFC)

The rest of this chapter consists of three sections. First, I will discuss the region that is common to various forms of self-control, a brain region called right ventrolateral prefrontal cortex (RVLPFC), and summarize some of the evidence demonstrating this region's contribution. Second, I will explore an unexpected consequence of this region's role in the brain's braking system in a study from our lab, which suggests that when we try to engage in a targeted form of self-control (e.g., motor self-control), we may unintentionally induce self-control in other domains (e.g., emotional self-control) because the brain's braking system will regulate all kinds of impulses when it is active. Third, I will discuss how putting feelings into words can unintentionally tap into this RVLPFC self-control system, and how certain forms of mental training, such as meditative practice, can improve the effectiveness of this system. From my own perspective, the first section highlights something that fMRI does particularly well: it shows that psychological processes that feel quite different from one another can share a common neural bases. This sets up and helps explain the interesting but paradoxical phenomena that follow.

Varieties of self-control

As I discuss each kind of self-control, bear in mind that there are always networks of brain regions involved. My main point is simply that the RVLPFC is the one brain region that seems to be present across all the different kinds of self-control.

Motor self-control

The neural basis of self-control has been studied most extensively in the domain of motor self-control. Anytime your body seems to "want" to do one thing but you know you need to do another, that's motor self-control. Driving on the opposite side of the road in foreign countries is certainly one kind of self-control, but scientists use a much simpler analog of this to study motor self-control within the confines of an MRI scanner. Typically, neuroscientists will use some variant of a go/no-go task.

In a typical go/no-go task, participants see a series of letters appear on the computer screen one at a time (i.e., each letter replaces the one that was there before it). They are instructed to hit a button for any letter that appears other than one particular letter (e.g., "R"). These are the go trials, and usually 80% or more of the trials in a go/no-go study are go trials. The letters occur about one every second, and so a participant gets into a rhythm of tapping the same button once a second. In other words, a button-pressing habit forms, and the brain's tendency to want to keep pressing the button is described as a prepotent response. Nearly all forms of self-control involve overriding some kind of prepotent response (i.e., a response the brain assumes should follow and thus is prepared to make), and in motor self-control this is certainly the case. This is where the no-go trials come in. Every so often (but not too often), the "R" appears, and the participant is instructed to *not* press a button when this happens. For the participant doing the task, this feels decidedly like withholding a response—the prepotent response that was all ready to go.

Anytime your body seems to "want" to do one thing but you know you need to do another, that's motor self-control.

This task and others that are conceptually similar (e.g., stop-signal task) have now been examined dozens of times with fMRI. Results do vary a bit from study to study, but the one near constant across these studies is that RVLPFC is more active during no-go trials (when self-control is needed) than during go trials. Other regions have certainly been observed as well, including left ventrolateral prefrontal cortex (PFC), supplementary motor area, and basal ganglia.

Demonstrating that particular brain regions are active during a particular form of self-control is important, but it does not tell us whether those brain regions are actually doing anything necessary to have successful self-control occur. Examining patients with brain damage—lesions to particular brain structures—can help remedy this situation. Adam Aron conducted the best neuropsychological study of motor self-control to date to figure out what brain structures are truly necessary for motor self-control. Aron and colleagues (2003) examined behavior performance on a stop-signal task in a variety of patients with damage in different brain regions. The extent of damage in different brain regions was related to performance on the motor self-control task, but only damage in the RVLPFC predicted impaired performance on the task. No other damage in the brain was associated with task impairment. Thus, the evidence for RVLPFC involvement in motor self-control is clear and uncontroversial. It shows up in nearly every fMRI study and is the one region that has been causally linked to motor self-control deficits in patients with brain damage.

Cognitive self-control

There are fewer studies of cognitive self-control than of motor self-control. During cognitive self-control, individuals try to modulate their own thoughts in terms of what does or does not come to mind, or try to influence how one thought or belief might influence other cognitive processes that logically should be kept separate. At this point we can say that a number of these studies, though not all, suggest RVLPFC involvement in cognitive forms of self-control.

In one study (Mitchell et al. 2007), participants were instructed to try not to think of a white bear. This turned out to be a very challenging task (try it!), but while participants were doing this, rather than engaging in free thinking, they generated increased activity in the RVLPFC. Similarly, in another study (Depue, Curran, and Banich 2007), individuals learned to associate pairs of pictures together and later were shown one picture and asked not to think of the other; their success at this was associated with RVLPFC activity.

In a different kind of study, Goel and Dolan (2003) examined the capacity to inhibit a belief in order to provide the logical answer to a question. In their study, participants were shown syllogisms and had to indicate whether the conclusion logically followed from the premises. Critically, a conclusion can logically follow from the premises even if the premises are not actually true. For instance, suppose you were shown the syllogism: (1) only expensive things are addictive, (2) cigarettes are inexpensive, (3) therefore, cigarettes are not addictive. Logically, the conclusion follows from the premises, even though the first premise is false. To answer this question accurately, one must suppress the belief that the conclusion is factually false. When individuals in the study were able to suppress their belief and provide the correct answer regarding the logical flow of the argument, the only brain region that demonstrated increased activity was the RVLPFC.

During cognitive self-control, individuals try to modulate their own thoughts in terms of what does or does not come to mind...

Financial self-control

Adults are quite good at passing Mischel's marshmallow test; however, they fail an analogous test easily. In studies of temporal discounting, individuals indicated whether they would prefer to receive $10 right now or $15 in a month. In these studies, individuals reliably preferred the smaller, sooner reward to the larger, later reward, even when the best possible returns on one's investment could not match the increased financial benefit of waiting for the later reward.

The first neuroimaging study to examine temporal discounting (McClure et al. 2004) observed increased activity in the RVLPFC when individuals selected the larger, later reward, presumably inhibiting the impulse to take the immediate reward. A subsequent study (Boettiger et al. 2007) created an index for each participant based on their overall tendency to take one kind of reward or the other. In this study, the only region associated with the tendency to take the larger, later reward was the RVLPFC. Although there have only been a few studies on financial self-control, they suggest that the RVLPFC plays a key role.

Emotional self-control

Emotional self-control is more typically described as emotion regulation and, along with motor self-control, is one of the most researched forms of self-control, both behaviorally and neurally. People use several different strategies to regulate their emotions, including distraction, detachment, reappraisal, and suppression (Ochsner and Gross 2008). Across the few dozen neuroimaging studies that have been conducted, three regions are pretty reliably associated with attempts at emotion regulation and the success of those attempts: RVLPFC, left ventrolateral PFC, and dorsomedial PFC. In one review of this literature (Berkman and Lieberman 2009), the RVLPFC was found to be most frequently associated with emotion-regulation processes.

Perspective-taking self-control

In some ways, the self-control involved in certain forms of perspective taking is the most intriguing form of self-control to consider. It is intriguing because it is so different from the others forms of self-control and could easily be forgotten as a form of self-control. A good deal of perspective taking does not involve self-control, but at least one relatively common form of perspective taking does. Self-control is involved when you, the perspective taker, have a competing perspective with the person you are trying to take the perspective of.

The data on this is still very sparse, with the main finding coming from a single study with a patient who has selective damage to the RVLPFC. This patient was tested on various forms of perspective taking, and its clear that his basic capacity for perspective taking was intact. However, when the patient had his own immediate perspective on something that needed to be inhibited in order to appreciate someone else's perspective that differed from his own, he was at a loss. For instance, if he was told that two people were watching a soccer match, with Ben rooting for Team A while Dan rooted for Team B, he had no problem at all identifying how each would feel after Team A scored a goal—as long as he had no stake in the outcome. If it turned out that Team A was the team he himself roots for, he then mistakenly believed that both Ben and Dan would feel the same way he feels when Team A scores. So he could engage in perspective taking, but only if it did not require setting aside his own perspective on things. Given that his damage is almost exclusively to the RVLPFC, this is important evidence that the RVLPFC is involved in this rather abstract form of self-control.

A recent fMRI study backs up the results of the patient study. In this new study, participants looked at images of needles or cotton swabs being applied to another person's hand. The needles looked like they would hurt, whereas the cotton swabs did not. However, on some trials of the experiment, participants were told that the hand was anesthetized and thus the needle would not hurt, and on other trials participants were told that the cotton swabs contained a chemical that would be painful to the skin. So on most trials, one's own perspective was aligned with and would not compete with the target's—needles hurt and cotton swabs do not. However, on some trials, the participants needed to inhibit their own immediate response to be able to empathize with those receiving the painful cotton swab and to not be so concerned over the needle going into the anesthetized hand. On these latter trials, RVLPFC activity increased. In other words, when participants needed to inhibit their own prereflective responses to appreciate another's perspective, they recruited the same brain region involved in all the other forms of self-control we have considered.

The brain's braking system

The results across all of these domains of self-control clearly point to the RVLPFC as a hub involved in virtually every form of self-control, no matter how different the forms of self-control feel or how distinct the demands necessary to achieve self-control in each. Consequently, it is appropriate to refer to the RVLPFC as the brain's braking system. As I mentioned earlier, while different brain regions are involved in each type of self-control, only the RVLPFC seems to be involved in every identified form of intentional self-control.

The results across all of these domains of self-control clearly point to the RVLPFC as a hub involved in virtually every form of self-control...

If this account is correct, it suggests that each time we engage in self-control, we are activating a system that might cause several kinds of self-control simultaneously. Turning on this system might put the brakes on any prepotent responses or cognitions that are currently active. Of course, this is not how self-control feels. When we try to inhibit one of our responses, it feels like we target just that response to be controlled and others are unaffected. Elliot Berkman, Lisa Burklund, and I (2009) conducted a study to find out what was really happening.

In our study, participants performed a go/no-go task similar to the ones described earlier. In some trials, participants were trying to inhibit a motor response, and in others they were not. Instead of using letters to cue go and no-go trials, we used faces: in any block of trials, one gender was the go cue and other gender was the no-go cue. Critically, the faces were emotionally expressive and thus likely to produce limbic activity (e.g., amygdala activity). At no time were participants trying to inhibit their emotional response to the pictures, and the emotionality of the pictures had nothing to do with the go/no-go task (i.e., paying attention to the emotions would not help a participant figure out if the trial was a go or no-go trial). Nevertheless, when participants saw a no-go cue that happened to include a negative emotional expression, their attempt at inhibiting their motor response produced an unintentional side effect—their amygdala response to the negative expression was also inhibited. Moreover the magnitude of the amygdala decrease was associated with the magnitude of the RVLPFC response during motor inhibition.

Thus, even though participants felt as if they were only inhibiting a motor response, they unintentionally inhibited their emotional response as well. This finding makes perfect sense if the RVLPFC is a common mechanism in the brain's braking system. Turning on the braking system for any reason is likely to have broad self-control effects beyond the particular response one is hoping to inhibit.

Putting feelings into words turns on the brakes

If turning on the brain's braking system can have effects beyond those intended, then perhaps turning on the braking system completely by accident could set self-control processes in motion as well.

Using your words

Parents and teachers have long told children to "use your words" because it is assumed that helps calm the child down when he or she is overly emotional or overaroused. It turns out this is surprisingly good advice.

Putting feelings into words turns on the brain's braking system.

We conducted a study (Lieberman et al. 2007) in which we showed emotional pictures to participants. Sometimes they were asked to choose an emotion word that described the target's emotion (affect labeling), sometimes they chose a gender-appropriate name (gender labeling), and sometimes they just looked at the picture (observe). What we found is that a single region of the brain, the RVLPFC, was more active during affect labeling compared with gender labeling (see fig. 2). In other words, putting feelings into words turns on the brain's braking system.

Indeed we also found evidence that affect labeling led to self-control effects. When people engaged in affect labeling, RVLPFC activity increased, but activity throughout the limbic system in general and in the amygdala in particular diminished. Putting feelings into words diminished participants' emotional responses to emotional pictures, even though putting feelings into words involves attending to the emotional aspects of the pictures. This is a paradoxical result, but it makes sense once we understand the role of the RVLPFC in the brain's braking system and in putting feelings into words. In the absence of this neural connection, such results sound a bit magical, but neuroscience allows us to the see the brain's trick behind the magic.

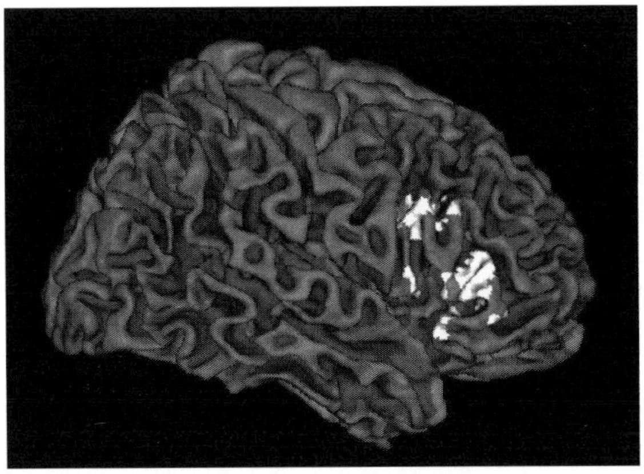

Figure 2. RVLPFC activity during affect labeling

Unintentional emotion regulation

The affect-labeling data suggests that putting feelings into words is a form of emotion regulation. The problem with this account is that affect labeling does not feel like emotion regulation. When you try to suppress your emotions, you know you are doing it—it is quite conscious. Although people sometimes put their feelings into words in order to generate new insights and improve their emotional well-being, we often put our feelings into words without any expectation that mere affect labeling will have an emotional benefit. Indeed, in three studies now (Lieberman et al., under review) we have found that people predict that looking at an emotionally evocative image will be more distressing if they are asked to label it. This has led us to conclude that affect labeling is a form of unintentional emotion regulation.

Learning to use your words

Can we learn to regulate our emotions better through "using our words"? The evidence suggests that we already do as we go through the preschool years. As students improve in their ability and tendency to use emotional words to describe their feelings, they evidence fewer emotional outbursts and gain a range of benefits, from classroom popularity to better academic performance (after statistically controlling for general language improvements).

What about us adults? Can we make meaningful strides in this area? There is only a little bit of data in this area, but the results are promising. We have been examining whether mindfulness meditative practice can increase the neurocognitive benefits of putting feelings into words. Mindfulness involves a nonjudgmental awareness of what one is thinking, feeling, and experiencing, which bears some strong resemblances to affect labeling. In our first study (Creswell et al. 2007), we found that those who report being higher in dispositional mindfulness showed greater RVLPFC activity and less amygdala activity while affect labeling, compared with those reporting being lower in dispositional mindfulness. We are following this up in a second study during which we are providing mindfulness training to individuals who are not experienced in this form of meditation, and thus far it appears that those getting the training are showing increased RVLPFC activity from pre- to posttraining, whereas those not getting the training are not showing increases.

Conclusions

In this review, we have examined work that together suggests that the RVLPFC is a central part of the brain's braking system, supporting self-control in its various forms. Neuroscience makes an important contribution here because the different forms of self-control feel so different from one another that it would be easy to assume the underlying processes supporting self-control in each case have little in common. We have also demonstrated evidence suggesting that putting feelings into words serves as an unexpected gateway into the brain's braking system, setting self-control processes in motion without the individual intentionally trying to engage in self-control.

The RVLPFC is a central part of the brain's braking system, supporting self-control in its various forms.

Lastly, we have found some promising evidence that people can strengthen the impact of putting feelings into words through mindful meditative practice. Of course, we may just be scratching the surface. The fact that mindfulness training may produce benefits in no way means that this is the only route or the best route toward improving the functioning of this process. Nevertheless, it's important to find out that this process is malleable, allowing for future investigations to examine other ways in which the brain's braking system can be made to work to our benefit.

References

Aron, A. R., Fletcher, P. C., Bullmore, E. T., Sahakian, B. J., and Robbins, T. W. 2003. "Stop-Signal Inhibition Disrupted by Damage to Right Inferior Frontal Gyrus in Humans." *Nature Neuroscience* 6: 115–116.

Berkman, E. T., Burklund, L., and Lieberman, M. D. 2009. "Inhibitory Spillover: Intentional Motor Inhibition Produces Incidental Limbic Inhibition Via Right Inferior Frontal Cortex." *Neuroimage* 47: 705–712.

Berkman, E., and Lieberman, M. D. 2009. "Using Neuroscience to Broaden Emotion Regulation: Theoretical and Methodological Considerations." *Social and Personality Psychology Compass* 4(3): 475–493.

Boettiger, C. A., Mitchell, J. M., Tavares, V. C., Robertson, M., Joslyn, G., D'Esposito, M., and Fields, H. L. 2007. "Immediate Reward Bias in Humans: Fronto-Parietal Networks and a Role for the Catechol-O-Methyltransferase 158(Val/Val)genotype." *Journal of Neuroscience* 27(52): 14383–14391.

Creswell, D., Way, B., Eisenberger, N. I., and Lieberman, M. D. 2007. "Neural Correlates of Dispositional Mindfulness During Affect Labeling." *Psychosomatic Medicine* 69: 560–565.

Depue, B. E., Curran, T., and Banich, M. T. 2007. "Prefrontal Regions Orchestrate Suppression of Emotional Memories Via a Two-Phase Process." *Science* 317: 215–9.

Goel, V., and Dolan, R. J. 2003. "Reciprocal Neural Response Within Lateral and Ventral Medial Prefrontal Cortex During Hot and Cold Reasoning." *Neuroimage* 20: 4314–4321.

Lieberman, M. D., Eisenberger, N. I., Crockett, M. J., Tom, S., Pfeifer, J. H., and Way, B. M. 2007. "Putting Feelings into Words: Affect Labeling Disrupts Amygdala Activity to Affective Stimuli." *Psychological Science* 18: 421–428.

Lieberman, M. D., Inagaki, T., Tabibnia, G., and Crockett, M. J. (under review). "Affect Labeling is a Form of Incidental Emotion Regulation: Subjective Experience During Affect Labeling, Reappraisal, and Distraction."

McClure, S. M., Laibson, D. I., Loewenstein, G., and Cohen, J. D. 2004. "Separate Neural Systems Value Immediate and Delayed Monetary Rewards." *Science* 306(5695): 503–507.

Mitchell, J. P., Heatherton, T. F., Kelley, W. M., Wyland, C. L., Wegner, D. M., and Neil Macrae, C. 2007. "Separating Sustained from Transient Aspects of Cognitive Control During Thought Suppression." *Psychological Science* 18(4): 292–297.

Ochsner, K. N. and Gross, J. J. 2008. "Cognitive Emotion Regulation: Insights from Social Cognitive and Affective Neuroscience." *Current Directions in Psychological Science* 17(1): 153–158.

11. The neuroscience of mindfulness

Dr. Yi-Yuan Tang[1,2,3,4] and Dr. Michael I. Posner[2]

[1]Institute of Neuroinformatics, Dalian University of Technology, Dalian, China

[2]Department of Psychology, University of Oregon, USA

[3]Institute of Psychology, the Chinese Academy of Sciences, Beijing, China

[4]Center for Social and Organizational Behavior, Graduate University of Chinese Academy of Sciences, Beijing, China

Introduction

Mindfulness is awareness of one's present thoughts, emotions, or actions. Right mindfulness (often also termed right meditation) involves bringing one's awareness back (i.e., from the past or the future) to the present moment. Recent studies indicated mindfulness meditation improves attention and self-regulation, which has the potential for stress reduction, well-being, performance improvement, and the like. The neural mechanism underlying mindfulness is not clearly known. This chapter focuses on recent research findings related to the neural basis of mindfulness. We take the Integrative Body-Mind Training (IBMT) as an example to explore possible brain mechanisms and their application. Future directions in the field are also addressed.

Mindfulness defined

More than a hundred years ago, the term "mindfulness" was translated from the Pali word "sati" by the British scholar T. H. Rhys Davids. This translation was derived from a Christian perspective (Thanissaro Bhikkhu 2002). However, mindfulness is understood in different ways depending on one's theoretical and practical viewpoint. For example, mindfulness can mean paying attention with purpose and in the present moment. Mindfulness may include strong self-awareness and self-observation, or "waking up" and seeing things as they are. But in our perspective, mindfulness is an experience rather than a precisely defined abstract concept. We are concerned about the essence and core of mindfulness and how to apply it in daily life, so we focus on the key points of mindfulness: awareness of the present, nonjudgment, and acceptance.

Right mindfulness (often also termed right meditation) involves bringing one's awareness back (i.e., from the past or the future) to the present moment. The mental process of mindfulness requires paying attention and self-regulation, and so it is reasonable to suggest that the underlying neural mechanism of mindfulness may involve similar brain regions and networks as these mental processes. Attention can be viewed as a system of anatomical areas that consists of three or more specialized networks. These networks carry out the functions of alerting, orienting, and executive control. Figure 1 illustrates what is known of the anatomy of attention networks. These three attention networks are involved in mindfulness practice, especially the executive control network. The executive control network plays a key role in resolving conflicting thoughts and thus maintaining a tranquil state in the often very restless mind.

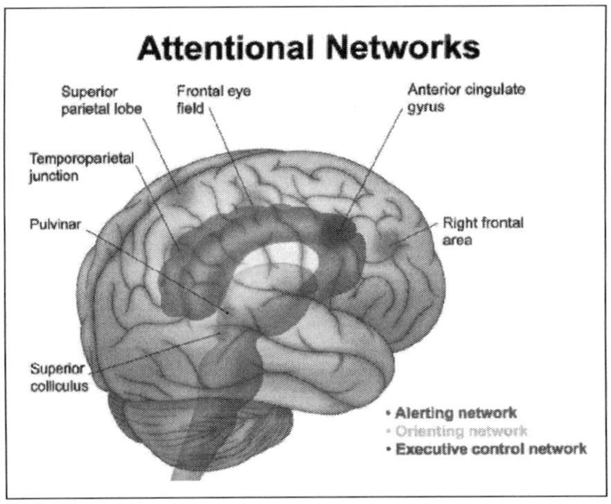

Figure 1. The anatomy of attention networks.

Brief review for possible brain mechanism of mindfulness

A previous study indicated that long-term meditators showed high-amplitude gamma-band oscillations and phase-synchrony of the EEG during meditation. These electroencephalogram patterns differ from those of controls, in particular over lateral fronto-parietal electrodes. This high level of gamma-band electrical activity may reflect brain regions becoming more interconnected during mindfulness meditation (Lutz et al. 2004). One recent study compared expert meditators (who had 10,000–54,000 hours of practice) with novices, who participated in meditation one hour per day by using three different techniques. Both groups showed activation of a large overlapping network of attention-related brain regions such as prefrontal, midfrontal, and parietal cortex. This result clearly demonstrated the involvement of attention changes after long-term mindfulness meditation practice (Brefczynski-Lewis et al. 2007).

The mental process of mindfulness requires paying attention and self-regulation...

The information-processing capacity of the human mind is limited. One source of evidence is the so-called "attentional blink." When two targets (T1 and T2) embedded in a rapid stream of events are presented in close temporal proximity, the second target is often not seen. This deficit is believed to result from competition between the two targets for limited attentional resources. A recent study compared an experimental group of people who'd had mindfulness meditation training with a control group with no training. The results indicated that three months of intensive mental training resulted in a smaller attentional blink and reduced brain-resource allocation to the first target, suggesting that mental training can result in increased control over the distribution of limited brain resources and cause an improvement in the executive attention network (Slagter et al. 2007). However, problems of subtle differences between control and experimental groups remain in the studies discussed above because the two groups were not completely randomly assigned, and meditators differed greatly in styles of meditation previously practiced.

What do the perception of pain, either physical (Rainville et al. 1997) or social (Eisenberger et al. 2003), processing of reward (Hampton and O'Doherty 2007), monitoring of conflict (Botvinick et al. 2001), error detection (Dehaene et al. 1994), and theory of mind (Kampe et al. 2003) all have in common? They all activate an area of midfrontal cortex that includes the anterior cingulate cortex (ACC). Is there a single function that requires all these important input signals? We have argued that the role of this brain area is to regulate the processing of information from other networks, serving as a part of an executive attention network involved in the control of both cognition and emotion. Executive attention is a brain network that includes the ACC and is often activated in adult studies by requiring a person to withhold a dominant response to perform a subdominant response (Posner and Rothbart 2007a; 2007b). In developmental psychology, the ability to control our thoughts, feelings, and behavior is called self-regulation. This self-regulatory perspective helps us understand how brain networks relate to important real-life functions.

We believe that self-regulation is a natural function of brain networks, designed to control the influx of information from the environment through orienting, to avoid conflicting responses in behavior (Rueda et al. 2004). A good example is the Stroop effect, in which word reading is a highly overlearned response that must be ignored to respond with the conflicting ink color. Neuroimaging presents strong evidence that conflict tasks like the Stroop effect activate common areas of the anterior cingulate gyrus (Botvinick et al. 2001; Bush et al. 2000; Fan et al. 2003). Support for the voluntary exercise of self-regulation comes from studies that examined either the instruction to control affect or the connections involved in the exercise of that control. For example, being instructed to avoid arousal during processing of erotic events (Beauregard et al. 2001) or to ward off emotion when looking at negative pictures (Ochsner et al. 2001) produced a locus of activation in midfrontal and cingulate areas. If people were required to select an input modality, the cingulate showed functional connectivity to the selected sensory system (Crottaz-Herbette and Menon 2006). Similarly, when involved with emotional processing, the cingulate showed a functional connection to limbic areas (Etkin et al. 2006). These findings support the role of cingulate areas in the control of cognition and emotion. There is also evidence for anatomical connectivity between the ventral cingulate and limbic areas and the dorsal cingulate, parietal, and frontal areas (Posner et al. 2007).

Taken together, we argue that the ACC plays an important role in executive function and self-regulation during mindfulness practice.

The Integrative Body-Mind Training

To test this idea of the role of the ACC in mindfulness, we applied the Integrative Body-Mind Training (IBMT). IBMT was developed in the 1990s, and its effects have been studied in China since 1995. Based on results from hundreds of adults and children ranging in age from 4 to 90 years in China, IBMT practice improves emotional and cognitive performance and social behavior (Tang 2005; 2007; 2008). We randomly assigned 80 Chinese undergraduates to an experimental group or a control group (40 in each group). The experimental group was given 5 days of training in IBMT for 20 minutes per day, while the control group was given the same amount of time in muscle-relaxation training, which is very popular in the West.

The two groups were given a battery of tests one week before training and immediately after the final training session. The battery included the Attention Network Test (ANT), the Raven's Standard Progressive Matrix, the Profile of Mood States (POMS), and a stress challenge of a mental arithmetic task that was followed by measures of cortisol and secretory IgA (sIgA). The ANT (Fan et al. 2002) is a standard computerized attention test measured orienting, alerting, and the ability to resolve conflict (executive attention). The task involves responding to an arrow target surrounded by flankers that point in either the same or opposite direction. Cues provide information on when a trial will occur and where the target will be. The Raven's Standard Progressive Matrix is a standard culture fair intelligence test. The cortisol and sIgA test reflects the stress and immunoreactivity response to a three-minute arithmetic task. The ANT, Raven's, and cortisol and sIgA are standard assays scored objectively by people blind to the experimental condition.

The POMS is an assay of mood state, providing a self-report of a person's mood. The IBMT group showed a significantly greater improvement than the control group on the ANT conflict scores as shown in figure 2.

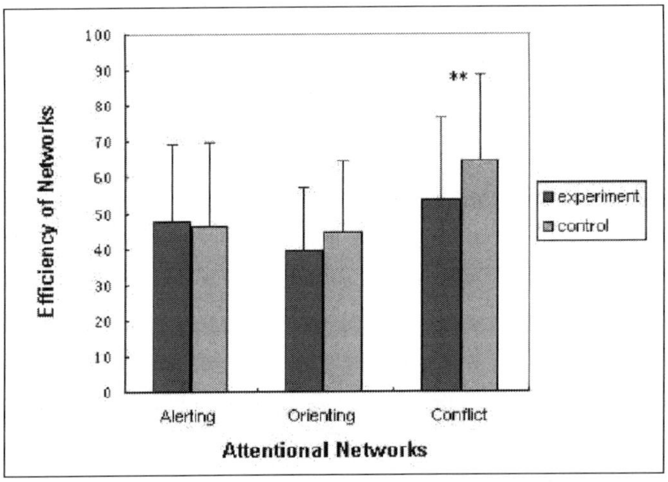

Figure 2. Performance of the ANT after 5 days of IBMT or control. Error bars indicate 1 SD. Vertical axis indicates the difference in mean reaction time between the congruent and incongruent flankers. The higher scores show less efficient resolution of conflict.

Because the efficiency of executive attention improved in the IBMT group, we expected better self-regulation of emotion. We compared the POMS scores of the experimental group to the control group and found lower anxiety, depression, anger, and fatigue, and higher vigor on the Profile of Mood States scale in the experimental group. The results indicated that short-term IBMT can enhance positive moods and reduce negative ones (see fig.3).

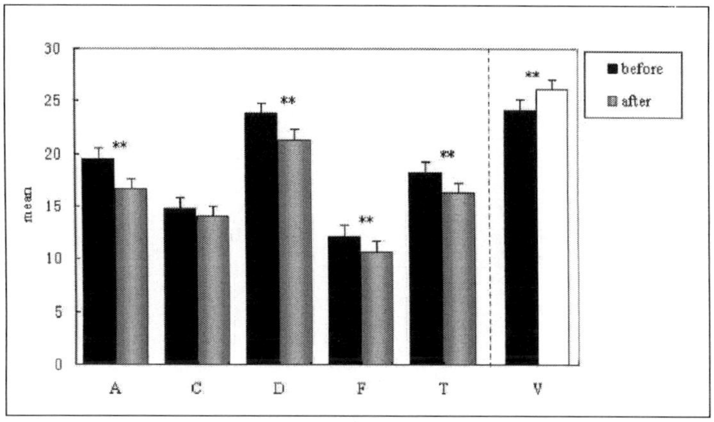

Figure 3. Comparison of six scales of the POMS before and after training for the experimental group. Black bar: five negative moods and one positive mood pretraining; gray bar: five negative moods posttraining; white bar: one positive mood posttraining. Significance was found in POMS scales of anger–hostility (A), depression–dejection (D), fatigue–inertia (F), tension–anxiety (T), and vigor–activity (V) posttraining in the experimental group. No significant difference was found in POMS scale C (confusion–bewilderment) posttraining.

We also tested the hypothesis that improvement of efficiency of attention accompanies higher intelligence scores. The result revealed that short-term IBMT can improve the Raven's score in the experimental group, although only marginally more so than in the control group.

We believe future research will help understand the underlying mechanism and enhance this type of mental training.

If self-regulation of emotion and cognition improved in the IBMT training group, members of the group should also show reduced reaction to stress as measured by cortisol and immunoreactivity. Cortisol and sIgA are indexes of the amount of stress induced by a cognitive challenge. We applied 3 minutes of mental arithmetic as an acute stress after 5 days of IBMT or relaxation. Compared with the relaxation group, the IBMT group showed a significant decrease in stress-related cortisol (fig. 4A) and an increase in immunoreactivity (fig. 4B).

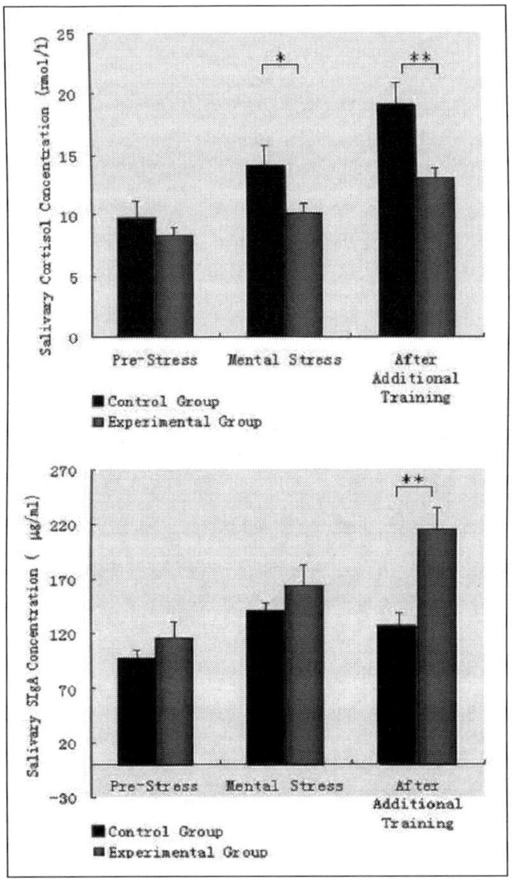

Figure 4. Physiological changes before and after stress. (A) Comparison of cortisol concentration between the experimental group (gray bars) and control group (black bars) in three different stages after 5 days of training. More cortisol secretion indicates higher levels of stress. (B) Comparison of sIgA concentration between experimental group (gray bars) and control group (black bars) at three different stages after 5 days of training. Higher immunoreactivity indicates a better response to stress. *, $P < 0.05$; **, $P < 0.01$. Error bars indicate 1 SEM.

Our latest neuroimaging results for healthy patients indicated more activation in midfrontal regions (ACC) in the IBMT group compared with the relaxation group after the same amount of training, which sheds light on the brain mechanism of IBMT (Tang et al., in process).

In summary, IBMT is an easy, effective way for improvement in attention and self-regulation in cognition, emotion, and social behavior. It may have implication in schools, workplace, and personal life. Our study indicated that attention, affective processes, and the quality of moment-to-moment awareness are flexible skills that can be trained.

Future directions

Although the meditation studies draw lots of attention and demonstrate training effects and possible neural mechanism, the neuroscientific study of meditation is still in its infancy. These findings will need to be supplemented with more data, most crucially from longitudinal studies examining changes over time within the same individuals randomized either to meditation training or to an active control group. Future work will need to address at least the following questions:

1. Which factors would help and facilitate the mindfulness? These may include appropriate attention and effort, optimal body-mind states, enjoyable attitude, and so on.
2. When is the critical period (i.e., age or length of training) for mindfulness practice? What are the critical ages (if any) for mindfulness training to have its greatest impact?
3. What is the optimal dose of particular types of meditation at different ages?
4. How are individual differences matched to meditation methods? Or how might gene and environment interactions affect the meditation practice?
5. What is the relationship between mindfulness and other states, such as flow and so on.
6. What are the peripheral biological consequences of different forms of meditation?

Mindfulness is not difficult; what's difficult is remembering to be mindful. Mindfulness meditation needs an open mind, patience, and acceptance. It's an experiential learning journey in which you must trust the process and listen your heart. We believe future research will help understand the underlying mechanism and enhance this type of mental training.

Acknowledgments

This work was supported by the Program for New Century Excellent Talents in University NCET-06-0277, National 863 Plan Project 2006AA02Z431 in China, and the James S. Bower Foundation.

References

Beauregard, M., Levesque, J., and Bourgouin, P. 2001. "Neural Correlates of Conscious Self-Regulation of Emotion." *Journal of Neuroscience* 21: RC165.

Brefczynski-Lewis, J. A., Lutz, A., Schaefer, H. S., Levinson, D. B., and Davidson, R. J. 2007. "Neural Correlates of Attentional Expertise in Long-Term Meditation Practitioners." *Proceedings of the National Academy of Sciences, USA* 104(27): 11483–11488.

Botvinick, M. M., Braver, T. S., Barch, D. M., Carter, C. S., and Cohen, J. D. 2001. "Conflict Monitoring and Cognitive Control." *Psychological Review* 108: 624–652.

Bush, G., Luu, P., and Posner, M. I. 2000. "Cognitive and Emotional Influences in Anterior Cingulate Cortex." *Trends in Cognitive Sciences* 4: 215–222.

Crottaz-Herbette, S., and Menon, V. 2006. "Where and When the Anterior Cingulate Cortex Modulates Attentional Response: Combined fMRI and ERP Evidence." *Journal of Cognitive Neuroscience* 18: 766–780.

Dehaene, S., Posner, M. I., and Tucker, D. M. 1994. "Localization of a Neural System for Error Detection and Compensation." *Psychological Science* 5 303–305

Eisenberger, N. I., Lieberman, M. D., and Williams, K. D. 2003. "Does Rejection Hurt? An fMRI Study of Social Exclusion." *Science* 302: 290–292.

Etkin, A., Egner, T., Peraza, D. M., Kandel, E. R., and Hirsch, J. 2006. "Resolving Emotional Conflict: A Role for the Rostral Anterior Cingulate Cortex in Modulating Activity in the Amygdala." *Neuron* 51: 871–882.

Fan, J., Flombaum, J. I., McCandliss, B. D., Thomas, K. M., and Posner, M. I. 2003. "Cognitive and Brain Consequences of Conflict." *Neuro Image* 18: 42–57.

Fan, J., McCandliss, B.D., Sommer, T., Raz, M., and Posner, M. I. 2002. "Testing the Efficiency and Independence of Attentional Networks." *Journal of Cognitive Neuroscience* 3(14): 340–343.

Hampton, A. N., and O'Doherty, J. P. 2007. "Decoding the Neural Substrates of Reward-Related Decision Making with Functional MRI." *Proceedings of the National Academy of Sciences, USA* 104: 1377–1382.

Kampe, K. K. W., Frith, C. D., and Frith, U. 2003. "'Hey John': Signals Conveying Communicative Intention Toward the Self-Activated Brain Regions Associated with "Mentalizing," Regardless of Modality." *Journal of Neuroscience* 23: 5258–5263.

Lutz, A., Slagter, H. A., Dunne, J. D., and Davidson, R. J. 2008. "Attention Regulation and Monitoring in Meditation." *Trends in Cognitive Sciences* 12(4): 163–169.

Ochsner, K. N., Kossyln, S. M., Cosgrove, G. R., Cassem, E. H., Price, B. H., Nierenberg, A. A., and Rauch, S. L. 2001. "Deficits in Visual Cognition and Attention Following Bilateral Anterior Cingulotomy." *Neuropsychologia* 39: 219–230.

Posner, M. I., and Rothbart, M. K. 2007a. *Educating the human brain*. Washington, DC: American Psychological Association.

Posner, M. I., and Rothbart, M. K. 2007b. "Research on Attention Networks as a Model for the Integration of Psychological Science." *Annual Review of Psychology* 58: 1–23.

Posner, M. I., Rothbart, M.K., Rueda, M. R., and Tang, Y-Y. (Forthcoming). "Training Effortless Attention. In Effortless Attention: A New Perspective in the Cognitive Science of Attention and Action."

Rainville, P., Duncan, G. H., Price, D. D., Carrier, B., and Bushnell, M. C. 1997. "Pain affect Encoded in Human Anterior Cingulate but not Somatosensory Cortex." *Science* 277: 968–971.

Tang, Y. Y., Ma, Y., Wang, J., Fan, Y., Feng, S., Lu, Q., Yu, Q., Sui, D., Rothbart, M. K., Fan, M., Posner, M. I. 2007. "Short-Term Meditation Training Improves Attention and Self-Regulation." *Proceedings of the National Academy of Sciences, USA* 104(43): 17152–17156.

Posner, M. I., Rothbart, M. K., Sheese, B. E., and Tang, Y. 2007. "The Anterior Cingulate Gyrus and the Mechanism of Self-Regulation." *Cognitive, Affective & Behavioral Neuroscience* 7(4): 391–395.

Slagter, H. A., Lutz, A., Greischar, L. L., Francis, A. D., Nieuwenhuis, S., Davis, J. M., and Davidson, R. J. 2007. "Mental Training Affects Distribution of Limited Brain Resources." *PLoS Biology* 5(6): e138.

Tang, Y. Y. 2005. *Health from Brain, Wisdom from Brain*. Dalian, China: Dalian University of Technology Press.

Tang, Y. Y. 2007. *Multi-Intelligence and Unfolding the Full Potential of Brain*. Dalian, China: Dalian University of Technology Press.

Tang, Y. Y. 2008. *Exploring the Brain, Optimizing the Life*. China: Science Press.

Thanissaro, Bhikkhu. 2002. *The Karma of Questions: Essays on the Buddhist Path*. Insight Edition. USA: Metta Forest Monastery.

Tang, Y. Y., Ma, Y. H., Feng, H. B., Hu, B., Lin, Y., and Fan, M. (In process). "Brain Mechanism for Short-Term Meditation Training."

About the authors

Dr. Yi-Yuan Tang is a professor in neuroscience; the director of Institute of Neuroinformatics, Dalian University of Technology, Dalian; adjunct professor in psychology of the Chinese Academy of Sciences; and adjunct professor in management of the Graduate University of Chinese Academy of Sciences, Beijing, China. He is currently a visiting professor (with Michael Posner) at the Department of Psychology, University of Oregon, USA.

Dr. Tang's research applies the tools of neuroimaging (fMRI, PET/SPECT, ERP), psychosocial and physiological measures, as well as genetic analysis, and covers the topics in cultural neuroscience, body-mind medicine, affective and social neuroscience, computational neuroscience, and neuroleadership. He is the founder of the Integrative Body-Mind Training (IBMT) and once trained many thousands of children and adults to improve their attention, self-regulation, and performance. Website: www.yi-yuan.net.

Dr. Michael I. Posner is professor emeritus at the University of Oregon and adjunct professor at the Weill Medical College in New York (Sackler Institute). He is a member of the National Academy of Sciences and the American Academy of Arts and Sciences.

Dr. Posner's outstanding research contributions to the nature of attention and related areas have been widely recognized. He has been one of the foremost figures in the endeavor of investigations of the human mind and its relation to the functions, and he has set in motion cognitive approaches to neuroscience that have resulted in a series of fundamental discoveries about mind and brain and made him one of the world leaders in this field. His recent work explores the interaction of genes and experience in normal and atypical development of attention and self-regulation.

12. Mindfulness, well-being, and performance

Dr. Craig Hassed, MBBS, FRACGP
Craig Hassed, Senior Lecturer, Department of General Practice, Victoria, Australia
craig.hassed@med.monash.edu.au

Introduction

Mindfulness is increasingly being promoted as a tool for maintaining health, improving performance, and treating serious illnesses including depression. An exponential increase in the level of interest among clinicians and researchers, particularly in the field of neuroscience, is certainly accelerating this process. This chapter establishes some background about stress and its effects on mind and body and then explores, scientifically, practically, and philosophically, how mindfulness might be used as a tool to promote well-being and optimal performance of mind and body.

Mental health today

Figures suggest that the stress of modern life is increasing rapidly. Some show a 45% increase over the last 30 years (Miller et al. 1997). Explanations could include an increased awareness about stress, people leading more stressful and busy lives, more people seeing happiness as being more dependent on material circumstances, and the level of change and instability in modern life. The answer is probably a combination of all these. If trends continue, mental health issues, particularly anxiety and depression, are predicted to be the single major burden of disease within the next two decades (Mathers et al. 2000). Chronic stress and anxiety are, of course, inextricably linked to mood and depression. This is reflected in the fact that stress reduces serotonin levels in the brain, the main neurotransmitter linked to mood (Porter et al. 2004). By the year 2030, it is predicted, depression will easily surpass the second major burden of disease—heart disease (Mathers et al. 2006).

Our modern pharmacological treatments of depression are all aimed at increasing the level of a neurotransmitter called serotonin in the brain. They are not aimed at changing thought or behavior patterns, and they have more limited success in treating depression and preventing relapse than many people think. When one reviews unpublished as well as published data on the effectiveness of antidepressants, it is found that the commonly used drugs to treat depression are no better than a placebo (Kirsch et al. 2008).

Stress response and effects on mind, brain, and body

To understand the mind-body relationship, it is best to take a metaphysical view. Awareness or consciousness is primary. Next is the mind, with its contents of thought and emotion. The mind uses awareness to empower and enliven thought and emotion. The physical manifestations are the end result of this creative process. Thus, if awareness is given to a happy thought, it produces one set of effects in the body and behavior; given to an angry thought, it produces another.

If meditation is defined as the focusing of attention on a particular thought or object, it may be said that the whole of humanity meditates on something or other. The only difference is what we "meditate" on. Unknowingly, we spend so much time meditating on resentment, anger, fear, depressive thoughts, and regrets. In principle, the physical body—and that includes the brain—will reflect or express whatever is going on in the mind, like the relationship between the driver and the car. The body has the capacity to increase performance when it needs to avert danger. We call this the "fight-or-flight response." This response is a natural, necessary, healthy, and appropriate physiological response to an exceptional and threatening situation—for example, if we were about to be attacked by a lion. In such instances, one needs to respond quickly. The response is aimed at preserving life. The physiological are described below.

Physiological changes associated with the fight or flight response:

- A surge of adrenaline leading to an elevation of blood pressure and heart rate aimed at increasing cardiac output to meet the challenge and also, in case of blood loss, to maintain circulation
- An increase in respiration—the intake of oxygen and removal of carbon dioxide—because of an anticipated increase in energy expenditure
- Mobilization of blood glucose and fats as fuel for this sustained energy expenditure
- An increase in sweating to assist with keeping the body cool while exerting itself
- Diversion of blood flow to muscles and away from the gut, with the gut's motility almost ceasing
- An increase in platelet adhesiveness, which means the blood becomes "stickier" to be better able to stop bleeding
- A short-term mobilization of white blood cells to protect the body if its defenses are breached
- Activation of inflammatory hormones (e.g., cortisol, cytokines, interleukins, etc.) that play a role in healing damaged tissues, including accelerating cell replication and laying down new blood vessels

These changes, activated appropriately based on a clearly perceived and significant threat and allowed to switch off when they are no longer needed, are, generally speaking, not damaging to the health. However, when activated inappropriately and frequently, these changes not only cause short-term anxiety-related problems but also become a significant risk factor for a range of chronic illnesses, including detrimental effects on the brain.

It is important to note that the brain will activate the response when told to by the mind; it does not matter if the stressor does not exist—that is, if the stressor exists only in our imagination. Thus, imagination, rumination, anticipation, exaggeration, and dreaming—all forms of misperception—can all activate the fight-or-flight response. In fact, in the vast majority of times we activate this response, it is based on one or other form of misperception: imagining things to be happening that aren't or perceiving things to be far larger threats than they are in reality.

The prolonged activation of the fight-or-flight response, mediated through the sympathetic nervous system, leads to physiological and neurological wear and tear called "allostatic load" (McEwen 2004). The brain is not static, as medical science once thought it to be. It can be wired and rewired (called neural plasticity) depending on how it is being used. This has implications for the promotion or reduction of stress. If we practice dwelling (meditating) on a particular thought, emotion, or desire, or if we reinforce a pattern of behavior by repeating it, the mind reinforces those neural circuits, like forming deeper and deeper ruts that are increasingly difficult to get out of. Although unhelpful thoughts, emotions, and behaviors can be wired in, it also means, from a therapeutic perspective, they can be wired out. It is much like programming and reprogramming a computer.

To understand the mind-body relationship, it is best to take a metaphysical view.

Prolonged allostatic load leads to a range of effects, including increased inflammation, impaired immunity (increased risk and severity of infections), accelerated atherosclerosis ("hardening of the arteries"), increased risk of type-2 diabetes, and increased bone demineralization (osteoporosis), and can also lead to atrophy or loss of nerve cells in some vulnerable regions of the brain that are targeted by stress hormones. These regions include the hippocampal formation (important for learning and memory) and the prefrontal cortex (the "frontal lobe" plays a role in working memory, decision making, reasoning, impulse control, and emotion regulation). Thus, chronic stress and depression are risk factors for chronic illness, poor performance, cognitive decline, and dementia. Mindfulness protects the brain from these damaging effects.

The level of emotional reactivity to events, thoughts, desires, and memories determines to a large extent the speed and degree to which this wiring takes place. Learning to be less automatically and habitually reactive to unhelpful thoughts, emotions, and impulses is possibly a prime way in which mindfulness helps to remodel the brain and thereby protect the body from the damaging effects of chronic stress and depression.

Importance of attention

How we develop our ability to pay attention is an important issue. Some people report that attention spans have steadily decreased in recent decades as the pace of life accelerates and the bombardment of rapid-fire banal and mind-numbing stimuli increases. Television watching in particular is not the best way to enhance our ability to pay attention. Apart from it being linked to ADHD in children, it also has cumulative effects on adults. Throughout one's life, the way we use our leisure time has an effect on cognitive decline. Those who have less than average diversity in leisure activities, spend less time on them, and practice more passive leisure activities (principally TV viewing) are nearly four times as likely to develop dementia over a forty-year follow-up, compared with those who rate higher than average on these parameters (Friedland et al. 2001; Scarmeas et al. 2001). "Among leisure activities, reading, playing board games, playing musical instruments, and dancing were associated with a reduced risk of dementia" (Verghese et al. 2003).

Attention has a number of facets: arousal, orientation, and focus (Carter 2002). The brain's "reticular activating system" activates relevant task-oriented parts of the brain and closes down unnecessary parts of brain activity (Kubota et al. 2001; Rees 1998). Thus the focused or alert brain is a relatively quiet brain. The peaceful but attentive state cultivated through mindfulness is different from what most people associate with relaxation—that is sleepy and inattentive. This meditative state is reflected in the term "restful alertness." When attention is aroused, other parts of the brain associated with orientation and focus activate, and these communicate with frontal lobes for higher-level decision making and appraisal. These attention centers are activated with concentration and meditative exercises (Lazar et al. 2000) and are also associated with down-regulating the stress response because attention is being diverted less to anxious rumination.

> *Throughout one's life, the way we use our leisure time has an effect on cognitive decline.*

Interestingly, it has recently been demonstrated through brain-scanning techniques (MRI) that cortical thickness (the "gray matter") in the brain regions associated with attention, interoception (being aware of oneself), and sensory processing (proprioception) are thicker in meditators than in nonmeditators. It seems that mindfulness looks to offset age-related cortical thinning and provides "evidence for experience-dependent cortical plasticity associated with meditation practice" (Lazar et al. 2005). This has been confirmed in subsequent studies. "The regular practice of meditation may have neuroprotective effects and reduce the cognitive decline associated with normal ageing" (Pagnoni et al. 2007). That means we may be able to change the brain anatomically and preserve many functions that are otherwise lost as a part of the aging process.

Stress and performance[1]

Stress is often used to motivate and to drive performance, and hence, many people are reluctant to reduce stress for fearing this will undermine productivity. As stress becomes habituated, and our awareness of it drops, our whole life can become pervaded by tension, even in the most mundane daily activities.

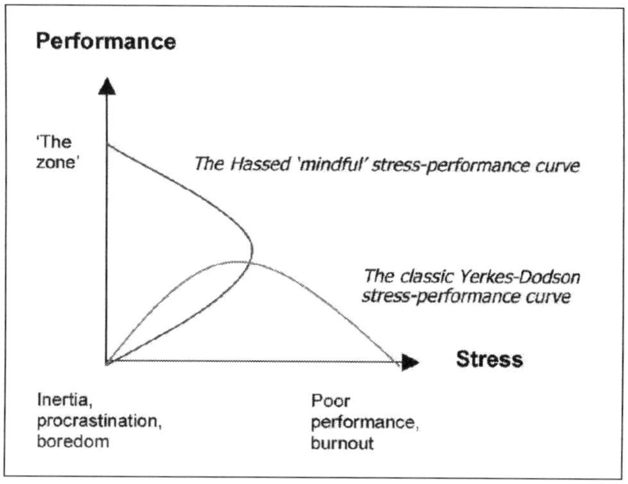

Figure 1

As the classic "stress-performance curve" illustrates, inertia, procrastination, or boredom are, initially at least, low-stress states—no stress means no performance. As stress increases, however, perhaps before an exam or at the approach of a deadline, performance tends to improve. If the stress is not too high or prolonged, then we tolerate the temporary increase in pressure and are able to maintain performance, albeit at a price. If, however, we are performing somewhere near the peak of this curve but the demands escalate further, then, having conditioned ourselves to driving performance with stress, we push harder. This presents the danger of running into more significant problems as stress escalates, especially since it has the effect of leading to a drop in performance. This is a "lose-lose" situation when, despite higher stress and energy expenditure, our performance starts to drop off rather than rise to a new level.

If this is prolonged, then sooner or later we burn out and are much more likely to make mistakes, as illustrated by studies on hospital-based medical staff. An Australian study found that 8 months into their intern year, 75% of interns qualified as having burnout (Willcock et al. 2004). Burnout is associated with such things as depersonalization, emotional exhaustion, lack of motivation, and little personal

[1] This section is adapted from the book *The Essence of Health* (Hassed 2008).

accomplishment. Burnout in demanding and responsible occupations is not an uncommon occurrence, nor is it a sign of being "weak"; but it may be a sign of a system that is not friendly to the people working in it, or of personal issues such as inattention, inefficiency, lack of self-awareness, and poor self-care. Another study of US hospital pediatric residents found that depressed doctors were six times more likely to make drug-prescribing errors than their nondepressed colleagues (Fahrenkopf et al. 2008). By contrast, "People who are put into a good mood select higher goals, perform better, and persist longer" (Marks et al. 1999). So self-care and promoting good mental health is as much an issue for those we serve as it is for our own well-being.

Taking the time to settle and focus before engaging in an activity is something that most people tend to ignore.

Anxiety leads to smaller working-memory spans. Working, otherwise known as short-term, memory relates to the brain structures and processes used for temporarily storing and manipulating information. It is not dissimilar to a computer's memory being used for working on documents on the desktop as opposed to what is stored on the hard disk. Specific parts of the brain responsible for working memory include the frontal cortex and the reticular activating system. ADHD is associated with impairment of the functioning of the frontal lobe, the same areas that are activated by attention training through mindfulness. Improving working memory helps increase IQ and treat ADHD (Klingberg et al. 2002), whereas reduced working memory capacity leads to a pronounced increase in reaction time and errors (Ashcraft et al. 2001). "Performance pressure harms individuals most qualified to succeed by consuming the working memory capacity that they rely on for their superior performance" (Beilock et al. 2005). Thus, the ability to maintain focus while under pressure is a vital skill when demands are high.

Taking the time to settle and focus before engaging in an activity is something that most people tend to ignore. Increasingly we live in a busier and faster world, and we are bombarded by stimuli from more fronts and with less time to assimilate them. Decrease in attention spans has consequent effects on performance. Modern media have a large part to play in conditioning this short and distractible state of the attention. Some have even suggested that a new neurological phenomenon exists: "attention deficit trait" (ADT) (Hallowell 2005). This is a close cousin of the phenomenon of "multitasking." If we pay careful attention to what takes place when we multitask, we may observe that rather than paying attention to many things, we are mostly on automatic pilot and not really paying attention to anything very well. This not only affects our performance but also our enjoyment of what we are doing. ADT—as opposed to ADHD—is a conditioned response to an overly busy or hyperkinetic environment, such as many people might experience at work and home. Those who coined the term ADT suggest that in trying to deal with too much input, we tend to become hyperreactive; adopt black-and-white thinking; and find it difficult to stay organized, set priorities, and manage time. A constant low level of panic and guilt also exists with ADT. This, the authors suggest, can be managed by learning to regulate attention, lifestyle maintenance, changing the environment to be less frenetic, and learning how to switch off when the opportunity presents.

Many people associate being "relaxed" with being apathetic, unmotivated, unresponsive, or unaware. From a mindfulness perspective, this represents a significant misunderstanding of the mindful state. There is an important distinction to draw between agitation and awareness, as well as distinguishing being "relaxed" as in apathetic and relaxed as in inwardly calm, because one is focused. This focused but responsive state is illustrated by the "attentional blink" demonstration online.[1] We all have a limitation in information processing in terms of the time gap between identifying and then consolidating a stimulus or piece of data in memory. This attentional blink is for many people more than half a second long, which means it is upward of half a second before the mind is free to receive a second stimulus. As a result, stimuli (information or data) are often not detected, particularly when they are coming at us rapidly and especially when we are anxious. We literally don't see things when they are coming at us. People also vary in their vulnerability to distractor interference.

When, however, people were given 3 months of mental or attentional training in the form of mindfulness, the training not only helped people be calm "under fire" but also reduced their attentional blink and improved their ability to select goal-relevant information from distractors (Slagter et al. 2007). Probably the most important distractor is the self-preoccupation that comes with the default state of mind and brain, such as rumination, worry, reliving the past, and day-dreaming (Gusnard et al. 2001).

When demands are high, as illustrated by the "mindful" stress-performance curve, we have the better option of enhancing performance through improved attention or focus. This, as a side effect will reduce stress, rather than increase it. Relaxation is therefore seen as a side effect of attention training, rather than the primary goal. Athletes talk about being in "the zone." Others talk about being in "the flow" (Sugiyama et al. 2005). In this state there is no stress. We feel calm, in touch, responsive, efficient, and energized. This is the most enjoyable and sustainable level of performance. Increasing focus through attention regulation has two significant effects. First, because attention is being less drawn to anxieties, fears, ruminations, and concerns, there is a reduction in stress. This is associated with a feeling of inward calmness. Second, because of this "effortless concentration" or "restful alertness," we are alert and responsive to the situation we are in and the mind is less agitated and distracted.

---

1 Available at http://www.cs.kent.ac.uk/people/rpg/pc52/AB_Webscript/blink.html.

Mindfulness, healing, and happiness

Apart from helping to facilitate healthy lifestyle change (Ornish et al. 2005), mindfulness has many other effects conducive to health and happiness. Meditation "research" began thousands of years ago when wise sages observed directly and intently their own experience during and, more importantly, after meditation. Modern science seems to be catching up with what many have known for a long time: meditation is a powerful healing agent for mind and body.

> *"The faculty of voluntarily bringing back a wandering attention over and over again, is the very root of judgment, character, and will. No one is* compos sui *if he have it not. An education which should improve this faculty would be the education par excellence."* —William James, *Principles of Psychology*, 1890

What we can directly explore from within, science can also explore from without. Modern meditation research began with measuring a range of physiological and psychological effects associated with the so-called "relaxation response," a term coined by Harvard researcher Herbert Benson. Over the last one to two decades, however, research has increasingly shifted to looking at the clinical outcomes for various illnesses. Following is a summary of some of the findings from early meditation research.

Physiological effects of stress reduction:

- Decrease in oxygen consumption and metabolic rate
- Lowering of cortisol and catechol (adrenaline) receptor sensitivity
- Reduction in cortisol levels
- Reduction in blood pressure and heart rate
- Reduction in serum cholesterol
- Increase in skin resistance
- Decrease in blood lactate
- EEG changes (increase in alpha and theta waves and EEG coherence)
- Reduction in epileptic seizure frequency
- Changes in neurotransmitters, including high serotonin and dopamine
- Selective increase in cerebral blood flow
- Reduced thyroid hormone levels (TSH and T3 levels)

- Improved immune function and reduction of inflammation
- Reduced calcium loss secondary to lowered cortisol
- Psychological effects of stress reduction:
- Improved response time and reflexes
- Improvement in perceptiveness of hearing and other senses
- Decreased anxiety
- More optimism, decreased depression
- Greater self-awareness, self-actualization, and autonomy
- Improved coping capabilities
- Adjunct to psychotherapy
- Reduced addiction, reliance on drugs or alcohol
- Improved sleep: more restful, less insomnia, and in time less sleep needed
- Reduced aggression and criminal tendency
- Improved IQ and learning capabilities (various age groups)
- Greater efficiency and output and reduced stress at work
- Better time management and improved concentration and memory
- Ability to change undesired personality traits

Other research looked at the overall effect of meditation—in this case Transcendental Meditation (TM)—on health-care utilization and medical expenses. This field of research is of particular interest to insurance companies. One study over 11 years that compared 600,000 nonmeditators with 2,000 meditators found significant reductions in illness and a 63% reduction in health-care costs (i.e., 63 cents of the health dollar saved) among meditators (Orme-Johnson 1997). They also found 11.4 times fewer hospital admissions for cardiovascular disease, 3.3 times less cancer, 6.7 times less mental disorders, and lower rates of substance abuse. This study did not control for all relevant lifestyle and personality factors, and so self-selection, healthy lifestyle change, and direct physiological benefits would all play a part in the measured health outcomes. Nevertheless, on the strength of the data, a number of insurance companies in the United States and Europe now offer 30% reductions in health-insurance premiums for regular meditators.

Another interesting area of research relates to the relationship between mindfulness and emotional intelligence (EI) as described by Daniel Goleman.

The five domains of EI:	Definition:
Self-awareness	Ability to recognize and understand emotions, drives, and effects
Self-regulation	Can control or redirect disruptive impulses; can think before acting
Motivation	Passion for work that goes beyond money or status, energy, and persistence
Empathy	Ability to understand emotions of others; skill in interacting with others
Social skill	Can manage relationships and build networks; can find common ground, rapport

It seems that people who rate highly on mindfulness scales also rate highly on EI and vice versa (Baer et al. 2004). This is not surprising when one considers such aspects of EI as self-awareness and self-regulation. Long-term mindfulness practice has also been shown through brain imaging and self-report measures to enhance the ability to feel compassion (Lutz et al. 2008).

Mindfulness meditation

Of all the practitioners and teachers of mindfulness around the world, Jon Kabat-Zinn is probably the most widely known and respected. He described mindfulness as "a way of being."

Mindfulness, used as an adjunct to individual psychotherapy, results in more rapid alleviation of symptoms...

Another, slightly more wordy definition is that mindfulness is "characterised by dispassionate, non-evaluative and sustained moment-to-moment awareness of perceptible mental states and processes" (Grossman et al. 2004). "Dispassionate" relates to being nonreactive or nonjudgmental about the contents of one's consciousness as one meditates and, indeed, in day-to-day life. Experience teaches us repeatedly that being reactive to an anxious thought or feeling amplifies its effect, but we rarely stop to notice this and learn the lesson that reduced reactivity reduces the intrusiveness of such thoughts and feelings. "Non-evaluative" means a person is trying not to intellectually dissect or analyze their thoughts but rather to simply view them as passing events with which one could choose to engage with or not. This puts mindfulness-based cognitive therapy (MBCT), which was developed from Kabat-Zinn's work, at variance with conventional cognitive therapy. "Moment-to-moment" relates to the importance of being in the now. The present moment is the only moment in which we ever really live, and it is the only moment we can respond to. Mindfulness therefore teaches us that the past and future are only ever ideas or imaginings held in the mind now. "Awareness" implies consciousness—that part in us that is looking, as distinct from that part of us we are looking at. What we view when we practice mindfulness are the ever-changing "perceptible mental states and processes."

A number of basic assumptions are ascribed to mindfulness practice and theory (Gusnard et al. 2001):

1. People generally operate on automatic pilot and are unaware of moment-to moment experience.
2. We are capable of developing sustained attention.
3. Development of this ability is gradual and progressive and requires practice.
4. Awareness makes life richer and more vivid and replaces unconscious reactiveness.
5. Awareness gives rise to veridicality (truthfulness or accuracy) of perceptions.
6. Awareness enhances perceptiveness, effective action, and control.

The evidence base behind the claimed effectiveness of mindfulness-based therapies for a range of conditions is confirming its therapeutic potential. A recent meta-analysis revealed 64 empirical studies, although the quality of those studies varied (Gusnard et al. 2001). Acceptable studies covered a wide spectrum of clinical populations (e.g., those with pain, cancer, heart disease, depression, and anxiety) and found consistent evidence of significant benefit.

But it is really in the field of psychotherapy where mindfulness is attracting the most interest. Mindfulness, used as an adjunct to individual psychotherapy, results in more rapid alleviation of symptoms, increased achievement of therapeutic goals, and a decrease in the number of therapy sessions compared with psychotherapy alone (Weiss et al. 2005). The mindfulness group also showed a significant decrease in psychological distress and greater goal achievement and needed fewer sessions than the comparison group.

Meditators also seem to have better capabilities to regulate emotions and moderate intensity of emotional arousal when having negative emotions experimentally induced (Aftanas et al. 2005). The most challenging emotion for many people is depression, and at least 20–25% of people will experience a major depressive episode during their life. In people with a history of severe relapsing depression, MBCT reduced relapse from 78% to 36% over the following two years in patients with 3 or more previous episodes (Ma et al. 2004). Suicidal thoughts are often a feature of depression and are "likely to be reactivated as part of a suicidal mode of mind whenever sad mood reappears" (Williams et al. 2006). MBCT may reduce relapses by changing relationships to negative thoughts rather than by changing belief in thought content (Teasdale et al. 2002). Put another way, we don't have to control thoughts, but also we don't have to be controlled by them. To use an analogy, we cannot necessarily control whether "trains of thought" keep coming into our minds, but we can control the decision about whether to get on the train.

The moment-by-moment attitude of nonjudgment and acceptance helps people to be able to see thoughts as mental events rather than facts. This is sometimes called metacognitive awareness—that is, we are able to stand back from our thoughts and view them more objectively. Our common approach to the thoughts, feelings, sensations, and experiences we find unpleasant is to try and block them out, suppress them, distract ourselves from them, or numb ourselves to them. Meditation teaches us a way of accepting them if they arise and learning to be at peace with them. It is not the presence of a thought, feeling, or sensation that determines the response we feel, but rather the attitude we take toward it. We potentially make stressors out of internal and life events or make stressors larger than they need to be.

As an adjunct to therapy for cancer patients—an example of dealing with a major adversity—mindfulness has been demonstrated to lower scores on mood disturbance (depression, anxiety, anger, and confusion) and increase vigor (Speca et al. 2000). Patients experience fewer physical symptoms and symptoms of stress. The overall reduction in total mood disturbance was 65%, with a 31% reduction in stress. Mindfulness also assists with chronic pain (Kabat-Zinn et al. 1985; Singh et al. 1998) and improves sleep, with better sleep quality, faster sleep latency, longer sleep duration, and less use of sleep medications (Cohen et al. 2004).

Happiness is natural and restores itself given the right conditions...

Mindfulness has also been demonstrated to produce effects on the brain (more left frontal lobe activity associated with better mood and optimism) and enhanced immune function (improved response to immunization) (Davidson 2003).

Mindfulness at Monash University

Mindfulness has been finding its way into medical education. At Monash University, a limited amount of mindfulness teaching has been a part of the core curriculum for all medical students since 1992. Since 2002 the new curriculum at Monash has included a 6-week mindfulness-based stress-management program based on the Stress Release Program outlined in the book *Know Thyself* (Hassed 2002). This program is now also being piloted at Harvard University as a part of the student support programs for medical students (Rosenthal 2005).

Medical students, as with other professional groups, experience various stresses and many poor health behaviors as a result. Although many studies have consistently shown that student well-being is at its lowest preexam, medical education has largely ignored the need for programs to promote student well-being as a part of the core curriculum. A recently published paper described the development, implementation, and outcomes of the Health Enhancement Program (HEP) at Monash University (Hassed et al. 2008). This program is part of personal and professional development and comprises a mindfulness course and the ESSENCE lifestyle program (Hassed 2008). It is experientially based, integrates with biomedical sciences and clinical skills, and is an assessable component of the medical course.

The cohort study performed on the 2006 first-year Monash medical course intake measured the effects of the HEP on various markers of well-being. Instruments used were the depression, anxiety, and hostility subscales of the Symptom Checklist-90-R, incorporating the Global Severity Index (GSI) and the WHO Quality of Life (WHOQOL) questionnaire. Precourse baseline data (T1) was gathered midsemester, and postcourse data (T2) corresponded with preexam week. It would normally be expected that markers of mental health and quality of life should be significantly worse at T2 than T1. What we found was, however, very encouraging. Over 90% of students reported personally applying the mindfulness practices. Furthermore, improved student well-being was noted on all measures and subscales.

This program is the first of its type to be integrated into the core curriculum, and this study is the also the first to demonstrate an overall improvement in medical student well-being during a high-stress period such as the preexam period. The findings indicate the potential for improving student well-being at the same time as enhancing sustainable performance and meeting important learning objectives. The notion that high levels of stress are inevitable and are required to drive performance needs to be questioned, and similar models need to be implemented and evaluated in other settings.

Conclusion

In summary, for better or for worse, our state of mind and emotion is reflected in the body and brain. A happy, focused, and peaceful mind, and a contented and open heart are conducive to a healthier state of physical health, enhanced social functioning, and improved performance. Happiness is natural and restores itself given the right conditions; thus, meditation does not produce an artificial state of mind and emotion but allows a natural state to reassert itself. We all "meditate" on something or other most of the time; unfortunately, we meditate on anger, stress, worry, depression, and the like. The effect of this indiscriminate, unconscious, habitual, and harmful form of "meditation" is a testament to the power of attention, because consciousness powers, or gives life to, thoughts and feelings. It is indiscriminate, and it is an act of intelligence or reason to decide what is worth giving attention to and what is not. Therefore, we almost constantly think our way out of happiness. As mindfulness gently refocuses the attention, it enables a more intelligent and constructive use of our awareness, allows us to see our experiences as transitory, and offers the potential to gently unhook the attention from unhelpful thoughts and feelings. To do this, it is important to learn to be accepting of, and not reactive to, the thoughts and feelings we wish to be free of. Reactivity and judgment only draws us deeper into the very thing we wish to be free of.

It is likely that in the future we will see mindfulness as an increasingly recognized and practiced life skill as well as a treatment for a wide range of conditions. It may be the most natural, simple, and gentle way we know of to attain the peace, freedom, health, and happiness we all seek. That it helps us to know ourselves better is probably just another way of saying the same thing.

References

Aftanas, L., and Golosheykin, S. 2005. "Impact of Regular Meditation Practice on EEG Activity at Rest and During Evoked Negative Emotions." *International Journal of Neuroscience* 115(6): 893–909. Doi:10.1080/00207450590897969.

Ashcraft, M.H., and Kirk, E.P. 2001. "The Relationships Among Working Memory, Math Anxiety, and Performance." *Journal of Experimental Psychology: General* 130(2): 224–237.

Baer, R.A., Smith, G.T., and Allen, K.B. 2004. "Assessment of Mindfulness by Self-Report: The Kentucky Inventory of Mindfulness Skills." *Assessment* 11(3): 191–206.

Beilock, S.L., and Carr, T.H. 2005. "When High-Powered People Fail: Working Memory and "Choking Under Pressure" in Math." *Psychological Science* 16(2): 101–105.

Carter, R. 2002. *Mapping the Mind*. London: Weidenfeld and Nicolson.

Cohen, L., Warneke, C., Fouladi, R.T., Rodriguez, M.A., and Chaoul-Reich. A. 2004. "Psychological Adjustment and Sleep Quality in a Randomized Trial of the Effects of a Tibetan Yoga Intervention in Patients with Lymphoma." *Cancer* 100(10): 2253–2260.

Davidson, R.J., Kabat-Zinn, J., Schumacher, J., Rosenkranz, M., Muller, D., Santorelli, S.F., Urbanowski, F., et al. 2003. " Alterations in Brain and Immune Function Produced by Mindfulness Meditation." *Psychosom Medical* 65(4): 564–570.

Fahrenkopf, A.M., Sectish, T.C., Barger, L.K., Sharek, P.J., Lewin, D., Chiang, V.W., et al. 2008. "Rates of Medication Errors Among Depressed and Burnt-Out Residents: Prospective Cohort Study." *British Medical Journal* 336(7642): 488–491. doi:10.1136/bmj.39469.763218.BE.

Friedland, R.P., Fritsch, T., Smyth, K. Koss, E., Lerner, A.J., Chen, C.H., Petot, G.J., et al. 2001. "Patients with Alzheimer's Disease have Reduced Activities in Midlife Compared with Healthy Control-Group Members." *Proceedings of the National Academy of Sciences, USA* 98: 3440–3445.

Grossman, P., Niemann, L., Schmidt, S., and Walach, H. 2004. "Health-Related Benefits of Mindfulness-Based Stress Reduction: A Meta-Analysis." *Journal of Psychosomatic Research* 57: 35–43.

Gusnard, D.A., Akbudak, E., Shulman, G.L., and Raichle, M.E. 2001."Medial Prefrontal Cortex and Self-Referential Mental Activity: Relation to a Default Mode of Brain Function." *Proceedings of the National Academy of Sciences, USA* 98(7): 4259--4264.

Hallowell, E.M. 2005. "Overloaded Circuits: Why Smart People Underperform." *Harvard Business Review January* 83(1): 54–62, 116.

Hassed, C. 2002. *Know Thyself: the Stress Release Programme*. Melbourne: Michelle Anderson Publishing Pty Ltd.

Hassed, C., de Lisle, S., Sullivan, G., and Pier, C. 2008. "Enhancing the Health of Medical Students: Outcomes of an Integrated Mindfulness and Lifestyle Program." *Advances in Health Sciences Education: theory and Practice* 14(3): 387-398. doi.org/10.1007/s10459-008-9125-3.

Hassed, C. 2008. *The Essence of Health: The Seven Pillars of Well-Being*. Sydney: Random House.

Kabat-Zinn, J., Lipworth, L., and Burney, R. 1985. "The Clinical use of Mindfulness Meditation for the Self-Regulation of Chronic Pain." *Journal of Behavioural Medicine* 8(2): 163–190.

Kirsch, I., Deacon, B.J., Heudo-Medina, T.B., Scoboria, A., Moore, T.J. et al. 2008. "Initial Severity and Antidepressant Benefits: A Meta-Analysis of Data Submitted to the Food and Drug Administration." *PLoS Medicine* 5(2): e45. doi:10.1371/journal.pmed.0050045.

Klingberg, T., Forssberg, H., and Westerberg, H. 2002. "Training of Working Memory in Children with ADHD." *Journal of Clinical and Experimental Neuropsychology* 24: 781–791.

Kubota, Y., Sato, W., Toichi, M., Murai, T., Okada, T., Hayashi, A., and Sengoku, A. 2001. "Frontal Midline Theta Rhythm is Correlated with Cardiac Autonomic Activites During the Performance of an Attendtion Demanding Meditation Procedure." *Cognitive Brain Research* 11(2): 281–287.

Lazar, S.W., Bush, G., Gollub, R.L., Fricchione, G.L, Khalsa, G., and Benson, H. 2000. "Functional Brain Mapping of the Relaxation Response and Meditation." *Neuroreport* 11(7): 1581–1585.

Lazar, S.W., Kerr, C.D., Wasserman, R.H., Gray, J.R., Greve, D.N., Treadway, M.T. et al. 2005. "Meditation Experience is Associated with Increased Cortical Thickness." *Neuroreport* 16(17): 1893–1897.

Lutz. A., Brefcaynski-Lewis, J., Johnstone, T., and Davidson, R.J. 2008. "Regulation of the Neural Circuitry of Emotion by Compassion Meditation: Effects of Meditative Expertise.". *PLoS ONE* 3(3): e1897. Doi:10.1371/journal.pone.0001897.

Ma, S.H,, and Teasdale, J.D. 2004. "Mindfulness-Based Cognitive Therapy for Depression: Replication and Exploration of Differential Relapse Prevention Effects." *Journal of Consulting and Clinical Psychology* 72(1): 31–40.

Mathers, C.D., and Loncar, D. 2006. "Projections of Global Mortality and Burden of Disease from 2002 to 2030." *PLoS Medicine* 3(11): e442. doi:10.1371/journal.pmed.0030442.

Mathers, C.D., Vos, E.T., Stevenson, C.E., and Begg, S.J. 2000. "The Australian Burden of Disease Study: Measuring the Loss of Health from Diseases, Injuries and Risk Factors." *Medical Journal of Australia* 172(12): 592–596.

Marks, N.F., and Flemming, N.1999. "Influences and Consequences of Wellbeing Among Australian Young People:1980-1995." *Social Indicators Research* 46: 301–323.

McEwen, B.S. 2004. "Protection and Damage from Acute and Chronic Stress: Allostasis and Allostatic Overload and Relevance to the Pathophysiology of Psychiatric Disorders." *Annals of the New York Academy of Sciences, USA* 1032: 1–7.

Miller, M., and Rahe, R. 1997. "Life Changes Scaling for the 1990's." *Journal of Psychosomatic Research* 43(3): 279–292.

Orme-Johnson, D.W., and Herron, R.E. 1997. "An Innovative Approach to Reducing Medical Care Utilization and Expenditures." *American Journal of Managed Care* 3: 135–144.

Ornish, D., Weidner, G., Fair, W.R., Marlin, R., Pettengill, E.B., Raisin, C.J. et al. 2005. "Intensive Lifestyle Changes May Affect the Progression of Prostate Cancer." *Journal of Urology* 174: 1065–1070.

Pagnoni, G., and Cekic, M. 2007. "Age Effects on Gray Matter Volumne and Attentional Performance in Zen Meditation." *Neurobiology of Ageing* 28(10): 1623–1627.

Porter, R.J., Gallagher, P., Watson, S., and Young, A.H. 2004. " Corticosteroid-Serotonin Interactions in Depression: A Review of the Human Evidence." *Journal of Psychopharmacology* 173(1–2): 1–17.

Rees, G. 1998. "Too Much for our Brains to Handle." *New Scientist* 158(11): 2128.

Rosenthal, J.M., and Okie, S. 2005. "White Coat, Mood Indigo-Depression in Medical School." *New England Journal of Medicine* 353(11): 1085–1088.

Singh, B.B., Berman, B.M., Hadhazy, V.A., and Creamer, P. 1998. "A Pilot Study of Cognitive Behavioral Therapy in Fibromyalgia."*Alternative Therapies in Health and Medicine* 4(2): 67–70.

Slagter, H.A., Lutz, A., Greischar, L.L, Francis, A.D., Nieuwenhuis, S., Davis, J.M., et al. 2007. *PLOS Biology* 5(6): e138. doi:10. 1371/journal.pbio.0050138

Speca, M., Carlson, L.E., Goodey, E., et al. 2000. "A Randomized, Wait-List Controlled Clinical Trial: The Effect of a Mindfulness Meditation-Based Stress Reduction Program on Mood and Symptoms of Stress in Cancer Patients." *Psychosomatic Medicine* 62(5): 613–622.

Sugiyama, T., and Inomata, K. 2005. "Qualitative Examintation of Flow Experience Among Top Japanese Athletes." *Perceptual and Motor Skills* 100(3 Pt 2): 969–982.

Teasdale, J.D., Moore, R.G., Hayhurst, H., Pope, M., Williams, S., and Segal, Z.V. 2002. "Metacognitive Awareness and Prevention of Relapse in Depression: Empirical Evidence." *Journal of Consulting and Clinical Psychology* 70(2): 275–287.

Verghese, J., Lipton, R.B., Katz, M.J., Hall, C.B, Derby, C.A., Kuslansky, G. et al. 2003. "Leisure Activities and the Risk of Dementia in the Elderly." *The New England Journal of Medicine* 348(25): 2508–2516.

Weiss, M., Nordlie, J.W., and Siegel, E.P. 2005. "Mindfulness-Based Stress Reduction as an Adjunct to Outpatient Psychotherapy." *Psychotherapy and Psychosomatics* 74(2): 108–112.

Willcock, S.M., Daly, M.G., Tennant, C.C., and Allard, B.J. 2004. "Burnout and Psychiatric Morbility in New Medical Graduates." *Medical Journal of Australia* 181(7): 357–360.

Williams, J.M., Dduggan, D.S., Crane, C., and Fennell, M.J. 2006. "Mindfulness-Based Cognitive Therapy for Prevention of Recurrence of Suicidal Behavior." *Journal of Clinical Psychology* 62(2): 201–210.

13. Mindsight at work: an interpersonal neurobiology lens on leadership

Dr. Daniel Siegel and Dr. Debra Pearce-McCall

Daniel Siegel, Clinical Professor of Psychiatry, UCLA School of Medicine
Executive Director, The Mindsight Institute, California, USA
info@drdansiegel.com

Debra Pearce-McCall, Psychologist and Consultant
Board Member, Editor of Quarterly *GAINS—Global Association for Interpersonal Neurobiology Studies*
Adjunct Professor—PSU Certificate Program in Interpersonal Neurobiology, Arizona, USA
dpearcemccall@gmail.com

Introduction

This chapter provides an overview of the framework of interpersonal neurobiology (IPNB) and its applications to leadership. Combining scientific rigor with an appreciation for subjective ways of knowing, IPNB is shaped by a wide array of sciences and emphasizes interdisciplinary inclusiveness. The framework emerged from consideration of consilient empirical findings from many disciplines, including neuroscience, complexity theory, relationship and developmental studies, social relations, examinations of consciousness, and studies of psychological and neuroplastic change.

Consilience is a way of discovering parallel findings shared across independent disciplines (Wilson 1998), and here IPNB creates a common ground, with a welcoming integrative perspective that offers a compassionate and hopeful view of human potential. IPNB allows us to consider what common factors contribute to healthy minds and well-being across multiple relational endeavors, including leadership, consulting, education, medical and therapeutic work, coaching, and our personal lives.

In the decade since the publication of *The Developing Mind: How Relationships and the Brain Interact to Shape Who We Are* (Siegel 1999), the IPNB perspective has been applied by a diverse range of people interested in the potential of the human mind, including psychotherapists and physicians, educators and administrators, scientists and artists, religious leaders and policy makers, attorneys and consultants, leaders and change agents. Pivotal to success across these endeavors is the human ability to see and shape the mind—a process called "mindsight"—that can be harnessed to help individuals and human groups function with more efficiency, vitality, and creativity. We will discuss how mindsight, well-being, and integration apply to each of us across a range of settings, to leading in the workplace, and to our organizations in their larger contexts.

Interpersonal neurobiology framework

Our understanding of human experience has expanded exponentially in recent decades, with the development of new frames of reference and sophisticated methods of measurement. Ideas from complex systems theory greatly facilitated the potential for cross-discipline pollination and the resultant interdisciplinary revolution, while the analytic power of computers and data from new tools like the fMRI informed our advancing investigations of being human. We began to see, describe, and research the interconnections, the interactional interdependencies within and among living systems.

In 1999, one of us (DJS) proposed the idea of "interpersonal neurobiology" to describe a way of considering mind, brain, and relationships as three interrelated, interacting, and irreducible elements of human experience, creating a conceptual framework for understanding how the human mind develops from the interactions of neurophysiologic processes and interpersonal relationships. Through the years (Siegel and Hartzell 2003; Siegel 2007; 2010), the framework expanded to also emphasize the importance of our intrapersonal connection—our relationship to our self. In this chapter, we present an overview of interpersonal neurobiology (IPNB) and discuss some of the implications for the field of leadership studies and the development of a leading mind.

To some, the multilevel perspective of IPNB is new, while for others it solidifies something they've subjectively sensed for some time. Through the expansion of interdisciplinary research, more evidence of the interacting complexity of mind, brain, and relationships continues to accumulate, moving us far beyond the simpler argument "is it nature or nurture?" to starting with the synthesis of genetics and experience and then asking additional questions from there. Examples are now numerous.

What can we do, as individuals, in our relationships and in our organizations, to help create and maintain healthy minds, to facilitate health and well-being on small and large scales?

Research in developmental psychology has documented that to develop well our neural systems and our minds require relationships involving attention and contingent interactions and that we are born wired to relate (for an extensive research review, see Cozolino 2006). Social neuroscience studies have shown that our neural circuitry responses for physical and social pain overlap (Eisenberger and Lieberman 2004) and that a comforting relational presence can decrease physical sensations of pain—on self-report and in brain activity (Coan, Schaefer, and Davidson 2006). Mindful awareness practices have been demonstrated to improve immune system functioning and impact neural patterns (Davidson et al. 2003), and just five days of Integrative Body-Mind Training has been shown to improve regulation of the autonomic nervous system by increasing brain-body information flow (Tang et al. 2009). The field of epigenetics, which investigates how experience affects gene expression, is uncovering how nature and nurture collaborate in outcomes, including our physiological and emotional responses to stress (McGowan et al. 2009).

From this interwoven view of human experience, IPNB focuses a lens of inquiry on mind and well-being and asks: "What can we do, as individuals, in our relationships and in our organizations, to help create and maintain healthy minds, to facilitate health and well-being on small and large scales? How can we develop organizations that not only function well but also are creative and flourishing?"

IPNB and leadership

How relevant to the study and practice of leadership is a way of knowing that looks at awareness and attention, compassion and connection, resilience and well-being? Locally and globally, current events continually show us the power that political and business leaders have, from affecting details of our everyday lives to influencing the course of humanity and our planet. Warren Bennis (2007) stated that one of the four major threats to our world is the leadership of our human institutions and that only exemplary leadership can solve the other three key threats: nuclear/biological catastrophe, pandemic, and tribalism/assimilation. Bennis called for the field of leadership studies to attend to how we can develop leaders who understand relationships and communication, who can manage themselves and others with wisdom, creativity, and values. We invite you to consider how the ideas of IPNB might contribute to this urgent need.

IPNB concepts are congruent with many existing and developing approaches to organizations and leadership. Paralleling its impact in the fields of psychotherapy and education, IPNB does not present a new intervention protocol or a set of specific techniques; instead, it provides a way of examining different models within a coherent framework through a lens that focuses on process, healthy development and change, and the potential in the commonly shared ingredients of numerous "best practices."

In attempting to understand how leaders exerted top-down influence on groups, past theories in the leadership field focused on charisma, authority, personality style, and other individual variables, but newer views of leadership consider the relationship between leader and follower as a mutual and emergent process. This move from a "single-skull" to a "multiskull" perspective is a hallmark of the IPNB perspective, as we seek to understand our minds and our social brains in interaction with each other. Other congruent advances in business perspectives include the wide-ranging impact of systems theory, originally through the major impact of the concept of "the learning organization" (Senge 1990); recognition of the vital importance of emotional intelligence and social intelligence at work (Goleman 1995; 2006); descriptions of ways that neuroscience can inform leaders and enhance their performance (Rock and Schwartz 2006); and the potentially world-changing implications of well-being and sustainability receiving serious economic and cultural consideration (Diener and Seligman 2004; Eisler 2007; Hawken 1993).

Bennis (2007) stated the field of leadership studies must advance by seeing leadership as grounded in relationship rather than located in an individual, becoming interdisciplinary, collaborative, and more inclusive in its methodologies. In their review, Avolio, Walumbwa, and Weber (2009) similarly summarized the important trends in the leadership field: movement toward a more holistic view of leaders/followers/context, examinations of the actual process of leadership, and an expansion of the methods of inquiry considered valid (for example, integrating qualitative research with the dominant quantitative strategies). These qualities—relational, holistic, interdisciplinary, focusing on process, and valuing subjective and objective data—are ingredients of the IPNB perspective.

Integration and the triangle of well-being

The recognition of a "triangle of well-being" and the full extent of the interdependence and connections among our neurobiology, our interpersonal world, and qualities of our minds, arose from the realization of concordance among attuned relationships, a neurally integrated brain, and a coherent mind (Siegel 1999; 2010). These are the three points of the triangle through which IPNB examines the movement toward healthy functioning. Relationships in this model are viewed as the sharing of energy and information flow; "brain" refers to the mechanism of that flow as it extends in the nervous system distributed throughout the whole body; and the "mind" is, in part, a process that regulates the flow of energy and information. For an extensive review of research supporting this thesis, including empirical findings demonstrating the correlations among the outcomes of secure attachment, the integrative functions of the prefrontal cortex, and the impacts of mindful awareness practices, see Siegel 2007.

Interpersonal, neural, or subjective: these three aspects of well-being rely on integration. Integration is the key to moving toward the flexibility, harmony, and adaptability that accompany complexity and the promotion of health in living systems (Siegel 2010). We can define integration as the linking together of differentiated elements of a system into a more complex whole. Differentiation means that each element is individuated and can attain and maintain specialized functions and retain some degree of sovereignty. The linkage of these parts involves functional connections, exemplified by neurons growing into associative networks through neuroplastic changes; an internal story-making process combining facts, feelings, memory, and meaning; or co-workers engaging in dialogue, knowing they have a shared vision and mission while respecting the unique perspectives of each. Integration occurs when we label an emotion and use the regulatory skill of the prefrontal cortex to calm the activity of limbic brain regions, or when we construct a coherent life narrative that weaves emotion with autobiographical themes, or in the decision-making process of an executive team as they collaborate on a strategic plan while expressing multiple perspectives and priorities.

We can define integration as the linking together of differentiated elements of a system into a more complex whole.

In IPNB, we consider nine specific domains of integration that can be cultivated to promote well-being, which we will review below. These domains are being applied in psychotherapy, education, program development, leadership training, and organizational development. In addition, many professionals find the frame lends itself to personal as well as work-relevant applications, a natural extension of its integrative perspective.

Complexity theory and research illuminate the ways in which linking differentiated elements of a system to one another—integration—catalyzes the emergence of a state of continued health and well-being. This movement toward integration generally occurs when a system remains balanced yet reorganizing, a synthesis of stability and change, adaptively developing through time. The outcome of such flow is the creation of new combinations that move between familiarity and disorder. We can visualize this process as a river bounded by the banks of rigidity and chaos. Though they may veer toward one side or the other, our neural nets, a healthy mind, a safe and loving relationship, or a well-led organization will each move from those stuck or unstable places back into a forward flow through time, in an integrative state with qualities that can be summarized in the acronym FACES: flexible, adaptive, coherent, energized, and stable (Siegel 2006).

Imagine how an organization in this mode can respond to internal and external shifts and demands in ways that maintain its core identity, while reinforcing the self-organizing development of the entity toward complexity and integration. Creativity and innovation often require some trolling near the chaos bank—but with enough order, familiarity, and sense of mission to return to a FACES flow. Rigid organizations that fail to "change with the times" rarely last. If we use the metaphor of an organization moving across time as a boat on this river, then exemplary leaders are those who risk charting the course toward the unknown and take responsibility for attuning with others, eliciting commitment and collaboration among the crew, and facilitating regulation and integration onboard and through the currents. In addition, the wisest leaders invite self-leadership in others—enabling and encouraging their differentiation while cultivating their linking communication with one another—and thus create favorable conditions for integration and the appearance of the coherence, creativity, and emergent order that can occur in self-organizing systems. To extend the metaphor, leaders and consultants help organizations stay on course, riding through rapids and pushing away from shoals as necessary, returning to the integrative FACES flow—a kind of emergence management (Pearce-McCall 2007).

Defining the mind

To understand how each of us can actually influence the course of integrative processes, we first need to consider the definition of "mind" used in IPNB. This definition itself emerged from an integrative leadership process. In 1992, Dan had organized an interdepartmental group representing a diversity of academic disciplines from across UCLA, ranging from natural and social sciences to computer technology. The 40 participants shared an interest in studying the connections between the mind and the brain, but all the experts held their own view or descriptions for the mind, formed by their specific academic disciplines—that is, the mind as an operating system, as brain activity, as thoughts and feelings, as shared social process. The tension among these differing views could have ended the meetings, but linkage among these differentiated disciplines came through construction of a definition of mind that all present could endorse while maintaining their particular perspectives. This established a common ground for multidisciplinary brain/mind discussions that continued for years.

The updated integrative definition, which continues to bring agreement among neuroscientists, anthropologists, psychologists, educators, and many more, is that mental activities emerge from patterns in the flow of energy and information within and between brains, and that a core feature of the human mind is a relational and embodied process that regulates the flow of energy and information.

Energy refers to all forms of the capacity for action studied in physics, such as kinetic, radiant, or chemical; information is any representation of something other than itself, such as words and ideas. This flow of information and energy across time is what connects the three aspects of the triangle of well-being. In our relationships, we share and exchange energy and information through actions, expressions, and words; our brain (what we use as a term for our entire nervous system distributed throughout the body) is the physical mechanism through which energy and information flow; and our mind regulates this flow, whether we are reacting with automaticity or reflecting and responding with intention.

Our individual mind can influence this flow of energy and information in our subjective experiences of emotion and perception, our brain/body, and our relationships. One easily apparent way we do this is with the focus of our attention. Pause and focus on your fingers, noticing how they look from the outside. Now close your eyes (after completing this sentence) and feel and sense your fingers from inside. These intentional shifts in focus can be seen in neural activity as we use our minds to regulate energy and information flow. In other words, the mind can drive the brain to become active in specific patterns. Ethical, exemplary leaders are responsible for developing their own minds in ways that help them regulate the flow of information and energy in integrative patterns, in their coworkers or group members and their organizations as well as in themselves.

Ethical, exemplary leaders are responsible for developing their own minds in ways that help them regulate the flow of information and energy in integrative patterns...

One of us (DJS) has now surveyed over 80,000 therapists from every major discipline of mental health in four continents. Consistently, over 95 percent of these mental-health professionals report not receiving a single lecture defining the mind or mental health during their training. It has also become apparent that even in other fields directly focusing on the mind—such as education, philosophy, and neuroscience—that the "mind" as a term and as an entity is not defined.

Defining the mind as having a core aspect of regulation enables consideration of some of the mind's components...

Some leaders in each of these fields have stated that the mind should not and cannot be defined, that it is a "mystery" beyond definition, a concept that shouldn't be limited by defining it in words. Others consider mind reducible to merely an outcome of neural circuitry. IPNB uses a working definition of the mind, and of mental health, to operationalize the subjective heart of our lives and has benefited over the last fifteen years through this approach. Defining the mind as having a core aspect of regulation enables consideration of some of the mind's components and ways we can develop these inherent monitoring and modifying aspects. Once we've taken the step of identifying the regulatory features of the mind, we can focus our interventions on how we can promote the capacity to see and shape energy and information flow in a positive direction.

Defining mindsight

People can be taught to monitor their internal world with more acuity and depth, and they can also be trained to modify energy and information flow with more specificity and strength. These skills of developing our monitoring and modifying abilities are a part of the learnable capacity for mindsight. In sum, one promising result of defining the mind as having a regulatory function is that we can learn ways to very practically strengthen the mind itself and cultivate mindsight to promote integration in our individual and collective lives.

The qualities of mind that promote intentional focus, self-regulation, and attuned relationship are neurally associated with the prefrontal cortex, particularly the middle aspects of the prefrontal cortex that functionally link the brainstem, limbic, and cortical regions of the brain. These integrative middle-prefrontal regions, which include the anterior cingulate, orbitofrontal, and medial and ventrolateral prefrontal zones, are also essential in self-observation and social communication. They receive from the entire brain and body input that becomes data about bodily states and emotion and serve as a central hub in the social or resonance circuits of the brain (Siegel 2007). Thus, this integrative middle-prefrontal region links the differentiated input from the cortex, limbic area, brainstem, body proper, and even the social world of other brains.

The nine specific functions that correlate with integrative neural activity in the middle areas of the prefrontal cortex are body regulation, attuned communication, emotional balance, fear modulation, response flexibility, insight, empathy, morality, and intuition. These nine functions are also the established outcomes and process of the intrapersonal attunement developed through the reflective skill of looking inward. We know the first eight on the list are also empirically proven outcomes of the interpersonal attunement of secure attachment, such as a parent-child relationship filled with love, congruence, and compassion; the research on intuition has not been completed yet with respect to attachment history between infant and parent. (For an extensive discussion of these nine functions and the research about each, see Siegel 2007; 2010.)

The principles of IPNB have proven descriptive and useful in examinations of individuals, relationships, organizations, and cultures. We suggest that the best leaders may function like the middle-prefrontal region for an organizational brain/body and that these nine middle-prefrontal functions point to qualities of effective leadership. This proposition requires further examination and application in the field of leadership studies.

Interestingly, some key leadership qualities that overlap with this list are those highlighted in the developing neuroleadership literature, where the four focus areas for leadership development are decision making and problem solving, emotion regulation, collaborating with and influencing others, and facilitating change (Ringleb and Rock 2008). These all involve the "firing up" of the integrative prefrontal cortex within a leader's brain and provide examples of how a leader's organizational role involves applying those prefrontal functions to self and to the whole organization.

Though little research has examined effective leadership and its similarity to the process or outcomes of secure attachment, the existing literature has found that transformational leadership styles correlate with secure attachment styles (Popper and Mayseless 2003), highly effective leaders function as a "secure base" for their followers (Davidovitz et al. 2007), and those with secure attachment styles are more often perceived by others as the emerging leaders (Berson, Dan, and Yammarino 2006). A similar need exists for research directly investigating the impact on leadership skill of developing traits of mindfulness. Those who have worked extensively with emotional intelligence and leadership have identified mindfulness, along with compassion and hope, as the qualities of "resonant leadership" that can be intentionally developed (Boyatzis and McKee 2005). From an IPNB perspective, secure attachment, mindfulness, and both social and emotional intelligence involve the integrative functions of a well-honed middle-prefrontal cortex (see Dan Goleman's foreword in Siegel 2010).

> *Years have passed since ground-breaking studies began to reveal that measurable neural changes correlated with developing a more coherent mind.*

What already has substantial empirical support is that we can all develop these prefrontal functions by developing our skills of reflection and relationship, and that we can intentionally use our minds to influence the function and structure of the brain itself to create more neural integration and promote these prefrontal capacities. The more we can develop these, the more we facilitate all the points of the triangle of well-being: a coherent healthy mind, positive empathic relationships, and continued neural integration.

From this understanding comes the proposal for a new version of the 3Rs: Reflective and Relational skills, in combination, create Resilience (Siegel 2007). Imagine a world where we regularly teach this to our children in schools and at home. Bennis (2007) nominated resilience as the most important quality in a leader (or anyone interested in leading a healthy and meaningful life). Can the application of an IPNB framework guide us toward ways in which all kinds of organizations can integrate reflective and relational skills to develop and maintain the entire triangle of health and well-being, creating sustainable resilience?

Years have passed since ground-breaking studies began to reveal that measurable neural changes correlated with developing a more coherent mind. Perhaps the earliest example is Jeffrey Schwartz and colleagues' 1992 study demonstrating that a "talking therapy" with mindful reflection and brain-teaching as components effectively reduced symptoms in those with obsessive-compulsive disorder, as well as actually altering brain functioning (Baxter et al. 1992). Mindful awareness practices now have a burgeoning literature supporting their positive effects in many measurable ways. Numerous research laboratories now include technology that allows measurement of neural and physiological changes to be analyzed in tandem with behavioral, emotional, cognitive, and/or relational variables.

From an IPNB perspective, we look toward emerging research that supports the notion that health is cultivated by focusing our attention in specific ways or having certain relationship experiences that nurture neural integration, that through stimulating neural activation and growth toward differentiation and linkage, neural integration is created. The neuroplasticity of the brain suggests that a leader who promotes neural integration will be harnessing the capacity to experience specific and repeated neural firing that can lead to gene expression, protein production, and changes in both the genetic regulation of neurons and the structural connections in the brain that create and reinforce integrated circuitry.

While trying to explain to psychotherapy clients how focusing our attention can create neuroplastic change, Dan began using the descriptive term "mindsight" for our reflective capacity to become aware of our own minds, as well as our empathic ability to recognize the intentions and emotional states of others, to truly understand "where they are coming from." Many kinds of reflective-awareness practices can develop our mindsight, increasing the potential to link separate, differentiated neural areas by literally using our focus of attention to direct the flow of energy and information through specific neural pathways.

Mindsight makes it possible for us to see the internal world and then to shape the flow of energy and information by focusing on the three points of the triangle of well-being: we cultivate empathic relationships, an integrated brain, and a coherent mind that can make sense of ongoing experience. Harnessing the power of awareness to strategically stimulate the brain's firing, mindsight enables us to voluntarily change a firing pattern, even one laid down involuntarily. The more we have the regulation to become aware of ourselves in our relating—and pause—the more we can notice the states of others and develop empathy. Synaptic linkages are strengthened, the brain becomes more interconnected, and the mind becomes more adaptive because it has more integrative neural circuits to ride. And when we practice noticing others with compassion, we develop the resonance circuitry in our social brains and increase our capacity to bring an empathic attention to our own internal complexity as well. Practices that support neural integration, attuned relationships, and coherence of mind can all move us toward an integrative flow at the heart of living a life of well-being and meaning. Mindsight permits us to intentionally move our lives toward such integrative states.

Mindsight illuminated

Mindsight is the basic skill that underlies what we mean when we speak of having emotional and social intelligence, and it can be developed throughout our life. Early in life we learn to name the five senses through which we perceive the outside world—we see, hear, smell, taste, and touch; this is termed exteroception. Less often we learn about what could be considered our sixth sense, interoception, which allows us to perceive our internal states, noticing the muscle tension that can make us shift in our seats or the rapid heartbeat of excitement or fear, and can include proprioception and nociception—our abilities to sense the position of our body in space and to experience pain. Mindsight is our seventh sense, our ability to perceive the workings of our minds and the minds of others. It allows us to see and shape the inner workings of our minds, to perceive a feeling or a thought, and to know it as an activity of our mind rather than be overtaken by it or flip into reactivity. Exercising our mindsight in relationships means we develop our abilities to attend more fully to the nonverbal levels of communication and to the ways we perceive information about another's internal state and intentions through our own interoception. Developing mindsight, which involves being more open and accepting toward the full panoply of human experience, seems to intrinsically increase our compassion and sense of connection to humanity.

Mindsight is our seventh sense, our ability to perceive the workings of our minds and the minds of others.

To see clearly, we must first strengthen and stabilize the lens through which we view the internal world. Three specific reflective skills are like the legs of a metaphorical tripod that stabilizes the lens of mindsight and enables us to see with more clarity, depth, and focus. These fundamental components of mindsight are openness or receptivity (to whatever thoughts, feelings, or memories come into awareness), observation (seeing the fuller context than just this event or this moment), and objectivity or reflexivity (developing an awareness of awareness itself, called meta-awareness). These legs of the tripod allow us to consider our minds and the minds of others with compassion and clarity. From the IPNB perspective, leadership is developing and applying mindsight to promote integration in oneself, in others, and in organizations.

Learning about the brain helps in the development of mindsight...

Minding your brain

The field of neuroleadership formed from the belief that human enterprise and performance can be enhanced greatly by incorporating understandings gained through neuroscience research about how our brains work. In IPNB, we call this learning about "minding your brain." Being able to conceptualize even some basics of our neurobiology inherently accomplishes two tasks: being able to think about these physiological processes creates a mindful separation between reaction and response, the pause of observation and reflection; and information about our brains often makes empathy, patience, and compassion more accessible, whether directed toward self or another. In other words, learning about the brain helps in the development of mindsight, which empowers people to become active authors of their own life stories, rather than merely passive scribes. This is one reason we always carry a model of the brain with us—ready for demonstration and reminders.

Look at the end of your arm, and you'll find you have one handy, as well. This "hand model" of the brain, originally described in *The Developing Mind* (1999), is now used by many, including parents, children, psychotherapists, doctors, patients, leaders, educators, students, prisoners, and prison staff, to help them keep the brain in mind. We will offer only a brief description here and refer you to any of Dan's books for lengthier and more complete descriptions and illustrations. Imagine your wrist as the top of your spinal cord, on which your brain sits, with the back of your head oriented toward the back of your hand. Place your thumb across your palm and curl all your fingers around it. Can you begin to see how it roughly resembles the brain? Your arm serves as a reminder that the "brain" includes the whole of our distributed nervous system as well, from peripheral nerves to the neural nets around our hearts and guts. The palm of your hand represents the inner brainstem; your thumb represents the limbic regions, including the hypothalamus, pituitary, hippocampus, and amygdala (ideally for this model we'd have two thumbs, representing the left and right sides of the brain); and your fingers are the cortex, with the occipital, parietal, and temporal lobes located from the middle knuckles back, and the frontal lobes from the knuckles forward. The area we have focused on, the prefrontal cortex, is the most forward part of the brain, located behind our forehead. On the hand model, the prefrontal region is represented by the area from your fingertips to your first knuckles. The outer two fingertips represent the dorsolateral (or just "side") prefrontal cortex, which participates in generating the conscious form of attention, sometimes also referred to as the chalkboard of the mind. Even in this simple hand model, you can notice something anatomically unique about the middle prefrontal cortex, represented by the top segments of your middle two fingers—it connects to numerous other areas, resting on top of the limbic-thumb and touching the brainstem-palm, as well as linking to the rest of the cortex fingers.

The hand model of the brain helps us visualize how the middle prefrontal area is literally one synapse away from neurons in the cortex, the limbic areas, and the brainstem. This model helps us reflect on what is happening when we become reactive and dysregulated (lift your fingers up—you can visualize "flipping your lid") and what the reflective skills and relational compassion of mindsight do (wrap your fingers gently back around your limbic thumb), helping the prefrontal cortex balance, coordinate, and integrate multiple areas of neural activity. When integration occurs, the brain functions in harmony. Without integration, neural function moves toward rigidity, chaos, or both.

When integration occurs, the brain functions in harmony.

Domains of integration

One of the central tenets of IPNB is that the development of mindsight allows us to purposefully attend to the various domains of integration that contribute to well-being. Having a beginning capacity for reflection, adequate functioning of the middle prefrontal regions, and some attuned relationship(s) is probably needed to traverse these domains. Recall that these forms of integrative process can be applied to ourselves, our relationships, groups, organizations, even cultures and societies, and that integration is the linkage of differentiated elements of a system. If we can discern when and how integration is insufficient or absent—by detecting areas of a workplace, for example, that have rigidity or chaos—we can then focus on developing strategies to increase differentiation, create connections, and promote integration and well-being. Enhanced integration in the workplace would be associated with increased productivity and job satisfaction and with other measures of organizational and personal well-being.

Being receptive is in stark contrast to being reactive...

Consciousness integration

The first type of integration, on which all the others rest, is that of consciousness. The capacity to move into a receptive state, which most people can do fairly easily with a little guidance, is the initial skill in stabilizing mindsight's lens through the integration of consciousness. Being receptive is in stark contrast to being reactive, in which we enter a fight-flight-or-freeze mode of processing incoming perception. In the receptive state, we become open to the inner and interpersonal world in a more flexible and adaptive manner. This is the integrative core of this domain of consciousness.

If you imagine a metaphoric "wheel of awareness," the hub of consciousness is the center from which we can open our receptive awareness or direct our focused attention to anything on the "rim"—information about the external world from our five senses; information about our internal world through our interoceptive sixth sense; or information about awareness, our mind, and other minds, seen through our mindsight. All mindful-awareness practices that help us develop our attention, focus, and intentionality can be seen as developing this hub. The shared attention, attunement, and resonance between people can also invite the spaciousness that comes from a receptive mind.

Developing this hub is what allows us to decouple automaticity, to discern different streams of awareness, and to be able to differentiate between our sensory bottom-up processing and the secondary top-down influences of prior learning and cognition (Siegel 2007). This core also permits us to make sense of mirror neuron and interoceptive information, enabling us to "feel for another" and yet distinguish our emotions from what we empathically sense another person is feeling. From this hub, we learn to focus and refocus our attention among multiple streams of information, and we develop the tripod skills of openness, observation, and objectivity. The integration of consciousness helps stabilize our minds within the constant internal and external streams of information and energy that fill our internal lives.

Leaders need to inhabit this hub to develop mindsight and all the qualities needed to provide integrative leadership to others, such as emotion regulation and response flexibility. They also need this hub of consciousness to be aware of the multiple aspects of self, coworkers and employees, the organization, and the larger context in which they reside, and to learn to focus and direct their attention among competing priorities.

Horizontal integration

On a neural level, horizontal integration refers to linkages between the left and right brain hemispheres with their broad tendencies toward specialization, or "modes," that have existed for millions of years. The "Ls" of the left mode—linear, logical, linguistic, and literal—and the more holistic, nonverbal, imagery-based relational and emotional processing of the right mode create a vital, rich, and broadened spectrum of our inner experience that colors our sense of ourselves and our interpersonal lives when integrated. For example, imagine reading a story with just the facts, or one with only emotional images; neither would make quite as much sense or have as much meaning as the full, combined version.

Our relational experiences during times of major neural development for our social brains may actually create adaptations that decrease horizontal or bilateral integration, leaving one hemispheric mode dominant. Many forms of therapy are attempts to help the mind travel back and forth in these modes, promoting neural integration and a deepened life experience.

In an organization, horizontal integration can be seen in the challenge of coordinating different departments, divisions, or locations, often each with its own modes and methods, or in the choices around the best positioning of a company in a marketplace of others.

Vertical integration

On an individual level, vertical integration involves bringing somatic input into awareness, via the distributed nervous system, and bringing the energy and information flowing through the spinal cord and bloodstream into the brainstem, limbic areas, and cortex—and back around. When we develop vertical integration, we can intentionally focus our attention on body sensations, and we are less likely to avoid awareness of bodily input (rigidity) or be flooded with sensation and emotion (chaos). Bodily awareness makes it more likely that we will be able to recognize and calm these energies, so we can consider and choose our responses.

Not surprisingly, many people have little experience with this awareness and can be amazed at the difference in information they receive just by sitting quietly, breathing, and sensing their bodies. Leaders can easily ignore cues for hunger, rest, or renewal when they are tuning out somatic input and attending to the business at hand, heightening their chances of developing stress-related illnesses or burnout. A lack of intrapersonal attunement—not being tuned into and accepting of your own internal world—may make you blind to an escalating torrent of physiological arousal/stress and can result in inappropriate and ineffective expressions of frustration and anger that can permanently scar working relationships. Anyone can go down this "low road" and temporarily lose integration. The key is to have enough presence of mind to note the warning signs of such an impending meltdown and take action to avoid its full enactment and thus the common destructive consequences it carries for all involved.

Vertical integration is extremely important on an organizational level, as well, ensuring, for example, that those at the "top" do not make decisions or design policies without considering information from those who will need to implement them. Leaders attend to vertically integrating energy and information flow up (higher levels of management, the board, regulatory agencies) and down (lower levels of management, employees). When done well, the use of 360-degree degree feedback for evaluations and goal setting is a concrete example of utilizing horizontal and vertical integration in an organizational process.

Memory integration

Several different types of memory have been identified, some volitional and others effortless, and a main task of memory integration involves assembling basic pieces into coherent wholes. Our earliest form, termed implicit memory, is present even before birth.

Our sensations, perceptions, emotions, and actions create the foundation for the way we "remember" our experiences.

Our sensations, perceptions, emotions, and actions create the foundation for the way we "remember" our experiences. These building blocks of memory become generalized as implicit mental models, shaping our expectations of how the world works. Sometime in toddlerhood, as brain development proceeds, we become able to have implicit memories linked to one another via the hippocampus, becoming woven together as explicit memories—the autobiographical and factual information that forms the foundation for our knowledge of the self and the ways of the world. However, throughout our lives we can sometimes experience implicit-only representations as though they are "here and now," which can be a source of misinterpretation and miscommunication. Mindsight increases our capacity to discern the current impact of implicit memory and to make these memories explicit, freeing us from some internal constraints and allowing us to live more fully in the present. In consultations, one of us (DPM) has found that recognition of negative implicit memories can quickly defuse their impact and improve leadership capacities or executive team collaboration.

An organizational form of memory integration can be seen in what has been called knowledge transfer or knowledge management. These require employees to be able to make explicit what they know about policies, best practices, client relationships, or organizational culture and to find ways to communicate and share this information with coworkers, especially during times of transition.

When organizations create their mission-vision-values-goals, they are developing an integrating narrative.

Narrative integration

We humans have a clear preference for creating and telling stories, and narrative integration is the weaving of the facts and felt experiences of our lives into coherent stories that make sense of our inner and outer worlds. A major attachment-research finding is that the most robust predictor of whether a child will have a secure attachment to his or her parent is the degree of coherence (what IPNB views as integration) in that parent's telling of his or her own life story. The amount of coherence is an indication of whether the parent has "made sense" of how early life events have impacted his or her life. Narrative integration shapes our lives, our families, and our cultures.

When leaders have a coherent story to tell—in the form of history, vision, mission, and values—this has a significant impact on the integration and resilience of the organization. Sternberg (2008), describing his WICS model of leadership, suggested that it is through compelling stories that successful leaders synthesize wisdom, intelligence, and creativity, and that leaders' stories must fit the needs of their followers. When organizations create their mission-vision-values-goals, they are developing an integrating narrative. Marketers and publicists have long realized the worth of a good story in attracting attention and selling to the public, a form of narrative integration between an organization and its larger context (Heath and Heath 2007).

Stories are not just fun ways of learning—they are the biological foundation for how the brain learns and remembers best.

State integration

State integration is necessary because we all experience a multiplicity of internal states, organized by our emotions, desires, or needs. A state of mind correlates with a cluster of neural firing patterns assembled into a functional unit. Our states of mind can contain their own habitual patterns and history, and involve increased accessibility to certain memories. With mindsight, we can learn to accept the diverse, shifting, and sometimes conflicting nature of our states of mind, which can help decrease shame and fear and open us to authenticity, integrity, and possibility.

Effective leaders may learn to use mindsight to integrate their own internal states and to influence the states in others. They do not avoid emotion and conflict (rigidity), nor are they overwhelmed by it (chaos); effective, inspiring leaders are emotion-informed, which requires comfort with and differentiation or linkage of multiple states.

Mindsight-informed awareness and regulation is not simply about calm or pleasant states; it encompasses the full range of emotional experience, from the organizational leaders who purposefully incorporate play to the educator who uses the Socratic method to increase anxiety, motivation, and attention.

Organizations may be more resilient when leaders can help employees make sense of and integrate the ebb and flow of states that vary with the cycles of the marketplace and the economy or the life cycles of their products. The realities of aggressive competition in the world beyond a company, for example, need to be balanced with states of cooperation and collaboration within the company's walls (even as those states may involve harnessing the charge of competitiveness for some). State integration entails embracing the diversity of states within each of us and promoting internal coherence within the varied and changing contexts of the work environment.

Interpersonal integration

Interpersonal integration involves the "neurobiology of we" (Siegel 2008)—the delightful and deeply rewarding human experience of "feeling felt" by another person, the resonant connection of two minds joining in energy and information flow. Research into the activity of the mirror neurons suggests a possible mechanism of the neural reality of close relationships. Neuroscientist Marco Iacoboni (2008), who investigates the role mirror neurons may play in bonding, learning, morality, consumer choices, and political affiliations, has summarized research findings as clearly demonstrating that we are wired for empathy. Mirror neurons may play an important role in phenomena such as emotional contagion, the power of imitation, the interrelationship of leaders and followers, and the experience of mindsight.

Those with well-developed mindsight are more able to create and maintain interpersonal integration and may be more likely to recognize and avoid the full impact of emotional contagion, or resonance. This social spreading, particularly of negative and disabling emotions, can be detrimental to motivation, performance, and job satisfaction. A leader's level of mindsight can be pivotal in connecting with this resonant potential and, rather than merely being overtaken by it, remaining reflective and able to move it in positive directions. Charismatic leaders are possibly those who excite our mirror neurons successfully with their words and their delivery, but these interpersonal skills can also be developed.

Organizations need interpersonal integration for successful coordination of people on work teams or across divisions or regions, each with differing personalities, cultures, perspectives, and roles.

Temporal integration

The need for temporal integration comes from our mental capacity to leave the present moment and "live" in the past or the future. Most of us are surprised to reflect on our mind's location in time and realize how infrequently we reside in the here and now. Temporal integration also involves the need this prefrontal cortex capacity for "time-travel" creates, even as we long for certainty, permanence, and immortality.

Finding a way to embrace these understandable desires—uncertainty, impermanence, and mortality—as well as their counterparts in the reality of existence is an aspect of this form of integration. Aside from the personal existential issues this raises, leaders must be the representatives of clarity about where their organization was, is, and can go, integrating current certainties with risks and changes for the future. As Senge (2006, 15) said, "To be an effective visionary you must also be connected to the realities of today." The pace of change in our world, markets, information technologies, and knowledge requires leaders who anchor their decisions in current perceptions while embracing ongoing adaptation and improvement.

Leaders are addressing temporal integration when they help others move away from the stuck place of "that's how it's always been done" to the uncertainty of new procedures and responsibilities. Letting go of the past and moving into the present to free the possibilities of the future combines many forms of integration, from temporal to narrative, as leaders create a more fluid and integrated flow of their organizations across developmental phases.

Emergence of transpirational integration

Attending to the development of these eight domains of integration often allows a new form of integration to emerge. This spontaneous development feels like it breathes life and energy across all the other domains, so Dan termed it "transpirational" integration. This is the expansive feeling of being part of a much larger whole, a connection to the essence of being human and to all of humanity, to the precious rhythms of the global pulse of life. In the many and various research explorations of happiness and wisdom, this awareness of interconnection seems to be at the heart of living a life of meaning and purpose.

Those organizations that somehow find ways to invite these feelings into employees' lives at work have lower turnover, higher productivity, and happier people. If we hope to have ethical leaders who value and promote well-being and sustainability, we need leaders who experience this form of integration. These leaders, with well-developed mindsight, will naturally help their businesses strive for "ecological intelligence" (Goleman 2009), considering our organizations, products, and purchases in terms of their real impact on the consumption of the earth's nonrenewable resources and on all people, locally and globally, now and in the future. True sustainability requires much more than the institution of "green practices," though the exponential interest in recycling, carbon offsets, and energy efficiency is a sign of progress (when not just a marketing device).

Commitment to an ongoing focus on human and planetary health and well-being requires a shift in our subjective and relational capacities toward appreciation, balance, and compassion, a shift that can occur through the development and application of mindsight to all the processes of integration.

Conclusion

Information and technology will continue to expand at an accelerating pace. Our growing knowledge of the brain, and ways to use this knowledge for learning, change, and social influence, will be put to use. What can help ensure that leaders apply these advances in positive ways that avoid rigidity and chaos and encourage adaptive and healthy development? True neuroleadership involves addressing the ethical responsibilities inherent in leading minds and brains.

When utilized in coaching, consulting, or leading, the IPNB perspective focuses on developing mindsight and the integrative processes that facilitate reflection, relationship, and resilience. Attending to these processes can promote the full triangle of well-being within our workplaces and in the energy and information flow of commerce, with its pivotal circulatory role in human and planetary health. With the cultivation of mindsight, leaders naturally consider long-term as well as short-term outcomes, collaboration instead of domination, and business practices that enhance profit, people, and the planet. Imagine what might become possible for all of us if we consistently applied mindsight and reflective, compassionate, and integrative leadership to ourselves, our relationships, our organizations, and our countries.

References

Avolio, B. J., Walumbwa, F. O., and Weber, T. J. 2009. "Leadership: Current Theories, Research, and Future Directions." *Annual Review of Psychology* 60: 8.1–8.29.

Baxter, L. R., Schwartz, J. M., Bergman, K. S., Szuba, M. P., Guze, B. H., and Mazziotta, J. 1992. "Caudate Glucose Metabolic Rate Changes with Both Drug and Behavior Therapy for Obsessive-Compulsive Disorder." *Archives of General Psychiatry* 49(9): 681–689.

Bennis, W. 2007. "The Challenges of Leadership in the Modern World." *American Psychologist* 62(1): 2–5.

Berson, Y., Dan, O., and Yammarino, F. J. 2006. "Attachment Style and Individual Differences in Leadership Perceptions and Emergence." *Journal of Social Psychology* 146(2): 165–182.

Boyatzis, R., and McKee, A. 2005. *Resonant Leadership: Renewing Yourself and Connecting with Others through Mindfulness, Hope, and Compassion*. Boston: Harvard Business School Press.

Coan, J. A., Schaefer, H. S., and Davidson, R. J. 2006. "Lending a Hand: Social Regulation of the Neural Response to Threat." *Psychological Science* 17(12): 1032–1039.

Cozolino, L. J. 2006. *The Neuroscience of Human Relationships: Attachment and the Developing Social Brain*. New York: W. W. Norton.

Davidovitz, R., Mikulincer, M., Shaver, P., Izsak, R., and Popper, M. 2007. "Leaders as Attachment Figures: Leaders' Attachment Orientations Predict Leadership-Related Mental Representations and Followers' Performance and Mental Health." *Journal of Personality and Social Psychology* 93(4): 632–650.

Davidson, R. J., Kabat-Zinn, J., Schumacher, J., Rosenkranz, M., Muller, D., Santorelli, S., Urbanowski, F., Harrington, A., Bonus, K., and Sheridan, J. F. 2003. "Alterations in Brain and Immune Function Produced by Mindfulness Meditation." *Psychosomatic Medicine* 65(4): 564–570.

Diener, E., and Seligman, M. 2004. "Beyond Money: Toward an Economy of Well-Being." *Psychological Science in the Public Interest* 5(1): 1–31.

Eisenberger, N. I., and Lieberman, M. D. 2004. "Why Rejection Hurts: A Common Neural Alarm System for Physical and Social Pain." *Trends in Cognitive Sciences* 8(7): 294–300.

Eisler, R. 2007. *The Real Wealth of Nations: Creating a Caring Economics*. San Francisco: Berrett-Koehler.

Goleman, D. 1995. *Emotional Intelligence*. New York: Bantam Books.

Goleman, D. 2006. *Social Intelligence: The New Science of Human Relationships*. New York: Bantam Dell.

Goleman, D. 2009. *Ecological Intelligence: How Knowing the Hidden Impacts of What We Buy Can Change Everything*. New York: Broadway Books.

Goleman, D. 2010. Foreword. In D. J. Siegel, *Mindsight: The New Science of Personal Transformation*. New York: Bantam.

Hawken, P. 1993. *The Ecology of Commerce*. New York: HarperCollins.

Heath, C., and Heath, D. 2008. *Made to Stick: Why Some Ideas Survive and Others Die*. New York: Random House.

Iacoboni, M. 2008. *Mirroring People: The New Science of How We Connect with Others*. New York: Farrar, Straus, and Giroux.

McGowan, P. O., Sasaki, A., D'Alessio, A. C., Dymov, S., Labonte, B., Szyf, M., Tureck, G., and Meaney, M. J. 2009. "Epigenetic Regulation of the Glucocorticoid Receptor in Human Brain Associates with Childhood Abuse." *Nature Neuroscience* 12: 342–348.

Pearce-McCall, D. 2007. "Mindsight at Work: Our Organizations, Ourselves. Connections and Reflections." *GAINS Quarterly* (Autumn) 12–17.

Popper, M., and Mayseless, O. 2003. "Back to Basics: Applying a Parenting Perspective to Transformational Leadership." *Leadership Quarterly* 14: 41–65.

Ringleb, A. H., and Rock, D. 2008. "The Emerging Field of NeuroLeadership." *NeuroLeadership Journal* 1: 3–19.

Rock, D., and Schwartz, J. M. 2006. "The Neuroscience of Leadership." *Strategy+Business Magazine* 43: 71–81.

Senge, P. M. 1990. *The Fifth Discipline: The Art and Practice of the Learning Organization*. New York: Doubleday.

Senge, P. M. 2006. "Business as a Human Community: An Interview with Peter Senge." *Society for Organizational Learning*. Accessed February 2, 2007. http://www.solonline.org/news/item?item id=9000239.

Siegel, D. J. 1999. *The Developing Mind: Toward a Neurobiology of Interpersonal Experience*. New York: Guilford.

Siegel, D. J. 2006. "An Interpersonal Neurobiology Approach to Psychotherapy: Awareness, Mirror Neurons, and Neural Plasticity in the Development of Well-Being." *Psychiatric Annals* 36(4): 247–258.

Siegel, D. J. 2007. *The Mindful Brain: Reflection and Attunement in the Cultivation of Well-Being*. New York: W. W. Norton.

Siegel, D. J., and McNamara, S. 2008. *The Neurobiology of "We": (How Relationships, The Mind, and The Brain Interact to Shape Who We Are).* Boulder, CO: Sounds True, 7 compact discs.

Siegel, D. J. 2010. *Mindsight: The New Science of Personal Transformation*. New York: Bantam.

Siegel, D. J., and Hartzell, M. 2003. *Parenting From the Inside Out: How a Deeper Self-Understanding Can Help You Raise Children Who Thrive*. New York: Penguin Putnam.

Sternberg, R. 2008. "The WICS Approach to Leadership: Stories of Leadership and the Structures and Processes that Support them." *Leadership Quarterly* 19: 360–371.

Tang, Y. Y., Ma, Y., Fan, Y., Feng, H., Wang, J., Feng, S., Lu, Q., et al. 2009. "Central and Autonomic Nervous System Interaction is Altered by Short-Term Meditation." *Proceedings of the National Academy of Sciences, USA* 106(22): 8865–8870.

Wilson, E. O. 1998. *Consilience: The Unity of Knowledge*. New York: Knopf.

14. The potential contribution of neuroscience to authentic leadership

Dr. Paul McDonald

Paul McDonald, Senior Lecturer, Victoria Management School, Victoria University of Wellington, New Zealand

paul.mcdonald@vuw.ac.nz

Introduction

A synergy is emerging between neuroscience and organizational research that includes theoretical and practical implications for authentic leadership. This chapter reviews four facets of authentic leadership—self-awareness, relational transparency, balanced processing, and internalized moral perspective—against the theoretical and empirical backdrop of neuroscience, with particular attention to social-cognitive and affective neuroscience. A number of insights as to theoretical propositions and developmental initiatives are offered to advance our understanding of authentic leadership.

Widening the exploration of effective leadership

Against the backdrop of financial turmoil, ethical scandals of global proportions, and clashes of culture across age, ethnicity, and socioeconomic status, the need for effective leadership has become increasingly salient and is now recognized as critical (Charan 2009). The efficacy of leadership development has been called into question (Haines 2009), with the suggestion that new skills need to be considered—in particular the ability to cope with stress and uncertainty while maintaining a positive focus on the future (Nicholson 2009). In addition to new skills, there is a requirement for leadership development to adopt more holistic methodologies beyond traditional emphasis on behavioral change, including emotional and neuroendocrine aspects of learning (Boyatzis, Smith, and Blaize 2006).

Turbulence, uncertainty, and complexity have impelled research in leadership theory and leadership development to become more eclectic at organizational (Darling and Heller 2009), group (Nemanich and Vera 2009; Rowland and Parry 2009) and individual (Avolio, Walumbwa, and Weber 2009) levels of analysis. There is much more latitude for exploration beyond behavior into the realms of biology, cognition, emotion, and spirituality. For example, recent studies have researched the development of leaders from a variety of perspectives, including authenticity (Avolio and Gardner 2005; Manz et al. 2008), courage (Treasurer 2009), dialogue (Mazutis and Slawinski 2008), emotional intelligence (McEnrue, Groves, and Shen 2009; Samad 2009), interpersonal communication (Love 2008), mythodrama (Olivier and Verity 2008), passion (Khan 2009), physical health (Macik-Frey, Quick, and Cooper 2009), pride (Michie 2009), spiritualism (Ferguson and Milliman 2008) and wisdom (McKenna, Rooney, and Boal 2009).

There is a requirement for leadership development to adopt more holistic methodologies...

At the same time, in a different realm of science, advances in theory accelerated by technological innovation—functional magnetic resonance imaging (fMRI), positron emission tomography (PET), and qualitative electroencephalography (QEEG)—have enabled neuroscience, and in particular social-cognitive and affective neuroscience, to provide tangible research insights into the biological and physiological underpinnings of social interaction. Ochsner and Lieberman (2001) define social-cognitive neuroscience as an emergent interdisciplinary field that aims to understand human interactions at the intersection of social, cognitive, and neural spheres of science.

Social-cognitive neuroscience is both eclectic and novel in its exploration of the human condition.

Similar to the current state of evolution in leadership development, social-cognitive neuroscience is both eclectic and novel in its exploration of the human condition. Recent examples include the following research: Adolphs (2009) proposed a neural basis to the construction of social knowledge, in particular the manner in which social inferences about the feelings, thoughts, and intentions of others are formed. Beauregard (2007) utilized neuroimaging to provide an explanation for the human process of self-regulation. Pallesen and colleagues (2009) applied neuroscience to explore goal-directed behavior. Kounios (2008) and colleagues studied neural antecedents to human insight. Tabibnia and colleagues (2008) studied brain activity in relation to perceptions of fairness and unfairness. Zahn and colleagues (2009) demonstrated the impact of neural architecture on the communication and meaning attached to social values.

The contribution of cognitive neuroscience to organizational research has been recognized in the literature. In November 2007, the *Annals of the New York Academy of Sciences* devoted an entire issue (1118) to the social-cognitive neuroscience of organizations. Butler and Senior (2007) discussed the benefits and limitations of cognitive neuroscience and defined the field of organizational cognitive research. A variety of topics were covered, including rewards and social information (Caldu and Dreher 2007), fairness and cooperation (Tabibnia and Lieberman 2007), teamwork (Levine 2007), change (Yeats and Yeats 2007), and strategy (Klein and D'Esposito 2007).

This chapter is based on three propositions: First, there is a need to recognize emotion in the workplace as an emergent and relevant field of study, including current relevance to leadership development (Antonakis, Ashkanasy, and Dasborough 2009; Ashkanasy and Daus 2002; George 2003). Second, teaching and research in leadership will benefit from access to the best available scientific evidence, in particular from access to the cumulative knowledge of the physical and social sciences that manifests convergent evidence of pervasive causal relationships (Rousseau and McCarthy 2007). Third, neuroscience has the potential to inform leadership research, including leadership development, with novel theoretical propositions as well as provide the substantiation of tangible, hard, scientific evidence (Peterson et al. 2008; Ringleb and Rock 2008).

Neuroleadership's potential contribution to authentic leadership

Ringleb and Rock (2008) propose an emergent field of scientific inquiry at the nexus of neuroscience and leadership called "neuroleadership." They define neuroleadership and its purpose as follows:

> This interdisciplinary field explores the neural basis of leadership and management practices, effectively bringing about the interface between the tools of social cognitive and affective neuroscience, cognitive neuroscience, integrative neuroscience, neurobiology and other domains within neuroscience, and questions and theories from the leadership and management social sciences. The research objective of this field is to improve leadership effectiveness within institutions and organizations by developing a science for leadership and leadership development that directly takes into account the physiology of the mind and the brain. (3)

My purpose here is to hypothesize about the potential contribution of neuroleadership to increased insight and understanding of authentic leadership, including the future development of leaders with greater authenticity and self-awareness.

Authenticity is not a new construct. Inscribed in the stone at the Oracle of Delphi was the admonition: **γνωθι σεαυτόν** (gnothi seauton = know thyself). In the middle ages, Polonius (Shakespeare's Hamlet) advises his son who is leaving for France, "To thine own self be true." Within the corporate world, the writings of American business executive Chester Barnard (1938) have been used as exemplary perspectives on authentic leadership (Novicevic et al. 2006). There has, however, been a marked increase in the salience of this construct in light of recent catastrophic leadership failures, including Bernie Ebbers at Worldcom (Scharff 2005), Kenneth Lay and Jeffrey Skilling at Enron (Stein 2007), and more recently and perhaps most tragically, Bernard Madoff and his $65 billion Ponzi fraud (Kranacher 2009). The resurgence of interest in authentic leadership has been evident in both applied (George et al. 2007) and academic management literatures (Gardner et al. 2005; see also the *Leadership Quarterly* 2005, vol. 16, no. 3).

Harter (2002) defines authenticity as "owning one's personal experiences, be they thoughts, emotions, needs, preferences, or beliefs, processes captured by the injunction to know oneself" and behaving in accordance with the true self. Luthans and Avolio (2003) define authentic leadership as "a process that draws from both positive psychological capacities and a highly developed organizational context, which results in both greater self-awareness and self regulated positive behaviors on the part of leaders and associates, fostering positive self-development." A general consensus in the literature is that the construct of authentic leadership is multidimensional; however, debate ensues as to its component elements. Prominent in the literature is a four-component model (Ilies, Morgeson, and Nahrgang 2005) building from Kernis's (2003) conceptualization. This model comprises the capabilities of self-awareness, unbiased processing, authentic behavior/acting, and authentic relational orientation.

The central proposition is that neuroscience has the potential to contribute to our understanding of authentic leadership.

This chapter relies on the development and validation of a theory-based measure of authentic leadership by Fred Walumbwa, Bruce Avolio, and their colleagues (2008), which builds on the earlier work of Ilies and colleagues (Ilies et al. 2005). Walumbwa et al. (2008) developed and tested a theory-based measure of authentic leadership called the Authentic Leadership Questionnaire (ALQ). The theory of a multidimensional construct has been supported by confirmatory factor analysis. Four factors were confirmed: self-awareness, relational transparency, balanced processing, and internalized moral perspective. To address cross-cultural validity and generalizability, Walumbwa and colleagues used five separate samples from China, Kenya, and the United States. Their resultant conceptualization of authentic leadership is as follows:

> Authentic leadership is a pattern of leader behavior that draws upon and promotes both positive psychological capacities and a positive ethical climate, to foster greater self-awareness, an internalized moral perspective, balanced processing of information, and relational transparency on the part of leaders working with followers, fostering positive self-development. (Walumbwa et al. 2008)

In this research each of the four facets of authentic leadership were examined against the neuroscience literature with the goal of identifying relevant theoretical propositions and developmental insights. The central proposition was that neuroscience has the potential to contribute to our understanding of authentic leadership. With respect to this central proposition, neuroscience has shown that the brain characterizes the opposing attributes of neural plasticity and rigidity. In status quo, the brain, in its comfort zone, favors well-worn neural pathways (a.k.a. habits). However, there is significant evidence (Alvaro et al. 2005) that the brain is plastic and capable of creating new patterns.

A lot of the research has to do with teaching individuals the practice of focused attention. One tangible methodology in this regard is neurofeedback, in which participants are hooked up to an EEG device that monitors brain and central nervous system activity and asked to watch a video screen (Peterson et al. 2008). Through a prescribed set of exercises participants can learn to reinforce positive neural networks and extinguish negative/dysfunctional neural networks. The research of Robert Thatcher et al. (2003) is exemplary in this area. EEG methodology is now being applied to leadership development. For example, Arizona State University offers brain mapping as part of its leadership development for MBA students (Peterson et al. 2008).

Self-awareness and authentic leadership

The first component of authentic leadership is self-awareness. A defining characteristic of humans is that they are cognitively self-aware. Each individual is capable of building a mental model of self within his or her environment, one that has meaning and influences day-to-day behavior. This mental model is multidimensional. It includes a sense of positive and negative attributes. Self-awareness is informed internally through introspection and personal insight and externally through social interaction and attention to one's social impact. Kernis (2003) defines self-awareness as "awareness and trust in one's motives, feelings and desires, and self-relevant cognitions. It includes, but is not limited to, being aware of strengths and weaknesses, trait characteristics and emotions."

A considerable body of literature in neuroscience is devoted to the concept of self-awareness. Gusnard (2005) reviews functional imaging in the representation of self and concludes that there is empirical convergence on "a set of brain areas that appear to play a significant role in permitting conscious access to representational content having reference to self as an embodied and independent experiencer and agent." Morin (2006) provides conceptual clarity of self-awareness by reconciling levels of consciousness from a neurocognitive perspective. In his work, self-awareness spans from meta-self-awareness (being aware that one is self-aware) to self-awareness to consciousness to unconsciousness. Focquaert, Braeckman, and Platek (2008) integrate evolutionary and neuroscience perspectives on self-awareness. They propose that humans have an evolutionary edge in self-awareness due to our unique ability for introspection.

Humans have an evolutionary edge in self-awareness due to our unique ability for introspection.

The following sections discuss the neuroscience literature in three specific areas relevant to self-awareness and leadership theory—self-knowledge, mindfulness, and personal insight— and makes recommendations as to how neuroscience can be applied to develop greater self-awareness in leaders.

Self-knowledge

Self-knowledge emanates from a variety of sources. We rely on direct appraisals that involve introspection into firsthand experiences and specific life events. In addition, we use reflected appraisals based on interpretations of how we are seen by others. Ochsner et al. (2005) conducted two fMRI experiments into the neural correlates of direct and reflected self-knowledge. They found evidence that neural systems mediate how we use direct and reflected knowledge; "The neural systems...involved in direct appraisals of self and close others may have more in common than those supporting direct appraisals of self and non-close others."

The implication for leadership development is that we are prone to ignore data about self from people we don't know in favor of data about self from those close to us. Furthermore, there is evidence that direct and reflected appraisals of self use the same neural pathways to create self-knowledge, indicating that reflected appraisals may be interpreted and biased through the cognitive filter of our own beliefs about self.

We are prone to ignore data about self from people we don't know in favor of data about self from those close to us.

In parallel with the concept of self-knowledge, leadership development aimed at enhanced authenticity needs to be aware of the concept of self-deception. Self-deception is defined as a dispositional or unconscious tendency toward an unrealistic or overly positive self-image (Sackeim 1983). While there are positive aspects of self-deception (Taylor 1989), the ability to deceive oneself may be instrumental in the enactment of evil and atrocious behavior (Morton 2005).

Within the organizational context, empirical evidence suggests, self-deception can negatively affect leader-follower relational authenticity (Gray and Densten 2007). On a similar note, Litz (2003) articulates the negative implications of self-deception, both in terms of executive mental health and organizational performance, including, for example, the NASA *Challenger* disaster. Litz recommends that leaders reduce their propensity toward self-deception by acknowledging its possibility, assessing future consequences, and encouraging realistic feedback.

In his insightful book *The Mindful Leader*, Carroll (2008) offers practitioner perspectives on leadership self-deception. Carroll proposes four reasons why leaders engage in self-deception: (1) relentless attention to future success rather than focusing on the flow of the present, (2) relying on external praise (or blame) over one's own internal sense of accomplishment, (3) attempting to maintain the illusion of full control over one's life, and (4) allowing routines to constrain behavior within the limits of one's comfort zone.

Therefore, authentic-leadership development needs to address the issue of self-deception, as well as emphasizing the importance of reflected data about self, including data from unfamiliar sources, and to instill a sense of caution about potential bias from existing self beliefs.

Mindfulness

The neuroscientific study of mindfulness has theoretical and practical implications for developing enhanced self-awareness in leaders. Mindfulness is defined as "awareness of one's present thoughts, emotions, and actions" (Tang and Posner 2008). These researchers go on to state, "Mindfulness may include strong self-awareness and self-observation, or 'waking up' and seeing things as they are." Subsumed under mindfulness is the practice of meditation, sometimes called "right-mindfulness," which emphasizes focus on the present moment.

Meditation—focused attention on a particular thought or object—is now being taught to medical professionals to improve performance and alleviate stress (Hassed 2008; Saunders et al. 2007). It is reasonable to suggest that similar programs should be available to business professionals as part of authentic-leadership development. To this end, Carroll (2008) provides a practical framework for leaders who wish to develop greater mindfulness.

Personal insight

Personal insight is a requirement of self-awareness. Neurological research (Jung-Beeman, Collier, and Kounios 2008; Kounios et al. 2008) has shown that positive mood and rest are the best conditions to facilitate insight. In this regard, one might wonder whether stressed executives, dealing real-time with complexity and competing external demands, have the physiological capacity to attend to internal thoughts and achieve valuable personal insights.

Added to this, neuroscience research has shown that the brain needs a good supply of glucose to work well. When glucose levels drop, our ability to make decisions and self-regulate deteriorates (Rosenthal et al. 2001). Further research needs to be conducted as to whether physiological deficits (stress, lack of sleep, low blood sugar) in the intense, complex, and fiercely competitive financial sector had causal implications for the current financial crisis and the paucity of authentic leadership.

Relational transparency

The second component of authentic leadership is relational transparency. This component defines the degree to which individuals are willing to be open and truthful with others about the real motives, thoughts, and feelings behind their personality and behavior. Kernis (2003) defines relational transparency as being genuine and allowing others to see "the real you," including both positive and negative aspects of oneself. It requires the ability to trust others, to develop intimacy and share personal knowledge. Avolio and Gardner (2005) note that leaders need to be authentic with their followers, which demands trust through personal disclosure.

The concept of relational transparency is cognitively complex, as there are competing motives at play. On one hand, people want to be accepted and liked. To this end, fear of rejection can motivate individuals to engage in duplicity and deception. On the other hand, people, and particularly people with a high sense of self-worth, have a need to be cognitively consistent, minimizing dissonance, thereby remaining true to internal thoughts, feelings, and emotions.

Traditionally, neuroscience research stayed away from explicated modeling of human social interactions, but this trend has reversed in recent years (Kosfeld 2007). There are now significant advances in our understanding of social relationships from a neuroscience perspective. The neuroscientific research streams of particular interest to relational transparency include neural basis of social knowledge, neurobiology of trust, genuineness and transparency, theory of mind, and neural responses to rejection and loneliness.

Social knowledge may be biased toward visual modality, which may explain why visually attractive people are more likely to be perceived as competent leaders.

Neural correlates to social knowledge

Ralph Adolphs (2009) has conducted extensive research in social neuroscience. He proposes that the brain organizes knowledge in three domains: nonsocial knowledge, knowledge of the minds of others, and knowledge of one's own mind. Social thinking in the brain can be both automatic (reflexive) and conscious (reflective), and neural processes mediate between the two (Lieberman 2007). Social knowledge may be biased toward visual modality, which may explain why visually attractive people are more likely to be perceived as competent leaders (Criswell and Campbell 2008; Zebrowitz and Montepare 2005).

Adolphs (2009) summarizes the social neuroscience literature as follows: Insight into how others think may be a unique human capacity. This insight has enabled human civilization to grow. There are automatic and controlled social thinking processes. The brain processes social information differently than it does nonsocial information. The amygdala maintains social vigilance and can be activated by negative/fearful visual patterns. The orbitofrontal cortex helps humans delay immediate social gratification to gain longer-term rewards. The insula controls empathy for others. And context is important in how the brain makes social judgments.

Building on this neuroscientific foundation from a leadership-development standpoint, further research is called for to understand the impact of a leader's visual salience in a manner that does not trigger an emotional threat response.

Neurobiology of trust

Trust is an essential element to facilitate social interaction, including the ability of authentic leaders to trust their followers, which in turn promotes openness, transparency, and truthfulness. In the field of neurobiology, the peptide oxytocin found in the brain has been shown to be a chemical antecedent to trust (Zak, Kurzban, and Matzner 2005). A deficit in this simple molecule, as a result of loneliness, anxiety, and/or stress, can decrease one's capacity to trust. In addition, fMRI studies have shown that the brain has automatic schema to evaluate others. For example, certain facial characteristics can activate a fear response in the amygdala, which in turn produces a judgment that someone is untrustworthy (Bar, Neta, and Linz 2006; Said, Baron, and Todorov 2009). Given these findings, authentic leadership research may benefit from the study of first impressions, including a leader's ability to establish personal warmth and demonstrate professional competence early on during interpersonal interactions.

The peptide oxytocin found in the brain has been shown to be a chemical antecedent to trust...

Genuineness and transparency

An abstract model of associative cognition and emotion has been developed (AMACE) to explain person-centered communications as defined by Carl Rogers (Motschnig and Nykl 2003). This model builds from a variety of cognitive perspectives, including cognitive neuroscience (long-term memory, working memory, emotional salience, brain region activation, emotional contagion, feelings, and consciousness). These research findings suggest neural correlates to congruence, genuineness, realness, and transparency—all of which are relevant to improved understanding of relational transparency as it pertains to authentic leadership.

Theory of mind

Theory of mind refers to the distinction between what one knows, thinks, intends, or feels versus what others know, think, intend, or feel (Premack and Woodruff 1978). In a study of the neurobiological functioning of interpersonal processes, Heisel and Beatty (2006) recognized theory of mind as essential to interpersonal communication and social relationships. Their research measured changes in electrical activity in two regions of the cortex (orbitofrontal cortex and dorsolateral prefrontal cortex) associated with theory of mind operations.

Empirical findings support the fact that individuals produce distinct neurological signatures when they think about others' mental states. This research may facilitate theoretical advancements such that a variety of scenarios might be empirically tested to gauge the degree to which individuals envision others' mental states as part of their own thinking processes. In this manner, future research may be able to empirically address a leader's efficacy in constructing cognitive representations of the state of mind of his or her followers.

Neural responses to rejection and loneliness

Neuroimaging has been used to investigate differences in neural patterns among individuals with different rejection sensitivity (Kross et al. 2007). It appears that individuals who are highly sensitive to rejection may have difficulty in accessing prefrontal cortex (PFC) regions of the brain that provide conscious cognitive control of social behavior. Therefore, with respect to relational transparency, it may be illustrative to study a subset of leaders who manifest high sensitivity to rejection.

A second mediating variable influencing social-cognitive processes is social isolation (loneliness). An fMRI study on loneliness in relation to neural patterns found evidence of individual differences (Cacioppo et al. 2009). These research findings suggest that pleasant social stimuli produce less activation in the brain reward centers of lonely people than in those of others. Therefore, lonely individuals will be less motivated to attend to social group exchange. From a neurological perspective, loneliness shapes expectations of what we expect from and think about others. Given these findings from neuroscience, further leadership research is recommended to understand loneliness as a leadership phenomenon, one that may be an inherited trait, and its implications for creating relational transparency with followers.

Balanced processing

The third component of authentic leadership is balanced processing. When a leader makes a decision, he or she accesses a variety of perspectives, both internal and external. The relevant consideration with respect to balanced processing is the degree to which the individual avoids denial, distortion, and/or exaggeration and remains objective in his or her analysis of all relevant data. Kernis (2003) noted that ego defense mechanisms may compel individuals to engage in self-delusion, in terms of both private self-knowledge and externally based evaluative information. Gardner et al. (2005) proposed that an authentic leader will solicit views that challenge his or her own deeply held positions. Balanced processing is critical if the leader is to achieve congruence between his or her ideal and actual self.

Ego defense mechanisms may compel individuals to engage in self-delusion, in terms of both private self-knowledge and externally based evaluative information.

Neuroscience can enlighten theoretical and developmental aspects of balanced processing with findings about what constitutes relevant data from a neurological viewpoint, neural impediments to balanced processing, and the brain's limitations regarding the scope and span of human attention.

Relevant data

Balanced processing, according to authentic-leadership theory, requires the objective analysis of data. For example, one of the ALQ scale items measures the degree to which a leader will "analyze relevant data before coming to a decision" (Walumbwa et al. 2008). Note the adjectival emphasis in the words "relevant data." In this regard, neuroscience can provide valuable theoretical and empirical insights into how the human brain determines relevance. In our sensory world, relevant data are construed as hard data, which means phenomena we can physically see, hear, touch, and so forth. In the corporate world, we appreciate hard facts to make good decisions.

Consider for the sake of example the hypothetical case of two employees, both of whom have requested a lighter workload during the next few weeks. One employee suffered a broken leg while skiing on the weekend. The other employee broke up with his long-term girlfriend on the weekend. The question here is, what does the authentic leader in the role of decision maker deem relevant data? It is suggested that the employee with the broken leg will fare much better than the employee with the broken relationship. However, neuroscience has shown that the brain processes soft, intangible data in the same way as hard, tangible data. Specifically, emotional pain (i.e., social rejection) is represented in the brain in the same manner as physical pain (i.e., a broken leg) (Lieberman and Eisenberger 2008). In addition, Izuma, Saito, and Sadato (2008) demonstrated that social reward (i.e., enhanced reputation) is processed in the brain in the same manner—anatomically and functionally—as monetary reward.

In light of these neuroscientific findings, further leadership research of an applied nature is recommended to understand how leaders utilize various types of data in their decision making—in particular the distinction between social data and nonsocial data.

Neural impediments to balanced processing

Aside from neuroscience research, decision-making research has shown that humans rely on the efficiency of heuristics rather than extensive analytical processes (Gilovich, Griffin, and Kahneman 2002). Of particular interest in neuroscience are affect heuristics emergent from emotions. Neurobiology presents evidence to suggest that there are neural impediments to balanced processing. The brain's limbic system—in particular, the amygdala—has been shown to be instrumental in a number of studies of decision biases. Fear and threat can trigger the amygdala, which in turn causes considerable disruption to cognitive processing (Davidson 2001).

For example, fMRI scans have shown that individuals have an emotional reaction to risk, which distorts the logic of their decisions (De Martino et al. 2006). Hsu et al. (2005) found neural distinctions between risk (probabilities known) and ambiguity (relevant information missing). Such results refute standard decision theory's unified treatment of these two uncertainty conditions. Peterson (2007) applied recent findings from neuroscience to study affective influences on financial decisions. He concluded that risk-seeking behavior (e.g., gambling) and risk-averse behavior (e.g., buying insurance) may be driven by two distinct neural mechanisms. For example, the nucleus accumbens Nacc—a part of the brain that mediates positive affect—can be cued by situational variables (free drinks, food, gifts in a casino setting) to trigger an increase in risk-seeking behavior.

Such conceptual distinctions found at the level of brain neurology have implications for the development of authenticity in leaders. Neuroscience research suggests that the situational and emotional context in which balanced processing takes place are of significant relevance and worthy of further research.

Neurological limits to attention

Implicit in the definition of balanced processing is the notion of an expansive scope and span of attention. Neuroscience suggests there are neural correlates that mediate the scope and span of our attention. For example, anxiety can truncate attention, including disruption to the functioning of the prefrontal cortex and working memory (Shackman et al. 2006). Neurobiology has shown that the brain is not capable of attending to its environment in a distributed, equal manner. Items in our environment with an emotional tag receive attention priority (Vuilleumier and Huang 2009). Items that follow too quickly behind earlier information tend to be missed via a neural process called "attentional blink" (Martens and Valchev 2009). Positive emotions increase span of attention, including seeking out new information (Rowe, Hirsh, and Anderson 2007). Negative emotions reign in attention, causing it to concentrate on limited actions and stimuli (Fredrickson and Branigan 2005). Individuals for whom information becomes routine and repetitive suffer from mental satiation, which manifests itself in the brain as reduced activity in reward centers and increased activity in centers controlling aversion (Mojzisch and Schulz-Hardt 2007).

From a leadership-development perspective, there may be benefit in training leaders to explicitly direct the focus of their thinking (metacognition) while recognizing and accommodating neural propensities such as attentional blink. In addition, further research might shed light on the developmental value of simple attention-control exercises such as "pause and redirect" as a means to enhance balanced processing.

Positive emotions increase span of attention, including seeking out new information.

Internalized moral perspective

The final component of authentic leadership is internalized moral perspective. This component comprises the theoretical amalgamation of two prior subelements: self-regulation with reference to the degree to which an individual behaves in accordance with internal values, beliefs, and moral standards, as opposed to external social pressures from relevant organizational, group, and societal spheres; and positive moral perspective whereby an individual has reserves of moral capacity, efficacy, courage, and resiliency to sustain behavior in an authentic and moral manner (Avolio and Gardner 2005). Internal moral perspective manifests itself in the leader's behavior, in particular the consistency of behavior in support of a set of internal values and standards.

There is debate in the leadership literature about requirements for a moral dimension. Luthans and Avolio (2003) propose that authentic leadership must include an inherent ethical/moral dimension. Shamir and Eilam (2005) take the counterposition that a leader can be authentic ("true to self") without that referent self being moral or displaying high standards of ethical behavior. Sparrowe (2005) advises that in the case of narcissistic or dysfunctional personalities, it might actually be undesirable for leaders to achieve authenticity.

Neuroscience has much to offer to our understanding of the concept of internalized moral perspective.

Neuroscience has much to offer to our understanding of the concept of internalized moral perspective. The following topics are considered from a neuroscience perspective: self-regulation, the neurological basis for morality, and the brain in relation to ethical decision making.

Self-regulation

The ability to consciously regulate one's responses to one's environment is a critical function, one that enables productive social interaction and the progression of human civilization. Self-regulation becomes even more critical for leaders who exist under the spotlight of social attention and who are expected to be exemplary role models. Moss and colleagues (2009) focused on self-regulation in relation to leadership. They proposed self-esteem as an antecedent variable. Individuals with "fragile," as opposed to "secure," self-esteem tend toward lower adaptability and social cohesion, particularly in diverse, unfamiliar contexts.

From the perspective of neuroscience, the consensus is that the conscious control functions of the brain, the so-called executive brain, are located in the frontal lobes (Goldberg 2001). This area is responsible, in coordination with other regions, for behavior, including moral behavior. This is the neural region where future actions are assessed, decisions between "good" and "bad" are made, and unacceptable social responses are controlled. Ochsner and Gross (2008) note that functional imaging has permitted the development of multilevel models of emotion regulation (behavior, information processing, and neural substrate) such that neuroscience data can inform and support behavioral data. In their study of reappraisal—rethinking the meaning of affectively charged stimuli to alter emotional impact—they recognize the efficacy of tactics such as reinterpretation and distancing.

Neuroscience data can inform and support behavioral data.

In a related, and subsequent, regulatory thought process—suppression of expressive behavior—Ohira et al. (2006) demonstrated the centrality of the prefrontal regions. Future research will be necessary to articulate the efficacy of various suppression strategies.

In addition, the propensity to ruminate, to focus on negative aspects of self or one's life, diminishes the individual's ability to self-regulate by reducing access to prefrontal regions implicated in self-focused thought (Ray et al. 2005). Neuroimaging studies empirically support the effectiveness of conscious and voluntary use of metacognition and cognitive recontextualization to enhance self-regulation (Beauregard 2007). These research studies are indicative of neuroscience's strong empirical foundation and implications for self-regulation with respect to authentic-leadership behavior. Future research has the potential to demonstrate the efficacy of teaching regulatory strategies as part of leadership-development programs, including the ability to reinterpret stimuli, distance oneself psychologically, suppress expressive behavior, and refocus attention away from the negative aspects of self and life.

The neurological basis for morality

Neuroscience is a recent and valuable addition to our understanding of moral reasoning. Not only is this research relevant to authentic-leadership theory but it has become quite salient in legal studies, with *Behavioral Sciences and Law* devoting a recent issue to the topic (Erickson and Felthous 2009). Neuroimaging has found evidence of three anatomical locations in the prefrontal cortex (PFC) involved in moral judgment (Knabb et al. 2009). The medial-frontal cortex (MFC) processes moral emotions such as compassion and guilt. The orbital-frontal cortex (OFC) is involved with emotions such as indignation. The dorsolateral prefrontal cortex (DLPFC) is implicated in evaluations of fairness. Dysfunction in these locations can result in a variety of moral deficiencies, including apathy, impulsiveness, lack of consideration, and inability to maintain goal-directed behavior. Knabb et al. (2009) recommend Moll et al.'s (2005) EFEC (Event-Feature-Emotion Complexes) model, which is based on the proposition that "moral cognitive phenomena emerge from both content-dependent and context-independent representations in the cortical as well as limbic networks." The EFEC model allows for prediction of moral emotions, moral values, and long-term goals. Future advances in this research have the potential to empirically substantiate that some people may be anatomically less capable than others of moral behavior.

Brain processes have been shown to mediate the degree to which a person decides between abstract principles for the greater good and their own individual needs...

In addition, brain processes have been shown to mediate the degree to which a person decides between abstract principles for the greater good (a utilitarian moral response) and their own individual needs (a personal moral response). There is an element of cognitive conflict in this regard (Greene et al. 2004). Control processes in the lateral prefrontal cortex compete with affective/emotional processes in the superior temporal sulcus (STS), posterior cingulated cortex (PCC), and medial-frontal cortex (MFC).

From the perspective of developing authentic leaders, recent research linking neuroscience and moral cognition shows considerable promise. Moral values can be predicted using neuroimaging technology based on activation of different brain regions (Moll et al. 2005). In this manner, future advances in neurofeedback may enable leaders to explore, using hard empirical data, their own moral thinking processes, including their propensity to engage in utilitarian moral behavior versus personal moral behavior.

Brain and business ethics

In their review of theoretical developments and empirical evidence from cognitive neuroscience research on ethical decision making, Salvador and Folger (2009) suggest that "neuroethics, the study of cognitive and neural mechanisms underlying ethical decision making, is a growing field of study." Their summary of the neuroethics literature produced several informative conclusions.

First, decision making in general, including ethical decision making, is a distributed function within the brain, relying on the interplay of several regions. However, it is important to note that ethical decision making has a unique neuroimaging signature such that it is considered an independent intellectual ability distinct from other forms of cognitive decision making. In terms of Rest's (1986) ethical decision sequence of identification-judgment-intention-behavior, neurological evidence supports distinctive neural patterns characterizing each element of the sequence except for intention.

Second, neuroscientists (Satpute and Lieberman 2006) have proposed separate reflective (conscious) and reflexive (unconscious) systems within brain anatomy. Ethical concerns based on stimuli can be triggered unconsciously and, in the case of high pattern similarity against stored memory, the whole decision sequence right out to behavior may remain unconscious (Reynolds 2006). When high pattern similarity does not occur, then the issue becomes reflective and active judgment takes place. These findings suggest that some ethical judgments may not be well thought out in the conscious sense. They may result from instantaneous and unconscious processes (Haidt and Bjorklund 2008). Paradoxically, attempts to circumvent unconscious processes using rule-based ethical decision-making protocols may result in normatively worse decisions (Woodward and Allman 2007).

It is clear that neuroscience research makes a valuable contribution to the moral dimensions of authentic leadership, both in terms of its future research agenda and the practicality of leadership development. Neuroscientific findings suggest that prescriptive approaches to ethical decision making, especially those that ignore affect (mood and emotion), may be suboptimal. From the perspective of authentic-leadership development, further research is called for to determine whether training interventions to develop moral awareness and judgment should be treated as distinct from general analytical interventions under the related concept of balanced processing. Neuroscience research appears to suggest that moral competence should not be treated singularly as rational and utilitarian. Recent studies show interesting potential. For example, Immordino-Yang and Damasio (2007) have developed a process in which participants can reflect on body sensations, perceptions, and emotions when faced with ethical dilemmas.

Concluding comments

This chapter has focused on the contribution of neuroscience to four factors of authentic leadership: self-awareness, relational transparency, balanced processing, and internalized moral perspective. For each factor, a number of research intersections have been recognized with both theoretical and developmental implications. It is important to recognize that authentic-leadership research (Walumbwa et al. 2008) devotes considerable attention to additional constructs, such as organizational culture, climate, and the nature of relations between authentic leaders and their followers. It is beyond the scope of this writing to explore these additional constructs in detail, save to note, in closing, their potential for future research.

For example, neuroscience research on mirror neurons (Gazzaniga 2004) has the potential to inform the development of authentic followers. Mirror neurons exist throughout the brain. The interesting point is that they fire not only when we behave but also when we observe the behavior of others. Watching an action creates the same neural signatures as doing the action ourselves. Therefore, the challenge to authentic leaders is to develop followers in a manner that utilizes our knowledge of mirror neurons, including acting as a mentor, being visible as a role model and coach, and using salient visual (as well as auditory and word) data to communicate expectations (Goleman and Boyatzis 2008).

The application of social-cognitive and affective neuroscience to organizational theory is a novel field of inquiry that holds much promise for theoretical integration and empirical substantiation. In particular, the emergent realm of neuroleadership has a valuable contribution to make to our understanding of authentic leadership and the practicalities of enhancing authenticity in leaders. It is still early, both in terms of theory development and empirical generalizability, but the potential is evident.

On a closing note, in addition to the evident potentiality of neuroscience as outlined here, it is important to anticipate the potential contribution of novel, synergistic research intersections that will further illuminate leadership and organizational theory. Of significant research interest in the future will be the three-way integration of neuroscience, genetics, and leadership research (Mattay, Meyer-Lindenberg, and Weinberger 2006). Early evidence (Lee and Chamberlain 2007) indicates that genetic markers may influence brain processes such as efficiency of the prefrontal cortex and sensitivity of the amygdala, which in turn affect leadership behaviors. Future research may be able to inform social scientists about the age-old question concerning the degree to which leaders are "born versus made," as well as the efficacy of leadership development versus innate, natural ability.

References

Adolphs, R. 2009. "The Social Brain: Neural Basis of Social Knowledge." *Annual Review of Psychology* 60(1): 693–716.

Alvaro, P., Amir, A., Felipe, F., and Lotfi, B. M. 2005. "The Plastic Human Brain Cortex." *Annual Review of Neuroscience* 28: 377–402.

Antonakis, J., Ashkanasy, N. M., and Dasborough, M. T. 2009. "Does Leadership Need Emotional Intelligence?" *Leadership Quarterly* 20(2): 247–261.

Ashkanasy, N. M., and Daus, C. S. 2002. "Emotion in the Workplace: The New Challenge for Managers." *Academy of Management Executive* 16(1): 76–86.

Avolio, B. J., and Gardner, W. L. 2005. "Authentic Leadership Development: Getting to the Root of Positive Forms of Leadership." *Leadership Quarterly* 16(3): 315–338.

Avolio, B. J., Walumbwa, F. O., and Weber, T. J. 2009. "Leadership: Current Theories, Research, and Future Directions." *Annual Review of Psychology* 60: 421–449.

Bar, M., Neta, M., and Linz, H. 2006. "Very First Impressions." *Emotion* 6(2): 269–278.

Barnard, C. I. 1938. *The Functions of the Executive*. Cambridge, MA: Harvard University Press.

Beauregard, M. 2007. "Mind Does Really Matter: Evidence from Neuroimaging Studies of Emotional Self-Regulation, Psychotherapy, and Placebo Effect." *Progress in Neurobiology* 81(4): 218–236.

Boyatzis, R. E., Smith, M. L., and Blaize, N. 2006. "Developing Sustainable Leaders Through Coaching and Compassion." *Academy of Management Learning and Education* 5(1): 8–24.

Butler, M. J. R., and Senior, C. 2007. "Toward an Organizational Cognitive Neuroscience." *Annals of the New York Academy of Sciences* 1118(1): 1–17.

Cacioppo, J., Norris, C., Decety, J., Monteleone, G., and Nusbaum, H. 2009. "In the Eye of the Beholder: Individual Differences in Perceived Social Isolation Predict Regional Brain Activation to Social Stimuli." *Journal of Cognitive Neuroscience* 21(1): 83–92.

Caldu, X., and Dreher, J. 2007. "Hormonal and Genetic Influences on Processing Reward and Social Information." *Annals of the New York Academy of Sciences* 1118(1): 43–73.

Carroll, M. 2008. *The Mindful Leader: Awakening Your Natural Management Skills through Mindfulness Meditation*. Boston: Trumpeter.

Charan, R. 2009. *Leadership in the Era of Economic Uncertainty: The New Rules for Getting the Right Things Done in Difficult Times*. New York: McGraw-Hill.

Criswell, C., and Campbell, D. 2008. "Image Counts: Building an Authentic Leadership Presence." *Leadership in Action* 28(2): 13–17.

Darling, J. R., and Heller, V. L. 2009. "Organization Development in an Era of Socioeconomic Change: A focus on the Key to Successful Management Leadership. *Organization Development Journal* 27(2): 9–26.

Davidson, R. J. 2001. "Toward a Biology of Personality and Emotion." *Annals of the New York Academy of Sciences* 935(1): 191–207.

De Martino, B., Kumaran, D., Seymour, B., and Dolan, R. J. 2006. "Frames, Biases, and Rational Decision Making in the Human Brain." *Science* 313(5787): 684–687.

Erickson, S. K., and Felthous, A. R. 2009. "Introduction to this Issue: The Neuroscience and Psychology of Moral Decision Making and the Law." *Behavioral Sciences and the Law* 27(3): 119–121.

Ferguson, J., and Milliman, J. 2008. "Creating Effective Core Organizational Values: A Spiritual Leadership Approach." *International Journal of Public Administration* 31(4): 439–459.

Focquaert, F., Braeckman, J., and Platek, S. 2008. "An Evolutionary Cognitive Neuroscience Perspective on Human Self-Awareness and Theory of Mind." *Philosophical Psychology* 21(1): 47–68.

Fredrickson, B. L., and Branigan, C. 2005. "Positive Emotions Broaden the Scope of Attention and Thought-Action Repertoires." *Cognition and Emotion* 19(3): 313–332.

Gardner, W. L., Avolio, B. J., Luthans, F., May, D. R., and Walumbwa, F. 2005. "Can You See the Real Me?" A Self-Based Model of Authentic Leader and Follower Development. *Leadership Quarterly* 16(3): 343–372.

Gazzaniga, M. S. 2004. *The Cognitive Neurosciences*. Cambridge, MA: Bradford Books.

George, B. 2003. *Authentic Leadership: Rediscovering the Secrets to Creating Lasting Value*. 1st ed. San Francisco, CA: Jossey-Bass.

George, B., Sims, P., McLean, A. N., and Mayer, D. 2007. "Discovering Your Authentic Leadership." *Harvard Business Review* 85(2): 129–138.

Gilovich, T., Griffin, D. W., and Kahneman, D. 2002. *Heuristics and Biases: The Psychology of Intuitive Judgement.* Cambridge, UK: Cambridge University Press.

Goldberg, E. 2001. *The Executive Brain: Frontal Lobes and the Civilized Mind.* Oxford, UK: Oxford University Press.

Goleman, D., and Boyatzis, R. E. 2008. "Social Intelligence and the Biology of Leadership." *Harvard Business Review* 86(9): 74–81.

Gray, J., and Densten, I. 2007. "How Leaders Woo Followers in the Romance of Leadership." *Applied Psychology* 56(4): 558–581.

Greene, J. D., Nystrom, L. E., Engell, A. D., Darley, J. M., and Cohen, J. D. 2004. "The Neural Bases of Cognitive Conflict and Control in Moral Judgment." *Neuron* 44(2): 389–400.

Gusnard, D. A. 2005. "Being a Self: Considerations from Functional Imaging." *Consciousness and Cognition* 14(4): 679–697.

Haidt, J., and Bjorklund, F. 2008. "Social Intuitionists Answer Six Questions about Moral Psychology." *Moral Psychology* 2: 181–217.

Haines, S. 2009. "Bankrupt Leadership Development?" *Training* 46(5): 64.

Harter, S. 2002. "Authenticity." *Handbook of Positive Psychology* 382–394.

Hassed, C. 2008. "Mindfulness, Well-Being, and Performance." *NeuroLeadership Journal* 1: 53–60.

Heisel, A. D., and Beatty, M. J. 2006. "Are Cognitive Representations of Friends' Request Refusals Implemented in the Orbitofrontal and Dorsolateral Prefrontal Cortices? A Cognitive Neuroscience Approach to "Theory of Mind" in Relationships." *Journal of Social and Personal Relationships* 23(2): 249–265.

Hsu, M., Bhatt, M., Adolphs, R., Tranel, D., and Camerer, C. F. 2005. "Neural Systems Responding to Degrees of Uncertainty in Human Decision Making." *Science* 310(5754): 1680–1683.

Ilies, R., Morgeson, F. P., and Nahrgang, J. D. 2005. "Authentic Leadership and Eudaemonic Well-Being: Understanding Leader–Follower Outcomes." *Leadership Quarterly* 16(3): 373–394.

Immordino-Yang, M. H., and Damasio, A. 2007. "We Feel, Therefore We Learn: The Relevance of Affective and Social Neuroscience to Education." *Mind, Brain, and Education* 1(1): 3–10.

Izuma, K., Saito, D. N., and Sadato, N. 2008. "Processing of Social and Monetary Rewards in the Human Striatum." *Neuron* 58(2): 284–294.

Jung-Beeman, M., Collier, A., and Kounios, J. 2008. "How Insight Happens: Learning from the Brain." *NeuroLeadership Journal* 1: 20–25.

Kernis, M. H. 2003. "Toward a Conceptualization of Optimal Self-Esteem." *Psychological Inquiry* 14(1): 1–26.

Khan, O. 2009. "Liberating passion: How the World's Best Leaders Produce Winning Results." *Leader to Leader* 52: 18–22.

Klein, H. E., and D'Esposito, M. 2007. "Neurocognitive Inefficacy of the Strategy Process." *Annals of the New York Academy of Sciences* 1118(1): 163–185.

Knabb, J. J., Welsh, R. K., Ziebell, J. G., and Reimer, K. S. 2009. "Neuroscience, Moral Reasoning, and the Law." *Behavioral Sciences and the Law* 27(2): 219–236.

Kosfeld, M. 2007. "Trust in the Brain. Neurobiological Determinants of Human Social Behaviour." *EMBO Reports* 8(S1): 44–47.

Kounios, J., Fleck, J. I., Green, D. L., Payne, L., Stevenson, J. L., Bowden, E. M., et al. 2008. "The Origins of Insight in Resting-State Brain Activity." *Neuropsychologia* 46(1): 281–291.

Kranacher, M. 2009. "Accounting for the Madoff Fraud." *CPA Journal* 79(4): 80.

Kross, E., Egner, T., Ochsner, K., Hirsch, J., and Downey, G. 2007. "Neural Dynamics of Rejection Sensitivity." *Journal of Cognitive Neuroscience* 19(6): 945–956.

Lee, N., and Chamberlain, L. 2007. "Neuroimaging and Psychophysiological Measurement in Organizational Research: An Agenda for Research in Organizational Cognitive Neuroscience." *Annals of the New York Academy of Sciences* 1118(1): 18–42.

Levine, C. 2007. "Neural Correlates of Corporate Camaraderie and Teamwork." *Annals of the New York Academy of Sciences* 1118(1): 102–108.

Lieberman, M. D. 2007. "Social Cognitive Neuroscience: A Review of Core Processes." *Annual Review of Psychology* 58: 259–289.

Lieberman, M. D., and Eisenberger, N. 2008. "The Pains and Pleasures of Social Life: A Social Cognitive Neuroscience Approach." *NeuroLeadership Journal* 1: 38–43.

Litz, R. 2003. "Cheating at Solitaire: Self-Deception, Executive Mental Health, and Organizational Performance." *Business and Society Review* 108(2): 235–261.

Love, M. 2008. "Why Preparation is Key to Leadership Communication." *Strategic Communication Management* 12(3): 12.

Luthans, F., and Avolio, B. J., eds. 2003. *Authentic Leadership: A Positive Developmental Approach*. San Francisco, CA: Berrett-Koehler.

Macik-Frey, M., Quick, J., and Cooper, C. 2009. "Authentic Leadership as a Pathway to Positive Health." *Journal of Organizational Behavior* 30(3): 453–458.

Manz, C. C., Anand, V., Joshi, M., and Manz, K. P. 2008. "Emerging Paradoxes in Executive Leadership: A Theoretical Interpretation of the Tensions Between Eorruption and Virtuous Values." *Leadership Quarterly* 19(3): 385–392.

Martens, S., and Valchev, N. 2009. "Individual Differences in the Attentional Blink." *Experimental Psychology* 56(1): 18–26.

Mattay, V. S., Meyer-Lindenberg, A., and Weinberger, D. R. 2006. *Imaging Genetics.* In *Methods in Mind*, edited by C. Senior, T. Russell, and M. S. Gazzaniga, 263–290. Cambridge, MA: MIT Press.

Mazutis, D., and Slawinski, N. 2008. "Leading Organizational Learning Through Authentic Dialogue." *Management Learning* 39(4): 437–456.

McEnrue, M. P., Groves, K. S., and Shen, W. 2009. "Emotional Intelligence Development: Leveraging Individual Characteristics." *Journal of Management Development* 28(2): 150–174.

McKenna, B., Rooney, D., and Boal, K. B. 2009. "Wisdom Principles as a Meta-Theoretical Basis for Evaluating Leadership." *Leadership Quarterly* 20(2): 177–190.

Michie, S. 2009. "Pride and gratitude: How Positive Emotions Influence the Prosocial Behaviors of Organizational Leaders." *Journal of Leadership and Organizational Studies* 15(4): 393–403.

Mojzisch, A., and Schulz-Hardt, S. 2007. "Being Fed Up: A Social Cognitive Neuroscience Approach to Mental Satiation." *Annals of the New York Academy of Sciences* 1118: 186–205.

Moll, J., Zahn, R., de Oliveira-Souza, R., Krueger, F., and Grafman, J. 2005. "The Neural Basis of Human Moral Cognition." *Nature Reviews Neuroscience* 6(10): 799–809.

Morin, A. 2006. "Levels of Consciousness and Self-Awareness: A Comparison and Integration of Various Neurocognitive Views." *Consciousness and Cognition* 15(2): 358–371.

Morton, A. 2005. "Atrocity, Banality, Self-Deception." *Philosophy, Psychiatry, and Psychology* 12(3): 257–259.

Moss, S. A., Dowling, N., and Callanan, J. 2009. "Towards an Integrated Model of Leadership and Self Regulation." *Leadership Quarterly* 20: 162–176.

Motschnig, R., and Nykl, L. 2003. "Toward a Cognitive-Emotional Model of Rogers's Person-Centered Approach." *Journal of Humanistic Psychology* 43(4): 8–45.

Nemanich, L. A., and Vera, D. 2009. "Transformational Leadership and Ambidexterity in the Context of an Acquisition." *Leadership Quarterly* 20(1): 19–33.

Nicholson, N. 2009. "Leading in Tough Times." *Business Strategy Review* 20(2): 38–41.

Novicevic, M. M., Harvey, M. G., Ronald, M., and Brown-Radford, J. A. 2006. "Authentic Leadership: A Historical Perspective." *Journal of Leadership and Organizational Studies* 13(1): 64–76.

Ochsner, K. N., Beer, J. S., Robertson, E. R., Cooper, J. C., Gabrieli, J. D. E., Kihsltrom, J. F., et al. 2005. "The Neural Correlates of Direct and Reflected Self-Knowledge." *NeuroImage* 28(4): 797–814.

Ochsner, K. N., and Gross, J. J. 2008. "Cognitive Emotion Regulation: Insights from Social Cognitive and Affective Neuroscience." *Current Directions in Psychological Science* 17(2): 153–158.

Ochsner, K. N., and Lieberman, M. D. 2001. "The Emergence of Social Cognitive Neuroscience." *American Psychologist* 56(9): 717–734.

Ohira, H., Nomura, M., Ichikawa, N., Isowa, T., Iidaka, T., Sato, A., et al. 2006. "Association of Neural and Physiological Responses During Voluntary Emotion Suppression." *NeuroImage* 29(3): 721–733.

Olivier, R., and Verity, J. 2008. "Rehearsing Tomorrow's Leaders: The Potential of Mythodrama." *Business Strategy Series* 9(3): 138–143.

Pallesen, K. J., Brattico, E., Bailey, C. J., Korvenoja, A., and Gjedde, A. 2009. "Cognitive and Emotional Modulation of Brain Default Operation." *Journal of Cognitive Neuroscience* 21(6): 1065–1080.

Peterson, R. L. 2007. "Affect and Financial Decision Making: How Neuroscience Can Inform Market Participants." *Journal of Behavioral Finance* 8(2): 70–78.

Peterson, S. J., Balthazard, P. A., Waldman, D. A., and Thatcher, R. W. 2008. "Neuroscientific Implications of Psychological Capital: Are the Brains of Optimistic, Hopeful, Confident, and Resilient Leaders Different?" *Organizational Dynamics* 37(4): 342–353.

Premack, D., and Woodruff, G. 1978. "Does the Chimpanzee have a Theory of Mind?" *Behavioral and Brain sciences* 1(4): 515–526.

Ray, R. D., Ochsner, K. N., Cooper, J. C., Robertson, E. R., Gabrieli, J. D. E., and Gross, J. J. 2005. "Individual Differences in Trait Rumination and the Neural Systems Supporting Cognitive Reappraisal." *Cognitive, Affective, and Behavioral Neuroscience* 5(2): 156–168.

Rest, J. R. 1986. *Moral Development: Advances in Research and Theory*. New York: Praeger.

Reynolds, S. J. 2006. "A Neurocognitive Model of the Ethical Decision Making Process: Implications for Study and Practice." *Journal of Applied Psychology* 91(4): 737.

Ringleb, A. H., and Rock, D. 2008. "The Emerging Field of Neuroleadership." *NeuroLeadership Journal* 1: 3-19.

Rosenthal, J. M., Amiel, S. A., Yaguez, L., Bullmore, E., Hopkins, D., Evans, M., et al. 2001. "The Effect of Acute Hypoglycemia on Brain Function and Activation: A Functional Magnetic Resonance Imaging Study." *Diabetes* 50(7): 1618–1626.

Rousseau, D. M., and McCarthy, S. 2007. "Educating Managers from an Evidence-Based Perspective." *Academy of Management Learning and Education* 6(1): 84–101.

Rowe, G., Hirsh, J. B., and Anderson, A. K. 2007. "Positive Effect Increases the Breadth of Attentional Selection." *Proceedings of the National Academy of Sciences, USA* 104(1): 383–388.

Rowland, P., and Parry, K. 2009. "Consensual Commitment: A grounded Theory of the Meso-Level Influence of Organizational Design on Leadership and Decision Making." *Leadership Quarterly* 20(4): 535–553.

Sackeim, H. 1983. "Self-Deception, Self-Esteem, and Depression: The Adaptive Value of Lying to Oneself." *Empirical Studies of Psychoanalytic Theories* 1: 101–157.

Said, C. P., Baron, S. G., and Todorov, A. 2009. "Nonlinear Amygdala Response to Face Trustworthiness: Contributions of High and Low Spatial Frequency Information." *Journal of Cognitive Neuroscience* 21(3): 519–528.

Salvador, R., and Folger, R. 2009. "Business Ethics and the Brain." *Business Ethics Quarterly* 19(1): 1–31.

Samad, S. 2009. "The Influence of Emotional Intelligence on Effective Leadership Among Managers in Malaysian Business Organizations." *The Business Review*, Cambridge, 13(1): 164–170.

Satpute, A. B., and Lieberman, M. D. 2006. "Integrating Automatic and Controlled Processes into Neurocognitive Models of Social Cognition." *Brain Research* 1079(1): 86–97.

Saunders, P. A., Tractenberg, R. E., Chaterji, R., and Amri, H. 2007. "Promoting Self-Awareness and Reflection Through an Experiential Mind-Body Skills Course for First Year Medical Students." *Medical Teacher* 29(1): 778–784.

Scharff, M. M. 2005. "Understanding WorldCom's Accounting Fraud: Did Groupthink Play a Role?" *Journal of Leadership and Organizational Studies* 11(3): 109–118.

Shackman, A. J., Sarinopoulos, I., Maxwell, J. S., Pizzagalli, D. A., Lavric, A., and Davidson, R. J. 2006. "Anxiety Selectively Disrupts Visuospatial Working Memory." *Emotion* 6(1): 40–61.

Shamir, B., and Eilam, G. 2005. "What's Your Story?" A Lifestories Approach to Authentic Leadership Development. *Leadership Quarterly* 16(3): 395–417.

Sparrowe, R. T. 2005. "Authentic Leadership and the Narrative Self." *Leadership Quarterly* 16(3): 419–439.

Stein, M. 2007. "Oedipus Rex at Enron: Leadership, Oedipal Struggles, and Organizational Collapse." *Human Relations* 60(9): 1387–1410.

Tabibnia, G., and Lieberman, M. D. 2007. "Fairness and Cooperation are Rewarding." *Annals of the New York Academy of Sciences* 1118: 90–101.

Tabibnia, G., Satpute, A. B., and Lieberman, M. D. 2008. "The Sunny Side of Fairness: Preference for Fairness Activates Reward Circuitry (and disregarding unfairness activates self-control circuitry)." *Psychological Science* 19(4): 339–347.

Tang, Y., and Posner, M. I. 2008. "The Neuroscience of Mindfulness." *NeuroLeadership Journal* 1: 33–37.

Taylor, S. 1989. *Positive Illusions: Creative Self-Deception and the Healthy Mind.* New York: Basic Books.

Thatcher, R. W., Walker, R. A., Biver, C. J., North, D. N., and Curtin, R. 2003. "Quantitative EEG Normative Databases: Validation and Clinical Correlation." *Journal of Neurotherapy* 7(3): 87–121.

Treasurer, B. 2009. "Courageous Leadership: Modeling the Way." *Leader to Leader* (52): 13–17.

Vuilleumier, P., and Huang, Y. M. 2009. "Emotional Attention: Uncovering the Mechanisms of Affective Biases in Perception." *Current Directions in Psychological Science* 18(3): 148–152.

Walumbwa, F. O., Avolio, B. J., Gardner, W. L., Wernsing, T. S., and Peterson, S. J. 2008. "Authentic Leadership: Development and Validation of a Theory-Based Measure." *Journal of Management* 34(1): 89–126.

Woodward, J., and Allman, J. 2007. "Moral Intuition: Its Neural Substrates and Normative Significance." *Journal of Physiology-Paris* 101(4-6): 179–202.

Yeats, R. M., and Yeats, M. F. 2007. "Business Change Process, Creativity and the Brain: A Practitioner's Reflective Account with Suggestions for Future Research." *Annals of the New York Academy of Sciences* 1118(1): 109–121.

Zahn, R., Moll, J., Paiva, M., Garrido, G., Krueger, F., Huey, E. D., et al. 2009. "The Neural Basis of Human Social Values: Evidence from Functional MRI." *Cerebral Cortex* 19(2): 276–284.

Zak, P. J., Kurzban, R., and Matzner, W. T. 2005. "Oxytocin is Associated with Human Trustworthiness." *Hormones and Behavior* 48(5): 522–527.

Zebrowitz, L. A., and Montepare, J. M. 2005. "Psychology: Appearance Does Matter." *Science* 308(5728): 1565–1566.

15. Mindfulness as capacity: at the threshold of leadership's next wave?

Dr. Angela Love and Julie Maloney, MA

Angela Love, Principal and Founder, The Daymark Group
angela.love@daymarkgroup.net

Julie Maloney, CEO, High Potential Executive Coaching
julie@juliemaloney.com

Introduction

The authors of this chapter, Love and Maloney, met through their work as leadership-development consultants working with the Microsoft Corporation. With the sponsorship of Lela Panagides, director of People and Organizational Capability, they are developing a pilot program to introduce the concept of "mindfulness" as a mental capacity that can be learned and cultivated to enhance personal and leadership satisfaction and results. The authors share a combined forty years of experience in leadership roles and as organization-development consultants and executive coaches, primarily in Fortune 500 companies, including AT&T, Ernst & Young, GE, GlaxoSmithKline, Johnson & Johnson, Merck & Co., MetLife, the Coca-Cola Company, Wells Fargo, and Tyco International. Love and Maloney work with leaders in positions ranging from midlevel to C-Suite level roles.

Our intent is to propose a new framework for leadership development, one that builds on best practices in the field of leadership development, yet raises the bar to consider what might be next in the theory and practice of leadership, particularly in light of research taking place in the field of neuroscience. We propose the idea and the possibility of a "mindfulness threshold": an emerging level of readiness/willingness of leaders to explore more powerful methods of expanding their own "mental capacity" (i.e., as in the findings of neuroscience related to mindfulness and the brain's ability to function at optimum, more objective, creative, and broader levels). We hope to raise additional questions for research that will both further the current understanding of the impact of mindfulness training and deepen the ability of leadership-development practitioners to design training that targets specific areas of the brain for measurable results.

Need for great leadership

Management research has long documented the far-reaching impact leaders have on organizations, business, and society. Recently, the reality of shortsighted and unethical leadership became the headlines of nightly news about the Wall Street debacles, bank failures, and auto company bankruptcies. Given this context, the need for a better pool of leaders who can think and act broadly and ethically may be one of the imperatives of our time. Yet, two key factors threaten our collective ability to source and deploy our best and brightest, just when they are needed most.

The first factor is a drain on the pool of available leadership talent. Global demographic trends are generating a talent deficit that will continue for at least a decade or more. For professionals in the age category of 35 to 49;—the traditional pool from which emerging and future leaders are sourced—forecasts are for minimal to negative growth in this cohort. By 2015, demographic shifts are expected to result in a 15% reduction in ready talent (Lombardo and Eichinger 2004).

The second factor is that talent is being drained—physically, emotionally, mentally, and spiritually (Loehr and Schwartz 2003). Across the globe, people today deal with a veritable tsunami of chronic high stress, increasing complexity, information and communication overload, rapidly evolving technologies, and a hypercompetitive, 24/7 work world (Hallowell 2006). Anecdotal feedback from leaders who engage with us in coaching and training work across multiple companies and industries is that they too often feel they are operating at "the limit" or near a "breaking point." Even the smartest, most senior leaders are struggling to keep up, to the point that they often don't know what decisions to make or actions to take (Welbourne 2006). Leaders are trying to achieve more with much less, primarily by defaulting to various forms of multitasking and hoping that technology (from their ever-present BlackBerrys to their Outlook e-mail and calendar) will save them. These tools will only take leaders so far; what is really required is a fundamental rethinking of how leaders value and use their mental capacity (Rock 2009).

Just as the world is demanding exponentially more of leaders, the tools and methods of leadership development must expand as well. Especially if demographically the pool of leaders is indeed smaller, it makes sense to ask how we can leverage that talent most efficiently, effectively, and for maxim impact. Our professional experience suggests that while a majority of leadership training programs focus appropriately enough on increasing leadership capabilities (skills), too few address this growing need for increased leadership capacity. The dictionary definition of "capacity"—"the ability to receive or contain" and "the actual or potential ability to perform, yield, or withstand"—leads us to an Internet analogy: too many leaders today are operating with the capacity equivalent of dial-up, when their world requires them to have the mental speed and bandwidth of DSL.

Building on the foundation: self-awareness and self-management

For several decades, the commonly accepted strategy and best practices in leadership development have included the cultivation of self-awareness and self-management abilities in leaders. That standard suite of leadership-development tools and methods includes 360-degree feedback instruments and executive coaching.

Once considered trendy or solely for poor performers, executive coaching has become one of the most widely used processes in leadership development (Goldsmith, Lyons, and Freas 2000; Thach 2002) and has garnered respect both in public consciousness and with the neuroscientific community (Rock 2006; Ringleb and Rock 2008). Executive coaching frequently is driven by "objective" data gathered from one or more sources, including performance appraisals, assessment tools, and feedback on an individual leader's strengths and weaknesses. Feedback is usually geared toward creating greater self-awareness in individual leaders, as a necessary precursor to skill building around predefined leadership competency models and measurable behavioral change. Additionally, over the years there has been extensive adoption of EI (emotional intelligence) and SI (social intelligence) tools and training (Goleman, McKee, and Boyatzis 2002; Goleman 2006) and recently a growing attention to a brain-based approaches to leadership coaching (Rock 2006).

Once considered trendy or solely for poor performers, executive coaching has become one of the most widely used processes in leadership development...

Consequently, we hypothesize that the current pool of leadership talent has attained some degree of self-awareness and ability to self-manage (i.e., ability to self-regulate their thoughts, emotions, and behaviors). This level of readiness, we hypothesize, could be better leveraged than we see being done currently, to take leaders to a new level of development. While the work done around self-awareness and self-management has laid a powerful foundation for future growth in leaders, the current level of leadership development can also be viewed as having hit a plateau. What might motivate leaders and leadership practitioners alike to leave their comfort zone in search of the next big leap in leadership? We think one answer may lie in the second factor impacting leadership talent discussed earlier: the sustained and significant levels of stress impacting leaders' well-being, thinking, and performance.

Stress: the problem and the opportunity

While the relationship between leadership and stress, recovery, performance, and creativity is well documented (Yerkes and Dodson 1908; Benson 1975; 2005; Csikszentmihalyi 1990; Loehr and Schwartz 2003), only a small number of corporations today systematically address (in their leadership programs) stress management and/or best practices in expanding one's physical, emotional, mental, and spiritual capacities.

In terms of mental capacity specifically, leaders self-report to us that they are particularly struggling with their ability to focus, be present, and think as creatively and deeply as their business requires. Linda Stone, lecturer and former Apple and Microsoft executive, describes part of this mental struggle as an issue of "continuous partial attention"; the habit of continually trying to focus on multiple things at once. On her website, she suggests that:

> Like so many things, in small doses, continuous partial attention can be a very functional behavior. However, in large doses, it contributes to a stressful lifestyle, to operating in crisis management mode, and to a compromised ability to reflect, to make decisions, and to think creatively.

Deep breathing was taught as a means to expand an individual leader's mental capacity...

In response to client requests for help around such issues and challenges, Maloney has taught a series of workshops to more than 600 high-potential leaders within Microsoft. These workshops included a simple deep-breathing technique. The deep breathing was taught as a means to expand an individual leader's mental capacity in two primary ways: (a) to reduce the impact of stress (shift out of limbic into higher-brain functioning); and (b) to increase mental focus by returning to the present moment, person, or task at hand. This particular technique was chosen because it could be used as both a stress-reduction technique and as very simple mindfulness practice (breath awareness). As Maloney continues to train and coach inside the company, she has heard anecdotally and tracked through simple participant feedback surveys that the deep-breathing technique is the most valuable tool workshop participants take away and continue to use postworkshop.

Maloney's experience is in alignment with a growing body of mindfulness research, including the benefits of mind-based relaxation and mental training. Tang and Posner (2007) tested a type of mind-body meditation training against a control group taught only stress reduction. They found that the mind-body meditation (IMBT) not only reduced stress more than the stress-reduction technique but also boosted performance on mental tasks. The authors concluded that:

> IBMT is an easy, effective way for improvement in self-regulation in cognition, emotion and social behavior. It may have implications in schools, workplace and personal life. Our study is consistent

> with the idea that attention, affective processes and the quality of moment-to-moment awareness are flexible skills that can be trained.

In terms of the effectiveness of mindfulness, researchers have historical precedence to stand upon as well. As Hassed (2008) states:

> Meditation "research" began thousands of years ago when wise sages observed directly and intently their own experience during and, more importantly, after meditation. Modern science seems to be catching up with what many have known for a long time: meditation is a powerful healing agent for mind and body.

Much is yet to be tested and researched, including the underlying brain mechanism related to mindfulness, which is not yet understood (Tang and Posner 2008). However, the potential applications of mindfulness as a leadership-development tool for increasing mental capacity, at a minimum, is intriguing and of high value. Further research on mindfulness and its relationship to cultivating mind states that enhance leadership performance is an exciting, and perhaps even necessary, call to action.

Mindfulness—leadership's next wave?

It has been suggested that the research on mindfulness and its impact has been inhibited by the lack of an operational definition of meditation or mindfulness (Lutz et al. 2008). Lutz and colleagues have proposed an operational definition or theoretical framework based on traditional meditation texts and their own neuroscientific conceptions. They group standard meditation into two broad categories: FA, or focused-attention, and OM, or open-monitoring meditation.

FA meditation involves directing and sustaining focus on a selected object (e.g., breath sensation) while detecting and monitoring distracters. During FA meditation, one would disengage attention from distracters and shift back to the object (breath) while appraising the distraction in a nonjudgmental manner. OM meditation does not require explicit focus on an object, but rather nonreactive metacognitive monitoring (e.g., labeling the experience). There is a nonreactive awareness of automatic cognitive and emotional interpretation of stimuli. OM is seen as the representative of mindful meditation, which Lutz et al. cite as having received multiple meanings. These two types of meditation represent several meditative traditions, including Zen, Vipassana, and Tibetan Buddhism.

The practice of OM, or mindful meditation, has been cited by Lutz et al. (2008) as showing preliminary support for the possibility that continued practice may disrupt or inhibit automatic responses in appraisal systems, diminishing intensity or duration of negative thoughts or rumination. They suggest that neurophysiologic changes induced by meditation training can be correlated with improvements in behavioral measures of sustained attention, such as functioning in continuous-performance tasks.

Despite the definitional challenges, scientific research on mindfulness has expanded significantly over the past two decades. Brown, Ryan, and Creswell (2007) found that mindfulness-based reporting in the psychological and medical research arenas had increased from 80 reports in 1990, to over 600 reports in 2006. Recent reviews and meta-analyses of the empirical literature suggest that interventions that incorporate mindfulness lead to clinically significant improvements in psychological functioning in varying populations (Baer 2003; Grossman et al. 2004; Salmon et al. 2004; Hayes et al. 2006). Benefits associated with the practice of mindfulness have included enhanced positive mood and reduction in negative moods (Tang and Postner 2008). Preliminary evidence also suggests that mindfulness is associated with enhanced attentional control and other indicators of concentrative capacity (Brown 2006).

Mindfulness and meditation have gone mainstream in medicine and popular culture.

Concurrent with the growth of mindfulness research, mindfulness and meditation have gone mainstream in medicine and popular culture. Few mindfulness experts have advanced the acceptance of mindfulness as much as Jon Kabat-Zinn. Kabat-Zinn and his colleague Saki Santorelli are widely recognized for their 30-year body of work related to Mindfulness-Based Stress Reduction (MBSR) at the University of Massachusetts Center for Mindfulness in Medicine, Health Care, and Society. The center is a natural outgrowth of the acclaimed Stress Reduction Clinic founded in 1979 at the UMass Medical School and has successfully taught secular meditative practice to over 17,000 attendees of its programs, with research indicating that meditation increases relaxation ability, reduces pain, increases ability to handle stress, and facilitates long-lasting decreases in physical and psychological pain (Santorelli 2000; Kabat-Zinn 2005). Another hypothesis we propose here is that leaders may be more interested in and/or open to mindfulness-based techniques in part because they may have been exposed to these techniques already through the media, taking yoga or martial-arts classes, and participating in health-management programs through their doctor or corporate-wellness initiatives.

The monks referred to mindful meditation as an antidote for stress and depression...

Looking specifically at the relationship between mindfulness and leadership, Love (2008) based her doctoral dissertation on her qualitative research with monks and lamas who practice Tibetan Buddhism and held roles that require management and leadership. The monks referred to mindful meditation as an antidote for stress and depression, the differentiating factor in happiness versus unhappiness, the way to calm down, the way to gain wisdom, and a way to find purity and clarity. The monks reported that mindfulness helped them slow down the decision-making process and find key questions from which to generate positive action.

Love found that the monks interviewed cited issues similar to those of corporate executives she works with, including stress related to finances, fundraising, cultural diversity, and working with people in direct-reporting relationships and on committees. The monks perceived mindful meditation as contributing to their effectiveness by clearing, calming, focusing, and stabilizing their minds as these issues arose. Their practice was seen as fostering improved relationships and control of negative emotions.

The monks also reported that mindfulness not only was the act of mindful meditation but was in fact a capacity developed as a result of meditation that allowed for the continued "watching of the mind." This consistent mind watching, or self-monitoring, was seen as a way to align thoughts with actions and ethical beliefs. When incorporating simple mindfulness techniques into her work with individual leaders at Microsoft and elsewhere, Love has had positive feedback related to an increased sense of well-being and ability to redirect attention. Although anecdotal, this feedback, along with the self-reporting feedback given to Maloney, has been the impetus to develop the pilot mindfulness program for Microsoft executives.

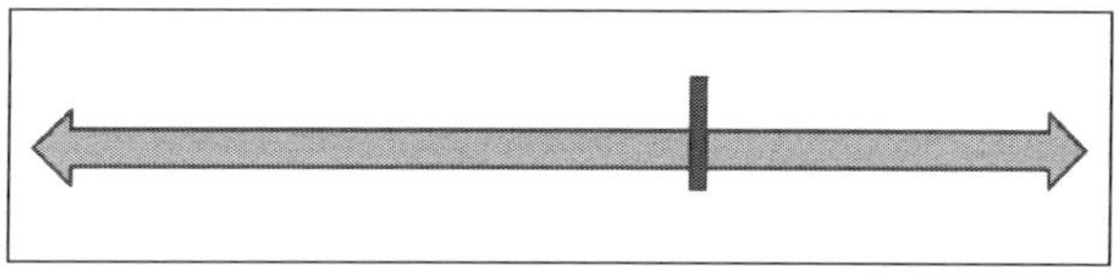

Figure 1. Mindfulness threshold framework

Mindfulness threshold: a proposed framework for leadership development

Given the historical focus of leadership development (on self-awareness and self-management), the current mindfulness practice and research (as cited previously), and the authors' own experience helping corporate leaders deal with stress-overload in their work and lives, we have come to some fundamental questions:

- Is the "pull" factor of increased self-awareness/self-management meeting the "push" factor of chronic /high stress levels in a way that can motivate fundamental change in leaders?
- Could that change include a new transition point in their evolution as leaders—a "mindfulness threshold" to more expansive and effective ways of thinking and leading?
- Conversely, what will happen if leaders don't change, but continue to try to function from the level of capability and capacity at which they now operate?

As a visual, we can propose the framework above for further dialogue, research, and application with leadership practitioners and neuroscientists interested in mindfulness and leadership.

Summary of the framework's key points:

- Widespread use of 360-degree feedback, executive coaching, and EI training over the past 20 years has created a pool of relatively self-aware leaders.
- These tools have moved leaders from a state of "unconsciousness" about who they are and how they impact others, to some degree of "self-awareness." (An unconscious leader could also include a leader who has not yet had had the benefit of the assessments and training that are the foundation for the EI and mindfulness training.)
- By applying increased self-awareness to better self-management of their own behavior, leaders achieve some degree of self-regulation.
- However, chronic overstress that goes unaddressed may drive leaders back toward less conscious thinking and behavior. But stress that is acknowledged and proactively managed (including using deep-breathing and mindfulness techniques) may help motivate leaders to move across a "mindfulness threshold," to develop an increased ability to access and apply higher-functioning mental states.

These tools have moved leaders from a state of "unconsciousness" about who they are and how they impact others, to some degree of "self-awareness."

- These higher mental states may reflect key characteristics attributed historically and through scientific research to "mindfulness," such as a greater capacity for present-moment awareness, compassion, ethical decision making, and systemic/integrative thinking. Behaviorally, this may look like, for example: learning how to exercise more control over their thinking processes; increasing ability to focus and minimizing distractions; slowing down emotional reactions to negative stimuli; and self-shifting mind-body into healthier states that support the objective, creative, executive functioning of the prefrontal cortex.
- If leaders do in fact arrive at this point (this threshold) both highly capable (self-aware and self-managed) and highly motivated (stress-driven), what then is required to help them make the leap? How could leadership-development methods and tools most easily and effectively move them to the next level of leadership? These and other questions require further research.

In summary, we hypothesize that at the Mindfulness Threshold (with some introduction to mind training, mindfulness, and/or meditation techniques), leaders might cross a breakthrough point on a continuum of higher mental states of leadership. This leadership continuum we believe is not unlike what the Mind and Life Institute, an ongoing dialogue between the Dalai Lama and neuroscientists, describes as "the cultivation of positive human qualities—mindful awareness, self-control, social responsibility, and concern for the welfare of others (Mind and Life Institute 2009).

In terms of leadership, we propose for further exploration, through this Mindfulness Threshold framework, a parallel continuum of characteristics for leaders, such as increasing levels of self-regulation, emotional intelligence, systemic/integrative thinking, compassion, and ethical leadership. At this point, in terms of leadership, what lies beyond mindfulness is still unproven and yet quite hopeful.

Call for further research

We have offered an imperative for change in how we develop leaders and proposed several hypotheses about what that change might look like—questions that require further research. In terms of future research, if a question can be considered a "bottom line," the following would be ours: could mindfulness training help leaders not only reduce stress and increase their mental performance but also make them more compassionate and ethical leaders?

Leaders and leadership teams who practice mindfulness will be the ones who show breakthrough results.

Our hope is that this will serve as a catalyst for many more such questions for research and study, by neuroscientists alone and in partnership with leadership practitioners. Future research could help leaders and leadership practitioners as well by also considering:

- How to measure the "threshold"—that is, exactly when and how does a self-aware and self-regulating leader become "mindful"?
- The "dosage" of mindfulness training required and the degree of lasting change it can produce
- Developing best-in-class techniques to teach executives the practice of mindfulness in ways that respect the limited time and resources available to executives
- Measuring changes in body-mind behavior during and after mindfulness practice
- Measuring business and organizational ROI related to the development/application of mindfulness

We believe that such research would find a willing and grateful audience. Speaking from the front lines of leadership, Ms. Panagides of Microsoft says: "I predict that leaders and leadership teams who practice mindfulness will be the ones who show breakthrough results. These will be the teams that create healthier organizations, tap into innovation and creativity, and who inspire those who work for them to know their passion—which all lead to a bigger place." Only research, practice, and time will tell. But perhaps the time to try is indeed now.

> *Attention is the most powerful tool of the human spirit. We can enhance or augment our attention with practices like meditation and exercise, or diffuse it with technologies like email and Blackberries, or alter it with pharmaceuticals. In the end, however, we are fully responsible for how we choose to use this extraordinary tool.* —Linda Stone (n.d.)

About the authors

Angela Love is the principal and founder of the Daymark Group, an organization development and executive coaching firm dedicated to serving Fortune 500 companies internationally. Dr. Love has over twenty years of experience in Fortune 500 corporation management, consulting, and leadership development. Her doctoral research and dissertation focused on mindfulness and ethics, and she often incorporates mindfulness and meditative practices in her work with corporate executives and teams.

Julie Maloney is CEO of High Potential Executive Coaching, a leadership training company that specializes in developing top talent, from green (high potentials) to great (high achievers). For over two decades, Ms. Maloney has coached and trained leaders across the spectrum of requirements for executive maturity and peak performance, including managing successful role transitions/first-ninety-days challenges, using 360-degree feedback to improve current job performance, developing new leadership skills, increasing self-awareness and interpersonal skills, and sustaining performance through greater work/life balance. Her passion is expanding leaders' mental capacity through the practices of mindfulness and mental downtime (white space).

References

Baer, A. R. 2003. "Mindfulness Training as Clinical Intervention: A Conceptual and Empirical Review." *Clinical Psychology: Science and Practice* 10: 125–143.

Benson, H. 2005. "Are You Working Too Hard?" *Harvard Business Review* 83(11): 53–58,165.

Benson, H. 2001. *Relaxation Response*. New York: Quill.

Boyatzis, R. E., and McKee, A. 2005. *Resonant Leadership: Renewing Yourself and Connecting with Others through Mindfulness, Hope, and Compassion*. Boston: Harvard Business School Press.

Brown, K. W. 2006. *Mindfulness and Attentional Control*. Manuscript, University of Rochester: Rochester, NY.

Brown, K. W., Ryan, R. M., and Creswell, J. D. 2007. "Mindfulness: Theoretical Foundations and Evidence for its Salutary Effects." *Psychological Inquiry* 18(4): 211–237.

Cherniss, C., and Goleman, D. 2001. *The Emotionally Intelligent Workplace: How to Select for, Measure, and Improve Emotional Intelligence in Individuals, Groups, and Organizations*. San Francisco, CA: Jossey-Bass.

Gauthier, R., and Giber, O. 2006. *Coaching business leaders.* In *Coaching for Leadership: The Practice of Leadership Coaching from the World's Greatest Coaches* (2nd ed.), edited by Goldsmith, M., and Lyons, L., 116–125. San Francisco, CA: John Wiley & Sons.

Goldsmith, M., Lyons, L., and Freas, A. 2000. *Coaching for Leadership: How the World's Greatest Coaches Help Leaders Learn*. San Francisco, CA: Jossey-Bass.

Goleman, D., McKee, A., and Boyatzis, R. E. 2002. *Primal Leadership Realizing the Power of Emotional Intelligence*. New York: Harvard Business School Press.

Goleman, D. 2006. *Social Intelligence: The New Science of Human Relationships*. New York: Bantam.

Grossman, P., Niemann, L., Schmidt, S., and Walach, H. 2004. "Mindfulness-Based Stress Reduction and Health Benefits. A Meta-Analysis." *Journal of Psychosomatic Research* 57(1): 35-43.

Hallowell, E. M., MD. 2006. *CrazyBusy: Overstretched, Overbooked, and About to Snap*. New York: Ballantine Books.

Hassed, C. 2008. "Mindfulness, Well-Being, and Performance." *NeuroLeadership Journal* 1(1): 53–60.

Hayes, S. C., Luoma, J., Bond, B., Masuda, F. W., and Lillis, J. 2006." Acceptance and Commitment Therapy: Model, Processes, and Outcomes." *Behaviour Research and Therapy* 44: 1–25.

Kabat-Zinn, J. 2005. *Full Catastrophe Living: Using the Wisdom of Your Body and Mind to Face Stress, Pain, and Illness*. New York: Delta Trade Paperbacks.

Loehr, J., and Schwartz, T. 2003. *The Power of Full Engagement: Managing Energy, Not Time, Is the Key to High Performance and Personal Renewal*. New York: Free Press.

Lombardo, E., and Eichinger, R. W. 2004. *The Leadership Machine*. 3rd ed. Minneapolis, MN: Lominger.

Love, A. 2008. *The Lived Experience of Tibetan Buddhist Monks in Managerial Leadership Roles*. PhD diss., Capella University. Ann Arbor, MI: ProQuest UMI.

Lutz, A., Slagter, H. A., Dunne, J. D., and Davidson, R. J. 2008. "Attention Regulation and Monitoring in Meditation." *Trends in Cognitive Sciences* 12(4): 123–170.

Mihaly, C. 1991. *Flow: The Psychology of Optimal Experience*. New York: Harper Perennial.

Mind and Life Institute. Accessed July 14, 2009. http://www.mindandlife.org.

Peltier, B. 2001. *The Psychology of Executive Coaching: Theory and Application*. New York: Taylor and Francis Group.

Ringleb, A. H., and Rock, D. 2008. "The Emerging Field of Neuroleadership." *NeuroLeadership Journal* 1(1): 3–19.

Rock, D. 2006. "A Brain-Based Approach to Coaching." *International Journal of Coaching in Organizations* 4(2): 32–43.

Rock, D. 2009. *Your Brain at Work: Strategies For Overcoming Distraction, Regaining Focus, and Working Smarter All Day Long*. New York: HarperBusiness.

Salmon, P., Sephton, S. E., Weissbecker, I., Hoover, K., Ulmer, C., and Studts, J. 2004. "Mindfulness Meditation in Clinical Practice." *Cognitive and Behavioral Practice* 11: 434–446.

Santorelli, S. 2000. *Heal Thyself: Lessons on Mindfulness in Medicine*. New York: Harmony/Bell Tower.

Stone, L. (n.d.) The Attention Project. LindaStone.net (blog). Accessed July 1, 2009. http://www.lindastone.net.

Stone, L. "Continuous Partial Attention." http://lindastone.net/qa/continuous-partial-attention/. Accessed June 28, 2013.

Tang, Y., and Posner, M. I. 2007. "Body-Mind Meditation Boosts Performance, Reduces Stress." *ScienceDaily*. October 9, 2007. http://www.sciencedaily.com/ releases/2007/10/071008193437.htm.

Tang, Y., and Posner, M. I. 2008. "The Neuroscience of Mindfulness." *NeuroLeadership Journal* 1(1): 33–37.

Tang, Y. Y, Ma, Y., Wang, J., Fan, Y., Feng, S., Lu, Q., Yu, Q., et al. 2007. "Short-Term Meditation Training Improves Attention and Self-Regulation." *Proceedings of the National Academy of Sciences, USA* 104(43): 17152–17156.

Thach, E. 2002. "The Impact of Executive Coaching and 360 Feedback on Leadership Effectiveness." *Leadership & Organization Development Journal* 23: 205–214.

Welbourne, T., MD. 2006. "Stacking Work: The Leadership (and HR) Dilemma." *International Association for Human Resource Information Management website*. Accessed November 2009. www.ihrim.org.

Yerkes, R. M., and Dodson, J. D. 1908. "The Relation of Strength of Stimulus to Rapidity of Habit-Formation." *Journal of Comparative Neurology and Psychology* 18: 459–482.

SECTION IV:
Collaborating with Others

16. The pains and pleasures of social life: a social-cognitive neuroscience approach

Dr. Matthew Lieberman and Dr. Naomi Eisenberger
Matthew Lieberman, University of California, Los Angeles, USA
lieber@ucla.edu

Introduction

Imagine business partners Gil and Sarah who have always split the work and the resulting rewards, evenly, right down the middle. Now Gil lines up three new clients, one of whom will be an easy client, both because he is personable and because Gil and Sarah have amassed great expertise in handling his needs. Each of the other two clients will be more difficult. One is known for being a bit of a bully who seems to change what he wants as a client as his whims change. The second is easy enough to get along with but has demands that really stretch Gil and Sarah's existing expertise. Because Gil has brought in the clients, he feels it is his prerogative to divide the work between them. He chooses to take the first client for himself and assign the two difficult clients to Sarah.

Naturally, Sarah finds this arrangement unfair. She is annoyed at just how much more work she is going to have to do than Gil. She also feels insulted that Gil thought it was acceptable to treat her this way. Her anger at the situation mounts, and she must figure out how to respond. Should she bring this up overtly with Gil and potentially jeopardize their collegial relationship? Should she find a way to respond in kind? Or should she just try to "suck it up" and accept what has happened?

Psychologically, this scenario raises a number of interesting questions. How do common psychological processes determine what one would feel and do in Sarah's position? How does she weigh the costs and benefits of lashing out versus holding her tongue? How do we determine whether her bad feelings are really due to the insult or to the amount of work she has been given? Self-report is notoriously unreliable in these kinds of situations. People are good at reporting how they feel but often quite poor at reporting on the reasons why they feel a certain way (Nisbett and Wilson 1977). How would Sarah have responded to a fairer division of labor? Over the past decade, brain scientists have begun to answer exactly these kinds of questions.

More broadly, a field called social-cognitive neuroscience (Lieberman 2007; Ochsner and Lieberman 2001) has examined both the painful and the pleasurable aspects of social living. To give away our conclusion right at the outset, social pains and pleasures bear a surprising resemblance to physical pains and pleasures. The brain uses similar circuits to handle the social and physical variants of pain and pleasure. This has enormous consequences as we think about the feelings of others and ourselves. It is easy to imagine that Sarah's pain comes primarily from the extra work she will have to do if she accepts Gil's proposal, but brain science suggests that her pain may well come from the social hurt of not being treated like an equal. And this social injury may affect her brain in much the same way as physical injury does.

In this review, we will survey the neuroscience of social pain and social pleasure. We will begin by examining the consequences of being excluded from a group, which is probably a rare event in everyday life but a truly painful one when it occurs and one that we commonly fear in an anticipatory way. Then, we will turn from social pain to social pinches, which refer to the more minor but more frequent types of social pain (e.g., unfair treatment). Finally, we will discuss social pleasure, which activates the brain's reward circuitry far more than most would have guessed.

Social pains

When one is on the receiving end of a relationship breakup, it is not uncommon to describe this to others in terms of one's hurt feelings or one's broken heart. It is striking to notice that the language we use to describe this social pain is in fact the language of physical pain. Indeed, a review of social pain terminology in 15 different languages found that social pain words are almost exclusively borrowed from the physical pain domain in each language (MacDonald and Leary 2005). This could be a coincidence, but mounting evidence suggests that the connection is much deeper.

The brain's physical pain system consists of three regions in the cortex. The somatosensory cortex codes for where in the body a painful stimulation has occurred, particularly for pain on the outer surface of the body. For instance, it can differentiate between pain applied to the left or the right hand. The insula responds to painful stimulation, particularly internal or visceral forms of pain, and seems to provide the brain with a representation of the body's overall state. Lastly, the dorsal anterior cingulate cortex (or dACC for short) is the region that's associated with the distress of physical pain.

It is striking to notice that the language we use to describe this social pain is in fact the language of physical pain.

The dACC is associated with how much a particular pain stimulation bothers an individual. Although the intensity of the stimulation and the subjective distress experienced by an individual are often highly correlated, they can be separated. For instance, through hypnotic suggestion, the same physical stimulus can be experienced as more or less distressing, and it is this experience of distress that is correlated with activity in the dACC (Rainville et al. 1997). Similarly, patients who have tissue surgically removed from their dACC to deal with chronic pain report that they can still identify where painful stimulation occurs and its level of intensity, but they also report that it no longer seems to bother them (Foltz and White 1968).

We were particularly interested in the dACC with regard to social pain because, in addition to its role in physical pain processing, evidence from animal research shows that it may play a role in social pain as well. One primate study found that when the dACC was electrically stimulated in monkeys, these monkeys produced distress vocalizations that are specifically associated with being separated from a caregiver (MacLean and Newman 1982). Similarly, surgical lesions of the dACC led to diminished distress vocalization production in monkeys when separated from their mothers (Kirzinger and Jurgens 1982).

To examine whether social pain in humans uses the same neural circuitry as physical pain uses, we conducted the first functional magnetic resonance imaging (fMRI) study of social exclusion (Eisenberger, Lieberman, and Williams 2003). fMRI is a technique that allows us to assess which regions of the brain are relatively more active when processing a stimuli of interest, performing a task, or having a particular experience. One of the major limitations of fMRI research is that the subject needs to lay absolutely still inside the scanner, not speaking, only pressing buttons on a small 4-button keyboard to provide responses. Under these circumstances, socially rejecting an individual can be quite a challenge.

We convinced subjects that while they were lying in an fMRI scanner in one location, two other subjects were lying in scanners elsewhere on campus and that the three of them were going to play a game together over the Internet while they all had their brains scanned. In fact, there were no other players; participants played with a preset computer program, but this cover story allowed us to set up an experience for the subject that was truly experienced as social and allowed us to control the events to create the experience of social pain.

While in the scanner, subjects played a game called Cyberball (Williams, Cheung, and Choi 2000), in which the subject and two other supposed players played a virtual game of "catch." The two computer players were programmed to throw the ball equally to everyone for a while but then to only throw the ball to each other after that, leaving the one real subject excluded from the game from that point on. It was quite obvious from self-reports that being left out of the game really bothered most of the subjects, but to quantify this social pain, subjects answered questions regarding how much social pain they felt ("I felt rejected," "I felt meaningless") after getting out of the scanner.

What we found was striking. Subjects showed greater activity in the dACC when they were excluded compared with when they were included. Moreover, subjects who reported feeling more social pain also showed greater activity in the dACC during the exclusion phase of the game.

In contrast, right ventrolateral prefrontal cortex (RVLPFC), a brain region involved in pain regulation (Weich et al., forthcoming), was also more active during exclusion than inclusion, though this region was more active to the extent that people reported feeling less social pain. In other words, RVLPFC appeared to be helping to regulate or cope with the social pain, and to the extent that it was active, subjects felt less distressed. Figure 1 displays the results of this study side by side with the results of another study of physical pain regulation (Lieberman et al. 2004). As can be seen, the regions involved in these social and physical pain studies are quite similar, and the relations between them, as indicated by the correlation values next to the arrows, are quite similar as well.

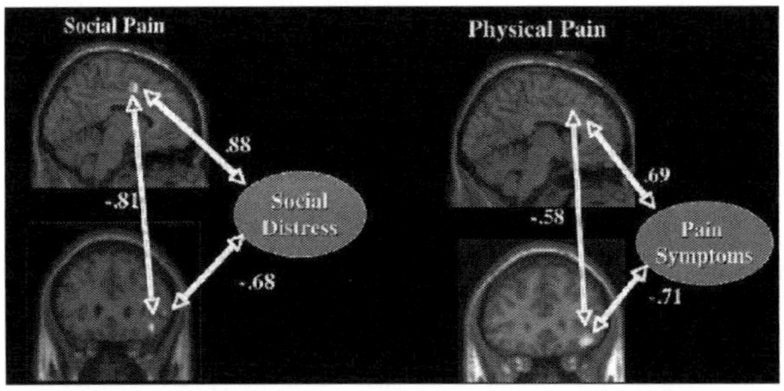

Figure 1. Social and physical pain. In the left panel, the neural responses to social pain and their relation to self-reported distress are shown, with dorsal anterior cingulate cortex (dACC) shown at the top and right ventrolateral prefrontal cortex (RVLPFC) shown at the bottom (from Eisenberger, Lieberman, and Williams 2003). In the right panel, the neural responses to physical pain and their relation to self-reported pain symptoms are shown, with dACC at the top and RVLPFC at the bottom (from Lieberman et al. 2004). The brain regions and the interrelationships between the brain regions and the experience are very similar in social and physical pain.

Why would our brain be organized this way? We believe that the social pain system in the brain may have piggybacked onto the physical pain system during mammalian evolution (Eisenberger and Lieberman 2004; Panksepp 1998), borrowing the pain signal to indicate broken social bonds. Although people generally agree that our basic survival needs are food, water, and shelter, because mammalian young are born immature, incapable of providing for their own physical needs, they must stay connected to their caregivers. In young mammals, the need for this social connection actually supersedes the need for food, water, and shelter, because without a caregiver to provide for these needs, young mammals would not survive. Just as evolution has wired us to feel pain when we lack food (e.g., hunger), water (e.g., thirst), or shelter (e.g., freezing, sunburn), perhaps evolution has wired us to feel pain when we lack or anticipate a lack of social connection.

Several follow-up studies have been conducted to further examine this possible connection between social and physical pain. First, the basic correlational pattern of activity in dACC, RVLPFC, and self-reported social pain during exclusion has been replicated (Eisenberger et al. 2007). Second, we have shown disapproving faces to subjects who vary in their self-reported rejection sensitivity and found that those who are more sensitive to rejection produced greater dACC activity when viewing the disapproving faces (Burklund, Eisenberger, and Lieberman 2007). We have also found that individuals who have a higher tolerance for physical pain also have a higher tolerance for social pain (Eisenberger et al. 2006), such that these individuals are less sensitive to both physical and social pain experiences. Lastly, we have observed that those who show greater dACC activity during social rejection in the scanner also report greater feelings of social disconnection in their real-life daily social interactions (Eisenberger, Gable, and Lieberman 2007).

Social pinches

People rarely experience the kind of full-blown social exclusion that we examined with the Cyberball game. How do the more minor slings and arrows of everyday social living affect us? Do social pinches hurt like social pains? A number of investigators have used economic bargaining games such as the Ultimatum Game to examine how the brain responds to the social pinch of being treated unfairly. Unfair treatment occurs frequently in daily life and thus may represent an important complement to the social rejection research.

In the Ultimatum Game, two individuals must split a sum of money, called the stake, between them. One player, the proposer, proposes a way to split the money. The other player, the responder, then chooses whether to accept the offer. If the offer is accepted, both players receive what the proposer proposed. If the offer is rejected, both players receive nothing. Thus, from a $10 stake, the proposer might propose to keep $8 and pass on $2 to the responder. If the responder feels sufficiently insulted, this offer would be rejected, and both individuals would leave with nothing. Even when subjects know they will only play one time, and thus there is no need to create a particular reputation for themselves, subjects typically reject offers that are less than 20–30% of the total stake (Guth, Schmittberger, and Schwarze 1982).

In the first fMRI study of the Ultimatum Game (Sanfey et al. 2003), subjects played 10 rounds of the game, each round with a new partner. In all rounds, the subject played the role of the responder. Approximately half of the offers were fair ($5 out of $10) and half were unfair ($1 or $2 out of $10). Subjects produced greater activity in the anterior insula and the dACC when confronted with unfair, relative to fair, offers. Both of these regions are part of the physical pain system in the brain. Additionally, the anterior insula has been associated with physical disgust sensations and thus was interpreted as reflecting the degree of insult or disgust the subject felt upon being treated unfairly. Critically, the magnitude of the insula activity predicted the likelihood that the offer would be rejected.

In a follow-up study (Crockett et al. 2008), some subjects played the Ultimatum Game after drinking a pharmaceutical cocktail that put them in a "low serotonin" state. To give a bit of context, low serotonin has been associated with anxiety, depression, impulsivity, and aggression. When people take selective serotonin reuptake inhibitors (SSRIs) such as Zoloft, Paxil, and Prozac, the pharmacological effect is, roughly speaking, to move the individual's brain chemistry from a low-serotonin state to a high-serotonin state. Crockett and colleagues found that when people were put in a low-serotonin state pharmacologically, people were more likely to reject unfair offers. These results suggest that fairness is truly in the eye of the beholder and that eye can change from day to day as one's brain chemistry changes.

In both of these Ultimatum Game studies, it is difficult to separate out the sense of insult from the desire for retribution. Another study using a similar game (de Quervain et al. 2004) separated out the phases of feeling insulted and deciding whether to punish, and observed that punishing a partner that was unfair activated one of the reward regions of the brain. Justice, it appears, can feel sweet indeed.

Sometimes it is necessary to hold one's tongue after unfair treatment. The ability to regulate one's responses to social insults can be critical for managing long-term goals and relationships. This was investigated in a study of the Ultimatum Game that included financially desirable but unfair offers (Tabibnia, Satpute, and Lieberman 2008). Recall that in the previous fMRI study (Sanfey et al. 2003), offers were either fair and desirable ($5 out of $10) or unfair and not very desirable ($1 out of $10). We added in trials that were unfair but financially desirable ($5 out of $20). A typical college undergraduate finds this a desirable amount of money; however, it is still insulting as it represents only 25% of the stake. Tabibnia and colleagues found that some subjects were far more likely to accept these desirable but unfair offers. These individuals tended to activate RVLPFC more, the region we previously described as playing a role in the regulation of physical and social pain distress. In addition, as RVLFPC activity increased, anterior insula activity decreased, suggesting the possible regulation of the insulted feelings associated with this region in the earlier study (Sanfey et al. 2003).

Thus, social pinches such as unfair treatment do appear to activate the social pain system. Additionally, regulation of these responses activates the same RVLPFC region involved in the regulation of social pain from full-blown social rejection.

Social pleasures

If being treated unfairly activates the social pain and disgust circuitry, what does being treated fairly do? One might expect it to have little effect on the brain, since fairness seems like the baseline treatment we expect, with only deviations from this baseline requiring attention and reaction. Others have argued that fair treatment represents an important social reward of its own. In our evolutionary past, and to some extent still today, being accepted and valued by one's group is important because it means access to critical resources for survival and thriving. Signs that one is accepted by a group indicate that one is likely to continue to be treated well by the group and share in that group's successes.

A series of studies have now begun to demonstrate that the brain's reward system, particularly the ventral striatum, reacts as strongly to social rewards in the form of social recognition as it does to one of the most ubiquitous human rewards—money. In the Ultimatum Game study by Tabibnia, Satpute, and Lieberman (2008), the brain's response to fair relative to unfair offers was examined. In a typical Ultimatum Game, and in life in general, fair offers are usually of greater material benefit than unfair offers. Thus it is difficult to know whether the brain's reward response to an offer of $5 out of $10 (relative to an offer of $1 out of $10) is due to the fairness component or the financial reward. To address this, we included fair and unfair offers with equivalent material benefit. For instance, a fair offer of $5 out of $10 could be compared with an unfair offer of $5 out of $20. After controlling for the financial benefit in this manner, we still observed robust activity in the ventral striatum, a reward structure, when subjects were presented with fair, relative to unfair, offers (see fig. 2).

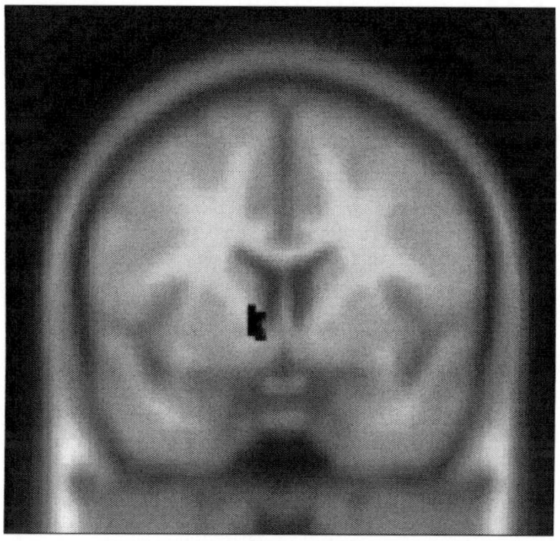

Figure 2. Being treated fairly activates the reward system. This figure shows activation in the ventral striatum when subjects were treated fairly, compared with when they were treated unfairly (Tabibnia, Satpute, and Lieberman 2008).

A second study examined the effects of social reputation (Izuma, Saito, and Sadato 2008). In this study, subjects performed one task in which money could be earned on each trial. In a second task, subjects received feedback from others about their personality that varied in positivity. They observed that rewards in both tasks, financial and social, led to equivalent levels of ventral striatum activity. In other words, our brain's reward system responds to positive feedback about us from others in the same manner that it responds to monetary incentives.

Finally, another group of researchers asked directly whether it is truly better to give than to receive. In this study (Moll et al. 2006), in some trials, subjects chose whether to give a certain portion of their payment to real charities around the world and on other trials received the money themselves. They found that donating to charity led to more activity in the ventral striatum than did receiving the money themselves. In addition, the extent to which the ventral striatum was active when deciding whether to donate was associated with how often during the task subjects chose to donate. Thus, in some cases, giving to others can be more rewarding than receiving a financial reward.

Conclusions

For decades now, we have been hearing about the parts of the brain that support language, vision, memory, and higher cognitive skills such as math and reasoning. Because of this, it is not surprising that the human brain has been conceptualized as a computer or a machine that can be optimized in the workplace by increasing processing efficiency or correcting errors through feedback. These new findings from social-cognitive neuroscience suggest that bringing out the best in people in the workplace depends at least as much on optimizing a person's social and emotional well-being as it does on those cognitive processes.

We would never expect someone who has a broken leg to run from one meeting to the next. But when someone is in social pain, we often treat this as if it should be compartmentalized and kept outside the office. Even worse, we sometimes think people should simply "get over" their hurt feelings, despite the fact we would never think someone should "get over" their broken leg. The evidence we reviewed clearly demonstrates strong similarities in how the brain reacts to social and physical pain. Accordingly, we need to appreciate that however much reality we accord to physical pain should also be extended to social pain.

When our social needs are being satisfied, the brain responds in much the same way as it responds to other rewards that are more tangible.

On the other side of the equation, when our needs are met, we feel pleasure. Eating when hungry, drinking when thirsty, and coming in from the cold are all pleasurable experiences that occur while a need is being satiated. The need for social regard may seem less immediate and real than other needs, but it is a basic need (Baumeister and Leary 1995). When our social needs are being satisfied, the brain responds in much the same way as it responds to other rewards that are more tangible.

This suggests that the exclusive premium put on financial rewards as an incentive around the office may be overstated. Being treated with respect and as a valued member of the organization may activate reward systems in the brain that promote stronger learning of behaviors that predict more of these social rewards in the future. And obviously, providing social rewards is an extremely cost-effective measure, requiring only a bit of time and thoughtfulness.

More generally, these results highlight what has been described as the human tendency toward affective forecasting errors (Gilbert 2005). People have strong beliefs about what will make them more or less happy, and, since we all want to maximize our positive feelings and minimize our negative feelings, we choose our careers, home, spouses, and friends on the basis of these emotional predictions .

Unfortunately, these forecasts of what will make us happy are often wrong. Most people would not predict that social rewards could be as pleasurable as financial rewards, and most would not predict that social pain can hurt like physical pain in many ways. Consequently, in both our professional and private lives, we make many choices that do not adequately take into account how much the human brain is sensitive to these factors. As we learn more about the brain, it may help people to better appreciate how their well-being and the well-being of those around them is affected by the pains and pleasures of social living.

References

Baumeister, R. F., and Leary, M. R. 1995. "The Need to Belong: Desire for Interpersonal Attachments as a Fundamental Human Motivation." *Psychological Bulletin* 117: 497–529.

Burklund, L. J., Eisenberger, N. I., and Lieberman, M. D. 2007. "The Face of Rejection: Rejection Sensitivity Moderates Dorsal Anterior Cingulate Activity to Disapproving Facial Expressions." *Social Neuroscience* 2: 238–253.

Crockett, M. J., Clark, L., Tabibnia, G., Lieberman, M. D., and Robbins, T. W. 2008. "Serotonin Modulates Behavioral Reactions to Unfairness." *Science* 320(5884): 1739.

De Quervain, D. J., Fischbacher, U., Treyer, V., Schelhammer, M., Schnyder, U., Buck, A., and Fehr, E. 2004. "The Neural Basis of Altruistic Punishment." *Science* 305: 1254–1258.

Eisenberger, N. I., and Lieberman, M. D. 2004. "Why it Hurts to be Left Out: The Neurocognitive Overlap Between Physical and Social Pain." *Trends in Cognitive Sciences* 8: 294–300.

Eisenberger, N. I., Gable, S. L., and Lieberman, M. D. 2007. "fMRI Responses Relate to Differences in Real-World Social Experience." *Emotion* 7: 745–754.

Eisenberger, N. I., Jarcho, J. J., Lieberman, M. D., and Naliboff, B. D. 2006. "An Experimental Study of Shared Sensitivity to Physical Pain and Social Rejection." *Pain* 126: 132–138.

Eisenberger, N. I., Lieberman, M. D., and Williams, K. D. 2003. "Does Rejection Hurt? An fMRI Study of Social Exclusion." *Science* 302: 290–292.

Eisenberger, N. I., Way, B., Taylor, S. E., Welch, W. T., and Lieberman, M. D. 2007. "Understanding Genetic Risk for Aggression: Clues from the Brain's Response to Social Exclusion." *Biological Psychiatry* 61: 1100–1108.

Foltz, E.L, and White, L.E. 1968. "The Role of Rostral Cingulotomy in "Pain" Relief." *International Journal of Neurology* 6: 353–373.

Gilbert, D. T. 2005. *Stumbling on Happiness*. New York: Vintage Books.

Guth, W., Schmittberger, R., and Schwarze, B. 1982. "An Experimental Analysis of Ultimatum Bargaining." *Journal of Economic Behavior and Organization* 3: 367–388.

Izuma, K., Saito, D. N., and Sadato, N. 2008. "Processing of Social and Monetary Rewards in the Human Striatum." *Neuron* 58: 294–294.

Kirzinger, A., and Jurgens, U. 1982. "Cortical Lesion Effects and Vocalization in the Squirrel Monkey." *Brain Research* 233: 299–315.

Lieberman, M. D. 2007. "Social Cognitive Neuroscience: A Review of Core Processes." *Annual Review of Psychology* 58: 259–289.

Lieberman, M. D., Jarcho, J. M., Berman, S., Naliboff, B., Suyenobu, B. Y., Mandelkern, M., and Mayer, E. 2004. "The Neural Correlates of Placebo Effects: A Disruption Account." *NeuroImage* 22: 447–455.

MacLean, P. D., and Newman, J. D. 1988. "Role of Midline Frontolimbic Cortex in Production of the Isolation Call of Squirrel Monkeys." *Brain Research* 450: 111–123.

MacDonald, G., and Leary, M. R. 2005. "Why Does Social Exclusion Hurt? The Relationship Between Social and Physical Pain." *Psychological Review* 131: 202–223.

Moll, J., Krueger, F., Zahn, R., Pardini, M., de Oliveira-Souza, R., and Grafman, J. 2006. "Human Fronto-Mesolimbic Networks Guide Decisions about Charitable Donation." *Proceedings of the National Academy of Sciences, USA* 103: 15623–15628.

Nisbett, R. E., and Wilson, T. D. 1977. "Telling More Than We Can Know: Verbal Reports on Mental Processes." *Psychological Review* 84: 231–259.

Ochsner, K. N., and Lieberman, M. D. 2001. "The Emergence of Social Cognitive Neuroscience." *American Psychologist* 56: 717–734.

Panksepp, J. 1998. *Affective Neuroscience*. New York: Oxford University Press.

Rainville, P., Duncan, G. H., Price, D. D., Carrier, B., and Bushnell, M. D., 1997. "Pain Affect Encoded in Human Anterior Cingulate but not Somatosensory Cortex." *Science* 277: 968–971.

Sanfey, A. G., Rilling, J. K., Aronson, J. A., Nystrom, L. E., and Cohen, J. D. 2003. "The Neural Basis of Economic Decision-Making in the Ultimatum Game." *Science* 300: 1755–1758.

Tabibnia, G., Satpute, A. B., and Lieberman, M. D. 2008. "The Sunny Side of Fairness: Preference for Fairness Activates Reward Circuitry (and Disregarding Unfairness Activates Self-Control Circuitry)." *Psychological Science* 19: 339–347.

Weich, K., Farias, M., Kahane, G., Shackel, N., Tiede, W., and Tracy, I. 2008. "An fMRI Study Measuring Analgesia Enhanced by Religion as a Belief System." *Pain* 139(2): 467–476.

Williams, K. D., Cheung, C. K. T., and Choi, W. 2000. "Cyberostracism: Effects of Being Ignored Over the Internet." *Journal of Personality and Social Psychology* 79: 748–762.

17. SCARF: a brain-based model for collaborating with and influencing others

Dr. David Rock

Dr. David Rock, CEO, NeuroLeadership Group, New York, USA

Faculty, CIMBA; Cofounder, NeuroLeadership Institute; Editor, *NeuroLeadership Journal*

david@neuroleadership.com

Introduction

In a world of increasing interconnectedness and rapid change, there is a growing need to improve the way people work together. Understanding the true drivers of human social behavior is becoming ever more urgent in this environment.

The study of the brain, particularly within the field of social, cognitive, and affective neuroscience is starting to provide some underlying brain insights that can be applied in the real world (Lieberman 2007). Social neuroscience explores the biological foundations of the way humans relate to each other and to themselves and covers diverse topics that can be operationalized and unambiguously tested to different degrees. Topics include: theory of mind, the self, mindfulness, emotion regulation, attitudes, stereotyping, empathy, social pain, status, fairness, collaboration, connectedness, persuasion, morality, compassion, deception, trust, and goal pursuit.

From this diversity, two themes are emerging from social neuroscience: first, that much of our motivation driving social behavior is governed by an overarching organizing principle of minimizing threat and maximizing reward (Gordon 2000); and second, that several domains of social experience draw on the same brain networks to maximize reward and minimize threat that are used for primary survival needs (Lieberman and Eisenberger 2008). In other words, social needs are treated in much the same way in the brain as the need for food and water.

The SCARF® model summarizes these two themes within a framework that captures the common factors that can activate a reward or threat response in social situations. This model can be applied (and tested) in any situation where people collaborate in groups, including all types of workplaces, educational environments, family settings, and general social events.

The SCARF model refers to five domains of human social experience: Status, Certainty, Autonomy, Relatedness, and Fairness.

Status is about relative importance to others. Certainty concerns being able to predict the future. Autonomy provides a sense of control over events. Relatedness is a sense of safety with others, of friend rather than foe. And fairness is a perception of fair exchanges between people.

These five domains activate either the "primary reward" or "primary threat" circuitry (and associated networks) of the brain. For example, a perceived threat to one's status activates brain networks similar to those activated by a threat to one's life. In the same way, a perceived increase in fairness activates the same reward circuitry as does receiving a monetary reward.

The SCARF model enables people to more easily remember, recognize, and potentially modify the core social domains that drive human behavior. Labeling and understanding these drivers draws conscious awareness to otherwise nonconscious processes, which can help in two ways. First, knowing the drivers that can cause a threat response enables people to design interactions to minimize threats. For example, knowing that a lack of autonomy activates a genuine threat response, a leader or educator may consciously avoid micromanaging employees or students. Second, knowing about the drivers that can activate a reward response enables people to motivate others more effectively by tapping into internal rewards, thereby reducing the reliance on external rewards such as money. For example, a line manager might grant more autonomy as a reward for good performance.

Foundations of the SCARF model

Before exploring the domains of SCARF individually, let's look at a brief context of the underlying science of the SCARF model—namely, the approach (reward)–avoid (threat) response and the impact of this response on mental performance.

The approach (reward)–avoid (threat) response: a survival instinct

According to integrative neuroscientist Evian Gordon, the "minimize danger and maximize reward" principle is an overarching, organizing principle of the brain (Gordon 2000). This central organizing principle of the brain is analogous to a concept that has appeared in the literature for a long time: the approach-avoid response. This principle represents the likelihood that when people encounter a stimulus, their brain either will tag the stimulus as "good" and they will engage in the stimulus (approach), or will tag the stimulus as "bad" and they will disengage from the stimulus (avoid). If a stimulus is associated with positive emotions or rewards, it will likely lead to an approach response; if it is associated with negative emotions or punishments, it will likely lead to an avoid response. The response is particularly strong when the stimulus is associated with survival. Other concepts from the scientific literature are similar to approach and avoidance and are summarized in table 1.

Table 1. Concepts similar to approach and avoidance

Response	Synonyms in literature	Which traditional primary factors activate the response	What social factors/ situations activate the response
Approach	Advance, attack, reward, resource, expand, solution, strength, construct, engage	Rewards in the form of money, food, water, sex, shelter, physical assets for survival	Happy, attractive faces; rewards in the form of increasing status, certainty, autonomy, relatedness, fairness
Avoid	Withdraw, retreat, danger, threat, contract, problem, weakness, deconstruct	Punishment in the form of removal of money or other resources, or threats like a large hungry predator or a gun	Fearful, unattractive, unfamiliar faces; threats in the form of decreasing status, certainty, autonomy, relatedness, fairness

The approach-avoid response is a survival mechanism designed to help people stay alive by quickly and easily remembering what is good and bad in the environment. The brain encodes one type of memory for food that tasted disgusting in the past and a different type of memory for food that was good to eat. The amygdala, a small, almond-shaped object that is part of the limbic system, plays a central role in remembering whether something should be approached or avoided. The amygdala (and its associated networks) are believed to activate proportionally to the strength of an emotional response.

The limbic system can process stimuli before it reaches conscious awareness. One study showed that subliminally presented nonsense words that were similar to threatening words, were still categorized as possible threats by the amygdala (Naccache et al. 2005). Brainstem-limbic networks process threat and reward cues within a fifth of a second, providing you with ongoing nonconscious intuition of what is meaningful to you in every situation of your daily life (Gordon et al. 2008). Such studies show that the approach-avoid response drives attention at a fundamental level—nonconsciously, automatically, and quickly. It is a reflexive activity.

It is easy to see that the ability to recognize primary rewards and threats, such as good versus poisonous food, would be important to survival and thus a part of the brain. Social neuroscience shows us that the brain uses similar circuitry for interacting with the social world. Lieberman and Eisenberger explored this finding in detail in the previous chapter, "The pains and pleasures of social life: a social-cognitive neuroscience approach" (Lieberman and Eisenberger 2008).

Effects of approaching versus avoiding

The significance of the approach-avoid response becomes clearer when one discovers the dramatic effect these states can have on perception and problem solving, and the implications of this effect on decision-making, stress-management, collaboration, and motivation.

In one study, two groups of people completed a paper maze that featured a mouse in the middle trying to reach a picture on the outside. One group had a picture of cheese on the outside, the other a predator—an owl. After completing the maze both groups were given creativity tests. The group heading toward the cheese solved significantly more creative problems than those heading to the owl (Friedman and Foster 2001). This study, supported by several other similar studies, showed that even subtle effects of this approach-avoid response can have a big impact on cognitive performance.

Translating this effect to the social world, someone feeling threatened by a boss who is undermining his or her credibility is less likely to be able to solve complex problems and more likely to make mistakes. This reduced cognitive performance is driven by several factors. First, when a human being senses a threat, resources available for overall executive functions in the prefrontal cortex decrease. A strong negative correlation exists between the amount of threat activation and the resources available for the prefrontal cortex (Arnsten 1998). The result is literally less oxygen and glucose available for the brain functions involved in working memory, which impacts linear, conscious processing. When feeling threatened by one's boss, it is harder to find smart answers because of diminished cognitive resources. Second, when people are threatened, the increased overall activation in the brain inhibits them from perceiving the more subtle signals required for solving nonlinear problems—involved in the insight or "aha!" experience (Subramaniam et al. 2009. Third, with the amygdala activated, the tendency is to generalize more, which increases the likelihood of accidental connections. There is a tendency to err on the safe side, shrinking from opportunities, as they are perceived to be more dangerous. People become more likely to react defensively to stimuli. Small stressors become more likely to be perceived as large stressors (Phelps 2006). When the boss appears threatening—perhaps he or she just doesn't smile that day—suddenly a whole meeting can appear threatening, and the tendency can be to avoid taking risks.

Clearly the threat or avoid response is not an ideal state for collaborating with and influencing others. However, this response is often the default situation in teams. Because of the overly vigilant amygdala, which is more tuned to threats than rewards, the threat response is often just below the surface and easily triggered. Just speaking to one's supervisor or someone of higher status is likely to activate this response. Thus, it is much easier to cause aggravation (activate an avoid response) than it is to help others think rationally and creatively (approach response). Many psychological and brain studies now support this idea, showing that the avoid response generates far more arousal in the limbic system, more quickly, and with longer-lasting effects than an approach response (Baumeister 2001). This discovery—that our brain is inherently attuned to threatening stimuli—helps explain many disquieting aspects of life, from why the media focuses on bad news to why people are self-critical. It also points to the need to understand the social nature of the brain and proactively minimize common social threats.

On the other hand, an approach response is synonymous with the idea of engagement. Engagement is a state of being willing to do difficult things, to take risks, to think deeply about issues and develop new solutions. An approach state is also closely linked to positive emotions. Interest, happiness, joy, and desire are approach emotions. This state is one of increased dopamine levels, important for interest and learning. A large and growing body of research indicates that people experiencing positive emotions perceive more options when trying to solve problems (Fredrickson 2001), solve more nonlinear problems that require insight (Jung-Beeman 2007), collaborate better, and generally perform better overall.

In summary, the SCARF model is an easy way to remember and act on the social triggers that can generate both the approach and avoid responses. The goal of this model is to help minimize the easily activated threat responses and maximize positive engaged states of mind during attempts to collaborate with and influence others.

SCARF model

While the five domains of the SCARF model appear to be interlinked in many ways, there is also value in separating out and understanding each domain individually. Let's look now at some of the supporting research for each domain and then explore how threats and rewards might be managed in each.

Status

In researcher Michael Marmot's book *The Status Syndrome: How Social Standing Affects Our Health and Longevity*, Marmot makes the case that status is the most significant determinant of human longevity and health, even when controlling for education and income. This finding is supported by Sapolski's work with primates (Sapolski 2002). Sapolski found that in primate communities, status equals survival: higher-status monkeys have lower baseline cortisol levels, live longer, and are healthier.

Status is about relative importance, "pecking order," and seniority. Humans hold a representation of status in relation to others when in conversations, and this affects mental processes in many ways (Zink et al. 2008). The brain thinks about status using similar circuits for processing numbers (Chiao, Bordeaux, and Ambady 2003). One's sense of status goes up when one feels "better than" another person. In this instance the primary reward circuitry is activated, in particular the striatum, which increases dopamine levels. One study showed that an increase in status was similar in strength to a financial windfall (Izuma, Saito, and Sadato 2008). Winning a swimming race, a card game, or an argument probably feels good because of the perception of increased status and the resulting reward circuitry being activated.

The perception of a potential or real reduction in status can generate a strong threat response. Eisenberger and colleagues showed that a reduction in status resulting from being left out of an activity lit up the same regions of the brain as physical pain did (Eisenberger, Lieberman, and Williams 2003). While this study explores social rejection, it is closely connected to the experience of a drop in status.

Reducing status threat

It can be surprisingly easy to accidentally threaten someone's sense of status. A status threat can occur through giving advice or instructions or simply suggesting someone is slightly ineffective at a task. Many everyday conversations devolve into arguments driven by a status threat, a desire to not be perceived as less than another. When threatened, people may defend a position that doesn't make sense to avoid the perceived pain of a drop in status.

In most people, the question "can I offer you some feedback?" generates a response similar to hearing fast footsteps behind you at night. Performance reviews often generate status threats, explaining why they are often ineffective at stimulating behavioral change. If leaders want to change others' behavior, more attention must be paid to reducing status threats when giving feedback. One way to do this is by allowing people to give themselves feedback on their own performance.

Increasing status reward

Organizations know all about using status as a reward, and many managers feel compelled to reward employees primarily via a promotion. This may have the unfortunate side effect of promoting people to the point of their incompetence. The research suggests that status can be increased in more sustainable ways. For example, people experience a status increase when they feel they are learning and improving and when attention is paid to this improvement. This probably occurs because individuals think about themselves using the same brain networks they use for thinking about others (Mitchell, Macrae, and Banaji 2006). For example, when beating one's own best time at a task or sporting activity, the reward circuitry from a sense of being "better than" is activated, but in this case, the person one is "better than" is oneself in the past.

Many everyday conversations devolve into arguments driven by a status threat, a desire to not be perceived as less than another.

Status can go up when people are given positive feedback, especially public acknowledgment. One study showed activation of the reward circuitry in children being as strong as money when they are told "that's correct" by a repetitive computer voice. (Scott et al., under review). Leaders can be afraid of praising their people for fear of the request for promotion. However, given the deeply rewarding nature of status, giving positive feedback may actually reduce the need for constant promotions, not increase it.

Finally, status is about one's relative position in a community of importance, such as a professional group or social club, based on what is valued. While society—especially advertising and the media—would have people spend money to be "better than others," it doesn't have to be a zero-sum game. Status can be increased without cost to others or affecting relatedness. As well as playing against oneself, one can also change the community one focuses on, as when a low-level mailroom clerk becomes the coach of a junior baseball team. Or, one can change what is important—for example, deciding that the quality of one's work is more important than the quantity.

Certainty

The brain is a pattern-recognition machine that is constantly trying to predict the near future. For example, the motor network is useless without the sensory system. To pick up a cup of coffee, the sensory system, sensing the position of the fingers at each moment, interacts dynamically with the motor cortex to determine where to move your fingers next. Your fingers don't draw on fresh data each time; the brain draws on the memory of what a cup is supposed to feel like in the hand, based on expectations drawn from previous experiences. If it feels different, perhaps slippery, you immediately pay attention (Hawkins and Blakeslee 2004). The brain likes to know the pattern occurring moment to moment; it craves certainty so that prediction is possible. Without prediction, the brain must use dramatically more resources, involving the more energy-intensive prefrontal cortex, to process moment-to-moment experience.

Even a small amount of uncertainty generates an "error" response in the orbital frontal cortex (OFC). This takes attention away from one's goals, forcing attention to the error (Hedden and Gabrieli 2006). If someone is not telling you the whole truth or is acting incongruously, the resulting uncertainty can fire up errors in the OFC. This is like having a flashing printer icon on your desktop when paper is jammed—the flashing cannot be ignored, and until it is resolved, it is difficult to focus on other things. Larger uncertainties, such as not knowing your boss's expectations or whether your job is secure, can be highly debilitating.

The act of creating a sense of certainty is rewarding. Examples are everywhere in daily life: music that has simple repeating patterns is rewarding because of the ability to predict the flow of information. Meeting expectations generate an increase in dopamine levels in the brain, a reward response (Schultz 1999). Going back to a well-known place feels good because the mental maps of the environment can be easily recalled.

Reducing the threat from uncertainty

Any kind of significant change generates uncertainty. Yet uncertainty can be decreased in many simple ways. This is a big part of the job of managers, consultants, and leaders. As people build business plans, set strategies, or map out an organization's structure, they feel increasing levels of clarity about how an organization might better function in the future. Even though it is unlikely things ever go as planned, people feel better because certainty has increased. Breaking a complex project down into small steps does the same. Another key tool involves establishing clear expectations of what might happen in any situation, as well as expectations of desirable outcomes.

Increasing the reward from certainty

Some examples of how to increase certainty include making implicit concepts more explicit, such as agreeing verbally on how long a meeting will run or stating clear objectives at the start of any discussion. In learning situations, the old adage is "tell people what you are going to tell them, tell them, then tell them what you told them," all of which increases certainty.

The perception of certainty can be increased even during deeply uncertain times. For example, when going through an organizational restructuring, providing a specific date when people will know more information about a change may be enough to increase a sense of certainty. Much of the field of change management is devoted to increasing a sense of certainty where little certainty exists.

Autonomy

Autonomy is the perception of exerting control over one's environment, a sensation of having choices. Mineka (1985) showed that the degree of control organisms can exert over a stress factor determines whether the stressor alters the organism's functioning. Inescapable or uncontrollable stress can be highly destructive, whereas the same stress interpreted as escapable is significantly less destructive. (Donny, Bigelow, and Walsh 2006). The difference in some rodent studies was life and death (Dworkin, Mirkis, and Smith 1995).

An increase in the perception of autonomy feels rewarding. Several studies in the retirement industry find strong correlations between a sense of control and health outcomes (Rodin 1986). People leave corporate life, often for far less income, because they desire greater autonomy.

A reduction in autonomy—for example, when being micromanaged—can generate a strong threat response. When one senses a lack of control, the experience is of a lack of agency or an inability to influence outcomes.

Reducing autonomy threat

Working in a team necessitates a reduction in autonomy. In healthy cultures, this potential threat tends to be counteracted with an increase in status, certainty, and relatedness. With an autonomy threat just below the surface, it can be helpful to pay attention to this driver. The statement "Here's two options that could work—which would you prefer?" will tend to elicit a better response than "Here's what you have to do now."

Increasing rewards from autonomy

Providing significant autonomy in an organization can be difficult. Yet even a subtle perception of autonomy can help—for example, by having self-directed learning portals, where employees get to design their own learning curriculum, and self-driven human resource systems.

Allowing people to set up their own desks, organize their workflow, even manage their working hours, can all be beneficial if done within agreed parameters. Sound policy establishes the boundaries within which individuals can exercise their creativity and autonomy. Sound policy should enable individual point-of-need decision making without consultation with or intervention by leaders. In this regard, sound policy hard-wires autonomy into an organization's processes.

Relatedness

Relatedness involves deciding whether others are "in" or "out" of a social group, whether someone is friend or foe. Relatedness is a driver of behavior in many types of teams, from sports teams to organizational silos; people naturally like to form "tribes" where they experience a sense of belonging. The concept of being inside or outside the group is probably a by-product of living in small communities for millions of years, where strangers were likely to be trouble and should be avoided.

In the absence of safe social interactions, the body generates a threat response...

The decision that someone is friend or foe happens quickly and impacts brain functioning (Carter and Pelphrey 2008). For example, information from people perceived as "like us" is processed using similar circuits for thinking one's own thoughts. When someone is perceived as a foe, different circuits are used

(Mitchell 2006). Also, when treating someone as a competitor, the capacity to empathize drops significantly (Singer et al. 2006).

Neuroscientist John Cacioppo talks about the need for safe human contact being a primary driver, like the need for food (Cacioppo and Patrick 2008). In the absence of safe social interactions, the body generates a threat response—also known as feeling lonely. However, meeting someone unknown tends to generate an automatic threat response. This explains why one feels better at a party knowing three people rather than one. Alcohol helps to reduce this automatic social threat response, enabling strangers to communicate more easily, hence its use as a social lubricant the world over. In the absence of alcohol, getting from foe to friend can be helped by an oxytocin response, an experience of connecting with the other person. Oxytocin is a hormone produced naturally in the brain, and higher levels of this substance are associated with greater affiliative behavior (Domes et al. 2007). Studies have shown far greater collaboration when people are given a shot of oxytocin through a nasal spray (Kosfeld 2005). A handshake, swapping names, and discussing something in common—be it just the weather—may increase a feeling of closeness by causing the release of oxytocin (Zak, Kurzban, and Matzner 2005). The concept of relatedness is closely linked to trust. One trusts those who appear to be in one's group, who one has connected with, generating approach emotions. And when someone does something untrustworthy, the usual response is to withdraw. The greater that people trust one another, the stronger the collaboration and the more information that is shared.

Reducing threats from lack of relatedness

Increasing globalization highlights the importance of managing relatedness threats. Collaboration between people from different cultures, who are unlikely to meet in person, can be especially hard work. The automatic foe response does not get diminished by social time together. This response can be mitigated by dedicating social time in other forms—for example, using video to have an informal meeting or ensuring that people forming teams share personal aspects of themselves via stories, photos, or even social-networking sites. In any workplace it appears to pay off well to encourage social connections. A Gallup report showed that organizations that encourage "water cooler" conversations increased productivity (Gallup 2008).

Increasing the rewards from relatedness

Positive social connections are a primary need; however, the automatic response to new social connections involves a threat. The key to increasing the reward response from relatedness is to find ways to increase safe connections between people. Some examples include setting up clearly defined buddy systems, mentoring or coaching programs, and small action learning groups. Small groups appear to be safer than large groups. The Gallup organization's research on workplace engagement showed that the statement "I have a best friend at work" was central to engagement in their "Q12" assessment (Gallup 2008). Perhaps even having one trusting relationship can have a significant impact on relatedness.

Fairness

Studies by Golnaz Tabibnia and Matthew Lieberman at UCLA showed that 50 cents generated more of a reward in the brain than $10.00 when it was 50 cents out of a dollar and the $10 was out of $50 (Tabibnia and Lieberman 2007). This study and a number of others illustrate that fair exchanges are intrinsically rewarding, independent of other factors. The need for fairness may be part of the reason why people experience internal rewards for doing volunteer work to improve their community; it gives a sense of decreasing the unfairness in the world.

Unfair exchanges generate a strong threat response (Tabibnia and Lieberman 2007). This sometimes includes activation of the insula, a part of the brain involved in intense emotions such as disgust. Unfair situations may drive people to die to right perceived injustices, such as in political struggles. People who perceive others as unfair don't feel empathy for their pain, and in some instances, they will feel rewarded when unfair others are punished (Singer et al. 2006).

Reducing the threat from unfairness and increasing the reward from fairness

A threat response from a sense of unfairness can be triggered easily. The following statements are examples of what employees might say in reaction to a threat to fairness:

- "He has a different set of rules for Mike and Sally than for the rest of us."
- "Management tell us that we need to lose headcount, but our sales are carrying the other division and they don't have to cut anyone."
- "They do all this talk about 'values,' but it's business as usual at the top."

The threat from perceived unfairness can be decreased by increasing transparency and the level of communication and involvement about business issues. For example, organizations that allow employees to know details about financial processes may have an advantage here.

Establishing clear expectations in all situations—from a one-hour meeting to a five-year contract—can also help ensure fair exchanges occur. A sense of unfairness can result from a lack of clear ground rules, expectations, or objectives. Allowing teams to identify their own rules can also help. In an educational context, a classroom that creates the rules of what is accepted behavior is likely to experience less conflict. Examples of the success of self-directed teams in manufacturing abound (Semler 1993). Much of what these self-driven teams do is ensure fairness in grassroots decisions, such as how workloads are shared and who can do which tasks.

The issue of pay discrepancies in large organizations is a challenging one, and many employees are deeply unhappy to see another person working similar hours earning a hundred times their salary. Interestingly, it is the perception of fairness that is key, so even a slight reduction in senior executive salaries during a difficult time may go a long way toward reducing a sense of unfairness.

Wider implications of the SCARF model

Managing oneself

The SCARF model helps individuals both minimize threats and maximize rewards inherent in everyday experience. For minimizing threats, knowing about the domains of SCARF helps one label and reappraise experiences that might otherwise reduce performance. Labeling (Lieberman et al. 2007) and reappraisal (Ochsner and Gross, 2005) are cognitive tools that have been verified in brain studies to be effective techniques for reducing the threat response. These techniques have been shown to be more effective at reducing the threat response than the act of trying to suppress an emotion (Goldin et al. 2007). Knowing about the elements of SCARF helps you understand such issues as why you can't think clearly when someone has attacked your status, instead of just trying to push the feeling aside.

Knowing the domains of SCARF also allows individuals to design ways to motivate themselves more effectively. An example might be focusing attention on increasing one's sense of autonomy during a time of uncertainty, such as focusing on the thrill of doing whatever you like when suddenly out of work.

Education and training

Successful educators, trainers, and facilitators intuitively use the SCARF model. They know that people learn best when they are interested in something. Interest is an approach state. Teaching children who feel threatened, disconnected, socially rejected, or treated unfairly is an uphill battle. For example, educators can create a nurturing learning environment by pointing out specifically how people are improving, which increases a sense of status. This is particularly important when learning anything new, which can create a threat response. Educators can also create certainty by presenting clear outlines of what is being learned, and provide a perception of some autonomy by introducing choice into the classroom. The key here is for educators, trainers, and coaches to value the approach state as the necessary state for learning, and to put effort and attention into maintaining this toward state.

Coaching

Personal and executive coaching can increase all five SCARF domains. Status can be increased through regular positive feedback, attention to incremental improvements, and the achievement of large goals. Certainty can be increased by identifying central goals and subsequently reducing the uncertainty inherent in maintaining multiple focuses. Breaking down large goals into smaller steps increases certainty about how a goal can be reached. Finding ways to take action when challenges appear insurmountable can increase autonomy. Relatedness can be increased through the relationship with the coach. Fairness can be reduced through seeing situations from other perspectives. The SCARF model helps explain why coaching can be so effective at facilitating change and points to ways of improving its delivery.

The SCARF model points to more creative ways of motivating that may be not just cheaper but also stronger and more sustainable.

Leadership development

The SCARF model provides a robust scientific framework for building self-awareness and awareness of others among leaders. Many new leaders may negatively impact the SCARF domains by accident. They may know how things should be done and subsequently provide too much direction and not enough positive feedback, thereby affecting people's status. They often don't provide clear expectations, impacting certainty. They micromanage, impacting autonomy. They want to maintain a professional distance, impacting relatedness. And they may impact fairness by not being transparent enough. When the opposite happens and you meet someone who makes you feel better about yourself, provides clear expectations, lets you make decisions, trusts you, and is fair, you will probably work harder for that person because you feel intrinsically rewarded by the relationship itself. Spending time around a leader like this activates an approach response and opens up people's thinking, allowing others to see information they wouldn't see in an avoid state.

Organizational systems

SCARF has many implications for how organizations are structured, including reward systems, communications systems, decision processes, information flow, and remuneration structures. We will explore just one of these here—reward systems. Techniques for motivating and rewarding staff are largely based on the carrot-and-stick principle, with the carrot mostly involving money or a promotion. The SCARF model points to more creative ways of motivating that may be not just cheaper but also stronger and more sustainable. For example, success could be rewarded by increasing people's autonomy through allowing them to have greater flexibility in their work hours. Or rewards could be provided via increasing the opportunity for learning new skills, which can increase a sense of status. Or people could be rewarded through increasing relatedness by allowing more time to network with peers during work hours.

Summary

The five domains of SCARF reflect core brain networks of greatest significance when it comes to collaborating with and influencing others. Understanding these drivers can help individuals and organizations function more effectively, reducing conflicts that occur so easily among people and increasing the amount of time people spend in the approach state, a concept synonymous with good performance.

Understanding the domains in the SCARF model and finding personalized strategies to effectively use these brain insights can help people become better leaders, managers, facilitators, coaches, teachers, and even parents.

In the early 2000s, the philosopher Theodore Zeldin said, "When will we make the same breakthroughs in the way we treat each other as we have made in technology?" These findings about the deeply social nature of the brain and the deep relevance of the domains of SCARF in everyday life may provide some small steps in the right direction.

Suggestions for future research

An abbreviated list of potential research issues includes the following questions:

- Which of the domains of SCARF generate the strongest threats or rewards?
- Which domains have the longest-term impact?
- What are the links between the domains?
- How can studies be designed to identify individual domains?
- What are the best techniques for minimizing threat and maximizing reward in each domain?
- Do people vary in the importance of the five domains, and if so, are there patterns across men and women, age groups, or cultures?
- Is there value in assessing these domains in individuals or culturally in organizations?
- What are the organizational implications of this model for how systems are set up?
- What aspects of the model are most effective to which individual leaders?

Acknowledgments

This was written with the help of several reviewers, including Rachel Sheppard, Dr. Evian Gordon, Joanne Capritti, and Karen Jayne Eyre. I am grateful for the dozens of interviews with many of the scientists referenced for their input as well, with special thanks to Dr. Jeffrey M. Schwartz, Dr. Matthew Lieberman, Dr. Mark Jung-Beeman, and Dr. Yi-Yuan Tang for their informal mentoring over recent years on these topics.

References

Arnsten, A. F. T. 1998. "The Biology of Being Frazzled." *Science* 280: 1711–1712.

Baumeister, R. F., Bratslavsky, E., and Vohs, K. D. 2001. "Bad is Stronger Than Good." *Review of General Psychology* 5(4): 323–370.

Baumeister, R. F., and Leary, M. R. 1995. "The Need to Belong: Desire for Interpersonal Attachments as a Fundamental Human Motivation." *Psychological Bulletin* 117: 497–529.

Cacioppo, J. T., and Patrick, B. 2008. *Loneliness: Human Nature and the Need for Social Connection*. New York: W. W. Norton.

Carter, E. J., and Pelphrey, K. A. 2008. "Friend or Foe? Brain Systems Involved in the Perception of Dynamic Signals of Menacing and Friendly Social Approaches." *Journal of Social Neuroscience* (3)2: 151–163.

Chiao, J. Y., Bordeaux, A. R., and Ambady, N. 2003. "Mental Representations of Social Status." *Cognition* 93: 49–57.

Domes , G., Heinrichs, M., Gläscher J., Büchel, C., Braus, D., and Herpertz, S. 2007. "Oxytocin Attenuates Amygdala Responses to Emotional Faces Regardless of Valence." *Biological Psychiatry* 62(10): 1187–1190.

Donny, E. C., Bigelow, G. E., and Walsh S. L. 2006. "Comparing the Physiological and Subjective Effects of Self-Administered vs. Yoked Cocaine in Humans." *Psychopharmacology* 186(4): 544–552.

Dworkin, S. I., Mirkis, S., and Smith, J. E. 1995. "Response-Dependent Versus Response-Independent Presentation of Cocaine: Differences in the Lethal Effects of the Drug." *Psychopharmacology* 117(3): 262–266.

Eisenberger, N. I., and Lieberman, M. D. 2004. "Why it Hurts to be Left Out: The Neurocognitive Overlap Between Physical and Social Pain." *Trends in Cognitive Sciences* 8: 294–300.

Eisenberger, N. I., Lieberman, M. D., and Williams, K. D. 2003. "Does Rejection Hurt? An fMRI Study of Social Exclusion." *Science* 302: 290–292.

Fredrickson, B. L. 2001. "The Role of Positive Emotions in Positive Psychology: The Broaden-and-Build Theory of Positive Emotions." *American Psychologist* 56: 218–226.

Friedman, R., and Foster, J. 2001. "The Effects of Promotion and Prevention Cues on Creativity." *Journal of Personality and Social Psychology* 81: 1001–1013.

Gallup. 2008. "Newsflash: Workplace Socializing is Productive." Employee engagement page on Gallup website. November 13, 2008. http://www.gallup.com/consulting/52/Employee-Engagement.aspx.

Gilbert, D. 2006. *Stumbling upon Happiness*. New York: Knopf.

Goldin, P. R., McRae, K., Ramel, W., and Gross, J. J. 2007. "The Neural Bases of Emotion Regulation: Reappraisal and Suppression of Negative Emotion." *Biological Psychiatry* 63: 577–586.

Gordon, E. 2000. *Integrative Neuroscience: Bringing Together Biological, Psychological, and Clinical Models of the Human Brain*. Singapore: Harwood Academic Publishers.

Gordon, E., Barnett, K.J., Cooper, N.J., Tran, N., and Williams, L.M. 2008. An "Integrative Neuroscience" Platform: Application to Profiles of Negativity and Positivity Bias. *Journal of Integrative Neuroscience* 7(3): 345-366.

Hawkins, J., and Blakeslee, S. 2004. *On Intelligence*. New York: Times Books.

Hedden, T., and Gabrieli, J. D. E. 2006. "The Ebb and Flow of Attention in the Human Brain." *Nature Neuroscience* 9: 863–865.

Izuma, K., Saito, D., and Sadato, N. 2008. "Processing of Social and Monetary Rewards in the Human Striatum." *Neuron* 58(2): 284–294.

Jung-Beeman, M. 2007. "*The Neural basis of insight*." Presented at the NeuroLeadership Summit, Asolo, Italy.

Kosfeld, M., Heinrichs, M., Zak, P. J., Fischbacher, U., and Fehr, E. 2005. "Oxytocin Increases Trust in Humans." *Nature* 435: 673–676.

Lieberman, M. D. 2007. "Social Cognitive Neuroscience: A Review of Core Processes." *Annual Review of Psychology* 58: 259–289.

Lieberman, M.D., Eisenberger, N.I., Crockett,M.J., Tom, S.M., Pfeifer, J.H., and Way, B.M. 2007. "Putting Feelings into Words: Affect Labelling Disrupts Amygdala Activity in Response to Affective Stimuli." *Psychological Science* 18(5): 421–428.

Lieberman, M.D., and Eisenberg, N. I. (2008). "The Pains and Pleasures of Social Life." *NeuroLeadership Journal* 1: 3–9.

Mason, M. F., Norton, M. I., Van Horn, J. D., Wegner, D. M., Grafton, S. T., and Macrae, C. N. 2007. "Wandering Minds: The Default Network and Stimulus-Independent Thought." *Science* 315: 393–395.

Mather, M., Mitchell, K. J., Raye, C. L., Novak, D. L., Greene, E. J., and Johnson, M. K. 2006. "Emotional Arousal can Impair Feature Binding in Working Memory." *Journal of Cognitive Neuroscience* 18: 614–625.

Mineka, S., and Hendersen, R. W. 1985. "Controllability and Predictability in Acquired Motivation." *Annual Review of Psychology* 36: 495–529.

Mitchell, J. P., Macrae, C. N., and Banaji, M. R. 2006. "Dissociable Medial Prefrontal Contributions to Judgments of Similar and Dissimilar Others." *Neuron* 50: 655–663.

Naccache, L., Gaillard, R. L., Adam, C., Hasboun, D., Clemenceau, S., Baulac, M., Dehaene, S., and Cohen, L. 2005. "A Direct Intracranial Record of Emotions Evoked by Subliminal Words." *Proceedings of the National Academy of Sciences, USA* 102: 7713–7717.

Ochsner K. N., and Gross, J. J. 2005. "The Cognitive Control of Emotion." *Trends in Cognitive Sciences* 9(5): 242–249.

Ochsner, K. N., and Lieberman, M. D. 2001. "The Emergence of Social Cognitive Neuroscience." *American Psychologist* 56: 717–734.

Phelps, E. A. 2006. "Emotion and Cognition: Insights from Studies of the Human Amygdala." *Annual Review of Psychology* 57: 27–53.

Rodin, J. 1986. "Aging and Health: Effects of the Sense of Control." *Science* 233: 1271–1276.

Sapolski, R. M. 2002. *A Primate's Memoir: A Neuroscientist's Unconventional Life among the Baboons*. New York: Simon and Schuster.

Schultz, W. 1999. "The Reward Signal of Midbrain Dopamine Neurons." *News in Physiological Sciences* 14(6): 249–255.

Scott, A.A., Dapretto, M., Ghahremani, D., Poldrack, R.A., and Booheimer, S.Y. (Under review, 2008). "Social Learning Deficits Relate to Decreased Neural Response to Rewards." *Social Cognitive and Affective Neuroscience Journal.*

Semler, R. 1993. *Maverick: The Success Story Behind the World's Most Unusual Workplace.* New York: Warner Books.

Seymour, B., Singer, T., and Dolan, R. 2007. "The Neurobiology of Punishment." *Nature Reviews Neuroscience* 8: 300–311.

Singer, T., Seymour, B., O'Doherty, J. P., Stephan, K. E., Dolan, R. J., and Frith, C. D. 2006. "Empathic Neural Responses are Modulated by the Perceived Fairness of Others." *Nature* 439: 466–469.

Subramaniam, K., Kounios, J., Bowden, E. M., Parrish, T. B., and Jung-Beeman, M. 2009. "Positive Mood and Anxiety Modulate Anterior Cingulate Activity and Cognitive Preparation for Insight." *Journal of Cognitive Neuroscience* 21: 415-432.

Tabibnia, G., and Lieberman, M. D. 2007. "Fairness and Cooperation are Rewarding: Evidence from Social Cognitive Neuroscience." *Annals of the New York Academy of Sciences* 1118: 90–101.

Zak, P. J., Kurzban, R., and Matzner, W. T. 2005. "Oxytocin is Associated with Human Trustworthiness." *Hormones and Behavior* 48(5): 522–527.

Zink, C. F., Tong, Y., Chen, Q., Bassett, D. S., Stein, J. L., and Meyer-Lindenberg, A. 2008. "Know Your Place: Neural Processing of Social Hierarchy in Humans." *Neuron* 58: 273–283.

18. SCARF in 2012: updating the social neuroscience of collaborating with others

Dr. David Rock and Dr. Christine Cox

David Rock, CEO, NeuroLeadership Group, New York, USA

Faculty, CIMBA; Cofounder, NeuroLeadership Institute; Coeditor, *NeuroLeadership Journal*

david@neuroleadership.com

Christine Cox, Postdoctoral Fellow, Phyllis Green and Randolph Cowen Institute for Pediatric Neuroscience, New York University Langone Medical Center, New York, USA Christine.Cox@nyumc.org

Introduction

The SCARF® model stands for Status, Certainty, Autonomy, Relatedness, and Fairness. SCARF defines the five domains of experience that activate strong threats and rewards in the brain, thus influencing a wide range of human behaviors. In the five years since its introduction in 2008, SCARF has become a widely discussed model in management circles, including being highlighted as one of the "Best Ideas of 15 Years" by *strategy+business* magazine.

Students in the NeuroLeadership Institute's postgraduate and master's programs are conducting a wide range of research studies based on SCARF concepts, and hundreds of thousands of people have learned about the model through blogs, videos, and training programs. Since SCARF was first published, social neuroscience research has contributed to a more in-depth understanding of the SCARF domains, providing support for the model and motivating further exploration of each domain.

In this chapter, we begin by proposing a conceptual model for how SCARF enables people to exhibit more adaptive behaviors, based on how mental experiences occur over time. We then update the research supporting the SCARF model that has been conducted in the five years since it was published, starting with the importance of social processing in the brain and then highlighting recent social neuroscience findings relevant to each of the SCARF domains. Finally, we explore interactions between the domains and issues such as individual variation and SCARF, the ideas of the multiplying and offsetting effects, as well as SCARF and leadership, culture, engagement, and reward.

Conceptual model: how SCARF can improve thinking, performance in individuals, teams

The SCARF model improves people's capacity to understand and ultimately modify their own and other people's behavior in social situations, thus being more adaptive. The model is especially relevant for organizational leaders and managers, organizational learning and development professionals, facilitators, trainers, coaches, consultants, and teachers, as well as social workers, community aid workers, or anyone looking to influence others. We collectively call these types of people "change agents." SCARF is also helpful for understanding and improving the quality of everyday interactions with colleagues, friends, or family.

The SCARF model enables people to be more adaptive by providing a clear, easy-to-remember language.

How does SCARF specifically help? The SCARF model enables people to be more adaptive by providing a clear, easy-to-remember language. This language improves our ability to label or reappraise our emotions, which helps regulate social threats and rewards (Ochsner 2008). Social threats in particular, such as a fear of looking bad in front of one's peers, can inhibit high-quality perception, cognition, critical thinking, creativity, and collaboration. Having a memorable language for social threats and rewards allows us to notice these experiences at several points we may not have otherwise noticed: before, during, and after an emotion-producing event.

Before: prediction

The language of SCARF can help us predict whether a threat is going to happen and modify our activities or choices accordingly. In James Gross's model of how emotions unfold, this is called "situation modification" (Gross 2003). This is being introduced here as the PRE (Prediction, Regulation, Explanatory) model by David Rock.

Before an emotional event occurs, SCARF enables people to predict the impact an action may have on others. For example, before announcing the reorganization of a team, a manager might recognize that the team could sense this as a status threat. He or she could then offset this threat by increasing people's sense of certainty about the situation by providing more information, and increasing their sense of autonomy by providing some choice in how the process occurs. Before a SCARF threat kicks in, knowing SCARF enables us to mitigate or take away the threats that an interaction might bring about.

The language of SCARF can help us notice a threat occurring while it is happening in real time and look to regulate our emotions.

During: regulation

The language of SCARF can help us notice a threat occurring while it is happening in real time and look to regulate our emotions. Many studies show that labeling or reappraising emotions can help reduce the emotion and increase executive functions (Lieberman 2009). During an arousal-producing event, SCARF provides people with an easy-to-recall framework for labeling and reappraising their responses.

Regulating emotions during an event is not easy because strong emotions reduce the capacity for self-regulation (Ochsner 2008). With an easy-to-recall framework like SCARF, people are able to identify the cause of a threat response better through labeling. They can also then change their response to an event through reappraising, which is easier to do after labeling has allowed them to reduce the overall threat response. Reappraisal can also occur by changing their opinion of other people's reactions to events. For example, when people feel their work is being attacked by others during a meeting, knowing SCARF can help them identify (label) their response as a status threat, and then look to see which threats others might be feeling that could be driving their reactions (for example uncertainty). In this way SCARF can help with the two main planks of self-regulation: both labeling and reappraisal. Doing this in the heat of the moment, when possible, can help people make better choices and reduce social conflict.

After: explanatory

After an emotional event, such as a team meeting that went wrong because a comment generated a sense of unfairness, SCARF can also help people explain and therefore understand a situation. This does not necessarily increase adaptive responses in the moment, but it can reduce uncertainty and ongoing conflict over time. With this knowledge, people may choose different strategies in the future for interacting with others. Using SCARF to explain a situation after the event may be the easiest and most likely use of SCARF. However, with sufficient awareness, people may be able to move from using SCARF after, to during, and then before an event—from explanatory to regulatory to predictive—as the distinctions become more easily accessed from moment to moment. More research would be useful on this issue.

PRE model summarized

In summary, understanding SCARF can impact people in these ways:

Before an event: prediction—SCARF can provide an increased ability to minimize negative and maximize positive emotions ahead of time in oneself and others, thereby mitigating distracting threats and increasing overall motivation.

During an event: regulatory—SCARF can increase the ability to regulate one's own and others' emotions in the moment, thereby increasing perception, cognition, creativity, and collaboration.

After an event: explanatory—SCARF can increase one's ability to understand strong emotions after the fact, thereby decreasing uncertainty and enabling different choices in the future.

In short, SCARF is a cognitive tool, a heuristic, for quickly and easily recalling the potential impact of your actions on others (and others' actions on you), thus enabling the possibility of different choices. The fact that it is simple to recall makes it especially useful as it can be easily accessed when cognitive resources are low.

Five domains of SCARF

We begin with a brief review of the five domains of the SCARF model (Rock 2008):

- **Status** refers to one's sense of importance relative to others (e.g., peers, coworkers, friends, supervisors).
- **Certainty** refers to one's need for clarity and the ability to make accurate predictions about the future.
- **Autonomy** is tied to a sense of control over the events in one's life and the perception that one's behavior has an effect on the outcome of a situation (e.g., getting a promotion, finding a partner).
- **Relatedness** concerns one's sense of connection to and security with another person (e.g., whether someone is perceived as similar or dissimilar to oneself, a friend, or a foe).
- **Fairness** refers to just and nonbiased exchange between people (e.g., praise for or acknowledgment of one's efforts, equivalent pay for equivalent work, sharing a candy bar with everyone, etc.).

All five of these domains can have an impact on a person's perception of a social situation, be it threatening or rewarding. For example, uncertainty about the way one's boss is evaluating one's performance can be threatening in the same way as uncertainty about whether the dark, elongated shape in one's peripheral field of view is a snake. Conversely, being acknowledged for one's hard work and effort by a supervisor can be rewarding in the same way that finding money on the street is rewarding.

Importance of social processing in the brain

Since 2008, advances in social neuroscience research have supported the basic tenets of the SCARF model: the view that social concerns are a primary motivator for human behavior and that the human brain is primed to attend to and process social information in a privileged manner.

Specifically, research has shown that humans have a fundamental need to belong, are incredibly sensitive to their social context, and are strongly motivated to remain in good standing with their social group and avoid social exclusion (Heatherton 2011). There is compelling evidence that the experiences people perceive as both the best and the worst in their lives are not individual achievements, such as winning awards, but social experiences, such as beginning and ending close relationships (Jaremka, Gabriel, and Carvallo 2011). Understanding others' minds and emotions is central to the way our brains process information.

Social pain is processed in the brain in much the same way as physical pain. Being excluded from a game or looking at a picture of someone who broke up with you "hurts" and also engages very similar brain regions as when you are physically hurt, such as when something hot touches your arm (Eisenberger 2012). Similarly, social rejection or ostracism can lead to increased inflammation in the body (Slavich et al. 2010) and negative mental health consequences such as depression (Williams and Nida 2011). Recent evidence has taken this even further, showing that people who took acetaminophen, a physical pain reliever, for three weeks reported reduced levels of social pain and showed reduced neural responses in the brain regions involved in the pain associated with social rejection, compared with those who took a placebo (DeWall et al. 2010). Just as the direct experience of social rejection activates pain circuits in the brain, so too does watching someone else being socially rejected (Masten et al. 2010).

Research has shown that humans have a fundamental need to belong, are incredibly sensitive to their social context, and are strongly motivated to remain in good standing with their social group and avoid social exclusion.

The processing of threat and reward in the brain is also affected by social context. Bault et al. (2011) showed that beating a peer in a lottery is more rewarding than winning alone, that this is associated with greater activity in the brain regions that process reward and social information, and that social winning increases the likelihood that people will take more risks and be more competitive.

These and other social neuroscience findings, further detailed below, make a strong argument that consideration of the social and emotional responses and needs of others plays a role in helping people successfully collaborate and understand one another. This is especially relevant for individuals in leadership roles, since fostering and supporting rewarding experiences, such as a sense of connectedness among employees, is crucial for well-being and job satisfaction. In fact, recent research cites coworker incivility as not only a cause of increased distress and problems in the workplace but also leading to a carryover effect in which stress from work is transferred to the home, negatively impacting personal relationships—for example, by reducing marital satisfaction (Ferguson 2012).

The social abilities of team members are of the utmost importance in enhancing performance. "Collective intelligence," or how well a group performs across a wide range of tasks, does not depend on having one or many smart people in the group, but instead is directly related to factors such as the social sensitivity of the group members and how much time is spent giving everyone in the group equal time to talk (Woolley et al. 2010).

The social abilities of team members are of the utmost importance in enhancing performance.

Most recent social neuroscience of SCARF

The wide reach and influence of SCARF has motivated an exploration of the most recent social neuroscience research and how findings from the last five years can update and provide a more in-depth understanding of the SCARF domains and their influence on human social behavior. The following sections highlight results from recent studies relevant to each of the five SCARF domains.

Status

People are acutely sensitive to their social status—that is, their importance relative to others—and tend to be accurate judges of where they fall on the social ladder (Srivastava and Anderson 2011). Even though people have a good sense of their own social status, comparing oneself with another person with higher status can elicit a threat response. Stronger envy when comparing oneself with someone of higher social status is associated with activation in the dorsal anterior cingulate cortex, a region of the brain implicated in processing pain (Takahashi et al. 2009). Conversely, stronger *Schadenfreude*, or pleasure derived from another's misfortune, is associated with activation in the striatum, which is involved in processing reward (Takahashi et al. 2009).

Status-confirming information can elicit activation in reward neural circuitry.

Sensitivity to one's own social status can also be seen in small-group settings, where a perception of lower status in the group is associated with reduced cognitive capacity (lower IQ), increased responses in the amygdala, and decreased responses in the prefrontal cortex relative to perceived higher group status

(Kishida et al. 2012). Making social status salient can also influence large-scale brain activity. Priming high social power (think of a situation in which you had power over someone) versus low social power (think of a situation in which someone had power over you) was associated with increased left frontal brain activity, previously shown to be related to a tendency toward an approach-related orientation and seeking of reward (Boksem, Smolders, and De Cremer 2012).

Status-confirming information can elicit activation in reward neural circuitry. Izuma, Saito, and Sadato (2008) showed common activity in the striatum when a person received a monetary reward and when he or she acquired a social reward—namely, when perceiving that he or she was acquiring a good reputation with others. Izuma (2012) further argues that reputation-based decision making drives many aspects of human social behavior and engages not only the striatum, but also the medial prefrontal cortex, temporal parietal junction, and amygdala, further highlighting the importance of status in threat, reward, and social processing.

Actively and consciously considering status-related information, such as when we compare ourselves to someone more affluent or with a more prestigious job, affects both our behavior and threat/reward neural activation.

However, our predisposition toward valuing status-related information operates on a more nonconscious level as well. Terburg et al. (2011) showed that people who tend to be more dominant took longer to avert their eyes from a subconsciously presented angry face. In the same study, people who were less dominant and more sensitive to reward took longer to look away from happy faces, also presented without conscious awareness. These findings support the idea that the importance of status for an individual may be a basic personality trait and can influence social interactions even if he or she is not aware of it. Someone who highly values status may be more likely to react to status-threatening situations in an aggressive and confrontational manner.

The tendency to perceive changes in social status as threatening also appears to be related to a person's baseline levels of testosterone. After losing a competitive task, both men and women with higher levels of testosterone exhibited increases in cortisol, a stress hormone released during a threat response, compared with low-testosterone losers (Mehta, Jones, and Josephs 2008). More recent work highlights the critical interplay between hormones and stress in dominance and social status. People who are high in testosterone but low in cortisol (low stress) seek to gain more social dominance, whereas high testosterone paired with high cortisol (high stress) is actually associated with seeking lower status (Mehta and Josephs 2010).

The tendency to perceive changes in social status as threatening also appears to be related to a person's baseline levels of testosterone.

Together, these studies support and extend prior work, showing that threats to or confirmation of status influence the way people perceive others and interact in social settings.

Certainty

Imagine how you would feel if your flight had been delayed and you were sitting in the plane on the runway. Would you feel less anxious and annoyed if the pilot gave you constant updates, or would you be just as happy if you did not have any of that information? People differ in their need for certainty and their ability to tolerate uncertain or ambiguous situations. Specifically, intolerance of ambiguity is the tendency for one to perceive ambiguous or uncertain situations as sources of threat.

People differ in their need for certainty and their ability to tolerate uncertain or ambiguous situations.

In general, increasing certainty is perceived as rewarding and increases activation in reward neural circuitry (e.g., ventral striatum). Although previous research has shown that unexpected rewards increase activation in reward-related brain regions more than expected rewards, just receiving information about an upcoming reward also activates these reward regions. Dopamine neurons in monkeys have been shown to fire during not just the expectation of a reward but also the expectation of information about that reward (Bromberg-Martin and Hikosaka 2009). Conversely, increased ambiguity or uncertainty decreases activation in reward circuits and increases activation in threat neural circuitry (e.g., the amygdala).

Individual differences in various personality traits can also affect the way people process and respond to uncertain or ambiguous situations. Ambiguous social situations can cause a large amount of stress, especially if someone is worried about being negatively evaluated, and this anxiety and stress is amplified by low self-esteem. People with low self-esteem who experience ambiguous social rejection engage in more negative self-appraisal and self-blame and also show greater cortisol reactivity than do people with high self-esteem (Ford and Collins 2010).

These studies highlight the rewarding nature of certainty and the threatening nature of uncertainty and ambiguity. An individual's ability to tolerate ambiguity has profound implications for whether uncertain social situations, such as the restructuring of a company or having to work with a new team of people, will be met with manageable or overwhelming levels of anxiety and stress.

Autonomy

The perception of having autonomy—that is, of having control over the things that happen in one's life—has long been known to increase well-being and cognitive functioning and to improve health. Across the globe, psychological prosperity (such as a sense of autonomy), as opposed to economic prosperity, better predicts feelings of well-being (Diener et al. 2010).

People have a fundamental need for personal control.

People have a fundamental need for personal control. In a recent study by Leotti and Delgado (2011), people reported that they liked a cue that signaled they could make a choice in the future more than a cue that predicted no choice. In the same study, anticipation of making a choice increased activity in the reward regions, specifically the ventral striatum, supporting the idea that a sense of autonomy is inherently rewarding.

Autonomy can be closely linked to the concept of agency, which is typically defined in neuroscience research as behavior that is self-generated (i.e., moving a joystick oneself versus another person moving the joystick). Thus, the focus of much of this research is on who initiates a behavior, not why a person does so. However, Lee and Reeve (2012) were interested in the latter question, which is pertinent to a discussion of the social neuroscience of autonomy: what are the neural correlates of being motivated to do something because you are intrinsically motivated and choose to do it (autonomy), compared with being motivated by extrinsic factors such as incentives? Intrinsically, as opposed to extrinsically, motivated behaviors activated the anterior insula, which is implicated in integrating information about internal bodily states and emotional evaluations. This insula activation was found to be highly correlated with the level of perceived autonomy and satisfaction that people reported experiencing in their lives. Extrinsic motivations, such as performance-based monetary incentives, have actually been shown to reduce intrinsic motivation to perform a task, a phenomenon termed the "undermining effect," which is associated with reduced activation in the striatum and prefrontal cortex (Murayama et al. 2010).

Inesi et al. (2011) showed that when people lack a sense of power (i.e., control over what other people do), they seek out a sense of choice (i.e., control over their own outcomes), and vice versa. People can be content with only a sense of power, only a sense of control, or both, but having neither power nor control leads to dissatisfaction.

These findings have specific implications for the workplace: leaders should be able to increase the satisfaction of individuals with a relatively powerless or low-level job by giving them a greater perception of choice, thereby increasing autonomy. In fact, Wood and de Menezes (2011) showed that this was the case; employees with a greater sense of autonomy reported greater job satisfaction and reduced anxiety. Social neuroscience research highlights the cognitive and neural mechanisms underlying this phenomenon—since the perception of autonomy is processed in the brain as a reward and fostering intrinsic motivation is also rewarding, implementing leadership practices that increase autonomy and intrinsic motivation in employees will increase productivity and promote collaboration.

People can be content with only a sense of power, only a sense of control, or both, but having neither power nor control leads to dissatisfaction.

Relatedness

The degree to which people feel a sense of connectedness and similarity to those around them is directly related to whether people feel they are engaging in safe or threatening social interactions. The phenomena known as "ingroup preference" and "outgroup bias" refer to the consistent finding that people feel greater trust and empathy toward people who are similar to them and are part of their same social circles, and greater distrust and reduced empathy toward those who are perceived as dissimilar and members of other social groups.

People even process information about ingroup members and outgroup members in different parts of the brain (Mitchell 2009; Jenkins, Macrae, and Mitchell 2008). Ingroup preference and outgroup bias are not only human phenomena but observed in monkeys as well (Mahajan et al. 2011).

People feel greater trust and empathy toward people who are similar to them...

It appears that the definition of ingroup and outgroup members is not limited to racial, ethnic, or political distinctions, but that arbitrarily assigning people to different teams can have the same effects of increasing liking for members of one's own team and decreasing liking for members of the other team, which is reflected in brain activity (Van Bavel, Packer, and Cunningham 2008). Mitigating ingroup bias and outgroup prejudice is an important consideration when facilitating collaboration among individuals who may perceive outside individuals as a threat (e.g., an independent consultant, a new team of coworkers, etc.). Walton et al. (2012) showed that providing minimal social links to another person or group increases motivation and performance. Equally important is the fact that increasing intergroup contact can reduce the prejudice observed toward outgroup members (Dhont, Roets, and Van Hiel 2011). If two groups or teams of people need to work together, fostering more social contact between groups is one way to increase relatedness and decrease a sense of threat.

Oxytocin, a neuropeptide involved in social cognition and behavior in mammals, is involved in increasing relatedness. It has been shown to reduce social stress, reduce amygdala activation, improve the processing of social and emotional information, and increase attachment and empathy toward others

(Meyer-Lindenberg et al. 2011). New research, however, has questioned this "love drug" role of oxytocin; instead, it may play a more general role by increasing all approach-related social behavior (e.g., positive as well as negative emotions such as anger and jealousy) and reducing social withdrawal (Kemp and Guastella 2011). Interestingly, oxytocin not only promotes ingroup trust and cooperation but also increases aggression toward outgroups (de Dreu et al. 2010).

Several research studies have shown that the size of one's social network is related to the structure and function of the brain. Among monkeys, living in larger social groups is associated with increased gray-matter volume and increased functional coupling between brain regions important for processing social information—the temporal and prefrontal cortices (Sallet et al. 2011). Pertinent to the ever-increasing prominence of social media and the debate about its effects on social relationships and relatedness, Kanai et al. (2012) showed that the more friends people have on Facebook, the greater the size of their amygdala and temporal cortex. Tamir and Mitchell (2012) recently reported that people are highly motivated to share information about themselves and that self-disclosure is related to increased activation in reward regions of the brain. It is interesting to speculate whether this motivation for self-disclosure is an underlying factor in the popularity of social networking sites such as Facebook and whether greater self-disclosure is related to larger social networks and an increased perception of social support.

Relatedness isn't just about feeling good. New studies show that having stronger social relationships increases your chance of living longer. A meta-analysis across 148 studies concluded that people with stronger social relationships have a 50% increased likelihood of survival than those with weaker social relationships (Holt-Lunstad, Smith, and Layton 2010). Similarly, people who feel they have high levels of social support at work are at a reduced risk of mortality (Shirom et al. 2011).

Relatedness isn't just about feeling good...having stronger social relationships increases your chance of living longer.

Fairness

The perception of the fairness of any situation is not based on "cold," rational thought processes; instead, emotions are integral to judging fairness, and those judgments emerge over time through social experiences with others (Barsky, Kaplan, and Beal 2011).

Unfair offers in neuroeconomic games, in which one person has to divide money between him- or herself and another player and does so in an unequal manner (e.g., $9/$1), elicit strong negative emotional reactions and increase anterior insula activation (Rilling and Sanfey 2011). Recent research has also shown that the amygdala is activated during the rejection of these unfair offers (Gospic et al. 2011). Even when fair and unfair offers are made equally valuable (i.e., equal monetary value), people are happier to receive fair offers than unfair ones, and receiving fair versus unfair offers activates reward regions in the brain (Tabibnia, Satpute, and Lieberman 2008).

Even when fair and unfair offers are made equally valuable...people are happier to receive fair offers than unfair ones...

Not only receiving, but also making fair offers activates brain regions related to reward and to theory of mind (Weiland et al. 2012). Tricomi et al. (2010) reported that people who gave more money to others than to themselves—that is, acted prosocially and reduced inequality—showed increased activity in the ventral striatum and ventromedial prefrontal cortex, reward-sensitive brain regions. The authors claim this is evidence for inequality-averse social preferences in the brain.

Results from a meta-analysis showed that perceptions of unfairness in the workplace can negatively affect employees' physical and mental health (Robbins, Ford, and Tetrick 2012). Accordingly, increasing the perception of fairness and reducing unfairness will promote satisfaction and well-being, especially in social situations in which sensitivity to interpersonal equality and inequality is heightened.

Interactions between SCARF domains

Although much can be said about each SCARF domain on its own, recent social neuroscience research points to several ways in which these domains relate to one another. Two of the most prominent are the connections between status and relatedness and between certainty and relatedness.

Status and relatedness

Social status can influence the way we relate to, behave toward, and interact with others. Lount and Pettit (2012) showed that people with high status are more trusting of others than are people with lower status and that this is because high-status individuals believe that others have positive (benevolent) intentions toward them. One's own social status can influence activity in reward-related brain regions when processing information about the social status of others. People with lower social ranking (i.e., lower socio-economic status) showed increased activation of the ventral striatum when answering questions about a low-status individual, and people with higher social ranking showed increased activation in the same brain region when answering questions about a high-status individual (Ly et al. 2011).

In a highly publicized paper, Piff et al. (2012) showed that upper-class (high social status) individuals are more likely to behave unethically than lower-class individuals. These behaviors included cutting people off while driving, cheating, stealing office supplies, taking candy that was intended for children, and viewing greed more positively. Further research suggests that higher social class people are worse than lower social class people at reading others' emotions—that is, they are lower in empathy (Kraus et al. 2011).

Individuals who experience high levels of anxiety in social situations (social anxiety disorder), perceive themselves as having low social rank but also low perceived closeness with others, including peers, friends, and romantic partners (Weisman et al. 2011). Difficulties relating to others are associated with perceptions of reduced social status.

Economic status can at times reduce relatedness...

We have discussed how perceptions of high status and greater relatedness are rewarding. Recent work takes this one step further and purports that a particular kind of status, sociometric status—that is, respect and admiration from peers—is much more predictive of a person's well-being than socioeconomic status (Anderson et al. 2012). This highlights the integral relationship between status and relatedness; increased social status that grows from better relatedness to others appears to be more rewarding than economic status is. We suspect that economic status can at times reduce relatedness (think of wealthy people in homes with big walls, cut off from people), whereas sociometric status involves being in a community of others.

Certainty and relatedness

Relating to and understanding others usually involves some degree of uncertainty or ambiguity because we have to guess or deduce what other people are thinking or feeling. Activity in the medial prefrontal cortex is sensitive to the amount of ambiguity involved when making decisions about what a person thinks or feels, reflecting greater computational demands in the part of the brain implicated in simulating different possible scenarios (Jenkins and Mitchell 2010).

In addition, personality characteristics such as a need for cognitive closure (i.e., a high need for certainty and to avoid ambiguity) are related to prejudice. People who have very low tolerance for ambiguity exhibit higher levels of race- and gender-based prejudice (Roets and Van Hiel 2011). Promisingly, however, increasing contact between ingroups and outgroups is effective in reducing prejudice, especially in people who have a high need for cognitive closure. Uncertainty can undermine relatedness (increase prejudice), but increasing one type of relatedness (intergroup contact) can mitigate the threat caused by uncertainty and reduce its negative impact on relatedness (reduce prejudice).

Individual variation and SCARF

The SCARF model provides an intuitive and easily remembered framework for conceptualizing the main factors that influence the way people perceive and respond to social situations. The five factors of the model—Status, Certainty, Autonomy, Relatedness, and Fairness—all affect the extent to which a person feels threatened or rewarded in social settings and therefore the extent to which a person is able to collaborate effectively with others. Going beyond these general descriptions, the SCARF framework has also been used to characterize individuals in terms of their sensitivity to each of the five domains, effectively creating custom SCARF profiles. This individual-differences approach highlights the ways in which people with different SCARF styles require different approaches when managing or collaborating with others. For example, a person who is highly anxious in uncertain situations will likely need more clarity and concrete detail than a person who is more tolerant of uncertainty.

In informal studies within SCARF workshops run by the NeuroLeadership Group (a consulting firm that draws on the NeuroLeadership Institute's work), people appear to have widely different orders in which the SCARF domains are important to them. For example, an individual may feel most passionately about fairness and least passionately about status, with the other domains spread in between. This individual variation is likely to be influenced by the environment at the time and could perhaps change over one's lifetime; however, it also appears to be relatively static. An individual who values fairness can usually track back through their life history and see how this domain informed their life and career choices over time. This is an area for substantial future research, with individual variation studied over time in relation to different career paths and in connection with genetic variability.

Contrasting with data from informal studies are findings from a large-scale research study conducted by the NeuroLeadership Group in which SCARF profiles from over 6,300 individuals were collected. Table 2 summarizes these findings, highlighting the most prevalent profile types and demographic variables associated with each. What is striking here is that 46% of responders indicated that the most important domain was Certainty, followed by Relatedness, which 27% of responders rated as the most important domain.

	S	C	A	R	F
Total (out of 6239)	791 (12%)	2898 (46%)	190 (3%)	1684 (27%)	766 (12%)
Gender: M, F	313 (40%), 478 (60%)	1077 (37%), 1821 (63%)	77 (41%), 113 (59%)	671 (40%), 1013 (60%)	325 (42%), 441 (58%)
Age (under 18)	67 (8%)	188 (6%)	24 (13%)	175 (10%)	120 (16%)
Age (18–25)	47 (6%)	168 (6%)	8 (4%)	124 (7%)	63 (8%)
Age (26–35)	244 (31%)	601 (21%)	48 (25%)	395 (23%)	216 (28%)
Age (36–45)	234 (30%)	842 (29%)	47 (25%)	448 (27%)	180 (23%)
Age (46–55)	146 (18%)	766 (26%)	44 (23%)	390 (24%)	135 (18%)
Age (56–65)	47 (6%)	305 (11%)	17 (9%)	136 (8%)	47 (6%)
Age (over 65)	6 (1%)	28 (1%)	2 (1%)	16 (1%)	5 (1%)
Top Industry	Banking/ Finance 80 (10%)	HR 326 (11%)	HR 28 (15%)	Education 198 (12%)	Education 104 (14%)
2nd Industry	HR 80 (10%)	Education 291 (10%)	Accounting, Education, Engineering 17 (9%)	HR 176 (10%)	HR 66 (9%)

Table 2. Findings from 6,300 SCARF profiles

Without some kind of awareness of other people's motivators, managers and peers will tend to try to motivate in the way they themselves would be motivated.

Understanding individual variation can have many benefits. Identifying an individual's SCARF profile can help tailor both engagement and reward programs to the individual by focusing on his or her key drivers rather than all domains at once. This kind of assessment can be helpful because of our tendency to think that others perceive the world as we do, a bias called the "false consensus effect" (Ross, Greene, and House 1977; Krueger and Clement 1994). Without some kind of awareness of other people's motivators, managers and peers will tend to try to motivate in the way they themselves would be motivated.

SCARF and culture

While there appears to be some individual variation in SCARF profiles, there is likely to also be a cultural influence in terms of both ethnic culture and the culture of someone's organization or community.

Studies from cultural neuroscience, summarized by Rockstuhl et al. (2010), suggest a genetic basis to a number of our tendencies that ties closely to SCARF. For example, there is a gene that alters the uptake of oxytocin in the brain, which makes some cultures feel social rejection and social support more acutely. This genetic variation may be behind variations in collectivism versus individualism, pushing some cultures to value relatedness and fairness more and others to value autonomy and status. Further research should be done on whether cultures have any consistent tendencies in terms of the SCARF framework itself, something that could help with intercultural understanding and communication.

Organizations are likely to have their own SCARF profiles. An organization such as a start-up technology company, which values creativity and innovation and requires an overall approach state, is likely to focus on issues such as autonomy, relatedness, and fairness, and try to reduce the status gap between people. However, the downside is that with so much autonomy and relatedness, certainty can suffer by having so much individual choice in how things are done and so many people involved in decision making.

An organization that needs people to follow preexisting systems may focus on using created status differentials to motivate others, as well as on the need for certainty with an emphasis on rigor and controls. An example of this might be a government office, where people may have high certainty but low autonomy. More research needs to be done on organizational SCARF profiles, the relevance of these, and how they can be altered over time.

People experience the strongest sense of engagement when they have rewards occurring in multiple domains...

SCARF and workplace engagement

In their paper "Neuroscience of Engagement," Rock and Tang (2009) outlined how the SCARF domains are likely to be the underpinning drivers of workplace engagement. They showed how several of the more popular engagement assessments were measuring various domains of SCARF, but with an uneven weighting and without all domains being measured. We propose that a more accurate measurement of engagement will be assessments that test evenly across all domains of SCARF. More research is needed in this area.

In noting that the SCARF domains drive threat and reward, it is useful to note that the reward or threat response can be either an expectation of or an actual positive increase in a domain. That is because expectations of rewards (or threats) are as strong as or stronger than actual rewards (Rock 2009).

Minimizing disengagement is perhaps the first rule of thumb, as threat responses tend to be the most intense experiences.

Rock and Dixon propose that people experience the strongest sense of engagement when they have rewards occurring in multiple domains, termed the "multiplier effect" (Rock, Dixon, and Ochsner 2010). For example, someone who is given a promotion may be rewarded by a greater sense of control over their work, an increased sense of status, and a perception of fairness if they worked hard to get the promotion. A feeling of making progress on a task, which was shown in a 2010 study (Amabile and Kramer 2010) to be the most engaging experience at work, is likely to increase one's sense of status, certainty, and autonomy all at once, another example of the multiplier effect.

The opposite is also likely to be true: someone will be highly disengaged via the multiplier effect if their sense of uncertainty goes up as a result of a change in their team that they have less control over than they expected, and is seen as unfair. Minimizing disengagement is perhaps the first rule of thumb, as threat responses tend to be the most intense experiences. This is best done ahead of time through better planning of organizational initiatives to minimize SCARF threats and by offsetting threats that may be necessary.

SCARF and change

The SCARF model explains in part why change can be so hard and points to ways of making change easier. Unless carefully managed, an organizational change is likely to affect all five domains of SCARF for a wide range of people. Managing a change carefully would involve using the offsetting effect (Rock, Dixon, and Ochsner 2010) to create a perception of increases in the domains where increases are easiest to execute. For example, a team that is reorganizing functions could offset SCARF threats by involving people in some aspect of choice about the process, which would increase a sense of autonomy. Also, information could be provided about the wider context so that people sense increases in certainty.

SCARF and leadership

There are many links between SCARF and leadership. In this brief summary, we have explored a few of the links between SCARF and individual variation, culture, engagement, and change. Another issue involves self-management as a leader, or how a leader manages his or her own behavior.

The relationship between people and their boss is a troubled one, on average. One study showed that people trust a stranger in the street more than their boss (Segalla 2009). This challenge may be explained by SCARF and the multiplier effect. Having a boss creates a status threat through being the lower-status person. A boss tends to create uncertainty by not setting clear expectations and by continuously seeking improvements, which are seen as changes and therefore uncertain. A boss has the control and the final say, reducing one's autonomy. Bosses tend to keep themselves separate, putting themselves in a different group—in this case the outgroup—resulting in a threat to relatedness. Finally, bosses are likely to be seen as unfair simply because they appear to be paid more money than their team while not doing the direct work. With all five domains under threat, the result may be minimal sharing of information, reduced accurate perception of the others' thoughts and intentions, and reduced creativity.

The threat that leaders inherently create needs to be offset for successful collaboration. Successful leaders do this by increasing relatedness, which can come from identifying and focusing on shared goals, and also by being authentic and open so that people share positive human experiences (George 2003). Alternatively, a leader may increase a sense of certainty through extensive sharing of information or be clear about where people have authority and thus autonomy. Leadership may easily devolve into threat-producing experiences; however, with attention, leaders can learn to offset these threats and develop a relationship with their teams built on moderate, rather than high, stress.

Conclusions

Economic theory that purports that individuals are purely rational decision makers is clearly false; people are also significantly driven by social information and social motivations in the form of both threats and rewards. Leaders who acknowledge this and take advantage of being able to reduce threat and foster reward in each of the SCARF domains are going to be much more successful than those who expect people to suppress their emotions and social needs. Suppression is, after all, a strategy that tends to make emotions worse and further reduce cognitive functioning (Ochsner 2008).

Leaders are under social magnification; everyone is watching them...

Leaders are under social magnification; everyone is watching them, looking for meaning, and even taking on their emotions nonconsciously. All social interactions for a leader are meaningful and must be done with care. This is why it is so important for leaders to take advantage of psychology and social neuroscience research and to be aware of implicit or unconscious influences on behavior, especially social signals and biases. Understanding and internalizing the SCARF model can help leaders become more socially sensitive and socially adaptive, helping them use social rewards and threats in more deliberate, useful ways that are in line with an organization's objectives. Christine Williams, a leadership development practitioner at NASA once said, "We can predict what will happen to a tiny space craft in ten years and a million miles away, but we can't seem to predict what will happen at a meeting tomorrow." SCARF may be only one small step in the journey toward understanding social interactions, but it appears to be a step in the right direction.

References

Amabile, T. M., and Kramer, S. J. 2010. "The HBR list: Breakthrough Ideas for 2010." *Harvard Business Review* (January).

Anderson, C., Kraus, M. W., Galinsky, A. D., and Keltner, D. 2012. "The Local-Ladder Effect: Social Status and Subjective Well-Being." *Psychological Science* 23(7): 764–771.

Barsky, A., Kaplan, S. A., and Beal, D. J. 2011. "Just Feelings? The Role of Affect in the Formation of Organizational Fairness Judgments." *Journal of Management* 37(1): 248–279.

Bault, N., Joffily, M., Rustichini, A., and Coricelli, G. 2011. "Medial Prefrontal Cortex and Striatum Mediate the Influence of Social Comparison on the Decision Process." *Proceedings of the National Academy of Sciences, USA* 108(38): 16044–16049.

Boksem, M. A., Smolders, R., and De Cremer, D. 2012. "Social Power and Approach-Related Neural Activity." *Social Cognitive and Affective Neuroscience* 7(5): 516–520.

Bromberg-Martin, E. S., and Hikosaka, O. 2009. "Midbrain Dopamine Neurons Signal Preference for Advance Information about Upcoming Rewards." *Neuron* 63(1): 119–126.

De Dreu, C. K., Greer, L. L., Handgraaf, M. J., Shalvi, S., Van Kleef, G. A., Baas, M., Ten Velden, F.S., Van Dijk, E., and Feith, S. W. 2010. "The Neuropeptide Oxytocin Regulates Parochial Altruism in Intergroup Conflict Among Humans." *Science* 328(5984): 1408–1411.

DeWall, C. N., Macdonald, G., Webster, G. D., Masten, C. L., Baumeister, R. F., Powell, C., Combs, D., et al. 2010. "Acetaminophen Reduces Social Pain: Behavioral and Neural Evidence." *Psychological Science* 21(7): 931–937.

Dhont, K., Roets, A., and Van Hiel, A. 2011. "Opening Closed Minds: The Combined Effects of Intergroup Contact and Need for Closure on Prejudice." *Personality and Social Psychology Bulletin* 37(4): 514–528.

Diener, E., Ng, W., Harter, J., and Arora, R. 2010. "Wealth and Happiness Across the World: Material Prosperity Predicts Life Evaluation, Whereas Psychosocial Prosperity Predicts Positive Feeling." *Journal of Personality and Social Psychology* 99(1): 52–61.

Eisenberger, N. 2012. "The Pain of Social Disconnection: Examining the Shared Neural Underpinnings of Physical and Social Pain." *Nature Reviews Neuroscience* 1: 421–434.

Ferguson, M. 2012. "You Cannot Leave it at the Office: Spillover and Crossover of Coworker Incivility." *Journal of Organizational Behavior* 33(4): 571–588.

Ford, M. B., and Collins, N. L. 2010. "Self-Esteem Moderates Neuroendocrine and Psychological Responses to Interpersonal Rejection." *Journal of Personality and Social Psychology* 98(3): 405–419.

George, B. 2003. *Authentic Leadership: Rediscovering the Secrets of Creating Lasting Value*. San Francisco, CA: Jossey-Bass.

Gospic, K., Mohlin, E., Fransson, P., Petrovic, P., Johannesson, M., and Ingvar, M. 2011. "Limbic Justice: Amygdala Involvement in Immediate Rejection in the Ultimatum Game." *PLoS Biology* 9(5): e1001054.

Gross, J. 2003. "The Social Consequences of Expressive Suppression." *Emotion* 3(1): 48–67.

Heatherton, T. F. 2011. "Neuroscience of Self and Self-Regulation." *Annual Review of Psychology* 62: 363–390.

Holt-Lunstad, J., Smith, T. B., and Layton, J. B. 2010. "Social Relationships and Mortality Risk: A Meta-Analytic Review." *PLoS Medicine* 7(7): e1000316.

Inesi, M. E., Botti, S., Dubois, D., Rucker, D. D., and Galinsky, A. D. 2011. "Power and Choice: Their Dynamic Interplay in Quenching the Thirst for Personal Control." *Psychological Science* 22(8): 1042–1048.

Izuma, K. 2012. "The Social Neuroscience of Reputation." *Journal of Neuroscience Research* 72(4): 283–288.

Izuma, K., Saito, D. N., and Sadato, N. 2008. "Processing of Social and Monetary Rewards in the Human Striatum." *Neuron* 58(2): 284–294.

Jaremka, L. M., Gabriel, S., and Carvallo, M. 2011. "What Makes us Feel the Best also Makes us Feel the Worst: The Emotional Impact of Independent and Interdependent Experiences." *Self and Identity* 10(1): 44–63.

Jenkins, A. C., Macrae, C. N., and Mitchell, J. P. 2008. "Repetition Suppression of Ventromedial Prefrontal Activity During Judgments of Self and Others." *Proceedings of the National Academy of Sciences, USA* 105(11): 4507–4512.

Jenkins, A. C., and Mitchell, J. P. 2010. "Mentalizing Under Uncertainty: Dissociated Neural Responses to Ambiguous and Unambiguous Mental State Inferences." *Cerebral Cortex* 20(2): 404–410.

Kanai, R., Bahrami, B., Roylance, R., and Rees, G. 2012. "Online Social Network Size is Reflected in Human Brain Structure." *Proceedings of the Royal Society B: Biological Sciences* 279(1732): 1327–1334.

Kemp, A. H., and Guastella, A. J. 2011. "The Role of Oxytocin in Human Affect: A Novel Hypothesis." *Current Directions in Psychological Science* 20(4): 222–231.

Kishida, K. T., Yang, D., Quartz, K. H., Quartz, S. R., and Montague, P. R. 2012. "Implicit Signals in Small Group Settings and their Impact on the Expression of Cognitive Capacity and Associated Brain Responses." *Philosophical Transactions of the Royal Society of B: Biological Sciences* 367(1589): 704–716.

Kraus, M. W., Horberg, E. J., Goetz, J. L., and Keltner, D. 2011. "Social Class Rank, Threat Vigilance, and Hostile Reactivity." *Personality and Social Psychology Bulletin* 37(10): 1376–1388.

Krueger, J., and Clement, R. W. 1994. "The Truly False Consensus Effect: An Ineradicable and Egocentric Bias in Social-Perception." *Journal of Personality and Social Psychology* 67(4): 596–610.

Lee, W., and Reeve, J. 2012. "Self-Determined, but not Nonself-Determined, Motivation Predicts Activations in the Anterior Insular Cortex: An fMRI Study of Personal Agency." *Social Cognitive and Affective Neuroscience* (April 17) doi: 10.1093/scan/nss029.

Leotti, L. A., and Delgado, M. R. 2011. "The Inherent Reward of Choice." *Psychological Science* 22(10): 1310–1318.

Lieberman, M. D. 2009. "The Brain's Braking System (and How To "Use Your Words" To Tap Into It)." *NeuroLeadership Journal* 2: 9–14.

Lount, R. B., and Pettit, N. C. 2012. "The Social Context of Trust: The Role of Status." *Organizational Behavior and Human Decision Processes* 117(1): 15–23.

Ly, M., Haynes, M. R., Barter, J. W., Weinberger, D. R., and Zink, C. F. 2011. "Subjective Socioeconomic Status Predicts Human Ventral Striatal Responses to Social Status Information." *Current Biology* 21(9): 794–797.

Mahajan, N., Martinez, M. A., Gutierrez, N. L., Diesendruck, G., Banaji, M. R., and Santos, L. R. 2011. "The Evolution of Intergroup Bias: Perceptions and Attitudes in Rhesus Macaques." *Journal of Personality and Social Psychology* 100(3): 387–405.

Masten, C. L., Eisenberger, N. I ., Pfeifer, J. H., and Dapretto, M. 2010. "Witnessing Peer Rejection During Early Adolescence: Neural Correlates of Empathy for Experiences of Social Exclusion." *Social Neuroscience* 5(5–6): 496–507.

Mehta, P. H., Jones, A. C., and Josephs, R. A. 2008. "The Social Endocrinology of Dominance: Basal Testosterone Predicts Cortisol Changes and Behavior Following Victory and Defeat." *Journal of Personality and Social Psychology* 94(6): 1078–1093.

Mehta, P. H., and Josephs, R. A. 2010. "Testosterone and Cortisol Jointly Regulate Dominance: Evidence for a Dual-Hormone Hypothesis." *Hormones and Behavior* 58(5): 898–906.

Meyer-Lindenberg, A., Domes, G., Kirsch, P., and Heinrichs, M. 2011. "Oxytocin and Vasopressin in the Human Brain: Social Neuropeptides for Translational Medicine." *Natural Reviews Neuroscience* 12 (9): 524–538.

Mitchell, J. P. 2009. "Inferences about mental states." *Philosophical Transactions of the Royal Society B: Biological Sciences* 364(1521): 1309–1316.

Murayama, K., Matsumoto, M., Izuma, K., and Matsumato, K. 2010. "Neural Basis of the Undermining Effect of Monetary Reward on Intrinsic Motivation." *Proceedings of the National Academy of Sciences, USA* 107(49): 20911-20916.

Ochsner, K. 2008. "Staying Cool Under Pressure: Insights from Social Cognitive Neuroscience and their Implications for Self and Society." *NeuroLeadership Journal* 1: 26–32.

Piff, P. K., Stancato, D. M., Cote, S., Mendoza-Denton, R., and Keltner, D. 2012. "Higher Social Class Predicts Increased Unethical Behavior." *Proceedings of the National Academy of Sciences, USA* 109(11): 4086–4091.

Rilling, J. K., and Sanfey, A. G. 2011. "The Neuroscience of Social Decision-Making." *Annual Review of Psychology* 62(62): 23–48.

Robbins, J. M., Ford, M. T., and Tetrick, L. E . 2012. "Perceived Unfairness and Employee Health: A Meta-Analytic Integration." *Journal of Applied Psychology* 97(2): 235–272.

Rock, D. 2008. "SCARF: A Brain-Based Model for Collaborating with and Influencing Others." *NeuroLeadership Journal* 1: 78–87.

Rock, D. 2009. *Your Brain at Work: Strategies for Overcoming Distraction, Regaining Focus, and Working Smarter All Day Long*. New York: HarperBusiness.

Rock, D., Dixon. P., and Ochsner, K. 2010. "Turn the 360 Around: Why Feedback Doesn't Work and How to do it Better." *NeuroLeadership Journal* 3: 78–86.

Rock, D., and Tang, Y. 2009. "Neuroscience of Engagement." *NeuroLeadership Journal* 2: 15–22.

Rockstuhl, T., Hong, Y., Ng, K. Y., Ang, S., and Chiu, C. 2010. "The Culturally Intelligent Brain: From Detecting to Bridging Cultural Difficulties." *NeuroLeadership Journal* 3: 22–36.

Roets, A., and Van Hiel, A. 2011. "The Role of Need for Closure in Essentialist Entitativity Beliefs and Prejudice: An Epistemic Needs Approach to Racial Categorization." *British Journal of Social Psychology* 50(1): 52–73.

Ross, L., Greene, D., and House, P. 1977. "False Consensus Effect: Egocentric Bias in Social-Perception and Attribution Processes." *Journal of Experimental Social Psychology* 13(3): 279–301.

Sallet, J., Mars, R. B., Noonan, M. P., Andersson, J. L., O'Reilly, J. X., Jbabdi, S., Croxson, P.L., et al. 2011. "Social Network Size Affects Neural Circuits in Macaques." *Science* 334(6056): 697–700.

Segalla, M. 2009. "How Europeans do Layoff." Harvard Business Review website, June 9. http://appli7.hec.fr/ hrm/diversity/HBR_HEC_Executive_Survey1.htm.

Shirom, A., Toker, S., Alkaly, Y., Jacobson, O., and Balicer, R. 2011. "Work-Based Predictors of Mortality: A 20-year Follow-Up of Healthy Employees." *Health Psychology* 30(3): 268–275.

Slavich, G. M., Way, B. M., Eisenberger, N. I ., and Taylor, S. E. 2010. "Neural Sensitivity to Social Rejection is Associated with Inflammatory Responses to Social Stress." *Proceedings of the National Academy of Sciences, USA* 107(33): 14817–14822.

Srivastava, S., and Anderson, C. 2011. "Accurate When it Counts: Perceiving Power and Status in Social Groups." In *Managing Interpersonal Sensitivity: Knowing When—and When Not—to Understand Others*, edited by J. L. Smith, W. Ickes, J. Hall, S. D. Hodges, and W. Gardner, 41–58. Hauppage, NY: Nova Science Publishers.

Tabibnia, G., Satpute, A. B., and Lieberman, M. D. 2008. "The Sunny Side of Fairness: Preference for Fairness Activates Reward Circuitry (and Disregarding Unfairness Activates Self-Control Circuitry)." *Psychological Science* 19(4): 339–347.

Takahashi, H., Kato, M., Matsuura, M., Mobbs, D., Suhara, T., and Okubo, Y. 2009. "When Your Gain is My Pain and Your Pain is My Gain: Neural Correlates of Envy and Schadenfreude." *Science* 323(5916): 937–939.

Tamir, D. I ., and Mitchell, J. P. 2012. "Disclosing Information About the Self is Intrinsically Rewarding." *Proceedings of the National Academy of Sciences, USA* 109 (21): 8038–8043.

Terburg, D., Hooiveld, N., Aarts, H., Kenemans, J. L., and Van Honk, J. 2011."Eye Tracking Unconscious Face-to-Face Confrontations: Dominance Motives Prolong Gaze to Masked Angry Faces." *Psychological Science* 22(3): 314–319.

Tricomi, E., Rangel, A., Camerer, C. F., and O'Doherty, J. P. 2010. "Neural Evidence for Inequality-Averse Social Preferences." *Nature* 463(7284): 1089–1091.

Van Bavel, J. J., Packer, D. J., and Cunningham, W. A. 2008. "The Neural Substrates of Ingroup Bias: A Functional Magnetic Resonance Imaging Investigation." *Psychological Science* 19(11): 1131–1139.

Walton, G. M., Cohen, G. L., Cwir, D., and Spencer, S. J. 2012. "Mere Belonging: The Power of Social Connections." *Journal of Personality and Social Psychology* 102(3): 513–532.

Weiland, S., Hewig, J., Hecht, H., Mussel, P., and Miltner, W. H. 2012. "Neural Correlates of Fair Behavior in Interpersonal Bargaining." *Society for Neuroscience* 7(5): 537–551.

Weisman, O., Aderka, I. M., Marom, S., Hermesh, H., and Gilboa-Schechtman, E. 2011. "Social Rank and Affiliation in Social Anxiety Disorder." *Behaviour Research and Therapy Journal* 49(6–7): 399–405.

Williams, K. D., and Nida, S. A. 2011. "Ostracism: Consequences and Coping." *Current Directions in Psychological Science* 20(2): 71–75.

Wood, S., and de Menezes, L. M. 2011. "High Involvement Management, High-Performance Work Systems, and Well-Being." *International Journal of Human Resource Management* 22(7): 1586–1610.

Woolley, A. W., Chabris, C. F., Pentland, A., Hashmi, N., and Malone, T. W. 2010. "Evidence for a Collective Intelligence Factor in the Performance of Human Groups." *Science* 330(6004): 686–688.

19. Neuroscience of engagement

Dr. David Rock and Dr. Yi-Yuan Tang
David Rock, CEO, NeuroLeadership Group, New York, USA
Faculty, CIMBA; Cofounder, NeuroLeadership Institute; Editor, *NeuroLeadership Journal*
david@neuroleadership.com

Dr. Yi-Yuan Tang, Institute of Neuroinformatics, Dalian University of Technology, Dalian, China
Department of Psychology, University of Oregon, USA
Institute of Psychology, the Chinese Academy of Sciences, Beijing, China
Center for Social and Organizational Behavior, Graduate University of Chinese Academy of Sciences, Beijing, China
yiyuan@uoregon.edu

Introduction

Workplace engagement involves the degree to which people put discretionary effort and care into their jobs. Until now, research on engagement has focused mostly on the degree to which engagement impacts organizational performance (Conference Board 2006). Also, there has been research into the way engagement varies across different organizations and different countries (Gallup, n.d.). However, no research has been done to identify the underpinning neurological drivers of engagement, its effects on various brain networks, and how we might measure engagement more objectively through neural or biological markers. Recent neuroscience research has begun to provide insights into the neurological drivers of behavior in the social environment (Lieberman 2008; Ochsner and Lieberman 2001; Rock 2008; Ringleb and Rock 2008; Tang and Posner 2008). We will draw on this neuroscience research to explore these five questions:

1. What is the neural basis of engagement?

2. What are the neural drivers that enhance and decrease engagement?

3. What are the levels of engagement from a neural perspective?

4. What effect does increasing or decreasing engagement have on the brain and our wider biology?

5. What neural markers might be used to more accurately measure engagement and the effects of engagement interventions?

Overall, we believe that understanding the neuroscience of engagement is more than just an interesting discussion, that it will open up insights into how to more accurately and effectively measure and improve employee engagement across all types of organizations. While there is much research still to do, the theoretical foundation described below can help shape future research.

Engagement is something the employee has to offer: it cannot be "required" as part of the employment contract.

Neural basis of engagement

Engagement as used here relates to the idea of workplace engagement. A definition of engagement from a US-based organizational research firm is:

> A heightened emotional connection that an employee feels for his or her organization, that influences him or her to exert greater discretionary effort to his or her work. (Conference Board 2006)

A definition from a UK-based organizational research firm is:

> A combination of commitment to the organisation and its values, plus a willingness to help out colleagues (organisational citizenship). It goes beyond job satisfaction and is not simply motivation. Engagement is something the employee has to offer: it cannot be "required" as part of the employment contract. (CIPD 2008)

Neuroscientist Evian Gordon, in one of the largest meta-analyses of brain research in the world, proposed that the organizing principle of the brain is to minimize danger and maximize reward (Gordon 2008). We propose that the neural basis of engagement is closely linked to this threat/reward function. The basis for this belief is the extensive literature emerging about the reward/threat response (Elliot 2008) and the fairly obvious common themes emerging when comparing engagement research to neuroscience research. For example, in the reward state (versus the threat state), people:

- Experience increased cognitive resources (Arnsten 1998)
- Are generally more creative (Friedman and Förster 2001)
- Solve more problems with the insight phenomenon, which is required for complex problem solving (Jung-Beeman et al. 2009)

- Come up with more ideas for actions (Fredrickson 2001)
- Have a wider field of perceptual view (Schmitz, De Rosa, and Anderson 2009)

These findings are consistent with definitions of engagement, where people are more capable overall at making decisions and solving problems (Conference Board 2006).

An employee of a bank who has a high level of engagement would experience high levels of activation of their reward and self-regulation circuitry when at work...

We propose that the neural basis of engagement can be defined by the average levels of activation of the brain's reward and self-regulation circuitry when people are thinking about or participating in their work. For example, an employee of a bank who has a high level of engagement would experience high levels of activation of his or her reward and self-regulation circuitry when at work; when at work, he or she would have good levels of dopamine in the executive attention or self-regulation networks and reward circuitry, including prefrontal region, anterior cingulate cortex (ACC), and striatum, and only moderate levels of activation of the threat circuitry. When an employee is engaged, activation is increased in his or her brain's reward and self-regulation circuitry—for example, what is released by the striatum and maintained by the self-control networks. The striatum releases dopamine directly into the prefrontal cortex, ACC, and other associated regions, positively affecting a wide range of cognitive and emotional functions through increasing brain resources and functional connectivity (Arnsten 1998; Tang and Posner 2009; Tang et al. 2009). We will explore the impact of engagement and disengagement in detail below.

The same principle can apply not only to thinking about an overall job but also to participating in any particular task. It is possible that an employee could be not engaged overall, but have one specific task he or she finds engaging. Perhaps the bank employee doesn't like dealing with his or her boss or the paperwork but is engaged when dealing with customers and is able to help them solve their problems. In this way, overall engagement can be thought of as the average level of reward experienced by employees in their jobs, but individual tasks could also be measured as well, both one-off and averaged over time. It should be noted that an individual's overall engagement in life could be assessed, which would include levels of engagement when at work, at home, or during leisure activities. It would be interesting in future research to see whether people had consistent levels within these domains and the impact that increasing engagement in one area may have on others.

We propose that the neural basis of disengagement can be defined by the average levels of activation of the brain's threat circuitry. Threat circuitry is not just fear. It includes anything that is an avoid response, including sadness, anxiety, lack of safety, depression, and mind wandering (which at the extreme involves attention deficit disorders, or ADD). Activation of threat circuitry has a surprising effect at very low levels (Friedman and Förster 2001), including when subtly primed, thus impacting subconscious awareness. This disengagement state can take large amounts of brain resources and decrease the efficiency of attention resources.

Disengagement, like engagement, can be measured across an entire job or within a specific task. We recognize that threat can indeed be effective for increasing noradrenaline levels and thereby focusing attention (Arnsten 1998). This type of engagement would not be considered within this framework as a positive engagement; it would involve the activation of the stress response, with the attendant effects (see below). This type of engagement can be effective in the short term for executing specific projects, but tends to be narrow in view, inhibiting creative thinking (Beeman 2009) and inducing mental fatigue (Tang and Posner 2009), and comes with long-term consequences such as negatively impacting overall health due to increased cortisol (Boudarene, Legros, and Timsit-Berthier 2002).

Threat circuitry is not just fear. It includes anything that is an avoid response...

Neural drivers that enhance and decrease engagement

With the idea of the threat/reward response as the basis of engagement, the question becomes, what are the issues that generally create high levels of rewards or threats, especially in social environments? The answer to this question, we propose, is largely to be found in the social-cognitive and affective neuroscience literature. The SCARF® model (Rock 2008) summarizes a wide range of social-cognitive and affective neuroscience findings into five domains of threat or reward: Status, Certainty, Autonomy, Relatedness, and Fairness. These five domains are environment factors that people keep track of—in a similar way to tracking levels of food or water and using similar circuits in the brain (Lieberman 2008). We propose that engaged employees are experiencing high levels of positive rewards in the SCARF domains and that disengaged employees are experiencing high levels of threats in the SCARF domains.

The research that supports this proposition involved looking over engagement models and metasummaries of engagement models and finding that the elements of each model fit into one of the SCARF domains. For example, in one of the most common engagement models—the Gallup organization's Q12—six out of 12 questions related to status, one to certainty, one to autonomy, two to relatedness, and one to fairness (see appendix 1).

On the other hand, engagement is also indexed by a balanced brain-body state, including occupied, effortless, joyful feeling, and being flow (Tang 2009), which we will discuss below.

What are the levels of engagement from a neural perspective?

Gallup organization (Gallup, n.d.) has identified three levels of engagement:

- Actively disengaged
- Not engaged
- Engaged

We propose a model with five levels that link to the threat/reward response:

Actively disengaged	*A high average threat state*
Disengaged	*An average threat state*
Neutral	*Midway between threat and reward states*
Engaged	*On average a reward state*
Deeply engaged	*A strong average reward state*

We have added "disengaged" and "neutral" to have a more robust model for researching engagement. We propose adding "deeply engaged" to take into account a higher level of engagement that may be necessary to offset the deep levels of the threat response that leaders experience, called "power stress" (Boyatzis, Smith, and Blaize 2006). By experiencing deep engagement, which is a strong average reward response, leaders develop a type of resilience to power stress, similar to the ideas of *Psychological Capital* (Luthans, Youssef, and Avolio 2007). Deep engagement is a level of engagement often seen in entrepreneurs who are inspirational, visionary leaders or in people who are highly successful at engaging others.

Deep engagement is a level of engagement often seen in entrepreneurs who are inspirational, visionary leaders...

We propose that deep engagement is an experience that occurs when people experience rewards from all five domains of SCARF. One way to achieve this is to undertake tasks you perceive to improve the greater good, by improving some kind of social condition. In doing so, you are improving your status in the eyes of yourself and others. You are decreasing uncertainty by solving some kind of social problem. You are acting autonomously, making choices instead of complaining about the social problem. You are connecting with other people to facilitate change, and you are reducing unfairness in the world in some way. These "social problems" can be as simple and local as improving the way people communicate in a lunchroom such that people start to share personal histories and connect more. Or they can be projects that deeply affect the well-being of communities.

Organizations committed to improving the world achieve more than those with a vision to just beat the competition...

This idea of socially valuable projects as being deeply rewarding links to organizational research on high-performing cultures, showing that organizations committed to improving the world achieve more than those with a vision to just beat the competition (Logan, King, and Fischer-Wright 2008). It also links to research on "socialized visionary communication" (Waldman et al. 2008) and to the concept of leaders being more inspiring when they focus people on a social change (Brown and Trevino 2006).

Numeric scale for measuring engagement

We propose the creation of a numerical scale that can be used to summarize average engagement levels for a project, an individual in a role, or a team or larger organization. This will facilitate more accurate research about the impact of engagement. While further work needs to be done to link these levels to specific biological markers, we propose that this framework will enable more accurate thinking about engagement in the future.

What effect does increasing or decreasing engagement have on the brain and our wider biology?

Engagement involves the central and autonomic nervous system to maintain the internal attention and rewarding states (Csikszentmihalyi 2008; Posner et al. 2009). We propose that five brain networks are impacted by the threat-reward response and thus by engagement levels. These are:

1. **Cognitive networks:** Lateral PFC and ACC provide the capacity for clear thinking and better executive attention, suggesting these have optimal cognitive function during engagement (Posner et al. 2007).

2. **Limbic system:** The reward experience and positive emotion require the involvement of the central and autonomic nervous system, indexed by higher immune function and body coordination—in other words, the central and autonomic nervous system interaction termed as "being state" (Tang et al. 2009).

3. **Social network:** In the workplace, collaboration and understanding others are the vital abilities for success and survival; in this regard, MPFC is the core region (Fair et al. 2008).

4. **Self-regulation network:** ACC is responsible for the regulation of both cognition and emotion (Tang and Posner 2008). Dorsal ACC serves for cognitive regulation and conflict resolution, whereas ventral ACC is involved in emotion regulation (Posner et al. 2007). If strong conflict occurs, the PFC may also participate.

5. **Learning and habit circuits:** Positive experience of engagement facilitates and enhances and strengthens working memory (WM). Repeated WM forms long-term memory, then habits via basal ganglia/striatum and PFC, ACC, etc. (Tang 2009).

In sum, we propose the brain networks including PFC, ACC, mPFC, and striatum are the main engagement circuits, and these brain networks are regulated or impacted by various levels of engagement.

Let's explore the states of deep engagement, neutral, and disengagement as examples to link the related networks with mental experiences involved in engagement. During the deep engagement state, a person accomplishes with the absence of subjective effort a task or goal that might at another time or by another person seem effortful. The person feels totally occupied with the present task so as to suspend evaluations and has strong pleasure and rewarding feelings, which involves being completely in the current moment.

Actively disengaged	Disengaged	Neutral	Engaged	Deeply engaged
100	-50	0	50	100

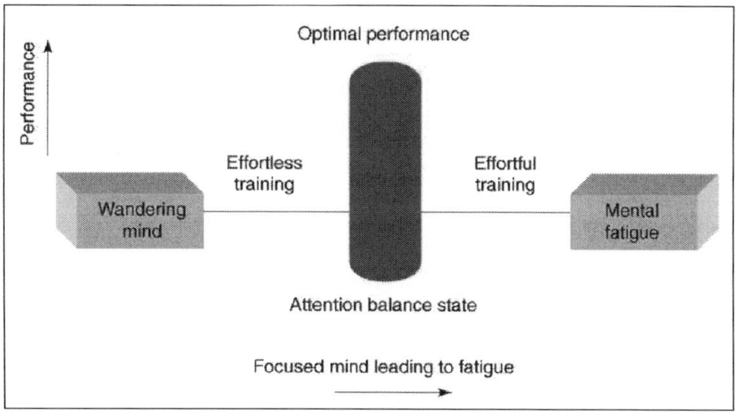

Figure 1. Training and Performance. Mind wandering and mental fatigue are two extremes of the untrained mind (left and right gray rectangles). Attention training requires effortful control to improve performance, whereas attention state training changes body-mind state through effortless practice. Optimal balance (attention balance state) is hypothesized to trigger the most efficient performance (middle cylinder area); see Tang and Posner (2009). If the process requires teamwork, mPFC will be involved to support the group dynamics and collaboration.

Given the effortful control, the PFC is dominant in the early stage of deep engagement, whereas the ACC and striatum take the role with less effort during the mid- or late-stage of deep engagement. Then the person attains an attention balance state showing optimal performance (Posner et al. 2009; Tang et al. 2009).

During a neutral state, we propose the person is in the default mode of network, or brain resting states, involved in the ACC, mPFC, and PCC circuit (Raichel et al. 2001). This state maintains the self-referential, introspective mental activity. In contrast, disengagement includes fear or other negative emotions and involves amygdala-related networks. This state uses large amounts of brain resources and decreases attentional efficiency. It also activates the autonomic and central nervous system, which triggers the stress response. As a consequence, it will reduce creativity and productivity, will induce mental fatigue (Tang and Posner 2009), and comes with long-term health problems.

In this threat state, people are likely to want to continue doing the same things, since change is harder because of overall fewer prefrontal resources. Insights are harder (Subramaniam et al. 2009), making difficult problems seem insurmountable. It will be harder to stay cool under pressure with a high baseline threat level. Others may be less inclined to collaborate.

Clearly the level of engagement or disengagement of an individual, a team, an organization, or even a country can impact performance in tangible ways. The level of engagement has a very real impact on one's ability to solve problems, make decisions, stay cool under pressure, collaborate with others, and deal with change—all four domains of neuroleadership.

The level of engagement or disengagement of an individual, a team, an organization, or even a country can impact performance in tangible ways.

States	**Brain networks**	**Functions**
Deep engagement	PFC, ACC, striatum, mPFC	Reward, attention, flow
Neutral	mPFC, ACC, PCC	Self-referential and introception
Disengagement	Amygdala, limbic system	Negative emotional feelings

What biological markers might be used to more accurately measure engagement and the effects of engagement interventions?

As mentioned above, engagement involves diverse central and autonomic nervous system networks, including cognitive networks (lateral PFC), limbic system (ACC, insula, etc.), social network (mPFC), self-regulation network (PFC and ACC), and learning and habit circuits (striatum). To measure the engagement state accurately and test the effects of engagement interventions, we propose the following brain-body biological markers (Tang et al. 2009; Tang and Posner 2008):

1. **Brain:** The activations of PFC, ACC, mPFC, and striatum using neuroimaging (fMRI, PET, SPECT and EEG, MEG) would be the neural markers to measure and evaluate engagement.

2. **Physiology (body):** The involvement of the autonomic nervous system indexed by heart-rate variability (HRV) and skin conductance response (SCR) would be ideal physiological biomarkers to measure engagement (Tang et al. 2009). To measure the stress level in the autonomic system (body), cortisol is one of the best indexes (Tang et al. 2007; 2009).

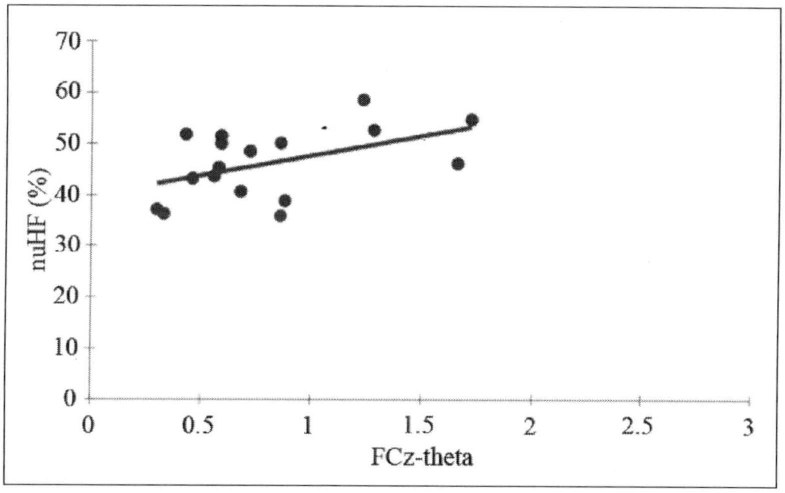

Figure 2. Correlation between high-frequency HRV and FCz-Theta in IBMT after five days of training: The horizontal axis indicates the percent change in frontal midline theta power (in FCz) and the vertical axis indicates percent change in normalized unit of high-frequency (nuHF) HRV. A positive Pearson's correlation was observed ($r = 0.551$, $P = 0.033$).

3. **Brain-body interaction:** Engagement requires the coordination and balance between body and brain systems. Attention and meditation-training literature indicated the theta band in the brain (self-regulation circuits, including ACC, PFC) correlates with HRV (autonomic system), suggesting the optimal state of body and mind engagement and flow states. This connection between body and brain may provide the inner psych-physiological foundation of engagement (Tang et al. 2009).

In organizations, if you could not use fMRI, you could work with a neuroscientist before and after interventions to test changes in skin conductance response (SCR), a simple technique and index to measure the employees' relaxation and calm state of body and mind. You could also use heart rate to analyze the heart-rate variability (HRV), another sensitive index for sympathetic and parasympathetic activity during different stages of engagement (Tang et al. 2009). (See appendix 3.)

Summary

In summary, by looking at engagement through the lens of neuroscience, we can develop a deeper understanding of the impact of levels of engagement on human performance, as well as measure engagement levels before and after various interventions. In time, the idea of employee engagement may be able to shift from a "soft" metric to something with data behind it.

References

Arnsten, A. F. T. 1998. "The Biology of Being Frazzled." *Science* 280: 1711–1712.

Boudarene M., Legros J. J., and Timsit-Berthier, M. 2002. "Study of the Stress Response: Role of Anxiety, Cortisol, and DHEAs." *Encephale* 2: 139–146.

Boyatzis, R., Smith, M., and Blaize, N. 2006. "Developing Sustainable Leaders Through Coaching and Compassion." *Academy of Management Learning and Education* 5(1): 8–24.

Brown, M. E., and Trevino, L. K. 2006. "Socialized Charismatic Leadership, Values Congruence, and Deviance in Work Groups." *Journal of Applied Psychology* 91: 954–962.

CIPD. 2008. *Employee engagement: A CIPD factsheet (2007)*. London: The Chartered Institute of Personnel Development.

Conference Board. 2006. *Employee Engagement: A Review of Current Research and its Implications*. New York: Conference Board.

Csikszentmihalyi, M. 2008. *Flow: The Psychology of Optimal Experience*. New York: HarperCollins.

Elliot, A., ed. 2008. *Handbook of Approach and Avoidance Motivation*. New York: Psychology Press.

Fredrickson, B. L. 2001. "The Role of Positive Emotions in Positive Psychology: The Broaden-and-Build Theory of Positive Emotions." *American Psychologist* 56: 218–226.

Friedman, R. S., and Förster, J. 2001. "The Effects of Promotion and Prevention Cues on Creativity." *Journal of Personality and Social Psychology* 81(6): 1001–1013.

Gallup. Employee Engagement page on, Gallup website. Accessed August 13, 2009. http://www. gallup.com/consulting/52/Employee-Engagement.aspx.

Gordon, E. 2008. "Neuroleadership and Integrative Neuroscience: 'It's About Validation Stupid!'" *NeuroLeadership Journal* 1: 71–80.

Lieberman, M.D. 2008. "Thank Yous and Welcomes: SCAN Turns Two." *Social Cognitive and Affective Neuroscience* 3(3): 191.

Lieberman M., and Eisenberg, N. 2008. "The Pains and Pleasures of Social Life." *NeuroLeadership Journal* 1: 38–43.

Logan, D., King, J., and Fischer-Wright, H. 2008. *Tribal Leadership: Leveraging Natural Groups to Build a Thriving Organization*. New York: HarperBusiness.

Luthans, F., Youssef, C., and Avolio, B. 2007. *Psychological Capital: Developing the Human Competitive Edge*. Oxford, NY: Oxford University Press.

Ochsner, K. N., and Lieberman, M. D. 2001. "The Emergence of Social Cognitive Neuroscience." *American Psychologist* 56: 717–734.

Posner, M. I., Rothbart, M., Rueda, M. R., Tang, Y. Y. 2009. *Training effortless attention. In Effortless Attention: A New Perspective in the Cognitive Science of Attention and Action*. Cambridge, MA: MIT Press.

Posner, M. I., Sheese, B., Rothbart, M., and Tang, Y. Y. 2007. "The Anterior Cingulate Gyrus and the Mechanism of Self-Regulation." *Cognitive, Affective, and Behavioral Neuroscience* 7: 391–395.

Raichle, M. E., MacLeod, A. M., Snyder, A. Z., Powers, W. J., Gusnard, D. A., and Shulman, G. L. 2001. "A Default Mode of Brain Function." *Proceedings of the National Academy of Sciences, USA* 98: 676–682.

Ringleb, A., and Rock, D. 2008. "The Emerging Field of Neuroleadership." *NeuroLeadership Journal* 1: 3–19.

Rock, D. 2008. "SCARF: A Brain-Based Model for Collaborating with and Influencing Others." *NeuroLeadership Journal* 1: 44–52.

Schmitz, T. W., De Rosa, E., and Anderson, A. K. 2009. "Opposing Influences of Affective State Valence on Visual Cortical Encoding." *Journal of Neuroscience* 29(22): 7199–7207.

Subramaniam, K., Kounios, J., Parrish, T. B., and Jung-Beeman, M. 2009. "A Brain Mechanism for Facilitation of Insight by Positive Affect." *Journal of Cognitive Neuroscience* 21: 415–432.

Tang, Y. Y., Ma, Y., Wang, J., Fan, Y., Feng, S., Lu, Q., Yu, Q., et al. 2007. "Short-Term Meditation Training Improves Attention and Self-Regulation." *Proceedings of the National Academy of Sciences, USA* 104: 17152–17156.

Tang, Y. Y., and Posner M. I. 2008. "The Neuroscience of Mindfulness." *NeuroLeadership Journal* 1: 33–37.

Tang, Y. Y. 2009. *Exploring the Brain, Optimizing the Life*. Beijing: Science Press.

Tang, Y. Y., and Posner, M. I. 2009. "Attention Training and Attention State Training." *Trends in Cognitive Sciences* 13: 222–227.

Tang Y. Y., Ma, Y., Fan, Y., Feng, H., Wang, J., Feng, S., Lu, Q., et al. 2009. "Central and Autonomic Nervous System Interaction is Altered by Short Term Meditation." *Proceedings of the National Academy of Sciences, USA* 106: 8865–8870.

Waldman, D. A, and Galvin, B. M. 2008. "Alternative Perspectives of Responsible Leadership." *Organizational Dynamics* 37: 327–341.

Appendix 1

The most widespread research about engagement has been done by Gallup and their "Q12" assessment. It comprises the following questions, which Gallup believes are the most central to engagement:

- Do you know what is expected of you at work?
- Do you have the materials and equipment you need to do your work right?
- At work, do you have the opportunity to do what you do best every day?

- In the last seven days, have you received recognition or praise for doing good work?
- Does your supervisor, or someone at work, seem to care about you as a person?
- Is there someone at work who encourages your development?
- At work, do your opinions seem to count?
- Does the mission/purpose of your company make you feel your job is important?
- Are your associates (fellow employees) committed to doing quality work?
- Do you have a best friend at work?
- In the last six months, has someone at work talked to you about your progress?
- In the last year, have you had opportunities at work to learn and grow?

The most widespread research about engagement has been done by Gallup...

Here is Gallup's survey, put into SCARF categories:

Status: 6

In the last seven days, have you received recognition or praise for doing good work?

1. At work, do you have the opportunity to do what you do best every day?
2. Does the mission/purpose of your company make you feel your job is important?
3. In the last six months, has someone at work talked to you about your progress?
4. In the last year, have you had opportunities at work to learn and grow?
5. At work, do your opinions seem to count?

Certainty: 1

1. Do you know what is expected of you at work?

Autonomy: 1

1. Do you have the materials and equipment you need to do your work right?

Relatedness: 2

1. Does your supervisor, or someone at work, seem to care about you as a person?
2. Is there someone at work who encourages your development?
3. Do you have a best friend at work?

Fairness: 1

1. Are your associates (fellow employees) committed to doing quality work?

Appendix 2

The meta study of twelve other large studies by the Conference Board found eight themes for what seems to create engagement:

- **Trust and integrity**

  How well managers communicate and "walk the talk."

- **Nature of the job**

  Is it mentally stimulating day-to-day?

- **Line of sight between employee performance and company performance**

  Does the employee understand how his or her work contributes to the company's performance?

- **Career growth opportunities**

  Are there future opportunities for growth?

- **Pride about the company**

  How much self-esteem does the employee feel by being associated with the company?

- **Coworkers/team members**

  Significantly influence one's level of engagement.

- **Employee development**

  Is the company making an effort to develop the employee's skills?

- **Relationship with one's manager**

  Does the employee value his or her relationship with his or her manager?

Gallup's survey is heavily weighted to status. Look at the Conference Board's study broken into the SCARF categories:

Status

1. **Employee development**

   Is the company making an effort to develop the employee's skills?

2. **Career growth opportunities**

   Are there future opportunities for growth?

3. **Pride about the company**

   How much self-esteem does the employee feel by being associated with the company?

4. **Nature of the job**

   Is it mentally stimulating day-to-day?

Certainty

1. **Line of sight between employee performance and company performance**

   Does the employee understand how his or her work contributes to the company's performance?

Autonomy

Relatedness

1. **Relationship with one's manager**

   Does the employee value his or her relationship with his or her manager?

2. **Coworkers/team members**

   Significantly influence one's level of engagement.

Fairness

1. **Trust and integrity**

   How well managers communicate and "walk the talk."

Appendix 3

1. **Skin conductance response (SCR):** SCR is one of the most robust and well studied physiological responses. It is caused by sympathetic nervous system activation, which changes the levels of sweat in the eccrine sweat glands and has been shown to be linked to measures of emotion, arousal, and attention. The lower score of SCR shows more parasympathetic activity with a calm and relaxed state.

The lower score of SCR shows more parasympathetic activity with a calm and relaxed state.

2. **Heart-rate variability (HRV):** HRV is a noninvasive technique that allows for a reliable and accurate measure of sympathetic and parasympathetic functions. Calculated by heart rate, HRV has three frequencies: high frequency (HF; 0.16–0.45 Hz), low frequency (0.04–0.15 Hz), and very low frequency (VLF; 0–0.03 Hz). More HF-HRV indicates the relaxed and calm state with parasympathetic activity dominance, which is close to an engagement state, whereas more LF-HRV indicates the excited and active state with sympathetic activity dominance.

20. Applying empathy and mirror neuron concepts to neuroleadership

Dr. Marco Iacoboni and Dr. Roger W. McHaney

Marco Iacoboni, Professor of Psychiatry and Biobehavioral Science
Director of the Transcranial Magnetic Stimulation Lab, Ahmanson-Lovelace Brain Mapping Center, David Geffen School of Medicine, UCLA, California, USA
iacoboni@ucla.edu

Roger W. McHaney, Professor of Management Information Systems,
Department of Management, Kansas State University, Manhattan, Kansas, USA
mchaney@k-state.edu

Introduction

Advances in the field of neuroscience have resulted in renewed interest in understanding empathy and how this very human capability of being able to share, sympathize, understand, and experience another person's emotional state might be explained through the concept of mirror neurons. From a neuroscience perspective, a variety of new literature suggests that empathy could stem from activity in the neural structures that were created during an individual's firsthand experience and then are revisited when observing others in a similar situation. If empathy is formed this way, it stands to reason that intentionally invoking and developing calculated responses using these same mechanisms is possible. In the context of leadership, social-cognitive neuroscience can provide insights for becoming more effective and working in a way that naturally coincides with inherent human capabilities. This chapter explores the connection between empathy and mirror neurons, and how neuroleadership training might be improved through the use of this naturally occurring human capability.

Through the lens of social-cognitive neuroscience

Social-cognitive neuroscience draws on commonalities found in social-cognition theory and cognitive neuroscience (Posner and Rothbart 1994; Ross and Nisbett 1991). While both of these disciplines seek to develop insights related to information-processing activities in the human brain, the manner in which these understandings are approached are very different. For instance, cognitive neuroscience often is concerned with physically describing brain structures to help link mental capabilities to underlying neural systems. On the other hand, social cognition seeks to explain human behavior through external social and affective forces that may trigger certain information processing within the brain. The marriage of these two disciplines, known as social-cognitive neuroscience, has resulted in a broader understanding of how both physical brain structures and external forces play important roles in explaining human behavior and decision making.

Empathy "cuts to the heart of what it means to be human"...

In recent years, empathy increasingly has been examined through the lens of social-cognitive neuroscience. This examination is important because empathy "cuts to the heart of what it means to be human" (Rameson and Lieberman 2009), making this capability one of the most important behavioral constructs to understand. To truly be human is to have the capability to experience the joys and sorrows of others. Some studies suggest that a lack of empathy is a telling component of various mental disorders (Farrow and Woodruff 1997).

Empathy

From a classical perspective, empathy has been viewed as an intellectual process in which a person consciously attempted to understand someone else's situation through his or her own experiences. This "theory of mind" approach attributed mental states, such as beliefs, desires, intentions, and knowledge, to a specific individual who realized others have their own unique beliefs, desires, intentions, and knowledge (Premack and Woodruff 1978). That classic view began to shift with the discovery and understanding of neurons. It became evident that humans have a hard-wired system in the brain that reflexively facilitates interpersonal connections, and this neural system may form the basis for empathy and other mental capabilities (Rameson and Lieberman 2009).

A person involuntarily simulates what others are going through using neural structures and internal interactions with the limbic system...

Mirror neurons

In 1996, researchers from the University of Parma published findings revealing that the same brain cells fired when a monkey watched humans or other monkeys eat a peanut as when it ate a peanut itself

(Rizzolatti et.alet al. 1996). Rizzolatti and colleagues called these brain cells "mirror neurons" since they reflect the action of others. Subsequent studies have revealed that human brains possess much more advanced mirror neurons adapted to understanding others' actions together with their intentions and emotional state (Iacoboni 2008a). While the mirror neural system has not definitely been shown to regulate empathy, several independent research studies have indicated its involvement (Preston and de Waal 2002; Decety and Jackson 2004; Gallese and Goldman 1998; Gallese 2001).

The concept of mirror neurons has led to the idea that a person involuntarily simulates what others are going through using mirroring neural structures interacting with the limbic system (which includes emotional brain centers). For example, when someone is crying, those same feelings are modeled with neural structures that were formed at an earlier time from direct experiences of a similar event. This internal simulation allows the observer to better understand what the subject is going through, thereby becoming capable of making better decisions about the next action to take.

It has been hypothesized that the mirror neurons that fire up when an observer sees someone crying are the same cells that fire up when actual crying takes place. In a sense, the observer is simulating the action of crying internally. This simulation causes a signal to be sent through the emotional brain centers to the limbic system, and this evokes a feeling in the observer's own brain that is associated with crying. Without any conscious inferring, an observer can put him- or herself in someone else's shoes and experience what they are going through (Iacoboni et al. 2005). Published research has reported the existence of mirror neurons in both inferior frontal and inferior parietal regions of the brain (Gallese et al. 1996; Fogassi et al. 2005), and recent fMRI studies suggest that even more areas of the brain exhibit mirror-neuron properties (Keysers and Gazzola 2009).

Viewed from the neural-structure level, human brains clearly react to other people's experiences in involuntary ways. For instance, when someone cuts a finger, those around the injured person wince (Smith 2002). Neuroscientists have attributed this phenomenon to a mirror-neuron system (Rizolatti 1999; Gallese, Keysers, and Rizzolatti 2004). So when a person observes an action performed by another, the observer's mirror-neuron system is activated, causing a similar reaction in the observer's brain. In addition to being activated through observing a physical act, the mirror-neuron system can be triggered through facial expressions associated with various emotions (Wicker et al. 2003). While the theory of mirror neurons has received a great deal of support and has even been called one of the most important recent discoveries in neuroscience (Ramachandran 2006), much debate concerning its nature continues (Lingnau, Gesierich, and Caramazza 2009; Kilner et al. 2009).

Applications of mirror-neuron concepts in leadership

Social-cognition neuroscience can be applied to leadership and used to understand its nature and improve its execution. For instance, a competent, socially aware leader generally exhibits the ability to understand others. An effective leader is able to 'put [him- or herself] in other people's shoes,' sense their emotions, and understand their perspective" (Ringleb and Rock 2008). The examination of these traits from the perspective of mirror-neuron concepts can provide valuable insight in a variety of ways. First, a leader's perceptiveness can be enhanced through interpreting and understanding facial expressions, speech intonation, body language, and a variety of other affective cues related to empathy. This allows a leader to form an impression of other people from a social perspective that helps detect fears and problems and direct motivations. Since mirror neurons may work in automatic ways that draw on hard-wired experiences deep within the brain, actively modeling responses to particular situations could potentially embed leadership traits as second nature.

Actively modeling responses to particular situations could potentially embed leadership traits as second nature.

A better understanding of mirror neurons may also result in improvements in employee feedback. Daft, in *The Leadership Experience* (2008), calls empathy one of the leader's most powerful tools during the feedback process. If this is true, then a more sophisticated understanding of mirror neurons and their role in empathy can only improve the employee-feedback process. Other cues that can improve with a better understanding of mirror neurons may include detecting an employee's social pain or anxiety during performance evaluations. By recognizing these experiences, mitigating techniques might be developed to improve leadership effectiveness.

Additionally, with a better understanding of mirror neurons, leaders may be able to improve their use of e-mail, texting, and richer forms of communication, such as video conferencing. Although it appears mirror neurons may work best in real-life, face-to-face situations (Iacoboni 2008a), a 2006 study (Murray et al.) found that watching violent television programs triggered activity in several brain regions. This finding is consistent with mirror-neuron activity brought about through mediated technology use and may indicate that as technology improves, it could be possible to fine-tune its uses to either maximize or minimize mirror-neuron response as desired in training or communication venues.

Mindsight and mirror neurons

Mindsight is the capacity for insight and empathy. This term. coined by neuroscientist Daniel Siegel, is based on the ability of the human mind to see itself, to know its own mind, and to be able to perceive the minds of others (Siegel 2001). Consistent with research on mirror neurons and empathy, studies of the medial prefrontal cortex have shown that similar brain circuits are used to know both oneself and others

(Pfeifer et al. 2008). This physical nexus could provide further incentive for leaders to improve their ability to understand and lead others by better understanding themselves.

The idea that increasing self-awareness also increases social awareness is not new and is becoming more accepted in the neuroscience literature (Block-Lerner et al. 2007). Practical applications of these ideas further demonstrate the development of mindfulness as a technique to increase empathy (Hassed 2008). If the neural brain circuitry used to develop one's own self-understanding is strengthened, it stands to reason that the same structures may improve a leader's capability for empathy and ultimately his or her ability to understand others (Baron-Cohen 1997).

Brains contain structures that enable empathy and may help simulate potential intentions to act. It is important that people do not imitate all the time.

Regulating responses

Another area of research with potential impact in neuroleadership is to better understand the mechanisms that keep the unwanted imitation potentially enabled by mirror neurons under control. Brains contain structures that enable empathy and may help simulate potential intentions to act. It is important that people do not imitate all the time. That means a structure must be in place to allow people to control their tendency to imitate others. This control mechanism creates a self–other distinction. If the cells in an observer's brain fire when he grasps a cup of tea and also when the observer sees a different person grasp a cup of tea, then that observer will have a problem unless a distinction can be made. The observer's brain has to determine who is grasping the cup of tea. Is it the observer or a different person? With this self–other distinction, the opposite behavior may occur—where neurons fire up when the observer grasps a cup and fire down when the observer sees someone else grasping.

This research is ongoing and has lead to various ideas. For instance, there may be super mirror neurons which suppress the firing of particular mirror neurons when actions are observed rather than directly engaged (Iacoboni 2008b). Super mirror neurons may be likened to on or off switches that prevent inappropriate actions from being activated. A better understanding of these mechanisms may enable leaders to better control negative behaviors and engage in more effective training.

Modulation of empathy

While research has shown that most people have a natural tendency to empathize with others, new studies have provided evidence that the level of empathy is moderated by prior social exchanges. In an experiment conducted by Singer and colleagues (2004), a sequential Prisoner's Dilemma game was played using actors but observed by subjects believing the game to be spontaneous. One actor used a fair strategy and reciprocated with cooperation. The other actor played unfairly and typically defected in response to first-mover cooperation. Ultimately, the experiment showed that observers tended to empathize more with the cooperators than with the defectors. This indicates that social context and previous experience with an individual may modulate or even suppress the automatic tendency to empathize.

From a neuroleadership perspective, this tendency means that if employees perceive their supervisor to be fair and equitable, they are more likely to empathize with the supervisor and perhaps yield a better performance. Leaders can improve their ability to be effective by managing employee impressions to prevent the suppression of the automatic tendency to empathize.

Interaction space

A recent study described different mirror-neuron responses based on where observed action occurs (Caggiano et al. 2009). In Caggiano and colleagues' work, the mirror neurons in rhesus monkeys activated by either execution or observation of physical acts were modulated by where in space the act took place. In other words, different neurons fired based on proximity. Some neurons appear to indicate whether interaction was possible, and other neurons appear to be used for understanding the behavior and preparation should future action be required. Space appeared to be divided into two zones, one being close (peripersonal space) and the other outside the observer's reach (extrapersonal space), and different neurons fired based on these two zones. These results could mean that some neurons relate to interaction and not just to recognition of what others are doing.

Although the study was conducted on monkeys, the findings suggest that actions performed by others can have different relevance for the observer, depending on the location. Different behavioral responses may be required, and the brain prepares for these contingencies. These neural responses are about what the observer can do with the actions of other people and point out the importance of interaction and how it appears to be hard-wired into a brain.

Neuroleadership lessons

Traditional research approaches by leadership theorists have long focused on power and influence, which fall clearly into the area of affective social behaviors. Early definitions of power as "an individual's ability to influence another person to bring about desired outcomes" and influence as "the affect a person's actions had on the attitudes, values, beliefs, or actions of others" (Burns 1978; Hitchner 1992/93; Dahl 1957; French and Raven 1960; Yukl and Taber 1983) positioned early work and research inquiries in areas such as small-group dynamics, social roles (Katz and Kahn 1978; Stewart and Barrick 2000), norms (Feldman 1984), cohesiveness (Bishop and Scott 1997), group size (Lawless 1972), and other topics. Within the context of leadership, theorists further explored collaboration by examining teams and teamwork.

Researchers have worked to understand why people form teams and what motivations underlie group behaviors.

Researchers have worked to understand why people form teams and what motivations underlie group behaviors (Shaw 1985). Others have explored group dynamics and the stages of group development (Tuckman 1965; Janis 1972). Using motivation research frameworks (Maslow 1943), researchers have developed behavioral models to describe leadership. Characteristics of effective and ineffective leaders have been examined and correlated with team performance and group dynamics (McGregor 1960). Starting in the early 1980s, research shifted toward participative management studies and concepts related to team building (McCarthy, Faerman, and Hart 1995). The concept of high-performance teams was developed (Katzenbach and Smith 1993; Pfeffer 1994).

Connections between people are complex and multilayered, resulting in a wide variety of interactions.

While this past research has significantly enhanced understanding of human workplace behavior, much remains to be understood from a variety of supporting perspectives. One such perspective is neuroleadership. By using neuroscience principles to explore processes within the brain that underlie and influence behaviors, leadership effectiveness within institutions and organizations can be improved.

Affective social behaviors aside, it becomes apparent that people in the workplace are connected and interact at a very basic level, with roots hard-wired in the brain. Humans have a tendency to empathize, and leadership awareness of this tendency will allow more meaningful connections to emerge in the workplace. By understanding concepts such as empathy and mirror neurons, leadership can become more than a top-down process; it becomes an interactive exchange, some of which takes place at a subconscious, physical level. Clearly, connections between people are complex and multilayered, resulting in a wide variety of interactions.

Understanding and applying neuroscience has the potential to change the way effective leaders connect with their followers. Employees look for cues from managers and mimic their behaviors, both consciously and subconsciously. For leaders, this implies the importance of maintaining a positive outlook and providing examples of positive, desirable behavior.

The field of neuroleadership can gain new insights by turning its attention to the neural mechanisms that govern empathy. An understanding of how people represent the minds of others and share in their experiences will result in improved team effectiveness and workplace relationships.

Conclusions

The following observations regarding empathy and mirror neurons can be applied to neuroleadership:

- **Leaders must become role models and exhibit positive, desirable behaviors.**

  Implications: Everyone has a hard-wired system in the brain that reflexively and involuntarily simulates what others are going through, using mirroring neural structures and internal interactions with the limbic system. Without any conscious thought, an observer can put him- or herself in somebody's shoes. If unwanted and undesirable behaviors are being constantly simulated, these brain circuits could be strengthened. Likewise, if positive, desirable behaviors are modeled, these could become the norm.

- **Leaders can better understand others by better understanding themselves.**

  Implications: Since the same neural structures developed during direct experience seem to be involved in empathy, the idea that increasing self-awareness also increases social awareness can result in more effective leadership and help detect fears and problems in the workplace.

- **Effective leaders recognize and embrace the natural human capability of empathy.**

  Implications: Competent, socially aware leaders seek to understand others and will increase their ability to sense followers' emotions and understand their perspectives. A leader's perceptiveness can be enhanced through capitalizing on the brain's natural ability to interpret and understand facial expressions, speech intonation, body language, and a variety of other affective cues related to empathy.

- **Social context and previous experience with an individual can suppress empathy.**

  Implications: If employees perceives their supervisor to be fair and equitable, they are more likely to empathize with the supervisor and to help achieve that leader's goals. A leader can improve his or her ability to be effective by managing employee impressions and ensuring a positive image is developed before substantial interaction.

- **Mediated technologies might be improved through better understanding mirror neurons.**

  Implications: With a better understanding of mirror neurons, leaders may be able to improve their use of e-mail, texting, and rich forms of communication such as video conferencing. Mirror neurons may work better in face-to-face situations, but research has shown these concepts apply to mediated technologies as well.

- **Understanding super mirror neurons may assist in moderating undesired behaviors.**

  Implications: Studies suggest super mirror-neural structures may play a role in determining when potential behaviors are enacted and when they are not. These super mirror neurons may be likened to "on" or "off" switches that may prevent inappropriate actions from being activated. Further knowledge in this area could be helpful in neuroleadership applications.

- **Understanding empathy and mirror neurons may help detect social pain or anxiety.**

  Implications: By better recognizing these employee experiences, mitigating techniques might be developed to improve leadership effectiveness in organizations.

- **Mirror neurons react differently based on proximity to motor actions.**

  Implications: Actions performed by others can have different relevance for the observer based on the location where they were performed. Different behavioral responses may be required, and the brain prepares for these contingencies. With a better understanding of these principles, training, learning, and reacting to various situations might be made more efficient.

Acknowledgments

Much of this article's content was derived from an interview with Marco Iacoboni, Department of Psychiatry and Biobehavioral Sciences, David Geffen School of Medicine, University of California, Los Angeles, California.

References

Baron-Cohen, S. 1997. *Mindblindness*. Cambridge, MA: MIT Press.

Bishop, J. W., and Scott, K. D. 1997. "How Commitment Effects Team Performance." *HR Magazine* 42(2): 107–111.

Block-Lerner, J., Adair, C., Plumb, J. C., Rhatigan, D. L., and Orsillo, S. M. 2007. "The Case for Mindfulness-Based Approaches in the Cultivation of Empathy: Does Nonjudgmental, Present-Moment Awareness Increase Capacity for Perspective-Taking and Empathic Concern?" *Journal of Marital and Family Therapy* 33(4): 501–516.

Burns, J. M. 1978. *Leadership*. New York: Harper & Row.

Caggiano, V., Fogassi, L., Rizzolatti, G., Thier, P., and Casile, A. 2009. "Mirror Neurons Differentially Encode the Peripersonal and Extrapersonal Space of Monkeys." *Science* 324(5925): 403–406.

Daft, D. 2008. *The Leadership Experience*. Boston: Thomson South-Western.

Dahl, R. A. 1957. "The Concept of Power." *Behavioral Science* 2: 201–215.

Decety, J., and Jackson, P. L. 2004. "The Functional Architecture of Human Empathy." *Behavioral and Cognitive Neuroscience Reviews* 3: 71–100.

Farrow, T. F. D., and Woodruff, P. W. R. 1997. *Empathy in Mental Illness*. Cambridge, UK: Cambridge University Press.

Feldman, D. C. 1984. "The Development and Enforcement of Group Norms." *Academy of Management Review* 9(1): 47–53.

Fogassi, L., Ferrari, P. F., Gesierich, B., Rozzi, S., Chersi, F., and Rizzolatti, G. 2005. "Parietal Lobe: From Action Organization to Intention Understanding." *Science* 308: 662–667.

French, J. R. P., and Raven, B. 1960. "The Bases of Social Power." In *Group Dynamics*, edited by Cartwright, D., and Zander, A., 453–473. Evanston, IL: Row Peterson.

Gallese, V. 2001. "The 'Shared Manifold' Hypothesis: From Mirror Neurons to Empathy." *Journal of Consciousness Studies* 8: 33–50.

Gallese, V., Fadiga, L., Fogassi, L., and Rizzolatti, G. 1996. "Action Recognition in the Premotor cortex." *Brain* 119: 593–609.

Gallese, V., and Goldman, A. I. 1998. "Mirror Neurons and the Simulation Theory." *Trends in Cognitive Sciences* 2: 493–501.

Gallese V., Keysers, C., and Rizzolatti, G. 2004. "A Unifying View of the Basis of Social Cognition." *Trends in Cognitive Science* 8(9): 396–403.

Hassed, C. 2008. "Mindfulness, Well-Being, and Performance." *NeuroLeadership Journal* 1: 53–60.

Hitchner, E. 1992/1993. "The Power to Get Things Done." *National Productivity Review* 12: 117–122.

Iacoboni, M. 2008a. *Mirroring People: The New Science Of How We Connect With Others.* New York: Farrar, Straus, and Giroux.

Iacoboni, M. 2008b. "Mesial Frontal Cortex and Super Mirror Neurons." *Behavioral and Brain Sciences* 31(1): 30.

Iacoboni M., Molnar-Szakacs, I., Gallese, V., Buccino, G., and Mazziotta, J. C. 2005. "Grasping the Intentions of Others with One's Own Mirror Neuron System." *PLoS Biology* 3(3): 79.

Janis, I. L. 1972. *Victims of Groupthink*. Boston: Houghton Mifflin Company.

Katz, D., and Kahn, R. L. 1978. *The Social Psychology of Organizations. 2nd ed*. New York: John Wiley & Sons.

Katzenbach, J. R., and Smith, D. K. 1993. *The Wisdom of Teams: Creating the High-Performance Organization*. New York: HarperBusiness.

Keysers, C., and Gazzola, V. 2009. "Expanding the Mirror: Vicarious Activity for Actions, Emotions, and Sensations." *Current Opinion in Neurobiology* (19)6.Accessed October 31, 2009. http://www.sciencedirect.com/science/article/B6VS3-4XK8S60-1/2/4abc92423d7a744bfc7e4a3f113b5207.

Kilner, J. M., Neal, A., Weiskopf, N., Friston, K. J., and Frith, C. D. 2009. "Evidence of Mirror Neurons in Human Inferior Frontal Gyrus." *The Journal of Neuroscience* 29(32): 10153–10159.

Lawless, D. J. 1972. *Effective Management: A Social Psychological Approach*. Englewood Cliffs, NJ: Prentice Hall.

Lingnau, A., Gesierich, B., and Caramazza, A. 2009. "Asymmetric fMRI Adaptation Reveals no Evidence for Mirror Neurons in Humans." *Proceedings of the National Academy of Sciences, USA* 106(24): 9925–9930.

Maslow, A. H. 1943. "A Theory of Human Motivation." *Psychological Review* 50: 370–96.

McCarthy, D. P., Faerman, S. R., and Hart, D. W. 1995. "The Appeal and Difficulty of Participative Systems." *Organizational Science* 6(6): 603–627.

McGregor, D. 1960. *The Human Side of the Enterprise*. New York: McGraw Hill.

Murray, J. P., Liotti, M., Ingmundson, P. T., Mayberg, H. S., Pu, Y., Zamarripa, F., Liu, Y., Woldorff, M. G., Gao, J., and Fox, P. T. 2006. "Children's Brain Activations While Viewing Televised Violence Revealed by fMRI." *Media Psychology* 8: 25–37.

Pfeffer, J. 1994. *Competitive Advantage through People: Unleashing the Power of the Work Force*. Cambridge, MA: Harvard Business School Press.

Pfeifer, J. H., Iacoboni, M., Mazziotta, J. C., and Dapretto, M. 2008. "Mirroring Others' Emotions Relates to Empathy and Interpersonal Competence in Children." *NeuroImage* 39(4): 2076–2085.

Posner, M. L., and Rothbart, M. 1994. "Constructing Neuronal Theories of Mind." In *Large Scale Neuronal Theories Of Mind*, edited by Koch, C., and Davis, J. L., 183–199 Cambridge,MA: The MIT Press.

Premack, D. G., and Woodruff , G. 1978. "Does the Chimpanzee Have a Theory of Mind?" *Behavioral and Brain Sciences* 1: 515–526.

Preston, S. D., and de Waal, F. B. M. 2002. "Empathy: Its Ultimate and Proximate Bases." *Behavioral and Brain Sciences* 25: 1–72.

Ramachandran, V. S. 2006. Mirror Neurons and Imitation Learning as the Driving Force Behind "The Great Leap Forward" in Human Evolution. *Edge Foundation*. Accessed November 23, 2009. http://edge.org/conversation/mirror-neurons-and-the-brain-in-the-vat

Rameson, L. T., and Lieberman, M. D. 2009. "Empathy: A Social Cognitive Neuroscience Approach." *Social and Personality Psychology Compass* 3(1): 94–110.

Ringleb, A., and Rock, D. 2008. "The Emerging Field of Neuroleadership." *NeuroLeadership Journal* 1: 1–17.

Rizzolatti G., Fadiga, L., Fogassi, L., and Gallese, V. 1999. "Resonance Behaviors and Mirror neurons." *Archives Italiennes de Biologie* 137: 85–100.

Rizzolatti, G., Fadiga, L., Gallese, V., and Fogassi, L. 1996. "Premotor Cortex and the Recognition of Motor Actions." *Cognitive Brain Research* 3(2): 131–141.

Ross, L., and Nisbett, R. E. 1991. *The Person and the Situation: Perspectives of Social Psychology*. New York: McGraw-Hill.

Shaw, M. E. 1985. *Group Dynamics: The Psychology of Small Group Behavior. 4th ed*. New York: McGraw-Hill.

Siegel, D. 2001. "Toward an Interpersonal Neurobiology of the Developing Mind: Attachment Mindsight and Neural Integration." *Infant Mental Health Journal* 22(1–2): 67–94.

Singer, T., Seymour, B., O'Doherty, J. P., Kaube, H., Dolan, R. J., and Frith, C. D. 2004. "Empathy for Pain Involves the Affective but not Sensory Components of Pain." *Science* 303(5661): 1157–1162.

Smith, A. 2002. *The Theory of Moral Sentiments*. Cambridge, UK: Cambridge University Press.

Stewart, G. L., and Barrick, N. R. 2000. "Team Structure and Performance: Assessing the Meditating Role of Intrateam Process and the Moderating Role of Task Type." *Academy of Management Journal* 43(2): 135–148.

Tuckman, B. W. 1965. "Developmental Sequence in Small Groups." *Psychological Bulletin* 63(6): 384–399.

Wicker, B., Keysers, C., Plailly, J., Royet, J. P., Gallese, V., and Rizzolatti, G. 2003. "The Common Neural Basis of Seeing and Feeling Disgust." *Neuron* 40(3): 655-654.

Yukl, G. A., and Taber, T. 1983. "The Effective use of Managerial Power." *Personnel* 60(2): 37–44.

21. The culturally intelligent brain: from detecting to bridging cultural differences

Thomas Rockstuhl,1 Dr. Ying-Yi Hong,1 Dr. Kok Yee Ng,1 Dr. Soon Ang,1 and Dr. Chi-Yue Chiu1

[1]Nanyang Business School, Nanyang Technological University, Singapore

Corresponding author: thom0003@e.ntu.edu.sg

Introduction

The aim of cultural neuroscience is to detect and explain the neurological underpinnings of cognitive and behavioral differences across cultures. Studies in cultural neuroscience are crucial for the education and development of global leaders. They raise awareness and appreciation of cultural differences in global leaders. Effective global leaders also bridge cultural differences.

In this chapter, we propose to extend cultural neuroscience research into intercultural neuroscience of the "culturally intelligent" brain. We define the intercultural neuroscience of the culturally intelligent brain as the intercultural neurological bases of the capability of an individual to function effectively in multicultural contexts (Earley and Ang 2003). We review briefly the existing research on cultural neuroscience and propose a critical new research agenda in intercultural neuroscience.

Cultural intelligence

Cultural psychology and neuroscience are closely interrelated disciplines. As Ames and Fiske (2010) aptly observed, "Culture is, after all, stored in people's brains." A number of scholars have recognized that the human brain possesses the unique ability to acquire basic cultural capacities such as language (Chomsky 1965). Conversely, without these neurobiological capacities, culture could not function (Ames and Fiske 2010). Therefore, the study of the culture-brain interaction, known as cultural neuroscience (Kitayama and Tompson 2010), offers many exciting research avenues with important theoretical and practical implications for understanding human diversity. It is not surprising, then, that the field of cultural neuroscience is gaining huge popularity, evidenced by three special journals published in 2009 and 2010 (*Progress in Brain Research* in 2009, *Social Cognitive and Affective Neuroscience* in 2010, and *Asian Journal of Social Psychology* in 2010).

Studies in cultural neuroscience are crucial for the education and development of global leaders.

What have we learned from the emerging field of cultural neuroscience so far? Broadly, neural research has demonstrated that "culture does indeed go under the skin" (Kitayama and Tompson 2010). For instance, neural research confirms previous cultural behavioral studies showing that Westerners tend to focus on objects while Asians tend to focus on contexts and relationships (Gutchess et al. 2006). Neural research also suggests that cultural practices shape habitual neurological activation and therefore require less attentional capacity from individuals engaged in culture-specific tasks (Corbetta and Shulman 2002; Gitelman et al. 1999). Another fascinating stream of neural research examined how people represent the self and others. Consistent with the interdependent view of the self by Asians (Markus and Kitayama 1991; Zhu et al. 2007), this research showed that thinking about a close other, such as one's mother, elicited preferential activation in the ventral medial prefrontal cortex (vmPFC) for Chinese participants but not for Western participants, indicating that Easterners view close others as part of the self.

Neural research has demonstrated that "culture does indeed go under the skin."

In summary, the emerging field of cultural neuroscience has achieved considerable success in uncovering neurological substrates of cultural differences in a number of basic psychological processes. These studies have enriched our understanding of culture's effects on human behaviors and offer tremendous practical implications for global organizations. According to a study of more than a thousand CEOs in more than fifty countries, a top concern is how to effectively bridge the cultural differences in a globalized workplace (PricewaterhouseCooper's 10th Annual Global CEO Survey). Cultural neuroscience, with its "hard" basis of research, can help create a deeper level of appreciation for cross-cultural differences in organizational leaders who work with people from different cultures.

However, effectively bridging cultural differences requires more than an understanding of how people in different cultures think and behave differently, which is the major focus of cultural neuroscience to date. We propose that expanding the current focus on cross-cultural comparison of neurological processes to intercultural capabilities can greatly contribute to the science and practice of global leadership. While the cross-cultural neuroscience perspective asks how neurological processes of individuals from different cultures differ, the intercultural perspective asks how neurological processes of individuals effective in bridging cross-cultural differences in intercultural interactions differ from those of the less effective individuals.

We propose that the theory of cultural intelligence offers a useful framework to direct cultural neuroscience research toward an intercultural perspective. Cultural intelligence (CQ) refers to the capability of individuals to function effectively in multicultural contexts (Earley and Ang 2003). Grounded in contemporary theories of intelligence as a multidimensional individual aptitude (Sternberg and Detterman 1986), the CQ construct provides a theoretical basis for examining neurological substrates of individuals effective in bridging cultures. Ultimately, we hope to integrate behavioral and neuroscience research on CQ to develop a deep and coherent body of knowledge on how individuals can be effective in bridging cultures.

Next, we will briefly review selected findings from cultural neuroscience research and their implications for global leadership. Then we will review cultural intelligence theory and recent work exploring the relationship between CQ and leadership in culturally diverse contexts. These reviews will ground our explorations into possible intercultural neuroscience of CQ. We will conclude these explorations by suggesting an agenda for future research on the culturally intelligent brain.

Findings from cultural neuroscience research

As organizations globalize and the work force becomes more diverse, it is increasingly important to understand how leaders can operate effectively in culturally diverse situations (Gelfand, Erez, and Aycan 2007). Leadership effectiveness depends on a leader's ability to solve complex social problems, such as the coordination of thoughts and behaviors within social groups (Mumford et al. 2000; Wong and Law 2002). In the culturally diverse context of global leadership, the social coordination problems a leader faces are especially complex because of the large cultural variations in the behaviors and expectations of various stakeholders.

It is increasingly important to understand how leaders can operate effectively in culturally diverse situations.

The current focus in cultural neuroscience studies is to document cultural variations in psychological, neural, and genomic processes. The research goal is to describe how cultural characteristics and neurobiology shape each other (Chiao et al. 2010). Cultural neuroscience studies have deepened global leaders' understanding of how cultural processes shape basic and higher-order cognitive processes and inspired optimism in uncovering the biological underpinnings of cultural differences in a range of cognitive processes (Ames and Fiske 2010; Chiao 2009). Such accomplishments are particularly remarkable in the research on the neurological basis of culturally characteristic perceptual styles and self-schemata and the ingroup advantage in emotion recognition. We will briefly review these accomplishments because of their potential relevance to global leadership.

Cultural differences in perceptual styles, such as those in the relative attention to objects versus contexts, have an impact on how leaders make sense of situations. For example, selective attention to focal events facilitates analytical processing of the inherent properties of these events at the risk of overlooking their situational embeddedness (Nisbett 2003).

How the individual views the self affects how he or she relates to others.

Considerable cross-cultural evidence shows that Westerners have a habitual tendency to selectively attend to focal events, whereas East Asians are more accustomed to focus on the embeddedness of the focal events in their physical and social environments (Chua, Boland, and Nisbett 2005; Kitayama et al. 2003; Nisbett and Miyamoto 2005). Cultural neuroscience evidence has reinforced this conclusion. Compared with East Asians, Westerners showed stronger neural activation in task-related regions of the brain during object processing (Gutchess et al. 2006; Lin, Lin, and Han 2008). Moreover, Westerners showed less activation in brain regions associated with attentional control during object processing (Hedden et al. 2008), indicating that object processing requires less mental control for Westerners than for East Asians. Nonetheless, brain-imaging results failed to reveal stronger neural activation among East Asians during context processing (Goh et al. 2007; Gutchess et al. 2006), calling into question whether Easterners have a greater habitual tendency to engage in contextual information processing.

How the individual views the self affects how he or she relates to others. Leadership research has provided ample evidence on how followers' self-views moderate the impact of leadership on follower attitudes and behavior (van Knippenberg et al. 2004). Cultures differ in the extent to which the self is seen as a self-contained entity (independent self-construal) or a socially embedded being (interdependent self-construal). Westerners are more likely to view the self as distinct from others, whereas East Asians are more likely to view the self as fundamentally related to others (Markus and Kitayama 1991). Cultural neuroscience has confirmed the preponderance of interdependent self-views among East Asians. For both Easterners and Westerners, thinking about the self activates an area of the ventral mPFC/anterior cingulate cortex (ACC) (Craik et al. 1999; Kelley et al. 2002; Zhang et al. 2006). However, thinking about significant others activates that same area only for individuals from Eastern cultures (Ng et al. 2010; Sui and Han 2007; Zhu et al. 2007). This finding implies that whereas Easterners engage the same region of the brain, Westerners engage different parts of the brain when processing information about the self and significant others.

Identifying emotions from facial expressions is an important people skill for effective leadership (Caruso, Mayer, and Salovey 2002; Rubin, Munz, and Bommer 2005). There is a well-documented "ingroup advantage" in emotion recognition (Elfenbein and Ambady 2002; Mesquita and Leu 2007). That is, people are more accurate in recognizing the emotions of people from their own culture than from others. Cultural neuroscience evidence corroborates this finding, showing greater activity in regions of the brain associated with emotion processing when people are asked to identify emotions of their conationals compared with those of foreigners (Adams et al. 2009; Chiao et al. 2008; Freeman et al. 2009). In summary, cultural neuroscience research has demonstrated its capability to inform global leaders of the neurological basis of many important cognitive differences across cultures.

Identifying emotions from facial expressions is an important people skill for effective leadership.

Implications for global leadership

A major discovery in cultural neuroscience concerns the plasticity and environmental responsiveness of brain functioning. Considerable evidence indicates that neurological activations can be changed as a function of adapting to or learning from a new culture (Hedden et al. 2008). Indeed, even a temporary, incidental exposure to another culture can change the brain-activation pattern when performing the same cognitive task (Ng et al. 2010; Sui and Han 2007). This implies that although individuals develop a habitual pattern of neurological behaviors after chronic (repeated) exposure to a certain culture, the brain retains its potential to adapt to new cultural influences. This is good news for global leadership development because through exposure to multicultural environments, global leaders can acquire cognitive habits that are useful for meeting distinct expectations from different cultures. Like balanced multilinguals who can flexibly switch languages and smoothly navigate diverse linguistic communities, global leaders may be able to appropriate the pertinent cognitive and neurological resources and flexibly switch cognitive habits in response to changing cultural demands in the current situation.

People are more accurate in recognizing the emotions of people from their own culture than from others.

Nonetheless, not all leaders with multicultural experiences are culturally savvy. Furthermore, as noted above, the primary challenge for global leadership is the coordination of cultural differences among their stakeholders (Mumford et al. 2000; Wong and Law 2002). A major gap in cultural neuroscience research is that it has not yet addressed the cognitive neurological basis of the competencies essential for effective leadership in culturally mixed environments. One such core competency is CQ (Earley and Ang 2003). In the next two sections, we seek to further connect the fields of cultural neuroscience and global leadership by elucidating the important role of CQ in global leadership and its possible neurological basis.

Cultural intelligence and global leadership

To explain why some individuals function more effectively than others in culturally diverse settings, Earley and Ang (2003) drew on Sternberg and Detterman's (1986) multidimensional perspective on intelligence to develop a conceptual model of CQ. Ang and colleagues (Ang and Van Dyne 2008; Ang et al. 2007) defined CQ as the capability of an individual to function effectively in situations characterized by cultural diversity and theorized that CQ is a multidimensional concept comprising mental (metacognitive and cognitive), motivational, and behavioral dimensions.

Not all leaders with multicultural experiences are culturally savvy.

The mental dimension of CQ consists of the metacognitive and the cognitive facets. The metacognitive facet refers to an individual's level of conscious cultural awareness during intercultural interactions. Metacognitive CQ involves higher-level cognitive strategies—those that allow individuals to develop new heuristics and rules for social interaction in novel cultural environments by promoting information processing at a deep level. Whereas metacognitive CQ focuses on higher-order cognitive processes, the cognitive facet reflects knowledge of norms, practices, and conventions in different cultures acquired from education and personal experience. Cognitive CQ includes knowledge of cultural universals as well as knowledge of cultural differences. It encompasses an individual's level of knowledge about culture, different cultural environments, and how the self is embedded in a cultural context.

The motivational dimension of CQ reflects the ability to direct attention and energy toward learning about and operating in culturally diverse situations. Kanfer and Heggestad (1997) argued that such motivational capacities "provide agentic control of affect, cognition, and behavior that facilitate goal accomplishment." According to the expectancy-value theory of motivation (Eccles and Wigfield 2002), the direction and magnitude of energy channeled toward a particular task involve two elements—the expectation of and the value associated with successfully accomplishing the task. Those with high motivational CQ can direct attention and energy toward cross-cultural situations because of their intrinsic interest in cultures (Deci and Ryan 1985) and their confidence in intercultural effectiveness (Bandura 2002).

Finally, the behavioral dimension of CQ reflects an individual's ability to exhibit culturally appropriate verbal and nonverbal actions when interacting with people from other cultures. It also includes judicious use of speech acts—the exact words and phrases used when communicating specific messages.

Although it is impossible for a person to master all the etiquette and rules of various cultures, certain new behaviors should be learned and certain old habits can be modified. This is important, because when a person initiates and maintains face-to-face interactions with culturally diverse others, they do not have access to the person's thoughts, feelings, and motivations. Yet they rely on what they see and hear in the person's verbal, vocal, facial, and other bodily expressions to form an impression of that person. In doing so, however, they are likely to depend on their own cultural lens to make sense of the person's behavior. Those with high behavioral CQ adapt their behaviors to culturally appropriate forms to facilitate effective interactions and to make culturally diverse others feel at ease.

The three dimensions of CQ are qualitatively different facets of the overall capability of functioning and managing effectively in culturally diverse settings (Ang and Van Dyne 2008; Ang et al. 2007). That is, mental, motivational, and behavioral CQ are distinct types of capability that together form the overall CQ construct.

Awareness during intercultural interactions allows leaders to understand the impact of their own culture and background...

CQ is related to global leadership effectiveness in three ways (Offermann and Phan 2002). First, awareness during intercultural interactions allows leaders to understand the impact of their own culture and background and their attendant values and biases on their behaviors in the workplace. It also makes them aware of the expectations they hold for themselves and others in leader/follower relationships. Second, their spontaneous predilection to verify the accuracy of their cultural assumptions, coupled with their knowledge of other cultures, helps them understand the values, biases, and expectations that others hold of them. Third, this understanding of self and others combined with behavioral flexibility enables them to adapt their leadership behaviors appropriately to concrete cross-cultural situations. In summary, CQ is highly useful to effective leadership in situations characterized by cultural diversity.

There is consistent empirical support for the unique contribution of CQ to global leadership effectiveness. Rockstuhl et al. (2009) studied the leadership effectiveness of Swiss military officers working in both domestic and international contexts. The investigators collected peer ratings of both general and cross-border leadership effectiveness to provide an objective measure of the leaders' effectiveness in these two contexts. Controlling for general intelligence, emotional intelligence, and personality, leaders' overall cultural intelligence predicted their cross-border but not general leadership effectiveness.

In another study, Rockstuhl et al. (2010) found that to be effective, global leaders require both mental and behavioral CQ. In an attempt to determine which team members in multicultural teams were most likely to emerge as team leaders, the investigators separately assessed the two CQ dimensions, using a newly developed performance-based measure of mental CQ and peer ratings of behavioral CQ. Again controlling for cognitive achievement, emotional intelligence, and personality, the joint effect of mental and behavioral CQ best predicted leadership emergence in multicultural teams. That is, individuals who had both high mental and behavioral CQ were more likely to emerge as leaders in multicultural teams. Together, these results suggest that CQ is a capability that is especially relevant to global leadership.

Next, we will explore the potential neurological basis of the different CQ components.

Neuroscience of cultural intelligence

The three (mental, motivational, and behavioral) dimensions of CQ map well onto the functional differentiation of the medial frontal cortex (MFC, including the ACC). Based on results from meta-analyses of MFC activities across a range of tasks (Amodio and Frith 2006; Koski and Paus 2000; Steele and Lawrie 2004), we propose that social-cognitive processes related to the mental dimension of CQ, such as self-reflection, person perception, or inference of others' thoughts, are associated with activity in the anterior rostral MFC (arMFC), which includes the paracingulate cortex. Processes related to the motivational dimension of CQ, such as the monitoring of gains and losses, engage the orbital MFC (oMFC). Finally, processes related to the behavioral dimension of CQ, such as the control and monitoring of actions, are associated with activity in the posterior rostral MFC (prMFC), including the dorsal ACC. We propose that individuals with high mental CQ are particularly likely to engage the associated region of the brain when they perform culturally relevant tasks or culturally neutral tasks in culturally mixed environments.

Neural correlates of the mental CQ

The arMFC is implicated in thinking about psychological attributes of both self and others, as well as in judgments about the dispositions and mental states of others. Thus, we propose that the arMFC also mediates mental CQ, which requires awareness of how leaders' and followers' cultural experiences shape their self-attributes and interpersonal expectancies.

Thinking about the self

Self-awareness requires differentiation of the self from other objects and recognizing the attributes and preferences related to the self. Research has shown the arMFC mediates a wide range of cognitive activities that demand self-awareness, including evaluation of self-related traits (Fossati et al. 2003; Kelley et al. 2002), monitoring one's emotional states (Ochsner et al. 2004), reflecting on others' perceptions of the self (Ochsner et al. 2005), and thinking about one's behavioral guides (e.g., hopes, aspirations, duties, and obligations) (Johnson et al. 2006).

Self-awareness requires differentiation of the self from other objects...

Fossati et al. (2003) obtained fMRI images of participants' brains while they processed positive and negative personality descriptors in one of three experimental conditions. In the self-referential processing condition, participants judged the extent to which they possessed a trait. In the other-referential processing condition, participants judged evaluative connotations of the descriptors. In the letter-recognition control condition, participants decided whether the descriptors contained a certain letter. The results showed that self-referential encoding evoked bilateral activation in the arMFC regardless of whether the descriptors referred to a positive or negative trait, whereas the other-referential condition evoked activation in lateral prefrontal areas. In another study, Ochsner et al. (2004) obtained whole-brain fMRI data from participants while they were viewing photos depicting a person in a positive, negative, or neutral scene. Participants were instructed to report their own emotional response to each photo, the emotional state of the central figure in each photo, or (in a baseline condition) whether the photo was taken indoors or outdoors. Judgments of one's own affective responses, relative to the baseline condition, evoked stronger activation of the arMFC region.

In yet another study, Ochsner et al. (2005) compared the neural mechanisms underlying both reflected self-appraisal (i.e., the participant's perception of how others view him or her) and direct self-appraisals (i.e., how participants view themselves) and found that both forms of self-appraisal activated the arMFC region. These investigators therefore concluded that the arMFC may mediate the metacognitive processes that are recruited for both direct and reflected self-appraisals. Finally, Johnson et al. (2006) examined fMRI brain images of people thinking about their behavioral guides (hopes, aspirations, duties, obligations) versus topics unrelated to the self. The results showed that self-related thoughts engaged the arMFC more.

Collectively, these studies indicate that the arMFC region plays a vital role in supporting self-awareness and that greater self-awareness correlates with stronger activity in the arMFC region. As we have discussed earlier, leaders high in mental CQ have greater self-awareness during their interactions with culturally diverse others than have leaders low in mental CQ. We, therefore, expect leaders with high mental CQ to exhibit stronger activity in regions of the arMFC associated with self-awareness when interacting with culturally diverse others compared with leaders with low mental CQ.

Thinking about others

The arMFC is also implicated in mentalizing others (i.e., understanding others' mental states and their correspondent behaviors; Frith and Frith 1999). A considerable body of evidence shows that mentalizing the self and others may rely on similar neural mechanisms (Lieberman 2007). For example, in an fMRI study, Lombardo et al. (2009) compared the neural mechanisms implicated in mentalizing the self and others. The investigators analyzed their fMRI data using functional connectivity analyses, which allowed them to characterize neural interactions between different neural regions during a particular task. Using this approach, they found that mentalizing the self and others produced identical functional connectivity patterns between the arMFC and areas distributed across low-level embodied neural systems, such as the frontal operculum/ventral premotor cortex, the anterior insula, the primary sensorimotor cortex, and the presupplementary motor area. These areas are generally associated with sensorimotor processes and subjective emotional experience. Based on these results, the investigators infer that the arMFC is responsible for integrating the low-level embodied simulation processes that support higher-level inferences while mentalizing the self or others.

Such findings raise the possibility that leaders can project their own private experiences to others or use their own thoughts and feelings as a starting point to simulate others' private experiences. Projection of personal thoughts and feelings to culturally dissimilar others could lead to ethnocentrism—an indication of low mental CQ. Thus, culturally intelligent leaders do not simply assume that culturally diverse others think and feel in the same way as they do. Instead, leaders high in mental CQ assess the cultural differences between the self and others and adjust their ideations of others based on these assessments (Offerman and Phan 2002).

Projection of personal thoughts and feelings to culturally dissimilar others could lead to ethnocentrism...

The arMFC is also responsible for making this kind of adjustment. Mitchell, Banaji, and Macrae (2005) measured neural activity while participants attended to either the mental or physical aspects of a series of faces. Later, they asked participants to rate targets' similarity to the participants themselves. Parametric analysis revealed that the level of activity in a region in the arMFC—previously found to be implicated in self-referencing tasks—correlated with the perceived self–other similarity, but only when the participants attended to the mental states of others. These results suggest that people project mental states of the self to others only when others are sufficiently similar to the self.

Vogeley et al. (2001) examined whether taking an egocentric perspective and attending to the mental states of others involve the same neural mechanisms. To answer this question, the investigators developed a task that allowed comparison of these two psychological processes in a two-way factorial design. They found that both processes involved self-projection (associated with activity in the area of the right temporoparietal junction) and adjustment (associated with activity in the anterior cingulate cortex). Most importantly, they found a strong interaction effect of the two processes in a region of the arMFC, indicating that this region is responsible for deciding which perspective (self or other) will be taken in a concrete situation.

Tamir and Mitchell (2010) also found that adjusting for dissimilarity of others involves a process of "anchoring and adjustment." According to the anchoring and adjustment hypothesis, perceivers make initial inferences based on their own introspection and subsequently use individuating information to refine their inferences. The investigators examined this hypothesis in an fMRI study in which participants judged the preferences of another person and their own preferences for the same items. Whole-brain parametric analyses showed that activity in a region in the arMFC was related linearly to the self–other discrepancy in ratings. Because a larger discrepancy reflects greater adjustment from the initial egocentric inference, these findings suggest that the arMFC region is responsible for using mental state inferences about dissimilar others to refine initial egocentric inferences.

Effective global leaders are inclined to consider similarities and differences in the cultural experiences of the self and others when judging others.

Taken collectively, the extant evidence indicates that areas of the arMFC are responsible for mentalizing others, for tracking similarity between the self and others, and for refining initial egocentric projections with readings of others' mental states when others are dissimilar to the self. Effective global leaders are inclined to consider similarities and differences in the cultural experiences of the self and others when judging others. This psychological quality—which is a hallmark of mental CQ (Offerman and Phan 2002)—protects leaders from rendering ethnocentric judgments. Because activity in the arMFC region mediates adjustment of judgments of others based on perceived differences between the self and others, we expect leaders with higher mental CQ to exhibit stronger activity in regions of the arMFC, particularly when interacting with culturally diverse others. Based on its role in mediating self-awareness and mentalizing others, we suggest that the arMFC region is likely to be the neural base underlying mental CQ.

Neural correlates of motivational CQ

Motivational capacities reflect a leader's "agentic control of affect, cognition, and behavior that facilitate goal accomplishment" (Kanfer and Heggestad 1997). Motivational CQ involves sensitivity to the incentive structure associated with various agentic behavioral choices in intercultural contexts.

The orbitofrontal cortex has been implicated in processing information related to rewards and punishments (Rolls 1996). Based on neuroimaging studies of learning and gambling tasks, Elliott, Dolan, and

Frith (2000) held that the oMFC is involved in monitoring the reward value of stimuli and responses. Similarly, Amodio and Frith (2006) contended that the oMFC guides behavior via the value associated with possible outcomes.

Motivational capacities reflect a leader's "agentic control of affect, cognition, and behavior that facilitate goal accomplishment."

Results from an fMRI study (Coricelli et al. 2005) support this view. In this multiple-trial study, participants chose between two gambles on each trial. At the end of each trial, the experimenters induced regret by providing information about the favorable outcome of the unchosen gamble. Over repeated implementations of the same procedures, participants became increasingly regret-averse, and this behavioral change was accompanied by enhanced activity within the oMFC and amygdala. Increased activities in these brain regions were also recorded just before the participants made a choice, indicating that the same neural circuitry mediates direct experience of regret and its anticipation. The investigators concluded that the oMFC modulates acquisition of adaptive emotional responses to anticipatory gain or loss in decision making.

Using event-related fMRI, Knutson et al. (2005) tracked the neural activities that occurred when participants anticipated monetary gains and losses of varying magnitudes and probabilities. They found that the level of activation in the oMFC varied systematically with the probability of anticipated gain. In addition, oMFC activation correlated with subjective estimates of the gain and loss probabilities. These results suggested that the oMFC mediates probabilistic estimates of expected outcomes and plays an important role in integrating affective valuation and probabilistic estimates of expected values.

Effective global leaders adapt their behaviors flexibly and discriminatively in response to changing cultural demands...

Taken together, these results are consistent with the idea that the oMFC represents and updates the value of possible future outcomes and the perceived probability of achieving them. Leaders high in motivational CQ enjoy intercultural interactions and are confident that they can achieve their goals during such interactions. Neuroscience research suggests that the intrinsic value and confidence in the achievement of goals correlate with activity in the oMFC region. Thus, this region may mediate a leader's preference for and confidence in intercultural interactions. In other words, we expect that leaders with higher motivational CQ would exhibit stronger activity in the oMFC region during intercultural interactions. We therefore suggest that the oMFC is the neural base underlying motivational CQ.

Neural correlates of behavioral CQ

We posit that effective global leaders adapt their behaviors flexibly and discriminatively in response to changing cultural demands in culturally diverse environments. Action monitoring is particularly important in culturally diverse contexts because it is often necessary for the leader to inhibit a prepotent but culturally ethnocentric response. Individuals with high behavioral CQ monitor and control their actions to ensure consistency with their intentions and the current situational context. Thus, behavioral CQ requires continuous internal monitoring of action and its situational appropriateness, which is known to be mediated by the prMFC and dorsal ACC (Botvinick, Cohen, and Carter 2004).

To elaborate, neuroimaging and event-related-potential research have linked the process of action monitoring to prMFC activity. In an extensive meta-analysis of functional imaging studies that included data from various action-monitoring tasks, Barch et al. (2001) found that the neural activities while performing these tasks generally cluster in the dorsal ACC.

Furthermore, a number of neuroimaging studies have examined the process whereby individuals intentionally override a prepotent response or impulse. Intentional regulation of behavior requires two components: (a) implementation of control, and (b) monitoring performance and signaling when adjustments in control are needed. MacDonald et al. (2000) used event-related fMRI and a task-switching version of the Stroop task to examine whether these components of behavioral control have distinct neural bases in the human brain. They found that the implementation of control is localized in a region of the prMFC—Brodmann's area 9 (BA9)—while performance monitoring is localized in the dorsal ACC. The inhibitory function of BA9/BA45 is also implicated in the ability of high-proficiency bilingual individuals to understand and speak one of their languages without apparent interference from the other (Rodriguez-Fornells et al. 2002), suggesting that it plays a crucial role in the ability to switch between alternative ethnolinguistic modes.

Culture influences a range of cognitive processes and their attendant neurological behaviors.

Consistent with the idea that the prMFC and dorsal ACC are responsible for different behavioral control functions, a number of studies have implicated the dorsal ACC in detecting the conflict between a current goal and a prepotent response (Botvinick, Cohen, and Carter 2004), whereas the prMFC has been more closely tied to maintaining the current goal in working memory and implementing the top-down control needed to produce appropriate responses (Aron, Robbins, and Poldrack 2004). In particular, Richeson et al. (2003) found that the activity in BA9 when white participants viewed faces of black people corresponded to the amount of cognitive depletion (due to cognitive control and suppression of inappropriate responses) these participants experienced after interacting with a black person.

In summary, whereas the oMFC represents and updates the value of possible future outcomes, the prMFC is involved in representing and continuously updating the value of possible future actions to regulate behavior (Holroyd and Coles 2002). These characterizations are also consistent with the anatomical connectivity of these regions, with the prMFC primarily connected to the motor system and the oMFC primarily connected to sensory association areas (Amodio and Frith 2006).

Cultural influences on neurological behaviors are not static.

Leaders with high behavioral CQ are able to adapt their behavioral responses based on the culture of their interaction partner. That is, they are better able than leaders with low behavioral CQ to inhibit their own culturally habituated response in favor of a culturally appropriate response. Neuroscience research suggests that activity in the prMFC (in particular BA9) correlates with inhibition of habituated behavioral responses. Hence we expect leaders with higher behavioral CQ to exhibit stronger activity in this prMFC region, particularly during interactions with culturally diverse others. We therefore suggest that the prMFC mediates behavioral CQ.

Neural tuning and overall cultural intelligence

The neuroscience evidence we have reviewed thus far suggests possible mappings of different CQ components onto different specific regions of the medial frontal cortex. In addition, higher overall CQ may correspond to a greater capability to tune one's patterns of neural activity to varying cultural contexts. Culture influences a range of cognitive processes and their attendant neurological behaviors. Nonetheless, it is important to note that cultural influences on neurological behaviors are not static. For example, neurological behaviors can change as individuals adapt to a new cultural milieu (Hedden et al. 2008; Goh et al. 2007; Maguire et al. 2000).

The malleability of neurological behaviors is further illuminated in the phenomenon of culture priming. Habitual use of a certain cultural orientation increases the overall likelihood of displaying culture-specific behaviors and their associated neurological activities. Yet, momentary priming (situational cuing) of a certain cultural orientation can also activate this orientation. Hence, cultural priming can elevate at least temporarily the likelihood of displaying the cognitive and neurological behaviors associated with the activated cultural orientation (Hong and Chiu 2001; Hong et al. 2000).

Individuals with higher overall CQ have greater cognitive and neurological flexibility in response to changing demands across cultural contexts.

Every culture has its iconic symbols, which, like magnets of meanings, can powerfully evoke other knowledge in that culture. The presence of such iconic cultural symbols in the immediate environment can call out from memory the dominant psychological orientation in the culture, as well as the cognitive and neurological behaviors that accompany the activated orientation. This view has received support from cultural neuroscience experiments that applied the priming procedures to bicultural individuals—individuals who have extensive exposure and hence knowledge of two cultures. In these experiments, incidental exposure to one or the other culture increases the likelihood of exhibiting the cognitive and neurological behaviors characteristic of the primed culture (Lin, Lin, and Han 2008; Ng et al. 2010).

These results suggest that many bicultural individuals can spontaneously switch their interpretive frame in response to shifting cultural expectations in the immediate context. Nonetheless, there are individual differences in the degree to which individuals can flexibly adapt their cognitive and neurological behaviors in response to variations in the cultural contexts. We contend that individuals with higher overall CQ have greater cognitive and neurological flexibility in response to changing demands across cultural contexts.

Agenda for future research

Having outlined potential neurological substrates of the culturally intelligent brain, we now turn our attention to an agenda for future research. Our recommendations for extending research on the culturally intelligent brain center on three research designs: (1) situating neuroscience research in intercultural contexts, (2) comparing intercultural novices and experts in intercultural interactions, and (3) tracking neurological changes associated with CQ development.

Situating neuroscience research in intercultural contexts

Global leadership, by definition, is necessarily situated in intercultural contexts (Ng, Van Dyne, and Ang 2009). Yet, to the best of our knowledge, little or no neuroscience research has focused on intercultural situations. Hence, we suggest that future intercultural neuroscience research should adopt intercultural research designs that could empirically validate the proposed neurological underpinnings associated with a culturally intelligent brain.

With regard to neurological substrates of mental CQ, we suggest that one fruitful approach would be to compare neurological activities of leaders solving monocultural vis-à-vis intercultural decision dilemmas. Previous CQ research has shown the importance of mental CQ for solving intercultural decision dilemmas (Ang et al. 2007; Rockstuhl et al. 2010). Yet we still understand little about the extent to which effectiveness in such dilemmas depends on general problem-solving skills and unique intercultural skills. Neuroscience methods of contrasting brain activity during decision making in domestic and intercultural contexts offer an elegant way to test our assertions about the neurological substrates of mental CQ. They also hold potential to inform theorizing on CQ by disentangling the effects of general problem solving and unique intercultural skills for such important leadership tasks.

Similarly, neuroscience research on choice behaviors to date has primarily studied economic rather than cultural choice games. We thus propose that future cultural neuroscience research would benefit from contrasting neurological predictors of culture-free choices (e.g., the choice between two local foods) with neurological predictors of intercultural choices (e.g., the choice between a local and an international food). The aim of such research would again be to disentangle general motivational factors from motivational CQ.

We further suggest that research on the behavioral dimension of CQ would benefit from comparing actual behaviors and their neurological substrates when leaders have to interact with someone culturally similar versus someone culturally dissimilar. Global leadership contexts most amenable to such studies could include contexts such as intercultural negotiations, global coaching and mentoring, leading multicultural teams, and resolving intercultural conflicts.

The cultural intelligence research further suggests two ways of behavioral adaptation in intercultural situations. The first approach is to match one's behavior to the cultural style of one's interaction partners (Earley and Ang 2003). Yet, as we know, flexing one's behavior chameleon-like is very difficult and cognitively taxing (Chartrand and Bargh 1999; Dalton, Chartrand, and Finkel 2010). The second approach is to adopt a general "behavioral sweet spot" that would work effectively across different cultures. For example, Imai and Gelfand (2010) found that in effective intercultural dyads, negotiators engage in a particular negotiation style that is between culturally preferred styles of the dyads. Future cultural neuroscience research that compares the neurological activity of leaders who flex their behaviors to match their counterparts with those that adopt a "sweet spot" behavior may further our understanding of the costs and benefits associated with both behavioral strategies.

Comparing intercultural novices and experts

Ever since Chase and Simon (1973) compared master and novice chess players to understand the cognitive structures associated with chess competence, comparisons of novices and experts have been instrumental in furthering our understanding of cognitive bases of competency (Chi, Glaser, and Farr 1988). In particular, the expertise approach has led to numerous advances in our understanding of the neurological bases of domain competencies (Bukach, Gauthier, and Tarr 2006; Grabner, Neubauer, and Stern 2006).

Global leadership, by definition, is necessarily situated in intercultural contexts.

Hence, another research design that can substantiate the links between the brain and cultural intelligence would be to compare the neurological activity of intercultural novices and experts engaged in the same intercultural tasks. An important goal for future research would be to discover the distinct neurological behaviors of intercultural novices and experts in representing culturally different groups. For example, regions in the arMFC have recently been implicated in the application of stereotypes when mentalizing others (Mitchell et al. 2008; Quadflieg et al. 2008). From what we know from cultural psychology, intercultural novices tend to rely on simple stereotypes (e.g., based on an irrational dislike of dissimilar people) whereas experts rely more on sophisticated stereotypes (e.g., based on theoretical concepts and lacking negative attributions) to characterize a culturally dissimilar group (Osland and Bird 2000). Neuroscience research on stereotype application to date has not distinguished between simple and sophisticated stereotypes. We encourage future neuroscience research into stereotypes to assess whether qualitatively different stereotypes (simple vs. sophisticated) are related to different neurological behaviors.

Research by Earley and Ang (2003) and Ang and Van Dyne (2008) further suggests that culturally intelligent individuals adopt sophisticated stereotypes about culturally diverse others as starting points but dynamically update their assumptions during intercultural interactions. Future research into the neuroscience of CQ could, therefore, trace the neural activities of initial anchoring through to the subsequent dynamic updating of stereotypes.

Examining neurological changes associated with CQ development

Another research design focuses on documenting changes in neurological activity as a result of CQ development or training. Here, intercultural neuroscience could be informed by two learning theories: experiential learning theory (Kolb 1984) and situated learning theory (Lave and Wenger 1991). Experiential learning theory is an adult-learning theory that highlights the critical role experience plays in affecting learning and change (Kolb and Kolb 2005). To date, experiential learning theory has received widespread attention in the global-leader-development literature (Kayes, Kayes, and Yamazaki 2005; Yamazaki and Kayes 2004). Initial evidence suggests that CQ does indeed improve as a consequence of developmental interventions that focus on experiential learning (Ng, Van Dyne, and Ang 2009; MacNab and Worthley

2010). We see great potential for future research that examines the neurological changes associated with CQ training or specific CQ developmental exercises.

CQ training exercises could also be grounded in the theory of situated learning (Collins, Brown, and Newman 1989; Lave and Wenger 1991; Ng, Tan, and Ang, forthcoming). Situated learning theory emphasizes the importance of exposure to "authentic" activities as a powerful source of learning and skill acquisition. Activities may be authentic with regard to the "ordinary practices of the culture" (Brown, Collins, and Duguid 1989), or they may be authentic with regard to the specific mental functions they activate (Fox 2006). Understanding which regions of the brain change as leaders develop their CQ allows trainers to design exercises that specifically target similar regions of the brain. Such exercises would be authentic in that they activate mental functions relevant to CQ and thus provide a platform for situated learning to occur. We therefore particularly encourage future research that tracks neurological changes associated with situated learning of CQ.

In increasingly globalized business environments, leaders are confronted with the complex role of managing people from diverse cultural backgrounds.

Conclusion

In increasingly globalized business environments, leaders are confronted with the complex role of managing people from diverse cultural backgrounds. Hence, effective global leaders are expected to not only understand but also bridge cultural differences. Studies in cultural neuroscience are crucial for the education and development of global leaders as they raise awareness and appreciation of cultural differences in global leaders. Levering off the recent advances in identifying the neurological substrates of different cognitive processes, we propose to extend cultural neuroscience research into intercultural neuroscience of the "culturally intelligent" brain. Specifically, we identify the theory of CQ (Ang and Van Dyne 2008), with its focus on intercultural capabilities, as a theoretical framework for charting a new research agenda into intercultural neuroscience.

References

Adams, R. B., Rule, N. O., Franklin, R. G., Jr., Wang, E., Stevenson, M. T., Yoshikawa, S., Nomura, M., et al. 2009. "Cross-Cultural Reading the Mind in the Eyes: An fMRI Investigation." *Journal of Cognitive Neuroscience* 22: 97–108.

Ames, D. L., and Fiske, S. T. 2010. "Cultural Neuroscience." *Asian Journal of Social Psychology* 13(2): 72–82.

Amodio, D. M., and Frith, C. D. 2006. "Meeting of Minds: The Medial Frontal Cortex and Social Cognition." *Nature Reviews Neuroscience* 7: 268–277.

Ang, S., and Van Dyne, L. 2008. "Conceptualization of Cultural Intelligence: Definition, Distinctiveness, and Nomological Network." In *Handbook of Cultural Intelligence: Theory, Measurement, and Applications*, edited by S. Ang and L. Van Dyne, 3–15. Armonk, NY: M. E. Sharpe.

Ang, S., Van Dyne, L., Koh, C. K. S., Ng, K. Y., Templer, K. J., Tay, C., and Chandrasekar, N. A. 2007. "Cultural Intelligence: Its Measurement and Effects on Cultural Judgment and Decision Making, Cultural Adaptation, and Task Performance." *Management and Organization Review* 3: 335–371.

Aron, A. R., Robbins, T. W., and Poldrack, R. A. 2004. "Inhibition and the Right Inferior Frontal Cortex." *Trends in Cognitive Sciences* 8: 170–177.

Bandura, A. 2002. "Social Cognitive Theory in Cultural Context." *Applied Psychology: An International Review* 51: 269–290.

Barch, D. M., Braver, T. S., Akbudak, E., Conturo, T., Ollinger, J., and Snyder, A. 2001. "Anterior Cingulate Cortex and Response Conflict: Effects of Response Modality and Processing Domain." *Cerebral Cortex* 11: 837–848.

Botvinick, M. M., Cohen, J. D., and Carter, C. S. 2004. "Conflict Monitoring and Anterior Cingulate Cortex: An update." *Trends in Cognitive Sciences* 8: 539–546.

Brown, J. S., Collins, A., and Duguid, P. 1989. "Situated Cognition and the Culture of Learning." *Educational Researcher* 18: 32–42.

Bukach, C. M., Gauthier, I., and Tarr, M. J. 2006. "Beyond Faces and Modularity: The Power of an Expertise Framework." *Trends in Cognitive Sciences* 10: 159–166.

Caruso, D. R., Mayer, J. D., and Salovey, P. 2002. "Emotional Intelligence and Emotional Leadership." In *Multiple Intelligences and Leadership*, edited by R. E. Riggio, S. E. Murphy, and F. J. Pirozzolo, 55–74. Mahwah, NJ: Lawrence Erlbaum Associates.

Chartrand, T. L., and Bargh, J. A. 1999. "The Chameleon Effect: The Perception-Behavior Link and Social Interaction." *Journal of Personality and Social Psychology* 76: 893–910.

Chase, W. G., and Simon, H. A. 1973. "Perception in Chess." *Cognitive Psychology* 4: 55–81.

Chi, T. H., Glaser, R., and Farr, M. J., eds. 1988. *The Nature of Expertise*. Hillsdale, NJ: Erlbaum.

Chiao, J. Y. 2009. "Cultural Neuroscience: A Once and Future Discipline." *Progress in Brain Research* 178: 287–304.

Chiao, J. Y., Hariri, A. R., Harada, T., Mano, Y., Sadato, N., Parrish, T. B., and Iidaka, T. 2010. "Theory and Methods in Cultural Neuroscience." *Social Cognitive and Affective Neuroscience* 5: 356–361.

Chiao, J. Y., Iidaka, T., Gordon, H. L., Nogawa, J., Bar, M., Aminoff, E., Sadato, N., and Ambady, N. 2008. "Cultural Specificity in Amygdala Response to Fear Faces." *Journal of Cognitive Neuroscience* 20(12): 2167–2174.

Chomsky, N. 1965. *Aspects of the Theory of Syntax*. Cambridge, MA: MIT Press.

Chua, H. F., Boland, J. E., and Nisbett, R. E. 2005. "Cultural Variation in Eye Movements During Scene Perception." *Proceedings of the National Academy of Sciences, USA* 102: 12629–12633.

Collins, A., Brown, J. S., and Newman, S. E. 1989. "Cognitive Apprenticeship: Teaching the Crafts of Reading, Writing, and Mathematics." In *Knowing, Learning, and Instruction: Essays in Honor of Robert Glaser*, edited by L. B. Resnick, 453–494. Hillsdale, NJ: Erlbaum.

Corbetta, M., and Shulman, G. L. 2002. "Control of Goal-Directed and Stimulus-Driven Attention in the Brain." *Nature Reviews Neuroscience* 3: 201–215.

Coricelli, G., Critchley, H. D., Joffily, M., O'Doherty, J. P., Sirigu, A., and Dolan, R. J. 2005. "Regret and its Avoidance: A Neuroimaging Study of Choice Behavior." *Nature Neuroscience* 8: 1255–1262.

Craik, F. I. M., Moroz, T. M., Moscovitch, M., Stuss, D. T., Winocur, G., Tulving, E., and Kapur, S. 1999. "In Search of the Self: A Positron Emission Tomography Study." *Psychological Science* 10: 26–34.

Dalton, A. N., Chartrand, T. L., and Finkel, E. J. 2010. "The Schema-Driven Chameleon: How Mimicry Affects Executive and Self-Regulatory Resources." *Journal of Personality and Social Psychology* 98: 605–617.

Deci, E. L., and Ryan, R. M. 1985. *Intrinsic Motivation and Self-Determination in Human Behavior*. New York: Plenum.

Earley, P. C., and Ang, S. 2003. *Cultural Intelligence: Individual Interactions across Cultures*. Palo Alto, CA: Stanford University Press.

Eccles, J. S., and Wigfield, A. 2002. "Motivational Beliefs, Values, and Goals." *Annual Review of Psychology* 53: 109–132.

Elfenbein, H. A., and Ambady, N. 2002. "On the Universality and Cultural Specificity of Emotion Recognition: A Meta-Analysis." *Psychological Bulletin* 12: 203–235.

Elliott, R., Dolan, R. J., and Frith, C. D. 2000. "Dissociable Functions in the Medial and Lateral Orbitofrontal Cortex: Evidence from Human Neuroimaging Studies." *Cerebral Cortex* 10: 308–317.

Fossati, P., Hevenor, S. J., Graham, S. J., Grady, C., Keightley, M. L., Craik, F., and Mayberg, H. 2003. "In Search of the Emotional Self: An fMRI Study Using Positive and Negative Emotional Words." *American Journal of Psychiatry* 160: 1938–1945.

Fox, S. 2006. "Inquiries of Every Imaginable Kind: Ethnomethodology, Practical Action, and the New Socially Situated Learning Theory." *Sociological Review* 54: 426–445.

Freeman, J. B., Rule, N. O., Adams, R. B., Jr., and Ambady, N. 2009. "Culture Shapes a Mesolimbic Response to Signals of Dominance and Subordination that Associates with Behavior." *NeuroImage* 47: 353–359.

Frith, C. D., and Frith, U. 1999. "Interacting Minds: A Biological Basis." *Science* 286: 1692–1695.

Gelfand, M. J., Erez, M., and Aycan, Z. 2007. "Cross-Cultural Organizational Behavior." *Annual Review of Psychology* 58: 479–514.

Gitelman, D. R., Nobre, A. C., Parrish, T. B., LaBar, K. S., Kim, Y. H., Meyer, J. R., and Mesulam, M. M. 1999. "A Large-Scale Distributed Network for Covert Spatial Attention: Further Anatomical Delineation Based on Stringent Behavioural and Cognitive Controls." *Brain* 122: 1093–1106.

Goh, J.O., Chee, M.W., Tan, J.C., Venkatraman, V., Hebrank, A., Leshikar, E. D., Jenkins, L., et al. 2007. "Age and Culture Modulate Object Processing and Object-Scene Binding in the Ventral Visual Area." *Cognitive, Affective, and Behavioral Neuroscience* 7(1): 44–52.

Grabner, R. H., Neubauer, A. C., and Stern, E. 2006. "Superior Performance and Neural Efficiency: The Impact of Intelligence and Expertise." *Brain Research Bulletin* 69: 422–439.

Gutchess, A. H., Welsh, R. C., Boduroglu, A., and Park, D. C. 2006. "Cross-Cultural Differences in the Neural Correlates of Picture Encoding." *Cognitive, Affective, and Behavioral Neuroscience* 6: 102–109.

Hedden, T., Ketay, S., Aron, A., Markus, H. R., and Gabrieli, J. D. E. 2008. "Cultural Influences on Neural Substrates of Attentional Control." *Psychological Science* 19: 12–16.

Holroyd, C. B., and Coles, M. G. 2002. "The Neural Basis of Human Error Processing: Reinforcement Learning, Dopamine, and the Error-Related Negativity." *Psychological Review* 109: 679–709.

Hong, Y. Y., and Chiu, C. Y. 2001. "Toward a Paradigm Shift: From Cross-Cultural Differences in Social Cognition to Social-Cognitive Mediation of Cultural Differences." *Social Cognition* 19: 181–196.

Hong, Y. Y., Morris, M. W., Chiu, C. Y., and Benet-Martinez, V. 2000. "Multicultural Minds: A Dynamic Constructivist Approach to Culture and Cognition." *American Psychologist* 55: 709–720.

Imai, L., and Gelfand, M. J. 2010. "The Culturally Intelligent Negotiator: The Impact of Cultural Intelligence (CQ) on Negotiation Sequences and Outcomes." *Organizational Behavior and Human Decision Processes* 112: 83–98.

Johnson, M. K., Raye, C. L., Mitchell, K. J., Touryan, S. R., Greene, E. J., and Nolen-Hoeksema, S. 2006. "Dissociating Medial Frontal and Posterior Cingulate Activity During Self-Reflection." *Social Cognitive and Affective Neuroscience* 1: 56–64.

Kanfer, R., and Heggestad, E. D. 1997. "Motivational Traits and Skills: A Person-Centered Approach to Work Motivation." *Research in Organizational Behavior* 19: 1–56.

Kayes, D. C., Kayes, A. B., and Yamazaki, Y. 2005. "Essential Competencies for Cross-Cultural Knowledge Absorption." *Journal of Managerial Psychology* 20: 578–589.

Kelley, W. M., Macrae, C. N., Wyland, C. L., Caglar, S., Inati, S., and Heatherton, T. F. 2002. "Finding the Self? An Event-Related fMRI Study." *Journal of Cognitive Neuroscience* 14: 785–794.

Kitayama, S., Dufy, S., Kawamura, T., and Larsen, J. T. 2003. "Perceiving an Object and its Context in Different Cultures: A Cultural Look at New Look." *Psychological Science* 14: 201–206.

Kitayama, S., and Tompson, S. 2010. "Envisioning the Future of Cultural Neuroscience." *Asian Journal of Social Psychology* 13(2): 92–101.

Knutson, B., Taylor, J., Kaufman, M., Peterson, R., and Glover, G. 2005. "Distributed Neural Representation of Expected Value." *Journal of Neuroscience* 25: 4806–4812.

Kolb, A. Y., and Kolb, D. A. 2005. "Learning Styles and Learning Spaces: Enhancing Experiential Learning in Higher Education." *Academy of Management Learning and Education* 4: 193–212.

Kolb, D. A. 1984. *Experiential Learning: Experience as the Source of Learning and Development*. Englewood Cliffs, NJ: Prentice-Hall.

Koski, L., and Paus, T. 2000. "Functional Connectivity of the Anterior Cingulate Cortex Within the Human Frontal Lobe: A Brain-Mapping Meta-Analysis." *Experimental Brain Research* 133: 55–65.

Lave, J., and Wenger, E. 1991. *Situated Learning: Legitimate Peripheral Participation*. Cambridge, UK: Cambridge University Press.

Lieberman, M. D. 2007. "Social Cognitive Neuroscience: A Review of Core Processes." *Annual Review of Psychology* 58: 259–289.

Lin, Z., Lin., Y., and Han, S. 2008. "Self-Construal Priming Modulates Visual Activity Underlying Global/Local Perception." *Biological Psychology* 77: 93–97.

Lombardo, M. V., Chakrabarti, B., Bullmore, E. T., Wheelwright, S. J., Sadek, S. A., Suckling, J., MRC AIMS Consortium, and Baron-Cohen, S. 2009. "Shared Neural Circuits for Mentalizing About the Self and Others." *Journal of Cognitive Neuroscience* 22(7): 1623–1635.

MacDonald, A. W., Cohen, J. D., Stenger, V. A., and Carter, C. S. 2000. "Dissociating the Role of the Dorsolateral Prefrontal and Anterior Cingulate Cortex in Cognitive Control." *Science* 288: 1835–1838.

MacNab, B., and Worthley, R. G. 2010. "An Experiential Education Approach to Teaching Cultural Intelligence: Individual and Contextual Influences." Paper presented at the Academy of Management Annual Meeting, (August) Montreal, Canada.

Maguire, E. A., Gadian, D. G., Johnsrude, I. S., Good, C. D., Ashburner, J., Frackowiak, R. S. J., and Frith, C. D. 2000. "Navigation-Related Structural Change in the Hippocampi of Taxi Drivers." *Proceedings of the National Academy of Sciences, USA* 97: 4398–4403.

Markus, H. R., and Kitayama, S. 1991. "Culture and the Self: Implications for Cognition, Emotion, and Motivation." *Psychological Review* 98: 224–253.

Mesquita, B., and Leu, J. 2007. "The Cultural Psychology of Emotion." In *Handbook for Cultural Psychology*, edited by S. Kitayama and D. Cohen 734–759. New York: Guilford.

Mitchell, J. P., Ames, D. L., Jenkins, A. C., and Banaji, M. R. 2008). "Neural Correlates of Stereotype Application." *Journal of Cognitive Neuroscience* 21: 594–604.

Mitchell, J. P., Banaji, M. R., and Macrae, C. N. 2005. "The Link Between Social Cognition and Self-Referential Thought in the Medial Prefrontal Cortex." *Journal of Cognitive Neuroscience* 17: 1306–1315.

Mumford, M. D., Zaccaro, S. J., Harding, F. D., Jacobs, T. O., and Fleishman, E. A. 2000. "Leadership Skills for a Changing World. Solving Complex Social Problems." *Leadership Quarterly* 11: 11–35.

Ng, K. Y., Tan, M. L., and Ang, S. (forthcoming). "Culture Capital and Cosmopolitan Human Capital: The Impact of Global Mindset and Organizational Routines on Developing Cultural Intelligence and International Experiences in Organizations." In *The Oxford Handbook of Human Capital*, edited by A. Burton and J. C. Spencer. New York: Oxford University Press.

Ng, K. Y., Van Dyne, L., and Ang, S. 2009. "From Experience to Experiential Learning: Cultural Intelligence as a Learning Capability for Global Leader Development." *Academy of Management Learning and Education* 8: 511–526.

Ng, S. H., Han, S., Mao, L., and Lai, J. C. L. 2010. "Dynamic Bicultural Brains: fMRI Study of their Flexible Neural Representation of Self and Significant Others in Response to Culture Primes." *Asian Journal of Social Psychology* 13(2): 83–91.

Nisbett, R. E. 2003. *The Geography of Thought: How Asians and Westerners Think Differently...and Why*. New York: Free Press.

Nisbett, R. E., and Miyamoto, Y. 2005. "The Influence of Culture: Holistic Versus Analytic Perception." *Trends in Cognitive Sciences* 9: 467–473.

Ochsner, K. N., Beer, J. S., Robertson, E. R., Cooper, J. C., Gabrieli, J. D., Kihlstrom, J. F., and D'Esposito, M. 2005. "The Neural Correlates of Direct and Reflected Self-Knowledge." *NeuroImage* 28: 797–814.

Ochsner, K. N., Knierim, K., Ludlow, D. H., Hanelin, J., Ramachandran, T., Glover, G., and Mackey, S. C. 2004. "Reflecting Upon Feelings: An fMRI Study of Neural Systems Supporting the Attribution of Emotion to Self and Other." *Journal of Cognitive Neuroscience* 16: 1746–1772.

Offermann, L. R., and Phan, L. U. 2002. "Culturally Intelligent Leadership for a Diverse World." In *Multiple Intelligences and Leadership*, edited by R. E. Riggio, S. E Murphy, and F. J. Pirozzolo 187–214. Mahwah, NJ: Lawrence Erlbaum Associates.

Osland, J. S., and Bird, A. 2000. "Beyond Sophisticated Stereotyping: Cultural Sense Making in Context." *Academy of Management Executive* 14: 65–76.

PricewaterhouseCoopers. 2010. 10th Annual Global CEO Survey London, UK: Nicholas Brealey Intercultural. Accessed February 11, 2010. http://www. swisseconomic.ch/pdf/wissen/10th_CEO_Survey_PWC.pdf accessed 2/11/2010.

Quadflieg, S., Turk, D. J., Waiter, G. D., Mitchell, J. P., Jenkins, A. C., and Macrae, C. N. 2008. "Exploring the Neural Correlates of Social Stereotyping." *Journal of Cognitive Neuroscience* 21: 1560–1570.

Richeson, J. A., Baird, A. A., Gordon, H. L., Heatherton, T. F., Wyland, C. L., Trawalter, S., and Shelton, J. N. 2003. "An fMRI Investigation of the Impact of Interracial Contact on Executive Function." *Nature Neuroscience* 6: 1323–1328.

Rockstuhl, T., Ang, S., Ng, K. Y., Van Dyne, L., and Lievens, F. 2010. "Cultural Intelligence in Multicultural Teams: Moderating Role of Behavioral Flexibility." Paper presented at the Society for Industrial and Organizational Psychology Annual Meeting (April), Atlanta, GA.

Rockstuhl, T., Ng, K. Y., Seiler, S., Annen, H., and Ang, S. 2009. "Emotional and Cultural Intelligence in Global Leadership Effectiveness." Paper presented at the Society for Industrial and Organizational Psychology Annual Meeting (April), New Orleans, LA.

Rodriguez-Fornells, A., Rotte, M., Heinze, H. J., Noesselt, T., and Muente, T. F. 2002. "Brain Potential and Functional MRI Evidence for How to Handle Two Languages With One Brain." *Nature* 415: 1026–1029.

Rolls, E. T. 1996. "The Orbitofrontal Cortex." *Philosophical Transactions of the Royal Society of London: Biological Sciences* 351: 1433–1443; discussion 1443–1444.

Rubin, R. S., Munz, D. C., and Bommer, W. H. 2005. "Leading From Within: The Effects of Emotion Recognition and Personality on Transformational Leadership Behavior." *Academy of Management Journal* 48: 845–858.

Steele, J. D., and Lawrie, S. M. 2004. "Segregation of Cognitive and Emotional Function in the Prefrontal Cortex: A Stereotactic Meta-Analysis." *NeuroImage* 21: 868–875.

Sternberg, R. J., and Detterman, D. K. 1986. *What Is Intelligence? Contemporary Viewpoints on Its Nature and Definition*. Norwood, NJ: Ablex.

Sui, J., and Han, S. 2007. "Self-Construal Priming Modulates Neural Substrates of Self-Awareness." *Psychological Science* 18: 861–866.

Tamir, D. I., and Mitchell, J. P. 2010. "Neural Correlates of Anchoring-and-Adjustment During Mentalizing." *Proceedings of the National Academy of Sciences, USA* 107: 10827–10832.

Van Knippenberg, D., van Knippenberg, B., De Cremer, D., and Hogg, M. A. 2004. "Leadership, Self, and Identity: A Review and Research Agenda." *Leadership Quarterly* 15: 825–856.

Vogeley, K., Bussfeld, S. P., Newen, A., Herrmann, S., Happé, F., Falkai, P., Maier, W., et al. 2001. "Mind Reading: Neural Mechanisms of Theory of Mind and Self-Perspective." *NeuroImage* 14: 170–181.

Wong, C. S., and Law, K. S. 2002. "The Effects of Leader and Follower Emotional Intelligence on Performance and Attitude: An Exploratory Study." *Leadership Quarterly* 13: 243–274.

Yamazaki, Y., and Kayes, D. C. 2004. "An Experiential Approach to Cross-Cultural Learning: A Review and Integration of Competencies for Successful Expatriate Adaptation." *Academy of Management Learning and Education* 3: 362–379.

Zhang, L., Zhou, T., Zhang, J., Liu, Z., Fan, J., and Zhu, Y. 2006. "In Search of the Chinese Self: An fMRI Study." *Science in China Series C: Life Sciences* 49: 89–96.

Zhu, Y., Zhang, L., Fan, J., and Han, S. 2007. "Neural Basis of Cultural Influence on Self-Representation." *NeuroImage* 34: 1310–1316.

22. Mapping leadership behaviors to neuroleadership models: a NASA case study

Ruth Donde and Christine R. Williams
Ruth Donde, Neuroleadership Group, Auckland, New Zealand
Christine R. Williams, NASA, Washington, USA

Background

The National Aeronautics and Space Administration (NASA) is a unique organization of almost 17,000 employees located on and off planet Earth. Its employees include nearly 11,000 engineers, among them systems engineers who are responsible for ensuring that hundreds of individuals and tens of thousands of parts all come together to ensure mission success.

Owing to the unique nature of the work done by each of NASA's ten centers, systems engineers have many different and unique responsibilities. In NASA, most systems engineers tend to be experts in one or two engineering disciplines and have experience in only those parts of the engineering life cycle on which their center focuses. In most cases it is difficult for an engineer to gain the broad experience needed to become a highly effective chief engineer without going beyond his or her home center.

In 2008, NASA's leadership identified systems engineering as a critical core competency. NASA leadership saw, in addition to most systems engineers not having broad experience, a number of factors that could have potentially adverse implications for future mission success. These factors included a large number of NASA's best systems engineers nearing retirement age; the fact that entire programs no longer resided in one culture or in a commonly understood set of processes; and underdeveloped leadership, creativity, communication, systems-thinking, and problem-solving skills in many systems engineers. It was these less tangible skills that NASA's leaders agreed were the key differentiators between good and great systems engineers.

The Office of the Chief Engineer was given responsibility for creating a program to accelerate the development of NASA's midlevel systems engineers, and within six months the first 16 competitively selected systems engineers were chosen for NASA's Systems Engineering Leadership Development Program (SELDP). The goals of SELDP were to develop both the science and the art of systems engineering.

The science [i]: Provide the hands-on technical experience not available at the participant's location and expand his or her understanding of how systems engineering processes vary across centers.

The art [ii]: Provide cross-agency experience to learn the engineering culture of other centers and build targeted leadership skills and capabilities, including creativity, flexibility, critical thinking, and dealing with complexity.

The art of systems engineering

To build systems engineering knowledge, NASA had a number of technical training courses designed. The acceleration of technical expertise in SELDP was to be gained through hands-on assignments at other NASA centers that could provide the unique experience missing in the individual's career up to that point. Teaching individuals the art of systems engineering was going to be harder. Not only did many engineers not have leadership skills and capabilities—including creativity, flexibility, critical thinking, and dealing with complexity—but most did not acknowledge these skills as critical components of their jobs. For NASA engineers to accept them as important, these skills had to be shown as relevant to their work and to enabling mission success.

To accomplish this, NASA conducted studies to ascertain the behaviors of highly regarded systems engineers, those whom their peers and NASA's leaders regarded as "go-to" people. The NASA Systems Engineering Behavior Study involved interviewing, shadowing, and observing thirty-eight of NASA's most highly regarded systems engineers to identify the behaviors that helped to make them successful. These behaviors were sorted into groupings, or competencies, which were further sorted into five prevailing themes:

- Leadership
- Attitudes and attributes
- Communication
- Problem solving and systems thinking
- Technical acumen

Identifying and understanding these competencies and their associated behaviors allowed NASA to align all elements of the program in a single framework.

The studies of people who were respected and known to achieve mission success gave these behaviors and associated skills the relevance and connection to mission success needed to engage systems engineers in learning these skills. However, this was just the start. The second phase was to show these engineers how to specifically enable their leadership capabilities by improving individual and team performance. This included relating effective behaviors to the SCARF® model and neuroleadership domains in order to identify specific behaviors and needs in the moment. The neuroscience research behind this work provided an additional level of credibility to the skills we were attempting to develop in these leaders.

Introduction to the case study

The purpose of this case study is to illustrate the way NASA's leadership behaviors were mapped to current neuroscience-of-leadership models. The aim is to better understand the impact of what leaders do in terms of either enabling or inhibiting employee performance. The benefit of such an analysis is the identification of displayed leadership behaviors that can be used to maximize employee reward-state response and improve employees' performance and organizational effectiveness.

This chapter reviews the neuroleadership domains and the SCARF model in particular, and then introduces NASA's executive leadership study from which the key leadership behaviors were sourced. In the implementation of the program, participants were taught how these behaviors either inhibited or enabled others, using an understanding of neuroscience.

For purposes of this case study, these behaviors were individually assessed through the lens of the neuroleadership domains and the SCARF model to better understand how and why they were effective. The analysis uncovers some interesting insights that both reinforce the expected and provide new learning. We will share learnings and the resulting adjustments made to the leadership-development training program. We will also address insights into what would be done differently when conducting future large-scale leadership studies of this type. We will conclude by asking for a consideration of the way these learnings may be applied in other organizations.

The aim is to better understand the impact of what leaders do in terms of either enabling or inhibiting employee performance.

Human resource training and organizational development business units are encouraged to look at their overall leadership-development frameworks in the context of SCARF and the neuroleadership domains as a way to improve their overall developmental strategy and increase their return on investment.

It is also hoped that this research will inspire organizations to assess leaders' behaviors in the context of the SCARF model, or similar neuroleadership frameworks, which show the link with brain-smart leadership development as a way to reduce the threat response and improve employee performance.

Neuroleadership domains

Neuroleadership is the intersection of neuroscience and the neural basis of leadership and management practices (Ringleb and Rock 2008). The field of neuroleadership has the objective of improving leadership effectiveness by evolving a science for leadership and leadership development, taking into account the physiology of the mind and the brain (Ringleb and Rock 2008). It is, therefore, well placed as a tool for reviewing NASA's leadership-behavior framework.

The neuroscience of leadership comprises four domains, which are commonly referred to as the neuroleadership domains (NLD):

- **Decision making and problem solving**

  This domain seeks to explore the way neuroscience can support and illuminate traditional leadership research on problem solving and decision making.

- **Emotion regulation**

  This domain refers to staying cool under pressure and being able to be mindful as opposed to reactive.

- **Collaborating with and influencing others**

  This domain refers to social interactions—that is, the way individuals get along with others and how to build trust.

- **Facilitating change**

  This domain is about the way individuals respond to and can navigate change and uncertainty.

SCARF model reviewed

The SCARF model has been discussed in this handbook on many occasions. This discussion, however, presents a practical use of the model in helping develop leaders. Let's first revisit the major components of this model to better understand the biology of how social behavior is driven. This is particularly important in relation to the way individuals collaborate with one another (Rock 2008).

The five perceptions listed in the SCARF model are shown in table 1.Statu

Table 1. The SCARF models

S	**Status**	**The interpretation of comparative position to others/self in all domains of life**
C	**Certainty**	**Feeling confident in the happenings of the future; predicting and managing expectations**
A	**Autonomy**	**The ability to influence and embark on self-determining actions; a sense of choice/control**
R	**Relatedness**	**The nature of the social relationship; a sense of connectedness or exclusion**
F	**Fairness**	**The perceived or actual interpretation of the equality of opportunity**

These same social perceptions are linked to the behaviors of effective leaders because, when activated, these elements result in threat or reward responses.

Table 2. Threat/reward response displays (Rock 2008)

Threat response	**Reward response**
• Reduces the resources available for executive function in the prefrontal cortex. This results in a literal reduction in visual capacity, which is associated with diminished creativity when collaborating or problem solving.	• Encourages a sense of engagement, a willingness to do things, think deeply about the issue at hand, and take risks.
• Reduces the capacity to receive perceived and subtle cues, which are beneficial in gaining insight and supporting complex problem solving.	• Closely linked to positive emotions, it increases dopamine levels, which are beneficial to learning and growth.

• Activates the amygdala, which results in a "tendency to generalise more, which increases likelihood of accidental connection" (Rock 2008, 3).	• Research indicates that people who are experiencing positive emotions are more creative and therefore perceive more options in problem solving, especially in relation to nonlinear problems. This research also indicates that people who experience positive emotions collaborate more successfully (Fredrickson 2009).

Research method used in NASA studies

Since October 2008, NASA has shown a commitment to investigating and identifying the characteristics and behaviors frequently observed in highly regarded technical and executive leaders. Two comprehensive studies have been undertaken; the data gathered seeks to explore answers to this question: what are the behaviors and attributes that enable individuals to become successful executives at NASA?

The two studies were:

- The NASA Systems Engineering Behavior Study, which included 38 people whom agency leadership considered highly regarded systems engineers.
- The Executive Leadership at NASA: A Behavioral Framework, which included 14 NASA executives whom agency leadership identified as highly effective in their roles and who possessed a technical background or systems orientation that contributed to their success.

The methodologies for both these studies were the same. Each study consisted of interviews and shadowing and/or observation of each of the executive participants.

The interviews were recorded and lasted 60 to 90 minutes. The questions posed in the interviews were vetted and approved by the NASA chief engineer before the start of the study. Participants were asked identical questions, with follow-up questions based on initial answers. Interview questions were divided into two categories: context and relation to self and personal awareness.

The shadow process included a minimum of one day of observing executives performing their day-to-day activities. In addition, study-team members were invited to meetings and events that executives were either leading or attending. The events observed included, but were not limited to, staff meetings; program, project or technical reviews; one-on-one discussions; brainstorming sessions; press interviews; and strategy meetings.

The data—that is, the observable behaviors/attributes that two or more executives exhibited or reported—were subsequently aggregated.

NASA study results

The results are clustered into elements within six broad themes, as shown in table 3. This table gives the broader themes used to categorize observable behaviors.

Table 3. NASA leadership behavior themes

Leadership	Deals with structure, organization, resourcing; including self-awareness and ability to build trust.
Attitudes and attributes	(Subtheme: executive presence) Personal characteristics that create an effective work environment and engage stakeholders in supporting the organization.
Communication	Ways of verbally and nonverbally engaging others and providing information to move the organization forward.
Problem solving and systems thinking	Ways of seeing the larger system at work and all its interconnected parts. Mostly applied to technical problems.
Political savvy	Ways of dealing effectively with outside stakeholders.
Strategic thinking	Maintaining the agency-wide view and the broader implications on near- and long-term decisions.

At the NeuroLeadership Conference held in 2010, NASA reported the results of these studies, as well as their initial efforts to align them with the SCARF model and to build training and development tools and techniques that are more brain-friendly and effective. That initial effort led to collaboration with the NeuroLeadership Group to expand this connection beyond the initial SCARF analysis and to also include the neuroleadership domains.

Research method of expanded study

The methodology for this developing this chapter involved cross-referencing the leadership behavior framework as developed by NASA with the SCARF model and the neuroleadership domains.

Both NASA and NeuroLeadership Group (NLG) contributors allocated the most appropriate domain(s) and SCARF model dimension(s) to each leadership behavior independently, based on the definitions in *NeuroLeadership Journal* articles on SCARF (Rock 2008) and the emerging field of neuroleadership (Ringleb and Rock 2008).

Based on field work carried out with various organizations, NLG contributors analyzed the element(s) of both SCARF and the NLD to determine what would be expected to be triggered by a particular behavior. On the other hand, NASA contributors asked what behavior was most likely to be triggered or not triggered in others. For example:

- Was his or her ego stroked?—Status
- Did the information answer a question/need he or she had?—Certainty
- Did the executive allow the individual to decide how to do his or her job?—Autonomy
- Did the executive create a feeling of belonging? Build teamwork? Get to know the person better?—Relatedness
- Did the behavior give everyone equal opportunity?—Fairness
- Each contributor's allocation was then cross-referenced and finalized for agreement.

The abbreviations used in table 5, NASA Representative Observable Behaviors, are defined in table 4. A full outline of the NASA Broad Themes and Observed Behavior Framework is available in the appendix. Table 6 shows the established allocation of both the neuroleadership domains and the SCARF model perceptions.

Table 4. Abbreviations

Abbreviation	Meaning
D&P	Decision making and problem solving
ER	Emotion regulation
C&I	Collaborating with and influencing others
FC	Facilitating change
S	Status
C	Certainty
A	Autonomy
R	Relatedness
F	Fairness

Table 5. Example of NASA Leadership Behaviors
(see appendix for complete Broad Themes and Observable Behaviors Framework)

Element	Representative Observable Behavior/Attribute
Leadership theme	
Develop employee capabilities (D&P) **(SCARF)**	• Provides resources, visible support, and encouragement for employees to develop knowledge, skills, and competencies. **Autonomy** • Identifies and encourages employees with talent, potential, and the ability to take a system-wide view to problem solving. **Certainty/Autonomy** • Provides employee work assignments and training opportunities that address critical developmental needs. **Certainty/Fairness** • Meets privately with employees to review performance and discuss work strategies. **Status/Relatedness** • Provides employees with constructive feedback on performance by exploring employees' thought and decision-making processes and helping them discover insights. **Autonomy** • Delivers corrective feedback on individual performance privately and in a manner that is objective and nonjudgmental. **Fairness/Relatedness**
Reduces distractions (ER) **(CR)**	• Deals personally with issues and problems that would otherwise be a source of distraction to project team members. Asks team members, "How can I help? What is getting in the way of your work?" **Certainty/ Relatedness** • Negotiates time and resource issues on behalf of project team members. **Certainty**
Attitudes and Attributes theme	
Lets go of current role to prepare for new one (FC) (ER) **(SA)**	• Intentionally chooses to move into leadership and to stop being technical expert. **Autonomy/Status** • Willing to relinquish familiar job functions and develop the skills and knowledge necessary to grow and advance to the next level of leadership. **Autonomy/Status**

Communication theme	
Strives for clarity and ensures understanding (C&I) **(CR)**	• Realizes that clarity is critical to providing facts in a way that ensures that understanding is reached. **Certainty** • Uses clear language to be sure everyone knows what is meant and has a shared understanding. **Certainty** • Compares and contrasts ideas (e.g., "if this then...if that then"). **Certainty** • Summarizes decisions and agreements at meetings. **Certainty** • Practices active listening. Solicits feedback to check that others receive messages that were transmitted. May ask staff to repeat in their own words what was said. When person is more senior, may check with that person's staff to ensure receipt of intended message. (HQ) **Certainty/ Relatedness** • Aligns verbal and nonverbal messages to ensure the meanings are clear and unambiguous. Ensures consistency between written charts and verbal communications. **Certainty** • Makes certain that meeting formats are consistent with their purpose (e.g., brainstorming, working an issue, information sharing, decision making, etc.). Ensures those in attendance know why they are there. **Certainty**
Problem Solving and Systems Thinking theme	
Finds connections and patterns (D&P) **(C)**	• Examines and explores the implications of the way technical decisions will affect the larger system architecture. **Certainty** • Observes system interfaces and the ripple effect of how changing requirements or how making a change to one element will affect other elements or the system. **Certainty** • Locates and corrects subsystem "disconnects" or "inconsistencies" that are having a negative impact on system performance. **Certainty**

Considers all options before deciding (D&P) **(CA)**	• Works to understand a problem from all perspectives. Actively seeks and weighs different perspectives. Open and willing to listen to multiple views. **Certainty/Autonomy** • Is highly inclusive, drawing on the full knowledge, skills, and experiences of the organization. **Certainty/Autonomy** • Considers all types of cost (e.g., technical, schedule, political, human, financial). **Certainty** • Identifies what will enable or inhibit the ability to accomplish goals. Looks at all aspects of the organizational system (e.g., facilities, budgets, policies, procedures, etc.). Asks: "What would happen if I did nothing?" "What is the worst thing that could happen?" **Certainty** • Understands there is always more than one solution. **Certainty/Autonomy** • Comes up with several solutions, defines the consequences of each and relates effects to managers and employees. **Certainty/Autonomy**
Political Savvy theme	
Knows how the political system works (D&P) **(SR)**	• Knows who makes decisions and what they need. Keeps up to date with new members of Congress and staff, and relies on NASA's Congressional experts to represent the agency in the best light. (HQ) **Status/Relatedness** • Has a keen sense of timing when opportunities arise. Understands how some opportunities are short-lived and quick action is needed. **Relatedness** • Knows how to present a design to show near-term gains that will meet current Administration and Congressional goals, while building on a longer-term accomplishment that might be realized over a number of Administrations. **Status/Relatedness**

Strategic Thinking theme	
Maintains an organization-wide view (D&P) **(CRF)**	• Ensures that NASA has a plan moving forward to maintain both the competencies and capabilities needed to be successful. **Certainty** • Intentionally selects people with different perspectives, talents, and knowledge to form a strong management team. **Certainty/Fairness** • Assimilates large amounts of information from across the agency. Makes decisions by keeping the big picture in mind. Considers all perspectives and proposed solutions before making a decision. **Certainty/Relatedness** • Balances decisions across programs and projects. **Fairness** • Works the larger agency-wide "trade space" to meet NASA's and the nation's highest priorities. Trades are made across missions and/or centers and may involve negotiations across federal agencies. **Fairness/Certainty**

Data analysis

The SCARF model allocations depict the perceptions that certain behaviors elicit, such as a sense of autonomy. The neuroleadership domains indicate the leadership behavior that was displayed to produce such a response. These are the behaviors that can be learned so as to engender the most conducive performance response in peers, subordinates, and the leaders themselves.

Table 6. SCARF and neuroleadership domains' frequency of appearance

Frequency of appearance		
SCARF	**No.**	**%**
Status	15	13
Certainty	41	37
Autonomy	17	15
Relatedness	30	27
Fairness	9	8
	112	

NL DOMAINS		
Decision making and problem solving	25	40
Emotion regulation	10	16
Collaborating with and influencing others	19	31
Facilitating change	8	13
	62	

As stated above, the behavior studies targeted NASA's high-performing executives with systems-engineering experience. The job of a systems engineer is to ensure that everything works together and to reduce the risk of failure.

The behavior studies targeted NASA's high-performing executives with systems-engineering experience.

Reducing risk and ensuring safety are paramount in NASA's high-risk environment; therefore, the fact that 37% of the leadership behavior in the SCARF model addresses the need for certainty is both expected and reassuring. Within NASA's leadership behavior theme of Problem Solving and Systems Thinking, close to 100% of the behaviors observed support a sense of certainty. These include:

- Thinks systemically and identifies and defines core issues/problems
- Actively probes for information and understanding
- Validates facts, information, and assumptions
- Acknowledges and manages uncertainty
- Remains open-minded and objective

Leadership theme behaviors—such as creates organizational structure, gauges resource needs to achieve mission objectives, acts decisively, and is aware of self and values—also support certainty. Within the Attitudes and Attributes theme, behaviors such as being patient and organized also strongly influence a certainty response. In addition, within the Communication theme, ensuring understanding and striving for clarity powerfully influence a sense of certainty, as do encouraging participation and leaders who link people, organizations, and ideas.

The second-highest SCARF perception identified in the leadership behaviors is relatedness, at 27%. All the work reflected in these studies is done in teams where relationships are essential, again an expected and encouraging outcome.

In the study "Executive Leadership at NASA: A Behavioral Framework," Williams et al. (2010) contend that the identified behaviors of highly effective NASA technical executives are mainly relational—an assertion that Boyatzis (2009) might agree with. In a *Journal of Management Development* special issue, he laid the theoretical groundwork for understanding competencies as a behavioral approach to emotional and social intelligence.

A large majority of the behaviors identified in the Political Savvy theme speaks to a perception of relatedness. This includes knowing how the political system works, having political staying power, managing multiple demands/opportunities, and providing historical perspective. In addition, many of these behaviors also address the need for certainty in the SCARF model.

It is interesting to observe that only 8% of observed behaviors associated with the SCARF model address the need for perceived fairness. This may perhaps be influenced by the culture of the organization or the nature of the work area observed. These results provide an opportunity for further investigation.

The plurality of behaviors assigned to the neuroleadership domains fall under decision making and problem solving, at 40%, with an additional 13% assigned to facilitating change. NASA's Leadership Development team sees a strong relationship between both of these areas and believes they require similar behaviors and skills. These behaviors logically fit under the themes of Leadership, Attitude and Attributes, and Problem Solving and Systems Thinking in NASA's leadership framework, whereas facilitating change lands firmly in the theme of Political Savvy.

Behaviors such as being patient and organized also strongly influence a certainty response.

There is also a connection between the neuroleadership domains and the SCARF model in that 31% of behaviors fall within the neuroleadership domain of collaborating and influencing others and 27% in the SCARF model's element of relatedness. Again, NASA's Leadership Development team confirmed these learnings as a trend it has observed in leaders, and it is promising to see this further confirmed by applying the neuroleadership domains and SCARF models to a live case study.

In this instance (and we are unsure if this is always the case), all leadership behaviors could be mapped to at least one of the SCARF elements and a neuroleadership domain. The nature of NASA as an organization is such that there is an overriding requirement for certainty, and, as this is so essential, it may be a reason for the dominance of this SCARF area. Similarly, sound decision making and problem solving is essential. It would be interesting to note the weighting of the SCARF elements in different types of organization.

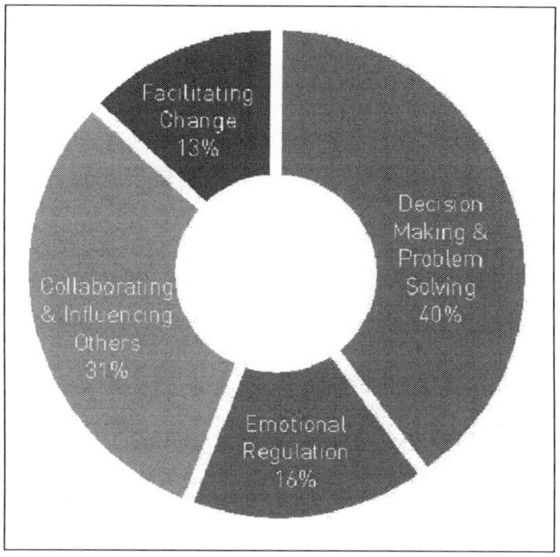

Chart 1. Neuroleadership domain percentages

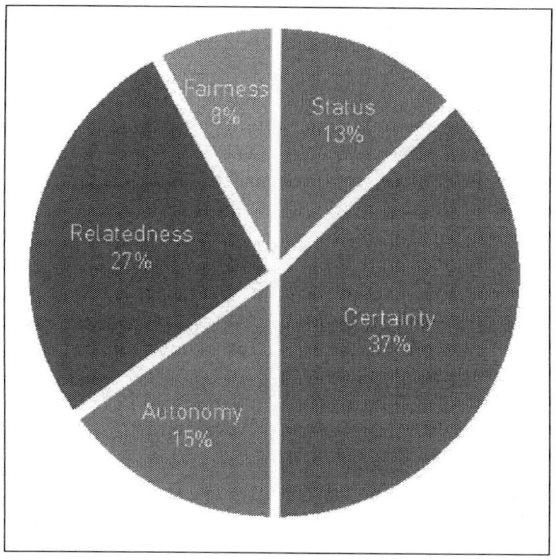

Chart 2. SCARF percentages

Discussion

The information harvested has aided in the development of leadership training initiatives that encourage the accelerated learning of these targeted and highly desirable skills and behaviors, creating proven future leaders for the organization. This framework provides a development and performance-management tool by means of which an individual's performance can be planned and tracked.

The behaviors cited in this study were seen to be effective in the NASA culture. These behaviors can be taught and used effectively in training situations, coaching, and mentoring, and have been incorporated into the NASA Systems Engineering Leadership Development Program (SELDP).

Taking a defined skill, such as communication, and breaking it down to what it specifically looks like when displayed well has been very effective. Seeing an actual behavior takes the guesswork out of the process. In the past, leaders might have been told, "You need to communicate more," and they would consequently have done more of what they already did, which may or may not be what was needed. Now leaders can be taught how to communicate. Since many of these behaviors are not what they do naturally, coaching and mentoring is helpful in providing practice and getting leaders comfortable with the new behavior.

The NASA Systems Engineering Behaviors Study formed the basis for a 360-degree assessment instrument that is used at the start of each program year. This assessment helps participants understand how extensively they are applying these effective systems-engineering behaviors. They then use the results of this assessment to identify areas for improvement, incorporating these into their coaching goals for the year.

Coaching and mentoring is helpful in providing practice and getting leaders comfortable with the new behavior.

Participants are also asked to take the SCARF assessment online to better understand what drives them personally, increasing awareness of any bias or blind spots. In the debrief of their SCARF results, participants discuss the systems-engineering behaviors in relation to the SCARF model to better understand those behaviors that motivate them and others. Participants also review behaviors that evoke the threat response and discuss the impact of that on productivity and creativity.

This brain-smart technique is only one of the many that the NASA SELDP has implemented. The idea was to change the way NASA provided information in order to help employees absorb and adopt it quickly. The goal was to work with, rather than against, people's biology.

Implications for designing learning activities

The NASA SELDP has not changed "what" but "how" leaders are trained and developed. In addition to the focus on behaviors, NASA has made other changes in the way it designed leadership development so as to align it to more recent neuroleadership learnings:

- In each element of the training, NASA explicitly connects the learning to what *it* has learned from the models, thus explaining how each piece is an extension of what was previously learned and how it fits together to create a learning system "picture" from a number of disconnected parts. Seeing the system has made it easier for participants to retain and use the information because they are not using cognitive short-term energy to learn something new each time. Using a systems approach that engineers are familiar with therefore makes for more effective retention and recall.
- Practice is paramount. NASA has participants read information that would normally be provided in a lecture ahead of time. The time with participants is then used to reintroduce the ideas and models and practice using the information or tools together. The idea is to push the information into long-term memory as quickly as possible through practice and in the process build relationships with classmates through the shared learning experience.
- At the start of the program, each participant is provided with a journal. Then, after a learning element has been completed, participants are given time to reflect and capture their ideas (insights) and identify their next steps.

- Sessions have been shortened, breaking elements down so they fit into 60–120-minute segments. This adds to participants' physical and mental comfort, thus relieving stress and enabling them to focus.
- Trainers facilitate solution-focused discussions, using coaching questions to shift the discussion from the problem to what could be. This change is intended to start focusing on capturing insights and designing a way forward, versus allowing the participants to get stuck in the problem.
- Relatedness is a central theme in the groundwork for each program, with significant time invested in participants getting to know each other. Discussions are focused on reinforcing the message that this is a practice field, a place to make all their mistakes and learn to improve (not a place where ego/status has a role). Participants are coached publicly to enhance trust in each other and reduce threat, which results in participants taking more chances and learning more quickly.
- Unsurprisingly, the threat response most common to engineers is the lack of certainty. This makes sense when appreciating that an engineer's world is focused on eliminating the unknown and thus reducing risk. As a result, an area that the program designers focus on is providing details, including schedules, processes, and program parameters. This has been found to help participants focus on the learning rather than worry about program logistics.

Trainers facilitate solution-focused discussions, using coaching questions to shift the discussion from the problem to what could be.

- The program has a number of elements that are common to everyone, but in two areas—developmental assignments and coaching— participants' individuality and unique needs are the primary focus. This is where their need for autonomy is addressed, and participants have a significant say in how these two elements are designed and executed. Coaching is based on a 360-degree assessment instrument that has been created from the effective behaviors identified.
- NASA also focuses on the actual physical learning environment. This includes a number of environmental factors, but the two that have shown to affect individuals' ability to focus are learning spaces with natural light (windows) and food that is "brain-friendly," including more protein, fewer carbohydrates, more water, and less coffee.

Lessons learned

The initial behavior study involved just 14 executives in one organization, NASA. Observation time with executives was limited, and observers were unable to see how all executives behaved in all relevant work situations. Accordingly, only those behaviors noted by all observers were included in the final report. Recently, a validation study of several hundred executives across the aerospace sector has been completed. This study, along with the other behavior studies noted above, can be found on the NASA website at http://www. nasa.gov/offices/oce/appel/seldp/resources/index.html.

Preliminary results from the validation study found that 80% or more of international technical leaders (including in government, industry, and nonprofit organizations) surveyed reported that the following seven behaviors were deemed important or very important (these behaviors are also highlighted in the appendix):

8. Develops employee capabilities (SCARF)(D&P)

21a. Strives for clarity (CR)(C&I)

38. Validates facts, information, and assumptions (C)(D&P)

41. Acknowledges and manages uncertainty (SC)(ER)

42. Remains open-minded and objective (CR)(ER)

50. Maintains organization-wide view (CRF)(D&P)

51. Manages near-term and long-term goals (CR)(D&P)

This would be a useful study to analyze further.

Implications for future research

Some key learnings from this study included the high need for certainty within NASA and the constant elimination of uncertainty—even more than was expected. It was also interesting to note that some behaviors crossed over multiple SCARF elements and NLDs. Moreover, some areas, such as innovation and creativity, seemed to be more complex to categorize. Questions to consider further include: Will different types of organizations emphasize different elements of SCARF? Will outcomes be similar for any organization? Are SCARF and the NLDs so generic that any leadership behavior could be linked to them? Could organizations use SCARF and the NLDs to prepare their leadership-development frameworks?

Will different types of organizations emphasize different elements of SCARF?

Conclusion

This case study has displayed how leadership behaviors can be successfully mapped to current neuroscience leadership models. Our aim has been to create a better understanding of the way leaders enable or inhibit employee performance and how these learnings can be incorporated into corporate training-development initiatives.

This purpose has been achieved by using the NASA Executive Leadership Behavior Framework as the focal point for comparison with both the SCARF model and the neuroleadership domains. The benefit of such an analysis is the identification of displayed leadership behaviors. The results of this analysis can be used to maximize employee reward-state response and improve productivity and organizational performance. Through training around models—for example, SCARF—and coaching and mentoring, more productive behaviors and greater organizational effectiveness can be achieved.

Acknowledgments

Thank you to the NASA executives and leadership team for being part of this case study and giving permission for the use of this data. In particular we would like to thank Dr. Michael Ryschkewitsch, NASA chief engineer, and Dr. Edward Hoffman, director of the NASA Academy of Program, Project, and Engineering Leadership. Also thank you to David Rock for the creation of NeuroLeadership and SCARF and to Annalise Roache for collaboration on the documentation of this initiative.

About the authors

Ruth Donde (MBA, BPharm) has extensive leadership experience across industry and corporate organizations. She is a global consultant, coach, and facilitator, and New Zealand regional director for the NeuroLeadership Group. She has conducted a number of wide-scale culture-change programs, and has written and presented papers at many global conferences. She is currently completing her studies in the neuroscience of leadership.

Christine R. Williams serves as the director of the NASA Systems Engineering Leadership Development Program. She also serves in the NASA Academy of Program, Project, and Engineering Leadership (APPEL). Her programs are considered world class, and she has been invited to speak internationally on the topics of leadership development, executive coaching, and the application of neuroscience to improving employee learning. Williams has a bachelor's degree in oceanography and a master's degree in organizational development and applied behavioral science.

References

Boyatzis, R. E. 2009. "Competencies as a Behavioral Approach to Emotional Intelligence." *Journal of Management Development* 28 (9): 749–770.

Fredrickson, B. 2009. *Positivity: Groundbreaking Research to Release Your Inner Optimist and Thrive*. Oxford, UK: Oneworld Publications.

Ringleb, A. H., and Rock, D. 2008. "The Emerging Field of Neuroleadership." *NeuroLeadership Journal* 1: 3–19.

Rock, D. 2008. "SCARF: A Brain-Based Model for Collaborating With and Influencing Others." *NeuroLeadership Journal* 1: 44–51.

Williams, C. R., Derro, M. E., Jarvis, M., and Morris, L. 2010. "Executive Leadership at NASA: A Behavioral Framework." *Executive Behavior Study-NASA* 3–24.

Appendix

Table 7. NASA Leadership Behaviors Table
(Note: Behaviors observed only in executives located at headquarters are noted by HQ.)

Element		Representative Observable Behavior/Attribute
Leadership theme		
1.	Creates organizational infrastructure (D&P) **(SCF)**	• Identifies the specific combination of skills, talents, and technical competencies required to achieve mission success. **Certainty** • Defines the roles and responsibilities of team members. **Status/ Certainty** • Assigns roles and responsibilities and evaluates performance based on team members' current capabilities and prior work experiences. **Fairness** • Designs and implements standard operating procedures that enable a smooth, consistent, and coordinated workflow. **Certainty**
2.	Gauges resource needs to achieve mission objectives (D&P) **(SC)**	• Identifies human, financial, and material resource requirements in consultation with subject matter experts and project owners. **Certainty/Status** • Ensures that mission goals and outcomes are achievable given available resources. **Certainty**
3.	Manages at the appropriate level (D&P) (C&I) (FC) **(SCAF)**	• Makes executive-level decisions, but delegates problem solving to the appropriate functional teams and system owners. **Autonomy/ Status** • Enables others to get work done. **Autonomy** • Holds others accountable for their assigned deliverables. **Autonomy/ Fairness** • Gathers information from stakeholders and experts at all levels when making decisions that can only be made at the executive level. **Autonomy** • Sets the context for decisions—the "what" and the "how." **Certainty**

4.	Accepts change and is resilient (MC) **(CA)**	• Demonstrates flexibility and responsiveness to changing priorities and critical needs. **Autonomy** • Monitors the environment for changes in required outcomes, critical assumptions, available resources, or other factors that could necessitate a change in strategy. **Certainty/Autonomy** • Adjusts direction, strategy, roles, responsibilities, and/or schedules to ensure critical organizational needs are met. **Certainty/Autonomy**
5.	Acts decisively (D&P) **(CA)**	• Identifies decisions that are critical, noncritical, and important to avoid. **Certainty/Autonomy** • Identifies and puts parameters around the amount of information needed to make a given decision. **Certainty/Autonomy** • Makes timely decisions based on experience, resource constraints, and available information. **Certainty**
6.	Inspires and motivates team members to perform at peak performance (C&I) **(SCARF)**	• Encourages team members to accept new challenges and perform to the best of ability in finding solutions to seemingly insurmountable problems. **Autonomy/Relatedness** • Promotes creativity and intelligent risk taking. **Autonomy** • Challenges others to ask questions and think "outside the box." **Autonomy** • Helps team members maintain a positive attitude and progress toward goals and outcomes when facing adversity while acknowledging threats and challenges. **Relatedness** • Monitors, tracks, and communicates progress. **Certainty** • Evaluates strategies on the basis of outcomes. **Fairness** • Publicly acknowledges team members' accomplishments and areas of expertise. **Status** • Provides informal praise (verbal, e-mail, thank you card, etc.) for individual and group accomplishments. **Status/Relatedness** • Provides appropriate formal rewards and recognition for good performance. **Fairness/Status**

7.	Builds trust and respects confidentiality (C&I) **(SCARF)**	• Trusts others' expertise and judgment. **Autonomy/Relatedness** • Re-evaluates assumptions, judgments, and strategies based on input from subject matter experts and stakeholders. **Fairness / Status** • Designs and implements communication processes that ensure the fair and objective evaluation of ideas and opinions. **Fairness / Certainty** • During individual and group discussions, identifies proprietary information and reaches agreement with participants on how the information should be managed. **Certainty/Relatedness**
8.	Develops employee capabilities (D&P) **(SCARF)**	• Provides resources, visible support, and encouragement to employees to develop knowledge, skills, and competencies. **Autonomy** • Identifies and encourages employees with talent, potential, and the ability to take a system-wide view of problem solving. **Certainty/ Autonomy** • Provides employee work assignments and training opportunities that address critical developmental needs. **Certainty/Fairness** • Meets privately with employees to review performance and discuss work strategies. **Status/Relatedness** • Provides employees with constructive feedback on performance by exploring employees' thought and decision-making processes and helping them discover insights. **Autonomy** • Delivers corrective feedback on individual performance privately, and in a manner that is objective and nonjudgmental. **Fairness/ Relatedness**
9.	Reduces distractions (ER) **(CR)**	• Deals personally with issues and problems that would otherwise be a source of distraction to project team members. Asks team members: "How can I help? What is getting in the way of your work?" **Certainty/Relatedness** • Negotiates on time and resource issues on behalf of project team members. **Certainty**

10.	Is aware of self and values (ER) **(SCR)**	• Knows personal strengths, limitations, and motivations. **Status** (because they rely on other's expertise where they are weak) • Knows when others need to be consulted. Understands that "getting it right" is always more important than "being right." **Certainty/Status** • Is aware that blind spots or biases might exist in own thinking and asks others to keep him/her aware of other perspectives. **Certainty/Status** • Adheres to a strong set of values that align with agency's mission and purpose. **Certainty/Relatedness** (knows where he/she stands and engages others with shared values) • Articulates values so others understand one's perspectives and positions. **Certainty/Relatedness**
11.	Develops self (D&P) **(SCAR)**	• Maintains basic working knowledge of technical disciplines. **Autonomy** • Maintains contact with current engineers and engineering projects. Seeks opportunities to interact with them and perform limited "hands-on" work. **Autonomy/Relatedness/Status** • Conducts benchmarking of engineering organizations performing cutting-edge engineering work and asks, "How do they do that?" **Autonomy/Certainty** (creating a way forward for the future) • Judiciously learns what is required in each new position and what it takes to be a successful government executive. Talks to and observes those who do the job best. **Certainty** • Develops a learning plan to gain the knowledge, skills, and abilities needed to be successful at each new level. **Certainty**
12.	Lets go of current role to prepare for new one (FC)(ER) **(SA)**	• Intentionally chooses to move into leadership and stop being a technical expert. **Autonomy/Status** • Is willing to relinquish familiar job functions and develop the skills and knowledge necessary to grow and advance to the next level of leadership. **Autonomy/Status**

Attitudes and Attributes theme		
13.	Remains inquisitive and curious (D&P) (C&I) **(A)**	• Has an ongoing passion for learning, enhancing knowledge, skills, and experience in both technical and nontechnical subjects. **Autonomy** (designing their own future) • Participates in a wide variety of formal and informal learning opportunities. **Autonomy** • Continually asks questions and probes for information. **Autonomy**
14.	Is patient (ER) **(SCA)**	• Understands that high-performing social and technical systems take time to develop. **Certainty** (managing expectations) • Manages and oversees key system functions, but allows other elements of the system to evolve and stabilize over time. **Autonomy** • Maintains commitment to chosen path or strategy, even when long-term results are not yet evident. **Certainty** • Is patient and open-minded when presented with new approaches or problem-solving strategies. **Status**
15.	Is organized (D&P) **(C)**	• Can manage large and complex systems, process extensive amounts of data, and rapidly explore the costs and benefits of a number of alternative strategies. **Certainty** • Effectively compartmentalizes, prioritizes, schedules, delegates, completes, and evaluates the outcome of activities associated with the executive role. **Certainty** • Makes full use of IT tools and technologies to help organize calendar and decisions. **Certainty**

Executive Presence (subtheme)		
16.	Displays self-confidence and courage (C&I) **(SCARF)**	• Exhibits confidence in technical knowledge, skills, and ability to lead and achieve goals. **Status** • Identifies the difficult issues, e.g., "the elephant in the room." **Certainty/Relatedness** • Is willing to be controversial. Fearlessly questions decisions even when in the minority or standing alone. Willing to disagree or push back on senior leadership. **Autonomy/Relatedness Status** • Is willing to make difficult decisions by listening to others and then acting as final arbiter. **Fairness**
17.	Remains calm under pressure (ER) **(CR)**	• Manages organizational pressures while maintaining team and organizational momentum by identifying the difficult issues and focusing on the solution. **Certainty/Relatedness** • Maintains perspective and a positive attitude in the face of adversity and avoids being defeated by setbacks by focusing on solutions. Holds the belief that "we will get past the problem, in the best way possible, to achieve the greater good." **Certainty/Relatedness**
18.	Is aware of how personal presence and behavior affects others (ER)(C&I) **(SAR)**	• Maintains a high degree of physical energy throughout the day. **Status/Relatedness** • Walks in with a no-nonsense style, e.g., "We have a job to do. Let's not waste time." Friendly, but to the point. **Status** • Is aware that others will tend to defer based on executive's position. Encourages others to state opinions in order to get the best solution. **Autonomy/Relatedness/Status** • Creates a safe environment that helps others feel comfortable by, for example, shaking hands, smiling, addressing people by their first names, referring to their previous work, showing humility, letting others take the lead, and engaging others by asking questions. **Relatedness**

Communication theme		
19.	Communicates throughout the organization (C&I) **(SCA)**	• Ensures important information is communicated to stakeholders throughout organization. **Certainty** • Communicates downward and laterally by disseminating information on priorities, interdependencies, impacts, and lessons learned. **Certainty/Autonomy** • Communicates appropriate amount and type of information upward. **Status** • Where appropriate, helps individuals and organizations gain access to information needed to perform their work effectively. **Autonomy**
20.	Tailors messages (C&I) **(SR)**	• Understands how different audiences interpret information. **Relatedness** • Expertly tailors and delivers messages to meet the needs of specific audiences such as the media, Capitol Hill, or other key stakeholders. **Relatedness/Status** • Can speak the language of multiple disciplines, i.e., finance, personnel, legal, etc. Consciously and continually learns to communicate with representatives from all functional areas. (HQ) **Relatedness** • Knows how to translate information on complex technical programs into nontechnical language. Talks to a congressional staffer in the language of Congress; talks to OMB staff in the language of the budget, etc. (HQ) **Relatedness** • Uses audience-appropriate analogies from discipline when speaking to engineers and analogies from home and office when communicating with nontechnical people. **Relatedness**

21.	a. Strives for clarity (C&I) (CR) b. Ensures understanding	• Realizes that clarity is critical to providing facts in a way that ensures that understanding is reached. **Certainty** • Uses clear language to be sure everyone knows what is meant and has a shared understanding. • Compares and contrasts ideas, e.g., "if this then...if that then." **Certainty** • Summarizes decisions and agreements at meetings. **Certainty** • Practices active listening. Solicits feedback to check that others receive the messages that were transmitted. May ask staff to repeat in their own words what was said. When person is more senior, may check with that person's staff to ensure receipt of intended message. (HQ) **Certainty/Relatedness** • Aligns verbal and nonverbal messages to ensure the meanings are clear and unambiguous. Ensures consistency between written charts and verbal communications. **Certainty** • Makes certain that meeting formats are consistent in their purpose, e.g., brainstorming, working an issue, information sharing, decision-making, etc. Ensures those in attendance know why they are there. **Certainty**
22.	Assesses context (ER) **(AR)**	• Knows when and how often to communicate. Assesses the context before speaking. Senses others' needs to argue a point, vent a frustration, solicit feedback, etc., and responds accordingly. **Relatedness/Autonomy** • Knows what the right level of communication is for each situation. Strikes the right balance in communicating what is needed, but not more. **Relatedness**

23.	Uses humor (C&I) **(R)**	• Uses humor to build rapport with individuals and groups and to reduce fear and anxiety among team members. **Relatedness** • Keeps the atmosphere light as appropriate when dealing with difficult or challenging issues. **Relatedness** • May joke, share personal or humorous anecdotes, or make self-effacing comments during or starting meetings. **Relatedness** • Smiles and remains energetic, animated, and attentive during discussions. **Relatedness**
24.	Practices effective speaking and listening skills (C&I) **(SCAR)**	• Continually demonstrates effective speaking and listening skills (e.g., turn-taking, paraphrasing, asking questions, etc.) to ensure a productive exchange of information and ideas. **Relatedness** • Listens effectively and gives individuals full attention. Ends conversations with a summary of actions, due dates, and who is responsible. **Relatedness/Certainty** • Sits back and lets the debate happen. Listens to all the various perspectives and then takes action. **Relatedness/Status/Autonomy** • Mentors others to help them become better communicators. Explains how others could potentially misinterpret an imprecise statement. **Relatedness/Status**
25.	Communicates through storytelling and analogies (C&I) **(R)**	• Uses personal experience, organizational stories, and analogies to explain challenges, issues, and situations. **Relatedness** • Uses historical references (e.g., Lewis and Clark and their scientific and research goals). **Relatedness** • Discusses the history of NASA (e.g., how the field centers came into being) to illustrate the importance of cultural differences and approaches. **Relatedness**

26.	Links people, organizations, and ideas (C&I) **(SC)**	• Makes transition from a program- or project-level systems engineer who concentrates on how technical systems interface to an executive who focuses primarily on how to get people to connect and work effectively together. **Status** of self • Establishes a common infrastructure and provides necessary resources. **Certainty** • Conducts effective meetings. Knows who should be at meetings (individuals/groups) and inquires about those who are missing. Avoids making final decisions until key stakeholders are available. **Certainty/Status** of others • Uses a variety of communication channels to maintain contact with individuals/groups throughout the day. Will track down experts mentioned in meetings to get their opinion on an issue. **Certainty/Status** of others • For important decisions requiring consensus, asks each stakeholder to confirm support and/or present objections until consensus is reached. **Certainty/Status** of others
27.	Encourages participation (C&I) **(SCARF)**	• Uses facilitation, coaching, and dialogue skills to ensure all opinions are solicited, points of view are shared, and everyone has the opportunity to participate. **Certainty/Fairness** • Asks open-ended questions, e.g., "What do you think?" vs. "Do you agree or disagree?" **Certainty/Status /Autonomy** • Uses authority (positional, expert, etc.) to facilitate the structure and flow of meetings to provide opportunities for all to participate. **Certainty/Fairness** • Senses when opinions are being suppressed; takes steps to solicit that input. **Certainty/Relatedness** • Avoids overusing e-mail or any one mode of communication. **Certainty/Relatedness**

28.	Seeks expert opinion (D&P) **(SAR)**	• Willing to admit what one does not know and seek out technical experts for their opinion. Openly says, "I don't know." **Status** • Intentionally identifies and builds networks of experts to call on. Takes time to determine the best expert for a particular problem. **Relatedness/Status** • Provides approaches, ideas, and strategies to help others reach their goal but leaves the decision to those responsible. Does not dictate solutions. **Autonomy**
29.	Builds consensus (C&I) **(CR)**	• Connects people, organizations, and ideas to build shared understanding and consensus by ensuring participation and buy-in. Ensures all stakeholders participate. **Relatedness** • Facilitates discussion. Listens to different perspectives and ensures everyone is heard. Will restate or rephrase a point someone has made to ensure that everyone understands what was said. **Relatedness/Certainty** • Keeps the conversation going until there is a convergence of ideas. **Relatedness** • Does not assume understanding. Summarizes agreements and ensures they are communicated. **Certainty** • Looks for common, unifying goals. Integrates perspectives into the big picture. Openly and honestly explains the rationale for moving in a given direction. **Relatedness** • Strategically builds and utilizes formal and informal networks. **Relatedness**

30.	Builds relationships through interaction (C&I) (R)	• Enjoys interacting and working with other people. Has very good interpersonal skills. **Relatedness** • Uses "We need to..." to correct someone rather than "You need to..." (HQ) **Relatedness** • Devotes a portion of conversations to nonwork issues. **Relatedness** • Stays focused on the individual/speaker and shows genuine interest. **Relatedness** • Rarely holds side conversations or lets BlackBerry be distractive. **Relatedness** • Strives to end meetings and conversations on an upbeat/positive note. **Relatedness**
31.	Demonstrates accessibility (ER)(C&I) **(SCARF)**	• Expresses availability to discuss issues, questions, and concerns. **Relatedness** • Has a strong focus on schedule and being available for important events. (HQ) **Status** of self • Gives people the time they need to explain the issue, tell their story, etc. Does not rush others. Does not show impatience. Willing to engage in hallway or parking lot conversations. **Relatedness** • Includes staff in meetings. Ensures anyone who wants to be included is included. **Fairness** • When issues are brought up, ensures actions are taken to address them. **Certainty** • Makes room on calendar to meet with others. Finds "15 minutes on calendar" for same-day meetings. Allows for drop-ins and responds positively. Creates a climate where people feel they are allowed to "drop by." **Relatedness/Status/Autonomy**

Problem Solving and Systems Thinking theme		
32.	Uses a systems perspective (D&P) **(C)**	• Uses systems thinking in strategy development and to see entire agency-wide system. **Certainty** • Applies systems engineering principles to mission/programs that have significant political, social, and economic implications. **Certainty** • Applies a systems perspective in the performance of executive roles and responsibilities. **Certainty**
33.	Thinks systemically (D&P) **(C)**	• Can look at a problem within multiple frameworks (e.g. "change of variables'). **Certainty** • Is able to look deeply into a problem while remaining focused on the big picture. Sees the big picture while demonstrating an overall awareness of the details. **Certainty** • Is able to look at all the pieces individually and collectively to meet program, mission, and agency-wide needs and to identify gaps and overlaps/duplications. **Certainty** • Sees multiview representations of systems to understand how the pieces fit together and interact. Visualizes systems in 3-D. Draws a picture in the mind or on paper. **Certainty** • Focused on developing a system that meets end-item product objectives and successfully integrates the system's parts into the whole. **Certainty** • Understands how the system works, what it was designed to do, its functions and requirements. **Certainty** • Looks across the entire system and facilitates trades and compromises to get a balanced design. **Certainty** • Recognizes what is technically right among many good ideas by viewing a problem across system boundaries and comparing each design to others. **Certainty**

		• Thinks about how components were designed to interact and what other interactions could occur that were not considered in the design. **Certainty** • Is able to analyze the system's data. Traces implications of a problem in a step-by-step manner across the system. **Certainty** • If having difficulty understanding a scenario, finds a different vantage point that offers a fresh perspective. **Certainty**
34.	Identifies and defines core issues/problems (D&P) **(C)**	• Spends time up front to ensure that self and others understand, frame, and define the problem. **Certainty** • Identifies the real issue/problem (whether technical, infrastructure, administrative, executive resource, or other) by asking questions and identifying the key requirements. **Certainty** • Confirms that the problem is identified. (For example, asks: "Are we solving the right problem?" "Has the correct problem been identified?" "Have we defined the problem properly?" "Do we understand the problem?" "Do we understand the constraints?") **Certainty**
35.	Actively probes for information and understanding (D&P) **(C)**	• Seeks to understand all aspects of a challenge. **Certainty** • Probes for crucial and critical information that may be missing. **Certainty** • Considers all proposed solutions/perspectives before making a decision. **Certainty** • Continues to question thinking and extract data until all issues have been addressed and there is shared understanding. Asks questions such as: "What is the measure of goodness?" "What has not been looked at?" "Why?" "Does it still make sense?" **Certainty**

36.	Finds connections and patterns (D&P) **(C)**	• Examines and explores the implications of how technical decisions will affect the larger system architecture. **Certainty** • Observes system interfaces and the ripple effect of how changing requirements or how making changes to one element will affect other elements or the system. **Certainty** • Locates and corrects subsystem "disconnects" or "inconsistencies" that are having a negative impact on system performance. **Certainty**
37.	Assimilates, analyzes, and synthesizes data and information (D&P) **(C)**	• Approaches and solves problems in a systematic manner by using tools, processes, and procedures in order to find solutions. **Certainty** • Ensures decisions made are supported with data. Assimilates and distills large quantities of data from across the organization and ensures all of the data is on the table to solve a problem or make a decision. **Certainty** • Breaks data into smaller pieces or parameters, prioritizes, then synthesizes to reach an answer or solution. **Certainty** • Determines how to put together all available information in a way to rigorously test mathematically or physically that the problem is adequately understood. **Certainty**
38.	Validates facts, information, and assumptions (D&P) **(C)**	• Questions all assumptions that go into a design. **Certainty** • Anticipates and looks for problems or issues in the system. Knows where data is missing/needed. **Certainty** • Recognizes that seemingly minor miscalculations can lead to significant problems in system performance. **Certainty** • Identifies system elements that lack metrics or have metrics that are misleading. **Certainty** • Recognizes that data has limitations and does not rely on it as the only source of information. **Certainty**

39.	Considers all options before deciding (D&P) **(CA)**	• Works to understand a problem from all perspectives. Actively seeks and weighs up different perspectives. Open and willing to listen to multiple views. **Certainty/Autonomy** • Is highly inclusive, drawing on the full knowledge, skills, and experiences of the organization. **Certainty/Autonomy** • Considers all types of costs (e.g., technical, schedule, political, human, financial). **Certainty** • Identifies what will enable or inhibit the ability to accomplish goals. Looks at all aspects of the organizational system, e.g., facilities, budgets, policies, procedures, etc. Asks: "What would happen if I did nothing?" "What is the worst thing that could happen?" **Certainty** • Understands there is always more than one solution. **Certainty/Autonomy** • Comes up with several solutions, defines consequences of each and relates impacts to managers and employees. **Certainty/Autonomy**
40.	Identifies, assesses, and manages risk (D&P) **(C)**	• Understands that managing risk is an ongoing process. Asks probing questions to ensure risks have been adequately explored. **Certainty** • Uses past experiences to anticipate potential problems that may affect the system. Identifies worst-case scenario and works from that point back. **Certainty** • Focuses on identifying and assessing risks by creating plans for dealing with those risks effectively. Identifies key indicators and methods of testing for each type of problem. **Certainty** • Applies and demands sufficient rigor in the application of analytical processes. **Certainty** • Develops mitigation strategies for addressing problems, should they arise. **Certainty**

41.	Acknowledges and manages uncertainty (ER) **(SC)**	• Works to remove as much uncertainty as possible by questioning everything. **Certainty** • Analyzes failures (what went wrong) and successes (what went right). **Certainty** • Ensures lessons learned are captured. **Certainty** • Lets others know of own willingness to be comfortable with uncertainty. **Certainty** • Openly and honestly discusses personal and programmatic successes, failures, and lessons learned. **Certainty/Status**
42.	Remains open-minded and objective (ER) **(CR)**	• Receptive to hearing diverse and dissenting opinions. Is willing to rethink/rework an issue or to change direction when new information or a better idea is presented. **Certainty/Relatedness** • Evaluates decisions objectively. Maintains flexibility by avoiding attachment to a particular strategy or point of view. **Certainty**
43.	Uses creativity in solving problems (D&P) **(CA)**	• Possesses passion for problem solving and takes initiative to solve problems. Enjoys and is energized by fully concentrating on a problem for long stretches, until solutions are formed and implemented. **Certainty/Autonomy** • Does not adhere to rigid rules or formulas for system design, but may create new ideas and approaches that are necessary to deal successfully with system constraints. **Autonomy** • May use intuition and past experiences to solve problems. Supplements traditional problem-solving strategies with those that are creative and nonlinear. **Certainty**

44.	Draws on past experience (D&P) (C&I) **(CA)**	• Knows good intuition is based on experience and works to expand that experience. **Certainty** • Uses experience, history, intuition, and sensing to assess situations and develop solutions. **Autonomy/Certainty** • Draws on past successes and failures to develop the proper approach. Knows when something looks right. **Autonomy** • Solves problems with a balance of innovative developments and proven heritage products. May rely on experience and existing design as guides, but sees each opportunity as a canvas to design new solutions. **Autonomy**
Political Savvy theme		
45.	Knows how the political system works (D&P) **(SR)**	• Knows who makes decisions and what they need. Keeps up to date with new members of Congress and staff and relies on NASA's Congressional experts to represent the agency in the best light. (HQ) **Status/Relatedness** • Has a keen sense of timing when opportunities arise. Understands how some opportunities are short-lived and quick action is needed. **Relatedness** • Knows how to present a design to show near-term gains that will meet current Administration and Congressional goals, while building on a longer-term accomplishment that might be realized over a number of Administrations. **Status/Relatedness**
46.	Has political staying power (FC) **(R)**	• Able to maintain momentum over many years and several Administrations. Quickly learns the priorities of new Administrations and effectively communicates how NASA is meeting those needs. **Relatedness** • Assesses the current political agenda to determine the likelihood of obtaining the budget needed. Assesses the political and budget realities in context of the design, requirements and potential trades. **Relatedness**

47.	Represents/promotes organization's programs across the political spectrum (FC) **(CR)**	• Understands and effectively communicates with government leadership on how programs meet agency and national needs. (HQ) **Relatedness** • Explains consequences and implications of NASA decisions and how the Administration and Capitol Hill may interpret the agency's actions. Helps others understand what the Administration is looking for so they can work more effectively within those constraints. (HQ) **Relatedness** • Explains the probable reactions of NASA's stakeholders to decisions that are made or put on hold. **Relatedness** • Is responsive to upper management's needs. Sends notes, calls, and updates as activities occur and issues emerge. **Relatedness** • Meets commitments in order to gain credibility and trust. Only makes commitments that NASA can meet. **Relatedness** • Lets Administration/Congress know when problems arise; notifies them early. (HQ) **Relatedness/Certainty**
48.	Manages multiple demands/opportunities (FC) **(CR)**	• Balances the needs and political interests of internal and external stakeholders, weighing what is best for the program against what is best for the agency. Makes decisions based on what is best for both. **Certainty/Relatedness** • Considers effects of executive decisions and actions on organizations inside and outside NASA before taking action. **Certainty/Relatedness** • Continually monitors these decisions and makes course corrections to meet high-priority goals and objectives. **Certainty** • Asks, "What is my boss and what is the Administration worried about?" **Relatedness** • Is aware of what is important to the NASA administrator and other key players, and keeps them informed. **Relatedness**

49.	Provides historical perspective (FC) **(CR)**	• Knows it is important for those inside and outside the agency to know NASA's history. **Relatedness/Certainty** • Helps others see and understand the historical progression of strategies and decisions. Is mindful that NASA has a wealth of lessons learned and is always working to ensure that the agency does not repeat mistakes. **Relatedness/Certainty**
Strategic Thinking theme		
50.	Maintains an agency-wide view (D&P) **(CRF)**	• Ensures that NASA has a plan moving forward to maintain both the competencies and capabilities needed to be successful. **Certainty** • Intentionally selects people with different perspectives, talents, and knowledge to form a strong management team. **Certainty/Fairness** • Assimilates large amounts of information from across the agency. Makes decisions by keeping the big picture in mind. Considers all perspectives and proposed solutions before making a decision. **Certainty/Relatedness** • Balances decisions across programs and projects. **Fairness** • Works the larger agency-wide "trade space" to meet NASA's and the nation's highest priorities. Trades are made across missions and/or centers and may involve negotiations across federal agencies. **Fairness/Certainty**

51.	Manages near-term and long-term goals (D&P) **(CR)**	• Keeps the end state in mind while managing day-to-day activities. **Certainty** • Continually looks at near-term activities and assesses how they may affect long-term results. **Certainty** • Proactively anticipates and positions the organization years in advance. Focuses on five years and beyond. **Certainty/Relatedness** • Sets a path and has the ability to stick to that path for an extended period of time. **Certainty** • Is mindful of the critical timing of issues (e.g., "We have 12 hours to make this decision."). Will sometimes define decisions in terms of "shelf-life." **Certainty**
52.	Understands the broad implications of activities at multiple levels (D&P) **(CR)**	• Understands where NASA's mission connects to the missions of other federal agencies and foreign nations. Considers them potential partners, collaborators, and in some cases customers. **Certainty/ Relatedness** • Seeks to build and maintain connections and partnerships. Shares information and communicates on shared goals and projects. **Relatedness**
53.	Monitors the environment (D&P) **(CR)**	• Monitors the environment outside NASA to understand national and international priorities and issues that will have an impact on agency goals and missions. **Certainty/Relatedness** • Works to understand larger government-wide issues and problems and finds ways in which NASA's work can help solve these issues and problems. **Certainty** • Works with other federal agencies to leverage overall federal program investments (e.g., maturing another agency's technology for use in NASA's programs). **Certainty**

54.	Uses networks (C&I) **(CR)**	• Builds and uses informal networks to validate and gain additional information. **Relatedness** • Looks to many different sources to be sure issues are covered and there are no surprises. **Certainty** • Connects organizations and individuals that need to be connected to accomplish goals. **Relatedness** • Probes and tests assumptions by reaching out to individuals on the periphery. Uses the "fringe" (individuals outside of a program or project team but aware of issues and able to lend support) to gain information, test assumptions, and assess the size and scope of issues and problems. **Relatedness**

SECTION V: Facilitating Change

23. Turn the 360 around

Phil Dixon, Dr. David Rock, and Dr. Kevin Ochsner
Phil Dixon, Consultant
phildixon1@mac.com

David Rock, CEO, NeuroLeadership Group, New York, USA
Faculty, CIMBA
Director and Cofounder, NeuroLeadership Institute; Editor, *NeuroLeadership Journal*
davidrock@neuroleadership.org

Kevin Ochsner, Department of Psychology, Columbia University, New York, USA
ochsner@psych.columbia.edu

Turn the 360 around

"Bill should let go of the details and lead the 'big picture.'"

"Jessica can sometimes be too frank and rub people up the wrong way."

These are real examples of feedback recently given to managers. Performance reviews and 360-degree feedback processes, jointly referred to as feedback interventions (Kluger and DeNisi 1996), are widespread in Western corporations. Research data varies, but perhaps as many as 95 percent of Fortune 2000 companies use feedback interventions (Edwards and Ewen 1998). There are numerous processes, systems, and training programs specifically developed for how to give feedback effectively. Feedback interventions consume a significant amount of time, energy, and money and create anxiety, both for the giver and the receiver. Leaders and managers the world over shudder when they hear the phrase "annual performance review season," as they anticipate their organization almost grinding to a halt.

Organizational feedback interventions have four main objectives. These objectives are separate, but often linked.

First, feedback may be for talent-management purposes. In this instance, the organization seeks to identify patterns in the talent pool, looking for people who should be promoted and for those who should be removed from the organization. This might be an informal process or a more formal "forced-ranking" system such as the one GE and many other companies installed at the end of the last century (Blume et al. 2006). This kind of feedback may be used to determine people's performance, to assist in calculating an annual bonus from an incentive pool, to determine salary increases, and so forth.

A second objective involves an employee who is seen as underperforming or who has significant behavioral issues. In this context, feedback is often given within a legal framework to be able to terminate a person's employment or to give that person "fair warning" that his or her job is in peril if performance doesn't improve.

The past fifty years have seen a wide debate about whether feedback actually gives rise to improvement in performance...

A third objective of feedback interventions is developmental—that is, to help individuals improve their performance. This may be an annual event, part of a leadership or other development program, or a one-off feedback event to help with an individual's growth.

Lastly, feedback interventions are an inherent part of most companies' periodic performance-review processes.

While the ideas we present here have relevance to all four feedback objectives, we are going to focus primarily on the third one, where feedback is given to improve an individual's performance through a change in his or her behavior.

Although, according to Atwater and Waldman (1998), feedback interventions are "one of the most notable management innovations of the 1990s," their value and efficacy have yet to be proven. The past fifty years have seen a wide debate about whether feedback actually gives rise to improvement in performance or whether it has a neutral, or even a negative, impact. Each "side" cites examples that "prove" their case, but it is difficult to reach a definitive conclusion.

The current concept of performance feedback appears to have taken root in the late nineteenth and early twentieth centuries, with Arps (1917) being an example of an early paper. In the first half of the twentieth century, most of the papers seem to endorse the efficacy of performance feedback, culminating in Ammons's (1956) meta-analysis indicating that feedback interventions had a positive effect. By the late 1950s, however, the debate about the value of feedback was gaining traction (e.g., Kelly 1958; McGregor 1957; Meyer, Kay, and French 1965).

In a seminal meta-analysis, Kluger and DeNisi (1996) reported that feedback interventions, on average, improve performance only 41 percent of the time and make matters worse 38 percent of the time. Later (DeNisi and Kluger 2000) they illustrated that doubts about the positive relationship between feedback and performance have been around for a considerable time and questioned why the inconsistencies weren't more widely known. They surmised that most researchers rested their hypotheses on Ammons's (1956) paper, which they now called into question. They added that "subsequent findings that were inconsistent with (Ammons) were largely dismissed as flukes or the result of poor research design" (130). They believe the value of feedback and its positive link to performance has become widely, but incorrectly, accepted, primarily as a result of the wide acceptance and citations of Ammons's paper.

So how much is this potentially wasteful effort costing corporations? Direct, specific financial estimates on the amounts currently spent on feedback interventions are difficult to ascertain, especially given the recent economic climate and associated cutbacks. It is also unclear in the available research whether reported costs include internal costs, such as lost time and psychological costs. With regard to overall management and leadership development, Avolio and Hannah (2008), citing *Training Magazine*'s "Industry Report" (2007), state that corporations, in America alone, spend $12 billion on management and leadership development. It is reasonable to assume that a significant percentage of this amount is spent on feedback interventions of some sort. At the organizational level, Watson Wyatt (2002) carried out a study of over 750 large North American companies addressing the impact of their HR practices. This study throws "a cautionary flag in front of some conventional practices." See in particular:

> Multisource feedback continues to enjoy mass popularity, and many, if not most, businesses report that they feel it is successful. *Yet, when the impact on market value for evaluating superiors and evaluating peers is combined, our research suggests it is linked to a decrease of 10.6%.* The truth is that it is a challenge to get multisource feedback right. It succeeds when an open culture is already in place. It succeeds when participants have been well trained to give and receive feedback. It succeeds when there is valid and reliable instrumentation and appropriate follow-up. When one or more of these elements is missing, multisource feedback can be a lengthy distraction that interferes with teamwork and reduces productivity and, ultimately, shareholder value. (10; emphasis added)

"Multisource feedback continues to enjoy mass popularity, and many, if not most, businesses report that they feel it is successful."

According to Hogan (2007), organizational climate surveys routinely show that about 75 percent of working adults report that the most stressful aspect of their job is their immediate boss. Further, while exact differences vary across different studies over the past twenty-five years, they predict that between 40 percent and 70 percent of managers will fail through incompetence and that a large portion of these failures are due to "overriding personality defects" (Hogan, Hogan, and Kaiser 2010). One would think that the feedback systems in place in many corporations are intended to correct some of these personality defects and reduce the employee stress factor. When examined closely, however, there are two inherent conundrums in most feedback processes. The first concerns the focus of the feedback. DeNisi and Kluger (2000) warn that feedback directed at the behavioral (or self) level is likely to be ineffective. Indeed, most treatises on feedback recommend that the focus should be "problem oriented rather than person oriented" (e.g., Smither and Walker 2004). Yet the self, according to Hogan et al. (2010), is exactly where the change is required.

The second conundrum is with regard to the content of the feedback. Feedback comes primarily in two forms: quantitative and qualitative (the latter is also referred to as narrative feedback). While much of the literature addresses the quantitative aspects, overall there has been little attention to the narrative aspects of feedback. Smither and Walker (2004, reporting on work by Ferstl and Bruskiewicz) suggest that recipients pay more attention to narrative comments than to quantitative data and indicate surprise at how little attention has been paid to narrative comments. Brutus (2009) states, "There is an overall lack of consideration for narrative comments in performance appraisal research." Recent studies (Dixon and Underwood 2010) indicate that 66 percent of narrative comments regarding behavioral-change requests were oriented to the self—exactly the sort that DeNisi and Kluger (2000) suggest don't work!

"There is an overall lack of consideration for narrative comments in performance appraisal research."

Dalton (1996) and Ashford, Blatt, and VandeWalle (2003) warn that we should not be cavalier about feedback as it "may well strike at the very core of a person's identity" (Dalton 1996) and "Feedback is not like any other information. As information about self, it is more emotionally charged." (Ashford, Blatt, and VandeWalle 2003). Rock adds another dimension by likening the statement "Let me give you some feedback" to "the feeling that one gets when walking down a dark alley and hearing footsteps behind you." (Rock 2009). "Hence it is crucial to provide conditions such that the feedback can be heard, and the likelihood of change increased." (Dalton 1996).

The issue of taking care during the feedback process is brought into focus when one considers the brain functioning involved. Feedback is often perceived as "threatening," because of our fundamental need to maintain a sense of "status" (Rock 2008). When status is threatened, we experience what is known as social pain (Eisenberger, Lieberman , and Williams 2003; Eisenberger and Lieberman 2004; Lieberman et al. 2007). Social pain, it turns out, lights up brain regions that are largely the same as physical pain (Lieberman and Eisenberger 2008). The threat of an attack on one's sense of self is construed by the brain's biology in a similar way to the threat of physical pain, which explains the strong reaction to criticism that people experience.

So the central conundrum of feedback is that on the one hand, the feedback content suggests the need to address the self and behavioral issues, and on the other hand, best practices tell us not to focus there! Part of this conundrum is that we don't have a good working model for successfully focusing on the personal issues that are so often the focus of feedback requests.

For a process that is so embedded in the corporate world, it still amazes us that there is little proof the feedback process is actually a valid approach. The only real result of the research to date is that one cannot say that feedback never works, only that it won't always work. (DeNisi and Kluger 2000). If feedback doesn't always work, if there are good indicators that it is unlikely to be effective, if it is unreliable, if we have no good methodology of predicting when and why it is effective, and if it can be shown to be linked to a decrease in shareholder value, then why do we continue using feedback in such a central fashion? Shouldn't we be looking at drastically changing the feedback process or replacing it with something completely different?

In this chapter, we will identify some models and approaches that may lead to some much-needed improvements in the feedback process and thereby increase its chances of success.

What neuroscience tells us about change

The presumed purpose of giving feedback is some form of sustained performance improvement, typically a change of behavior or a change of task focus. For such an improvement to take place, the recipient needs to be aware of the need for change (probably via some form of feedback intervention) and to then elect to do something different from what he/she has done in the past—whatever has been his/her habitual behavior. Thus, the recipient needs to be aware of and interrupt his/her normal pattern and replace it with something new—presumably something in line with the feedback that was given and subsequently heeded. In this section, we will look at this interruption and replacement process.

Without any form of feedback intervention, life for feedback recipients would continue as normal. They would respond to the world using their habitual patterns with most of their behavior guided by systems that operate fairly automatically outside of their conscious awareness. These are the systems of habit (e.g., Dickinson 1985; Poldrack et al. 2001). These habit systems are optimized to quickly analyze what people say, what is happening in the greater world, and what is perceived through all the sense organs, and to then match these data to patterns that have already been stored. In response, these habit systems trigger whatever sort of behavior seems to be appropriate based on that stored past experience. The term "habit" here refers to a whole sequence of thoughts or actions, or the habitual way of doing something that involves a coordinated series of behaviors and/or thoughts. Using this definition, driving is a habit, typing is a habit, and how you might think about something is a habit. In addition, an emotional response is an emotional habit—the particular way we interpret information from the world leads us to have a particular kind of emotion. The critical thing about this "habit system" is that it all happens outside of awareness and doesn't really require any conscious monitoring. It is surmised that this is what the brain has evolved to do best. The brain didn't evolve to do best at conscious, deliberate thought; it evolved to do best at taking everything it could outside of awareness and make it as habitual, automatic, effortless, and seamless as possible—and it is very good at doing so. The brain is good at sensing a pattern and acting in a habitual way toward that pattern.

The brain didn't evolve to do best at conscious, deliberate thought...

The good news is that we are capable of interrupting this habit system. The brain has also evolved a large prefrontal cortex (PFC), which is able to exercise "top-down" control over this habit system so that it can deliberately control behavior. That's the good news. The bad news is that while the PFC is very powerful, it is very capacity-limited and easily disrupted. It will forget to do this task of interruption, and if the individual is stressed, hungry, low on sleep, or debilitated in any way, the PFC's ability to focus and interrupt is reduced even more. Thus, relying on this "top-down" mechanism to interrupt and impose a change of behavior is a risky strategy at best. Furthermore, to be at all effective with this intervention strategy, the feedback preceding the identified change needs to be delivered proximally to the behavioral act in question—that is, if someone is perceived to behave in a manner that needs improvement, then any feedback needs to be given very soon after the behavior or else the impact is lost. The current manner in which feedback is given in the corporate world makes this proximity unlikely. No doubt Bill and Jessica's behavior, which resulted in the feedback comments at the beginning of this chapter, occurred days, weeks, or months before this feedback was given.

In addition, the "habit system" has evolved to resist change; it takes the long view and regards individual "change requests" as likely to be anomalies and, as such, best ignored. The habit system learns and changes slowly and uses a long-lasting representation of what behavior should be adopted for the vast majority of times.

Hence, we have two systems with different strengths that are almost in opposition: first, a highly reliable, efficient, experience-driven, habit system that controls behavior automatically most of the time, and second, a "top-down" intervention system that is very powerful but easily distracted.

Expecting change through feedback

In general, we assume that giving feedback will initiate a change in the recipient. Indeed, "managers typically assume that providing employees with feedback about their performance makes it more likely that performance on the job will be improved" (DeNisi and Kluger 2000). All other things being equal, however, the two-system model outlined above will tend to ensure that old behaviors based on old habits continue. But the feedback-change link gets even more tenuous. Many more aspects of receiving feedback, compounded, make it even less likely that change will occur. Let's now examine the act of giving feedback.

> *Research has shown that it is significantly more difficult for people to self-regulate when they are in a threat state...*

Widely held are views that (a) people want to know how they are performing, and (b) the best way of letting them know is through feedback. It is common experience, however, that the feedback conversation is a difficult one to have, from both the deliverer's and the recipient's perspectives. It is easy for people to feel threatened when receiving feedback. In fact, we may have drastically underestimated the degree to which this threat is experienced. The threat response tends to take over, and the recipient typically responds to the threat defensively, rather than in a "what could I do differently" way. Research has shown that it is significantly more difficult for people to self-regulate when they are in a threat state (Rock 2009), and as a result, they will tend to resort to the habit system described above. In short, in the threat state, there is increased functioning in the brain of automatic motor function regions and decreased resources for high-cognitive functions. Also, in a threat state, people accidentally class information as threatening even when it is not and err on the side of withdrawing and not taking risks (Rock 2009).

Rock (2008) proposed the five-dimension SCARF® (Status, Certainty, Autonomy, Relatedness, and Fairness) model as a way of looking at these types of processes. We can use this model to examine the setup of a feedback conversation and the feedback conversation itself. Let's take a typical feedback situation, that of a performance review for Bill, one of the examples from the beginning of this chapter. Frequently, the prelude to such an event might go something like this: "Hey, Bill. It's time for your performance review. Let's meet in my office at two p.m. tomorrow, and I'll give it to you." Each of the five SCARF components has immediately been thrust into the threat state:

- The boss stating that there will be a review will raise Bill's status threat level because of the potential for a drop in his status. Just speaking to someone of higher status tends to create a threat response on its own. If the higher-status person provides information that makes someone look bad, a strong threat response can result.

- As a recipient, Bill has little knowledge of what to expect of the feedback process, and hence the certainty dimension is also in a threat state. He doesn't know about the nature of the upcoming feedback, so he wouldn't know if his job might be on the line or if the feedback will be insignificant.
- Bill has been given little or no input into the situation; hence, the autonomy dimension is also in threat. He has no say in when, where, or how the feedback has been collected or is being delivered.
- The relatedness dimension is possibly threatened because Bill's brain now perceives the boss as a foe. Additionally, knowing that others may have given feedback about him without him knowing, he may now class his peers as potential foes as well.
- Fairness issues are common in performance interventions, with people comparing themselves with others, so the fairness dimension could also be threatened.

Rock has also proposed the idea of the multiplier effect with SCARF. The multiplier effect occurs when individual threats—say, to status—are significantly increased if there are threats in other domains. So if feedback is being given that attacks someone's status, the threat response is going to be amplified if there is uncertainty and no autonomy, for example. The same attack on status, certainty, and autonomy will be worse again if there is no sense of relatedness between the giver and receiver of feedback. (Note: The multiplier effect is a hypothesis that is yet to be studied formally in the lab but from observations of behavior, appears to have validity.)

Now let's take a look at the conversation itself: "Hi, Bill. Take a seat. This shouldn't take us long, as I'm sure we both want to get this over with. I've spoken with a number of people, and there are several things we should focus on, but one that every one agrees on is that, for your position, you need to focus less on the detail and more on the big picture."

If we review this part of the conversation through the SCARF lens, then even within this brief monologue, the manager has again sent most, if not all, of the SCARF components into red alert.

- Status is in the threat state, partly as a result of Bill being reviewed as outlined above, but additionally with the dismissive way that his boss treats the review—as though it is not important and hence shouldn't take long.
- Certainty is also in the threat state, as Bill has no information about what is about to happen.
- Autonomy is also in the threat state, as Bill has had zero control over the process and zero control over what happens next.

- Relatedness will still be threatened, as the boss has done nothing to lessen Bill's internal but unconscious view of his boss as foe.

- Fairness is in the threat state, as Bill most likely feels that the whole process is unfair.

In a threat state, we act defensively and are not likely to agree with statements that make us look bad.

In a threat state that is overwhelming, someone receiving feedback is likely to discard the feedback as not being relevant to themselves. In a threat state, we act defensively and are not likely to agree with statements that make us look bad. For most of us, in such situations, the threat state is so activated that it is virtually impossible to learn—which is the whole point of the feedback. So one of the central challenges of feedback is that in many situations, people don't get to the first base of recognizing and accepting that there is a habit to change. Given that feedback interventions themselves create strong threats, someone giving feedback needs to be able to reduce these threats somehow. This brings us to the idea of the "offsetting effect," the flipside of the multiplier effect. Rock proposes that a threat response may be reduced by activating rewards in other domains to offset that threat. A common example is in a crisis: when certainty decreases, people tend to want to connect with others more, to increase their sense of relatedness, reducing the overall threat.

So if someone is feeling a status threat, it might be reduced by increasing their sense of autonomy, such as giving them aspects of a feedback session that they can make choices about: when and where it is held, for example, or who to get the feedback from. These small changes appear to help. You may not be able to reduce the status threat directly, but you might be able to offset the threat by focusing on creating the perception of reward in another SCARF domain.

There are deep-rooted, biological reasons why behavior and habit change are difficult.

Clearly, there are deep-rooted, biological reasons why behavior and habit change are difficult. It is also clear that our current approach of feedback/goal setting isn't bringing about the performance changes we are looking for. Another strategy needs to be invoked in order to provide a better mechanism for inducing change.

How to improve the chances of change

Let's assume that Bill has had a feedback session during which the SCARF domains were handled sufficiently well that Bill has been able to regulate his threat response enough to hear the need for a change in his behavior. Using the Transtheoretical construct (Prochaska, DiClemente, and Norcross 1992) for the stages of change—precontemplation, contemplation, preparation, action, maintenance, and termination—let's also assume that Bill is "ready" for the suggested change and has decided to take action.

In this case, for Bill to change behavior, he needs to develop a real intention to change. Gollwitzer (1993) refined the concept of "goal intentions" (e.g., Bill: "I am going to increase my focus on the big picture.") by adding in the concept of "implementation intentions" (e.g., Bill: "If I find myself distracted by details, I will ignore the distraction.") Gollwitzer et al. in many studies (e.g., 1993; 1997; 1999) suggested implementation intention as a method for increasing the chance of an individual achieving a goal or acting on an intent to change.

It is difficult for people to remember and identify in the moment that they should regulate and to recognize that this is the moment to implement their intention (in Bill's case, to not get into the details). Gollwitzer suggests that in addition to creating a goal statement, they should also create a statement in an "if-then" format: "If I am in circumstance *x* then I should do *y* in order to achieve goal *z*." In this statement, they specify the moment when they need to become aware—that's the "if" part; in other words, "Under these circumstances, I will..." The statement follows with a description of what the person should do when encountering that situation: "then I should do the following"—which is the "then" part. Gollwitzer has shown that, compared with holding only goal intentions, holding implementation intentions proves to be significantly more effective. By forming an implementation intention, the mental image of the specified situation or cue becomes highly activated and more readily accessible (Gollwitzer 1999). Gollwitzer refers to the process as "instant habit." He has also shown this increase in effectiveness is true in a variety of different situations. In addition, it also turns out to be effective, even if the individual doesn't remember that he or she was supposed to be doing this self regulatory act—that is, once the situation occurred, the response was immediate (Gollwitzer and Brandstätter 1997) and without deliberate intent (Achtziger, Gollwitzer, and Sheeran 2008, referencing Bayer et al. 2007). The act of making the statement seems to help the brain automatically trigger the top-down control when it needs to trigger it and removes or lessens the burden for the person to be continuously monitoring their behavior to check whether they are supposed to be regulating. To the PFC, the constant monitoring is taxing and burdensome and is likely to be quickly forgotten and taken over by some other short-term goal. Indeed, Einstein et al. (2003) suggested that this effort is expensive in terms of resources, even in the short term, especially if the individual is frazzled, stressed, interrupted, or has other goals in mind.

Gollwitzer and Brandstätter (1997) suggested that implementation intentions had greater impact for difficult goals, as opposed to easy goals. Dewitte, Verguts, and Lens (2003) argued that the effect for easy goals and difficult goals depends on external circumstances, and suggested that for difficult goals, implementation intentions may not have any impact unless they specify *what* action needs to be taken, rather then when or where.

Achtziger, Gollwitzer, and Sheeran (2008) also showed that the efficacy of the implementation intention remains, even if the cue or situation is internally driven (e.g., desires, cravings, or fears) rather than external situations or cues. They indicated that by creating an if-then statement around "inner states as initiators of goal-shielding responses," people had a self-regulating strategy that could be used across a variety of external contexts. This eliminates the need to anticipate multiple kinds of external cues and situations to form an implementation intention.

Henderson, Gollwitzer, and Oettingen (2007) refined the implementation intention process yet further, and suggested that the "then" portion of the if-then statement has greater impact if it is an action-oriented statement ("I will change my approach") rather than a reflection-oriented statement ("I will think about the approach I am using").

Imagining an action is equivalent to actually carrying it out…

Dholakia, Bagozzi, and Gopinath (2007) suggested that the formation of an implementation plan (of which implementation intentions are just one of four variables) is just one strategy to facilitate successful goal pursuits. A parallel strategy is to remember actions that have been performed successfully in the past to accomplish similar goals. They highlight the fact that these two strategies use different cognitive bases: formulating intention plans requires future thinking, while remembering past actions involves retrospective memory, an activity that is less effortful than future thinking.

In an empirical study, Knäuper et al. (2009) suggested that refining the use of implementation intentions by adding mental imagery resulted in a yet greater impact in goal success. As a possible explanation of this improvement, they referred to a recent theory that imagining an action is equivalent to actually carrying it out because it activates the same area of the brain.

In translating these concepts to the business world, it appears that a combination of all these aspects might be appropriate: First, have the individual construct an if-then statement and review when similar efforts have been made in the past and what caused their success. This review, in turn, might inform and refine the if-then statement. Once formed, the individual might be encouraged to imagine him- or herself executing the if-then statement.

Some of the latest research suggests that how good people are at performing this if-then intervention in the very first moments predicts how successful they will be over a subsequent longer period. The combination of the raw top-down horsepower an individual has (i.e., their PFC's capacity and inhibitory control), together with the if-then implementation intention method for action follow-through, can be a powerful way of changing behavior.

If this proves to be true, then it starts to become clear that not every strategy will work for everybody and that there are real individual differences in the best way to address the likelihood of someone adopting a behavioral change. For some people, the top-down control doesn't work very well; they're either too anxious and distractible, or, for whatever reason, they're not good at it. Where this method is not suitable, giving the individual in-the-moment feedback is a strategy to encourage behavioral change. Other people may be frustrated by in-the-moment feedback, finding it too slow, annoying, and irritating, as they are very top-down (i.e., they have a lot of top-down control).

When would this if-then approach be most likely to work? Recent work in the field of emotion regulation can help shed some light. Gross (1998a; 1998b) proposed a five-stage process model of emotion regulation. His model identifies five strategies that can be differentiated along the timeline of an emotional response. At its broadest level, the model distinguishes between antecedent strategies and response-focused strategies. John and Gross (2003) argue that antecedent regulation strategies are more effective than response-focused strategies—that is, it is better to rethink and reappraise what's going on *ahead* of a possible emotional "event" rather than try to suppress it after it has happened.

Let's take a look at the four antecedent strategies, using the example of someone getting upset at a baseball game:

- Situation Selection: select situations, in advance, that minimize the chances of this emotional event of occurring (e.g., don't go to the game).
- Situation Modification: change the topic of conversation to steer away from the emotional event (e.g., go with friends and sit in a corporate box).
- Attention Deployment: choose a change of focus of attention (e.g., read a book).
- Cognitive Change: choose to reassess the underlying meaning of what is happening (e.g., look at it as a way of connecting socially).

Having received legitimate feedback, if someone has volitionally indicated the intention to change, one could combine the if-then approach with the five-phases concept and build a series of if-then statements focused on each of the five different phases. Using the two examples (Bill and Jessica) of feedback, we could work with them to construct if-then statements they could use in each of the four success-oriented phases. These if-then statements could be a mixture of those based on inner states and those based on external situations and cues.

SCARF points to ways to minimize threat in a feedback intervention...

Table 1. Possible implementation intention statements

Antecedent strategies		
	"Bill should let go of the details and lead the "big picture.'"	*"Jessica can sometimes be too frank and rub people up the wrong way."*
Situation Selection	"If I am invited to a meeting, then I will determine the agenda in advance and will only attend those that address the big picture."	"If I anticipate that I will be faced with the need to voice a strong opinion in a meeting, then I will adopt an alternative method of putting my opinion across."
Situation Modification	"If I am in a meeting and the conversation starts to focus on the detail, then I will suggest that we move on to the next topic."	"If a situation arises when I feel like being frank and stating my opinion, then I will respond by asking if there are any other ideas."
Attention Deployment	"If I start to feel that I should enter into the detailed discussion, then I will make a note of the fact in my notebook but not speak out."	"If I feel the need to be frank with my coworkers, then I will simply stop and count to ten—slowly."
Cognitive Change	"If the conversation turns to detail, then I will review in my mind whether we have covered all the big-picture items."	"If I find myself getting worked up, then I will give myself ten seconds to focus on my breath."

Summary

1. Feedback as it stands doesn't work for individuals or organizations at creating change. It chews up a lot of resources.
2. We propose that one reason for this is that a lot of the time, people don't get to the point of being willing to change—that is, to "contemplation" in Prochaska's model. SCARF explains why this occurs through the multiplier effect.
3. SCARF points to ways to minimize threat in a feedback intervention through the "offsetting effect."
4. The if-then framework, focused on actions, improves the likelihood of behavior change.
5. The phases of self-regulation give us a framework for where in the emotional timeline an if-then formula can be used.
6. All this points to managers needing to be better trained at the process of giving feedback if organizations are going to invest time and money in the process.

References

Achtziger, A., Gollwitzer, P. M., and Sheeran, P. 2008. "Implementation Intentions and Shielding Goal Striving from Unwanted Thoughts and Feelings." *Personality and Social Psychology Bulletin* 34(3): 381–393.

Ammons, R. B. 1956. "Effects of Knowledge of Performance: A Survey and Tentative Theoretical Formulation." *Journal of General Psychology* 54: 279–299.

Arps, G. F. 191. "A Preliminary Report on 'Work with Knowledge Versus Work Without Knowledge of Results.'" *Psychological Review* 14: 449–455.

Ashford, S. J., Blatt, R., and VandeWalle, D. 2003. "Reflections on the Looking Glass: A Review of Research on Feedback-Seeking Behavior in Organizations." *Journal of Management* 29(6): 773–799.

Atwater, L., and Waldman, D. A. 1998. "360-Degree Feedback and Leadership Development." *Leadership Quarterly* 9(4).

Avolio, B. J., and Hannah, S. T. 2008. "Developmental Readiness: Accelerating Leader Development." *Consulting Psychology Journal: Practice and Research* 60(4): 331–347.

Blume, B. D., Baldwin, T. T., Rubin, R. S., and Bommer, W. 2006. "All Forced Ranking Systems Are Not Equal: A Policy Capturing Study." *Academy of Management Best Conference Paper.*

Brutus, S. 2009. "Words Versus Numbers: A Theoretical Exploration of Giving and Receiving Narrative Comments in Performance Appraisal." *Human Resource Management Review* doi:10.1016/j.hrmr.2009.06.003.

Dalton, M. 1996. "Multirater Feedback and Conditions for Change." *Consulting Psychology Journal: Practice and Research* 48(1): 12–16.

DeNisi, A., and Kluger, A. N. 2000. "Feedback Effectiveness: Can 360-Degree Appraisals Be Improved?" *Academy of Management Executive* 14(1): 129–138.

DeWitte, S., Verguts, T., and Lens, W. 2003. "Implementation Intentions Do Not Enhance All Types of Goals: The Moderating Role of Goal Difficulty." *Current Psychology: Developmental, Learning, Personality, Social* 22(1): 73–89.

Dholakia, U. M., Bagozzi, R. P., and Gopinath, M. 2007. "How Formulating Implementation Plans and Remembering Past Actions Facilitate the Enactment of Effortful Decisions." *Journal of Behavioral Decision Making* 20: 343–364.

Dickinson, A. 1985. "Actions and habits: The Development of Behavioural Autonomy." *Philosophical Transactions of the Royal Society of London. Series B: Biological Sciences* 308(1135): 67–78.

Dixon, P., and Underwood, W. 2010. "Narrative Comments in 360-Degree Feedback." *In development*.

Edwards, M.R., and Ewen, A.J. 1998. "Multisource Assessment Survey of Industry Practice." Paper presented at the 360-Degree Feedback Global Users Conference (May), Orlando, FL.

Einstein, G. O., McDaniel, M. A., Williford, C. L., Pagan, J. L., and Dismukes, R. K. 2003. "Forgetting of Intentions in Demanding Situations is Rapid." *Journal of Experimental Psychology: Applied* 9(3): 147–162.

Eisenberger, N. I., Lieberman , M. D., and Williams, K. 2003. "Does Rejection Hurt? An fMRI Study of Social Exclusion." *Science* 302: 290–292.

Eisenberger, N. I., and Lieberman, M. D. 2004. "Why Rejection Hurts: A Common Neural Alarm System for Physical and Social Pain." *Trends in Cognitive Science* 8(7): 294–300.

Gollwitzer, P. M. 1993. "Goal Achievement: The Role of Intentions." *European Journal of Social Psychology* 4: 141–185.

Gollwitzer, P. M. 1999. "Implementation Intentions: Strong Effects of Simple Plans." *American Psychologist* 54: 493–503.

Gollwitzer, P. M., and Brandstatter, V. 1997. "Implementation Intentions and Effective Goal Pursuit." *Journal of Personality and Social Psychology* 73: 186–199.

Gross, J. 1998a. "Antecedent and Response-Focused Emotion Regulation: Divergent Consequences for Experience, Expression, and Physiology." *Journal of Personality and Social Psychology* 74: 224–237.

Gross, J. 1998b. "The Emerging Field of Emotion Regulation: An Integrative Review." *Review of General Psychology* 2: 271–299.

Henderson, M. D., Gollwitzer, P. M., and Oettingen, G. 2007. "Implementation Intentions and Disengagement from a Failing Course of Action." *Journal of Behavioral Decision Making* 20: 81–102.

Hogan, R. 2007. *Personality and the fate of organizations*. Mahway, NJ: Erlbaum.

Hogan, J., Hogan, R., and Kaiser, R. B. 2010. "Management Derailment." In *American Psychological Association Handbook of Industrial and Organizational Psychology* edited by S.Zedeck, 3: 555–575. Washington, DC: American Psychological Association.

John, O.P., and Gross, J.J. 2007. "Individual Differences in Emotion Regulation." In *Handbook of Emotional Regulations* edited by J.J Gross, 351-372. New York: Guilford Press.

Kelly, P. R. 1958. "Reappraisal of Appraisals." *Harvard Business Review* 58–68.

Kluger, A. N., and DeNisi, A. 1996. "The Effects of Feedback Interventions on Performance: A Historical Review, a Meta-Analysis, and a Preliminary Feedback Intervention Theory." *Psychological Bulletin* 119(2): 254–284.

Knäuper, B., Roseman, M., Johnson, P. J., and Krantz, L. H. 2009. "Using Mental Imagery to Enhance the Effectiveness of Implementation Intentions." *Current Psychology: Developmental, Learning, Personality, Social* 28: 181–186.

Lieberman, M. D., and Eisenberger, N. I. 2008. "The Pains and Pleasures of Social Life: A Social Cognitive Neuroscience Approach." *NeuroLeadership Journal* 1: 38–43.

Lieberman, M. D., Eisenberger, N. I., Crockett, M. J., Tom, S. M., Pfeifer, J. H., and Way, B. M. 2007. "Putting Feelings into Words." *Psychological Science* 18(5): 421–428.

McGregor, D. 1957. "An Uneasy Look at Performance Appraisal." *Harvard Business Review* 89–94.

Meyer, H. H., Kay, E., and French, J. R. 1965. "Split Roles on Performance Appraisal." *Harvard Business Review* 43: 123–129.

Poldrack, R. A., Clark, J., Pare-Blagoev, E. J., Shohamy, D., Creso Moyano, J., Myers, C., and Gluck, M. A. 2001. "Interactive Memory Systems in the Human Brain." *Nature* 414: 546–550.

Prochaska, J. O., DiClemente, C. C., and Norcross, J. C. 1992. "In Search of How People Change." *American Psychologist* 47(9): 1102–1114.

Rock, D. 2008. "SCARF: A Brain-Based Model for Collaborating With and Influencing Others." *NeuroLeadership Journal* 1: 44-52.

Rock, D. 2009. *Your Brain at Work: Strategies for Overcoming Distraction, Regaining Focus, and Working Smarter All Day Long*. New York: HarperBusiness.

Smither, J. W., and Walker, A. G. 2004. "Are the Characteristics of Narrative Comments Related to Improvement in Multirater Feedback Ratings Over Time?" *Journal of Applied Psychology* 89(3): 575–581.

Watson Wyatt Worldwide 2002. "Human Capital Index: Human Capital as a Lead Indicator of Shareholder Value." *Towers Watson* 1–6.

24. Learning that lasts through AGES

Dr. Lila Davachi, Dr. Tobias Kiefer, Dr. David Rock, and Lisa Rock

Lila Davachi, Assistant Professor of Psychology, Department of Psychology, New York University, New York, USA
lila.davachi@nyu.edu

Tobias Kiefer, Director, Global Learning and Development, Booz and Company, Munich, Germany
tobias.kiefer@booz.com

David Rock, CEO, NeuroLeadership Group, New York, USA
Faculty, CIMBA; Cofounder, NeuroLeadership Institute; Editor, *NeuroLeadership Journal*
david@neuroleadership.com

Lisa Rock, COO, NeuroLeadership Group, New York, USA
lisa@neuroleadership.com

Introduction

With more to learn than ever, faster innovation cycles, and reduced training budgets, organizations everywhere are trying to get more from their learning programs. However, to increase the effectiveness of learning, some of our intuitive understanding about learning may need updating. For example, while people generally predict that concentrated learning in one block of time is more effective, neuroscience research is clearly showing that it is far better to break up learning interventions to facilitate successful long-term learning. This chapter outlines recent findings from neuroscience research about how we learn and how to optimize the formation of memory. These findings have been summarized in a four-part model for how to make learning stick—Attention, Generation, Emotion, and Spacing—that we are presenting here as the AGES model.

So much to learn, so little time

Increased organizational change is increasing pressure on learning. Every new product, distribution model, partnership, or organizational structure comes with new information and processes to remember. As well as having more to learn than ever, there is less time to learn it in, driven by a desire to get to market quickly. Then there is the challenge of the nature of work itself, where distractions and multitasking inhibit the ability to focus sufficiently to learn something new. Finally, budgets for learning today are under significant pressure. In short, the pressure is on for employees to learn more, faster, under tougher conditions, and within tight budgets.

One outcome of these forces is simply shorter training programs. Training programs that used to be run over two or three days are now run in half a day, and a significant number of organizations are shifting training from a formal company-driven approach toward more social and informal learning methods (Bersin and Associates 2011). Yet our ability to absorb new ideas is not dissimilar to our capacity to absorb food: there are physical limits to the digestion of both. To try to address this, more learning is being pushed to "prework," in the hope that participants arrive at a training program already knowledgeable about core ideas. This works only partially, due to the mixed level of focus people give to a prereading.

Increased organizational change is increasing pressure on learning.

Organizations are also experimenting with just-in-time learning, delivered by managers rather than trainers. The downside of this approach is that most managers are selected on their skill set and are not always optimal teachers. However, organizations consciously investing in their leaders to serve as trainers report good results (Bethof 2009). Other organizations, noting the impact of follow-through on learning (Bersin and Associates 2011; Zenger, Folkmann, and Sherwin 2005), are creating internal coaches to drive embedding of insights: one study of 358 companies about their use of coaching found that 67 percent were using internal coaches (Rule, Rock, and Donde 2011).

In summary, learning managers are attempting to evolve their learning offerings to meet the changed environment and needs. Yet, by and large, they are doing so based on guesswork, without a good theory to inform their experimentation.

Learning means retrieving easily

In the workplace much learning is declarative, or explicit learning, meaning information that needs to be recalled (Davachi and Dobbins 2008). This kind of learning involves encoding information in the brain sufficiently well for easy retrieval. In any learning experience, whether learning a new product description or organizational chart, a key outcome of the experience is that information is remembered and can be recalled easily.

With just the right amount of attention, generation, emotion, and spacing, learners intensely activate their hippocampus...

Neuroscientists have discovered that during an encoding task, the level of activation of the brain region called the hippocampus plays a significant role in whether people can recall what they learned (Davachi and Wagner 2002). Many studies (e.g., Davachi and Wagner 2002; Lepage, Habib, and Tulving 1998) have since explored the types of activities that do and don't activate the hippocampus. This new understanding of the biology of learning is providing rich insights into how we can more efficiently create long-term memories as part of a learning experience.

A number of surprises have emerged from this thread of research. It turns out that some of our long-held assumptions about learning, such as the importance of repetition, are incorrect. We have also begun to recognize the importance of overlooked factors in learning, such as the significant impact of spacing out a learning activity.

In this chapter, we draw together recent findings about memory formation into one easy-to-remember model, called AGES: Attention, Generation, Emotion, and Spacing. These four variables may be the key to maximizing learning interventions. With just the right amount of attention, generation, emotion, and spacing, learners intensely activate their hippocampus, which creates deep circuits for easy retrieval. This model can help learning designers improve their learning initiatives by focusing on, and experimenting with, the key variables of effective learning.

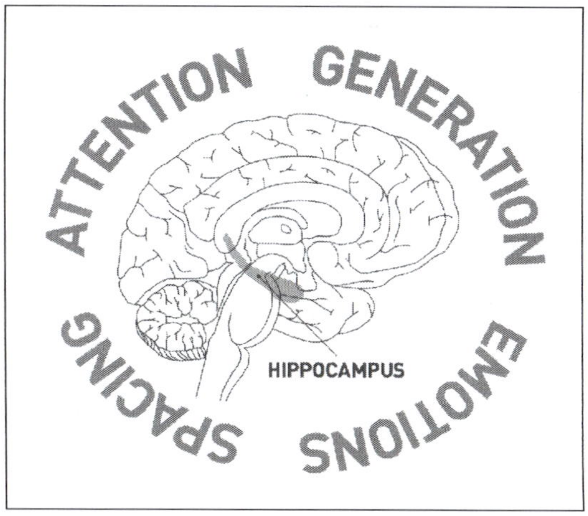

Figure 1. The AGES model for lasting learning impact

Attention

For the hippocampus to activate sufficiently for learning to occur, the learner needs to be paying full attention to the topic being learned. In a world with so many distractions (e.g., phones and other devices), this is easier said than done. Dividing attention between two tasks significantly decreases the quality of attention, and the likely sustainability of any learning, because the hippocampus is not engaged when attention is divided (Kensinger, Clarke, and Corkin 2003). This has been shown to occur with even small levels of distraction. Focusing on multiple streams of information, including trying to multitask in the learning environment, also results in neurons decreasing their firing, and hence learning decreases significantly (Arnsten 1998; 2009). Thus one of the foundational ideas for learning is ensuring you have "undivided attention"—that people are focused closely on the learning task at hand.

In a classroom, this is easier to manage through activities that focus people's thinking in one direction. In online learning, with the possibility of distraction from other devices being "on," or distractions inherent in the technology itself, attention can be harder to focus. The quality of attention paid and how to ensure maximum attention during online learning is an area for further research.

To pay close attention to something, the brain needs just the right amount of two important neurochemicals called catecholamines—specifically dopamine and norepinephrine—placed at huge numbers of synapses (Vijayraghavan et al. 2007). Dopamine is involved in a feeling of reward, of relevance, and is also released through novelty. It is released in the "toward" state (Rock 2008), when we are open, curious, in a goal-focused state, and/or working to gain something.

To increase dopamine levels in a learning situation, the content needs to be relevant—that is, the learner needs to see the value (e.g., potential reward) of focusing attention on the content. One way to do this is by making learning situations as "real" and "personal" as possible, such as with the use of advanced simulations, which also addresses other elements of AGES (e.g., increased arousal due to role-playing in front of a group).

Varying the learning techniques provides additional novelty that can help raise dopamine levels to keep the learner's attention in the learning environment. For example, the presentation of information can be mixed with group discussions, role-playing, or scenario planning.

Norepinephrine affects the chemistry of alertness, of feeling aroused and focused. This neurochemical tends to be released in greater quantities in the "away" state (Rock 2008), when we are alert to threat and our senses are heightened. Norepinephrine may be released during competitive activities (Pierce, Kupprat, and Harry 1976) or when we feel under pressure to perform, perhaps by a deadline.

We need good amounts, but not too much, of both these "chemistries" to pay good attention. Good learning states involve paying close attention to something relevant and interesting, with enough of a challenge to keep our attention. Both elements need to go hand-in-hand to allow an optimum level of attention. If an optimum attention level cannot be generated, the hippocampus will not fire sufficiently for memory encoding to occur. In short, making learning easy to digest, through chunking, visuals, and stories, and making it interesting and engaging are critical for optimizing retrieval of information.

To improve at any skill or competency, it helps to be able to measure that competency. How can we measure "attention" in learning? One approach comes from the *idea* of attention. Attention density technically means the number of observations (attention paid) to a particular idea per unit of time. Each time we activate a circuit, this further wires that circuit together (Hebb 1949). Taking this idea, we could, in theory and in time, be able to measure the quality of attention paid to specific circuits by measuring the level of activation of brain regions. While this would be cumbersome in a training room, it is technically feasible. For now, we could at least measure how long, perhaps in seconds, an idea is held in mind in the laboratory.

Varying the learning techniques provides additional novelty that can help raise dopamine levels to keep the learner's attention in the learning environment.

This brings up an interesting question: how much attention is paid to a core idea in a classroom, versus in other forms of learning—say in virtual learning—per hour spent in the learning experience? Counterintuitively, some forms of classroom learning have a high distraction factor, with attention going to what other people are doing and other social cues, rather than to the core ideas. On the other hand, some forms of virtual learning, such as games and other immersive experiences, can be more focused on the core ideas but carry the risk that other distractions come into play (such as e-mail or parallel Internet usage).

If attention is a key to learning, a question raised is, how do we maximize attention itself? The answer may come from research on the social brain (Lieberman and Eisenberg 2008). Studies are showing that we feel strongest about, and pay most attention to, social issues (Jaremka, Gabriel, and Carvallo 2010). Making learning a greater social experience (e.g., learning from best practices through storytelling) in some way may be a key to improve learning effectiveness. There does appear to be a movement toward making learning more social (Bersin and Associates 2010; 2011), but it also questions the self-paced learning approach of prereading and online learning.

Generation

Information is not expressly stored in the hippocampus as discrete memories, like in a hard drive. Instead, memories are made up of vast webs of data from across the brain all linked together (Davachi and Dobbins 2008). The more associations (or in other words, entry points linked to the original information) connected to a memory, the thicker the web is and, therefore, the easier it is to find a memory later. The hippocampus activates when we create these associations. Once sufficient attention has been paid to a learning task and an idea is being held in working memory, the question becomes, how do we maximize the likelihood of memories forming?

Despite being widely thought of as central for learning, research has shown that repetition has only a limited impact on creating lasting learning (Woiniak and Gorzelanczyk 1994). Repeating a new word 30 times does not necessarily add it to long-term memory. So what works? Both psychological and neuroscientific research have shown that the key to optimizing learning and building long-term memory is to create "ownership" of learning content (Jensen 2005; Poldrack et al. 2001). This ownership, or "generation of own learning," occurs when an individual is motivated to understand, contextualize, retain, and apply knowledge in their own way. Therefore, learners should be encouraged to take in the presented information and personalize it by transforming it in a way that is meaningful for them. This act itself creates a rich set of associations, activating the hippocampus.

Memories are made up of vast webs of data from across the brain all linked together...

One way to generate associations is to encourage the learner to evaluate the meaning of the information and compare it with their existing knowledge, or to think about the information in a "deep," versus "shallow," way (Davachi and Wagner 2002; Craik and Tulving 1975) (see fig. 2). One study showed a significant increase in memory when learners were asked to elaborate on three presented items, ordering them instead of purely rehearsing them. This enhanced memory was associated with greater activation of the hippocampus (Davachi and Wagner 2002).

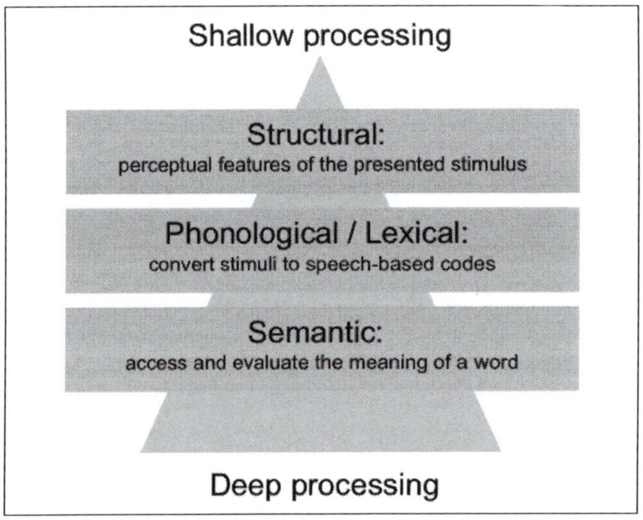

Figure 2. Levels of input processing

Learners may gain greater value if they are presented with data and then asked to formulate, organize, or add their personal experience to the learning content (Jensen 2005). An example would be to do the final development of a leadership model within the training session instead of being presented with a predefined model.

If we work on the assumptions that each brain is unique and that people need to generate associations to learn, then all learning should be, to some extent, self-directed. Individuals must map new learning to their existing knowledge and experiences and generate their own meaning and ways to apply the new knowledge.

Questioning the learner triggers retrieval of the recently learned information and improves long-term retention.

Questioning the learner triggers retrieval of the recently learned information and improves long-term retention. Asking the learner to visualize situations in which they could apply their new learning or to make decisions within the context of the new data also helps reinforce what has been learned. Again, these tasks increase associations in the brain. Immediate feedback on any errors also significantly increases accuracy of future retrieval (Guthrie 1971).

Structuring learning initiatives with these findings in mind might mean less teaching, or presentation of information, and more time dedicated to the self-generation of learning with the goal of building more personal associations with existing knowledge for easier retrieval. The more associations the learner generates, the higher probability over time that he/she will be able to find an access point to the data at a later date.

In terms of measuring the idea of generation, this is possible with current technologies by looking into which regions of the brain are active during learning, specifically the level of hippocampal activity. However, this is too cumbersome to be helpful in a training experience itself. For now, we could use self-report to identify how actively a person may be thinking about an idea for himself/herself, versus just listening passively. Additionally, if generation, rather than repetition or listening, is key, we can increase this by simply getting people talking to each other about ideas, versus just listening to presentations. In this way, we could measure the amount of "listening" versus "generating" in a classroom. Or we could encourage participants to invent their own terms and approaches based on the content learned and then collect their ideas to measure the "degree of generation."

Emotions

Learning happens in many complex layers, with emotion being one of the more important regulators of learning and memory formation. Studies show that the correlation of vividness of a memory and the emotionality of the original event is around 0.9 (Jensen 2005). The way in which emotion is thought to enhance memory is twofold. First, emotional content is thought to grab the attention of the individual and, hence, help focus attention on the emotional event or stimulus (LeDoux 1994; Damasio 1994). Second, it is known that emotion leads to activation of a brain structure called the amygdala, which sits directly in front of the hippocampus and can help signal the hippocampus that a particular event is salient and thus increase the effectiveness of encoding (Ochsner 2000; Cahill et al. 1994). When looking into current professional training design, emotions are a common tool used in behavioral change programs, such as leadership trainings (Kiefer 2009).

Emotions are a common tool used in behavioral change programs, such as leadership trainings...

Of course, one challenge of using emotion in a learning context is the difficulty of creating emotion-arousing events, especially ones that are positive. It is far easier to stimulate negative emotions, such as fear and threat (e.g., by presenting 360-degree assessment tools and reports), than to create a joy/pleasure response—especially when confronting individuals with novelty (Kohlrieser 2006). Simply presenting angry faces, for example, has been shown to increase arousal and be highly effective in engaging attention (Ohman, Flykt, and Lundquist 2000). Generating strong negative emotions such as fear in a training program is a commonly used strategy for burning memories.

For example, many sales, presentation, and negotiation programs are based on videotaped sessions that focus on the negatives of the presenters instead of their strengths. However, there are difficulties with using strong negative emotions to burn in memories: negative emotions also reduce creativity and innovation (Subramaniam et al. 2009), so while people may learn, they are less likely to innovate. Also, the brain's organizing principle is to minimize threat and maximize reward (Gordon 2000). As a result, people will not be inclined to turn up for training when the experience continues to use negative emotions, and they are likely to warn their colleagues to stay away too. However, if a learning experience is fun, they are likely to want to do more learning and tell others about the positive event.

Based on the SCARF model...there are ways to generate strong rewards by increasing people's sense of status, certainty, autonomy, relatedness, or fairness.

While it is easier to invoke negative emotions, positive emotion can also be invoked in a learning experience. Based on the SCARF® model (Rock 2008), there are ways to generate strong rewards by increasing people's sense of status, certainty, autonomy, relatedness, or fairness. The easy domains to generate rewards in a training program are most likely to be status and relatedness. An increase in a sense of status, which activates primary reward functions (Zink et al. 2008), can come from people learning new tasks and receiving positive feedback. It has been shown that positive feedback leads to an increase in dopamine neurotransmission that is thought to help learning stick (Schultz 1997). An increase in relatedness, which also activates primary reward functions (Cacioppo and Patrick 2008), can come from creating situations where people get to connect deeply with others and experience emotional "resonance" (Boyatzis 2001) in which they experience a sense of connectedness with others.

It may also be useful to have a training structure that includes novelty and entertainment, as this may stimulate positive emotions in the learner. In addition, strong evidence indicates that positive anticipation has an impact on the formation of new learning (Bradley and Lang 2000), so a good aim is to make learning enjoyable instead of just a mandatory event.

> *Positive anticipation has an impact on the formation of new learning...so a good aim is to make learning enjoyable instead of just a mandatory event.*

In terms of measuring emotions, we can use self-report to measure the level of intensity of emotions, whether positive or negative. We can also use devices to measure heart rate, skin conductance, and other biological markers for emotional arousal. As a general statement, social issues are the experiences we feel strongest about, so to increase emotions, clearly we should incorporate more social activities into learning experiences wherever possible. Positive social connections themselves may be one of the easier positive emotions that can be generated in a classroom setting.

Spacing

It has been known for some time that distributing learning over time is better than cramming learning into one long study session (Crowder 1976). Massing, defined as large blocks of learning in short periods of time, increases short-term performance, which guides learners to rate the learning impact of massing as superior to spacing (Baddeley and Longman 1978; Kornell and Bjork 2008; Simon and Bjork 2001; Zechmeister and Shaughnessy 1980). However, distributing learning over time leads to better long-term memory, which is the ultimate aim of organizational learning.

Spacing information over time leads to higher retrieval rates of new information and seems to build stronger long-term memory (Litman and Davachi 2008). Given all the positive research on spacing, why is massing the more common approach to learning? Putting aside the financial benefits of delivering learning in one block, there are other likely reasons why massing is the dominant approach.

There is evidence that initial testing of newly learned items, with a small delay after the learning event, will further drive the building of long-term memory...

The positive attitude by learners to massing may result from experience with cramming for exams. Cramming information is a successful strategy for exams where minimal retrieval is required in the future. Learning in the workplace has a different aim, with participants needing to build contextual understanding of the information presented as well as learn how to apply the information in the future. Spacing also leads to forgetting, and this can make the learning feel "harder." However, the more difficult the retrieval, the higher the learning effect (Bjork and Allen 1970; Cuddy and Jacoby 1982; Krug, Davis, and Glover 1990). There is evidence that initial testing of newly learned items a short time after the learning event, will further drive the building of long-term memory as this causes an additional retrieval effort (Karpicke and Roediger 2007).

In addition to the "active part" of the learning, spacing allows the brain to further digest new content and over time build and wire new connections, even when learners are at rest (Spitzer 2002; Tambini, Ketz, and Davachi 2010). Spacing enhances memory performance and the rate of forgetting drops due to enhanced hippocampally mediated memory consolidation (Litman and Davachi 2008). Another study showed that repeated testing is superior to repeated studying in the formation of maximum long-term memory (Roediger and Karpicke 2006).

Repeated testing is superior to repeated studying in the formation of maximum long-term memory...

One question that is difficult to answer is whether there is an optimum timing of spacing between learning. The best take-home message is that any spacing (whether it be minutes, hours, or days) is better than no spacing at all. Cepeda et al. (2008) examined the effect of this and suggested that the longer the time between the first and second learning sessions ("the gap"), the higher the retrieval rate (1-5 years) after the learning event. A recent study with 1,354 subjects examined the optimum gap lengths for testing subjects' recognition and recall rate. The project consisted of multiple combinations of gap lengths and RI (retention interval) lengths to examine the impact of the gap lengths on long-term memory foundation. For each RI, the recall and recognition performance rose with an increasing gap length and then decreased as the gap lengths further increased.

One question that is difficult to answer is whether there is an optimum timing of spacing between learning.

The Cepeda study showed a significant improvement of the recall rate when spacing information compared with a zero-day gap (see fig. 3). The Cepeda findings (Cepeda et al. 2008) underpin the notion that defining the optimum spacing is quite complex, since a couple of constraints and factors influence the design:

1. The RI gap: depending on the estimated recall date, the gap length first increases and then decreases since forgetting learned content comes into play.
2. As RI increases, the ratio of optimum gap to RI should decline.

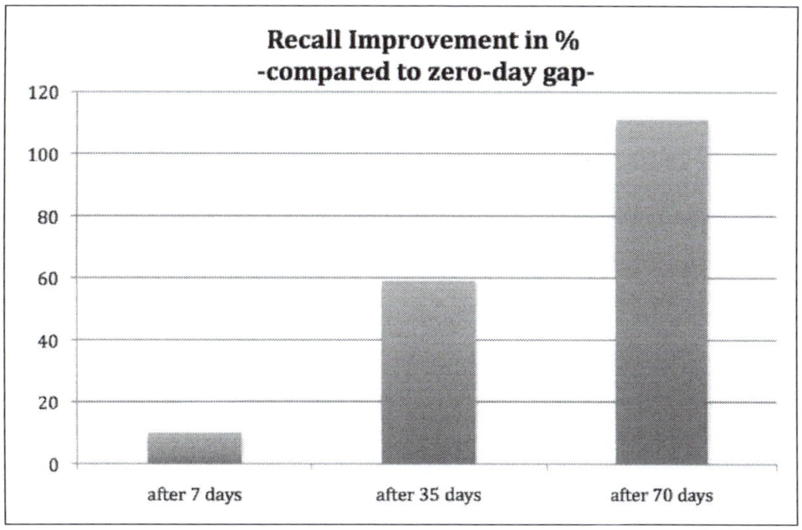

Figure 3, Spacing effect and learning improvement (recall improvement in percentage and days after initial learning). (The optimum learning gap was defined as d = 1 for seven-day recall test, d = 7 for thirty-five-day recall test, and d = 21 for seventy-day recall test.)

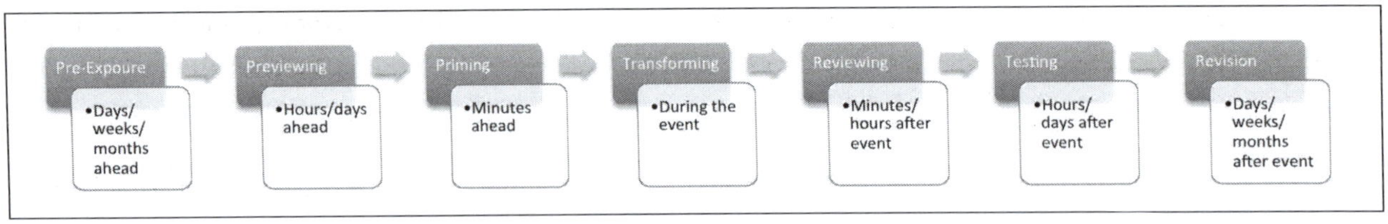

Figure 4. Spaced repetition (learning journey) and expansion of memory and associations

However, the data also suggest that it might be wise to avoid defining the "one" optimum gap between learning events, since it significantly depends on the RI. In other words, how long you want to remember newly learned content determines the optimum timing of the learning gap and the time studying new content.

Many studies have been published on optimization of learning intervals (number of repetitions and spacing) to ensure learning. As mentioned earlier, repetition itself has a limited impact on creating lasting learning (Woiniak and Gorzelanczyk 1994). However, repetition of new information, in a spaced manner, plays a role in building long-term memory. Taking the power of forgetting and the power of transformational learning into account, we follow Jensen's (2005) approach in using a variety of techniques to leverage repetition as a learning instrument. Incorporating this lesson, we suggest a "spaced repetition," which combines spacing and generating of learning over time.

Repetition itself is minimized since the content does not simply get repeated. Repetition happens through various techniques, such as priming, reviewing, or testing the content, during new learning generation (fig. 4).

Priming allows the brain to build the new concept into a larger contextual and semantic structure, increasing efficiency in learning (Martin and Van Turenout 2002; Cave 1997). Studies demonstrate that the use of priming as a repetition technique increases verbal fluency significantly (Mack and Rock 1998).

Priming allows the brain to build the new concept into a larger contextual and semantic structure...

Most training programs mass information in one or two days, without much attention to follow-up. This raises the question of how much we should be breaking up learning and instead delivering smaller bites of learning over time.

There is no current recipe of how much content can be taught and learned in a specific amount of time.

This is an important area for future research, and we cannot yet find any formal studies as a guide. However, it is important to note that brain function shows multiple constraints around learning limitations with regard to learning a lot of information, including:

- The limitations of the prefrontal cortex and its ability to process only three to seven information chunks at any one time (Linden et al. 2003).
- The time necessary to form new synaptic connections (Goda and Davis 2003).
- If the synapse gets disturbed before it "sets," the memory is lost (Milner 1999).
- The "rest time" needed to allow the brain to recycle protein in the neurons, which is crucial for building long-term memory (Bodzis et al. 2002; Schroth, Dötsch and Dörr 2001.
- The "digestion time" needed for the brain to reorganize, distribute, and consolidate new content through the hippocampus (Piegneux et al. 2001; Stickgold 1998; Siapas and Wilson 1998; Walker and Stickgold 2006) and awake rested (Tambini, Ketz, and Davachi 2010).

There is no current recipe of how much content can be taught and learned in a specific amount of time. However the indicators and data points are clear: building learning connections is time-consuming and requires maintenance.

Areas for further research

Many areas deserve significant further investigation. Questions to explore about learning from the brain perspective include: Which of the AGES variables is most significant, and what are the interactions between the variables? How much can people learn or digest at one time? What is the optimum interval for spacing to maximize learning? What is the impact of positive versus negative emotions in learning events? Answering these questions and more will go a long way toward enabling us to improve the impact of learning experiences in organizations.

Summary

Adult learning is highly complex. How do we ensure people are interested in learning what is presented, and how then do we present the information to ensure that the knowledge is sustainable, accessible, and easily applied in adaptive and contextual ways?

We suggest that learning designers should focus on:

- Creating maximum attention with a greater focus on learner motivation, ensuring one focus during learning events, and utilizing more novelty and change during learning experiences
- Encouraging significant generation of learning by participants when teaching new concepts to build learner ownership, rather than using presentation of information

- Creating a positive emotional environment, with opportunities for people to gain positive feedback and connect deeply with others

- Utilizing more spacing of learning instead of massing and repetition, with more dispersed content, such as turning a three-day learning event into six half-day events over a longer period

We encourage chief learning officers, learning consultants, and trainers to explore these new ways to reshape instructional design to ensure high-impact learning that lasts through AGES and that enables training departments to fully unleash the capabilities within their organizations.

References

Arnsten, A. F. T. 1998. "The Biology of Being Frazzled." *Science* 280: 1711–1712.

Arnsten, A. F. T. 2009. "Stress Signaling Pathways that Impair Prefrontal Cortex Structure and Function." *Nature Reviews Neuroscience* 10(6): 410–422.

Baddeley, A. D., and Longman, D. J. A. 1978. "The Influence of Length and Frequency on Training Sessions on the Rate of Learning to Type." *Ergonomics* 21: 627–635.

Baumeister, R. F., and Vohs, K. D. 2004. *Handbook of Self-Regulation: Research, Theory, and Applications*. New York: Guilford.

Bersin, J. 2010. *Informal Learning: What, Why, and How - The Economic Realities.* www.bersin.com/Lib/Rs/Details/aspx?docis=103312462&title=Informal-Learning-What-Why-and-How--The-Economic-Realities&id=.

Bersin, J. (2012) *The Corporate Learning Factbook.* Oakland, CA: Bersin & Associates.

Bethof, E. (2009). Leaders as Teachers: Unlock the Teaching Potential of Your Company's Best and Brightest. Baltimore, MD: United Book Press Inc.

Bjork, R.A., and Allen, T.W. 1970. "The Spacing Effect: Consolidation or Differential Encoding?" *Journal of Verbal Learning and Verbal Behavior* 9: 567–572.

Bódizs, R., Békésy M., SzĐcs A., Barsi P., and Halász P. 2002. "Sleep-Dependant Hippocampal Slow Activity Correlates with Waking Memory Performance." *Neurobiology of Learning and Memory* 78(2): 441–457.

Bor, D., Duncan, J., Wiseman, R. J., and Owen, A. M. 2003. "Encoding Strategies Dissociate Prefrontal Activity from Working Memory Demand." *Neuron* 37: 361–367.

Boyatzis, R. E. 2001. "How and Why Individuals are Able to Develop Emotional Intelligence." In *The Emotionally Intelligent Workplace: How to Select for, Measure, and Improve Emotional Intelligence in Individuals, Groups, and Organizations*, edited by C. Cherniss and D. Goleman, 234–253. San Francisco, CA: Jossey-Bass.

Bradley, M., and Lang, P. 2000. "Measuring Emotion: Behavior, Feeling, and Physiology." In *Cognitive Neuroscience of Emotion*, edited by R. Lane and L. Nadel, 242–276. New York: Oxford University Press.

Cacioppo, J. T., and Patrick, W. 2008. *Loneliness: Human Nature and the Need for Social Connection*. New York: W. W. Norton.

Cahill, C., Prins, B., Weber, M. and McGaugh. J.L. 1994. "Adrenergic Activation and Memory for Emotional Events." *Nature* 371: 702–704.

Cave, B. 1997. "Very Long-Lasting Priming in Picture Naming." *Psychological Science* 8: 322–325.

Cepeda, N. J., Vul, E., Rohrer, D., Wixted, J.T., and Pashler, H.2008. "Spacing Effects in Learning: A temporal Ridgeline of Optimal Retention." *Psychological Science* 19(11): 1095–1102.

Cepeda, N. J., Pashler, H., Vul, E., Wixted, J.T., and Rohrer, D. 2006. "Distributed Practice in Verbal Recall Tasks: A Review and Quantitative Synthesis." *Psychological Bulletin* 132: 354–380.

Craik, F. I. M., and Tulving, E. 1975. "Depth of Processing and the Retention of Words in Episodic Memory." *Journal of Experimental Psychology: General* 104: 27.

Crowder, R. G. 1976. *Principles of Learning and Memory*. Mahwah, NJ: Lawrence Erlbaum Associates.

Csikszentmihalyi, M. 1990. *Flow: The Psychology of Optimal Experience*. New York: Harper & Row.

Cuddy, L.J., and Jacoby, L.L. 1982. "When Forgetting Helps Memory: An Analysis of Effects." *Journal of Verbal Learning and Verbal Behavior* 21: 441–452.

Damasio, A. 1994. *Descartes' Error*. New York: Putnam.

Davachi, L., and Dobbins, I. G. 2008. "Declarative Memory." *Association for Psychological Science* 17(2): 112–118.

Davachi, L., and Wagner, A. D. 2002. "Hippocampal Contributions to Episodic Encoding: Insights from Relational and Item-Based Learning." *American Physiological Society* 88: 982–990.

Diamond, D., Park, C.R., Heman, K.L., and Rose G.M. 1999. "Exposing Rats to a Predator Impairs Spatial Working Memory in the Radial Arm Water Maze." *Hippocampus* 9: 542–552.

Goda, Y., and Davis, G. W. 2003. "Mechanisms of Synapse Assembly and Disassembly." *Neuron* 40(2): 243–264.

Gordon, E. ed. 2000. *Integrative Neuroscience: Bringing Together Biological, Psychological and Clinical Models of the Human Brain*. Singapore: Harvard Academic Publishers.

Gordon, E., Barnett, K.J., Cooper, N.J., Tran, N., and Williams, L.M. 2008. "An "Integrative Neuroscience" Platform: Application to Profiles of Negativity and Positivity Bias." *Journal of Integrative Neuroscience* 7(3): 345–366.

Guthrie, J.T. 1971. "Feedback and Sentence Learning." *Journal of Verbal Learning and Verbal Behavior* 10: 23–28.

Hebb, D. O. 1949. *The Organization of Behavior*. New York: John Wiley & Sons.

Jaremka, L., Gabriel, S., and Carvallo, M. 2010. "What Makes Us Feel the Best Also Makes Us Feel the Worst: The Emotional Impact of Independent and Interdependent Experiences." *Self and Identity* 10(1): 44–63.

Jensen, E. 2005. *Teaching with the Brain in Mind*. 2nd ed. Alexandria, VA: Association for Supervision and Curriculum Development.

Jung-Beeman, M., Collier, A., and Kuonis, J. 2008. "How Insight Happens: Learning From the Brain." *NeuroLeadership Journal* 1: 20–25.

Karpicke, J. D., and Roediger, H. L. 2007. "Expanding Retrieval Practice Promotes Short-Term Retention, but Equally Spaced Retrieval Enhances Long-Term Retention." *Journal of Experimental Psychology* 33(4): 704–719.

Kensinger, E. A., Clarke, R. J., and Corkin, S. 2003. "What Neural Correlates Underlie Successful Encoding and Retrieval? A functional Magnetic Resonance Imaging Study Using a Divided Attention Paradigm." *The Journal of Neuroscience* 23: 2407–2415.

Kirsch, I. 1999. *How Expectancies Shape Experience*. Washington, DC: American Psychological Association.

Kiefer, T. 2009. Leadership Development 3.0: IQ*EQ*XQ. Presented at Learntech 2009, Germany.

Kohlrieser, G. 2006. *Hostage at the Table: How Leaders Can Overcome Conflict, Influence Others and Praise Performance*. San Francisco, CA: Jossey-Bass.

Krug, D., Davis, T.B., and Glover, J.A. 1990. "Massed versus distributed repeated reading: A case of forgetting helping recall." *Journal of Educational Psychology* 82: 366–371.

Kuonis, J., Fleck, J. L., Green, D. L., Payne, L., Stevenson, J. L., Bowden, M., and Jung-Beeman, M. 2008. "The Origins of Insight in Resting-State Brain Activity." *Neuropsychologica* 46: 281–291.

Kopp, B., and Wolff, M. 2000. "Brain Mechanisms of Selective Learning: Event-Related Potentials Provide Evidence for Error-Driven Learning in Humans." *Biological Psycholog* 51: 223–246.

Kornell, N., and Bjork, R. A. 2008. "Learning Concepts and Categories: Is Spacing the "Enemy of Induction"?" *Psychological Science* 19: 585–592.

LeDoux, J. 1994. "Emotion, Memory, and the Brain." *Scientific American* 270(6): 50–57.

Lepage, M., Habib, R., and Tulving, E. 1998. "Hippocampal PET Activations of Memory Encoding and Retrieval: The HIPER model." *Hippocampus* 8: 313–322.

Lieberman, M., and Eisenberg, N. 2008. "The Pains and Pleasures of Social Life." *NeuroLeadership Journal* 1: 38–42.

Linden, D.E., Bittner, R.A., Muckli, L., Waltz, J.A., Kriegeskorte, N., Goebel, R., Singer,W., et al. 2003. "Cortical Capacity Constraints for Visual Working Memory: Dissociation of fMRI Load Effects in Frontoparietal Network." *Neuroimage* 20: 1518–1530.

Litman, L., and Davachi, L. 2008. "Distributed Learning Enhances Relational Memory Consolidation." *Learning and Memory* (September) 15(9): 711–716.

Mack, A., and Rock, I. 1998. *Inattentional Blindness*. Cambridge, MA: MIT Press.

Martin, A., and Van Turenout, M. 2002. "Searching for the Neural Correlates of Object Priming, in: Schachter, D., and Squire, L." *Neuropsychology of Memory* 239–247.

Milner, P. 1999. *The Autonomous Brain*. Mahwah, NJ: Lawrence Erlbaum Associates.

Ochsner, K. N. 2000. "Are Affective Events Richly Recollected or Simply Familiar? The Experience and Process of Recognizing Feelings Past." *Journal of Experimental Psychology: General* 129: 242–261.

Ohman, A., Flykt, A., and Lundquist, D. 2000. "Unconscious Emotion: Evolutionary Perspectives, Psychophysiological Data, and Neuropsychological Mechanisms." In *Cognitive Neuroscience of Emotion*, edited by R. Lane and L. Nadel. New York: Oxford University Press..

Pashler, H., Johnston, H. C., and Ruthruff, E. 2001. "Attention and Performance." *Annual Review of Psychology* 52: 629–651.

Paivio, A. 1969. "Mental Imagery in Associative Learning and Memory." *Psychological Review* 76: 23.

Pierce, D., Kupprat, I., and Harry, D. 1976. "Urinary Epinephrine and Norepinephrine Levels in Women Athletes During Training and Competition." *European Journal of Applied Physiology and Occupational Physiology* 36(1): 1–6.

Poldrack, R. A., Clark, J., Pare-Blagoev, E. J., Shohamy, D., Creso Moyano, J., Myers, C., and Gluck, M. A. 2001. "Interactive Memory Systems in the Human Brain." *Nature* 414: 546–550.

Pride, D. D., Verne, G. N., and Schwartz, J. M. 2006. "Plasticity in Brain Modulation and Modulation of Pain." *Progress in Brain Research* 117: 333–352.

Piegneux, P., Laureys, S., Delbeuck, X., and Maquet, P. 2001. "Sleeping Brain, Learning Brain: The Role of Sleep for Memory Systems." *Neuroreport* 12: A111–A124.

Rock, D. 2007. *Quiet Leadership*. New York: HarperCollins.

Rock, D. 2008. "SCARF: A Brain-Based Model for Collaborating With and Influencing Others." *NeuroLeadership Journal* 1: 129–142.

Rock, D. (2009). Your Brain at Work: Strategies for Overcoming Distraction, Regaining Focus, and Working Smarter All Day Long. New York: HarperBusiness.

Roediger, H. L., and Karpicke, J. D. 2006. "Test-Enhanced Learning: Taking Memory Tests Improves Long-Term Retention." *Psychological Science* 17: 249–255.

Rule, M., Rock, D., and Donde, R. 2011. Global Coaching Study 2011. Presented by NeuroLeadership Group, Sydney: NSW

Schroth, M., Dötsch, J., and Dörr, H.G. 2001. «Hypercalcemia and Idiopath Hypoparathyroidism." *Journal of Clinical Pharmacy and Therapeutics* 26 (6): 453–455.

Schultz, W. 1997. "Dopamine neurons and their role in reward mechanisms." *Current Opinion in Neurobiology* 7: 191–197.

Siapas, A. G., and Wilson, M. A. 1998. "Coordinated Interactions Between Hippocampal Ripples and Cortical Spindles During Slow Wave Sleep." *Neuron* 21: 1123–1128.

Simon, D. A., and Bjork, R. A. 2001. "Metacognition in Motor Learning." *Journal of Experimental Psychology: Learning, Memory, and Cognition* 27: 907–912.

Spitzer, M. (2002). Lernen: Gehirnforschung und Schule des Lebens. Heidelberg; Berlin: Spekrum Akademischer Verlag GmbH.

Stickgold, R. 1998. "Sleep: Off-Line Memory Processing." *Trends in Cognitive Sciences* 2: 484–492.

Subramaniam, K., Kounios, J.B., Bowden, E.M., Parrish, T.B., and Jung-Beeman, M. 2009. "Positive Mood and Anxiety Modulate Anterior Cingulate Activity and Cognitive Preparation for Insight." *Journal of Cognitive Neuroscience* 21: 415–432.

Tambini, A., Ketz, N., and Davachi, L. 2010. "Enhanced Brain Correlations During Rest Are Related To Memory For Recent Experiences." *Neuron* 65: 280–290.

Taylor, S. E. 1991. "Asymmetrical Effects of Positive and Negative Effects: The Mobilization—Minimization Hypothesis." *Psychological Bulletin* 110(1): 67–85.

Taylor, K., and Rohrer, D. 2010. "The Effects of Interleaved Practice." *Applied Cognitive Psychology* 24: 837–848.

Vijayragharan, S., Wang.M., Birnbaum, S.G., Williams, G.V., and Arnsten, A.F.T. 2007. "Inverted-U Dopaimine D1 Receptor Actions on Prefrontal Neurons Engaged in Working Memory." *Nature Neuroscience* 10: 376–384.

Walker, M. P., and Stickgold, R. 2006. "Sleep, Memory, and Plasticity." *Annual Review of Psychology* 57: 139–166.

Wills, T. W., Soraci, S. A., Chechile, R. A., and Taylor, H. A. 2000. "'Aha' Effects In the Generation of Pictures." *Memory and Cognition* 28: 939–948.

Woiniak, P. A., and Gorzelanczyk, E. J. 1994. "Optimization of Repetition Spacing in the Practice of Learning." *Acta Neurobiologiae Experimentalis* 54: 59–62.

Zechmeister, E. B., and Shaughnessy, J. J. 1980. "When You Know That You Know and When You Think That You Know But You Don't." *Bulletin of the Psychonomic Society* 15: 41–44.

Zenger, J., Folkman, J., and Sherwin, R. 2005. "The Promise Of Phase 3." *Training and Development* 59(1): 30–35.

Zink, C. F., Tong, Y., Chen, Q., Bassett, D. S., Stein, J. L., and Meyer-Lindenberg, A. 2008. "Know Your Place: Neural Processing Of Social Hierarchy In Humans." *Neuron* 58: 273–283.

25. Neuroleadership and the productive brain

Dr. Megan O'Connor,[1] Nicholas J. Cooper,[1] Dr. Leanne M. Williams,[2] Savannah DeVarney,[1] and Dr. Evian Gordon[1]

[1]Brain Resource International Database, Brain Resource Ltd., New South Wales, Australia

[2]BRAINnet.net Foundation
www.BRAINnet.net, California, USA
Corresponding author: evian.gordon@brainresource.com

Introduction

Global competition and tough economic challenges have converged to escalate the pressure on leaders and employees to find new solutions to achieve greater productivity. Adaptive resilience and enhanced productivity have become a survival imperative for many companies.

The field of neuroleadership has highlighted how important it is to understand the human brain when developing strategies to improve leadership skills and cultivate employee productivity (Rock 2008). These models also build on recent breakthroughs in brain science, which shows we are capable of changing our brain. Contrary to long-held assumptions, the brain is "plastic" and able to be trained to improve performance. This is the principle of "neuroplasticity" (Doidge 2007).

In our study, we focused on a core concept of adaptive brain function: self-regulation (SR). The study first asked whether better SR relates to increased productivity in employees. It then asked whether brain training can improve SR in these participants. The study found that self-regulation is a brain-based capacity that highly influences workplace productivity. With regular brain training using an online platform, an improvement of 14 percent in self-regulation was seen after thirty days. These results can provide neuroleaders and employees with new options to explore digital solutions to increase productivity and workplace outcomes.

The concept of SR has been the focus of research in psychology, medicine, and psychophysiology (Thayer, Newman, and McClain 1994; Thayer and Lane 2000; Gross and John 2003; Wing et al. 2006). A common focus in this research is that SR relies on self-awareness and our capacity to manage the way we think and feel and proactively develop positive thoughts and feelings. The outer cortical regions of the brain—particularly the frontal regions—have been implicated in SR (Damasio 1996; Davidson and Irwin 1999). SR is also reflected in the way our brain interacts with body activity in measures such as heart-rate variability (Thayer and Lane 2000).

In a framework called the INTEGRATE Model, we have integrated these common concepts of SR and their brain basis (Gordon et al. 2008; see fig. 1). From this framework, we have identified three facets of SR that can be assessed using self-report and correlate to brain and heart-rate function (Williams et al. 2009; Williams et al. 2010). These facets are: positivity-negativity bias (the tendency to expect the worst), emotional resilience (a "thick skin" and capacity for self-efficacy), and social skills (capacity to engage with others).

These concepts of self-regulation are being harnessed by neuroleaders. Seminal models of neuroleadership, such as SCARF® (Status, Certainty, Autonomy, Relatedness, Fairness), have highlighted how the capacity to regulate our behavior and our reactions to others in order to minimize perceived threats and maximize rewards is a central principle of the brain that has an impact on various aspects of team dynamics and work life (Rock 2008).

We had two main aims in this study. The first one was to test the hypothesis that SR will relate to employee productivity. SR and productivity were measured in 5,550 employees of corporations in the USA, Australia, and New Zealand.

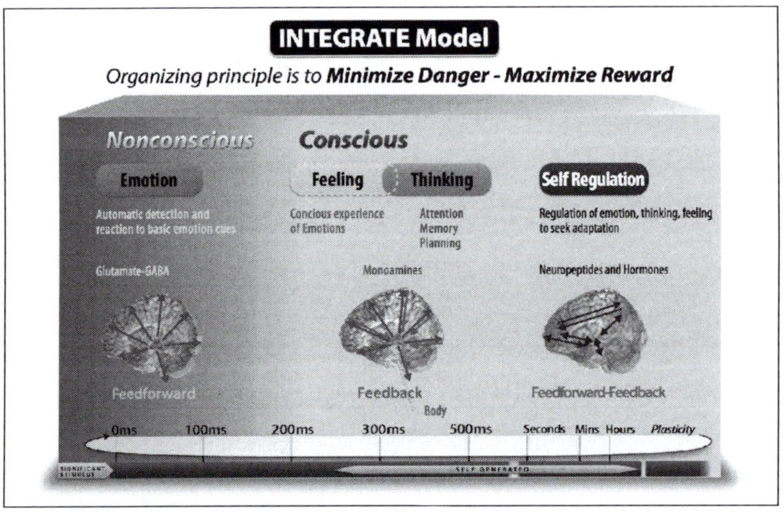

Figure 1. The INTEGRATE Model: The motivation to "minimize danger and maximize reward" is the key organizing principle of brain function and behavior. This motivation drives emotion, feeling, thinking, and self-regulation along a continuum of time (nonconscious to conscious) and associated brain and body activity.

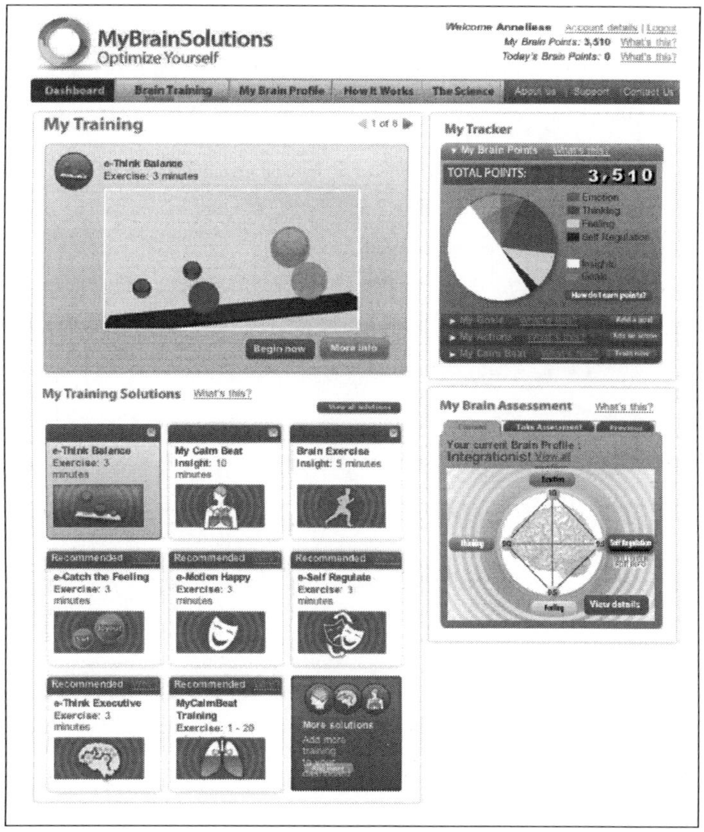

Figure 2. Brain-training program MyBrainSolutions™: MyBrainSolutions is an online program that consists of a suite of brain-training exercises and videos, as well as tools to track training and other personal goals.

Our second aim was to test the hypothesis that SR could be significantly improved within a "30-day challenge" period through online brain training. Employees in the study took part in a web-based brain-training program called MyBrainSolutions™ (fig. 2) based on the INTEGRATE Model (fig. 1). SR and productivity were then reassessed after this 30-day challenge of brain training.

Methods

Participants

Some 5,550 employees (mean ± SD: age 41 ± 11, education 16 ± 2) were recruited from ten corporations in the United States (n = 8), Australia (n = 1), and New Zealand (n = 1). These corporations had chosen to offer their employees participation in an integrated brain assessment and brain-training program known as MyBrainSolutions. This program encompasses a web-based assessment and holistic suite of brain-training games/exercises. Data were acquired directly via MyBrainSolutions in accordance with the accepted terms and conditions. Some employers offered incentives for employees to engage in the program, while others did not. Incentives included monetary rewards (gift cards and cash up to $130) or credits toward health-insurance benefits.

Study design, assessments, and brain training

Participants were given login codes to register with the online brain-training program MyBrainSolutions. After first logging in, participants were asked to complete a My Brain Assessment and the WHO Health and Productivity Questionnaire (HPQ) (Kessler et al. 2003; Kessler et al. 2004). The My Brain Assessment consisted of a validated neurocognitive assessment, WebNeuro™ (Silverstein et al. 2007),[1] and the BRISC (Brain Resource BRISC and WebNeuro™ Assessment Manual 2010). Participants then had access to the brain-training program MyBrainSolutions. Participants were encouraged to complete follow-up HPQ and My Brain Assessments. In some cases, incentives were provided for completing two assessments within a 30-day interval along with a minimum amount of brain training (4,000 "brain points," which was roughly equivalent to 20 minutes three times per week).

The My Brain Assessment consisted of a validated neurocognitive assessment...

BRISC is a forty-five-item, self-report test that assesses feeling and self-regulation brain processes. Items on the BRISC are converted to standardized scores so that low scores indicate poorer capacity (e.g., compromised SR) and higher scores indicate better capacity for SR (Gordon et al. 2005). Nonclinical norms used to standardize BRISC items have been established across a wide age range of six to ninety-two years (Williams et al. 2008). It has a test-retest reliability of 0.79.

In addition to the My Brain Assessment, participants completed the eleven-item WHO HPQ (Kessler et al. 2003; Kessler et al. 2004). The HPQ assesses workplace productivity, which is calculated using the measures of relative absenteeism and relative presenteeism. Relative absenteeism compares actual hours worked with the number of hours an employee is expected to work, while relative presenteeism is the ratio of an employee's work performance compared with that of other employees in the same job. A productivity score of 100 percent would represent someone who works exactly the hours expected of them and whose job performance matches the average employee's.

Participants were then able to access the brain-training component of MyBrainSolutions, which offers game-like exercises designed to train and improve brain processing in emotion, thinking, feeling, and self-regulation (fig. 4). MyBrainSolutions is underpinned by the Brain Resource International Database (the world's largest standardized and integrated brain database) and the training games/exercises that reflect core aspects of emotion, feeling, thinking, and self-regulation.

---

1 WebNeuro and BRISC form an integrated web-based brain assessment. Please note that analysis of WebNeuro results is beyond the scope of this study.

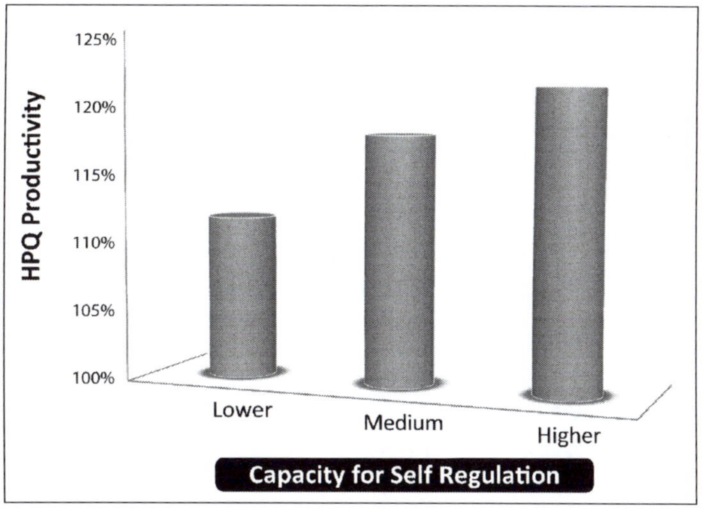

Figure 3. Self-Regulation and Workplace Productivity: Workplace Productivity is strongly influenced by an employee's capacity for self-regulation. Higher levels of self-regulation were found to align with higher levels of workplace productivity (Kruskal-Wallis: H = 84.203, d.f. 2, $p < 0.0001$).

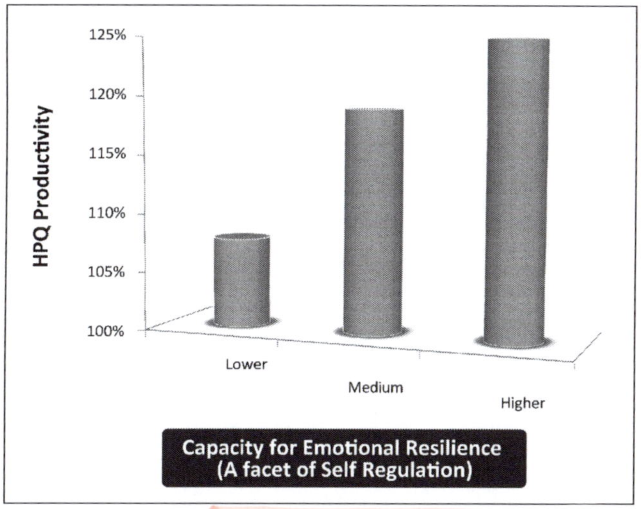

Figure 4. Emotional Resilience and Workplace Productivity: The self-regulation facet of emotional resilience was found to be the strongest factor influencing workplace productivity (Kruskal-Wallis: H = 188.366, d.f. 2, $p < 0.0001$).

The second assessment was completed after 30 days of training. Participants were encouraged to complete reassessment with the My Brain Assessment and the HPQ. With each game/exercise, participants received "brain points" on their personalized website "dashboard" to enhance engagement. It was recommended they target a minimum of a thousand brain points per week, based on an equivalent of training for 20 minutes three times per week.

Data analysis

Scores for SR and the facets of SR—emotional resilience, positivity–negativity bias, and social skills—were standardized with respect to gender and age. Scores were scaled from one to ten, where higher scores indicated better self-regulation capacity.

To investigate whether there was a relationship between SR and productivity, Kruskal-Wallis tests were performed. For this analysis, SR and its facet scores were classified as "lower" (score of below 3.5), "medium" (3.5 to 7.5), or "higher" (above 7.5) in terms of capacity for SR. Kruskal-Wallis tests were chosen after performing Levene's test for homogeneity of variances.

Not all facets of SR have the same influence on productivity. The facet that had by far the most influence on productivity was emotional resilience...

To assess whether 30 days of brain training with MyBrainSolutions changed scores on SR, a paired t-test was done. Cohen's d was also calculated to determine the size of the effect of training, and a test effect was taken into consideration.

Results

Analysis revealed a strong relationship between workplace productivity and SR. Workers with a higher capacity for SR scored significantly higher for workplace productivity ($H = 84.203$, d.f. 2, $p \leftarrow 0.0001$). On average, an employee with "higher" capacity for SR achieved 121 percent for workplace productivity, while those with "medium" and "lower" scores on capacity for SR had productivity scores of 118 percent and 112 percent respectively (fig. 3). (Note, a productivity score of 100 percent represented a worker who self-rated his/her job performance to match the average employee in his or her position.)

Further analysis of the relationship between SR and workplace productivity revealed that not all facets of SR have the same influence on productivity. The facet that had by far the most influence on productivity was emotional resilience ($H = 188.366$, d.f. 2, $p \leftarrow 0.0001$). People with "higher" capacity for emotional resilience had, on average, productivity scores of 125 percent, while those with "medium" and "lower" levels had productivity scores of 119 percent and 108 percent respectively (fig. 4). Social skills also had a positive influence on productivity but not as strongly as emotional resilience ($H = 11.16$, d.f. 2, $p = 0.004$). The SR facet of positivity–negativity bias did not seem to have any influence on productivity ($H = 0.197$, d.f. 2, $p \leftarrow 0.91$).

To see whether SR can improve, participants' SR scores after 30 days of MyBrainSolutions training were compared to their before-training scores. To be included in this analysis, participants had to have met the minimum training requirement of 4,000 brain points (approximately four hours of training). The number of people included in this analysis was 175. Encouragingly, we found that those who trained with MyBrainSolutions significantly improved their SR score after 30 days (p ← 0.0001; effect size 0.67; fig. 5).

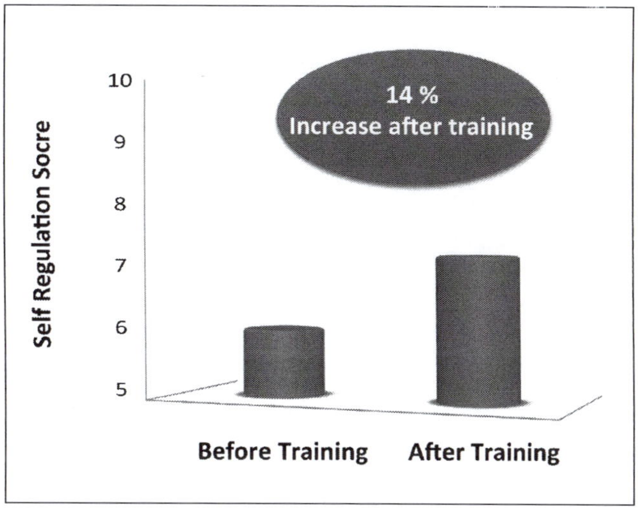

Figure 5. Self-regulation scores improved with MyBrainSolutions training. After 30 days of brain training, there was a 14 percent increase in self-regulation (effect size 0.67, $p < .0001$), over and above any practice effect due to repeat testing. Self-regulation scores are presented on the standardized STEN scale of 1 to 10, with 10 representing the best scores.

The average pretraining SR score was 6.8, while the average posttraining score was 7.8 (possible scores range from 1–10).

Discussion

The first new finding of this study was that higher SR relates significantly to higher workplace productivity. This relationship was particularly apparent for the SR facet of emotional resilience.

The second main finding was that brain training, using the online program MyBrainSolutions, significantly improves employees' SR capacity within 30 days.

These findings are consistent with the INTEGRATE Model framework. SR is the means by which we manage ourselves to minimize danger and maximize reward to achieve optimal adaption to our changing environment. In a work context, reward includes not only monetary goals but also having a sense of meaning and achievement in the work itself. The emotional resilience facet of SR relates to a personal self-efficacy and a sense of direction that is needed to achieve optimal adaption to the workplace.

The relationship between SR (and its emotional resilience facet in particular) and workplace productivity also accords with the aspects of the SCARF model (Rock 2008) and further highlights the importance of a personal sense of direction, planning and goals in creating reward, and minimizing danger (or risk) in our own behavior and in how we react to others.

Higher SR relates significantly to higher workplace productivity.

For leaders, these findings highlight the intrinsic brain processes that are important to workplace performance. Leadership strategies for building the capacity to self-regulate emotion, feeling, and thinking will help boost productivity of the leader and the employees being lead.

Online brain training is a relatively new concept that is quickly gaining interest. A number of studies report that training with computer programs can lead to improvement in real-world performance (Mahncke et al. 2006; Willis et al. 2006; Jaeggi et al. 2008; Smith et al. 2009). This study diverges from the previous literature in that the focus was on training of brain processes other than cognition.

Additionally, research on brain training to date has commonly focused on cohorts who have a disadvantage before the training sessions. In the present study, significant improvements were observed with a healthy sample from companies in which employees were already performing at a high level. This indicates that employees of all levels of functioning could likely benefit from scalable online and well-designed solutions.

Online brain training is a relatively new concept that is quickly gaining interest.

With evidence that SR can be improved via online brain training programs and that SR, in turn, relates to productivity, leaders may consider brain training on its own or in conjunction with leadership or coaching programs to optimize their own personal performance and the performance of their teams.

Given the cost-effectiveness of online programs such as MyBrainSolutions, the return on investment (ROI) is likely to be much higher when compared with more traditional training, such as intensive training seminars. Online training also offers scalability for employers to reach employees who may not be based in traditional centralized offices or workplaces. Given the sample size of more than five thousand in this study, the generalization of this benefit applied to a large work force is considerable. Future studies with larger samples completing reassessment after training would be valuable to seek replication of the findings.

The present study provides an encouraging demonstration that brain training has the potential to provide large-scale productivity benefits to innovative workplaces.

Overall implications of the findings:

- Self-regulation is a key brain-based capacity to cultivate in employees for optimal productivity.
- Self-paced online brain training is one means of boosting self-regulation and productivity.

Acknowledgments

MO, NJC, and SD have received income and stock options as employees with Brain Resource Ltd.

LMW has received consulting fees and stock options in Brain Resource Ltd. and is a stockholder in Brain Resource Ltd. She has received Advisory Board fees from Pfizer.

EG is founder of and receives income as chief executive officer and chairman of Brain Resource Ltd. He has stock options in Brain Resource Ltd.

References

Brain Resource BRISC™ and Assessment Manual. 2010. Brain Resource Ltd., V1.6.

Damasio, A. R. 1996. "The Somatic Marker Hypothesis and the Possible Functions of the Prefrontal Cortex." *Philosophical Transactions of the Royal Society B: Biological Sciences* 351(1346): 1413–1320.

Davidson, R. J., and Irwin, W. 1999. "The Functional Neuroanatomy of Emotion and Affective Style." *Trends in Cognitive Sciences* 3(1): 11–21.

Doidge, N. 2007. *The Brain that Changes Itself: Stories of Personal Triumph from the Frontiers of Brain Science.* New York: Viking.

Gordon, E., Barnett, K. J., Cooper, N. J., Tran, N., and Williams, L. M. 2008. "An "Integrative Neuroscience" Platform: Application to Profiles of Negativity and Positivity Bias." *Journal of Integrative Neuroscience* 7(3): 345–366.

Gordon, E., Cooper, N. J., Rennie, C., Hermens, D., and Williams, L. M. 2005. "Integrative Neuroscience: The Role of a Standardized Database." *Clinical EEG and Neuroscience* 36: 64–75.

Gross, J., and John, O. 2003. "Individual Differences in Two Emotion Regulations Processes: Implications for Affect Relationships and Well-Being." *Journal of Personality and Social Psychology* 85: 348–362.

Jaeggi, S. M., Buschkuehl, M., Jonides, J., and Perrig, W. J. 2008. "Improving Fluid Intelligence with Training on Working Memory." *Proceedings of the National Academy of Sciences, USA* 105(19): 6829–6833.

Kessler, R. C., Ames, M., Hymel, P. A., Loeppke, R., McKenas, D. K., Richling, D. E., Stang, P. E., and Ustun, T. B. 2004. "Using the World Health Organization Health and Work Performance Questionnaire (HPQ) to Evaluate the Indirect Workplace Costs of Illness." *Journal of Occupational Environmental Medicine* 46: S23–37.

Kessler, R. C., Barber, C., Beck, A., Berglund, P., Cleary, P. D., McKenas, D., Pronk, N., et al. 2003. "The World Health Organization Health and Work Performance Questionnaire (HPQ)." *Journal of Occupational Environmental Medicine* 45: 156–174.

Mahncke, H. W., Connor, B. B., Appelman, J., Ahsanuddin, O. N., Hardy, J. L., Wood, R. A., Joyce, N. M., et al. 2006. "Memory Enhancement in Healthy Older Adults Using a Brain Plasticity-Based Training Program: A Randomized, Controlled Study." *Proceedings of the National Academy of Sciences, USA* 103(33): 12523–12528.

Rock, D. 2008. "SCARF: A Brain-Based Model for Collaborating with and Influencing Others." *NeuroLeadership Journal* 1: 44–52.

Silverstein, S. M., Berten, S., Olson, P., Paul, R., Willams, L. M., Cooper, N. J., and Gordon, E. 2007. "Development and Validation of a World-Wide-Web-Based Neurocognitive Assessment Battery: Webneuro." *Behavior Research Methods* 39: 940–949.

Smith, G. E., Housen, P., Yaffe, K., Ruff, R., Kennison, R. F., Mahncke, H. W., and Zelinski, E. M. 2009. "A Cognitive Training Program Based on Principles of Brain Plasticity: Results from the Improvement in Memory with Plasticity-Based Adaptive Cognitive Training (IMPACT) study." *Journal of the American Geriatrics Society* 57: 594–603.

Thayer, J. F., and Lane, R. D. 2000. "A Model of Neurovisceral Integration in Emotion Regulation and Dysregulation." *Journal of Affective Disorders* 61: 201–216.

Thayer, R. E., Newman, J. R., and McClain, T. M. 1994. "Self-Regulation of Mood: Strategies for Changing a Bad Mood, Raising Energy, and Reducing Tension." *Journal of Personality and Social Psychology* 67(5): 910–925.

Williams, L. M., Gatt, J. M., Hatch, A., Palmer, D., Nagy, M., Rennie, C., Cooper, N. J., Morris, C., Grieve, S., Dobson-Stone, C., Schofield, P., Clark, C. R., Gordon, E., Arns, M., and Paul, R. H. 2008. "The INTEGRATE Model of Emotion, Thinking and Self Regulation: An Application to the 'Paradox of Aging.'" *Journal of Integrative Neuroscience* 7(3): 367–404.

Williams, L. M., Gatt, J. M., Schofield, P. R., Olivieri, G., Peduto, A., and Gordon, E. 2009. "'Negativity Bias' in Risk for Depression and Anxiety: Brain-Body Fear Circuitry Correlates, 5-HTT-LPR and Early Life Stress." *NeuroImage* 47(3): 804–814.

Williams, L. M., Hermens, D. F., Thein, T., Clark, C. R., Cooper, N. J., Clarke, S. D., Lamb, C., Gordon, E., and Kohn, M. R. 2010. "Using Brain-Based Cognitive Measures to Support Clinical Decisions in ADHD." *Pediatric Neurology* 42(2): 118–126.

Willis, S. L., Tennstedt, S. L., Marsiske, M., Ball, K., Elias, J., Koepke, K. M., Morris, J. N., Rebok, G. W., Unverzagt, F. W., Stoddard, A. M., and Wright, E. 2006. "Long-Term Effects of Cognitive Training on Everyday Functional Outcomes in Older Adults." *Journal of the American Medical Association* 296(23): 2805–2814.

Wing, R. R., Tate, D. F., Gorin, A. A., Raynor, H. A., and Fava, J. L. 2006. "A Self-Regulation Program for Maintenance of Weight Loss." *New England Journal of Medicine* 355: 1563–1571.

26. The neuroscience of motivation

Dr. Dean Mobbs[*] and Walter McFarland[*]
Dean Mobbs, Senior Investigator Scientist, MRC-Cognition and Brain Sciences Unit, Cambridge University, United Kingdom
dean.mobbs@mrc-cbu.cam.ac.uk

Walter McFarland, Senior Vice President, BoozAllen|Hamilton, Mclean, Virginia, USA
mcfarland.walter@gmail.com

Introduction

Human motivation has been a topic of keen interest to organizational scholars and practitioners since Fredrick Taylor (1911) and has been a featured topic in the disciplines of psychology, sociology, economics, political science, organizational development, leadership, management, and even philosophy. Each discipline has sought to better define what human motivation is, how it can be measured, and how it can be achieved and sustained. The result of this cross-disciplinary focus has been the development of numerous theories of motivation—many of which have contributed to our understanding of motivation in the context of the organization. However, after some hundred years of study, our understanding of human motivation remains limited—and this limitation is of particular concern as we enter the twenty-first century, for at least two reasons.

> *Human motivation has been a key focus of organizational science for the last hundred years.*

The first reason is more esoteric and concerns the notion of "meaning" in work. Since the days of Mary Parker Follett (1940), organizational scholars have imagined a new type of organization: one in which human needs for achievement and organizational needs for performance coincide. Scores on survey instruments measuring such things as job satisfaction and employee engagement are often regarded as indicators of both employee motivation and their meaning in work. Said another way, high levels of employee motivation are seen as being "good" both for organizations, because of the link to performance, and for people, because of the link to meaning in work.

The second reason is more practical and concerns the role of human motivation in providing organizations with competitive advantage. Organizations all over the world are preparing themselves to cope with unprecedented levels of competition and pressure to perform. These organizations face a legion of complex issues that include: the need to assume a more global stance, the need to become more innovative, the need to manage scarce resources better, and the need to deal with a growing set of issues over which they have no control. Examples include such things as energy constraints, climate changes, and political instability. For many organizations, the search for competitive advantage is focused on maximizing human performance, and the question of how to create and sustain a highly motivated work force is taking on new meaning and urgency.

For many organizations, the search for competitive advantage is focused on maximizing human performance...

Arguments for motivation as a source of competitive advantage tie to recent data related to employee engagement. As discussed later, "engagement" is one of a group of variables often used to measure employee motivation in an organization—and one that has grown in popularity in recent years. The return on investment (ROI) estimates on employee engagement paint a vivid picture of why engagement (i.e., motivation) matters in organizational performance. For example, Ulrich and Smallwood (2004) estimated that engaged employees are two to four times more productive than average employees; Pfeffer and Sutton (2006) stated that employee engagement matters even more in complex jobs and estimated that highly engaged software engineers are 12 times more productive than the average; and the Gallup organization estimated that disengaged employees cost an organization $3,400 for every $10,000 in salary. These and other data prompted human resources consulting firm Towers Perrin (2006) to conclude, "We are witnessing an era for businesses around the world in which engaging employees makes the difference between success and failure."

"We are witnessing an era for businesses around the world in which engaging employees makes the difference between success and failure."

Although motivation theory has come a long way in the last century, important gaps in our understanding remain. Further, we assert that the field of neuroscience can help fill some of these gaps by incorporating emerging information on how the human brain works. The study of the brain, particularly within the field of social, cognitive, and affective neuroscience, is starting to provide some underlying brain insights that can be applied in the real world (Lieberman 2007)—and, we believe, to increasing our understanding of motivation.

We begin with a brief review and critique of the current theories of motivation, then introduce the field of neuroscience, and conclude with a discussion of how breaking research in neuroscience may add important insight into human motivation in organizations.

Theories of motivation

Although there are numerous definitions of motivation, Robbins (1996, 2012) offers one that is particularly relevant to human motivation in the organizational context. He states that motivation is "the willingness to exert high levels of effort toward organizational goals, conditioned by the effort's ability to satisfy some individual needs." Although there are many theories of motivation, the major ones are often organized into five groups: need theories, goal-setting theory, reinforcement theory, equity theory, and expectancy theory. Each group will be briefly discussed.

Need theories

Much of how we now see human motivation began in the 1950s with the need theories, the most famous of which is Abraham Maslow's hierarchy of needs. Maslow (1954) asserted that internal to each of us is a hierarchy of five needs: physiological, safety, social, esteem, and self-actualization. As each need is met in succession, the next need becomes dominant. According to Maslow, although no need is ever fully gratified, a substantially satisfied need no longer motivates. To motivate an employee, managers must know what level of the hierarchy the employee is currently on and focus on satisfying needs at or above this level. Although Maslow's theory has received wide recognition, Maslow provided no empirical substantiation for it, and research does not generally validate it.

Much of how we now see human motivation began in the 1950s with the need theories...

Frederick Herzberg, Bernard Mausner and Barbara Bloch Snyderman (1959) proposed another famous needs theory referred to as motivation-hygiene theory. Simply put, motivation-hygiene theory states that both intrinsic and extrinsic factors relate to motivation. Intrinsic factors include things such as personal achievement; recognition; the work itself; and the opportunities for responsibility, advancement, and growth. Extrinsic factors include such things as company policy, supervision, work conditions, salary, relationship with peers, and status. Herzberg suggested that intrinsic factors relate to job satisfaction, while extrinsic factors are associated with job dissatisfaction. Herzberg also observed that removing dissatisfying factors from a job (company policy, supervision, salary, etc.) does not necessarily make the job satisfying. Instead, removal of these "hygiene" factors merely makes a job less dissatisfying. To Herzberg, the secret to increasing employee motivation was in focusing on improving intrinsic factors.

In the 1960s, Clayton Alderfer (1969) reworked Maslow's needs hierarchy theory to align it more closely with emerging research on motivation. He called his revised hierarchy ERG theory. ERG theory substitutes three levels (i.e., existence, relatedness, and growth) for Maslow's five. The existence need is concerned with providing our basic material requirements and combines Maslow's physiological and safety needs. Relatedness refers to the need we have for maintaining important interpersonal relationships and aligns with Maslow's social need and a portion of his esteem need. Growth needs are the intrinsic desire for personal development and incorporate portions of Maslow's esteem and self-actualization categories. Beyond the reduction in categories, ERG theory is different in other ways. Most importantly, ERG theory argues, like Maslow, that satisfied lower-order needs lead to the desire to satisfy higher-order needs. Unlike Maslow, however, ERG theory asserts that multiple needs can be operating as motivators at the same time and that frustration in attempting to satisfy a higher-level need can result in regression to a lower-level need.

David McClelland's (1961) theory of needs focuses on the motivating power of three needs: achievement, power, and affiliation. The need for achievement is the drive to excel, to achieve in relation to a set of standards, to strive to succeed. The need for power is the drive to make others behave in a way they would not have behaved otherwise. The need for affiliation is the drive for friendly and close interpersonal relationships. Of the three needs, the most research has been done on the need for achievement. This research suggests several things (Davidson et al. 2002). First, individuals with a high need to achieve are most motivated by jobs with personal responsibility, feedback, and an intermediate degree of risk. Second, high achievers are not necessarily good managers as their focus is on how they do personally. Third, the needs for affiliation and power are closely related in managerial success. The best managers are high in their need for power and low in their need for affiliation.

Relatedness refers to the need we have for maintaining important interpersonal relationships...

Goal-setting theory

Edwin Locke (1968) proposed that intentions to work toward a goal are a major source of work motivation. That is, goals tell an employee what needs to be done and how much effort will need to be expended. More specifically, we can say that specific goals increase performance; that difficult goals, when accepted, result in higher performance than do easy goals; and that feedback leads to higher performance. In addition to feedback, three other factors have been found to influence the goals-performance relationship: goal commitment, adequate self-efficacy, and national culture.

Reinforcement theory

Where goal-setting theory is a cognitive approach, proposing that an individual's purposes direct his actions—reinforcement theory—by contrast is a behavioristic approach (Skinner 1953) that argues that behavior is only about reinforcement and is environmentally caused. Said another way, behavior is a function of its consequences. Reinforcement theory ignores the inner state of the person (i.e., feelings, attitudes, expectations, etc.) and focuses on what happens to a person when he or she takes some action.

Reinforcement theory ignores the inner state of the person...

Equity theory

Equity theory (Knutson et al. 2001) states that individuals compare their job inputs and outcomes with those of others and then respond to eliminate perceived inequities. Equity theory recognizes that individuals are concerned not only with the absolute amount of rewards they receive for their efforts, but also with the relationship of this amount to what others receive. When people perceive an imbalance in their outcome-input ratio relative to others, tension is created. This tension provides the basis for motivation, as people strive for what they perceive as equity and fairness.

Expectancy theory

One of the most widely accepted explanations of motivation is Victor Vroom's (1964) expectancy theory. Expectancy theory argues that the strength of a tendency to act in a certain way depends on the strength of an expectation that the act will be followed by a given outcome and on the attractiveness of that outcome to the individual. Simply said, expectancy theory says an employee is motivated to exert a high level of effort when he or she believes effort will lead to a good performance appraisal; a good appraisal will lead to organizational rewards such as a bonus, salary increase, or promotion; and the rewards will satisfy the employee's personal goals.

Limitations of current theories

The five theories briefly discussed above provide some insight into the volume of work and research focused on human motivation in the 60 years since Maslow introduced his hierarchy of needs. Still, important limitations in motivation theory persist. For example, there is no common agreement on how motivation is defined and measured; some or all of the current motivational theories may be culturally biased; and most importantly, there is no single theory that best predicts motivation. Each of these limitations will be briefly discussed.

. . . current theories of motivation may be culturally biased—and therefore of limited use to organizations whose employees are increasingly multinational.

First, researchers commonly use different things to define and measure motivation in organizations. Common things include: productivity, absenteeism, turnover, and employee satisfaction. In recent years, the employee satisfaction variable is often redefined as employee engagement. What is motivation? Is it just one of these things or all?

Next, current theories of motivation may be culturally biased—and therefore of limited use to organizations whose employees are increasingly multinational. Most current motivational theories were created in the United States by and for Americans. Inherent in these theories is a strong emphasis on both individualism and "quality of life." For example, both the goal-setting and the expectancy theories emphasize the motivational power of goal accomplishment and individual effort.

Finally, an examination of research data notes that some theories are better at predicting some definitions of motivation than others. For example, Landy and Becker (1987) found: "Employee productivity is best predicted by Goal-Setting Theory followed by Expectancy Theory; absenteeism is equally predicted by Reinforcement Theory, Equity Theory, and Expectancy Theory; while employee satisfaction is best predicted by Expectancy Theory followed by Equity Theory." This observation leads to the second point: no single theory or combination of theories predicts motivation holistically.

In fact, as noted above, research has supported a number of the theories—at least in part. Each of the five theories has been shown to predict one or more of the motivation definitions listed, with some theories predicting more than one. Still, no theory has been found to be a good predictor of all definitions. The closest is probably equity theory, which is a strong predictor of absence and turnover and a weak predictor of employee productivity and satisfaction (Landy and Becker (1987). In fact, the theories discussed are not mutually exclusive but complementary. The challenge for the practitioner—often the chief human resources officer—is deciding when and how to use each, while understanding the limitations of all. This is a daunting task to say the least.

In summary, current theories of motivation are helpful but do not yet provide the insight needed to create and sustain a highly motivated work force. In their search for competitive advantage, twenty-first-century organizations need all the insight they can get. We believe that a neuroscience perspective on motivation can add an important and powerful perspective.

We believe that a neuroscience perspective on motivation can add an important and powerful perspective.

Neuroscience of motivation

Neuroscience is beginning to play a key role in creating new perspectives in several fields. Some examples include the popular field of neuroeconomics, as well as the lessser-known fields of neuroaccounting and neuromarketing. We propose that understanding how the brain responds to specific motivators will allow a fresh look at motivation theories.

The first step in understanding motivation is to understand how the brain has evolved. Our brains have evolved to detect biologically salient stimuli and to optimally pursue a course of action. Such simple mechanisms of motivation are seated in the oldest parts of our brains that are common to our mammalian cousins. In the field of neuroscience, the question of what brain systems motivate an organism to act was first addressed by Olds and Milner (1954). These neuroscientists showed that when the pleasure centers of the brain are electrically stimulated, the rodent's behavior is positively reinforced, illustrating that motivation and reinforcement have an underlying neural basis. After this study, researchers showed that stimulation of the brain can result in escape behaviors in the absence of any environmental threat (Moreau, Schmitt, and Karli 1986). These and other studies revolutionized psychology and reinforcement theory and set the stage for the modern neuroscience of motivation.

Understanding how the brain responds to specific motivators will allow a fresh look at motivation theories.

We now have an intricate picture of the neural systems associated with motivation. This has come about by advances in measuring brain responses, including single-cell recording, lesion mapping, and brain-imaging techniques such as positron-emission tomography (PET) and functional magnetic resonance imaging (fMRI). While each technique has its limitations, when the evidence is accumulated, it is clear that the midbrain, striatum, and prefrontal cortex are critical in eliciting reward- and punishment-related behaviors. Overall, these techniques have bridged the gap between human and animal physiology, showing overlapping neural systems relating to motivation. Below we discuss some of the theories of motivation in the context of recent developments in brain imaging. We specifically focus on the needs theories of Maslow and McCellend, as well as the equity and expectancy theories.

How does the brain motivate us?

The goal of the nervous system is to produce responses that yield the best possible inclusive fitness (Glimcher 2003). Evolution has created core motivation systems that, in their basic forms, manifest as approaching or retreating behaviors.

Approaching, in the form of exploration or foraging, is associated with reward processes. Under most circumstances, these behaviors are driven by the brain's dopaminergic system, which originates in the midbrain ventral tegmental area (VTA) and substantia nigra pars compacta (SNC). The VTA axons extend to the nucleus accumbens, amygdala, and hippocampus via the mesolimbic pathway, while the prefrontal cortex receives dopamine via the mesocoritcal pathway. The caudate and putamen receive dopamine via the nigostriatal pathway from the SNC. The dopamine system is associated with many types of rewards and is thought to increase motivation and vigor.

The goal of the nervous system is to produce responses that yield the best possible inclusive fitness...

Conversely, the motivation to avoid a stimulus, such as a predatory threat, activates a set of distinct neural systems. The major neurostransmitter associated with aversion is serotonin (5-HT). The core 5-HT cell bodies are found in the midbrain raphe nuclei with the dorsal (upper parts) of the raphe nuclei, which sends projections to the limbic system, including the amygdala and striatum as well as the cortex (Dayan and Huys 2008). In relation to aversion, McNaughton and Corr (2004) have proposed that defensive avoidance of a threat is associated with a cascade of regions that reflect distal and proximal danger. This network of systems associated with 5-HT expression involves the midbrain periaqueductal gray (PAG) and hypothalamus when the threat is close, and the amygdala and ventral prefrontal cortex when the threat is distant (Deakin and Graeff 1991; Mobbs et al 2007). While these reward and fear networks overlap (Daw, Kakade, and Dayan 2002; **Ö**ngür, Ferry, and Price 2003), neuroscientific research clearly illustrates that a set of hard-wired neural systems motivates avoidance and approach to stimuli.

Needs theory and neuroscience

Neuroscientists typically place rewards in the categories of primary (e.g., food) and secondary (e.g., money). Others, such as Berridge and Robinson (1995), have proposed that rewards can be further divided into the two components of *wanting* (motivation) and *liking* (pleasure). Liking is believed to be a hedonic reaction to the pleasure of a reward. Conversely, despite being a component of reward, wanting is not pleasure but the motivational drive to pursue a potential reward. Berridge has shown that dopamine is associated with wanting, while the opioid system modulates liking, and that both are differentially represented in a distinct subregion of ventral striatum known as the nucleus accumbens. Therefore, the needs theory is in harmony with the brain's "wanting" system.

At the basic level of primary rewards, physiological needs such as for food (Beaver et al. 2006) and sex (Komisaruk and Whipple 2005) activate the brain's reward circuitry. In most behavioral economic studies, however, secondary rewards such as money are typically used. Not surprisingly, money is a robust method of evoking the brain's reward system, and innumerable studies are testament to this (e.g., Mobbs et al. 2009; O'Doherty et al. 2003; Knutson et al. 2001). Another important part of Maslow's hierarchy is the need for safety. Using fMRI, Kim, Shimojo, and O'Doherty (2006) showed that the avoidance of punishment activates the reward circuitry itself, thus making it rewarding to escape punishment. At the highest level of the hierarchy of needs are cognitive rewards, such as curiosity and desire for knowledge. To test if such needs activate the brain's reward systems, Kang and coworkers (2009) conducted an experiment in which subjects read trivia questions while their brains were scanned. The level of curiosity for knowing the answer correlated with activity in the reward area of the caudate. Therefore, many of what Maslow termed "needs" seem to be closely associated with the brain's dopamine system.

It has been shown that affiliation activates the brain's reward network.

Fitting with a later model of needs (i.e., McClelland's theory (1961), it has been shown that affiliation activates the brain's reward network. Mobbs and coworkers (2009) created a game-show paradigm where subjects were introduced to two contestants who played a guessing game. First, subjects were asked to rate how similar they were to the contestants (on social, ethical, and personal preferences such as favorite movies or music). Next, subjects in the MRI scanner watched as the contestants took turns guessing the likelihood of a card being higher or lower than another unseen card. Results showed that when the subjects observed the similar contestant win money, activity increased in the ventral striatum. Such vicarious reward was not observed when the dissimilar contestant won money. Also supporting McClelland's idea that power is a basic need, Zink and colleagues (2008) showed that when subjects were rated higher in a social hierarchy (superior compared to inferior players in a game), activity increased in the ventral striatum. Taken together, we can speculate that the brain treats many needs as rewarding and motivates the individual to perpetually pursue the fulfillment of these needs.

Equity theory and social comparison

Adams's theory of equity proposes that employees aim to keep equity between themselves and coworkers (Adams 1965). It has been shown that social comparison can have a strong impact on perceived fairness. For example, how would you feel if you just got a pay raise, but then found out that your work colleague was given a smaller or bigger pay raise? Fliessbach et al. (2007) investigated this question by scanning pairs of subjects in two adjacent MRI scanners. During the scan, the subjects performed a simple task (guessing the number of dots on a screen) that entailed financial rewards for correct responses. Subsequently, the pair of subjects was told how much money they would be given for their correct response. When one was given more money than the other subject, there was increased activity in the ventral striatum. Thus, $10 means more when another person is given $5, compared with when another is given $15, suggesting that, under these circumstance, social comparison is as important as the actual amount of money.

Social comparison can also create negative emotions, such as envy and gloating at another's failures.

Similarly, we are particularly vulnerable to acting adversely to others being unfairly paid more or less. Known as inequity aversion, it is proposed that people act to reduce such inequity because it has a negative impact on experienced reward. In a recent study, Tricomi et al. (2010) used fMRI to examine the neural systems that underlie inequity-averse social preferences. Inequity was manipulated by recruiting pairs of subjects and dividing them based on how much money they were given ($50 or $0). Both the rich ($50) and poor ($0) subjects transferred money either to themselves or to the other person. Results showed that activity in the ventral striatum was most responsive when rich players transferred money to the poor others, therefore supporting the inequality-averse models. However, poor subjects showed the opposite pattern, with increased activity in this reward region when transferring money to themselves. Intriguingly, Brosnan and de Waal (2003) also showed inequality-aversion in nonhuman primates (capuchin monkeys), suggesting it is a basic and primitive sentiment.

The perception of fairness by a work force is believed to be a fundamental requirement for high levels of motivation and performance.

Social comparison can also create negative emotions, such as envy and gloating at another's failures. Takahashi et al. (2009) showed that when subjects were asked to imagine a self-relevant individual in an envious situation (e.g., gaining top scores on an exam), the brain's pain circuitry became active. However, when something bad happened to the self-relevant and envied individual, the subjects showed increased activity in the brain's reward circuitry. This suggests that when we are envious of a self-relevant individual, we gain more satisfaction when being told about that person's encounter with a terrible event (i.e., schadenfreude, or joy at another's misfortunes) than when told about an envious event. Fairness can also evoke schadenfreude. Tania Singer and colleagues (2006) showed that observing an unfair individual being shocked results in the reward systems being activated and that these reward areas were correlated with revenge scores. One explanation is that it is rewarding to experience another's failure because it reduces competition and teaches others that it is not acceptable to act in certain ways.

Given the negative emotions that go along with inequity and envy, it is not surprising to suggest that this may have a negative relationship to the organization. Adams proposed that employees will attempt to restore equity through a number of means. For example, employees who feel underpaid and underappreciated may attempt to restore equity in ways that are detrimental to the organization (Adams 1965). Both Adams's assertions and the neuroscience research point to the importance of perceived fairness in human motivation. This suggests that organizations seeking higher levels of employee motivation should focus significant attention and resources on designing performance-management systems that are perceived by employees as appropriate and fair. We believe there is no substitute for direct employee involvement in the design of these systems and that all stages of the design should be transparent to all. The perception of fairness by a work force is believed to be a fundamental requirement for high levels of motivation and performance.

Expectancy and the brain

Expectancy theory (Vroom 1964) is based on the idea that expectancy of a certain outcome (e.g., possibility of a pay rise) influences how we act. Expectancy is believed to increase motivation. Nearly eighty years ago, Hull (1932) offered the theory of goal-gradience, which states that the organism will show increased motivation and vigor with the higher likelihood of acquiring the goal. This is supported by later research showing that rats pull with more force on a harness when a reward is close, compared with distant (Haner 1955). Such increased motivation may relate to increased likelihood (or expectancy) of acquiring the goal.

Stopping people from acquiring their goals can have a detrimental effect on behavior and presumably the organization.

Research on rodents has shown that expecting an outcome is associated with the obitofrontal cortex (OFC). The OFC receives dense input from dopamine cell bodies via the mesocortical pathways and is believed to guide behaviors associated with generating outcome expectancies. Schoenbaum et al. (1998) showed that the OFC learns to discriminate between two odors based on outcomes they predict. One study conducted on patients with damage to the OFC showed that these patients exhibited an inability to discriminate between two competing stimuli and thus were unable to generate expectancy outcomes (Camille et al. 2004). From this and other studies, Schoenbaum and Roesch (2005) have proposed that outcomes generated by the OFC allow for the comparison between predicted and actual outcome, which in turn generates expectancies and motivates the organism to pursue a course of action.

What happens when our expectations are not met? B. F. Skinner was the first to suggest that the omission of a scheduled reinforcement results in rats showing subtle forms of aggression. The observation was taken further by Amsel, who showed that blocking rats from gaining rewards resulted in what he coined "frustrative non-reward" (Amsel 1958). Inspired by both Amsel's theory and Hull's theory of goal-gradience, we have recently examined the neural basis of expectancy and frustration (Yu et al., unpublished observation) showing that stopping people from acquiring their goals can have a detrimental effect on behavior and presumably on the organization.

By understanding how the human brain works to motivate people, we can start to think about how to enhance motivation...

From the brain to the organization

We began by asserting that human motivation is a key topic for twenty-first-century organizations that depend on a highly motivated work force for competitive advantage—and that current theories of motivation are a good starting point but fall short in several ways. We then suggested that the field of neuroscience could add a new perspective and, hopefully, some additional understanding of human motivation. The neuroscientific studies reviewed lend credence to many of the models of motivation. Most of these occupational motivations tap into the various theories of motivation, which have overlapping neural signatures.

By understanding how the human brain works to motivate people, we can start to think about how to enhance motivation (and productivity) in efficacious ways. What this review of the neuroscientific literature shows is that most motivators—from those entwined in the various needs, expectation, and equity theories—are modulated by the brain's wanting system, which is mediated by dopamine. We also know that negative situations such as inequity tap into the brain's aversive systems (Takahashi et al. 2009).

Summary

So how can we take this neuroscientific information and help organizations? Neuroscience provides clarity on the biology of motivation and how the aversive systems can easily be engaged. Thus, neuroscience can inform us about how to not engage the "aversive" system and better engage the "motivational" system. Below, we discuss some of the important implications of the neuroscientific research.

Neuroscience has taught us that motivations are more complex than previously thought. What is clear, however, is that different motivators tap into overlapping motivational systems. In HR systems, the role of neuroscience may help get the best out of employees by understanding their idiosyncratic motivations. What are the implications of a neuroscience finding that motivations are more complex than thought? One is that it's probably simplistic for managers to rely on any one theory of motivation because important considerations will then be missed. What would neuroscience have managers do instead? For example, is triggering the brain's aversive systems a profound mistake? Is it key for managers to know what *not* to do as much as what *to* do? Is another piece of advice the focus on the brain's wanting systems? So a neuroscience lens might suggest not relying on one theory, avoiding as a priority the demotivational aspects of triggering the brain's aversive systems, and focusing motivational strategy on the brain's wanting systems that include both extrinsic and intrinsic factors.

All of this suggests a new role for managers—not as people who memorize motivational theories and blindly apply them to an anonymous work force, but as enlightened leaders who understand that people are unique and that knowledge of the brain offers advice on motivating and demotivating them.

- People compare themselves with others. When people are satisfied with their own circumstances, they will act as better collaborators, willing to help others and work with more motivation. An important finding of neuroscience is that equity may have even more power to motivate and demotivate than previously thought. When the brain perceives inequity, despite the absolute value of a reward, it is profoundly demotivated. A more important consideration in using rewards to motivate is how the reward will be compared with that of others. An effective reward system has several features: the amount of the reward should be perceived as significant; how awards are distributed should be perceived as fair; and extrinsic awards should be complemented by intrinsic awards such as public recognition, managerial praise, and the like.

- Dissatisfaction based on inequity is furthermore a powerful way of evoking the aversive system through cynical emotions like envy, jealousy, and gloating at another's failures. Therefore, when inequity is high, the aversive system will be evoked and there may be increased job dissatisfaction and decreased motivation. This is the downside of the above discussion. It can be rolled into that or kept separate, but the point is that rewards used poorly can demotivate as much as motivate, or more. The implications of triggering the aversive systems are profound. The brain loses productivity and shuts down, and productivity is hard to regain. Said another way, triggering the aversive system has a deleterious effect on organizational productivity. It elicits both downtime and costs to fix.

- Expectancy plays a major role in motivation and job dissatisfaction. We know that people have expectations that motivate them and when blocked can result in the engagement of the aversive system (i.e., frustration) and work dissatisfaction. Therefore, job goals and aspirations should be clear between the individual and the organization. Making goals unclear or even blocking goals may tap into the brain's aversive system. In this way, managers become facilitators for employee achievement. Managers insist on clarity, agree to support, and actively help remove impediments to goal accomplishment. The impetus to accomplish goals remains with the employee.

The goal of the organization is to minimize engagement of the brain's aversive system and attempt to best engage the motivational system.

The goal of the organization is to minimize engagement of the brain's aversive system and attempt to best engage the motivational system. We believe the above knowledge can make valuable contributions to modern organizations by making important contributions to various parts of an organization's human resource management system. Some examples include the increased use of neuroscience technologies such as brain imaging to support leadership-development programs and leveraging neuroscience thinking to coach leaders on how to better communicate with employees—that is, to use language that is more inspirational and evokes less resistance.

It should also be noted that even with better integration of neuroscience principles, important challenges around human motivation remain. Examples include the lack of a common definition of what human motivation in the organizational context is and how to best measure it, ensuring that motivation enhancements are implemented without cultural bias (a real advantage for neuroscience), tailoring motivation enhancements to specific professional groups (neuroscience says different professions literally think differently), better understanding the impact of intrinsic motivators, and rethinking how neuroscience principles should be integrated across the entire HRM system life cycle.

References

Adams, J.A. 1965. "Inequity in Social Exchange." In *Advances in Experimental Psychology 2* edited by L. Berkowitz, 267–299 New York: Academic Press.

Alderfer, C. P. 1969. "An Empirical Test of a New Theory of Human Needs." *Organizational Behavior and Human Performance* 142–175.

Amsel, A. 1958. "The Role of Frustrative Nonreward in Noncoutinuous Reward situations." *Psycho! Bull* 55: 102–119.

Anderson, N. H. 1968. "Likableness Ratings of 555 Personality-Trait Words." *Journal of Personality and Social Psychology* 9: 272–279.

Beaver, J. D., Lawrence, A. D., van Ditzhuijzen, J., Davis, M. H., Woods, A., and Calder, A. J. 2006. "Individual Differences in Reward Drive Predict Neural Responses to Images of Food." *The Journal of Neuroscience* 26: 5160–5166.

Berridge, K.C., and Robinson, T.E. 1995. "The Mind of an Addicted Brain: Neuroal Sensitization of Wanting Versus Liking." *Current Directions in Psychological Science* 4:71–76.

Brosnan, S.F., and de Waal, F. 2003. "Monkeys reject unequals pay." *Nature* 425: 297–299.

Camille N., Coricelli, G., Sallet, J., Pradat-Diehl, P., Duhamel, J. R., and Sirigu, A. 2004. "The Involvement of the Orbitofrontal Cortex in the Experience of Regret." *Science* 304: 1167–1170.

Davidson, R. J., Lewis, D. A., Alloy, L. B., Amaral, D. G., Bush, G., Cohen, J. D., Drevets, W.C., et al. 2002. "Neural and Behavioral Substrates of Mood and Mood Regulation." *Biological Psychiatry* 52: 478–502.

Daw, N. D., Kakade, S., and Dayan, P. 2002. "Opponent Interactions Between Serotonin and Dopamine." *Neural Networks* 15: 603–616.

Dayan, P., and Huys, Q. J. M. 2008. "Serotonin, Inhibition, and Negative Mood." *PLoS Computational Biology* 4(2): e4 doi:10.1371/journal.pcbi.0040004.

Deakin, J. F. W., and Graeff, F. G. 1991. "5-HT and Mechanisms of Defence." *Journal of Psychopharmacology* 5: 305–315.

Easterbrook, J. A. 1959. "The Effects of Emotion on Cue Utilization and the Organization of Behavior." *Psychological Review* 66: 183–202.

Fliessbach, K., Weber, B., Trautner, P., Dohmen, T., Sunde, U., Elger, C.E., and Falk, A. 2007. "Social Comparison Affects Reward-Related Brain Activity in the Human Ventral Straitum." *Science* 318: 1305–1308.

Follett, M. P. 1940. "Constructive Conflict." In *Dynamic Administration: The Collected Papers of Mary Parker Follett*, edited by H. C. Metcalf and L. Urwick, 30–49. New York: Harper.

Glimcher, P. W. 2003. *Decision, Uncertainty, and the Brain: The Science of Neuroeconomics*. Cambridge, MA: MIT Press.

Haner, C. F., and Brown, P. A. 1955. "Clarification of the Instigation to Action Concept in the Frustration-Aggression Hypothesis." *Journal of Abnormal Psychology* 51: 204–206.

Herzberg, F., Mausner, B., and Snyderman, B. 1959. *The Motivation to Work*. New York: John Wiley.

Hull, C. L. 1932. "The Goal Gradient Hypothesis and Maze Learning." *Psychological Review* 39: 25–43.

Kang, M.J., Hsu, M., Krajbich, I.M., Loewenstein, G., McClure, S.M., Wang, J.T., and Camerer, C.F. 2009. "The Wick in the Candle of Learning: Epistemic Curiosity Activated Reward Circuitry and Enhances Memory." *Psychological Science* 20(8): 963-973.

Kim, H., Shimojo S., and O'Doherty, J. P. 2006. "Is Avoiding an Aversive Outcome Rewarding? The Neural Substrates of Avoidance Learning in the Human Brain." *PloS Biology* 4: e233.

Knutson, B., Adams, C. M., Fong G. W., and Hommer, D. 2001. "Anticipation of Increasing Monetary Reward Selectively Recruits Nucleus Accumbens." *Journal of Neuroscience* 21: RC159.

Komisaruk, B. R., and Whipple, B. 2005. "Functional MRI of the Brain During Orgasm in Women." *Annual Review of Sex Research* 16: 62–86.

Landy, F. J., and Becker, W. W. 1987. "Motivation Theory Reconsidered." In *Research in Organizational Behavior*, edited by L. L. Cummings and B. M. Staw. Greenwich, CT: JAI Press.

Lieberman, M. D. 2007. "Social Cognitive Neuroscience: A Review of Core Processes." *Annual Review of Psychology* 58: 259–289.

Locke, E.A. 1968. "Toward a Theory of Task Motivation and Incentives." *Organizational Behaviour and Human Performance* 3(2): 157–189.

Maslow, A. 1954. *Motivation and Personality*. New York: Harper & Row.

McClelland, D. 1961. *The Achieving Society. Princeton*. NJ: Van Nostrand.

McNaughton, N., and Corr, P.J. 2004. "A Two-Dimensional Neuropsychology of Defense: Fear/ Aniexty and Defensive Distance. *Neuroscience and Biobehavioural Reviews* 28, 285–305.

Mobbs, D., Petrovic, P., Marchant, J., Hassabis, D., Weiskopf, N., Seymour, B., Dolan, R. J., and Frith, C. D. 2007. "When Fear is Near: Threat Imminence Elicits Prefrontal—Periaqueductal Grey Shifts in Humans." *Science* 317(5841): 1079–1083.

Mobbs, D., Yu, R., Meyer, M., Passamonti, L., Seymour, B., Calder, A. J., Schweizer, S., Frith, C. D., and Dalgleish, T. 2009. "A Key Role for Similarity in Vicarious Reward." *Science* 324: 900.

Moreau, J., Schmitt, P., and Karli, P. 1986. "Ventral Tegmental Stimulation Modulates Centrally Induced Escape Responding." *Physiology and Behavior* 36: 9–15.

O'Doherty, J.P., Dayan, P., Friston, K., Critchley, H., and Dolan, R.J. 2003. "Temporal Difference Models and Reward-Related Learning in the Human Brain." *Neuron* 38: 329–337.

Olds, J., and Milner, P. 1954. "Positive Reinforcement Produced Byb Electrical Stimulation of the Septal Area and Other Regions of Rat Brains." *Journal of Comparative and Physiological Psychology* 47: 419–427.

Öngür, D., Ferry, A. T., and Price, J. L. (2003). Architectonic Subdivision of the Human Orbital and Medial Prefrontal Cortex. Journal of Comparative Neurology, 460, 425–449.

Pfeffer, J., and Sutton, R. I. 2006. *Hard Facts*. Boston: Harvard Business School Press.

Robbins, S. P. 1996. *Organizational Behavior: Concepts, Controversies, Applications*. Englewood Cliffs, NJ: Prentice Hall.

Schoenbaum, G., Chiba, A., and Gallagher, M. 1998. "Orbitfrontal Cortex and Basolateral Amygdala Encode Expected Outcomes During Learning." *Nature Neuroscience* 1: 155–159.

Schoenbaum, G., and Roesch, M.R. 2005. "Orbitaofrontal Cortex, Associative Learning and Expectancies." *Neuron* 47: 633-636.

Singer, T., Seymour, B., O'Doherty, J.P., Stephan, K.E., Dolan, R.J., and Frith, C.D. 2006. "Empathic Neural Responses are Modulated by the Perceived Fairness of Others." *Nature* 439(7075): 466–469.

Skinner, B. F. 1953. *Science and Human Behavior*. New York: Free Press.

Takahashi, H., Kato, M., Matsuura, M., Mobbs, D., Suhara, T., and Okubo, Y. 2009. "When Your Gain Is My Pain and Your Pain Is My Gain: Neural Correlates of Envy and Schadenfreude." *Science* 323: 937–939.

Taylor, F. W. 1911. *Principles of Scientific Management*. New York: W. W. Norton.

Tricomi, W., Rangel, A., Camerer, C.F., and Doherty, J.P. 2010. "Neural Evidence for Inequality-Averse Social Preferences." *Nature* 463: 1089–1091.

Ulrich, D., and Smallwood, N. 2004. "Capitalizing on Capabilities." *Harvard Business Review* (June) 119–127.

Vroom, V. H. 1964. *Work and Motivation*. New York: John Wiley & Sons.

27. Neuroscience of engagement and SCARF: why they matter to schools

Dr. Giselle O. Martin-Kniep
Giselle O. Martin-Kniep, President, LCI Learner-Centered Initiatives, Ltd., New York, USA
gisellemk@lciltd.org

Introduction

More than fifty years ago Professor James B. Conant, former president of Harvard, wrote that the education system "works, most of us like it, and it appears to be as permanent a feature of our society as most of our political institutions" Conant (1959). In the years of debate over the efficacy of the education system that ultimately ensued, it is probably fairest to say that at least the latter part of his statement remains true. With regard to the former, within a decade of Professor Conant's optimistic assessment, demands for education improvement, reform, and change began to be raised (Holt 1969; Silberman 1970; Illich 1971). A variety of both government and nongovernment studies brought to light system shortcomings in fundamental skill mastery (particularly in the sciences), school-to-work relationships, dropout rates, teacher turnover, school leadership, and other ailments (Goldberg 1996; US National Commission 1983; Ravitch 2010). The situation confronting the education system, and the stakeholders it was intended to serve, was perhaps best expressed by Mr. Silberman, who at the time of his writing was an editor at *Fortune* magazine:

> It is not possible to spend any prolonged period visiting public school classrooms without being appalled by the mutilation visible everywhere—mutilation of spontaneity, of joy in learning, of pleasure in creating, of sense of self. The...schools...are the kind of institution one cannot really dislike until one gets to know them well. Because adults take the schools so much for granted, they fail to appreciate what grim, joyless places most...schools are, how oppressive and petty are the rules by which they are governed, how intellectually and aesthetically barren the atmosphere. (Silberman 1970, 10)

In the decades that followed, educational reform took on a variety of forms, all intended to bring about needed changes. These reforms can be categorized generally as calling for changes in content (Evans 2005; Goodson 1993), expectations (Weinstein 2004), time (Kneese 2009), teaching and assessment (Martin-Kniep and Picone-Zocchia 2009), and infrastructure (Adelman and Taylor 2007; Donaldson 2006). Virtually all Western governments responded by enacting legislation and creating commissions intent on reforming the educational process (Boyd-Barret and O'Malley 1995; Ibáñez-Martín and Jover 2010). Despite these well-intended efforts and with educational improvement and reform a continuing priority worldwide, the search for viable solutions continues today.

A more recently proposed solution showing considerable promise is the application of neuroscience to the educational environment (Sousa 2010). Over the past decade, significant advances in brain-imaging technology, most specifically in the use of the fMRI, have provided neuroscientists, social psychologists, and instructional theorists with significant new insights into the functioning of the brain (Ochsner and Lieberman 2001; Geary 2007). In fact, back in 1997 there were just ten such studies published; in 2007, there were nearly eight per day (Editorial 2008).

Taken together, and particularly in the case of driving change, this neuroscience and social-psychology research has the potential to significantly advance our understanding of how school leaders can improve the quality of their areas of responsibility—improving both student and teacher productivity, creativity, and ability to solve problems. Despite its relative youth, neuroscience research and the tools it suggests have brought about considerable interest in neuroscience's applications to teaching (Jensen 2005), learning (Sousa 2005), the curriculum (Costa and Kallick 2009), and education science in general (Tokuhama-Espinosa 2010). Utilizing the lens of neuroscience, we look at the potential application of the Status, Certainty, Autonomy, Relatedness, and Fairness (SCARF®) model (Rock 2008; 2009) to the education system, specifically considering its ability to elevate the engagement level of the school learning and teacher working environments.

Notion of engagement in schools

In general, the term "engagement" refers to the degree to which a person is committed or dedicated to an organization or relationship (Rutledge 2005); Rock and Tang 2009). In the workplace, it refers to the degree of positive emotion employees attach to the organization, their job, and their colleagues. When people are engaged, they are attracted to, inspired by, committed to, and even fascinated by their work or their input to the relationship. Students are said to be "engaged" when they make a psychological investment in learning, are involved in their school and its activities, persist despite challenges and obstacles, and take visible pride in accomplishing learning objectives beyond grades (Newmann 1989; Newmann 1992; Gordon 2006). Student engagement in schools has been found to be one of the most robust predictors of student achievement (Guthrie, Schafer, and Huang 2001), regardless of the student's economic and social stature (Klem and Connell 2004).

In exploring the issue of the "engaged student," students fall into five main categories of engagement (see fig. 1):

- Actively disengaged: a high average threat state
- Disengaged: an average threat state
- Neutral: midway between threat and reward states
- Engaged: on average a reward state
- Deeply engaged: strong average reward state

Student engagement in schools has been found to be one of the most robust predictors of student achievement...

Students in the first category have the potential to undermine the learning environment. By contrast, an engaged student is positive for everyone—fellow students, teachers, administrators, and parents (Gordon 2006).

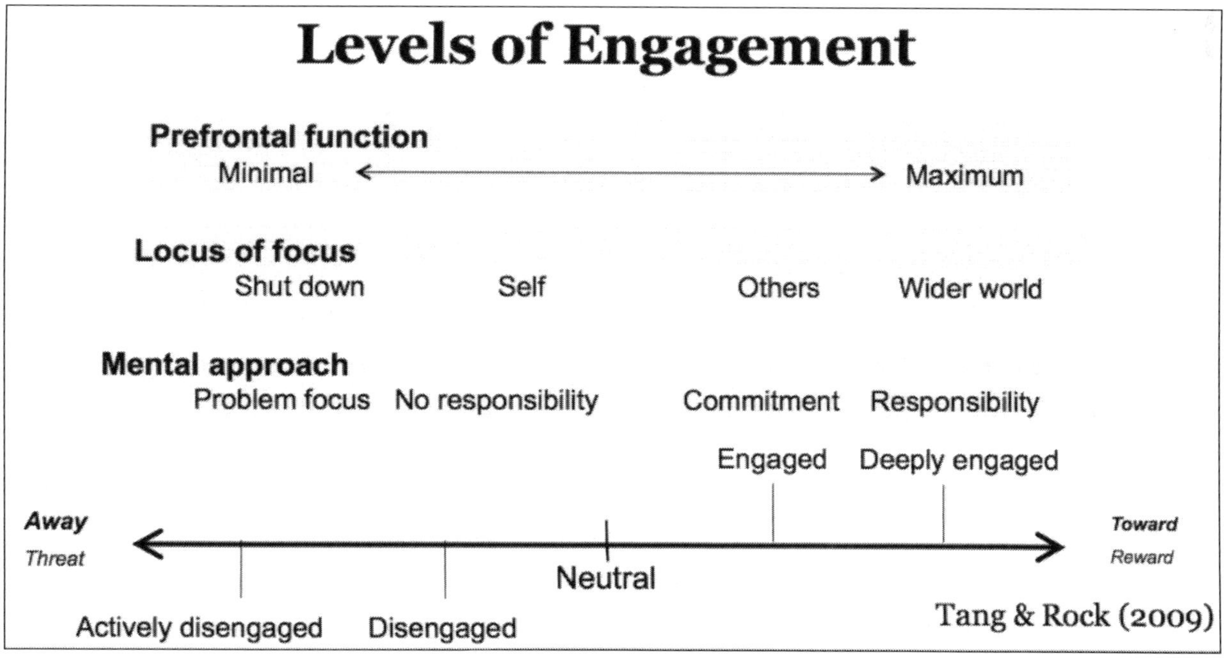

Figure 1. Levels of engagement

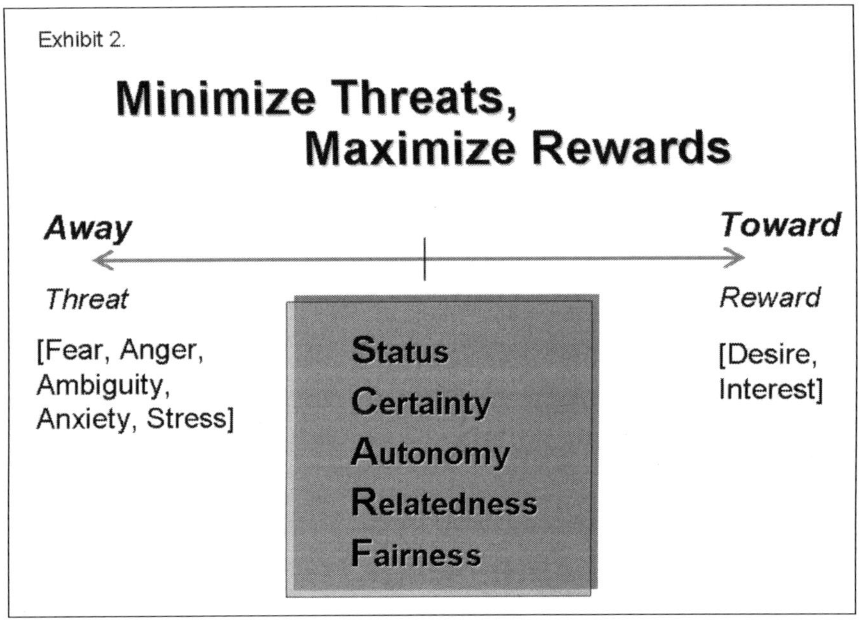

Figure 2. SCARF

Neuroscience of SCARF

The SCARF model is a summary of major findings in social, cognitive, and affective neurosciences that reflect a pattern in human behavior (Rock 2008; 2009). It includes five domains of human social experience that provide an organizing principle for the brain and its motivational circuitries. The brain considers these domains as important as "life and death," assessing them as either threatening or rewarding (Gordon 2000; Lieberman and Eisenberger 2008).

These five domains are *status* (Zink et al. 2008; Eisenberger and Lieberman 2003; Chiao, Bordeaux, and Ambady 2004), *certainty* (Hedden and Gabrieli 2006), *autonomy* (Donny, Bigelow, and Walsh 2006; Dworkin, Mirkis, and Smith 1995), *relatedness* (Cacioppo and Patrick 2008; Kosfeld et al. 2005; Mitchell, Macrae, and Banaji 2006), and *fairness* (Tabibnia, Satpute, and Lieberman 2008; Seymour, Singer, and Dolan 2007). As defined by Rock (2009): "Status is about relative importance to others. Certainty concerns our ability to predict the future. Autonomy provides a sense of control over events. Relatedness is a sense of safety with others, of friend rather than foe. And fairness is a perception of fair exchanges between people."

These domains activate either primary rewards, or primary threat circuitries of the brain. Reward states are associated with more cognitive resources (Arnsten 1998), more creativity (Friedman and Foster 2001), greater ability to solve problems with insight (Fredrickson 2001), and experiencing a wider perceptual field (Schmitz, De Rosa, and Anderson 2009). On the other hand, a threat state is associated with less creative thinking (Jung-Beeman, Collier, and Kounios 2009); mental fatigue (Tang and Posner 2009); and poor health and avoidance responses, such as sadness, anxiety, lack of safety, depression, and mind wandering (Rock and Tang 2009).

Self-regulation is a critical function of our brain and is central to our capacity to control our impulses, make strategic decisions, moderate our emotions, and pursue our goals (McDonald 2009; Diaz, Neal, and Amaya-Williams 1990). It enables us to set and adjust our goals and expectations as we face new events and situations (Paris, Byrnes, and Paris 2001). Self-regulation and motivation are intrinsically related. Motivating behavior is very much related to maximizing rewards and minimizing dangers as far as the brain is concerned. Since understanding the SCARF domains can increase our self-understanding and enhance our self-regulation, it may very well have an application for educators and students in schools.

SCARF in schools: an illustration

How might using SCARF increase students' ability to assume greater responsibility for their own learning? How might it help parents expand on their use of rewards for motivating their children? What role might SCARF play in the development and support of teachers' learning and work? Let's begin with a brief preview of how SCARF plays out in the world of schools from first the student perspective and then from that of teachers and administrators.

Self-regulation is a critical function of our brain and is central to our capacity to control our impulses, make strategic decisions, moderate our emotions, and pursue our goals.

SCARF elements and the student

Janira is a 12-year-old student in an urban middle school. She is an avid doodler in class. She is also prone to distractions and has a hard time sitting still during her teacher's lectures. She is articulate, opinionated, and passionate about lots of things, including art, music, animals, people, and culture, but has a difficult time connecting any of her interests with the actual classroom material provided by her teachers. Her disengagement reveals itself in constant acts of defiance, including talking back to her teachers and refusing to complete work, do homework, or finish tests. These acts have earned her a long-standing reputation of a rebel, if not a bully. In the past three months, she has gone to school detention ten times and has been suspended twice. Despite her parents' attempts to reason with her, or with the school, nothing has changed. Her parents mirror the school's punishments with curfews and loss of privileges, which Janira finds a way to defy on a regular basis. Janira feels increasingly alienated and disengaged. She has befriended a small group of peers who no longer attend school and who do all kinds of drugs, and has become the leader of that group.

Janira experienced very little status in her school, so she sought it elsewhere. The constant detentions and suspensions did little to change her negative outlook about school or to provide her with a sense of fairness. Her ability to relate to her peers at school was greatly diminished by her being singled out and separated from them, so she found relatedness with her new peers. She sought autonomy outside of the school setting since no one had legitimately involved her in shaping the scenarios that could lead her to experience a different reality at school. Her certainty was situational and was limited to the positive and negative consequences she could predict from her experiences in school and with her new friends.

Now, what might have happened if Janira's parents and the school had increased her autonomy by providing her with the opportunity to shape some of her work in school, perhaps by asserting greater control over what she learned or how she could demonstrate her learning? How might her sense of certainty and fairness have changed if she had been encouraged to define goals and accept the consequence for not meeting them, or if she could have defined and monitored the actions she was taking toward meeting her goals? How might her status have increased if her teachers or the school administrator had enabled her to share her talents and passion at school?

SCARF elements: teachers and administrators

While one may think that Janira represents a rather extreme case of a student, she is not unique. Many schools struggle to accommodate the needs of students who do not conform in one way or another. Furthermore, alienation such as Janira's is found among other school actors as well.

A few months ago, I was faced with a group of educators immobilized by a deep collective anxiety. The group included school superintendents, technology and data specialists, and school officials charged with helping schools use inquiry and data. The anxiety they displayed resulted from changes in city and state government legislation that called for a reorganization of the Department of Education. As a result, many of the people wondered what their new positions would be. Whereas one might consider that this situation warranted such anxiety, these individuals had deep familiarity with changing legislation and its consequences for schools. Approximately 85 percent of these individuals had experienced at least two reorganizations in the past, and most of them had been working in the educational system for over 15 years. However, despite their prior experiences with significant reorganizations, the group felt demoralized and anxious about their future. During my time with them, they struggled to assimilate the material we were exploring, arguing that they were not sure of the specific situations in which they could apply them.

On the morning of my third day with the administrators, I referred to SCARF as a means to help individuals reframe their thinking around the domains they had some control over. We determined that status, certainty, autonomy, and fairness were not rewards they could access or tap into in their present situation.

We then explored the role that relatedness had played in building the individual and collective resilience of this group, and brainstormed additional strategies for explicitly using relatedness to strengthen their motivation and increase their collective self-efficacy. We identified the givens and uncertainties of their positions, and the group was able to generate tangible strategies for strengthening their social and professional relatedness, including scheduled meetings, informal gatherings, and information-technology networks. Having SCARF as a framework for identifying coping strategies lightened the load everyone was carrying and changed the tenor of the room, thereby enabling them to operate as actors rather than reactors.

The case for SCARF in building engaged schools

I found my SCARF experience with administrators to be quite enlightening and insightful. What follows is a modest attempt at exploring the status and value of different SCARF rewards for different stakeholders in schools, along with some guiding questions they could pose as they consider those rewards within schools.

Recent studies have revealed that there is a positive relationship between our status and our dopamine receptors.

Status

Status refers to the ascribed position in which we place ourselves relative to others in our different communities. Recent studies have revealed that there is a positive relationship between our status and our dopamine receptors (Martineza et al. 2010). This suggests that people who have higher status have a greater ability to experience pleasure. For the most part, administrators possess high status among teachers and students in terms of defining the terms of engagement and enacting policies, programs, and practices. This status is higher for building and district leaders than for middle-level administrators. With ever-increasing external accountability requirements (Abernathy 2007), such status is threatened if the school is not meeting standards but can be enhanced when administrators are able to redirect their attention to the ways in which they inspire, enable, or influence the people they are responsible for. Administrators can increase the status of adults and students in the school by identifying formal leadership roles and providing them with greater autonomy.

Questions administrators could pursue if they wanted to develop distributed leadership structures in the school and increase status rewards for teachers and other adults include:

- How can teachers feel empowered? What actions would increase their status?

- What policies could result in a greater distribution of student status?
- How might the school leverage high-quality work in the school to increase the status of those who produce it?
- How might the teacher evaluation process be redirected toward a focus on growth and improvement?
- How might listening and communication behaviors be used to increase status among staff members, students, and parents?
- What routines or policies might increase our regard for parents' input or contributions toward their children's education?

Teachers tend to have high status among students in terms of enforcing rules and policies, enacting practices, and ascribing value to student work. Their status among peers is less dependent on seniority than on their perceived influence in school. Such status can be threatened by low student performance or by political strife among staff within the school. Teachers can increase the status of students in their classes by providing them with formal leadership roles, a structure that maximizes their choice and autonomy, and opportunities to excel in self-defined areas.

Some of the questions teachers can pursue as they consider enhancing their own status and the status of their students include:

- How can you use or disseminate your expertise about teaching and learning to help others?
- What projects, activities, or routines might reward students for their thinking, work, or values?
- What are the different ways in which students' talents and interests could be acknowledged and fostered?
- What activities or structures could you use to increase the status of students in your own classes and in the school at large?
- What grouping structures might increase students' ability to relate to each other in ways that could increase their status and interdependence?

Teachers tend to have high status among students in terms of enforcing rules and policies, enacting practices, and ascribing value to student work.

Parents have significant status at home, but their perceived status in schools varies, depending on a number of factors that include the school's culture and the ways in which schools invite and engage parental input and participation. In many schools students have low status in terms of making decisions about rules, norms, and work in the school. Their status with peers depends on the perceived pecking order of the traits that students in the school community value. Student status is increased by grades, awards, and excelling in behaviors that are valued. Status is threatened if they do not meet minimum standards or if they go against student-developed norms and behaviors.

Questions students and parents could consider to enhance their status include:

- What do you know, do well, or care about that could help your peers, teachers, or someone else in the school?
- How can you share or use your passions and interests to help others?
- How can your work help someone else learn or do something?
- In what ways could you share what you care about with others?
- Who can you support or help?

Certainty

Certainty refers to the ability to predict the future based on previous experiences and patterns. Access to new information is, in and of itself, highly connected to certainty and is rewarding to the brain. For both administrators and teachers, certainty is high in terms of job security when they are tenured, but it is often compromised in terms of knowing what is expected of them with increasing external accountability demands.

Middle-level managers and teachers experience more or less certainty depending on their specific school assignments since such assignments are sometimes made with limited input from them. Administrators can increase the certainty among those who work for them through transparent and continuous communication and by involving them in decision making, securing their input in terms of job-related responsibilities, and giving them greater control over the allocation or use of school and other resources.

Students' sense of certainty is high in terms of classes, school routines, and expectations. It is also high in terms of their anticipating future subjects, grades, and standards. When students' locus of control is external, or when their teachers are inconsistent in terms of their routines, standards, and expectations, their certainty in terms of predicting their ability to cope or succeed may be compromised.

School administrators and teachers can increase student certainty by ensuring that teachers share similar expectations for student behavior, performance, and work quality through access to explicit and attainable opportunities to learn and through the enforcement of consistent norms.

Questions that increase certainty for all school stakeholders include:

- What can we do to increase our sense of certainty about our values and commitments (at home or at school)?
- What are some nonnegotiables we want to abide by (in school, at home)?
- What policies, processes, and practices do we need to establish, and consistently enforce, to increase everyone's sense of certainty?
- Who can students, teachers, administrators, and others depend on for advice? Support? How can support be more accessible to others?
- In what contexts do individuals and group members feel safe?
- How do we increase the sense of safety for everyone?
- How can we manage information flow and exchanges to promote certainty?
- How can we create a bridge between the sense of certainty all stakeholders feel at home and at school?

Autonomy

Autonomy is the ability to have and make choices and, in a sense, to have the illusion of control. It is highly connected to our sense of efficacy. For administrators, autonomy very much depends on their specific job assignment. District and building leaders tend to have a high degree of autonomy in terms of hiring, allocating, and managing resources and setting policies. The autonomy of middle-level administrators and other staff members very much depends on their supervisors' leadership style and opportunities they provide related to the allocation of resources and the shaping and implementation of policies, processes, programs, and practices.

Teachers who are tenured operate mostly without significant oversight or supervision. Untenured teachers have far less autonomy and experience a great degree of oversight during their untenured period. Their autonomy is greatly increased when they have opportunities to design or revise curriculum and assessment and when they can provide input on policies, programs, and schedules. Both tenured and untenured teachers operate under the pressure of external accountability forces that greatly curtail their perceived autonomy.

Administrators and teachers can increase their own autonomy and the autonomy they provide others by addressing questions such as:

- How can teachers assume greater control and responsibility for curriculum, instruction, or assessment decisions while staying true to the mission and vision of the school?
- In what ways could teachers support each other's learning and work without administrative oversight?
- What school or classroom routines could be implemented and monitored by others? Could be self-monitored?
- How might we increase the amount of discretion or choice that teachers and other staff members have without compromising a unified vision?
- In what context could students have greater choice about what they learn, how they learn, or how they demonstrate their learning attainment?
- How can the evaluation process for both staff members and students incorporate greater attention to goal setting and strategic planning?
- How might teachers' and other staff members' goals become a greater focus of school-related activities and work?

In many schools, student autonomy is low in terms of determining what to learn, how to learn, and how to demonstrate such learning. Teachers and parents can greatly enhance student autonomy by enabling students to set learning goals and determine the means to attain them and then helping them monitor them. They can also increase students' autonomy by providing students with choice in terms of what they learn or how they can demonstrate an understanding of what they have learned.

Questions that can help elicit ways to increase student autonomy include the following:

- In what contexts could students have greater choice about what they learn or do, how they learn it or do it, and how they demonstrate their learning attainment?
- What culminating projects or experiences would increase students' choice and control over their work and presentations?
- How can classroom routines incorporate more and clearer options for students to exercise?
- How could students be encouraged to have greater control over how they spend time in class? At home?
- How can the student evaluation process incorporate greater attention to goal setting and strategic planning?

Relatedness

Relatedness has to do with whether we consider others friends or foes, and about who is in our "in group" and who is in our "out group." The degree to which relatedness is a reward in a school depends very much on the size and culture of the school. For the most part, much of the school day is structured in ways that minimize opportunities for significant adult-to-adult communication, so relatedness occurs informally and is fostered primarily among students and between teachers and students.

The degree to which relatedness is a reward in a school depends very much on the size and culture of the school.

Administrators can increase relatedness for teachers and other adults in the school with opportunities for teachers to work with their peers and with school staff and community members. Teachers can increase relatedness by providing students with varied learning configurations, including peer-to- peer, and varied forms of group work. Students' sense of relatedness varies in terms of their formal and informal opportunities for relationships with peers and family. Parents' sense of relatedness varies depending on the extent to which they feel welcomed and an integral part of the school community. Schools can increase relatedness through opportunities for students to learn and work collaboratively with peers and with other students and adults in the school and in the community.

Questions that increase relatedness between and among all school stakeholders include:

- Who has a sense of community in our school?
- What do we celebrate? When do we celebrate? How can we structure formal and informal opportunities to celebrate what we care about or value?
- What opportunities could we create for teachers, parents, students, and others to learn more about each other's interests, passions, and work?
- How might we increase our ability to work together toward shared goals and interests?
- In what ways and to what ends do we encourage collaboration?
- What can we collaborate on that might increase our regard for each other's expertise?
- How do we minimize cliques?

Fairness

Fairness is the perception of and need for equitable exchange and has to do with feeling that we are treated justly and equitably. According to various neuroscientists, the social pain system in the brain that relates to fairness may have been piggybacked onto the physical pain system during mammalian evolution (Eisenberg and Lieberman 2004; Panksepp 1998).

Depending on their position, administrators may experience a sense of fairness with respect to defining policies, processes, and practices that establish what is fair or not. Depending on their place within the school hierarchy, they may have more or less control related to transmitting or enforcing regulations and policies. They can increase a sense of fairness for adults and students with clear external expectations for policies and practices and by enforcing incentives and consequences consistently.

Teachers' sense of fairness may be different in terms of their perceptions of the school at large vis-à-vis their own classrooms, where they can generate and enforce rules, responsibilities, and expectations. They may have a low sense of fairness if they equate fairness with equal treatment and feel unfairly treated by externally driven policies and regulations. Their sense of fairness can be increased by clear expectations for practices and consistently enforced incentives and consequences and by opportunities to inform expectations and policies. Students are highly sensitive to "unfair" treatment by peers and others. Teachers and administrators can increase their sense of fairness with clear, explicit expectations and consistently applied norms, incentives, and consequences, and through opportunities to participate in the norm-setting or review processes.

The following questions might help teachers and administrators who want to engender a greater sense of fairness for themselves and other members of the school community:

- What social justice agendas do we want to promote?
- How do we help everyone understand the distinction between fair and equitable?
- What school initiatives, programs, or activities can we incorporate that include explicit opportunities for students and others to do good deeds?
- What appeals processes could we implement to promote fair treatment or a more equitable allocation of resources?
- How might we increase the transparency of our standards and expectations?
- How can we ensure a greater constancy in teacher or parent expectations?
- In what ways could we engage staff, student, or parent input in the development, review, or evaluation of policies or in the identification of standards?

Summary and conclusion

Learning occurs only if we are motivated to learn. SCARF enables us to better understand motivation, rewards, and threats in a far more sophisticated manner than the "carrot-and-stick" approach. If status, certainty, autonomy, relatedness, and fairness serve as stimuli to the brain's threat and reward circuitries, contributing to our motivation to learn, it is critical for individuals and schools to consider ways of allocating these rewards so as to maximize learning for all.

A growing body of neuroscience research shows that every action a teacher takes and every decision a teacher makes either supports or undermines the perceived levels of status, certainty, autonomy, relatedness, and fairness among students. In fact, this may be why teaching is so challenging—knowing that every word and glance carries with it social meaning. Sentences and gestures are noticed and interpreted, magnified, and combed for meanings the teacher often never intended. Neuroscience supports the notion that often what the teacher is saying may not be what the students are hearing.

The SCARF model provides a means of alerting the teacher (bringing conscious awareness) to students' core concerns (which they may not even understand themselves) and shows the teacher how to calibrate his or her words and actions to better effect. The process starts by reducing the threats inherent in the classroom and in teacher behavior. Students cannot think creatively, work well with others, or make informed decisions when their threat responses are on high alert. Skilled teachers understand this and act accordingly. The SCARF model also provides a means for students to become more aware of their own needs and the conditions that support their learning. Advancing school practices could enable students to appropriate this knowledge and use it to become more efficacious learners.

For years economists have argued that people will change their behavior if they have sufficient incentive. We now have reason to believe that economic incentives are effective only when people perceive them as supporting their social needs. The SCARF model thus provides students, teachers, and administrators with more nuanced and effective ways to expand the definition of reward. In doing so, SCARF principles also provide a more granular understanding of the state of engagement, in which students can give their best performance. Engagement can be induced when people working toward objectives feel rewarded by their efforts, with a manageable level of threat: in short, when the brain is generating rewards in SCARF-related dimensions.

References

Abernathy, S. 2007. *No Child Left Behind and the Public Schools*. Ann Arbor: University of Michigan Press.

Adelman, H. S., and Taylor, L. 2007. "Systematic Change for School Improvement." *Journal of Educational and Psychological Consultation* 17(1): 56–77.

Arnsten, A. F. T. 1998. "The Biology of Being Frazzled." *Science* 280: 1711–1712.

Boyd-Barret, O., and O'Malley, P. 1995. *Education Reform in Democratic Spain*. New York: Routledge Education.

Cacioppo, J. T., and Patrick, B. 2008. *Loneliness: Human Nature and the Need for Social Connection*. New York: W. W. Norton.

Chiao, J. Y., Bordeaux, A. R., and Ambady, N. 2004. "Mental Representations of Social Status." *Cognition* 93(2): 49–57.

Cohen, D. K., Hill, H. C., and Hill, H. 2001. *Learning Policy: When State Education Reform Works*. New Haven: Yale University Press.

Conant, J. B. 1959. *The American High School Today*. New York: Signet Books.

Costa, A. L., and Kallick, B.O. 2009. *Habits of Mind Across the Curriculum: Practical and Creative Strategies for Teachers*. Alexandria, VA: Association for Supervision and Curriculum Development.

Diaz, R. M., Neal, C. J., and Amaya-Williams, M. 1990. "The Social Origins of Self-Regulation." In *Vygotsky and Education: Instructional Implications and Applications of Sociohistorical Psychology*, edited by L. C. Moll, 127–154. New York: Cambridge University Press.

Donaldson, G. A. 2006. *Cultivating Leadership in Schools: Connecting People, Purpose, and Practice*. New York: Teachers College Press.

Donny, E. C., Bigelow, G. E., and Walsh, S. L. 2006. "Comparing the Physiological and Subjective Effects of Self-Administered vs. Yoked Cocaine in Humans." *Psychopharmacology* 186(4): 544–552.

Dworkin, S. I., Mirkis, S., and Smith J. E. 1995. "Response-Dependent Versus Response-Independent Presentation of Cocaine: Differences in the Lethal Effects of the Drug." *Psychopharmacology* 117(3): 262–266.

Editorial. 2009 "Connecting the Dots." *Nature Neuroscience* (February) 12(2): 99.

Eisenberger, N. I., and Lieberman, M. D. 2004. "Why it Hurts to be Left Out: The Neurocognitive Overlap Between Physical and Cognitive Pain." *Trends in Cognitive Sciences* 8: 294–330.

Eisenberger, N. I., and Lieberman, M. D. 2003. "Does Rejection Hurt? An fMRI Study of Social Exclusion." *Science* 302(5643): 290–292.

Evans, N. 2005. *Curriculum Change in Secondary Schools, 1957–2004: A Curriculum Roundabout?* New York: Routledge Education.

Fredrickson, B. L. 2001. "The Role of Positive Emotions in Positive Psychology: The Broaden-and-Build Theory of Positive Emotions." *American Psychologist* 56: 218–226.

Friedman, R. S., and Forster, J. 2001. "The Effects of Promotion and Prevention Cues on Creativity." *Journal of Personality and Social Psychology* 81(6): 1001–1013.

Geary, D. C. 2007. "Educating the Evolved Mind: Conceptual Foundations for an Evolutionary Educational Psychology." In *Psychological Perspectives on Contemporary Educational Issues*, edited by J. S. Carlson and J. R. Leven Charlotte. North Carolina: Information Age.

Goldberg, B. 1996. *Why Schools Fail: The Denial of Individuality and the Decline of Learning*. Washington, DC: Cato Institute.

Gordon, E. 2000. *Bringing Together Biological, Psychological, and Clinical Models of the Human Brain*. In Integrative Neuroscience, E. Gordon. Reading, UK: Harwood Academic Publications.

Gordon, G. 2006. *Building Engaged Schools: Getting the Most Out of America's Classrooms*. New York: Gallup.

Guthrie, J., Schafer, W. D., and Huang, C. 2001. "Benefits of Opportunity to Read and Balanced Instruction on the NAEP." *Journal of Educational Research* 94 (3):145–162.

Hedden, T., and Gabrieli, J. D. E. 2006. "The Ebb and Flow of Attention in the Human Brain." *Nature Neuroscience* 9: 863–865.

Holt, J. C. 1969. *The Underachieving School*. New York: Pitman.

Ibáñez-Martín, J. A., and Jover, G., eds. 2010. *Education in Europe: Policies and Politics*. New York: Springer.

Illich, I. 1971. *Deschooling Society: World Perspectives*. New York: Harper & Row.

Goodson, I. F. 1993 *School Subjects and Curriculum Change (Studies in Curriculum History)*. New York: Routledge Education.

Jensen, E. 2005. *Teaching with the Brain in Mind*. Alexandria, VA: Association for Supervision and Curriculum Development.

Jung-Beeman, M., Collier, A., and Kounios, J. 2009. "How Insight Happens: Learning from the Brain." *NeuroLeadership Journal* 2: 20–25.

Klem, A., and Connell, J. 2004. "Relationships Matter: Linking Teacher Support to Student Engagement and Achievement." *Journal of School Health* 74(7): 262–273.

Kneese, C. 2009. *Balancing the School Calendar: Perspectives from the Public and Stakeholders*. New York: Rowman and Littlefield Education.

Kosfeld, M., Heinrichs, M., Zak, P. J., Fischbacher, U., and Fehr, E. 2005. "Oxytocin Increases Trust in Humans." *Nature* 435(7042): 673–676.

Lieberman, M. D., and Eisenberg, N. I. 2008. "The Pains and Pleasures of Social Life: A Social Cognitive Neuroscience Approach." *NeuroLeadership Journal* 1: 48–43.

Martin-Kniep, G,. and Picone-Zocchia, J. 2009. *Changing the Way You Teach, Improving the Way Students Learn*. Alexandria, VA: ASCD.

Martineza, D., Orlowskaa, D., Narendranc, R., Slifsteina, R., Liua, F., Kumara, D., Brofta, A., Van Heertumb, R., and Klebera, H. D. 2010. "Dopamine Type 2/3 Receptor Availability in the Striatum and Social Status in Human Volunteers." *Biological Psychiatry* 67(3): 275–278.

Marzano, R. 2003. *What Works in Schools: Translating Research into Action*. Alexandria, VA: Association for Supervision and Curriculum Development.

McDonald, P. 2009. "The Potential Contribution of Neuroscience to Authentic Leadership." *NeuroLeadership Journal* 2: 53–63.

Mitchell, J. P., Macrae, C. N., and Banaji, M. R. 2006. "Oxytocin Increases Trust in Humans: Dissociable Medial Prefrontal Contributions to Judgments of Similar and Dissimilar Others." *Neuron* 50: 655–663.

Newmann, F. M. 1989. *Student Engagement and High School Reform: Educational Leadership*. Alexandria, VA: Association for Supervision and Curriculum Development.

Newmann, F. 1992. *Student Engagement and Achievement in American Secondary Schools*. New York: Teachers College Press.

Ochsner, K. N., and Lieberman, M. D. 2001. "The Emergence of Social Cognitive Neuroscience." *American Psychologist* 56(7): 717–734.

Panksepp, J. 1998. *Affective Neuroscience*. New York: Oxford University Press.

Paris, S. G., Byrnes, J. P., and Paris, A. H. 2001. "Constructing Theories, Identities, and Actions of Self-Regulated Learners." In *Self-Regulated Learning and Academic Achievement*, edited by B. J. Zimmerman and D. H. Schunk, 253–287. Mahwah, NJ: Lawrence Erlbaum Associates.

Ravitch, D. 2010. *The Death and Life of the Great American School System: How Testing and Choice Are Undermining Education*. New York: Basic Books.

Ringleb, A. H., and Rock, D. 2008. "The Emerging Field of Neuroleadership." *NeuroLeadership Journal* 1: 3–19.

Rock, D. 2009. *Your Brain at Work: Strategies for Overcoming Distraction, Regaining Focus, and Working Smarter All Day Long*. New York: HarperBusiness.

Rock, D. 2008. "SCARF: A Brain-Based Model for Collaborating with and Influencing Others." *NeuroLeadership Journal* 1: 44–52.

Rock, D., and Tang, Y. 2009. "Neuroscience of Engagement." *NeuroLeadership Journal* 2: 15–22.

Rutlege, T. 2005. *Getting Engaged: The New Workplace Loyalty.* Toronto, ON: Mattanie Press.

Sagor, R. 2002. "Lessons from Skateboarders." *Educational Leadership* (September) 60(1): 34–38.

Seymour, B., Singer, T., and Dolan, R. 2007. "The Neurobiology of Punishment." *Nature Reviews Neuroscience* 8: 300–311.

Schmitz, T. W., De Rosa, E., and Anderson, A. K. 2009. "Opposing Influence of Affective State Valence on Visual Cortical Encoding." *Journal of Neuroscience* 29(22): 7199–7207.

Silberman, C. 1970. *Crisis in the Classroom*. New York: Random House.

Skinner, E., and Belmont M. 1991. *A Longitudinal Study of Motivation in school: Reciprocal Effects of Teacher Behavior and Student Engagement*. University of Rochester, New York.

Sousa, D. A. 2005. *How the Brain Learns*. Thousand Oaks, CA: Corwin.

Sousa, D. A. 2010. *Mind, Brain, and Education: Neuroscience Implications for the Classroom*. Bloomington, IN: Solution Tree.

Stiver, J., and Cramer, S. F. 2009. *A Teacher's Guide to Change: Understanding, Navigating, and Leading the Process*. Thousand Oaks, CA: Corwin.

Tabibnia, G., Satpute, A. B., and Lieberman, M. D. 2008. "The Sunny Side of Fairness: Preference for Fairness Activates Reward Circuitry (and Disregarding Unfairness Activates Self-Control Circuitry)." *Psychological Science* 19: 339–347.

Tang, Y. Y., and Posner, M. I. 2009. "Attention Training and Attention State Training." *Trends in Cognitive Sciences* 13: 222–227.

Tokuhama-Espinosa, T. 2010. *Mind, Brain, and Education Science: A Comprehensive Guide to the New Brain-Based Teaching*. New York: W. W. Norton.

US National Commission on Excellence in Education. 1983. *A Nation at Risk: The Imperative for Educational Reform. A Report to the Nation and the Secretary of Education, United States Department of Education*. Washington, DC: US Government Printing Office.

Weinstein, R. S. 2004. *Reaching Higher: The Power of Expectations in Schooling*. Cambridge, MA: Harvard University Press.

Zink, C. R., Tong, Y., Chen, Y. O., Bassett, D. S., Stein, J. L., and Meyer-Lindenberg, A. 2008. "Know Your Place: Neural Processing of Social Hierarchy in Humans." *Neuron* 58: 273–283.

SECTION VI:
Case Studies

28. Application of neuroscience in executive team coaching: the WSR case

Carla Street

Carla Street, President, ROI Executive Coaching

Board Member, Georgia Coach Association (GCA), Atlanta, USA

pcstreet@comcast.net

Introduction

This case study describes how ROI Executive Coaching leveraged neuroscience to inform the design and implementation of a seven-month executive-team development program conducted for WSR, a company in the health and wellness industry. ROI, founded in 2001, is a consultancy in Atlanta, Georgia, that uses evidence-based methodology to leverage the latest research findings in brain science, integrating neuroscientific principles into the design of its coaching programs to optimize measurable results for individual leaders and their teams.

To expand the current literature regarding the practical application of neuroleadership and increase the probability of successful individual and organizational transformation, we will share in this case study how neuroscientific concepts were applied to an executive-team coaching engagement and the related impacts and results achieved.

In a 2006 McKinsey Quarterly online survey, only 38 percent of the global executives responding reported that a recent transformation had either a "completely" or "mostly" successful impact on the expected performance of their management team, while 10% acknowledged that the change effort their organization was involved with was either "completely" or "mostly" unsuccessful. In all, more than half of those who responded to the survey characterized their results as less than successful. These percentages indicate that there is significant opportunity for professional coaches to improve the transformation process.

Organizations undergo constant change. For executive coaches, it is helpful to clarify what clients mean by a desired "change." This case study suggests that organizations are now looking to transcend the popular definition of change as an "end point" and are seeking a more transformative, evidenced-based concept of dynamic stability as described by Rock and Page (2009): change that allows a system to adapt and evolve over time, rather than becoming rigid and then unable to respond—and doing so without becoming overwhelmed by chaos.

For executive coaches, it is helpful to clarify what clients mean by a desired "change."

The WSR program leveraged neuroscience to evoke and develop the thought patterns, feelings, and behaviors that would support transformation through the intentional creation of and commitment to dynamic stability.

Situation overview

ROI was engaged by WSR's chief executive officer to design and implement an executive-team coaching program. The CEO sensed that the company's Operating Committee (OC), consisting of the top six executives in the organization, was not performing at its highest level. When asked to describe his vision of the OC as a high-performing team, the CEO described a highly collaborative team whose members could manage conflict in a constructive manner and be more accountable to leadership. He also shared confidentially that the near future would bring an increased need for the team to "step up" the scope of its responsibilities. As he was considering ways to minimize his own role, including retirement, he was open to exploring various options for the future of the company.

ROI was hired for a seven-month executive-team coaching engagement. The executive coach defined the following overarching objectives:

1. Improve thinking and performance.
2. Achieve the specific goals as established by the client.
3. Capture pre- and postprogram metrics to document return-on-investment.
4. Create an intentional state of dynamic stability with the client.

"To minimize danger and maximize reward is an overarching organizing principle of the brain."

Discovery

The initial discovery phase included one-on-one interviews with the CEO and executive team, using evidence-based coaching skills. The coach used the Birkman Method® assessment and a high-performing team survey. The CEO was surveyed separately from the team to uncover the different perspectives, as well as the opportunities that could increase understanding and alignment.

Generally speaking, the initial stage of discovery offers a significant opportunity for the coach to establish the rapport and trust that are critical to the program. The SCARF® (Status, Certainty, Autonomy, Relatedness, Fairness) model, first presented by David Rock at the 2008 NeuroLeadership Summit, defines five domains of human social experience. When these domains are satisfied, the result is a reward (approach) response. When challenged, this is perceived as an instinctive threat (avoidance) response. As integrative neuroscientist Evian Gordon (2000) stated, "To minimize danger and maximize reward is an overarching organizing principle of the brain." Keeping this in mind, SCARF serves as a powerful point of reference that helps maximize the reward-approach response, establish rapport and trust, and create a generative flow for the engagement.

During the in-person individual and team coaching sessions, the coach remained cognizant of SCARF to mitigate potential amygdala triggers. These are described by author Daniel Goleman, Richard Boyatzis and Annie McKee (2002) as events that can interfere with the positive, productive frame of mind of individuals, as well as of the team.

Readiness and engagement

The neural drivers identified in the SCARF model have the capacity to either enhance or diminish both an individual's coaching readiness and his or her level of engagement in the process. When SCARF concerns are mitigated, a client's state of readiness appears to increase, and vice versa.

Readiness is a popular topic of discussion among clients and professional coaches. Potential clients want to know if they, along with their executives and managers, are coachable. Clients ask coaches to create readiness. What is readiness?

Readiness is an individual's degree of self-awareness and how motivated they are to increase their effectiveness and achieve a desired reality. While some individuals engage voluntarily in the coaching process, in team coaching, members are typically enrolled involuntarily by a supervisor or company policy. The latter can immediately trigger SCARF domains, so these individuals enter into the process feeling threatened and distressed. This is not an optimal state of readiness, or a desirable sense of engagement for coaching.

When SCARF concerns are mitigated, a client's state of readiness appears to increase, and vice versa.

Executive coach perspective and practical application of SCARF: the WSR case

Status

Status refers to an individual's feeling of relative importance compared with others. Related research by Eisenberger and colleagues showed that when individuals perceive a reduction in status, known as social pain, the same regions of the brain are lit up as occurs with physical pain (Lieberman and Eisenberger 2008). In this case, team and individual interactions focus on positive feedback and affirmations in an attempt to trigger the ventral striatum, the brain's social reward system, and increase feelings of satisfaction.

Certainty

The brain is a pattern-seeking device that constantly seeks outcomes that satisfy its craving for certainty. Even a blip in a predictive pattern can send an error signal to the orbital frontal cortex (OFC) and interrupt an individual's focus. In this case, the coach remained sensitive to any expression of uncertainty arising from issues such as role definition, hiring decisions, or financial transparency. To counter these uncomfortable thoughts and feelings, the coach used powerful questions to help the client find a place of increased certainty and calm the perceived threat.

Autonomy

Autonomy refers to the feeling and belief that individuals have choices as well as some control over their environment. Addressing the threats related to this domain comes most naturally to professional coaches. The professional coaching process empowers clients to discover their goals and cocreate their programs. This approach places the client in the driver's seat and consequently calms potential threats to the individual's autonomy. This is one of the many reasons why individuals find the coaching process pleasurable. A coach listens for instances in which team members perceive an external threat to their autonomy and counters with exploratory questions that help them discover options and regain a sense of control.

Relatedness

This became the most complex and challenging domain to manage during the WSR engagement. Relatedness refers to an individual's sense of belonging and how he or she determines whether someone is on the team—that is, friend or foe. This domain is closely related to trust. Viewing a teammate as a competitor has been shown to significantly reduce an individual's capacity to empathize. Witnessing these behaviors, the coach remains sensitive to the perceptions of individual competition that repeatedly trigger the threat response. The coach's explanation of the brain science behind these feelings helps normalize the individual emotions, thereby providing team members with the knowledge to relate more effectively.

Fairness

An individual's threat response is easily triggered by a sense of unfairness. Numerous SCARF infringements were detected throughout the engagement, many of these related to a perception of unfairness. To better address these infringements, the OC revisited its ground rules for behavior, and focused on process management and role clarification. This was useful in mitigating most feelings of unfairness among the team members.

Final thoughts on SCARF

When a coach tunes into the five domains, the expressions of these threats are quite distinctive and difficult to overlook.

One particular situation triggered all five domains for a team member, which catapulted her into significant distress and disengagement. During this individual's personal coaching session, the coach "teased out" the SCARF threats, helping the individual discover options and improved thinking to temper the concerns. This process significantly reduced her stress, enhanced her situation, and lessened the potential negative impact that her emotional distress might have transferred to the team.

The SCARF model is a practical, powerful tool that allows the coach to maximize the reward-approach response and cultivate a positive, productive, generative state of being at the individual and team level.

Workplace engagement is defined by the Conference Board (2006) as "the heightened emotional connection that employees feel for their organization, which then motivates them to exert greater discretionary effort." Also relevant here are Rock and Tang's (2009) findings related to the achievement of a neutral, engaged, or deeply engaged state. Through application of the SCARF model and in-person, individual coaching sessions (whereby team members realized they needed and desired change), the coach was able to cultivate and maintain readiness and an engaged or deeply engaged state with the WSR team and its members.

Neuroleadership program design

ROI designed a NeuroLeadership Executive Team Framework (see fig. 2) to depict the methods and application of neuroscientific principles planned for the engagement. Throughout the implementation process, the coach referenced a checklist (see fig. 1) of neuroscientific concepts to maintain attention on a brain-friendly approach. The thoughts of Siegel and McCall (2009) are relevant here and serve to articulate the overarching purpose of the program framework:

Wise leaders, and coaches, invite self-leadership in others—enabling and encouraging their differentiation while cultivating their linking communication with one another—and thus create favorable conditions for integration and the appearance of the coherence, creativity, and emergent order that can occur in self-organizing systems.

Neuroleadership concepts checklist
✓ Readiness ✓ Engagement ✓ Attention density ✓ Quantum zeno effect ✓ Dynamic stability ✓ Open-loop system ✓ Cognition and feeling ✓ Implicit learning ✓ ARIA faces of insight ✓ SCARF model ✓ Red, blue and green zones ✓ Neuroplasticity ✓ Neural Darwinism ✓ Amygdala hijack ✓ Visualization ✓ Feedback

Figure 1

The design of the program considered how an individual's mind is capable of influencing the collective mind of the team and, therefore, the need for integration. The findings of Siegel (2010) hold that integration must be the key to creating the flexible, harmonious, and adaptable environment needed to support complexity and the health of the team system. The coach's expectation was that attention to integration would support the overarching goal of dynamic stability.

During this process, the coach viewed each team member as an individuated element of the team system. Therefore, each team member was acknowledged and respected for their specialized roles and strengths, imparting a degree of sovereignty. With this in mind, the coach facilitated debriefs and exercises based on the Birkman Method assessment, which affirmed individual's strengths and encouraged insights from the team to best facilitate each of those assets to add value to the overall team. The coach continued to guide, facilitate, and witness the progress of integration during team workshops.

Mission, values, and goal setting

In session one, the coach assisted the executive team in revisiting the organization's mission and values (see fig. 3). The team set four team goals during this first workshop. Consistent with the findings of Rock and Page (2009), the mission, values, and goals became the integrating narrative, strange attractors, or points in a system that aided the elements (team members) in forming stable patterns.

The coach assisted the client in identifying the team's strange attractors, which helped achieve the overarching goal of dynamic stability. It was expected that at the end of the seven-month period, the coach could disengage and the system (team) would be able to retain its core identity and maintain a sense of intentional dynamic stability.

This neuroscientific perspective helps deepen the coach's commitment to a purpose-driven, values-based foundation for individuals and teams. Coaches can help clients identify the strange attractors: the purpose, beliefs, values, and ground rules that hold teams together both during times of positive growth and during crises.

Individual executive coaching

To emphasize the value and importance of each team member as a part of the system, the coach conducted individual engagements with team members the day before each team workshop. Individual team members received an initial, confidential debrief of their Birkman Method assessment. Each person designed their own outcome tracker and established the goals they expected to achieve by the end of the engagement. Initial measurements were taken for each goal. The coach also encouraged individuals to consider how their personal goals aligned with the goals of the overall team. ROI believes that the attention focused on each team member (individuated element) in the personal coaching sessions contributed significantly to the holistic success of the program.

Team coaching workshops

Integration was the overarching thought during the implementation of team workshops. Specifically, the coach considered how to link these individuated elements (team members) to one another so the process could lead to a state of continued health and well-being. Siegel and McCall (2009) addressed this in "Mindsight at Work: An Interpersonal Neurobiology Lens on Leadership." Movement toward integration occurs when a system reaches a state of balance despite disruptions; the synthesis of stability and change remain dynamic throughout the process.

Siegel and McCall (2009) suggested that integration be imagined as a river. They explained that a well-led organization moves from eddies back into the forward flow through time with flexibility, adaptiveness, coherence, energy, and stability.

With this concept of integration in mind, the key components of the team workshop design included:

- Goal setting
- Cognition and feeling
- Attention density
- Feedback
- ARIA
- Metrics

Goal setting

During the discovery phase, the coach aided the CEO in establishing personal goals and measuring and documenting these in his outcome tracker. This offered valuable insight into the leader's vision, expectations, and metrics for success. In addition, the coach held meetings with individual team members to establish their personal outcome trackers that clearly stated and measured their goals. During coaching sessions, the coach helped individual team members discover the extent and in what ways their goals aligned with the team and organization.

With the CEO and individual team member's personal goals established, it was time to create team goals. The intimate knowledge gained during the one-to-one meetings, including the results of the assessment and survey data, set the stage for the first team workshop.

The top three goals have a clear link with the four domains of neuroleadership.

The nonconfidential survey and assessment data were presented to the team, and through the coaching process, the team established four umbrella goals for the seven-month engagement. The WSR OC team established one umbrella goal related to a core value, two goals related to a high-performing team competency, and one business project goal.

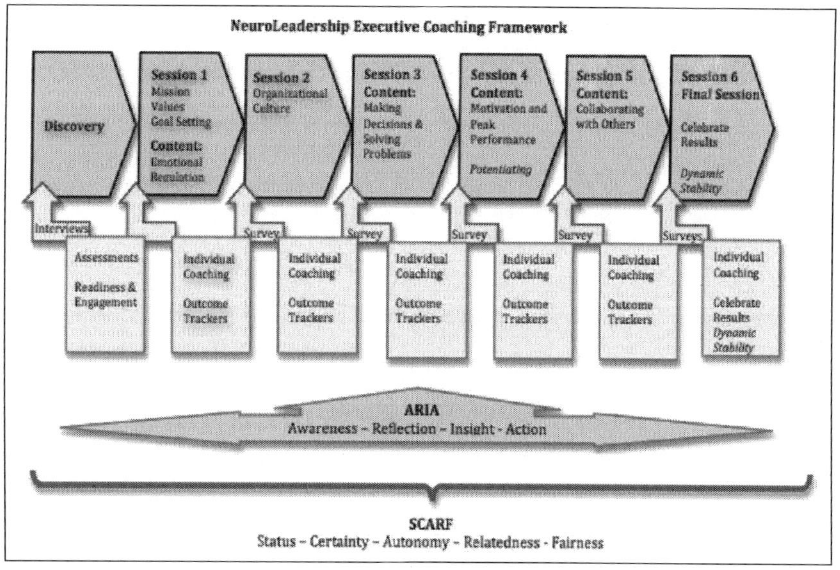

Figure 2. NeuroLeadership Executive Coaching Framework

The top three goals have a clear link with the four domains of neuroleadership. The business project, goal 4, offered the team an opportunity to practice and demonstrate their development of goals 1–3.

WSR Goal	
Neuroleadership domain	
1.Constructive conflict	• Staying cool under pressure • Collaborating with others
2. Process management	• Making decisions and solving problems • Collaborating with others • Facilitating change
3. Motivating others	• Staying cool under pressure • Collaborating with others
4. *Business project:* Operations manual	*Team practiced and demonstrated increased competency of goals 1–3.*

Figure 3

The coach asked brain-friendly questions, exploring both the current reality (CR) and the desired reality (DR) for each goal. A 1–10 scale was utilized to deepen thinking and monitor forward movement in a way that was meaningful to the client. The team established CR and DR measurements for the four goals. By the end of the first workshop, the team had created its first outcome tracker, stating its umbrella goals, initial measurements, and action steps.

When a coach asks a client to determine a number on a 1-10 scale for a current and desired reality, the typical response is reflection and visualization. If clients answer "8" they are asked to explore what that number means to them: "Describe an '8' to me. How will you know when it is an 'eight'?" Research shows that imagining a situation in detail helps prepare mental circuits in ways that are similar to the real experience. The pathways in the brain used to actually undertake an activity are the same pathways used when we merely picture this activity (Rock and Page 2009).

The format of team workshops, subsequent to the initial goal-setting session, followed a flexible structure that included a team outcome-tracker debrief, content, exercise, and the creation of a new outcome tracker. During one workshop, after a team exercise that focused on process management, the team members' main insight was: what is possible? This insight led the team to determine a desired reality of a "12" for an action item, surpassing "10" and saying, why not shoot for a "12"? What would that look like? What is possible?

Cognition and feeling

Coaches who acknowledge the role of emotion are more likely to succeed as change agents. Neuropsychologist Dr. Louis Cozolino (2002) underscored this fact when he noted, "Intellectual understanding of psychological problems in the absence of increased integration with emotion, sensation, and behavior does not result in change...There is a recognition that the evocation of emotion coupled with conscious awareness is most likely to result in...personal growth."

By the end of the first workshop, the team had created its first outcome tracker, stating its umbrella goals, initial measurements, and action steps.

The Birkman Method assessment is unique in its ability to report the potential emotional stress behaviors that may develop if underlying needs are not met. This assessment creates a complex and useful picture of individuals, placing the spotlight on their usual behaviors, underlying needs, and the resultant stress when their needs are not satisfied. The Birkman Method measures 11 components on a scale of 1 (low) to 99 (high) and additionally measures Usual Style (public self), Need (private self), and Stress (Red-Zone emotion) for each component. In Birkman terms, Green-Zone emotions, or the individual's usual, positive, most productive self, emerge when needs are met. Information shared on the CIMBA MBA Leadership

Process (Ringleb and Pagon 2009) relating to Red- and Green-Zone emotions support a more meaningful interpretation and implementation of the Birkman Method.

This assessment tool is particularly powerful, because it enables the coach and client to articulate triggers for Red-Zone emotions that might affect the person's performance and effectiveness on the team. These challenges were captured on individuals' outcome trackers and further explored during coaching sessions. By applying knowledge gained through the Birkman Method, individuals were able to combine emotion ("How did that situation make me feel?") with cognition ("Why did I feel that way?") to generate awareness and insights and create personal growth.

Attention density

An evidence-based coaching process leverages the power of attention. As a quantum environment, the brain is subject to the laws of quantum mechanics. The Quantum Zeno Effect (Stapp, Schwartz and Beauregard 2005) states that the mental act of focusing attention stabilizes the associated brain circuits. When a coach helps a client concentrate on a desired reality during a period of time, the coach helps maintain the client's brain state in association with that experience. These circuits eventually become not just chemical links but stable, physical changes in the brain's structure—in other words, hard-wired. So coaches help clients pay attention to concepts that continually reshape the patterns of clients' brains, indicating the hardwiring of desired thoughts, feelings, and behaviors.

The delivery and receipt of skillful, positive feedback is further endorsed by neuroscience research indicating that social and physical pain are similar...

During individual sessions and team workshops, the coaching process maintains attention density, or quality attention over time, on established goals and emerging positive behaviors. In addition to coaching, the main tools that help achieve this are the individual and team outcome trackers and intersession surveys. An online survey was sent to each team member to review and complete one week before team workshops. The survey asked members to rate progress on each umbrella goal and the related action items on the outcome trackers. The intersession surveys required each member to pay constant attention to their goals and focus on their commitments for change.

During one of the team workshops, a member suggested that the team establish the habit of asking, "What are we doing right?" and "How can we do more of that?" during their OC meetings. This self-directed feedback mechanism helped maintain and hard-wire the desired neural signatures to support the team's transformation.

Feedback

At the end of each workshop, ROI initiated a step-by-step practice to capture feedback. The key factors guiding this practice included allowing team members to offer their own observations first and keeping the feedback specific and focused on the positive. Follow-up questions such as "What did you do well and discover about yourself?" or "What went well, what impact did that have, and how do you think you could do more of that?" serve to reinforce positive neural patterns and create desired habitual behaviors.

The delivery and receipt of skillful, positive feedback is further endorsed by neuroscience research indicating that social and physical pain are similar (Lieberman and Eisenberger 2008). The findings suggest that bringing out the best in people in the workplace depends at least as much on optimizing a person's social and emotional well-being as it does on cognitive processes.

Lieberman and Eisenberger offer the analogy of "expecting someone who has a broken leg to run from one meeting to the next...But when someone is in social pain, we often treat this as if it should be compartmentalized and kept outside the office. We might tell them to 'get over' their hurt feelings despite the fact that we would never think someone should 'get over' their broken leg."

According to Lieberman and Eisenberger, specific, positive feedback that treats individuals as valued members of the organization may activate reward systems in the brain that promote stronger learning of those behaviors. When social needs are satisfied, the brain responds in much the same way as it responds to more tangible (monetary) rewards. Skillful feedback can be viewed by organizations as a highly cost-effective social-reward system.

When social needs are satisfied, the brain responds in much the same way as it responds to more tangible (monetary) rewards.

The neurocoach: coaching presence

If neuroscience informs and guides a professional coach's methodology, then the title of "neurocoach" is a helpful distinction. This "title" sends a signal to a client that the coach studies neuroleadership and integrates relevant neuroscientific findings in order to facilitate, augment, and optimize coaching programs. ROI approached the WSR engagement as a neurocoach might, keeping the brain and mind of the client omnipresent.

Credentialed professional coaches of the International Coach Federation (ICF) demonstrate 11 core competencies at a high level. One of these competencies, coaching presence, is defined as the ability to be fully conscious, intuitive...to be able to confidently shift perspectives and self-manage emotions without being overpowered by a client's needs (coachfederation.org).

To maintain a coaching presence, coaches must be aware of when and how their mind maps and beliefs enter the coaching space.

This mindfulness can signal the development of mindsight, the reflective capacity to become aware of our own minds, as well as our empathic ability to recognize the intentions and emotional states of others and to truly understand where they are coming from (Siegel and McCall 2010). Mindsight is considered our seventh sense, the ability to perceive the workings of our own minds in addition to the minds of others. Mindsight is a mission-critical competency for coaches. It ensures their minds and emotions connect with clients but do not become entrained. Being client-centered, or having a client focus in neurocoaching, takes on a deeper meaning when there is the potential to connect clients' neurons in new ways, leading to novel thoughts, beliefs, and feelings. When David Rock explained coaching to neuroscientist Jeffrey Schwartz (Rock and Page 2009), he responded, "Oh, I see, what coaching is...it is a way of facilitating self-directed neuroplasticity."

Mindsight is considered our seventh sense, the ability to perceive the workings of our own minds in addition to the minds of others.

The contagious nature of our emotions, as described by Goleman (2004), is addressed at the initial team workshop. Making the team aware of how two individual bodies operating at different rhythms can actually mirror each other's physiological profiles by the end of a simple fifteen-minute conversation sends a clear message of interdependence to the team. The topic of the open-loop system underscores the reason why each individual involved in the coaching engagement (coach included) is required to strive for and promote positive emotion regulation.

By understanding the science behind the "gut feeling" (Goleman, Boyatzis, and McKee 2004), the coach is able to ask powerful questions based on the belief that it is possible to tap into the individual and collective wisdom of team members. Learning the science behind this gut feeling is motivating and empowering to executives. When they understand how it works, they realize that they embody a well of valuable information that can be discovered through reflection and mindfulness.

A coach's presence has an impact on the dynamics of the system (CEO and team). Many coaches create rituals such as meditation, yoga, and visualization to prepare for coaching sessions. This preparation helps coaches monitor physical, auditory, and emotional signals to create a positive environment in an attempt to expand the client's peripheral vision and generate greater insight. The establishment of these rituals is supported by Fredrickson in her book *Positivity* (2009).

ARIA

ARIA—the four faces of insight: Awareness, Reflection, Insight, and Action—a model introduced by Rock as an improvement on the model he published in *Quiet Leadership* in 2006, was first published in a paper called "Coaching Leaders To Be Coaches at EDS" and informed the coaching methodology throughout the one-to-one meetings and team workshops. The coach set an intention to help the team generate and acknowledge insights in the moment, encouraging team members to write down relevant actions on both individual and team outcome trackers that could move the client closer to its desired reality. The coach was aware throughout the coaching sessions that serotonin is released during reflection, creating a "feel-good" state, and that adrenaline is triggered at the moment of insight, which supports action. The adrenaline rush is short-lived. If a coach misses the glimpse of an insight, it might be lost within minutes or sooner. Thus, it is essential to catch the insight and ask how it might be important. Is it worth writing down?

Metrics: return on investment

While there is skepticism surrounding measurements taken immediately after a program, metrics that are tracked and captured at the completion of a seven-month coaching engagement, versus a shorter-term project, can reveal more meaningful indications of transformation. It is difficult to tease out the commonly cited Hawthorn Effect, which attributes positive results to the fact that people received special attention during a program. But what is meant by "special attention"? If, from a neuroscientific perspective, this "attention" is applied with a brain-friendly, neurocoaching approach, then the positive results would be evidence-based and potentially powerfully transformative. ROI Executive Coaching uses the 1–10 scale for more qualitative goals and a different quantitative model to measure the extent of impact for numbers-based goals. The process of establishing initial measurements generates deeper thinking as the client reflects on the proper number to represent the status of the goal. This process alone can generate valuable insight.

The survey enables them (and the coach) to see the positive shift in alignment.

The CEO's pre- and postprogram results showed significant improvements (see fig. 4 and 5). He stated that he was unaware of what he didn't know at the beginning of the engagement and therefore believed that the initial measurements were too high. The team expressed the same thought regarding the four team goals and the initial measurement of satisfaction and effectiveness (see fig. 6 and 7). Therefore, ROI believes that the percentage improvement shown in these charts might be conservative and plans to address this insight with an additional layer to future postprogram surveys: "Knowing what you know now, how would you have rated these factors and goals at the beginning of the engagement?"

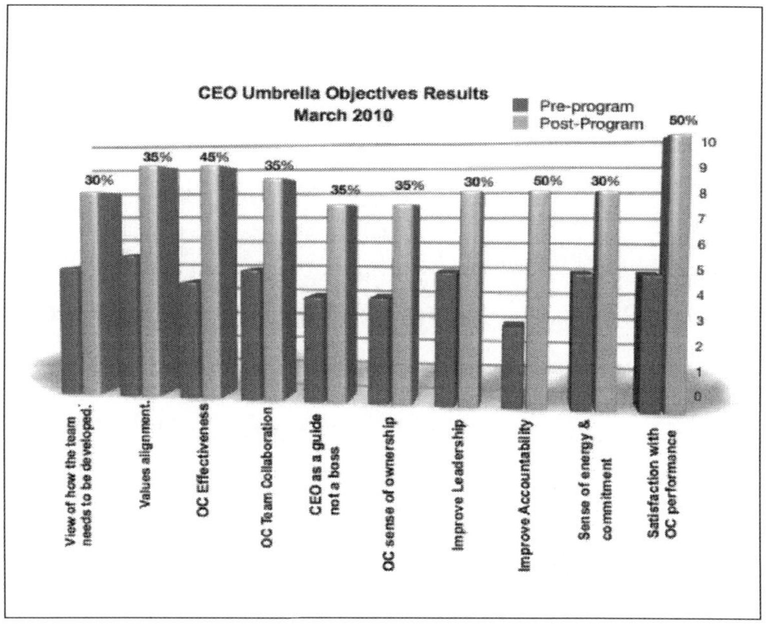

Figure 4. CEO umbrella objectives results, March 2010

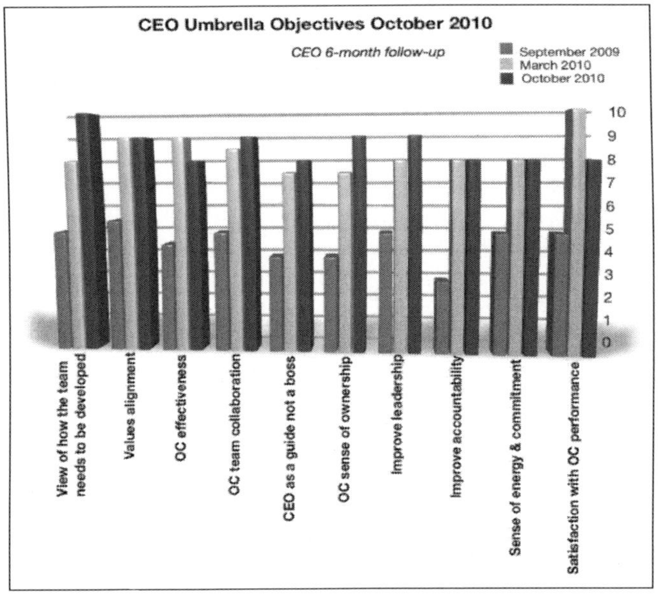

Figure 5. CEO umbrella objectives results, October 2010—CEO six-month follow-up

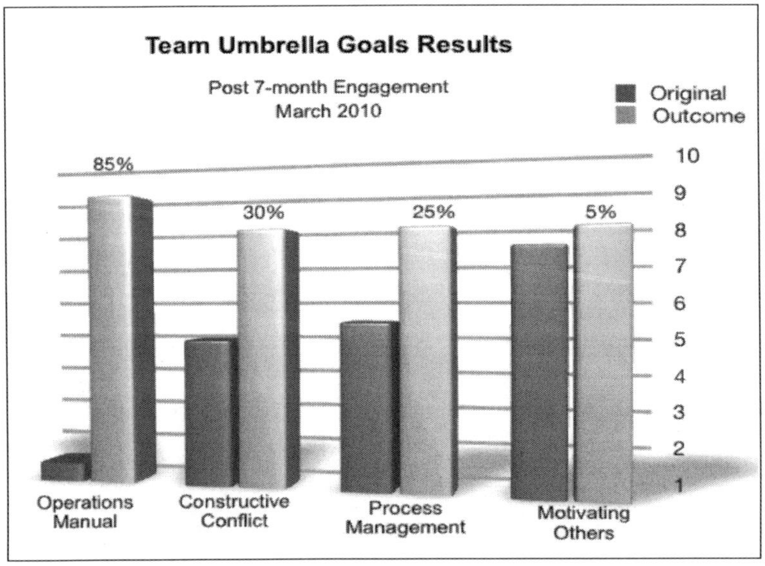

Figure 6. Team umbrella goals results, March 2010, post seven-month engagement

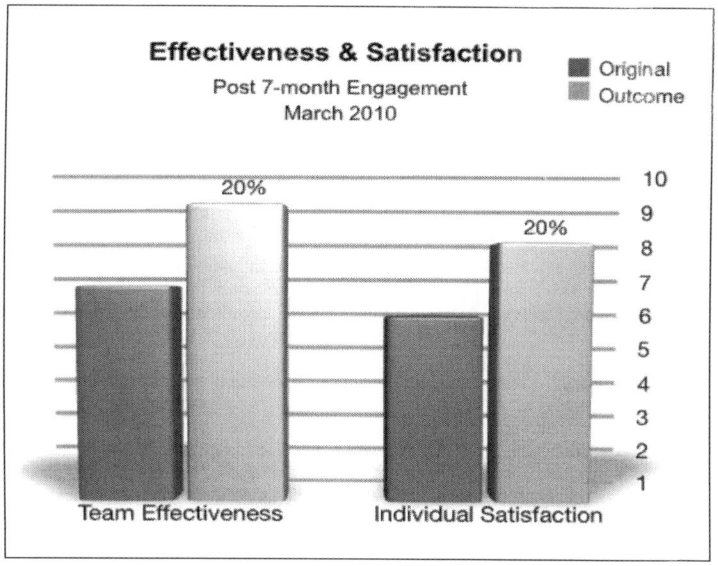

Figure 7. Effectiveness and satisfaction, March 2010, post seven-month engagement

The most striking finding revealed by the final measurements for this program is the new degree of alignment between the CEO and the executive team on the high-performing team survey (see fig. 8 and 9). The CEO and executive team expressed a newfound feeling of synchronicity and a sense of dynamic stability, but they could not articulate why. The survey enabled them (and the coach) to see the positive shift in alignment.

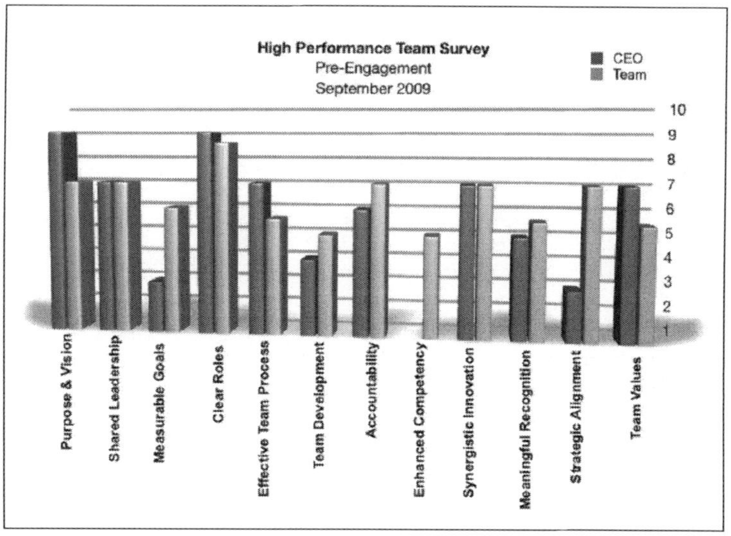

Figure 8. High-performance team survey—preengagement, September 2009

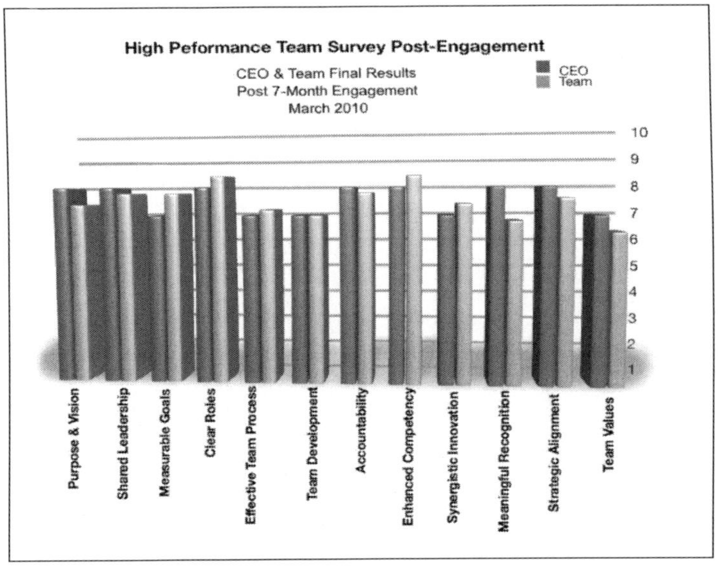

Figure 9. High-performance team survey postengagement—CEO and team final results, March 2010—post seven-month engagement

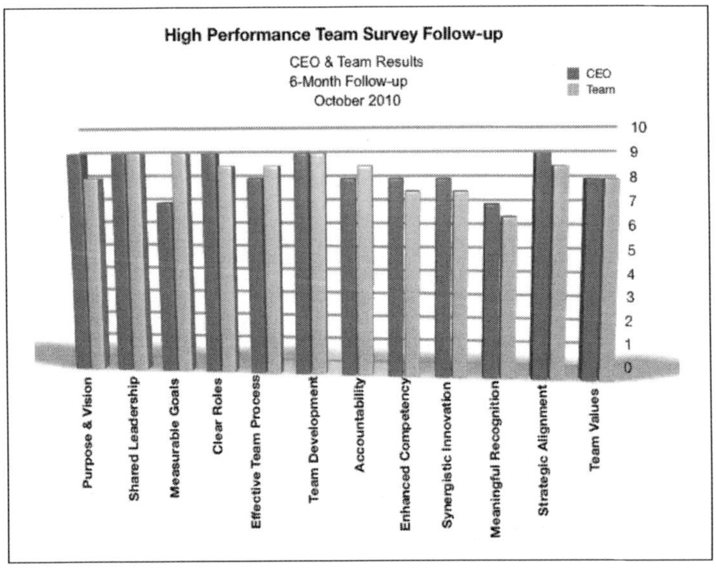

Figure 10. High-performance team survey follow-up, October 2010—CEO and team results. six-month follow-up

While the final metrics for the WSR project showed significant improvement and signs that the team achieved a state of dynamic stability at the seven-month mark, economic considerations precluded ROI from continuing with phase II, a proposed program to support and further document the transformation over an 18-month period. WSR placed phase II on temporary hold with the expectation of resuming in the spring of 2011.

Follow-up measurements

In lieu of phase II, ROI spoke with the CEO and redeployed two of the original surveys, the high-performing team survey and the CEO umbrella objectives, six months after the engagement, at the 13-month mark. The purpose was to obtain some indication of sustained behavioral change. When first asked to participate in the follow-up surveys, the CEO was willing though uncertain of what the results might be. He said, "I think it's fine, but this is a particularly stressful time for the team...a system conversion has not gone particularly well and people are feeling a little ornery. Also the OC changes are pretty significant." One team member had left to start her own company, another was repositioned within the organization and was no longer on the OC, and two new members had joined the team. In addition, the CEO shared that there had been a significant development, saying, "We reached a huge milestone for the company that we had been seeking for over three years." He further implied that this had allowed for expansion of the business.

The WSR study is one real-world example of how neuroscientific principles can be integrated into a coaching program to optimize measurable results for leaders and teams.

The high-performance team follow-up survey (see fig. 10) was deployed to those individuals who participated in the coaching program and who were still active on the OC. The survey suggested stability and indicated a slight improvement overall. The measurement of "team development" showed a 20 percent increase, while "meaningful recognition" slipped 10 percent from the CEO's perspective and 5 percent from team members' points of view. One of the four original team goals was "motivating others." The development of this competency involved efforts to improve "meaningful recognition." In the follow-up survey, one member commented on this area, "We still need work here."

The CEO umbrella objectives follow-up survey (see fig. 5) also indicated sustained change from original measurements taken 13 months previously. The CEO expressed a 20 percent improvement in his understanding of "how the team needs to be developed," whereas his "satisfaction with the OC performance" decreased 20 percent. Other objectives remained stable or increased slightly, though all showed a sustained, significant improvement over original measurements. When asked to comment on the experience of taking the follow-up survey, the CEO said, "It was of value. I was actually surprised at how positive I felt, despite the many changes occurring in the background, foreground, and on either side."

Perhaps the identification and continued focus on the team's strange attractors (mission, values, goals, strengths) has enabled the system (OC team) to adapt and evolve over time, responding positively to the changes that the CEO noted, rather than becoming rigid and overwhelmed. The surveys suggest that a state of dynamic stability has emerged and is being maintained by the OC team.

Conclusions

The WSR study is one real-world example of how neuroscientific principles can be integrated into a coaching program to optimize measurable results for leaders and teams. Organizations might be attracted to evidence-based programs for two main reasons: an increased probability of success, and the integrity and validity of a scientific foundation.

Coaching professionals who better understand the science of coaching have the ability to design and implement programs that are most likely to succeed. When coaches know why and how specific elements of methodologies work, it is possible to adjust practices accordingly to leverage the power of neuroscience and to maximize positive impacts.

Additionally, as organizations become more familiar with the emerging field of neuroleadership and neuroscience reveals the "secrets" of coaching, the profession has the opportunity to advance with greater integrity and effect. As a result of the WSR experience, ROI expects to be more transparent about the underlying neuroscientific principles at work in future coaching sessions. As neuropsychologist Dr. Louis Cozolino (2002) states, "There is a recognition that the evocation of emotion coupled with conscious awareness is most likely to result in...personal growth." ROI anticipates a clearer intention to combine emotion ("How did that situation make me feel?") with cognition ("Why did I feel that way?") during coaching programs to promote the understanding of the neuroscience at work, generate insights, and create personal growth.

Coaching professionals who better understand the science of coaching have the ability to design and implement programs that are most likely to succeed.

In hindsight, the concept of dynamic stability may best be addressed earlier in the program and emphasized to a greater degree. Initially, the concept was a "hidden" goal from the neurocoaching perspective. Dynamic stability is openly introduced in the sixth session, and the team works on a dynamic stability map in the seventh session, which proves challenging. In the future, dynamic stability as an overarching goal will be openly discussed at the beginning of a coaching program. ROI will work with clients to instill an expectation that they have the capacity to continue to create and maintain a state of dynamic stability after the coaching contract is completed, resulting in a longer-term return-on-investment.

As a final thought, to further the emerging field of neuroleadership, it is suggested that the NeuroLeadership Institute (NLI) consider identifying and publishing a list of core neuroscientific guidelines deemed to be foundational to brain-friendly coaching programs. Professional coaches may self-qualify or follow an NLI process to have program designs stamped "NeuroLeadership Institute (NLI) Approved" as a symbol of credibility and integrity. Coaches who have the discipline to obtain the NLI stamp would demonstrate their thought leadership and dedication to the design and delivery of optimal, evidence-based programs for clients. As the field of neuroleadership continues to enhance human enterprise and performance and neurocoaching becomes the gold standard, the momentum may challenge business schools, executive education providers, and professional coaches around the world to design more focused, evidence-based programs that cultivate dynamic stability and increase the probability of successful transformation.

References

Bennis, W., and O'Toole, J. 2005. "How Business Schools Lost Their Way." *Harvard Business* 83(5): 96–104.

Brothers, L. 1997. *Friday's Footprint: How Society Shapes the Human Mind.* Oxford, NY: Oxford University Press.

Busche, G. R. 2007. "Appreciative Inquiry is Not (just) About the Positive." *OD Practitioner* 39(4): 33–38.

Conference Board. 2006. *Employee Engagement: A Review of Current Research and its Implications.* New York: Conference Board.

Cozolino, L. 2002. *The Neuroscience of Psychotherapy: Building and Rebuilding the Human Brain.* New York: W. W. Norton.

Eisenberger, N., and Lieberman, M. 2008. "The Pains and Pleasures of Social Life: A Social Cognitive Neuroscience Approach." *NeuroLeadership Journal* 1: 38–43.

Fredrickson, B. 2009. "Positivity: Top-Notch Research Reveals the 3-to-1 Ratio that will Change your Life." *Broaden Your Mind* 4: 73.

Goleman, D. 2004. *Working with Emotional Intelligence.* New York: Bantam.

Goleman, D., Boyatzis, R., and McKee, A. 2002. *Primal Leadership: Learning to Lead with Emotional Intelligence.* Boston: Harvard Business School Press.

Gordon, E. 2000. Integrative Neuroscience: Bringing Together Biological, Psychological, and Clinical Models of the Human Brain. Singapore: Harwood Academic Publishers. Accessed on International Coach Federation website. http://coachfederation.org/research-education/icf-credentials/core-competencies.

Isern, J., and Pung, C. 2007. "Driving Radical Shange: Transforming an Organization Requires Clearly Articulated Aspirations, as well as the Ability to Generate Energy and New Ideas." *McKinsey Quarterly.com* (November).

Jung-Beeman, M., Collier, A., and Kounios, J. 2008. "How Insight Happens: Learning from the Brain." *NeuroLeadership Journal* 1: 20–25.

Lieberman, M., and Eisenberger, N. 2008. "The Pains and Pleasures of Social Life: A Social Cognitive Neuroscience Approach." *NeuroLeadership Journal* 1: 38–43.

Lewis, T., Amini, F., and Lannon, R. 2000. *A General Theory of Love*. New York: Random House.

Mintzberg, J. 2004. *Managers Not MBAs: A Hard Look at the Soft Practice of Managing and Management Development*. San Francisco: Berrett-Koehler.

Navarro, P. 2008. "The MBA Core Curricula of Top-Ranked US Business Schools: A Study in Failure?" *Academy of Management Learning and Education* 7(1): 108–123.

Pfeffer, J., and Fond, C.T. 2002. "The End of Business Schools? Less Success than Meets the Eye." *Academy of Management Learning and Education* 1(1): 78–95.

Ringleb, A. H., and Pagon, M. 2009. "The CIMBA MBA Leadership Process." *NeuroLeadership Journal* 2: 42–52.

Rock, D., and Page, L., 2009. *Coaching with the Brain in Mind: Foundations for Practice*. Hoboken, NJ: John Wiley & Sons.

Rock, D. 2008. "SCARF: A Brain-Based Model for Collaborating with and Influencing Others." *NeuroLeadership Journal* 1: 44–52.

Rock, D. 2006. *Quiet Leadership: Six Steps to Transforming Performance at Work*. New York: HarperCollins.

Rock, D. 2007. "Coaching Leaders to be Coaches at EDS." *Wiley InterScience* (September-October) 55–62.

Rock, D., and Tang, Y. 2009. "Neuroscience of Engagement." *NeuroLeadership Journal* 2: 15–22.

Siegel, D. 2010. *Mindsight: The New Science of Personal Transformation*. New York: Bantam.

Siegel, D., and McCall, D. 2009. "Mindsight at Work: An Interpersonal Neurobiology Lens on Leadership." *NeuroLeadership Journal* 2: 23–34.

Stapp, H.P., Schwartz J., and Beauregard, M. 2005. "Quantum Theiry in Neuroscience and Psychology: A Neurophysical Model of Mind-Brain Interaction." *Philosophical Transactions of the Royal Society of London, Series B* 360(1458): 1309–1327.

Thompson, R. 2008. "Harvard Business School Discusses Future of the MBA." *Working Knowledge* (November 24). Accessed on Harvard Business School website, http://hbswk.hbs.edu/item/6053.html.

29. Lead change with the brain in mind

Dr. Jim Whiting, Elizabeth Jones, Dr. David Rock, and Xenia Bendit
Jim Whiting, Global Organizational Development Program Manager, Texas, USA
whitingjim@gmail.com

Elizabeth Jones, NeuroLeadership Group, New York, USA
bethjones@neuroleadership.com

David Rock, CEO, NeuroLeadership Group, New York, USA
Faculty, CIMBA; Cofounder, NeuroLeadership Institute; Editor, *NeuroLeadership Journal*
david@neuroleadership.com

Xenia Bendit, Global Head of Organizational Development

Introduction

Organizational transformations are challenging, even under the best of circumstances, with overall success rates at about 30% (McKinsey Quarterly 2010). One of the toughest tasks is to maintain employee engagement and motivation in the midst of uncertainty created by wide-scale organizational change.

This case study discusses how one company incorporated key neuroscience principles into a major company-wide change initiative so that its leaders could minimize the impact of change while maintaining employee engagement and focus. The study also reviews survey results that measured whether positive statistically significant changes occurred in management behavior as a result of the training, from the perspective of both manager-participants who attended the training and manager-participants' subordinates.

The study took place in a global telecommunications organization with a presence in more than a hundred countries. Due to substantial competitive market forces, this organization was under intense pressure to transform performance quickly. The company was undergoing wide-scale change that included realigning resources for growth in profitable countries, regions, business lines, and markets; layoffs and divestitures in least-profitable countries, regions, business lines, and markets; labor union negotiations; and communication and implementation of additional cost containment and prioritizing of profit-making strategies.

The official spoken language of the company was English, although many managers and employees in the company were multilingual, commonly speaking two or more languages fluently. Team membership and working relationships often transcended geographical boundaries, with many teams commonly working in a virtual environment (not colocated at the same physical site). For example, managers and employees on a team often were based in different countries, meeting virtually via conference or video call, and very rarely meeting face-to-face (perhaps once or twice a year). Being able to work in a cross-cultural environment was considered a core competence at this company.

One of the toughest tasks is to maintain employee engagement and motivation in the midst of uncertainty...

Significant company change initiatives included shifts in business strategies, major reorganizations, and layoffs in all business functions globally. Given the wide scope of the change initiative and anticipated difficulties with the needed changes, the company was challenged with how to keep leaders, managers, and employees focused and productive.

Specifically, the company wanted to support leaders and managers by equipping them with skills to lead the organizational change powerfully and minimize the disruption of change. The client was willing to go beyond conventional leadership programs and was interested in helping their managers make new connections about how to manage change more effectively based on leadership theories related to neuroscience. The goal was to help leaders better understand and manage their own reactions to change from a brain-based perspective, as well as help them facilitate high-quality conversations about organizational changes with employees to maximize employee engagement and motivation. The client was also eager to continue to build leadership capabilities that would contribute to long-term effectiveness beyond the immediate needs of the restructure. This organization recognized the importance of "intentionally addressing the social brain in the service of optimal performance" (Rock 2009b) as an important leadership capability.

This organization recognized the importance of "intentionally addressing the social brain in the service of optimal performance" as an important leadership capability.

The company's goal was to quickly develop and roll out a highly effective program that could be delivered virtually to 700 managers worldwide while major organizational changes were in process.

The Focused Manager program highlighted in this case study was part of a larger company-wide initiative to provide employees at all levels skills to adapt to and work successfully in the changing environment.

Program overview and objectives

The Focused Manager program was delivered via five teleconference classes (1.5 hours each) in groups of 20–25 participants using the best practices approach of HIVE™ (High Impact Virtual Experience) technology developed by the NeuroLeadership Group (see more detailed description of HIVE below). This solution allowed program delivery to be scaled very quickly worldwide while minimizing costs. The aim of the program was to introduce neuroscience-based skills and models to equip managers to deal more effectively with the "people issues" of organizational change so that employees could maximize collaboration and maintain positive focus.

The Focused Manager program was designed to enable managers to lead change from a neuroscience perspective by understanding the following:

- How and why change is hard at a biological level
- How to turn overwhelming threats into manageable threats
- How to help others see the future in the face of change and potential threat
- How to regulate their own and other's emotions effectively
- How to have tough conversations in a brain-friendly way
- How to maintain attention, generation, emotion, and spacing to maximize engagement and learning

In addition to education, the program was designed to build skills in these areas so that managers could proactively increase individual and team engagement with the change initiative. Each teleconference class included theory, practical models, and then real-time practice using actual workplace scenarios. Between classes, participants completed reading and writing assignments, as well as partner exercises, to further embed their learning.

The three specific objectives of the Focused Manager program were to equip managers with the tools to:

1. Lead the restructure (both strategic and organizational changes)
2. Deal with conflict
3. Focus the team

The underpinning theory for the program was a three-step brain-based change model that addresses what it takes to create successful change:

1. Create a "toward" state—help people feel safe enough to think about the future

2. Facilitate new connections—help people think in new ways

3. Embed new wiring—help people develop new habits

This high-level change model was developed by David Rock and first presented at the NeuroLeadership Summit in Los Angeles in 2009.

Each of the five modules of the training program was designed to help managers understand the biology behind important brain functions and to provide them with useful tools so they could create new, more easily accessible mental maps for themselves about how to help themselves and their employees stay in a more positive mental state. The result would be improved thinking and better decision making for the entire organization.

Focused Manager modules and key neuroscience theory

What follows is a summary of the key ideas and underpinning theory covered in each module.

Module 1: Set the direction—conversation about what's ahead

Focus:

Create a "toward" state—help people feel safe enough to think about the future.

Synopsis:

Participants learned what the brain needs in order to change and how to have conversations about the future in the face of significant change. The brain's organizing principle—to minimize threat and maximize reward—was introduced in the context of organizational change. Participants completed the first session practicing the use of specific tools to support themselves and others to have more effective conversations about their own—and the company's—future during the change.

Key neuroscience theory:

Understanding the brain's organizing principle of minimizing danger and maximizing reward (Gordon 2000) helped managers gain a better appreciation of how difficult change can be for individuals. Wide-scale corporate change creates uncertainty and fear—messages that the brain interprets as threat. The result is that employees react with a fear response (fight or flight) and cannot contribute their best thinking (Arnsten 1998).

Organizational change is a complex topic and requires a lot of conceptual thinking about future events—a task that requires a lot of cognitive resources. Managers learned how to help themselves and others get into a more positive mental state (toward state) so they could engage much-needed cognitive resources for more effective problem solving, creativity, collaboration, and innovation.

The SCARF® model (Rock 2008) was introduced as an important model to help managers understand the five domains of social experience that the brain is always monitoring. Managers were able to relate organizational-change dynamics to its effects on the domains of SCARF, such as loss of status, high degree of uncertainty about the future, reduced autonomy, erosion of trust, and heightened perception of unfairness about decisions related to the change initiative. The result can be an overwhelming threat response from employees and strong resistance to change. Managers practiced using SCARF in team meetings and one-to-one conversations to help offset threats created by the change initiative. The goal was to help managers and their direct reports feel safe enough to have productive conversations about a vision for the future and next steps.

The SCARF model was introduced as an important model to help managers understand the five domains of social experience that the brain is always monitoring.

Module 2: Get into action—turn strategy into action

Focus:

Facilitate new connections—help people think in new ways.

Synopsis:

Participants were introduced to a framework that maps the flow of change conversations, from being stuck (impasse) to uncovering new thinking (insight) to generating actions likely to create change (action), and then embedding new behaviors over time (habit) (Rock 2006).

The framework can lead to shorter, more effective in-person or virtual conversations that help someone think more clearly and move more quickly into motivated action. Questioning skills to help facilitate insight in others were introduced as part of the framework.

Key neuroscience theory:

Successful organizational change requires that employees create new mental maps for how to move forward with a fresh perspective. In change conversations, the goal is to teach managers how to help employees think in new ways by skillfully facilitating insight in others when faced with challenging situations or problems, rather than simply "telling" direct reports the answers.

Although a manager's role is to share important information to set the direction during change, he/she can build commitment and create alignment by facilitating conversations that invite employees to think about the future for themselves—filling in the gaps and connecting to where they are going and what it might mean for them personally. The conversation framework introduced in this module helps structure a conversation in a "brain-friendly" way that respects the SCARF domains throughout the dialogue. Skills such as asking permission, providing a clear context for the conversation, and engaging the employee through skillful questioning can improve status, certainty, and autonomy. The framework also keeps the conversation "solution-focused" to minimize activation of strong emotions that can result from a problem-focused approach. The framework is a road map to help managers actively engage the other person in identifying ways to move forward from a challenging situation.

The active ingredient in facilitating change is supporting others to generate their own insights about how to move forward.

The active ingredient in facilitating change is supporting others to generate their own insights about how to move forward. Insight matters in change conversations because the moment of insight changes the brain in a way that linear problem solving does not (Ludmer, Dudai, and Rubin 2011). Research shows that learning through insight is also more memorable than noninsight. New networks are created in the brain that help us see a situation in a totally new way. It can positively affect SCARF domains such as status, since status increases as a result of solving a problem for oneself. Insights are rewarding because it gives the brain a boost of dopamine (novel connections) and releases energy. Because of the burst of energy and the satisfaction of solving a problem on one's own, insight creates a greater sense of ownership of the idea, as well as the motivation to put the idea into action. When managers and employees alike see their way forward in change as a result of their own insights, buy-in and support of the change are more likely to happen.

Module 3: Work through challenges—hard conversations

Focus:

Develop emotion-regulation strategies for self and others.

Synopsis:

Emotion regulation is one of the most important elements for managers in today's stressful and complex business environment—especially during times of wide-scale organizational change. Having the ability to "stay cool under pressure" is key for maintaining focus and clear thinking. In this module, participants reviewed the impact of stronger emotions on higher-level cognitive processes and the implications for managing effectively. They learned tools to regulate their own mental state so they could better manage their own emotional response to their world. Managers also discussed how to use these strategies to reduce conflict in difficult workplace conversations so that people could stay in a more positive mental state and reengage more quickly with their work.

Neuroscience theory:

As discussed earlier, the dynamics of organizational change can result in employees feeling quite threatened and resistant to change—just at a time when the organization most needs creativity and great decision-making from its employees.

Managers gained a greater understanding of the role of the limbic system as it tracks emotional responses common in change, such as anxiety, fear, anger, and uncertainty. The resulting threat-response impacts important cognitive capacity because resources such as oxygen and glucose are reduced in the prefrontal cortex (PFC). Reduced functioning happens quickly and, in many cases, without conscious awareness. When the limbic system is overaroused by threat, (Rock 2009a). We can certainly continue to make decisions, but the brain is drawing on more automatic responses easily accessible to it. Organizational change constantly presents managers with new situations and challenges they have not experienced in the past, so their automatic responses under pressure may not be the best solution. Also, when under threat, we take in less information from stimuli around us, so we may be more likely to miss information, such as key words spoken to us, since our attention is more likely to be focused inward. Threat responses also cause us to err on the side of pessimism in responding to our environment since the brain is on "heightened alert" for additional danger.

The emotion-regulation tools outlined in Gross's (2003) process model for emotion regulation were introduced so that managers could employ regulation strategies before and after an emotional response kicks in. Emphasis was placed on tools to help with cognitive change: labeling and reappraisal.

Finding the right word to identify an emotional sensation is a technique called labeling (Lieberman 2009). The act of searching for and identifying a word that describes a feeling activates the right ventrolateral prefrontal cortex, the region that is central to any type of braking in the brain. Labeling can damp down the limbic system and engage the brain's braking system so that critical resources increase in the PFC.

Emotion regulation is one of the most important elements for managers in today's stressful and complex business environment...

When stronger emotional responses are in play, cognitive reappraisal is a second tool for helping managers "stay cool" (Ochsner 2008). Engaging the PFC to think about a situation from a different, more positive perspective increases activation of the right and left ventrolateral prefrontal cortex. At the same time, the activation of the limbic system is reduced.

The third technique introduced was "direct experience"—the ability to be fully present in the moment without the interference of the brain's narrative circuitry (Farb et al. 2007). When the direct-experience network is activated, the body and brain are able to process more incoming data in "real time," so one is able to more accurately experience the reality of an event. The result is that one might take in more information that helps improve decision making. Helping managers learn to change the focus of their attention from the narrative network (our default) to the direct-experience network not only increases their ability to take in more external data, but also increases awareness of their own internal mental state. Increased internal awareness can lead to smarter choices about actions and quicker access to emotion-regulation techniques.

Module 4: Implement the change—even harder conversations

Focus:

Integrate key learnings from previous modules and apply to challenging one-on-one and team conversations occurring in person and virtually.

Synopsis:

A framework was introduced for managing team conversations about change so that team members felt connected and focused on what's next. This framework builds on the conversation framework introduced in module 2 and guides a team in dealing with an impasse, facilitating new insights, generating actions, and embedding new effective behaviors as habits. Participants practiced using this framework as well as emotion-regulation strategies with challenging workplace conversations. Best practices of working effectively in virtual environments were introduced, drawing on the HIVE (High Impact Virtual Experience) best practices also used by the facilitators of the Focused Manager sessions.

Neuroscience theory:

The conversation framework is designed to structure the thought processes and interactions of a team so that the threat response of a challenging meeting is offset for both the manager and employees. Managers learn to actively manage the SCARF domains throughout a meeting so that team members are in a toward state and actively engaged. This occurred through both labeling (Lieberman 2009) and the offsetting effect, which involves creating rewards in other SCARF domains to offset the total threat response (Dixon, Rock, and Ochsner 2010).

The framework guides the manager in how to be a facilitator—not a driver—of a meeting so that team status is built and autonomy protected. Inviting the group to set meeting expectations, add to agendas, and actively contribute their ideas helps create a greater sense of autonomy. The "solution focus" of the meeting framework creates certainty for a team that the conversation has a useful, positive direction. Managers also learn that helping the team generate "stretch" goals can add a just-enough "healthy threat" to inspire a team to find ways to work together. In organizational change, teams are often asked to work toward goals that are new to them—ones for which they do not have existing brain maps to rely on. Managers can facilitate insights from a group—just as in a one-on-one conversation—so that the team sees a new way forward. New ideas can increase team status as well as generate energy to move the team into setting actions.

The framework can be extremely useful for incorporating new team members so that all team members begin to relate to each other as "ingroup" (instead of "outgroup") members.

Module 5: Engage the change—move your team ahead

Focus:

Embed new wiring—help people develop new habits.

Synopsis:

Participants focused on three ways to support others to develop and sustain new ways of behaving as they work with the organizational change:

- Managing the flow of a change conversation to create greater accountability and ownership with self-directed feed-forward
- Setting actions and developing new habits with implementation intentions
- Deepening new learning and behavior with quality follow-up

This final module was also designed for participants to continue integrating the models learned in the previous four modules.

Neuroscience theory:

Giving feedback to others in order to improve performance and facilitate change often results in a strong threat reaction unless handled well. Threats to status, autonomy, relatedness, and fairness can be easily activated when a manager approaches a feedback conversation by telling an employee what is wrong and how to fix it. (Dixon, Rock, and Ochsner 2010). Focusing on the problem during a feedback conversation can also increase limbic arousal and negatively affect the cognitive resources available for effective problem solving.

Giving feedback to others in order to improve performance and facilitate change often results in a strong threat reaction unless handled well.

Changing behavior through feedback is also difficult because of the brain's strong "habit system," which has evolved to conserve energy via reacting to stimuli by drawing on stored past patterns and therefore resisting change (Dixon, Rock, and Ochsner 2010b).

Participants were introduced to the feedback process of "self-directed feed-forward" (Rock and Page 2009), which invites employees to first give themselves feedback on how to solve a problem or address a performance issue (Dixon, Rock, and Ochsner 2010). Employees are less likely to react defensively if given the opportunity to find their own solutions and raise their own status while doing so. Employees are also more likely to implement actions necessary to change as a result of increased ownership through generating their own insights about how to move forward. Managers learned that successful self-directed feed-forward requires them to use emotion-regulation techniques to inhibit the strong desire to give a solution to the employee, as well as manage the SCARF domains to create a toward state during the conversation.

Chances of change improve when an employee identifies a goal and creates the goal statement in an "if-then" format...

As a result of self-directed feed-forward, chances of change improve when an employee identifies a goal and creates the goal statement in an "if-then" format—an implementation intention. Implementation intentions give the brain a very specific cue to scan for—"If I find myself getting frustrated in a meeting"—and a very specific action to take—"I will take two deep breaths before sharing my thoughts."

"By forming an implementation intention, the mental image of the specified situation or cue becomes highly activated and more readily accessible" (Gollwitzer and Brandstaetter 1997). A more general goal intention to change, such as "I will handle my emotions more effectively in meetings," is too abstract for the brain to scan for effectively. The constant monitoring required for a more general goal is taxing to the brain's resources and may be easily overridden by other distractions, such as anxiety or a new short-term goal (McDaniel et al. 2003).

The third strategy for helping others embed new habits is quality follow-up in the form of acknowledgment. When managers give authentic positive feedback to an employee, they are highlighting the behaviors they want to see more of. Acknowledgment is a way of reinforcing new wiring and maps for that person and cuing the brain to "do more of that action." When a behavior is new, the brain circuits are fragile until the behavior is repeated often enough to be hard-wired. Acknowledgment can be very useful in helping an employee keep attention focused on new ideas and behaviors long enough to make strong neural connections.

Acknowledgment of others for how they are growing, learning, and challenging themselves can support a growth mind-set (Dweck 2006) that drives engagement and improved performance.

Many of us are our own "worst critics," and we easily find fault in ourselves—without the help of our colleagues or managers or the dynamics of organizational change. The result is a noisy brain that may be in a threat state as a result of our problem focus. Even mild threat states interfere with our ability to think and perform at our best. Acknowledgment can be a powerful tool to help managers shift others into a quieter, more positive brain state and better thinking.

Acknowledgment of others for how they are growing, learning, and challenging themselves can support a growth mind-set that drives engagement and improved performance.

Delivery methodology: HIVE (High Impact Virtual Experiences)

To be able to scale delivery of the Focused Manager program quickly without losing quality, HIVE methodology was used. HIVE technology is based on neuroscience research findings about how to optimize learning experiences so that information can be remembered and recalled easily. Attention, generation, emotions, and spacing are important components of what the brain needs to remember information (Davachi et al. 2010).

The overall strategy of scaling learning quickly using HIVE is to:

- Deliver virtual programs in real time (not recordings) with very high participant engagement.
- Focus participants' attention for short bursts (60–90 minutes) in small groups (12–24 people).
- Distribute class time over several weeks (i.e., once a week) to allow participants to more fully integrate information.

- Combine class time with structured "homework" assignments to further embed learning.

During the telecalls, HIVE best practices of facilitation hold the attention and focus of the learner so that valuable learning can take place. These best practices were shared during the Focused Manager program so that managers could run more efficient, effective virtual meetings—a valued skill in a global company.

Survey results study

Study design

This study used a quasi-experimental, quasi-prepost design with the intent of approximating whether positive statistically significant changes occurred in management behavior as a result of the training, from the perspective of both manager-participants who attended the training and manager-participants' subordinates.

For the sake of this study, quasi-experimental implies the lack of control-group measures, while quasi-prepost means the use of a Likert scale that recorded "before" and "after" measures at a single survey event, as measured by a one-tailed paired samples t-test. For example, manager-participants were asked to rate their own behavior before and after the training at one time in a single survey, compared with having manager-participants complete two surveys at two separate times (once before and then after the training); similarly, subordinates were asked to rate their manager's behavior change (if any) before and after the training at a single point in time as described above. The study design included having subordinates rate their managers as a way to cross-validate participant-manager survey results, as it was expected that managers could have inflated self-ratings due to reasons associated with social-desirability biases.

A quasi-prepost design was used because of the need to reliably maintain the confidentiality and anonymity of respondents. For example, within this organization's context, it was unacceptable to attempt to have survey respondents complete one survey at a certain point (pretest) and then to specially code (e.g., using a unique identifier) and later redistribute a second survey to the same set of survey respondents (posttest) to ensure valid prepost respondent survey data pairings for each respondent. Moreover, even if it were the case that surveys could have been administered reliably and separately on two distinct occasions to each respondent so the responses could be accurately paired for each respondent, a potential concern could have been the lower response rates associated with having each manager-participant and subordinate respond twice (instead of once) to yield usable data for a paired sample t test.

The sample of 544 manager-participants in the study was drawn from the organization, with an attempt to represent populations in various regions and at different managerial levels. All managerial levels, from frontline manager to executive, were represented in the study population. The study hypothesis was that training would result in a positive increase in manager performance; therefore one-tailed paired samples t-tests, with an alpha of .025, were used in SPSS to calculate potential shifts in manager behavior, as independently self-rated by manager-participants and rated by subordinates. To help control for potential problems associated with missing data, only fully completed surveys were used to calculate the findings below. The organization and NeuroLeadership Group collaborated on the definition of program effectiveness questions included in the manager-participant and subordinate surveys, as shown below in tables 1 and 2.

Table 1. Manager-participant survey program effectiveness questions

1	"I am well equipped to lead the restructuring, as it applies to my team."
2	"I am well equipped to deal with conflict in my team."
3	"I am well equipped to focus the team on the company's new direction."
4	"I am well equipped to drive accountability and discipline in my area of the organization."
5	"I am well equipped to have conversations with my team that help us deal with change in the workplace."
6	"I am well equipped to have conversations with my team that motivate us to take action."
7	"I am well equipped to manage my emotions when having challenging conversations."
8	"I am well equipped to help other people on our team to manage their emotions in challenging conversations."
9	"I am well equipped to help my team set actions that will develop new behaviors, which enhance accountability and discipline."

Note: Questions 1–3 were used as primary program-effectiveness measures.

Table 2. Subordinate survey program effectiveness questions

1	"My manager seems able to effectively lead the restructuring, as it applies to my team."
2	"My manager seems able to effectively deal with conflict on my team."

3	"My manager seems able to effectively focus the team on the company's new direction."
4	"My manager seems able to drive accountability and discipline in my area of the organization."
5	"My manager has effective conversations with my team that help us deal with change in the workplace."
6	"My manager has effective conversations with my team that motivate us to take action."
7	"My manager effectively manages his/her emotions when having challenging conversations."
8	"My manager effectively helps other people on our team to manage their emotions in challenging conversations."
9	"My manager effectively helps my team set actions that will develop new behaviors, which enhance accountability and discipline."

Note: Questions 1–3 were used as primary program-effectiveness measures.

All managerial levels, from frontline manager to executive, were represented in the study population.

Figure 1 shows the effectiveness scale used in the manager-participant and subordinate surveys. The effectiveness scale ranged from zero to ten, with zero being associated with the lowest rating and ten associated with the highest rating; a "don't know" rating was also included at the low end of the scale. Given the restructuring occurring in the company and sporadic changes in manager-subordinate reporting relationships, allowing subordinate respondents to respond with "don't know" (equal to a zero) was considered important, as some subordinates might not have had adequate time in which to form a valid opinion about a new manager.

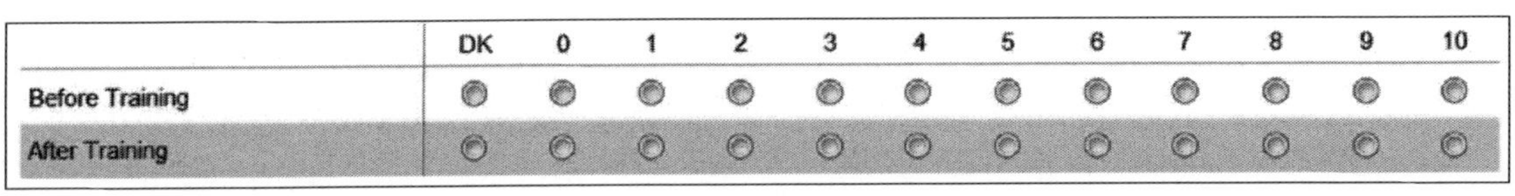

Figure 1. Likert scale used to measure training effectiveness ratings in manager-participant and subordinate surveys

Procedure for surveys

The 544 manager-participants who completed the training were surveyed to self-rate changes in their own behavior seven days after the conclusion of the last of five training modules, which were delivered over a five-week period. The seven-day delay before sending the survey allowed the managers to practice behaviors learned from all modules and was intended to attempt a balance between collecting timely and accurate manager-participant response data.

During the first and second week of the training, the manager-participants were encouraged to send a form e-mail to their subordinates, notifying their subordinates they were attending training and attempting to positively modify their management behavior in accordance with the concepts learned in training. Subordinates were surveyed 30 days after the conclusion of the training, to rate changes in their manager's behavior; the 30-day delay was intended to give an adequate observation period for subordinates before they rated their manager's potential behavior changes.

Findings

Effect sizes for all results are reported using Cohen's d, with the following effect size guidelines provided by Steinberg (2008, 365): "small effect = 0.4 standard deviation or less, medium effect = 0.5 to 0.7 standard deviation, and large effect = .8 standard deviation or more."

The manager-participant results of the study include 337 (of a possible 544) responses from manager-participant respondents. As shown in table 3, manager-participants' self-assessed behavior ratings before (pre) training and after (post) training indicated statistically significant positive mean score shifts for all three of the following primary program measures:

- "I am well equipped to lead the restructuring, as it applies to my team" before training ($M = 7.07$, $SD = 1.84$) and after training ($M = 8.14$, $SD = 1.59$), $t(336) = -15.60$, $p \leftarrow .001$, $d = -0.62$ (one-tailed), with Cohen's d (-0.62) indicating a medium effect size.

- "I am well equipped to deal with conflict in my team" before training ($M = 6.96$, $SD = 1.53$) and after training ($M = 7.87$, $SD = 1.30$), $t(336) = -16.79$, $p \leftarrow .001$, $d = -0.64$ (one-tailed), with Cohen's d (-0.64) indicating a medium effect size.

- "I am well equipped to focus the team on the company's new direction" before training ($M = 7.08$, $SD = 1.71$) and after training ($M = 7.73$, $SD = 1.56$), $t(336) = -11.61$, $p \leftarrow .001$, $d = -0.40$ (one-tailed), with Cohen's d (-0.40) indicating a small effect size.

Table 3 shows primary and secondary program-effectiveness measures related to manager-participants' self-assessed behavior change, and figure 2 shows a graphical depiction of the three primary program-effectiveness measures before (pre) and after (post) training for manager-participants.

The subordinates' results of the study include 1,244 (of a possible 4,220) responses collected from manager-participant respondents' subordinates. As shown in table 4 and figure 3, manager-participants' self-assessed behavior ratings before (pre) training and after (post) training indicated statistically significant positive mean score shifts for all three of the following primary program measures:

- "My manager seems able to effectively lead the restructuring, as it applies to my team" before training (M = 6.24, SD = 2.98) and after training (M = 6.87, SD = 3.06), t(1243) = -13.29, p ← .001, d = -0.21 (one-tailed), with Cohen's d (-0.21) indicating a small effect size.
- "My manager seems able to effectively deal with conflict on my team" before training (M = 6.11, SD = 3.17) and after training (M = 6.59, SD = 3.26), t(1243) = -10.85, p ← .001, d = -0.15 (one-tailed), with Cohen's d -0.15) indicating a small effect size.
- "My manager seems able to effectively focus the team on the company's new direction" before training (M = 6.58, SD = 2.84) and after training (M = 7.24, SD = 2.92), t(1243) = -13.34, p ← .001, d = -0.23 (one-tailed), with Cohen's d (-0.23) indicating a small effect size.

See table 4 for results of primary and secondary program measures and figure 3 for a graphical depiction of significant difference between subordinates' assessment of participant-managers before (pre) training and after (post) training effects (evidence of behavior change).

	Before Training		After Training				95% CI		
Variable	M	SD	M	SD	t(336)	p	LL	UL	Cohen's d
Lead restructuring*	7.07	1.84	8.14	1.59	-15.60	←.001	-1.21	-0.94	-0.62
Deal with conflict*	6.96	1.53	7.87	1.30	-16.79	←.001	-1.01	-0.80	-0.64
Focus the team*	7.08	1.71	7.73	1.56	-11.61	←.001	-0.76	-0.54	-0.40
Drive accountability and discipline	7.40	1.52	7.89	1.45	-9.27	←.001	-0.59	-0.38	-0.33
Conduct change conversations	7.08	1.53	8.05	1.36	-17.21	←.001	-1.07	-0.85	-0.67
Conduct motivational conversations	7.12	1.57	7.87	1.51	-12.58	←.001	-0.87	-0.63	-0.49
Manage my emotions in challenging conversations	6.93	1.51	8.02	1.24	-18.45	←.001	-1.20	-0.97	-0.79
Help others manage emotions in challenging conversations	6.61	1.53	7.58	1.56	-15.26	←.001	-1.10	-0.85	-0.63
Develop team behaviors of accountability and discipline	6.84	1.61	7.64	1.47	-14.62	←.001	-0.90	-0.69	-0.52

Table 3. Contrast of manager-participants' self-reported assessment of before (pre) and after (post) training behavioral effectiveness (N=337)

Note: *Indicates a primary program effectiveness variable; see table 1 for the complete question asked of respondents.

CI = confidence interval; LL = lower limit; UL = upper limit.

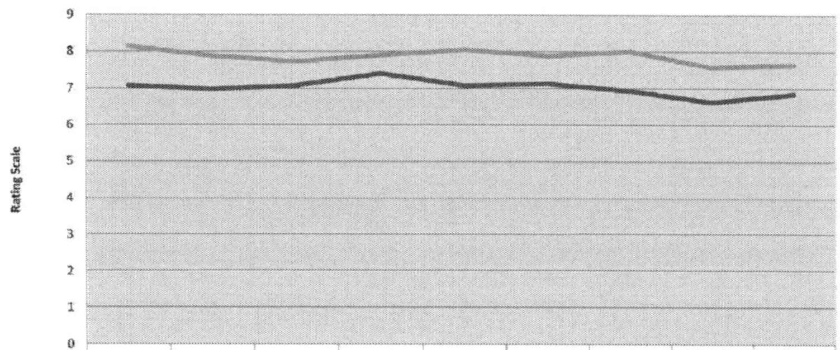

	Lead restructuring	Deal with conflict	Focus the team	Drive accountability and discipline	Conduct change conversations	Conduct motivational conversations	Manage my emotions in challenging conversations	Help others manage emotions in challenging conversations	Develop team behaviors of accountability and discipline
Before	7.07	6.96	7.08	7.40	7.08	7.12	6.93	6.61	6.84
After	8.14	7.87	7.73	7.89	8.05	7.87	8.02	7.58	7.64

Figure 2. Manager-participants' self-reported assessment of before (pre) and after (post) training behavioral effectiveness (N=337) (Note: Table indicates means scores.)

	Before Training		After Training			95% CI			
Variable	M	SD	M	SD	t(336)	p	LL	UL	Cohen's d
Manager seems able to lead restructuring*	6.24	2.98	6.87	3.06	-13.29	←.001	-0.72	-0.53	-0.21
Manager seems able to deal with conflict*	6.11	3.17	6.59	3.26	-10.85	←.001	-0.57	-0.39	-0.15
Manager seems able to focus the team*	6.58	2.84	7.24	2.92	-13.34	←.001	-0.76	-0.56	-0.23
Manager seems able to drive accountability and discipline	6.68	2.89	7.17	2.95	-10.35	←.001	-0.59	-0.40	-0.17
Manager has effective change conversations	6.30	2.94	6.85	3.07	-12.57	←.001	-0.63	-0.46	-0.18
Manager has effective motivational conversations	6.33	2.94	6.81	3.07	-11.24	←.001	-0.57	-0.40	-0.23
Manager manages own emotions in challenging conversations	6.74	3.00	7.18	3.07	-9.43	←.001	-0.53	-0.35	-0.14
Manager helps team manage emotions in challenging conversations	6.07	3.20	6.50	3.35	-10.31	←.001	-0.52	-0.35	-0.13
Manager develops team behaviors of accountability and discipline	6.24	2.96	6.78	3.09	-11.87	←.001	-0.63	-0.45	-0.18

Table 4. Contrast of subordinates' reported assessment of before (pre) and after (post) training effectiveness of their manager-participant's behavior (N=1244)

Note: *Indicates a primary program effectiveness variable; see table 2 for the complete question asked of respondents.

CI = confidence interval; LL = lower limit; UL = upper limit.

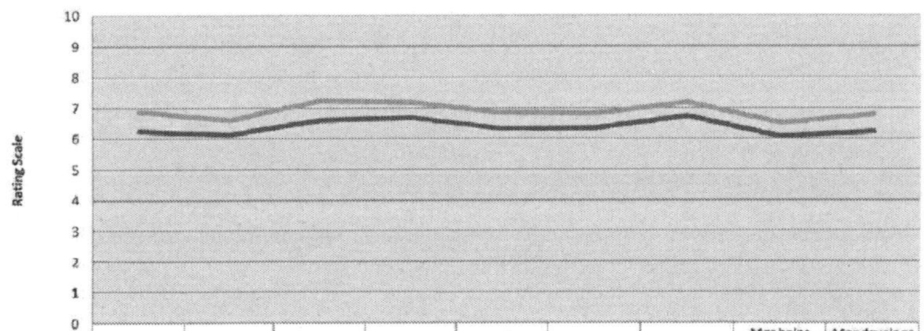

	Mgr seems able to lead restructuring	Mgr seems able to deal with conflict	Mgr seems able to focus the team	Mgr seems able to drive accountability and discipline	Mgr has effective change conversations	Mgr has effective motivational conversations	Mgr manages own emotions in challenging conversations	Mgr helps team manage emotions in challenging conversations	Mgr develops team behaviors of accountability and discipline
Before	6.24	6.11	6.58	6.68	6.30	6.33	6.74	6.07	6.24
After	6.87	6.59	7.24	7.17	6.85	6.81	7.18	6.50	6.78

Figure 3. Contrast of subordinates' reported assessment of before (pre) and after (post) training effectiveness of their manager-participant's behavior (N=1244)

Note: Table indicates means scores.

Discussion

The results of the study show that a well-designed and well-delivered virtual change-management training program delivered in real-time (live) with multiple (five) virtual sessions in a single course can be significantly effective from the perspective of manager-participants and their subordinates in the midst of a difficult organizational-change situation—even when the organization is global in nature and presents substantial challenges like cultural differences, including a multilingual manager-participant population base dispersed among many different physical locations across the world.

Similar training content could be perceived as very helpful to managers who find themselves in similar difficult organizational-change situations.

Remarkably, positive, statistically significant program-effectiveness results in manager-participant behavior change were observed for all primary and secondary effectiveness measures, according to both manager-participants' self-ratings and their subordinates' ratings.

Medium effect sizes were generally observed in the results of the manager-participants' self-ratings, and small effect sizes were observed from the subordinates' ratings. A notable large effect size in behavior change was observed in manager-participant self-ratings within the area of emotion-management during challenging conversations; the implication may be that similar training content could be perceived as very helpful to managers who find themselves in similar difficult organizational-change situations.

Perhaps manager-participants may have rated their own behavior change with larger effect sizes due to a social-desirability bias (a wish to be perceived as "getting better" at management); alternatively, perhaps managers were more keenly aware of their own successes in their attempts to change their behavior, compared with the levels of their subordinates' awareness. On balance, perhaps subordinates were less likely to rate manager-participant behavior changes more favorably due to the difficult organizational changes that were occurring when the study was conducted. Nevertheless, the evidence showed that subordinates did detect a positive and significant behavioral change in manager behavior; it is unclear whether subordinates would have been as aware of manager-participant behavior changes, where observed, if the subordinates were not primed to make such observations—this could be an area for future research.

There may likely be practical limits to the statistical assumptions that can be made using the quasi-experimental design in this study, such the use of one quasi-prepost measurement survey instead of two separate pre and post surveys. However, this design enabled a way to maintain the needed confidentiality and anonymity of respondents, and generated considerable sample sizes of matched-pair responses needed for paired-sample t-tests—this allowed for an innovative means to assess program effectiveness from a manager-participant perspective, with a cross-check from the perspective of subordinates, and allowed for a means to generalize and internally validate the results inside the organization.

Future research with this training content (particularly in the area of emotion management in challenging conversations) using this experimental design is recommended to enhance the generalizability to other organizations, and this study could be used as a baseline for such research. Increasing the behavioral capability of managers' emotion management when conducting challenging conversations could increase the performance and effectiveness of organizations undergoing difficult changes.

Evidence showed that subordinates did detect a positive and significant behavioral change in manager behavior...

References

Arnsten, A. F. T. 1998. "The Biology of Being Frazzled." *Science* 280: 1711–1712.

Davachi, L., Kiefer, T., Rock, D., and Rock, L. 2010. "Learning that Lasts Through the Ages: Maximizing the Effectiveness of Learning Initiatives." *NeuroLeadership Journal* 3: 53–63.

Dixon. P., Rock, D., and Ochsner, K. 2010. "Turn the 360 Around: Why Feedback Doesn't Work and How to do it Better." *NeuroLeadership Journal* 3: 77–82.

Dweck, C. S. 2006. *Mindset: The New Psychology of Success*. New York: Random House.

Farb, N. A. S., Segal, Z. V., Mayberg, H., Bean, J., McKeon, D., Fatima, Z., and Anderson, A. K. 2007. "Attending to the Present: Mindfulness Meditation Reveals Distinct Neural Modes of Self-Reference." *Social Cognitive Affective Neuroscience* 2: 313–322.

Gollwitzer, P. M., and Brandstaetter, V. 1997. "Implementation Intentions and Effective Goal Pursuit." *Journal of Personality and Social Psychology* 73: 186–199.

Gordon, E. 2000. *Integrative Neuroscience: Bringing Together Biological, Psychological, and Clinical Models of the Human Brain*. Singapore: Harwood Academic Publishers.

Gross, J. J. 2003. *Handbook of Emotion Regulation*. New York: Guilford.

Lieberman, M. D. 2009. "The Brain's Braking System (and How To "Use Your Words" To Tap Into It)." *NeuroLeadership Journal* 2: 9–14.

Ludmer, R., Dudai, Y., and Rubin, N. 2011. "Uncovering Camouflage: Amygdala Activation Predicts Long-Term Memory of Induced Perceptual Insight." *Neuron* 69: 1002–1014.

McDaniel, M. A, Einstein, G. O., Graham, T., and Rall, E. 2003. *Delay Execution of Intentions: Overcoming the Cost of Interruptions*. Published online in Wiley InterScience.

McKinsey Quarterly 2010. "What Successful Transformations Share: McKinsey Global Survey results." Accessed June 28, 2013 on McKinsey & Company website. http://www.mckinsey.com/insights/organization/what_successful_transformations_share_mckinsey_global_survey_results.

Ochsner, K. 2008. "Staying Cool Under Pressure: Insights from Social Cognitive Neuroscience and their Implications for Self and Society." *NeuroLeadership Journal* 1: 26–32.

Rock, D. 2006. "A Brain-Based Approach to Coaching." *International Journal of Coaching in Organizations* 4(2): 32–43.

Rock, D. 2008. "SCARF: A Brain-Based Model for Collaborating with and Influencing Others." *NeuroLeadership Journal* 1: 44–52.

Rock, D. 2009a. *Your Brain at Work: Strategies for Overcoming Distraction, Regaining Focus, and Working Smarter All Day Long*. New York: HarperBusiness.

Rock, D. 2009b. "Managing with the Brain in Mind: Neuroscience Research is Revealing the Social Nature of the High-Performance Workplace." *Strategy + Business* (Autumn) 56. http://www.strategy-business.com/article/09306?gko=5df7f.

Rock, D., and Page, L. J. 2009. *Coaching with the Brain in Mind: Foundations for practice*. Hoboken, NJ: John Wiley & Sons.

Steinberg, W. J. 2008. *Statistics Alive*. Thousand Oaks, CA: Sage.

30. Neurocoaching: leadership coaching using neurofeedback

Carol J. Kershaw and J. William Wade
Carol J. Kershaw, Brain Change International, Texas, USA
Corresponding author: carolkershaw@aol.com

Introduction

The human brain tends to entrain to the most dominant frequency to which it is exposed. Furthermore, entrainment—or emotional-state contagion—has been shown to have an impact on groups, particularly teams of people who are already focused on working in concert. To capitalize on this, leaders need to be in the state from which they would like their teams to function. By learning to shift into and maintain optimal brain states, executives gain the capacity to regulate their own physiology and enhance their performance and that of those around them.

Additionally, the ability to choose and hold an optimal brain state can help an executive avoid negative reactivity in difficult situations. The leadership coaching method we have found to be the most effective and efficient for this is neurofeedback training.

Traditionally, leadership coaching practice has been based largely on psychological principles and the observation of behavior and self-report. Using neurofeedback, a "neurocoach" may now view a leader's mental states in real time by observing his or her EEG as he or she trains on a system. Neurofeedback training, when incorporated into the executive coaching process, can be used to train brain-state flexibility and can allow the executive to reach agreed-upon goals more quickly.

Mental states and their implications for neurofeedback training

Mental states are reflected in the ratio of EEG frequencies that include gamma, beta, alpha, theta, and delta. Gamma ranges from 38–42 Hz; high beta is between 20 and 32 Hz; beta ranges from 13–21 Hz; sensorimotor rhythm is defined from 12–15 Hz; alpha runs from 8–12 Hz; theta is 4–7 Hz; and delta ranges from .05–3 Hz. Anxiety may be reflected in dominant states of high beta amplitudes, 21–25 Hz, and obsessive-compulsive ideation and rumination may be experienced in high beta around 26–35 Hz

(Demos 2005). An excess of beta brainwaves may also indicate a narrow focus of attention that activates the fight-flight-or-freeze response (Fehmi and Robbins 2007), while high amplitudes of delta may be suggestive of memory problems (Demos 2005). Mental states precede perspective, attitudes, beliefs, emotions, and behaviors. We therefore recommend that mental states should be the primary focus for change.

Neurofeedback is a targeted form of biofeedback that works directly on the central nervous system...

Neurofeedback is a targeted form of biofeedback that works directly on the central nervous system and, because it tunes the central nervous system, the mind-brain can be reorganized for optimal functioning (Lubar 1997; Othmer 2008; Demos 2005). As a brain-training exercise, neurofeedback improves focus and memory, promotes increased energy, calms rumination, loosens psychological defenses, shifts perspectives to more positive ones, and overall reduces stress and tension. Research suggests that people also learn to develop flexibility in mental-state change and stability in regulating their emotions and behavior (Lubar 1997; Hammond 2005; Demos 2005).

People who have excessive slow brain waves in the prefrontal areas of the brain relative to a population norm may exhibit excessive fear or anxiety or may be extremely reactive with little provocation.

The quantitative EEG (QEEG) analysis is an evaluation of brain functioning that is derived from information acquired during an electroencephalograph usually measured at 20 sites on the scalp and compared with a database of same gender and age normative scores. For example, people who have excessive slow brain waves in the prefrontal areas of the brain relative to a population norm may exhibit excessive fear or anxiety or may be extremely reactive with little provocation. Individuals who may be insensitive to others may also have frontal lobe issues. Neurofeedback can often normalize these problems, thereby improving leadership skills (Demos 2005). Note that if the QEEG reveals epileptiform activity (spikes and sharp waves observed in the alpha/theta range), these patterns are frequently indicative of previous head injury. When these forms are present, training in alpha/theta states is contraindicated.

Principles of neuro-organization and their application

Neuroscientists have identified the overarching organizing principle of the brain as one of moving toward reward and away from threat (Gordon et al. 2008). In other words, the brain literally organizes itself on the basis of "carrots" and "sticks." When we put it this way, executives understand it instantly. Leadership, they realize, functions at a neural level. Rewarding emotional states include happiness, curiosity, and contentment, while threatening emotional states include anxiety, discomfort, fear, and a sense of loss. Environments that maximize reward ("carrots") and minimize threat ("sticks") have been shown to lead to increased productivity and satisfaction. The underlying reason for that is located in the limbic system (Gordon 2000; Gordon et al. 2008).

Because of its survival value, the limbic system becomes more highly aroused when it senses danger than when it perceives reward. Positive feeling states are harder to maintain and are dislodged more easily. Unfortunately, the greater the degree of arousal, the more difficult it is to calm the system, and in an overaroused state, memory degrades, rational thinking devolves into survival thinking, performance deteriorates, and productivity falls.

In a study investigating how people order their moment-to-moment experience, researchers discovered that they switch between two types of thought processing: direct sensory experience and a personal narrative (Farb et al. 2007). The Farb study found that when subjects were mindfully aware of a direct experience, such as a light breeze on the face, rather than a mental narrative, they could keep their minds calmer. This was even more evident if the mental narrative involved self-judgment, such as "my presentation isn't polished enough." Switching one's attention toward a direct experience thus serves for self-calming. We suggest this practice to executives, both for themselves and as a method of stress management they can teach their teams.

The human brain tends to entrain to the most dominant frequency to which it is exposed.

As mentioned, the human brain tends to entrain to the most dominant frequency to which it is exposed, and that entrainment—or emotional-state contagion—has been shown to have an impact on groups and particularly on teams of people already focused on working together (Brewer and Hewstone 2004; Yapko 2009). In addition, teams are likely to be highly influenced by their leaders' states (Barsade 2002; Spoor and Kelly 2004). This virus-like experience is a process in which "a person or group influences the emotions or behavior of another person or group through the conscious or unconscious induction of emotion states and behavioral attitudes" (Schoenewolf 1990, 50). To capitalize on this, leaders must be in the state that they would like their team to function from.

The mental training we have found to be the most effective and efficient in achieving brain-state flexibility is neurofeedback.

The ability to shift into and maintain an optimal brain state for a particular activity allows executives to regulate their own physiology and performance, as well as that of those around them. There is, however, no single optimal brain state. Much work demands alert and focused thinking to support decision making. Creative problem solving is best approached from a "wide-angle" perspective, a brain state that is calm but unfocused. The goal is flexibility and balance. That is, the brain needs to be able to shift mental states quickly and easily to meet the needs of a situation.

Several forms of reappraisal promote optimal brain functioning. These include reframing a situation to emphasize the better of its negative aspects, normalizing a negative event so it does not become blown out of proportion, reordering or changing a hierarchy of important things, and making use of different perspectives to see other possibilities (Rock 2009). The ability to choose and hold an optimal brain state can help an executive to avoid being thrown into hasty reactivity in difficult situations. Equally, the ability to avoid or shift from states characterized by scattered thinking, anxiety, or depression—since these may be experienced either by other team members or the leader—is crucial to effective leadership.

We found neurofeedback to be the most effective and efficient form of mental training to achieve brain-state flexibility.

Leadership coaching program using neurofeedback

The neurofeedback coaching program begins with an initial assessment that includes taking a complete history of the executive's strengths and difficulties. Through discussion, we assist the executive in defining specific goals, and we identify the target mental states needed to achieve them. Such goals may include confidence, calmness, focus, motivation, persistence, and so on. Based on the goals, we develop behavioral and emotional-state markers for improvement—for example, becoming more empathic or less reactive or accomplishing a particular goal. Included in the training program are leadership skills, as well as business goal setting and future-vision training, which is a process of intuiting information about the best possible future. Many of the leadership skills are most easily acquired during alpha/theta neurofeedback training, especially when theta-dominant brain states (in the range 4–7 Hz) are present. Such theta states also serve to heal underlying emotional conflicts (Egner, Zech, and Gruzelier 2004).

Many of the leadership skills are most easily acquired during alpha/theta neurofeedback training...

Before beginning any neurocoaching, we evaluate the executive's general neural functioning using a QEEG. If the QEEG shows evidence of any brain trauma, we are very cautious about using alpha/theta neurofeedback training because the amplitudes may be problematic for the affected brain areas. The results of this evaluation inform the neurocoach of where an individual's brain operates in states of overarousal and underarousal, and where it is humming along in balance. Based on that information, the neurocoach can develop neurofeedback protocols for brain training, specifically selecting which frequency amplitudes to inhibit and which to reward. An explanation of the results can often assist the executive to better understand particular difficulties he or she may have. Additionally, the explanation frames the executive's issues as having an organic basis rather than simply being the result of "personal weaknesses." This often makes it easier for an executive to address the issues as a matter of developing a new skill set instead of changing "bad" behavior.

Using brain training to expand the sense of the possible

We begin by teaching individuals how to change the sensations in their hands and arms just by developing a focused attention and then noticing how the sensations might change. We use this process to elicit a state of empowerment and suggest that people have amazing abilities they may be unaware of. Many people can develop heaviness, lightness, numbness, warmth, or tingling in the arms and hands. The following is a sample script to elicit the sensory alteration:

> Sit comfortably and focus your attention on the back of one of your hands. As you observe your hand, you may notice that your hand's sensations change. You might be aware of a developing heaviness in your hand. You may be aware of warmth developing in your palm. You may be aware of a slight tingling in the fingers. Please keep staring at the back of your hand and tell me which sensations you notice.

After the executive reports which sensations he or she has experienced, the coach may suggest increasing the intensity of the sensations. For example:

> Now that you have noticed a feeling of heaviness, just allow that sensation to continue to develop. Everyone has picked up a heavy suitcase and felt its weight tugging against their arm. Notice how that warm feeling in the palm of your hand can spread. Perhaps it will move up your arm so that you now have a heavy warm feeling throughout your arm. If you like, the tingling sensation can increase, and you can begin to allow the hand to feel a little numb. Isn't it interesting to see how

you can develop these different sensations just by focusing on your hand? And there are many other abilities you have that you may not be aware of yet.

This exercise is designed to suggest to the client that if attention can change and direct physical sensations, executive performance might also be enhanced with attention.

Biofeedback trains the autonomic nervous system...

Whether we choose to employ neurofeedback training or not, we can use various types of biofeedback training to calm the nervous system. Biofeedback trains the autonomic nervous system and includes temperature training for relaxation, heart-rate variability training for controlling heart rate, and overall feelings of well-being outside the training environment (Kershaw and Wade 2012; Fehmi and Robbins 2007). Biofeedback training may utilize programs such as the eMWAVE from HeartMath, which trains a person in slowing the breathing rate to counteract stress, or a temperature trainer to increase temperature in the hands and facilitate the relaxation response.

Formal neurofeedback training

We begin formal neurofeedback work by using sensory motor rhythm (SMR) training. SMR is a brain rhythm of 12–15 Hz that calms the nervous system and was originally found to enable cats, which were trained to produce the rhythm, to resist drug-induced seizures (Sterman, Macdonald, and Stone 1974). This trains for alertness and brain stability. It also assists leaders in developing an easier access to the "flow state," described by Csikszentmihalyi (1997) as an optimal state for being in the "zone" of positive team learning and creative conversation, as well as a sense that a person can meet any situation with the best response. In this state, action and awareness blend together, and there is intense concentration on the present activity (Nakamura and Csikszentmihalyi 2002; Gruzelier et al. 2010).

"The target zone is a state of alpha brain resonance... while the interface, a state of hypnogogic reverie, is the bull's-eye of the deep healing process."

Using alpha/theta neurofeedback training for healing and insight

As long as it is not counterindicated by the QEEG results, alpha/theta (or "deep-state") neurofeedback training can be used to reach agreed-upon goals. To begin deep-state training, we explain that people fortunately have an innate healing system in the brain/body called the "alpha/theta healing system"

(Wisneski and Anderson 2005) and that the process of moving into deep theta states acts like a reset button to the brain. Depending on the executive, we may also explain that, when entering this deep state, the brain releases natural endocannabinoids, one of which is called anandimide, the "chemical of bliss" (Devane and Axelrod 1994). This is the "target zone" for the endogenous release of any of the family of neuropeptides of relaxation. Wisneski and Anderson (2005, 136) reported that "the target zone is a state of alpha brain resonance (8–13 Hz), while the interface, a state of hypnogogic reverie, is the bull's-eye of the deep healing process." In this deep state, creative insight, solutions, and future paths become clear. It is also the state in which trauma can be resolved and painful memories released, often without intense abreaction (Green and Green 1977; Panikashvili et al. 2001; Panikashvili et al. 2006; Peniston and Kukolsky 1989; Wisneski and Anderson 2005).

Neurofeedback training can be used to reach agreed-upon goals.

In our work with executives and coaching clients, we have found that consciousness is restructured in this breakthrough state; when the mind enters a profound calm, anxieties about the present and future dissolve, priorities shift, and the sense of not knowing what to do dissolves. Before a client begins alpha/theta neurofeedback training, we generally do between five and ten stabilization training sessions in SMR, rewarding the presence of 12–15 Hz cortical rhythms. In the actual alpha/theta work, we use two-channel training with active leads at Pz, O1, O2, A1, and A2 (scalp sites that have been mapped according to brain function). For software, we use the Cygnet™ system developed by the Othmers. All alpha/theta training is done with eyes closed using auditory rewards. Sessions are normally 30 minutes long, and we suggest the person allow the mind to drift to the edge of sleep in order to move into the deepest theta state. This facilitates the theta crossover (where theta "crosses over" and predominates over every other frequency).

When positive states are stimulated, people have more access to internal resources and an increased desire to be part of a team.

As we explain to executives, neither rewards nor threats have to be particularly overt to trigger significant neural responses. A "reward" may be as simple as a sincerely offered "thank you." A "threat" may be perceived in a minor but ambiguous comment.

We encourage executives to pay much closer attention to the actual messages they convey to those around them. Leaders have the ability to focus their team's attention in particular ways that influence their brain states and concomitant emotions and behaviors. In fact, we suggest that, to be effective, a leader must influence those around them in positive ways at a neurological level. When positive states are stimulated, people have more access to internal resources and an increased desire to be part of a team. Too often, positions of leadership and power, coupled with highly demanding business environments, make executives all too prone to "express their stress" at their direct reports, rather than mastering techniques of stress management and working to convey messages that will encourage staff members and, in turn, support the health of the enterprise.

Neither rewards nor threats have to be particularly overt to trigger significant neural responses.

Executive coaching case study

Howard, the CEO of a large oil company, was interested in managing stress and being less reactive with difficult employees. He stated that he wanted to enhance his performance in goal attainment, become more productive, and make better decisions around organizational strategy and financial challenges. In addition, he wanted to expand his intuition and insights to encompass unexpected problems. As we progressed with the initial evaluation, he also noted that he tended to drink too much and overeat when he was stressed, and he wanted to break these negative patterns.

After some initial sessions spent rewarding sensory motor rhythm, we started alpha/theta neurofeedback training with him, using Pz and O1 as active lead sites. We suggested he gently allow his mind to move all the way to the edge of sleep. If images appeared, it was important to just allow them to be. We explained that they were "oracles" offering information we would process later.

Over 20 sessions, Howard began to feel much less stressed. He began to develop insightful ideas about the company and learned that when his mind was calm, he could see much more clearly what solutions were needed. As his mind became generally calmer, he had less need to use food or alcohol to change mental states. He stopped drinking daily and found that he felt full on less food.

To his surprise, he noticed that he was more easily able to shift his focus of attention between intense concentration and a more open focus. Howard reported feeling as if he were flowing through the day, and the experience reminded him of his college days when he was in the zone on the football field.

What leaders learn through neurofeedback is that they are in charge of their mental states.

In one of the alpha/theta sessions, Howard described a three-dimensional image that appeared to him as a laughing Buddha who told Howard that he was rewiring his brain for happiness and success. The Buddha figure chuckled at the idea of calming an entrepreneurial mind that was always stressed and trying to gallop in many directions at once. The laughing Buddha became Howard's imaginary consultant as he set specific performance metrics for both himself and his employees and considered a potential corporate acquisition with his board of directors. It was, we suggested, his unconscious mind's wise guidance, stimulated by the alpha/theta training.

What leaders learn through neurofeedback is that they are in charge of their mental states. They learn that it is possible to recondition the brain and to turn certain neural circuits on or off by focusing their attention in particular ways. In doing so, executives fully realize that they have the capacity to create their own internal environment of calm and steady states—both for themselves and those they lead—and the ability to reach into their own quiet center for enhanced insight and problem-solving ability.

Discussion

This case study describes a method for leadership training that adds the use of neurofeedback to standard verbal coaching to enhance executive effectiveness and leadership skills. Since emotional-state contagion particularly affects teams of people who are already working in concert, the most effective leadership extends to the level of setting the dominant brain state for a workplace. Neurofeedback training can develop an executive's ability to consciously select and hold an optimal brain state relative to the needs of a given management situation or task. When an executive leader can bring narrowly focused attention to matters requiring the consideration of details, increased accuracy and efficiency result. When he or she can bring a diffused attention to the process of problem-solving in the context of a calm mind, flexibility in creative thinking occurs.

Alpha/theta training in particular can enhance the ability to attend to trains of thought, as well as archetypal imagery, that can direct and guide solution processes. Additionally, such training tends to integrate the emotions with cognitive processes in a way that often results in a sense of profound clarity.

The primary limitation in the application of neurofeedback training to leadership coaching is that, at present, there are very few clinicians who have the necessary equipment and are skilled in neurofeedback training. Even fewer clinicians have in-depth experience in the area of alpha/theta training.

A secondary limitation, but far easier to address, is that time-pressured executives tend to want results "yesterday." Neurofeedback training does not produce stable results in just a few sessions; an executive must be committed to a series of 20 to 30 sessions.

A third limitation is that neurofeedback training cannot readily be incorporated into group workshops or leadership conferences; the training is highly personalized and must generally be done one-on-one.

In fact, our equipment allows us to work with as many as four people at once so that working simultaneously with a small top-management team is possible. Our clinical work with more than one team member seems to enable people to feel more secure with each other—secure enough to offer ideas without fear of criticism. In fact, criticism is diminished. In interactions following the neurofeedback sessions, we typically have team members process the experience and then discuss their images of positive future scenarios for the team and the company. This process often generates ideas never before thought of or considered. This approach can be particularly effective with a management team of related individuals, such as are commonly found in small family-run businesses. In the case of larger teams, we would work with members either one at a time or in groups of up to four. In the latter instance, we recommend rotating the team members among the various groups so every person has an opportunity to work with all the different members of the team.

An important direction for further research would be to design and conduct larger studies using company teams and measuring the neurofeedback results. Identifiable variables—tracking aspects such as stability of mood, level of perceived stress, frequency of idea stimulation, and frequency of feeling threatened—could be measured pre- and posttraining. This would enable an analysis of quantifiable levels of improvement along the various parameters.

References

Barsade, S. 2002. "The Ripple Effect: Emotional Contagion and its Influence on Group Behavior." *Administrative Science Quarterly* 45: 197–231.

Brewer, M., and Hewstone, M. 2004. *Emotion and Behavior*. Malden, MA: Blackwell.

Csikszentmihalyi, M. 1997. *Finding Flow: The Psychology of Engagement with Everyday Life*. New York: Basic Books.

Demos, J. 2005. *Getting Started with Neurofeedback*. New York: W. W. Norton.

Devane, W., and Axelrod, J. 1994. "Enzymatic Synthesis of Anandamide, an Endogenous Ligard for the Cannabinoid Receptor, by Brain Membranes." *Proceedings of the National Academy of Sciences, USA* 91(14): 6698–6701.

Egner, T., Zech, T., and Gruzelier, J. 2004. "The Effects of Meurofeedback Training on the Spectral Topography of the Electroencephalogram." *Clinical Neurophysiology* (November) 115(11): 2452–2460.

Farb, N., Segal, Z. V., Mayberg, H., Bean, J., McKeon, D., Fatima, Z., and Anderson, A. 2007. "Attending to the Present: Mindfulness Meditation Reveals Distinct Neural Modes of Self-Reference." *Social Cognitive and Affective Neuroscience* 2: 313–322.

Fehmi, L., and Robbins, J. 2007. *Open-Focus Brain: Harness the Power of Attention to Heal Mind and Body*. Boston, MA: Trumpeter.

Gordon, E. 2000. *Integrative neuroscience: Bringing Together Biological, Psychological, and Clinical Models of the Human Brain*. Singapore: Harwood Academic.

Gordon, E., Barnett, K. J., Cooper, N. J., Tran, N., and Williams, L. M. 2008. "An "Integrative Neuroscience" Platform: Applications to Profiles of Negativity and Positivity Bias." *Journal of Integrative Neuroscience* 7(3): 345–366.

Green, E., and Green, A. M. 1977. *Beyond Biofeedback and Self-Control*. San Francisco, CA: Delacorte.

Gruzelier, J., Inoue, A., Smart, R., Steed, A., and Steffert, T. 2010. "Acting Performance and Flow State Enhances with Sensory-Motor Rhythm Neurofeedback Comparing Ecologically Valid Immersive VR and Training Screen Scenarios." *Neuroscience Letters* 480(2): 112–116.

Hammond, C. 2005. "Neurofeedback with Anxiety and Affective Disorders." *Child and Adolescent Psychiatric Clinics of North America* 14(1): 105–123.

Kershaw, C., and Wade, J. W. 2012. *Brain Change Therapy: Clinical Interventions for Self Transformation*. New York: W. W. Norton.

Lubar, J. 1997. "Neurobiological Foundation for Neurofeedback Treatment of Attention Deficit Hyperactivity Disorder (ADD/HD)." *Biofeedback* 25(4–5): 18–19.

Nakamura, J., and Csikszentmihalyi, M. 2002. "The Concept of Flow." In *Handbook of Positive Psychology*, edited by C. Snyder, and S. Lopez, 243–264. London: Oxford University Press.

Othmer, S. 2008. "Neuromodulation Technologies: An Attempt at Classification." In *Introduction to Quantitative EEG and Neurofeedback: Advanced Theory and Applications, 2nd ed.,* edited by T. Budzynski, H. Budzynski, J. Evans, and A. Abarbanel, 3–28. San Diego, CA: Academic Press.

Panikashvili, D., Shein, N., Mechoulam, R., Trembovler, V., Kohen, R., Alexandrovich, A., and Shohami, E. 2006. "The Endocannabinoid 2-AG Protects the Blood Brain Barrier after Closed Head Injury and Inhibits mRNA Expression of Proinflammatory Cytokines." *Neurobiology of Disease* 22(2): 257–264.

Panikashvili, D., Simeonidou, C., Ben-Shabat, S., Hanus, L., Breuer, A., Mechoulam, R., and Shohami, E. 2001. "An Endogenous Cannabinoid (2-AG) is Neuroprotective after Brain Injury." *Nature* 413: 527–531.

Peniston, E. G., and Kukolsky, P. J. 1989. "Alpha-Theta Brainwave Training and B-Endorphin Levels in Alcoholics." *Alcoholism: Clinical and Experimental Research* 13: 271–279.

Rock, D. 2009. *Your Brain at Work: Strategies for Overcoming Distraction, Regaining Focus, and Working Smarter All Day Long*. New York: HarperBusiness.

Schoenewolf, G. 1990. "Emotional Contagion: Behavioral Induction in Individuals and Groups." *Modern Psychoanalysis* 15: 49–61.

Spoor, J., and Kelly, J. 2004. "The Evolutionary Significance of Affect in Groups: Communication and Group Bonding." *Group Processes and Intergroup Relations* 7(4): 398–412.

Sterman, M., Macdonald, L., and Stone, R. 1974. "Biofeedback Training of the Sensorimotor Electroencephalogram Rhythm in Man: Effects on Epilepsy." *Epilepsia* 15(3): 395–416.

Wisneski, L., and Anderson, L. 2005. *The Scientific Basis of Integrative Medicine*. New York: CRC Press.

Yapko, M. 2009. *Depression Is Contagious: How the Most Common Mood Disorder Is Spreading around the World and How To Stop It*. New York: Free Press.

8773960R10323

Printed in Great Britain
by Amazon.co.uk, Ltd.,
Marston Gate.